DOMINICANS
IN THE MAJOR LEAGUES

Edited by
Bill Nowlin and Julio M. Rodriguez

Associate Editors
Len Levin and Carl Riechers

Society for American Baseball Research, Inc.
Phoenix, AZ

Dominicans in the Major Leagues
Copyright © 2022 Society for American Baseball Research, Inc.

Edited by Bill Nowlin and Julio M. Rodriguez
Associate Editors: Len Levin and Carl Riechers
Spanish translations by Reynaldo Cruz

Cover Photo Courtesy of Kathryn Riley and the Boston Red Sox

Library of Congress Control Number (LCCN) 2021917045

ISBN 978-1-970159-59-2
(Ebook ISBN 978-1-970159-58-5)

Book design: David Peng

Society for American Baseball Research
Cronkite School at ASU
555 N. Central Ave. #416
Phoenix, AZ 85004
Phone: (602) 496-1460
Web: www.sabr.org
Facebook: Society for American Baseball Research
Twitter: @SABR

Table of Contents

v	History of Dominican Baseball Julio M. Rodriguez G. with Cuqui Cordova	53	Pedro Borbón Jorge Iber
1	Felipe Alou Mark Armour	58	Rico Carty Wynn Montgomery
10	Jesús Alou Mark Armour	67	Luis Castillo Rich Bogovich
16	Matty Alou Mark Armour	78	César Cedeño John DiFonzo
25	Joaquín Andújar Malcolm Allen	88	José DeLeon Richard Cuicchi
34	Miguel Batista Cosme Vivanco	94	Miguel Diloné Seth Moland-Kovash
39	Tony Batista Scott Cummings	99	Juan Encarnación Paul Hofmann
43	George Bell Seth Moland-Kovash	106	Tony Fernández Tom Hawthorn
47	Rafael Belliard Joe Cox	111	Julio Franco Leslie Heaphy

DOMINICANS IN THE MAJOR LEAGUES

116	Dámaso García Paul Goodson		219	Pedro Martínez Norm King
121	César Gerónimo Jorge Iber		229	Ramon Martínez Gregory H. Wolf
126	Alfredo Griffin Justin Krueger		237	José Mesa Joseph Wancho
132	Pedro Guerrero Frank Morris		243	Raul Mondesi J. W. Stewart
143	Vladimir Guerrero Cosme Vivanco		249	Manny Mota Rory Costello
152	José Guillén Bill Johnson		260	Diómedes Olivo Rory Costello
157	Cristian Guzmán Gregg Omoth		268	David Ortiz Bill Nowlin
162	Rudy Hernández Rich Bogovich		282	Alejandro Peña Alan Cohen
171	Julián Javier Paul Geisler Jr.		291	Tony Peña Blake Sherry
177	Stan Javier Richard Cuicchi		298	Neifi Pérez Ralph Carhart
185	José Lima Rory Costello		306	Luis Polonia John Struth
193	Julio Lugo Justin Krueger		313	Manny Ramírez Bill Nowlin
199	Juan Marichal Jan Finkel		321	Rafael Ramírez Josh Sullivan
210	Horacio Martínez Rory Costello		331	José Rijo Charles Faber

346   Juan Samuel
Thomas Brown

351   Pedro Alejandro San
Julio M. Rodríguez G.

358   Elías Sosa
Rory Costello

363   Sammy Sosa
Eric Hanauer

371   Mario Soto
Gregory H. Wolf

381   Fernando Tatis
Chad Moody

389   José Uribe
Bill Johnson

393   Juan "Tetelo" Vargas
Julio M. Rodríguez G.

400   Ozzie Virgil
Ryan Brecker

406   Dominican Passion and Pride on Display in Sweep of 2013 World Baseball Classic
Richard Cuicchi

411   Contributor Biographies

Photo courtesy of Bill Nowlin

The History of Baseball in the Dominican Republic

By Julio M. Rodriguez G. with Cuqui Cordova

Baseball developed in the Northeastern United States in the nineteenth century and spread south, to Florida and from there to Cuba.

In 1891 the Alomá brothers, Ignacio and Ubaldo, left Cuba to live in the Dominican Republic. They organized the first teams to play the game regularly in the Dominican Republic.[1]

Dominicans liked the game and began to organize teams. In 1907 Licey was founded in Santo Domingo. In 1910 the Estrellas Orientales (Oriental Stars) were organized in San Pedro de Macorís. A number of other short-lived teams were organized over the years.

In 1911 Gimnasio Escolar, the first stadium for baseball and other sports, was built in Santo Domingo.

But the game really took off in the country during the American intervention of 1916-24.

Previous to the occupation, President Woodrow Wilson, disgusted with a revolution that took place in 1913, sent a delegate, James Mark Sullivan, to "teach Dominicans democracy."

Arriving in Montecristi, in September of 1913, Sullivan sent this observation to Secretary of State William Jennings Bryan: "I have noticed that the Dominicans are learning to play baseball and I foresee that in not a distant future, the stars of the game will replace the revolutionary leaders in the mind of the people."[2]

This was not quite so, but over time we have seen that many Dominicans turned out to become very good players.

During the years of the intervention, many games were played between Dominican teams and teams made of US Marines who came on Navy warships.

To see Dominican teams beat those American teams was one the greatest pleasures of the population during those years.

In 1917 La Primavera race track was built in Santo Domingo and, in the center of it, a baseball field was designed.

By 1922, baseball rivalry in Santo Domingo was intense. Licey was usually the usual winner of both the short series and games played on Sunday afternoons. A group of owners decided to fuse the best players of three teams into one that would play against Licey. This team was called Escogido (the chosen ones).

That year the first Dominican tournament was organized. In the scheduled 32 games, Escogido (23-9) beat Licey.

The following year, 1923, the second tournament (or series of games) could not be finished because the passion was so high that a big fight broke out on the field. This series was suspended to avoid serious and regretful consequences.

In 1924 another series was organized between Licey and Escogido, again 32 games. Licey won with a 17-15 record, winning in the last scheduled game of the tournament.

Five years later, in 1929, another tournament was also organized and Licey won again.

In September of 1930 Hurricane San Zenón destroyed both the Gimnasio Escolar and the Primavera race track.

Ginmasio Escolar was rebuilt in 1933 but was torn down in 1943 to open an avenue along Santo Domingo's Caribbean coastline.

In 1936 a tournament was organized, this time with four teams: Licey, Escogido from Santo Domingo (already renamed Ciudad Trujillo, or Trujillo City), Estrellas Orientales from San Pedro de Macoris, and the Santiago BBC from Santiago, representing the northern region of the country. (In 1937 this team changed its name to Aguilas Cibaeñas. Estrellas Orientales won the 1936 tournament.

Then came the famous tournament of 1937.

Dictator Rafael Trujillo's tyranny was in full swing by then and the name of Santo Domingo had been changed to Ciudad Trujillo in 1936. In order to make this name stick, Trujillo fused Licey and Escogido and called this team the Dragons of Trujillo City (Dragones de Ciudad Trujillo).

Initially in the tournament the Dragons were not doing well, so Trujillo dispatched Jose Enrique Aybar to the United States to bolster his team with the best players money could buy at that time.

The stars of the Negro Leagues were easier to contract than the ones in the white major leagues, so pretty soon the best Negro players were in Santo Domingo, not only with Trujillo's club, but in the other two as well. Their owners had, in response, also launched an economic effort to compete with Trujillo's ballclub.

Because of the drainage of its best players the Negro Leagues in the United Sates did not finish the series that year.

Trujillo's club finally won the championship, but the effort left the pride of the sportsmen hurt and their pockets empty, so baseball languished for the next 14 years. It was not until 1951 that the next tournament could be organized.

Photo courtesy of Bill Nowlin

Photo courtesy of Bill Nowlin

In 1944 another race track was built in Santo Domingo, the Perla Antillana, and as in the Primavera track, a baseball field was designed inside the track. Games were played there and in other parts of the country, but tournaments were short and without players from foreign countries participating.

In 1946 a stadium was built for the high school of Santo Domingo and was called El Estadio de la Normal, where Licey and Escogido played their games from 1951 to 1954.

In 1950 Dominicans won an international amateur baseball competition in Nicaragua and the enthusiasm for baseball was so high that in 1951 series began in the summer with foreign players rising the quality of the game. These summer series were played for four years.

In 1955 Trujillo built a new ballpark with lights. Dominican baseball joined what was then called Organized Baseball in the United States and the series began to be played in the winter from October through January, a practice that continues today.

The league had enlarged from the four traditional teams of Licey, Escogido, Aguilas Cibaeñas, and Estrellas Orientales to six teams with the addition of the Bulls of La Romana (Toros del Este) and the Giants (Gigantes) of San Francisco de Macoris. There are currently five baseball parks with lights.

After 1937, Trujillo did not interfere with baseball again until one day in January 1958 when during a playoff game between Licey and Escogido, his brother Petain came down to the field of play and slapped the face of Escogido shortstop Andre Rodgers. The turmoil that followed was so great that the next night Rafael Trujillo showed up at the ballpark himself to quell any possible disorder. At that time, he watched his first (and only) complete professional baseball game.

- In 1925 Mero Ureña was the first Dominican to play in the minor leagues.

- In 1926 the first Dominican player to play in the American Negro leagues was Pedro Alejandro San. After him came Tetelo Vargas and Horacio Martinez, a tremendous shortstop. Martinez participated in five Negro League All-Star Games.

- In 1934 and 1935 the Concordia team from Venezuela visited the Dominican Republic while on a goodwill tour of Caribbean countries.

- In the spring of 1936 a team of Cincinnati Reds players visited the Dominican Republic and played three games. Kiki Cuyler was in the squad that visited the Dominican Republic.

- In 1948 the Brooklyn Dodgers had their spring training in the Dominican Republic. It was in the swimming pool of their hotel that Jackie Robinson was, for the first time, in a swimming pool with white people.

There is a story in this spring training that tells you how much the Dominicans enjoyed baseball. Branch Rickey was going to a game and approaching the ballpark heard a big noise from the crowd. He was surprised because it was not time for the game to start yet. He asked what had happened. The answer was that Jackie Robinson and Pee Wee Reese were practicing the double play.

- In September of 1956 Osvaldo Virgil, from Montecristi, Dominican Republic, became the first Dominican to play in the major leagues, with the New York Giants. Today more than 700 players have played major-league baseball and the Dominican Republic is the foreign country that has sent more players to the big leagues than any other country.

- In 1983 Juan Marichal, also from Montecristi, became the first Dominican player to be inducted into the National Baseball Hall of Fame in Cooperstown.

- Dominican teams have competed in all four World Baseball Classics held to date, triumphing in the 2013 competition without being defeated.

NOTES

1 Cuqui Córdova, *Historia del beisbol dominicano desde 1891* (Santo Domingo, Republica Dominicana: MV Films, ca. 1982).

2 Ramon Marrero Aristy, La Republica Dominicana. *Origen y destino del pueblo cristiano mas antiguo de America*, Volume II (Ciudad Trujillo, Republica Dominicana: Editora del Caribe C por A, 1958), 344.

Photo courtesy of Bill Nowlin

Felipe Alou

by Mark Armour

Upon arriving in the United States in the spring of 1956, without knowing a single person, ignorant of the native language, customs, and food, and unaware of racism, Felipe Alou was armed with nothing but his mind, courage, determination and talent. No Dominican had ever played in the major leagues, and there were as yet only a handful of dark-skinned Latinos playing in the US. Over the course of the next five decades, Alou would become and remain one of the most respected figures in baseball, an All-Star player, a team leader, and a successful manager. While he was admired throughout baseball, among his fellow Dominicans, who would soon be plentiful, he was a revered hero.

"Felipe was really the first," remembered Manny Mota, "the guy who cleared the way. He was an inspiration to everybody [in the Dominican Republic]. He was a good example."[1] Juan Marichal, like Mota a fellow Dominican, agreed. "Everybody respects Felipe Alou," he recalled. "He was the leader of most of the Latin players."[2] Willie Mays, a teammate of all of these players, remembered, "It was like a family when they came over."[3] These men helped define the baseball of their time, and Alou was both a leader and a friend to many of them.

Photo courtesy of the National Baseball Hall of Fame

Felipe Rojas Alou was born on May 12, 1935 in Bajos de Haina, San Cristóbal, on the southern coast of the Dominican Republic, a few miles from Santo Domingo. (His nickname at home is *El Panqué* [Sweet Bread] *de Haina*.) The first child born to José Rojas and Virginia Alou, he was followed by María, Mateo, Jesús, Juan and Virginia. José also had two children with a previous wife who had died young.

Though José was dark-skinned and Virginia (descending from Spaniards) was white, Felipe did not give this much thought—race was not a big issue in his country.

José Rojas was a carpenter and blacksmith who built their small four-room house, and many of the other houses in the vicinity. The Rojas family had very little money, as they were often at the mercy of their neighbors' ability to pay their bills. World War II brought further hardship, causing José to turn to fishing to feed his family. Although they did not always have food, their well-built home afforded them shelter that not everyone in their neighborhood had.[4] Felipe swam in the nearby ocean, and was an avid fisherman—a hobby he kept up the rest of his life.

In keeping with the Latin custom, this man is known in full as Felipe Rojas Alou, with each parent contributing half of the double surname. The paternal half is normally used in everyday life, and in the Dominican people know Felipe, Mateo, and Jesús as the Rojas brothers. During Felipe's time in the American minor leagues he began to be called (incorrectly) Felipe Alou, rhyming (again incorrectly) with "lew" rather than "low." However, he did not feel empowered enough to correct the error. Two of his brothers, Mateo and Jesús, followed him to American baseball and also, because of the error with Felipe, assumed the surname Alou during their Stateside careers. Similarly, three of Felipe's sons played professionally, one becoming a star, and all of them used the name Alou even though it was not a part of their name at all (it being their grandmother's maiden name, not their mother's). For convenience, this biography will refer to the subject by the name most readers are familiar with: Felipe Alou.

Alou spent six years in local schools and went to high school in Santo Domingo, a 12-mile trip he often made on foot. He also worked on his uncle's farm and helped his father with his carpentry business. An excellent student, he became a member of the Dominican national track team, running sprints and throwing the discus and javelin. As a senior in high school, he participated in the 1954 Central-American Games in Mexico City. Though track kept him from playing high school baseball, he did play and star for local amateur teams.[5]

In 1954 Alou entered the University of Santo Domingo in its pre-med program, part of his parents' dream that he become a doctor. Alou batted cleanup for the team that won the 1955 collegiate championship. He returned to Mexico City for the Pan-American Games, intending to run sprints and throw the javelin, but at the last minute was removed from the track team and placed on the baseball team. He got four hits in the final game against the United States as the Dominican Republic won the gold medal.[6]

After the tournament Alou received many offers from the major leagues, which at first he had no intention of taking. His resolution lasted until his father and uncle both lost their jobs. As it happened, his university coach, Horacio Martínez, doubled as a bird dog scout for the New York Giants. "Rabbit" Martínez had played shortstop for Alex Pómpez, owner of the New York Cubans, and later a Giants scout. Alou signed in November 1955 for $200, which paid off his parents' grocery bill. More importantly, he had a job. Despite his parents' mixed feelings, "we needed somebody to start contributing some earnings to the house."[7]

Alou began his professional career in Lake Charles, Louisiana, helping to integrate the Evangeline League. Soon after he arrived, the league voted to expel Lake Charles and Lafayette (the two clubs that had black players).[8]

Instead, the blacks were shifted to other teams in other leagues; Alou, having just arrived in the United States, rode a bus to Cocoa, Florida to play in the Florida State

League. Desperately homesick, and stung by racism for the first time in his life, he pulled it together enough to hit a league-leading .380 with 21 home runs. On September 23, far away in New York, Ozzie Virgil made his debut with the Giants, becoming the first Dominican native to play in the major leagues. (Because Virgil had gone to high school in New York city, his path to the majors was different than Alou's.)

Alou began 1957 at Triple-A Minneapolis, but his .211 average in 24 games led to a demotion to Springfield, Massachusetts, where he recovered with a .306 average and 12 home runs. It could have been better—Alou was hitting over .380 in mid-season before injuring his right leg on a slide into home plate; he hobbled the rest of the year. Nonetheless, his season earned him an invitation to major league camp in 1958 and a raise to $750 a month. Alou spent very little of it—he kept enough to live on and sent the rest home to his family. During the offseason, the New York Giants moved to San Francisco, and their top minor-league affiliate was now in Phoenix, where Alou was ultimately assigned. Batting leadoff for the first time, he hit .319 with 13 home runs in just 55 games before the Giants brought him to the big leagues.

On June 8 Alou became the second Dominican major leaguer, playing right field and leading off at San Francisco's Seals Stadium. He singled and doubled off Cincinnati's Brooks Lawrence in his first two at-bats, and, three days later, got his first home run off Pittsburgh's Vernon Law. After a hot start that kept him over .300 for a month, he cooled down in July and finished at .253 with 4 home runs in 182 at-bats.

In his first few years Alou could never quite establish himself as a regular player, hampered mostly by the competition on his own team. Beginning in about 1958, a large wave of young players, mostly African-Americans and Latinos, arrived with the Giants. In just this single season, the Giants debuted Alou, Orlando Cepeda, Willie Kirkland, and Leon Wagner. Bill White had a fine rookie year in 1956, went into the Army, came back in late 1958 and had no place to play. Felipe Alou competed with all these guys, along with several others on their way; Willie McCovey and José Pagán joined the club in 1959.

Most of these players were outfielders and first basemen. Alou had the advantage of being athletic enough to play center field, but with the peerless Willie Mays on hand, that skill did not help Alou get on the field. He played as a fourth outfielder in 1959, but with McCovey hitting .372 with 29 home runs for Phoenix in late July, the Giants wanted to bring McCovey up and send Alou back down. With just a year's seniority under his belt, the 24-year-old told the Giants he would not go back to the minors. His wife was going through a difficult pregnancy, and Alou did not believe the move to Phoenix and the return to San Francisco in September would help. Instead, he told Giants manager Bill Rigney that they would go home. The Alous checked out of their apartment and booked flights to Santo Domingo. The Giants backed down, and instead made room for McCovey by making Hank Sauer a coach.[9]

Still, the addition of McCovey meant that either he or Orlando Cepeda had to play the outfield, and, with Willie Mays out there already, that left just one spot for Alou and several other qualified players to fight for. Over the 1959 and 1960 seasons combined, Alou hit .269 with 18 home runs in 569 at bats. In 1961, under new manager Al Dark, Alou played most of the time, got 447 at-bats, and responded with 18 home runs and a .289 average.

While Alou's star was rising in his profession, something else became even more central to his life. "The day I joined the Giants in San Francisco was one of the most important days of my life," recalled Alou. "That was the day my new teammate Al Worthington introduced me to Jesús Christ." Alou had often read the Bible in the minor leagues because he had a Spanish-language version and it became his only reading material. But because of Worthington, and later Lindy McDaniel ("who baptized me into the new faith"), Alou became one of the more devout Christians in baseball. His devotion caused some discomfort within his own family, but they remained very close.[10]

Felipe's brother Mateo, generally called Matty in the States, signed with the Giants before the 1957 season and began to work his way up through the minors. He debuted in late 1960, and reached the majors full time in 1961, hitting .310 in 200 at-bats. Although his presence was great for Felipe personally, Matty also was another outfielder—by September, Dark was platooning the two Alous in right field. Meanwhile, 19-year-old brother Jesús, yet another outfielder, was hitting .336 for a Giants affiliate in the Northwest League.

Felipe finally broke through as a full-time player in 1962, winning the right field job outright and keeping it all season. In 605 at-bats, Alou hit .316 with 25 home runs. He was selected to the NL All-Star team in July, coming in for Roberto Clemente and hitting a sacrifice fly in his only plate appearance. More importantly, the Giants won the NL pennant, overcoming a four-game deficit with seven games to go to tie the Dodgers, then winning a three-game pennant playoff. In the playoff series, Alou was 4-for-12 with two doubles.

The 1962 World Series was a classic seven-game affair pitting the Giants and the New York Yankees. Alou played every inning in right field, and managed 7 hits in 29 at-bats. But he has never forgotten his last chance, in the ninth inning of the final game, with the Giants trailing 1-0. Matty led off with a bunt single, and Felipe tried to sacrifice him to second base. "I was asked to bunt, and I bunted poorly and the ball went foul. Then, with the infield charging for the bunt, I swung at a bad pitch and fouled it off for strike two. Then I struck out."

"That was the lowest point of my career. This is something I am going to die with because I failed in that situation."[11] Alou was not often asked to bunt, but he did not blame Dark. He believed, then and later, that he should have been practicing bunting in case he was asked. Years later, as a manager, he obsessed over his clubs being capable of bunting. After another out, Willie Mays doubled Matty to third, but they were both stranded when McCovey lined out to second base, ending the game and Series.

The Giants fell back to third place in 1963, though Alou had another fine season—20 home runs and a .281 batting average. The highlight of the year came in September when his brother Jesús was recalled from Triple-A Tacoma to join Felipe and Matty. Late in the game on September 15, Jesús and Matty replaced Mays and McCovey, creating an all-Alou outfield. The brothers repeated this two more times that month, and appeared in the box score together a few other times. This feat has never been repeated in the regular season, and Felipe has a theory as to why. "Because people don't want to have children," he reasoned. The odds of three boys, all ballplayers, all on the same team, are quite remote.[12]

Meanwhile, in 1963 Alou found himself embroiled in some politics with the baseball establishment. Throughout his professional career, Felipe returned home every October and played baseball in the Dominican Winter League. On his way up to the majors, he won back-to-back batting titles in 1958-59 and 1959-60. A growing list of fellow major leaguers joined Alou, including his brothers, Manny Mota, Juan Marichal, and more. The Alous and Marichal usually played for Leones del Escogido in Santo Domingo, which won five of six championships beginning with the 1955-56 season. In 1956, Escogido club president Paco Martínez Alba—brother-in-law of Rafael Trujillo, the long-time Dominican strongman—formed a working agreement with the Giants.

Trujillo was assassinated in 1961, leaving the country in the hands of the military. The Winter League season was shortened in 1961-62, and cancelled outright in 1962-63. The Dominican government arranged a series of games with a touring team of Cuban players who were living in the US (exiled from their own country, and their own winter league). Among those who participated were Felipe Alou and Juan Marichal. Baseball commissioner Ford Frick, deeming these games "unauthorized," fined the players $250 each.

Many of the Dominican players were upset, but it was Alou who went public. In the spring of 1963, Alou suggested that Latin players have a representative in the commissioner's office, someone who understood Latin culture and politics, and could explain their unique set of problems. "They do not understand," Alou said, "that these are our people and we owe it to them to play for them."[13] In December 1965, Commissioner William Eckert hired Bobby Maduro to fill exactly this position.

Alou expanded on his people's grievances in a courageous first-person account in *Sport* (as told to Arnold Hano) that fall. "When the military junta 'asked' you to do something, you did it. If I had not played, I would have been called a Communist." Most Latin players came from very impoverished circumstances, and earning the extra money in the off-season (there were no other jobs available) helped feed huge extended families. In the US, the players were often isolated from their teammates by language, and often criticized or even disciplined for speaking Spanish amongst themselves. Alou was very complimentary of the United States, calling it a "wonderful country," but left no doubt where his heart lay. "I am a Dominican. It is my country. And I love it."[14] Alou pulled no punches, criticizing Frick and also Alvin Dark, his own manager. In the words of writer Rob Ruck, "Nobody had ever spoken so eloquently or forcefully about Latin ballplayers, much less prescribed how baseball could and should address their unique concerns."[15]

In early December, not long after the article in *Sport* appeared, the Giants traded Alou to the Milwaukee Braves as part of a seven-player trade. Whether the deal was related to Alou's outspokenness is unclear, but his Latino teammates, including Cepeda, Marichal, and Pagán, were devastated. "I think that was one of the biggest mistakes the Giants ever made," said Marichal decades later.[16] The Giants did have a surplus of outfielders, and needed the pitching they acquired. Jesús Alou, who many thought would surpass both his brothers, was anointed as the new Giants right fielder.

Alou spent the next six years with the Braves. Before reporting in 1964 he had injured his knee playing in the Dominican Winter League. He played through it, knowing that the Braves needed him to play center field, but he got off to a slow start hitting and fielding. In June manager Bobby Bragan (faced with an outfield surplus with the sudden emergence of Rico Carty, a rookie Dominican) asked Alou to play first base, and a few games later he tore cartilage in his knee reaching for a ground ball. He missed a month of action, and hit just .253 with nine home runs on the season. In 1965 he recovered nicely, alternating between first base and the outfield, hitting .297 with 23 home runs.

In 1966 the Braves moved to Atlanta, and Alou responded to the hot climate with his best season. Again playing first base and all three outfield positions, Alou hit .327 with 31 home runs, leading the NL with 218 hits, 122 runs scored, and 355 total bases. He lost out on the league batting title to his brother Matty (.342), who had been traded to Pittsburgh and was capitalizing on his first chance at regular playing time. Felipe returned to the All-Star Game, though he did not see any action.

The Atlanta writers named Alou the team MVP, and some of his teammates were in awe. "I've never seen anyone stand out head and shoulders the way Felipe did," said catcher Joe Torre. "I've never seen anyone hit so consistently well all season long," added Henry Aaron. Alou parried such talk: "If a team isn't going right, what can one man do to help? I think this stuff about leading a team, I wonder if that is really possible." But it was not just his ballplaying. Gene Oliver, a white teammate who lost his first base job to Alou, said, "He is the kind of man you hope your kid will grow up to be."[17]

Alou struggled in 1967, suffering from bone chips in his elbow and falling to .274 with just 15 home runs. He recovered to hit .317 in 1968 (a year that saw league averages plummet to .243), playing in the All-Star game again. His batting average was third highest in the league, and he tied Pete Rose for the lead with 210 hits. After three years of moving around the diamond, Alou played 156 times in center field under new manager Lum Harris.

Alou got off to a great start in 1969, hitting well over .300 through May. On June 2 he broke a finger and missed two weeks after he was hit by a pitch thrown by the Cardinals' Chuck Taylor. During his absence the Braves acquired Tony González from San Diego, and when Alou returned the two platooned in center field. During the Braves' successful drive for the division title, and the subsequent playoff loss to the Mets, Alou got little playing time. For the season he hit just .282 with five home runs. With an outfield surplus, Atlanta dealt the 34-year-old to Oakland for pitcher Jim Nash over the winter.

No longer a star player, in 1970 Alou was the elder statesman on a young A's team filled with up and coming stars. He hit .271 in 154 games. Just a few days into the 1971 season, Oakland dealt Alou to the Yankees for two young pitchers, making room for Joe Rudi in left field. Alou played most of the next three years in New York, hitting .289, .278 and finally .236, moving between the outfield and first base all three seasons. He played 19 games for Montreal in September 1973, and got three at bats for Milwaukee the next April before drawing his final release. Felipe was sad, saying he would "have to get used to the life of a man who can't play baseball."[18]

Alou joined the Montreal Expos organization as an instructor in 1976, but suffered the tragedy of his life in 1976 when his oldest boy, Felipe Jr., an aspiring ballplayer, jumped into a shallow pool and drowned. Alou was so broken up he did not work at all that season, and could not talk about the tragedy for many years. He rejoined the Expos the next year, and spent the next seventeen years as a minor league manager (with a few stints as a major league coach). In the minors, he piloted West Palm Beach, Memphis, Denver, Wichita, and Indianapolis, earning a reputation as a serious and respected teacher of young players. He apparently was offered the job in 1985 to manage the San Francisco Giants but turned it down out of loyalty to the Expos.

In the winter months, Felipe transitioned from player to manager of his longtime team, the Leones del Escogido in the Dominican Republic. Alou managed the club to four league championships (1980-81, 1981-82; 1989-90, 1991-92). Previously, he had also won two Venezuelan titles as skipper of the Caracas Leones (1977-78, 1979-80). In the mid-1980s, he managed Caguas in the Puerto Rican Winter League as well.

The genuinely devoted Alou, who did not drink or smoke or socialize much, has been married four times and has fathered eleven children. As a young man he married María Beltré, from his hometown, and the couple had four children: Felipe Jr., María, José and Moisés. He and Beverley Martin, from Atlanta, had three girls: Christia, Cheri, and Jennifer. His third wife was Elsa Brens, from the Dominican, and the couple had Felipe José and Luis Emilio. In 1985, he married Lucie Gagnon, a French-Canadian, and had two more children, Valerie and Felipe Jr.

"People ask how a man who likes to be home with his family gets married four times," Alou said in 1995. "All the evils that go on in life, the evils of the life of a traveling ballplayer, I wasn't immune to that. But I loved all my wives and children. ... I've been a lucky man. I had two children in my 50's, and God gave us other Felipes."[19] Among his children, José and Felipe José became minor league players, and Moisés made it to the Majors.

In 1986 Alou returned to manage at Single-A West Palm Beach, and remained there for six years, an eternity for a minor-league manager. In 1992 he returned to the major leagues as the bench coach for manager Tom Runnells. After a sluggish start (17-20), general manager Dan Duquette fired Runnells and hired Alou to finish the season. The young team responded with a 70-55 record to finish a strong second to the Pittsburgh Pirates. The 57-year-old Alou's job was secure. "The biggest mistake I've made in my career," said Duquette, "was not recognizing his ability then to be a terrific major league manager. He's one of the best in the game."[20] He was the first of his countrymen to manage a big-league team.

Alou took over a Montreal club filled with young talent, including Larry Walker, Marquis Grissom, Delino DeShields and Wil Cordero. One of the team's best relief pitchers was Mel Rojas, who was Felipe's nephew (the son of his half-brother). The team's left fielder was 25-year-old Moisés Alou, Felipe's son. Moisés had not grown up with Felipe (his parents had divorced when Moisés was two), but they talked frequently and saw each other occasionally over the winter months. "I was the happiest kid in the world," Moisés recalled. "He was the most famous player, maybe the most famous person, on the island, and *he was my father*."[21] Alou was a good young player who developed rapidly under his father's tutelage, turning into a six-time All-Star and one of the better hitters in the National League.

The Expos finished 94-68 in 1993, just three games behind the first-place Phillies. Over the off-season, Duquette traded second baseman DeShields to Los Angeles for 21-year-old pitcher Pedro Martínez, a Dominican who joined Ken Hill and Jeff Fassero to give Alou one of the league's best starting staffs. The fortified club soared to the best record in baseball in 1994, a great team that could hit, field, run and pitch. Unfortunately for Alou and his team, the season was ended in early August by a player's strike, and the club was not able to continue its quest for a championship. The club's 74-40 pace, if maintained over the full schedule, would have yielded 105 wins, the most since the 1986 Mets. Alou was named the National League Manager of the Year.

Compounding the tragedy, the team's ownership was not willing to spend the necessary money to keep the team intact. Before the 1995 season got underway, the Expos had lost Walker, Grissom, Hill, and John Wetteland. Alou's club fell all the way to last place in 1995, before clawing their way back to 88 wins and second place in 1996. But soon Cordero and Fassero departed, followed by Moisés Alou and Pedro Martínez. As the club continued to develop good players (Vladimir Guerrero, Rondell White, Orlando Cabrera, and Javier Vázquez arrived in the late 1990s), the club's five straight fourth-place finishes did not harm Alou's reputation as a manager. It was understood that Alou was doing a fine job with his youngsters, but that the team was not willing to keep them once they attained the seniority that allowed them to earn big money. After another mediocre start in 2001 (21-32), Alou finally was released as manager after nine years.

He spent 2002 as the bench coach for the Tigers (working under Luis Pujols, who had been Alou's bench coach in Montreal). After the 2002 season Alou returned to San Francisco to manage the Giants. Under Dusty Baker, the club had reached the World Series in 2002, but after the season Baker left the club in a contract dispute, joining the Chicago Cubs. The 67-year-old Alou took over.

The Giants' team and personality was dominated by the late-career Barry Bonds, who had set the single-season home record in 2001 and whose days were now filled with home runs, bases on balls and (ever increasingly) steroid allegations. Alou's first club won 100 games, an improvement on the World Series team that had won 95 and the NL wild card. Unfortunately, the 2003 club was upset in playoffs by the young Florida Marlins. Bonds missed 30 games but managed to hit .341 with 45 home runs and 148 walks. The next season Bonds walked a record 232 times and won the batting title, but the club fell to 91 wins, and then to 75 wins in 2005 with Bonds hurt. Moisés Alou rejoined his father in 2005, and had two pretty good seasons with the Giants. After the 2006 season, the 71-year-old Felipe Alou was released from his job as manager.

Alou remained a beloved figure in San Francisco, and was offered a job as a special assistant to general manager Brian Sabean. "I am truly overjoyed to have Felipe remain with the Giants organization," said Sabean. "As he was during his four years as our manager, Felipe will continue to be a huge asset to the ballclub going forward."[22] Alou has worked as a major-league scout, and minor-league instructor, helping Sabean on player evaluation. In 2010 Alou received his first championship ring after the Giants defeated the Rangers in the World Series.

In 2012 he was beginning his sixth season in this position, 57 years after signing his first contract with the Giants. He had begun his career as a stranger in a strange land, but had become one of baseball's most respected men. A three-time All-Star turned into an award-winning manager, who helped many of the game's greatest stars as they began their careers. But he remains most famous as the eldest in one of baseball's greatest families, the brother and father to fellow All-Stars. Very few men have left a greater mark on baseball than Felipe Rojas Alou.

SOURCES

Thanks to Rory Costello for his help, especially for his straightening out my understanding of Felipe Rojas Alou's name.

NOTES

1 Michael Farber, "Diamond Heirs," *Sports Illustrated,* June 19, 1985.

2 Rob Ruck, *Raceball–How the Major Leagues Colonized the Black and Latin Game* (Boston: Beacon Press, 2011), 164.

3 Rob Ruck, *Raceball*, 154.

4 Felipe Alou with Herm Weiskopf, *My Life and Baseball* (Waco, Texas: Word Books, 1967), 1-13.

5 Alou and Weiskopf, *My Life and Baseball*, 14-17.

6 Alou and Weiskopf, *My Life and Baseball*, 18-21.

7 Steve Bitker, *The Original San Francisco Giants: The Giants of '58* (Sports Publishing, Inc., 2001), 68.

8 *The Sporting News*, May 16, 1956, 37.

9 Steve Bitker, *The Original San Francisco Giants*, 68.

10 Steve Bitker, *The Original San Francisco Giants*, 66.

11 Steve Bitker, *The Original San Francisco Giants*, 69.

12 Steve Bitker, *The Original San Francisco Giants*, 70.

13 Bob Stevens, "Felipe Suggests Latins Have Rep in Frick's Office," *The Sporting News*, March 16, 1963: 11.

14 Felipe Alou with Arnold Hano, "Latin-American Ballplayers Need a Bill of Rights," *Sport*, November 1963: 21.

15 Rob Ruck, *Raceball*, 164.

16 Rob Ruck, *Raceball*, 164.

17 John Devaney, "Felipe Alou: The Gentle Howitzer," *Sport*, June 1967, 63.

18 Lou Chapman, "Brewers Salute Tom Murphy as Bullpen Savior," *The Sporting News*, May 18, 1974, 9.

19 Michael Farber, "Diamond Heirs."

20 Michael Farber, "Diamond Heirs."

21 Michael Farber, "Diamond Heirs."

22 Associated Press, "Alou returns to Giants as special assistant," ESPN.com, http://sports.espn.go.com/espn/wire?section=mlb&id=2721755, accessed February 27, 2012.

Jesús Alou

By Mark Armour

He enjoyed a 15-year career in the major leagues and today is well into his sixth decade working in baseball, but Jesús Alou is destined to be remembered as the third brother in an extraordinary baseball family. He might have accomplished less as a player than his two All-Star siblings, but those comparisons are unfair. Jesús had a fine career in his own right as part of the first great wave of Dominican players that came to the major leagues in the late 1950s and early 1960s. Jesús Alou was the 13th Dominican in the majors, though just third in his own family.

José Rojas and Virginia Alou raised six children (Felipe, María, Mateo, Jesús, Juan and Virginia) in their small home in Bajos de Haina, San Cristóbal, near Santo Domingo on the southern coast of the Dominican Republic. Rojas, a carpenter and blacksmith who built their home and others in the neighborhood, also fathered two children with a previous wife who had passed away. Though José was black and Virginia white, this was not unusual in the Dominican and the children knew little racism in their homeland—they were Dominicans. The family was poor, like most people they knew. "We all helped [our father] in the shop," recalled Jesús, "but no money was

Photo courtesy of the National Baseball Hall of Fame

coming in because everyone was poor around there. I was happy, though, just thinking about where my next meal might come from."[1]

Jesús María Rojas Alou was born on March 24, 1942. In keeping with the Latino custom, each parent contributed half of his double surname, but he is known in everyday life as

Jesús Rojas in his homeland. While Felipe was playing in the US minor leagues, a team official mistakenly began identifying him as Felipe Alou, and he did not feel empowered to correct the error. When Mateo and Jesús followed him to the States, they used the Alou surname in order to associate with Felipe.

If this were not enough, many American writers and broadcasters were uncomfortable with his first name (properly pronounced "hay-SOOS"). Although there have been more than a dozen players named Jesús in the major leagues, Jesús Alou was the first, and is still the most prominent. Before his first season with the Giants, a San Francisco writer asked local religious leaders about the situation, and they all agreed that he needed a nickname, that reading "Jesús Saves Giants" in the morning paper would not do. The paper asked readers to write in with their suggestions, which many did.[2] His Latino teammates often called him Chuchito, but the writers often called him Jay. "What," the subject asked in 1965, "is wrong with my real name, Jesús? It is a common name in Latin America like Joe or Tom or Frank in the United States. My parents named me Jesús and I am proud of my name."[3] Thankfully, by the end of his career, everyone, even the writers, called him Jesús.

When Jesús was born, Felipe was nearly seven years old, while Mateo (later known mainly as "Matty" in the U.S.) was three. Unlike his older brothers, Jesús came to baseball slowly and somewhat reluctantly. "I wouldn't even go and watch Felipe and Mateo play on the lots around our home," he recalled. "I went fishing."[4] When he did play, the brothers used bats that they made on their father's lathe.[5] In fact, it was mainly his brothers' success that led Frank (Chick) Genovese, who managed the other Rojas brothers on Leones del Escogido in the Dominican Winter League, to pressure Jesús to give baseball a try. Genovese's cause was joined by Horacio Martínez, a former Negro Leaguer who worked as a bird dog for New York Giants scout Alejandro Pómpez and helped run the Escogido team. In late 1958 the 16-year-old Jesús signed to be the team's batting practice pitcher.

At about the same time, Genovese signed Jesús for the San Francisco Giants organization, as he had done a few years earlier with Felipe and Mateo. The man who would now be known as Jesús Alou had very little organized baseball experience and the Giants' optimism was largely based on the talents of Felipe, who had made the major leagues, and Mateo, who had hit .321 for St. Cloud the previous year. Jesús was assigned to Hastings, Nebraska, which had a team in the short-season Nebraska State League. Alou pitched just two games, allowing 11 runs in five innings, though he did manage to finish 2-for-3 as a batter. "I don't win. I don't lose," Alou recalled of his summer in Nebraska. "I don't do much of anything except brood."[6]

The next winter Alou hurt his arm throwing batting practice for Escogido, and thought his reluctant baseball experiment might have ended before he turned 18. He reported to the minor league camp for the Giants in 1960, and was assigned to Artesia (New Mexico), a Class-D affiliate. Manager George Genovese, the brother of Chick, wanted Alou to give up pitching and play the outfield, like his brothers. Again Alou balked, suggesting instead that he just go home. He finally agreed, and played the entire year in center field. His hitting was great (.352 with 11 home runs and 33 doubles), though his outfield play was a bit raw due to his sore arm. "It was a tougher year on Gil Garrido, our shortstop, than it was for me," Alou remembered. "My arm was so bad that every time a ball was hit out to me Garrido had to race almost to my side to take the cutoff throw."[7]

Tough year or not, Garrido, a future major leaguer from Panama, hit .362 to win the batting title, while Alou led the league with 188 hits. Both were named to the league's postseason All-Star team. After the Artesia season was over, the 18-year-old Alou played a few games with Eugene (Oregon) of the Northwest League, where he hit .350 in 20 at-bats.

Alou's remaining years in the minor leagues were equally successful. Spending the 1961 season back in Eugene, he hit .336, led the league in hits, and was named a postseason All-Star. The next year in El Paso (Texas League), the 20-year-old Alou hit .346. Finally reaching the top rung of the ladder (Triple-A Tacoma) in 1963, Alou hit .324 with 210 hits (a total that broke Matty's former Tacoma all-time record). He was an All-Star at every level, and had done everything he could to earn a spot with the Giants. On September 10, 1963, he finally made it, pinch-hitting against the New York Mets, grounding out against Carlton Willey to lead off the eighth. Willey then retired Mateo and Felipe for a 1-2-3 inning. The three brothers also played the outfield together briefly five days later. During his call-up, Jesús hit .250 in 24 at-bats.

As his major-league career was starting, many people believed that he would surpass both his brothers as a player. Among the believers were his brothers. "Jesús represents our family now," said Felipe. "He has the right approach to baseball. Matty and I are, how you say it? We're satisfied. We're in the majors doing the best we can. But Jesús, he is a restless man. If he can't be supreme, he doesn't want to be at all. He has to be the greatest."[8] As evidence, people could point to his performance with Escogido, where the three brothers had formed the outfield over several winters. As early as 1961, Alejandro Pómpez had said, "Jesús Alou hits the curve ball twice as good as most kids who have been around much longer. The day will come when he'll outshine both Felipe and Matty."[9]

Jesús had already outgrown both of his brothers, reaching 6'2" and 190 pounds by the time of his debut. George Genovese, who had managed Jesús a few times in the minors, was optimistic. "He has live hands and a fast bat and he attacks the ball with great aggressiveness," he said. "When he puts on another 15 pounds, he will have more power than Felipe."[10] Added manager Al Dark, "We think young Alou is one of the finest players our farm system has developed in recent years."[11]

Thoughts of an all-Alou outfield in San Francisco were unrealistic, however. The team already had star performers in center field (Willie Mays), left field (Willie McCovey), and first base (Orlando Cepeda). Felipe Alou had established himself as a good player in right field, while Matty Alou was behind Harvey Kuenn among the extra outfielders. After the season, the Giants partly dealt with the logjam by trading Felipe to the Braves. They announced that Jesús, and not Matty, would get first crack at the right-field job.

The biggest flaw in Jesús's game, then and later, was his inability to take a walk. Even in the 1960s this was remarked upon, though more as a curiosity than a flaw. In 1963 baseball increased the dimension of the strike zone from the bottom of the knee to the top of the shoulders, which did not affect Jesús at all. As a Tacoma writer remarked, "Jesús has a personal strike zone which far exceeds anything considered by rulesmakers."[12] Teammate Juan Marichal remembered, "One time. . . a pitch [came in] about level with Jesús's head. Jesús swung at it and hit a home run to right field. He was that type of hitter."[13] But the Giants were ready to live with his approach. "He swings at quite a few bad balls," admitted farm director Carl Hubbell, "but I call him one of those 'they shall not pass' hitters. If he can reach a ball, he'll swing."[14]

Alou played fairly regularly in 1964, hitting .274 but with little power (three home runs) or plate discipline (13 walks). On July 10 he enjoyed the game of his career, when he went 6-for-6 with a home run in a Giant victory in Chicago's Wrigley Field. His season ended abruptly on September 4 when he was spiked at second base by New York's Ron Hunt, resulting in 91 stitches in his foot, ankle, and calf. He came back the next year to play 143 games, batting .298 with nine home runs. At a time when the league hit just .249, his average was impressive, but his 13 walks gave him only a .317 on-base percentage, just over the league average. With Alou's skill set, he was going to have to hit .320 to be a star, and most observers believed that he would. He turned just 23 in 1965.

Alou reported in 1966 determined to improve his batting eye. "I know pitchers are getting me to swing at bad pitches," he admitted. "I try to cut it down this year. Sometimes maybe I forget, but I am going to cut it way down, I think."[15] Instead, he took a step back, and when he was hitting just .232 with two walks in nearly full-time play on June 13, he was optioned to Phoenix for two weeks, ostensibly because of a sore arm. He hit better upon his return, and got his average up to .259. It was a big year for the other Alou brothers: Matty, traded to the Pirates the previous winter, hit .342 to capture the league batting title; and Felipe, playing for the Braves, finished second at .327 while also clubbing 31 home runs. The talk of Jesús being the best of the Alou brothers had quieted down.

After the 1966 season, Jesús allowed that he wanted to be traded, reasoning that his brothers had found success after leaving San Francisco's Candlestick Park, whose cold winds created difficulties for both hitters and outfielders. During the winter meetings, the Giants reportedly talked to other clubs about Alou, but held on to him.

In 1967 Alou played more or less full-time, and returned to his 1965 levels of hitting: .292 in 510 at bats, though again with little power (five home runs) and few walks (14). Oddly, the Giants used Alou as their primary leadoff hitter. As manager Herman Franks explained, Alou's swinging and missing at so many bad pitches made him a bad hit-and-run guy, so he didn't like him up with men on base. "So," said Franks, "the leadoff position is where he can do the least harm and definitely the most good."[16] Alou hit .308 as the leadoff batter, and hit .337 when leading off innings.

The 26-year-old Alou played left and right fields for the Giants in 1968, starting 97 games and playing parts of 23 others. He regressed a bit from his 1967 comeback, hitting just .263 with no home runs and nine walks in 436 plate appearances. This turned out to be his final go-round with the Giants, as on October 15 Alou was selected by the Montreal Expos in an expansion draft to stock the two new National League teams.

Montreal reportedly turned down several trade offers for Alou, including one from the Astros for Mike Cuellar. After several weeks of speculation, on January 22 the Expos dealt Alou and Donn Clendenon to the Astros for outfielder Rusty Staub. Six weeks later Clendenon announced that he would retire rather than report to Houston, nullifying the trade for a few weeks. Eventually the Expos substituted two pitchers and some money to get the deal done. Houston manager Harry Walker coveted Alou, as he wanted more speed in the outfield. Walker had long fancied himself a hitting guru, and his biggest success story had been Matty Alou, who became a consistent .330 hitter after joining up with Walker in Pittsburgh in 1966.

Jesús Alou began the 1969 season as the Astros' right fielder and leadoff hitter, and stroked three hits in his first game. He then went into a long slump that lasted most of the year, though his season was partly saved by a .328 final month. On June 10, while playing left field, Alou was involved in a brutal collision with shortstop Héctor Torres. His teammate's forehead hit Alou's face and caused him to swallow his tongue. Pirates trainer Tony Bartirome may have saved the unconscious Alou's life when he pried open his mouth, inserted a rubber tube and breathed into it, which opened his air passage enough so that Alou could resume breathing. Alou and Torres were each carried off the field and rushed to the hospital—both players suffered concussions while Alou fractured his jaw. He missed six weeks of action. For the season, he hit just .248.

Alou was not a regular to start the 1970 season, but his consistent hitting eventually got him an everyday role. He ended up hitting .306 in 115 games, with a career-high 21 walks. "To me, hitting .300 is not all that big an issue," he said late in the year. "What is important for me as the leadoff hitter is to get on base. I think I've been good, actually, ever since I came out of the hospital last year."[17] Once again he excelled as a leadoff hitter—he hit .392 leading off games, and hit .328 when leading off an inning. In 1971, he started even hotter, hitting over .350 into June, before slowly dropping off. A bad September left him at .279 for the season.

Through it all, baseball people liked having Jesús Alou around. Jim Bouton, an Astros teammate in 1969 and 1970, described him in his second book, *I'm Glad You Didn't Take It Personally*. "We called him J. or Jesús, never hay-soos. . . . J. is one of the most delicate, sensitive, nicest men I have ever met. He'd walk a mile out of his way to drop a coin in some beggar's cup." Bouton then went on to describe how Alou's sensitivity made him a comic foil for practical joker Doug Rader's most disgusting antics.

"Alou is popular with his teammates because of his inherent good nature and philosophical way of looking at things," said another writer in 1971. "And Alou is interesting to watch during a game." He drew much comment throughout his career for all his mannerisms in the batter's box—he held the bat vertical directly behind his right ear, then repeatedly rotated his neck. "People write letters asking why I jerk my neck," Alou said. "I can't answer except to say it's not a back problem. It's just a mental problem."[18] Early in his career Dodger pitcher Don Drysdale thought Alou might be trying to steal the catcher's signs, and subsequently knocked Alou down with a pitch.[19] Yet the habit remained.

Alou also had a very self-deprecating sense of humor. Late in his career he failed to reach a fly ball in the outfield, and observed, "Ten years ago, I would have overrun it."[20] When reminiscing about his years in the game, he would often recall moments when he forgot how many outs there were or the time he overran a base.[21] Despite his relatively modest accomplishments, he stayed in the game a long time because his managers and teammates liked him so much. He was quiet and dignified, and often could be seen reading a Bible at his locker.

As Jimmy Wynn recounted in his autobiography, though, Harry Walker's inveterate tinkering with hitters and their approach at the plate managed to infuriate even "The J. Alou"—as Jesús jocularly referred to himself. "The Hat" went so far as to break Alou's bat in order to make sure that his player used a Harry Walker model. Another clubhouse incident a few days later finally set Alou off, and Wynn later wrote, "We are laughing in shock over the discovery that he is capable of anger at this level."[22]

With the emergence of Bob Watson and Cesar Cedeño, and the presence of Wynn, Alou no longer had a regular job after the

1971 season. He hit .312 in 1972 as a reserve outfielder and pinch-hitter, but just .236 in the same role the following season. On July 31, 1973, his contract was sold to the Oakland Athletics.

The A's had won the World Series in 1972 and would repeat the next two seasons. Alou played 20 games over the last two months of the 1973 season, mainly in left field, and hit .306. When regular center fielder Bill North sprained his ankle that September, it opened the door for Jesús to play in the postseason. He hit 2-for-6 in the ALCS, but just 3-for-19 in the World Series. The next year he stayed with the A's the entire year and got 232 plate appearances, mainly as a designated hitter, hitting .262. He hit just twice in the postseason, including a pinch single in the first game of the ALCS. Matty Alou had helped win a World Series for the A's in 1972, and now Jesús had won back-to-back with the same club.

The next spring Alou was released. "Maybe I'm overrating myself," he said. "I think this team needs a guy who does the type of job I can do."[23] He was soon picked up by the New York Mets. "I was offered more money to play with my brother, Matty, in Japan," Alou said, "but I prefer to play in the United States." Alou served as a reserve outfielder and pinch-hitter, hitting .265 in 108 plate appearances.

In March 1976 he was released again, and this time he headed back to the Dominican, where he remained for two years. Besides playing winter ball in his homeland, he and a friend tried to start a business. "We were going to start a watch-assembly plant in the Dominican Republic," he recalled. "We would buy the parts in other countries and assemble the watches there. But the government down there didn't like the idea."[24] After two years away, Alou returned to the major leagues with the Astros in 1978, and hit .324 in a reserve role. When he returned the next year, the 37-year-old took on the added role of batting coach. He hit .256 this time around in just 43 at bats, though his relatively high walk total (6) gave him a respectable .349 on-base percentage.

After the 1979 season Alou drew his release, and his major-league career was over. He finished with a respectable .280 batting average, but his walk rate of just 3 per 100 plate appearances was the lowest in the 20th century for someone who played 1,000 games. He played parts of 15 seasons in the majors, and won two World Series. In the Dominican, he starred for many years for Escogido with his two brothers. He was Rookie of the Year in 1960-61. His lifetime stats at home were .302 with 20 homers and 339 RBIs in 20 seasons (12 for Escogido and 8 for archrival Licey). He played in five Caribbean Series (1973, 1974, 1977, 1978, and 1980), hitting .351 with two homers and 13 RBIs. One of his highlights in a Dominican uniform came during the 1973 edition in Caracas, Venezuela, when he was 12 for 24 (.500) as Licey won the tournament.[25]

Jesús Alou married Angela Hanley in the late 1960s, and the couple raised five children—Angela, Jesús Jr., María de Jesús, Claudia, and Jeimy—in the Dominican Republic. After his playing career ended, Alou moved back home and remained there, still fishing and swimming in the nearby waters in the summer. He lived not far from where he grew up, and not far from the homes of his brothers and sisters. "I guess we look much richer to the people here than we really are," he once observed.

Although he did some managing in the Dominican winter league, Alou turned to scouting when his pitching coach with Escogido, Bob Gebhard, became an executive with the Montreal Expos. Jesús said, "I imagine he saw me working with kids. Even when I was a player, I liked to work with kids." In typical form, he added, "I have very high blood pressure. I don't think I can stand managing."[26]

He continued to work for American baseball, moving from the Expos to the Marlins. Since 2002, he has been the Dominican scouting director for the Boston Red Sox. He has also served as director of the team's Dominican Summer League operations, much the same role as he had held with the Marlins' Dominican academy.

Jesús came back to San Francisco in 2003 for Opening Day, joined by his two brothers, one of whom (Felipe) was now managing the Giants. They had all accomplished so much in the game, forty years after playing in the same outfield. "I have never dreamed anything in baseball," Jesús said. "Everything has been a surprise. Every day is a new surprise. Felipe being manager in San Francisco makes me proud. It's another surprise."[27]

Dominicans have come to play a huge role in American baseball, following in the giant footsteps of Felipe, Mateo, and Jesús Alou. Late in his career, Jesús was asked to compare the skills of the three Alous. "Felipe is a very tough guy in baseball," he said, "tougher than all of us. Matty was smaller and had to take more advantage of his ability, the guy who does more thinking. Me, I wasn't as tough as Felipe or as thinking as Matty. One thing we had in common: we didn't like to strike out too much, maybe because we used to play with rubber balls in our backyard. As long as a guy didn't strike out, he could keep batting, and we all liked to bat."[28] The brothers played over 5,000 major-league games between them.

Jesús Alou spent many years in the game as a player, and is still involved in finding players for the Major Leagues. He was a vital part of a great baseball family, and his legacy will live on.

An updated version of this article appeared in Mustaches and Mayhem: Charlie O's Three Time Champions: The Oakland Athletics: 1972-74 *(SABR, 2015), edited by Chip Greene.*

ACKNOWLEDGMENTS

Thanks to Rory Costello for his editing and for adding a few additional stories to the article. Thanks also to Gabriel Schechter, Rod Nelson, and Matías Alou.

NOTES

1. Joséph Durso, "We Band of Brothers," *The New York Times*, August 14, 1975.

2. Prescott Sullivan, "Wanted—Name for New Right Fielder!" *San Francisco Examiner*, March 6, 1964.

3. Bob Stevens, "Jesús Alou Could Be the Best in Family," *The Sporting News*, July 3, 1965, 7.

4. Bob Stevens, "The Little Alou," *Sport*, September 1965, 81.

5. Jack McDonald, "No. 3 Alou May Gain No. 1 Spot," *The Sporting News*, April 6, 1963, 10.

6. Stevens, "The Little Alou," 81.

7. Stevens, "The Little Alou," 81.

8. Stevens, "The Little Alou," 80.

9. Jack McDonald, "Giants Phenoms Train in Lap of Luxury," *The Sporting News*, April 12, 1961, 9.

10. McDonald, "No. 3 Alou May Gain No. 1 Spot," 10.

11. Jack McDonald, "Giants," *The Sporting News*, February 22, 1964, 24.

12. Ed Honeywell, "Jesús Alou Gives Up Passes to Hit Away," *The Sporting News*, August 10, 1963, 33.

13. Juan Marichal with Low Froodman, *Juan Marichal: My Journey from the Dominican Republic to Cooperstown*, Minneapolis, Minnesota: MVP Books, 2011, 114. Marichal's memory was fuzzy about the details. He recalled it as being in San Francisco against Jim Bunning of the Phillies, but SABR's Home Run Log shows no such record.

14. Jack McDonald, "Giants Paint Pennant Picture With Jesús Alou and Jim Ray Hart." *The Sporting News*, January 4, 1964, 10.

15. Jack McDonald, "Those Bad Pitches Look Too Juicy for Jesús Alou to Resist," *The Sporting News*, April 2, 1966, 17.

16. Bob Stevens, "Alou a Goliath in Giant Leadoff Spot," *The Sporting News*, July 1, 1967, 16T.

17. John Wilson, "Jay Alou Giving Brothers Lesson in Swatting Art," *The Sporting News*, August 29, 1970, 17.

18. John Wilson, "A Sizzling Bat Pushes Alou Into Astros' Lineup," *The Sporting News*, June 26, 1971 24.

19. Stevens, "The Little Alou," 80.

20. Gordon Verrell, "Dodgers Tap Rookie Wall to Add Bullpen Depth," *The Sporting News*, January 10, 1976, 28.

21. Mike Mandel, *SF Giants. An Oral History* (Santa Cruz: self-published, 1979), 149.

22. Jimmy Wynn and Bill McCurdy, *Toy Cannon: The Autobiography of Baseball's Jimmy Wynn*, Jefferson, North Carolina: McFarland & Co., 2010, 121-122.

23. Ron Bergman, "Happy Charlie Does Jig Over Hippity-Hoppy," *The Sporting News*, April 19. 1975, 5.

24. Harry Shattuck, "Bat Artist Alou Doubles as Astro bat tutor," *The Sporting News*, March 17, 1979, 51.

25. Gustavo Rodríguez, "Jesús Alou: Ganó la triple corona en SC en 1973," *Hoy* (Santo Domingo, Dominican Republic, January 26, 2012.

26. Gordon Edes, "Alou Acts as Scout, Dreams as a Player," *South Florida Sun-Sentinel*, February 8, 1994.

27. Associated Press, "Alou reunion takes place in San Francisco," *Albany Times-Union*, April 8, 2003.

28. Joséph Durso, "We Band of Brothers," *The New York Times*, August 14, 1975.

Matty Alou

By Mark Armour

Most famous today for being the second of three baseball-playing brothers, Mateo Alou was part of the first wave of Dominicans who helped change the very culture of American baseball in the 1960s. After years of sporadic playing time, often competing with his brothers, he finally left them and became a batting champion, and one of baseball's unique and interesting stars.

Mateo Rojas Alou was born on December 22, 1938, in Bajos de Haina, San Cristóbal, not far from Santo Domingo on the southern coast of the Dominican Republic. His father, José Rojas, was a carpenter and blacksmith who built the family home and many of the others in the neighborhood. Rojas fathered two children with his first wife, who died young, then six more with Virginia Alou. Mateo was her second of four boys. Virginia was white, though Mateo and his siblings did not think of themselves as belonging to any race—they were Dominicans. They were also poor, as José's income was dependent on the local economy and the ability of his customers to pay him. The Rojas family had a house, but they did not always have food.

The subject is known in his home country as Mateo Rojas Alou, informally Mateo Rojas, and he and his brothers are known as the Rojas brothers. Early in Felipe's minor-league days he began to be called Felipe Alou (also mispronounced "Al-oo" instead of "Al-oh"), and the mistake was never corrected. The brothers Felipe, Mateo and Jesús are therefore all known in the US as Alou, and Mateo was often Anglicized to Matty in the States. For this article, the subject will be referred to as Mateo or Matty Alou.

Mateo later said that his father played baseball as a boy until he saw a friend die after being struck by a ball, though Felipe did not remember this. "I can say for sure my father never threw a ball to me," Felipe recalled.[1] The boys spent hours in the nearby ocean fishing for grouper or snapper, helping out their father in his shop, or playing ball in their yard. Their ball was often a coconut husk or half a rubber ball, their bat a tree limb, and their gloves made from strips of canvas. Unlike Felipe, who planned to be a doctor and spent a year in college, Mateo left school after eighth grade and hoped to become a sailor. In the meantime he caddied at the Santo Domingo Golf Club and played more baseball.

In 1956 the 17-year-old Mateo Alou played for Aviación Militar, the Dominican Air Force team, sponsored by General Ramfis Trujillo, the son of the Dominican dictator Rafael

Photo courtesy of the National Baseball Hall of Fame

Trujillo. Alou's teammates included future major-league teammates Juan Marichal and Manny Mota. Although they were all members of the Air Force, they were mainly ballplayers recruited because the younger Trujillo wanted to field the best baseball team in the Caribbean. "We were soldiers," laughed Mota. "The only thing, we have no guns." It was still serious business—when the team lost a double-header in Manzanillo, the General launched an investigation, and accused the players of drinking (a charge Marichal denies). The entire team was put in jail for five days.[2]

In late 1955 Felipe had signed a baseball contract with Horacio Martínez, a former Negro Leaguer who worked as a bird dog for the New York Giants scout Alejandro Pómpez. With the considerable help of Pómpez and Martínez, the Giants got a jump on the rest of baseball in the Caribbean, especially the fertile Dominican Republic, inking Marichal, Mota, and eventually all three Alou brothers. Mateo signed in the winter of 1956-57, at the age of 18.

Unlikely many blacks and Latinos of the era, Mateo Alou spent the bulk of his minor league days outside of the deep South. But even in Michigan City, Indiana, where he began his career in 1957, he and Manny Mota were turned away from a restaurant because of their skin color. During spring training in Florida one year, Mota and Alou were placed in a police lineup because a white woman said a black ballplayer had molested her.[3] The Dominicans had not encountered much racism in their own country, but in the US they had to do so while also not understanding the language. "The ballplayers always treat us good," Alou recalled. "The only trouble we had was in the streets, the restaurants, the hotels, all those things. We used to cry but we didn't fight."[4]

Alou hit just .247 for Michigan City in full-time play in 1957. He then played winter ball at home in the Dominican League for the first time. Promoted to St. Cloud of the Northern League in 1958, he recovered to hit .321 for the first-place club and made the postseason All-Star team as an outfielder. For 1959 he reached Single-A Springfield, Massachusetts, playing with several future major leaguers, including Mota, Marichal, and Tom Haller. Springfield won the Eastern League championship, with Alou contributing a .288 average and 11 home runs to the cause.

Unlike older brother Felipe, who grew to a chiseled 6-feet and 200 pounds, or his younger brother Jesús, who was even taller, Mateo was later listed officially at 5-9 and 160 pounds as a major leaguer (though he was likely shorter and lighter, especially in the minors).[5] Unlike his brothers, he was left-handed, and got a lot of bunt singles and infield hits. "Nobody taught me how to play ball, nobody taught me how to hit," Alou recalled. " But I practiced, I had good reflexes, was quick moving. Good eyes. And it came natural."[6]

Alou spent the 1960 season with the Tacoma Giants of the Pacific Coast League. This was another good club filled with future major-league players, and Alou hit .306 with 14 home runs as the center fielder. In September he earned a callup to San Francisco, and appeared in four games at the end of the year. In his first big league at-bat, he singled off the Dodgers' Larry Sherry.

Alou's rise to stardom was slow and sometimes frustrating, and he believed he was not given the opportunities he deserved. In truth, he faced some pretty stiff competition, including Willie Mays in center field (Alou's best position) and his brother Felipe in right field. In 1961 Alou made the club and played parts of 81 games in the outfield or as a pinch-hitter, batting .310 with six home runs in 200 at-bats. He was just 23 years old and behind a few other players on his team, but after the season farm director Carl Hubbell suggested he would not trade Matty Alou for the Dodgers stars Willie Davis *and Tommy Davis*.[7]

The next season he played the same role, batting .292 in 195 at-bats, and had a big part in the National League pennant chase. In the last seven games of the regular season, he played six complete games, and hit 14-for-27 (.510). In the decisive game of the three-game playoff series with the Dodgers, with the Giants trailing 4-2 in the ninth inning, Alou led off with a pinch-hit single that launched the game-winning rally. He played in six of the seven World Series games, getting four hits in 12 at-bats. In the ninth inning of the final game, with the Giants down 1-0 to the Yankees, Alou led off with a pinch-hit bunt single, advanced to third base on Willie Mays' two-out double, but was stranded there when Willie McCovey lined out. There was talk over that winter that third-base coach Whitey Lockman should not have held Alou at third on Mays' hit, but most observers, including Alou himself, felt that he would have been out easily at home plate.

Alou's transition to the big leagues was aided immeasurably by the presence of so many other Latino players on the Giants. Besides his brother Felipe, his teammates included Dominicans Marichal and Mota and Puerto Ricans José Pagán and Orlando Cepeda, all of whom were very close. When he first arrived in San Francisco Mateo and Marichal lived in the home of an older woman named Blanche Johnson, who taught them to speak English, and cooked both American and Dominican food for them.[8]

On October 24, 1962, Mateo married María Teresa Vásquez in the Dominican Republic. During the 1963 season he, Felipe, Marichal, and their three wives lived together in a house in San Francisco. "We got along very, very well together," recalled Marichal. "Felipe is the godfather of my oldest daughter, Rosie, and I am the godfather of a daughter of his. And Mateo is the godfather of my second girl, Elsie, while I'm the godfather of his daughter [Teresa]. That is a serious obligation for a Dominican, to be a godfather."[9] The couples spent a lot of time together away from the park. Mateo, the former caddy, taught the others to play golf, while the wives helped each other make their way in a strange country. After the season, they all returned to their homeland for the winter baseball season.

In spring training of 1963, working hard in hopes of earning more playing time, Alou badly hurt his knee running to first base during an exhibition game in El Paso, Texas. He played through it, but struggled all summer long. Felipe, who often acted as the reserved Mateo's spokesman with club management, urged the Giants to send his brother to a doctor. Instead, in early August, they sent him to Tacoma. He returned in September, but it was a lost year: 11 hits in 76 at-bats for a .145 batting average. The only good memory from the season came in September, when younger brother Jesús joined the Giants and helped form an all-Alou outfield late in the game on September 15. The three played in a same game a few other times, but their time as teammates was brief—after the season, Felipe was dealt to the Milwaukee Braves.

Heading into the 1964 season, Mateo had been passed by Jesús on the Giants depth chart. With Willie Mays and Willie McCovey in the outfield, and the veteran Harvey Kuenn still productive, Mateo returned to his fifth-outfielder/pinch-hitter role. Hitting just .219 on June 2, Alou was struck on the wrist by a pitch from Pittsburgh's Bob Veale, breaking a bone, and spent five weeks home in the Dominican Republic. He hit better upon his return (.282), so well that he was used fairly regularly in September. He managed to get into 110 games, including 49 starts, and hit .264. For a man who had very little power and drew few walks, the batting average was too low for an outfielder even in the 1960s.

Even so, based on his strong second half, in 1965 new manager Herman Franks gave Alou a lot of playing time—but he did not hit. "'65 was my worst year in baseball," recalled Alou, "because they gave me a chance and I didn't do anything." He hit just .231 in 324 at-bats. His most memorable game that season came on August 26 at Pittsburgh's Forbes Field when he pitched the final two innings of an 8-0 loss. He allowed no runs and struck out three, including Willie Stargell twice. "I just threw him slow curve, slow curve," Alou said. "And I know I would get him out again if I faced him."[10]

Despite his star turn on the mound, it came as no surprise when the Giants traded Alou to the Pirates on December 1, 1965. In later years the Giants were criticized for their handling of Alou, although they gave him 1,131 plate appearances and he had not contributed much since 1962. Alou welcomed the deal, later saying, "My brother didn't tell me anything about Willie Mays. I just signed because I liked to play the game."[11]

Pittsburgh manager Harry Walker had coveted Alou, and had big plans for him. Walker spent many years as a hitting instructor in the game, usually trying to get everyone to choke up, and hit the ball down and to the opposite field, as Walker himself had done as a player. This approach backfired with many people, but Alou was his best and most famous success story. "The Hat" worked tirelessly with Alou, getting him to stop trying to pull the ball and instead hit nearly everything up the middle or to left field. To force this, he gave Alou a much bigger bat—38 ounces—and asked him to stroke down on the ball and use his speed. As a pull hitter, Alou had held the bat low and swung with an uppercut. Walker had him hold the bat high and straight up, forcing him to swing downward on the ball. Walker set up a platoon in centerfield with Alou and old friend Manny Mota, giving the left-handed Alou most of the at-bats, and hit Alou in the leadoff position whenever he played.

Alou took to the new batting style extremely well. Bunting and slapping singles, Alou put up a league-leading .342 batting average, more than 100 points higher than his effort in 1965. Since Mota was also hitting very well, finishing at .332, the platoon in center field remained—Alou started 121 games, just twice against a left-handed starter, but managed 535 at-bats. Finishing second was Atlanta's Felipe Alou at .327. Mateo still did not walk much or hit for power, but at a time when the league's on-base percentage was .313, Alou's .373 mark was eighth highest in the league, and tops among players who primarily hit leadoff for their teams.

Alou's sudden fame raised a lot of questions about what had changed for him. He credited Walker's tutelage, escaping San Francisco's challenging Candlestick Park, and platooning with Mota, which allowed him plenty of rest. Late in the season, when it appeared that one of the Alous might win the batting title, Felipe allowed that he was rooting for his brother. "It would be a wonderful thing for Matty to win it," said Felipe. "Wonderful for the Alous, and wonderful for baseball in the Dominican Republic. We always sort of took care of Matty because he was so small. Now look at him leading all of us in hitting!"[12]

Alou's next two years were nearly carbon copies of 1966. He continued to platoon with Mota, his roommate and best friend, and both men continued to hit. In 1967 Alou hit .338 (third in the league) in 550 at bats, starting just four times against left-handers, while Mota hit .321, also backing up the other outfield positions. (Walker could not easily play both of them—his left fielder was Willie Stargell, and his right fielder was Roberto Clemente.) The acquisition of Maury Wills moved Alou out of the leadoff spot in the order, and by 1968 he was often hitting third or fourth. In 1968 Alou hit .332, just three points behind Pete Rose for the batting title, in 598 at-bats. He also played in his first All-Star Game, legging out an infield single off Sam McDowell in his only at-bat.

After the 1968 season the Pirates lost Mota to the Montreal Expos in the expansion draft. Although Alou had faced lefties a bit more in 1968, the next year he became a full-time player for the first time in his career. Playing 162 games, he led the league in at-bats, hits (231), singles (183), and doubles (41), while hitting .331 at the top of the order. He played the entire All-Star Game in center field, garnering two hits and a walk in five appearances in the NL's 9-3 win. The 30-year-old Alou, after hitting .330 or higher for four straight seasons, had become a full-fledged star and one of the more interesting players in the game. He was a leadoff hitter who did not walk much—just 42 times in 1969—yet he was valuable because he was able to maintain his high batting average. His 698 at-bats set a new major-league record, since broken.

Although he faced occasional criticism for his defense, especially for being shy about crashing into fences, Alou had a strong and accurate throwing arm and often was among the league leaders in outfield assists, finishing first with 15 in 1970. "I play deep because this is a big park and the ball carries deep. I'm not fence shy. They said that in San Francisco. You know, sometimes everybody want you to be Willie Mays. Sometimes they say, 'Why aren't you like Willie Mays?' Well, there is only one Willie Mays."[13]

In 1970 Alou slipped to .297, but still finished with 201 hits, fifth best in the league. The Pirates had been a good team for a few years but finally broke through and won the Eastern Division, and Alou finished 3-for-12 in the three-game loss to the Reds. During the offseason the Pirates, wanting to make room in center field for youngster Al Oliver, sent him to the Cardinals in a four-player deal. Thus, Alou missed out on the Pirates championship season of 1971. "I think of myself mostly as a Pirate," Mateo said years later. "Because they gave me confidence. They treat me good, and I had the best years of my life there."[14]

Alou spent most of the next two seasons for the Cardinals and played well. He hit .315 in 1971, with 192 hits, playing center field for half the season and (after the recall of rookie José Cruz) mostly first base in the second half. In 1972 he switched between first base and right field and hit .314. In late August he was traded to the Oakland A's, a young team on the verge of winning their first of three straight championships. He played nearly every day the rest of the season in right field, hitting .281. He played well in the ALCS (.381 with four doubles), but slumped in the World Series (just 1-for-24). Still, after just missing in 1962 Alou finally tasted the champagne of a World Series victory.

Not long after the Series, Alou was traded again, this time to the New York Yankees, reuniting with his brother Felipe. He hit well in New York, .296 in 123 games as the regular right fielder, but when the team fell out of contention they sold him back to the Cardinals, who were in contention for a division title, on September 6. (On the very same day, the club sold Felipe to the Montreal Expos.) Mateo was not thrilled with the trade, delayed reporting for a few days, and was used solely as a pinch-hitter in the waning weeks of the pennant race. After the season the Cardinals sold him to the San Diego Padres, but after hitting just .188 in 81 at-bats he drew his release in July 1974, ending his major-league career. He ended with a .307 career average over 14 seasons, with three All-Star appearances and two trips to the World Series.

The 35-year-old Alou next took his career to Japan, spending the rest of the 1974 season and two more with the Taiheiyo Club Lions in the Nippon Pro League. He hit .312 in his first half-season, then .282 and .261 his next two years. He finished with a .283 lifetime average in Japan. "I didn't like playing there really," Alou recalled. "I played there because I had to. I had three kids to support. It was too hard there. Too much practice, too much traveling, had to travel almost every day."[15]

Alou returned home. A star for 15 seasons with Leones del Escogido in the Dominican Winter League, his .327 career average is second only to Manny Mota's .333 in league history. He won batting titles in 1966-67 (.363) and 1968-69 (.390). He later coached and managed in the league for many years. While the Alou brothers gained fame for manning the same outfield for the Giants for a parts of a few games in 1963, this was not such a big deal to the Rojas brothers—in the Winter League, for many seasons they formed the Escogido outfield, and still dominate the all-time leader boards for the club. For the 1961-62 and 1962-63 winters, when political unrest shut down the Dominican league, Mateo played winter ball in Venezuela.

Although Alou spent most of his post-playing years in his homeland, he worked for several major league organizations over the years. He scouted for the Tigers for a while in the late 1980s. He also spent many years as the Dominican scouting supervisor for the San Francisco Giants. He coached a single season (1994) for a club in the Dominican Summer League (a circuit affiliated with the US minor leagues). In 2007 he was honored at San Francisco's AT&T Park, celebrating his induction to the Hispanic Heritage Baseball Museum Hall of Fame. Brother Felipe, then manager of the Giants, had been inducted in 2003.

Mateo remained a private person who was not often in the news in the States. His 1962 marriage to Teresa lasted the rest of his life. They raised three children—Mateo Jr., Matías, and Teresa—primarily in their homeland. Mateo died at age 72 in Santo Domingo, Dominican Republic on November 3, 2011, after suffering a stroke. He had stopped working for the Giants a few years earlier for health reasons. He was survived by his wife of 49 years, his three children, four grandchildren, three brothers and two sisters.

An updated version of this article appeared in *Mustaches and Mayhem: Charlie O's Three Time Champions: The Oakland Athletics: 1972-74* (SABR, 2015), edited by Chip Greene.

ACKNOWLEDGMENTS

Thanks to Rory Costello for his assistance.

NOTES

1. Michael Farber, "Diamond Heirs," *Sports Illustrated*, June 19, 1985.
2. Rob Ruck, *The Tropic of Baseball* (Lincoln: University of Nebraska, 1998), 70-71.
3. Rob Ruck, *Raceball–How the Major Leagues Colonized the Black and Latin Game* (Boston: Beacon Press, 2011), 153-4.
4. Mike Mandel, *SF Giants. An Oral History* (Santa Cruz: self-published, 1979), 123
5. Charles Einstein, "Alou Alou," *Sport*, September 1962: 25.
6. Mike Mandel, *SF Giants*, 123.
7. *The Sporting News*, May 2, 1962.
8. Juan Marichal with Charles Einstein, *A Pitcher's Story* (New York: Doubleday, 1967), 100-101.
9. Rob Ruck, *The Tropic of Baseball*, 78.
10. Mike Mandel, *SF Giants*, 124.
11. Mike Mandel, *SF Giants*, 123.
12. *The Sporting News*, September 24, 1966.
13. Lou Prato, "Matty Alou: 'Wait, Wait, Wait,' *Sport*, October 1968: 38.
14. Mike Mandel, *SF Giants*, 124.
15. Mike Mandel, *SF Giants*, 125.

Joaquín Andújar

By Malcolm Allen

Joaquín Andújar was a fierce competitor and entertaining showman for 13 major-league seasons. The hard-throwing right-hander was the first starting pitcher from the Dominican Republic to earn a World Series victory, and no big leaguer won more games in the 1984 and 1985 seasons combined. With his emotional, all-out style of play, Andújar also won a Gold Glove and homered from both sides of the plate, but his volcanic temper also led to an infamous World Series ejection that marred the four-time All-Star's reputation. Andújar was an unpredictable athlete whose career can perhaps best be described by his own signature quote: "One word in America says it all – youneverknow."[1]

Joaquín Andújar Sabino was born on December 21, 1952, in San Pedro de Macoris, a sugar mill town on the Dominican Republic's southeastern coast. He was the only child of José Joaquín Andújar and Clara Sabino, a short-lived couple who split up before he could walk. His paternal grandparents, Saturno and Juana Garcia Andújar, raised him in their zinc-roofed home between San Pedro de Macoris's famed Catedral San Pedro Apostol to the east, and the Iguamo River to the west.

During Andújar's formative years, the Dominican Republic was enduring the final trimester of Rafael L. Trujillo's three decades of dictatorship. Most of the country's resources were firmly controlled by "El Jefe," including the seasonal sugar industry, which was San Pedro de Macoris's chief employer. Andújar's grandfather worked at the Ingenio Porvenir, second oldest of the seven sugar mills dotting the city. Porvenir means "future" and, for Andújar and most of his peers, growing up to a life of labor there was indeed a probable outcome.

The 1960s were as turbulent in the Dominican Republic as they were in the United States. Andújar was 8 years old when Trujillo was assassinated in 1961. By the year he turned 13, tens of thousands of US troops occupied the country briefly to quell a Dominican civil war following a series of regime changes. "Trying to Prevent Another Cuba" was the snag line on a *Time* magazine cover story describing the events of 1965. Meanwhile, the first wave of Dominican ballplayers was establishing a pipeline that would soon see their country surpass Cuba as the majors' primary source of Latin American talent.

Andújar actually preferred basketball initially but, like much of his country, he was fascinated when the 1962 San Francisco Giants surged to the National League pennant

Photo courtesy of the National Baseball Hall of Fame

with four Dominicans on the roster. The first two big leaguers from San Pedro de Macoris – Amado Samuel of the Milwaukee Braves and Manny Jimenez of the Kansas City Athletics – debuted the same year. Baseball had been popular in the Dominican back to the late nineteenth century, but suddenly it was everywhere, and Andújar began playing as much as he could. "Without a good glove, a decent bat or a pair of cleats, because everybody is very poor," he recalled. "We used to make a rag ball, or we bought a rubber ball and played in the streets."[2]

Andújar's first amateur club was called Jabon Hispano and, when he got older, he played for a team managed by Pedro Gonzalez, the first Dominican to play for the New York Yankees. Andújar was a switch-hitting center fielder who usually hit cleanup, an all-or-nothing free swinger with a combustible temper. Once, he destroyed his own jersey when Gonzalez took him out of a game. It was a big deal, because the incident occurred around the same time Andújar quit attending José Joaquin Pérez High School because his family couldn't afford to buy him pants or shoes. With his grandfather nearing retirement age, the boiler room at Ingenio Porvenir looked increasingly like the setting for Andújar's future.

Tetelo Vargas Stadium opened in San Pedro de Macoris just before Andújar's 7th birthday. The Estrellas Orientales of the Dominican winter league played there, and Andújar spent a good chunk of his teen years shagging balls for them and studying major leaguers like Braves slugger Rico Carty up close. The facility was available to youth leagues, too, and it was there that Wilfredo Calvino noticed a particularly strong Andújar throw from center field. Calvino was a former minor-league catcher from Cuba who scouted for the Cincinnati Reds. "He asked me if I wanted to become a pitcher," Andújar said. "I told him that I didn't care, that the only thing I wanted was to go to the United States to make money and help my family and myself."[3]

Andújar signed with the Reds in November 1969, and reported to rookie league the following summer along with two other 17-year-old Calvino signees from San Pedro. Incredibly all three of them would play in the major leagues. Santo Alcala was a tall, happy pitcher who'd room with Andújar in the minors for most of the next five years, while Arturo DeFreites was a serious, muscular third baseman who'd wallop 32 homers one year in Triple A when he filled out. On a diet of hot dogs and French fries because he didn't know how to order anything else in English, Andújar struck out more batters than any right-handed pitcher in the Gulf Coast League in 1970, including a handful in the circuit's all-star game. Upon returning home, he joined the legendary Leones del Escogido – winner of half of the last dozen Dominican League championships—for seven appearances before his 18th birthday.

A promotion to the Northern League Sioux Falls Packers in 1971 proved extremely challenging, however. Tougher competition, real road trips, and a manager who didn't speak Spanish added up to a difficult season. Andújar led the team in wild pitches and was demoted to the bullpen. At the end of the season, manager Dave Pavlesic told the high-kicking Andújar, "You're not Juan Marichal. You'd better learn how to pitch."[4]

Andújar got 93⅓ innings of much-needed experience that winter for Escogido. He led the Dominican League in walks, but fashioned an impressive 2.93 ERA and the Reds noticed. While Alcala and DeFreites went to a co-op Single-A team to play for a Spanish-speaking manager, Cincinnati promoted Andújar to Double A. The Eastern League hitters were one challenge, but pitching for Les Aigles des Trois-Rivieres meant "home" games were played in the French-speaking Canadian province of Quebec. Against all odds Andújar thrived, winning seven of his first eight decisions before rolling his ankle and literally limping to a 7-6 final record.

Still hobbling in winter ball, Andújar was traded in midseason to the Estrellas Orientales. The four-player deal allowed Escogido to recover the contractual rights to Juan Marichal. Andújar was thrilled to pitch for his hometown team, which featured lots of Houston Astros through a working agreement with the National League franchise. César Cedeño and J.R. Richard were two of the club's stars that winter, but it was Estrellas manager (and Astros coach) Hub Kittle who'd have the biggest impact on Andújar's future. "Everything I have, I owe to Hub Kittle," Andújar remarked years later.[5]

The Reds invited Andújar to his first big-league spring training in 1973, but sent him to Triple A, where he didn't care for Indianapolis Indians skipper Vern Rapp. "I tell (Reds farm director Chief) Bender in spring training I no like to go to Indianapolis. I told them I no like manager. He gives you hell when you lose," Andújar explained.[6]

Andújar walked too many batters and in June was sent back to Trois-Rivieres, where he proceeded to show he had nothing left to prove in Double A by going 5-2 with a 1.98 ERA. He followed that up with a 2.53 mark in winter ball, where he cut down his leg kick and walk rate while learning from "El Coyote," Hub Kittle's nickname in the Dominican.

Back at Indianapolis in 1974, Andújar made 17 starts and 16 relief appearances as Rapp jerked him in and out of the rotation. The low point came in July when Andújar responded to an early hook by destroying a dugout water cooler, which prompted Rapp to suspend him. Andújar finished 8-8 with a 3.57 ERA and two saves as Indianapolis made it to the league finals before falling to the Tulsa Oilers. The championship series went the distance with several extra-inning contests, but Rapp used Andújar only as a pinch-runner.

Back in the Dominican, however, Kittle was more than happy to give him the ball. Andújar responded by winning six of seven decisions and the Dominican League's native-pitcher-of-the-year honors. "They said he had a million-dollar arm and a ten-cent head. But that's not true. He's a very intelligent person," Kittle observed.[7]

The Estrellas came up just short in their championship series as well, but Andújar was selected to accompany the triumphant Aguilas Cibaenas to Puerto Rico for the Caribbean Series. He beat Venezuela in his lone start.

Andújar arrived at spring training in 1975 with Reds manager Sparky Anderson hoping some special treatment would unlock his potential, as it had for another volatile

Dominican, Pedro Borbón, a few years before. Instead, Andújar began a third straight season in Indianapolis. Before he even got into a game, Rapp told him he was going back to Double A. "Vern Rapp grabs me and says if I don't like it I can fight him," Andújar said. "I think to myself, Joaquin, you be making wrong move fighting with Vern Rapp."[8]

Injuries limited Andújar to just 62 innings at Trois-Rivieres and, two days after the Reds won the World Series, they traded Andújar to the last-place Houston Astros for pitchers Luis Sanchez and Carlos Alfonso, neither of whom pitched a single inning for Cincinnati. Andújar went 7-2 for the Estrellas to repeat as native-pitcher-of-the-year in what proved to be his last winter with Kittle, who left the Astros organization as part of their organizational shakeup

On Opening Day 1976, Andújar made his major-league debut in—of all places—Cincinnati, walking the first two batters he faced to force in a run. He didn't pitch much for the first two months, but beat the Reds, 2-1, with a complete-game two-hitter on June 1 for his first major-league win. He became the first Dominican ever named Player of the Week after shutting out the Cubs in his next start. By mid-July, he'd beaten the Reds twice more with complete games, and pitched back-to-back 1-0 shutouts. Pitching for a sub-.500 club, Andújar finished his rookie season 9-10 with a 3.60 ERA.

Andújar got off to a slow start in 1977, but reeled off six straight victories. With a 10-5 midseason record, he was named to Sparky Anderson's National League All-Star squad. A pulled hamstring in his last start before the break kept him out of action, and Andújar won only once more after missing six weeks. He proved he was healthy in 14 starts that winter, rejoining the Leones del Escogido in the Dominican capital of Santo Domingo for the first time in five years. Andújar also married the former Walkiria Damaris Saez in the offseason, and expected big things from himself in 1978.

After predicting a 25-win season in spring training, Andújar pitched well early in 1978, though poor run support prevented his record from reflecting it. He hurt himself swinging for the fences during batting practice in May, however, then ticked off manager Bill Virdon by swinging too hard in his first game back and aggravating the injury. Andújar exited one game with a debilitating case of jock itch, then suffered another hamstring pull that knocked him out of action for nearly two months. After finishing a lost Astros season in the bullpen, he recovered to lead the Dominican League in complete games for Escogido and pitch in another Caribbean Series before spring training.

Andújar's antics didn't endear him to his manager, never mind opponents, but many fans got a kick out of his gunslinger routine in which he pointed his index finger at vanquished hitters like a pistol. In his early years, he'd even pretend to blow the gunsmoke away and return the gun to his holster.

The 1979 Astros got off to a great start with Andújar excelling in a swingman role. When he finally rejoined the rotation, he won Pitcher of the Month honors in June and returned to the All-Star Game with an 11-5 first-half record. Andújar pitched in the game at the Seattle Kingdome. Over the course of the next month, he became a father when son Jesse was born, and hit his first big-league home run, an inside-the-park blast with a man aboard at the Astrodome to beat Montreal's Bill "Spaceman" Lee, 2-1.

The Astros coughed up a 10-game division lead, however, as Andújar lost seven of eight decisions after the break and was sent back to the bullpen. Houston agreed to swap him to the World Series champion Pittsburgh Pirates for aging slugger Bill Robinson at the winter meetings, but Robinson nixed the deal by exercising his 10-5 rights. Andújar didn't know who he'd be pitching for on Opening Day, but he enjoyed another strong winter campaign for Escogido. In February he beat Venezuela in his only start to help the Dominican Republic win the Caribbean Series on their home turf.

Andújar had his first six-figure salary heading into 1980 after winning his arbitration case, but few opportunities to start after Houston signed Nolan Ryan to a free-agent contract. One year after pitching in the All-Star Game, Andújar failed to win a single game in a first half in which he rarely got to pitch at all. The Astros kept him as insurance in case somebody got hurt, which proved to be all too prescient when ace J.R. Richard suffered a tragic stroke in July. Andújar posted a 1.19 ERA in August when the Astros turned to him in desperation, but was returned to the bullpen for a third straight year by season's end. Houston survived a one-game tiebreaker to win the National League West. When the Astros finally won a tense NLCS Game Two in Philadelphia for the franchise's first-ever postseason victory, Andújar got credit for a save. They lost the NLCS in five games.

Andújar's winter season ended abruptly when he got into a dispute about complimentary tickets with Escogido's front office. The Leones won their first title in a dozen years without him, and the Astros kept making it abundantly clear that they weren't relying on Andújar either by acquiring two more proven starting pitchers. Andújar offered to pitch for free as he languished as the last man on the pitching staff for two months. His agents implored him to wait quietly for his impending free agency. Finally, in the first week of June, he was traded to the St. Louis Cardinals. Before he could even get into a game with his new team, major-league players walked out on strike for more than seven weeks.

When play resumed, however, Andújar won six of seven decisions for Cardinals manager Whitey Herzog and a St. Louis pitching coach he knew very well, Hub Kittle. "Before the Cardinals got me, I was like a plant that needed water," he said. "Whitey and Hub, they poured water on me, and I grew to be a tree."[9]

Andújar signed a three-year free-agent contract to return to St. Louis, and it paid immediate dividends in 1982. His control was better than ever and he was an important part of an exciting team that got off to a hot start. By the All-Star break, Andújar had the second-lowest ERA in the National League, but not enough victories to earn a spot on the team. Though he continued to pitch effectively, his record slipped to 8-10 by early August before he reeled off seven straight wins to close the regular season. His 5-0 record in September earned him NL Pitcher of the Month honors and helped the Cardinals win their division. Andújar won the pennant-clincher in Atlanta in the NLCS, then took on the high-scoring Milwaukee Brewers in the World Series.

Andújar was the only player on the field wearing short sleeves on a cold night as he carried a shutout into the seventh inning against the highest-scoring team in two decades. His evening ended abruptly when Ted Simmons hit a wicked one-hopper that caromed off Andújar's right knee into foul territory. Writhing and screaming in obvious agony, he nevertheless became the first pitcher from the Dominican Republic to win a World Series game when reliever Bruce Sutter nailed down the final outs.

Andújar spent several days on crutches, and it appeared unlikely that he'd be able to pitch if the Series went the distance. When Game Seven of the 1982 fall classic got underway at Busch Stadium, however, Andújar was back on the mound to demonstrate why he'd been calling himself "One Tough Dominican" all season. Andújar got through seven innings with a lead, then had to be hauled off the field by several teammates after Milwaukee's Jim Gantner profanely called him a hot dog. Six outs later, the Cardinals were World Series champions. Andújar figured his 2-0 series record and 1.35 ERA were Series MVP numbers, but the honors went to his catcher, Darrell Porter. Even one of the losing Brewers got more votes than Andújar.

In 1983 he won his first two decisions to extend his winning streak to 12 before his season unraveled due to too many overthrown, straight, high fastballs. In June the Cardinals lost leadoff hitter Lonnie Smith to drug rehab and star first baseman Keith Hernandez to a trade. Andújar was healthy enough to start 34 games, but finished the season with a miserable 6-16 record. "God is still my amigo," he insisted. "He must be someplace else. Maybe He's watching the American League."[10]

Andújar was one of the most aggressive, and unusual, hitters in baseball history. He struck out in more than half of his at-bats, usually swinging as hard as he could. He was a switch-hitter, but not in the usual sense. "If the pitcher has good control, I will bat left-handed against a right-handed pitcher. I bat right-handed against pitchers who don't have good control, or if I don't know them, because I don't want to get hit in the right arm. I bat right-handed with nobody on base because I'm a power hitter from that side. I bat left-handed with men on base so I can make better contact and drive in runs."[11]

In 1984, he homered both right-handed and left-handed – including a grand slam – and won a Gold Glove. Andújar also earned National League Comeback Player of the Year honors after winning his 20th game with just two games to play in the regular season. Andújar skipped the All-Star Game to be with his ailing grandfather, and finished a distant fourth in Cy Young voting despite being the league's only 20-game winner. After the season, he received a hero's welcome, however, when more than 10,000 Dominicans welcomed his flight back to Santo Domingo. "I grew up here. I never moved from here. People appreciate that," he explained. "I hope I die here, but you never know."[12]

St. Louis rewarded Andújar with a three-year contract that made him just the third Dominican to average more than $1 million annually. He was the Cardinals' Opening Day starter in 1985 and raced off to a 12-1 start that kept the Redbirds afloat in what would prove to be a season-long dogfight with the young New York Mets in the NL East. Andújar appeared on the cover of *The Sporting News* with his friend and fellow Dominican, Reds ace Mario Soto. Both pitchers had been involved in multiple bench-clearing incidents in recent seasons, and Andújar led the league in hit batters for the second consecutive year. In the article, titled "So Good... So Misunderstood," Andújar said: "Nolan Ryan pitches inside, and I don't see anybody fighting Nolan Ryan. Steve Carlton pitches inside to everybody, nobody says anything. But when Joaquín Andújar and Mario Soto pitch inside, everybody goes to the mound and fights. If they love to fight, they should go to war and fight. They should go to the Middle East."[13]

Andújar's record was 15-4 in the first half, but San Diego Padres manager Dick Williams decided to choose his All-Star Game starting pitcher based on a one-game showdown between Andújar and San Diego's LaMarr Hoyt. Andújar was so put off by the idea that he vowed never to attend another All-Star Game in his life. As unlikely as it was at the time, he'd never be invited back anyway. Andújar won a career-high 21 games in 1985, despite struggling through a 6-8 record in the second half. To make matters worse, in September, former Cardinals teammates Lonnie Smith and Keith Hernandez both identified him as a cocaine user in the sensational drug trial taking place in Pittsburgh.

The Cardinals went 101-61 to win the NL East and ousted the Los Angeles Dodgers in a six-game NLCS, but Andújar's struggles continued. He was bombed by the Kansas City Royals in Game Three of the World Series, which proved to be his last appearance in St. Louis as a Cardinal. The Redbirds nearly won their second World Series championship in four years, but blew a ninth-inning lead in Game Six following a controversial call by first-base umpire Don Denkinger. St. Louis was already trailing Game Seven, 9-0 in the fourth inning, when Whitey Herzog called on Andújar – whom he'd chosen not to start – to pitch mop-up relief with Denkinger calling balls and strikes. He gave up a single and a base on balls. The walk caused Andújar to lose his cool, charging and bumping Denkinger, and getting ejected.

Though Andújar's 41 wins over two seasons were unsurpassed in the majors, the Cardinals took the best offer they could get for him, sending him the Oakland A's for pitcher Tim Conroy and catcher Mike Heath in December of 1985. In addition to a 10-game suspension for his World Series outburst, Andújar faced up to a one-year ban from Commissioner Peter Ueberroth in the fallout from the drug trial. Unlike the six other players – including Smith and Hernandez – facing the most severe punishment, Andújar was never called to testify.

As it turned out, Andújar missed only the first five games of 1986 before a series of injuries caused him to spend time on the disabled list for the first time in eight seasons. He talked about retirement before coming on strong to go 12-7 for an Oakland club that finished 10 games under .500.

In 1987 he arrived late for spring training, which wasn't unusual, but injured himself going all out in his first day of drills, which was. The birth of his second son, Christopher, was about the only highlight in a season that saw him post a 6.08 ERA and average less than five innings in the 13 starts he was able to make. When Oakland general manager Sandy Alderson reflected on the trade he put together to acquire Andújar, he said, "Both teams got nothing, but our nothing was louder than theirs."[14]

Andújar took a substantial pay cut to return to the Houston Astros in 1988, but endured a pulled muscle in his side and knee surgery in April alone. In his first appearance back in St. Louis since being traded by the Cardinals, he surrendered a walk-off home run to fellow Dominican Tony Peña. When he drilled Peña with a fastball a few weeks later, he was fined and suspended by NL President Chub Feeney. "There is some guy, some big guy in United States baseball, he doesn't want me in baseball. He wants me out of the game," Andújar said.[15]

Andújar's 4.00 ERA wasn't terrible, but he couldn't go deep enough into games to stay in the starting rotation. He kept asking for his release, but faded quietly to the end of his major-league career with a lifetime 127-118 record.

In 1989 no team would guarantee Andújar a major-league roster spot, so he stayed home in the Dominican until the Gold Coast Suns of the newly formed Senior League of Professional Baseball offered him an opportunity. Just before his 37th birthday, Andújar went 5-0 with a minuscule 1.31 ERA to earn an incentive-laden deal and invitation to spring training from the Montreal Expos. A gimpy leg and an abscessed tooth limited him to two appearances, however, and the Expos released him before Opening Day when he made it clear he wouldn't pitch in the minors.

When Whitey Herzog became the California Angels' senior vice president after the 1991 season, he hired Andújar as a scout, but the arrangement proved to be short-lived. The Angels weren't willing to invest much in Latin scouting, and Andújar still wanted to pitch. Several teams expressed interest in signing him when he made a comeback attempt with the Estrellas in late 1993, but knee problems and a freak car accident convinced Andújar that he should retire once and for all after only two starts.

Andújar continued to help young players around San Pedro de Macoris, assisting the San Francisco Giants Dominican Summer Leaguers and the Estrellas, particularly when his old friend Arturo DeFreites was their skipper. The Chicago White Sox noticed his ability to help young pitchers and brought him to spring training one season, but he refused their offer of a job when he found out it would be at the expense of one of his friends. Instead Andújar coached informally, but consistently, and played softball to keep his swing in shape. Investments in a construction business, and later a trucking company, did little except drain his bank account, however. In 2003 Andújar returned to St. Louis for the first time in 15 years to throw out a ceremonial first pitch at Busch Stadium to a loud ovation. "I live in the Dominican, but my heart still is in St. Louis," he said.[16]

Two years later, Major League Baseball made Andújar one of 15 finalists for a Latino Legends team that would be chosen through fan voting. He finished 10th among pitchers. Andújar's last appearance at Busch came in 2007, for the 25th anniversary of the 1982 World Series champions. *St. Louis Post-Dispatch* columnist Rick Hummel described him as looking "smaller than we remembered him."[17]

The Hall of Fame of San Pedro de Macoris inducted Andújar as a member in 2011, and the Caribbean Series made him a member of its Hall of Fame a year later. Andújar missed both ceremonies for undisclosed health reasons. The truth was that diabetes was taking a toll on "One Tough Dominican." Andújar also went through a divorce, lost his big home and moved to an apartment in Santo Domingo, where he survived on his major-league pension.

Joaquín Andújar died on September 8, 2015. Many sports fans in the United States learned the news from the Instagram feed of Robinson Cano, the most prominent player from San Pedro de Macoris at the time. Cano called it a "big pain for all baseball fans, especially all Dominicans, but even more so for all of us who had the chance to know you and learn from your example."

Just over a month before Andújar's death, the Dominican Republic enjoyed a proud moment when Juan Marichal joined Pedro Martínez on stage at the latter's induction ceremony at the National Baseball Hall of Fame. Two of the only three Dominicans with multiple 20-win seasons stood smiling and holding their country's flag aloft. Precisely 15 years after Marichal's last 20-win season, and 15 years before Martínez's first, Andújar won 20 for the first of two consecutive years. "Andújar was in the middle of every dream I had because he was one of the best pitchers we ever had in the Dominican Republic," remarked Martínez.[18]

NOTES

1 Kenny Hand, "Andújar Gets Shot Against L.A. Tonight," *Houston Post*, September 9, 1980: 2D.

2 Julio Gonzalez, "Joaquin: Facing the Future With a View from the Past," *Oakland A's Magazine*, Volume 6, Number 2: 14.

3 Gonzalez: 12.

4 Dave Pavlesic, interview with author, May 31, 2006.

5 *The Sporting News*, November 5, 1984: 49.

6 Duke De Luca, "Andújar Slows Down Phils," *Reading Eagle*, June 30, 1973: 6.

7 Rick Hummel, "Andújar's Secret? Daddy Knows Best," *St. Louis Post-Dispatch*, June 3, 1982.

8 Kenny Hand, "Ayyyayyaya, Joaquin. Andújar Makes Astros Happy with Jokes, Pitching," *Houston Post*, May 22, 1977.

9 Steve Wulf, "Here's a Hot Dog You've Got to Relish," *Sports Illustrated*, January 24, 1983: 32.

10 Rick Hummel, "Andújar: God Is Still My Amigo," *St. Louis Post-Dispatch*, July 22, 1983: B1.

11 Rick Hummel, "Sport Interview: Joaquín Andújar," *Sport*, September 1985: 27.

12 Rick Hummel, "Youneverknow What to Expect From Cards' Ace," *The Sporting News 1985 Baseball Yearbook*, 120.

13 Rick Hummel, "So Good … So Misunderstood," *The Sporting News*, June 17, 1985: 3.

14 David H. Nathan, *The McFarland Baseball Quotations Dictionary* (Jefferson, North Carolina: McFarland), 2000.

15 Neil Hohlfeld, "Could 'Someone Big' Be Out to Get Andújar?" *The Sporting News*, June 27, 1988: 21.

16 Rick Hummel, "Andújar's Heart Remains in St. Louis," *St. Louis Post-Dispatch*, July 26, 2003.

17 Derek Goold, "Colorful Cardinals Ace Andújar Dies," *St. Louis Post-Dispatch*, September 8, 2015.

18 Joey Nowak, "Former All-Star Pitcher Joaquín Andújar Dies," mlb.com, September 8, 2015. mlb.com/news/joaquin-andujar-dies-at-62/c-148062060.

MIGUEL BATISTA

By Cosme Vivanco

Miguel Batista is regarded as one of the more interesting individuals to don a major-league uniform. Throughout his 18-year pitching career, Batista's travels took him to 11 different teams, for which he toiled as both a starter and a reliever. A deeply philosophical person, he stood out from the average ballplayer with his unquenchable desire to find something bigger and more fulfilling than baseball. Batista's athletic prowess brought him considerable wealth, but his outside interests brought out a new level of understanding the world beyond the ballpark. His love for the written word led him to publish a book of poetry in Spanish titled *Sentimientos en Blanco y Negro* (Feelings in Black and White) and a novel, *The Avenger of Blood*, a thriller about a serial killer. His many passions off the mound didn't exactly win over many of his teammates throughout his major-league career. And his career stats indicate a pitcher who was inconsistent. But Miguel Batista would like to be remembered as a decent human being who just happened to play major-league baseball. "When I die, I don't want people to remember me by saying, 'He was a great baseball player,' "Batista says. "I want them to say, 'He was a great man. A great human being.' That's how I want to be remembered."[1]

Miguel Descartes Batista Jerez was born on February 19, 1971, in Santo Domingo, Dominican Republic. Many of the young men who grew up in the Dominican Republic had dreams of playing major-league baseball, but Batista's first love was the written word. His grandmother instilled in him the maxim that the greatest investment in the world was a book. As an adolescent, Miguel scribbled thoughts into a journal to compensate for having no close friends while growing up in San Pedro de Macoris. "Writing started for me being a loner," Batista said in 2006. "As a kid, I had a problem. Kids my age didn't want to talk about things that interested me. That pushed me away. I started writing when I was 12 or 13."[2] By his mid-teens, he started to write poetry but mostly kept it to himself.

Batista didn't start playing baseball until he was 15. He developed an eye-popping fastball but had trouble controlling it. Two weeks after his 17th birthday, he had an encounter that would change his life. Israel Frias, a minor-league catcher with the Baltimore Orioles, told him of a tryout camp in nearby Ingenio Santa Fe. Of the 60 players at the tryout, Batista was the only pitcher,[3] and he was the only person to sign a deal; he inked a contract with the Montreal Expos.

Photo courtesy of the National Baseball Hall of Fame

The Expos sent Batista to their Rookie League team in the Gulf Coast League. In his second year, 1991, Batista posted an 11-5 record for Rockford of the Class-A Midwest League. After the season he was snapped up by the Pittsburgh Pirates in the Rule 5 draft. Batista opened the 1992 season with the Pirates and made his major-league debut on April 11, giving up a two-run home run in relief to Ruben Amaro as the Pirates lost to the Philadelphia Phillies, 7-4. Twelve days later, he was returned to the Expos. Before his next major-league appearance, Batista spent the next four years honing his craft in the minor leagues.

Batista spent the rest of the 1992 season with West Palm Beach of the Class-A Florida State League (7-7, 3.79 ERA). With Harrisburg of the Double-A Eastern League in 1993, he posted a 13-5 mark with an ERA of 4.34. In 1994 he pitched in only three games, and after the season he was released by the Expos.

Batista signed with the Florida Marlins and in 1995 at Triple-A Charlotte, he began to be used more as a reliever than a starter. In August 1996 Batista was called up by the Marlins and pitched out the bullpen in nine games. After the season Batista was sent to the Chicago Cubs on waivers.

Batista began the 1997 campaign with Triple-A Iowa. His command improved significantly, and the Cubs called him up in August. His first appearance for the Cubs was a start on August 11 in which he gave up two runs in seven innings as the Cubs lost to the Los Angeles Dodgers, 2-1.

Batista's next four appearances were out of the bullpen. He got five more opportunities to earn a spot in the Cubs rotation, but an 0-4 record with an 8.72 ERA in those five starts nixed that idea. After the season the Cubs traded Batista to the Montreal Expos for left fielder Henry Rodriguez.

For the next two seasons, Batista worked mostly out of the bullpen, but Expos manager Felipe Alou gave him some starts as well. His most notable victory came on April 14, 1999, when he pitched a complete game against the Milwaukee Brewers, striking out six and walking none as the Expos cruised to a 15-1 victory.

Three weeks into the 2000 season, the Expos sent Batista to the Kansas City Royals for right-hander Brad Rigby. Playing for his fifth club, Batista continued to struggle with his control. In his only season with the Royals he posted a 2-6 mark with a 7.74 ERA and a WHIP of 1.754. Combined with his 14.04 early-season ERA with Montreal, his ERA for the entire season ballooned to 8.54 and his WHIP increased to 1.867.

Released by the Royals after the season, Batista signed with the Arizona Diamondbacks. The Diamondbacks were looking to make a return trip to the postseason after winning the NL West division crown in 2000.

With Randy Johnson and Curt Schilling powering Arizona's pitching staff, it appeared that Batista would mostly be relegated to the same duties he'd become used to since he arrived in the big leagues.

The 2001 season was a dream year for the four-year-old Diamondbacks franchise. They defeated the New York Yankees in a dramatic seven-game World Series. Batista had the best season of his career, going 11-8 with an ERA of 3.36. His WHIP was 1.242 and his pitching WAR was 2.6. Batista started 18 games, going 6-6. Opponents hit .226 against him. He made the most of his first trip to the postseason. In Game Three of the NLDS, he struck out four Cardinals in six innings of a 5-3 victory. Batista started the fifth game of the World Series and said the Yankees mystique didn't faze him one bit. "I don't care if they're the angels of Jesus Christ," Batista said. "I still have to go out there, do my job and beat them."[4]

The decision to hand the ball to Batista for an important Game Five showdown was a gutsy move by Diamondbacks manager Bob Brenly. Diamondbacks ace Curt Schilling would have been a logical choice, but he had been moved up to start Game Four. However, Brenly was confident that Batista could cope with the pressure. "I hate to put anybody in that position, but Miguel has shown throughout the course of the season that he is not your regular run-of-the-mill pitcher," Brenly said. "He is able to handle things because of his resilient arm and resilient mind. He is able to pitch one day, come back and pitch two days in relief after that. It's an amazing quality I have not seen recently in any pitcher in the major leagues."[5]

Batista came through with a 7⅔-inning performance in which he struck out six, walked five, and allowed no runs. However, the Diamondbacks couldn't hold the 2-0 lead as they lost in extra innings.

Batista stood out among his teammates by being an iconoclast. He was likely the only big-league player to have a framed photo of Albert Einstein sitting on the top shelf of his locker. And while many players enjoyed, fishing, hunting, and playing golf, Batista enjoyed reading, writing, and going to museums. He enjoyed the game and the opportunities it provided him, but the search for truth in this complicated world was extremely important to him. "I have never been around anybody like Miguel Batista," Brenly said. "He is a refreshing breath of fresh air. Not that this a criticism, but if you are not talking about fantasy football or baseball or girls, most ballplayers don't have much to say. Miguel has got opinions on everything. He's extremely well read, extremely well spoken and a very thoughtful, caring human being. He's a great pitcher on top of it."[6]

In 2002, his second season with the Diamondbacks, Batista pitched in 36 games (29 starts) and finished the regular season with an 8-9 record, with a 4.29 ERA. In the NLDS, as the Diamondbacks were swept by the Cardinals, Batista started the deciding Game Three, giving up four runs in 3⅔ innings. The following year, *The Sporting News* named Batista its number one good guy in major-league baseball for his numerous charitable causes, specifically his $50,000 contribution to build a baseball field on tribal land in Arizona.[7] He also began an education-oriented program called Imagine That. Its objective was to encourage fourth- through sixth-graders to use their creativity to develop new ideas.

On the pitching mound, Batista finished the 2003 season tied for the Diamondbacks team lead in wins with 10. His WAR was 4.3, the best of his career. Batista's most notable pitching performance was an 11-strikeout effort in a 3-2 loss to the Florida Marlins on July 28.

Batista was a free agent after the season and signed a three-year, $13.1 million deal with the Toronto Blue Jays. In his first season, 2004, Batista pitched poorly and lost his job as a starter toward the end of the season. In 2005 he became the Blue Jays' closer and had 31 saves, but also eight blown saves. After the season it was back to the Diamondbacks, as the Blue Jays traded Batista and Orlando Hudson to Arizona for Troy Glaus and Sergio Santos.

With the Diamondbacks, Batista returned to the starting rotation. In his first start, he struck out 11 in seven innings on the third game of the season, as Arizona defeated the Colorado Rockies, 12-5. On September 12, as Batista made an unsuccessful start against the Washington Nationals, the English version of his novel *The Avenger of Blood* was published. The thriller centered on a 14-year-old boy accused of committing a series of brutal slayings. (It got mixed reviews.)

After the season the Diamondbacks offered Batista arbitration, but were not willing to commit to a long-term deal with the free-agent right-hander. On December 14, 2006, he signed a three-year, $24 million contract with the Seattle Mariners. In 2007, his first year with his new club, Batista won a career-high 16 victories. In 2008, however, he had one of the worst seasons of his career, posting a 4-14 mark with a 6.26 ERA. The next season the Mariners moved him to long relief. While Batista was adjusting to his new role, he was earning praise for his humanitarian work as the club recognized him as its candidate for the Roberto Clemente award.

Released by the Mariners after the season, Batista inked a minor-league contract with the Washington Nationals, and won a bullpen job in spring training. He made one start, though: On July 27, with just 10 minutes to go before the first pitch, Batista was called to pitch for injured right-hander Stephen Strasburg. The Nationals faithful peppered Batista with a chorus of boos as they hoped to see their talented ace. But Batista turned those jeers into cheers as he tossed five scoreless innings, striking out six and walking just one as the Nationals beat the Atlanta Braves, 3-0.

Batista understood the fans' frustration. "Imagine if you go to see Miss Universe, then you end up having Miss Iowa, you might get those kind of boos," Batista said. "But it's okay. They have to understand that as an organization we have to make sure that the kid is fine. You don't want to expose him out there and screw up his future."[8]

Batista's attempt at self-deprecating humor, offended Miss Iowa, Katherine Connors, who responded, "I know I can throw a pitch or two! The question is, can Miguel Batista walk the runway in a swimsuit?"[9]

Batista apologized to her and was her batterymate as she threw out the ceremonial first pitch at a Nationals game a couple of days later.

A free agent again after the season, Batista signed with the St. Louis Cardinals for 2011. He was released on June 22 after pitching only 29⅓ innings. The New York Mets picked him up, and Batista won his 100th major-league game in the majors on September 1, getting the 7-5 victory in a start against the Marlins. In the final game of the season, Batista started against Cincinnati and pitched a two-hit shutout. The 2012 season was not so successful: After posting a 1-3 mark with a 4.82 ERA, he was released by the Mets on July 26.

The next day Batista signed with the Atlanta Braves. After pitching in five games out of the bullpen, he was released. On January 19, 2013, Batista, now 41, signed a minor-league deal with the Colorado Rockies, but was released in spring training.

A year later, on April 9, 2013, Batista, in hopes of resuming his big-league career, signed a minor-league contract with the Blue

Jays and was assigned to the Triple-A Buffalo Bisons. He was released by the Jays on May 21. Until 2015 he pitched a few games in the Dominican Winter League.

Batista's career was filled with ups and downs. He posted a 102-115 record with a 4.48 ERA. One might argue, though, that a true measure of his success was what he accomplished off the field. In 2012 the Miguel Batista Foundation celebrated its 10th anniversary. The objective of the foundation is to promote both youth baseball and education in the Dominican Republic.

SOURCES

In addition to the sources cited in the Notes, the author consulted Baseball-Reference.com and Retrosheet.org.

NOTES

1. Geoff Baker, "M's Batista Striking the Right Notes," *Seattle Times*, August 17, 2007. https://www.seattletimes.com/sports/mariners/ms-batista-striking-the-right-notes/

2. "Batista Shows He Has the Write Stuff," *Seattle Times*, October 22, 2006. seattletimes.com/sports/baseball-notebook-batista-shows-he-has-the-write-stuff/.

3. Gustavo Olivo Peña, Acento.com. "Miguel Batista: 'Mi abuela decia que un libro era la mejor inversion del mundo,'" August 17, 2011. acento.com.do/2011/actualidad/6142-miguel-batista-mi-abuela-decia-que-un-libro-era-la-mejor-inversion-del-mundo/

4. Chris Baldwin, "Yanks' Aura Means Nothing to Batista," *Daily Record* (Morristown, New Jersey), November 1, 2001: D7.

5. David Heuschkel, "For Batista It's a No-Brainer," *Hartford Courant,* November 1, 2001: C5.

6. Heuschkel.

7. *The Sporting News*, July 7, 2003: 13.

8. Gene Wang, "Miguel Batista Turns Boos to Cheers as the Washington Nationals Beat the Atlanta Braves, 3-0," *Washington Post,"* July 29, 2010, washingtonpost.com/wp-dyn/content/article/2010/07/27/AR2010072706093.html.

9. Jim Caple, "Miss Iowa USA Sounds Off About Miquel Batista." ESPN.com, espn.com/espn/page2/index/_/id/5420051.

TONY BATISTA

By Scott Cummings

A picture of Tony Batista at the plate perhaps deserves some recognition in a corner of Cooperstown. When the right-handed batter came to plate, he had an open stance that caused his chest to face the pitcher. His left leg was nearly even with his right leg. His hands were at eye level with the bat. As the pitcher wound up, Tony brought his open left leg in and closed his stance, back to a natural baseball "open stance." This stance made him pull the ball to left field, hit for more power, help him stay in the major leagues and promote one of his passions, Christian missionary work, throughout his professional baseball career.

Batista's batting stance was so extreme that the Batting Stance Guy, Gar Ryness, blew out his back imitating it stance for his book, *Batting Stance Guy: A Love Letter to Baseball*. Ryness wrote, "He stands with his front foot planted in the far back corner of the box, body facing the pitcher, bat in the clouds. If a kid in T-ball did that, any self-respecting coach would be on him in a flash, rearranging just about everything."[1]

But that stance aided Batista during 11 major-league seasons spread among six teams, and one season in the Japanese Pacific League. Helped him make two All-Star Game appearances, and hit 221 career home runs. Batista split duties at third base, second base, shortstop, and DH; 807 out of his 1,188 games were played at third.

Leocadio Francisco Batista Hernandez was born on December 9, 1973, in Puerto Plata, Dominican Republic. According to Miguel Tejada, a friend, Batista's parents lived in Mao Valverde Province in the Dominican Republic. Their occupation was raising animals like goats, pigs, and cattle.[2]

Batista graduated from Liceo Juan de Jesus high school. He became interested in baseball by watching his two older brothers, Ramírez and Vicente, who eventually turned pro, play the game. "I learned from them, they both were professional players in the states but they only got to Double A," he said.[3]

In 1991, at the age of 17, Batista signed with the Oakland Athletics out of high school. His best season in the minors was 1994 for the Modesto A's in the Class-A California League, when he slugged 17 home runs and hit .281/.359/.459 in 119 games. In 1996, batting .322 for Triple-A Edmonton (Pacific Coast League), the 22-year-old Batista earned a call-up to the Athletics on June 3. In his major-league debut that night, Batista, playing third base and batting ninth, went 0-for-3 against Kansas City's Kevin Appier with two strikeouts. In 1996 and 1997, he bounced back and forth between Edmonton and Oakland.

Batista played some shortstop for the A's, but was dogged by his poor defensive play at the position, and in 1997 Miguel Tejada took over the position. After the season Batista was unprotected by Oakland and was taken in the expansion draft by the Arizona Diamondbacks as the 27th pick. Meanwhile, Batista, mired in a 0-for-28 hitless streak in the Dominican winter league, adopted his wide-open left-footed stance. He said he didn't know why he chose such a bizarre, unique stance. "I tried to do something different," he said. "And right away I got a hit with that kind of stance and it's been working for me since that day."[4]

The new stance gave him consistent major-league home run power. Batista slugged 18 home runs for the Diamondbacks in 1998. Defensively, he bounced between third base, shortstop, and second base in 106 games. He didn't settle into a full-time role and hit .273 with those 18 home runs. In 1999 he settled in at shortstop, playing in 44 games (.257, 5 home runs) for the Diamondbacks. On June 11 he was traded to the Toronto Blue Jays with right-handed pitcher John Frascatore for left-handed pitcher Dan Plesac. In 98 games for the Blue Jays he batted .285 with 26 homers.

With Toronto for the full 2000 season, Batista posted his best season, batting .263 with 41 home runs and 114 runs batted in. This earned Batista his first of two All-Star Game appearances. But in 2001 he regressed. Batting just .207 with 13 home runs in 72 games, Batista was sent to the Baltimore Orioles on waivers. This was Batista's fourth big-league club in just five seasons. For the Orioles the rest of the season, Batista batted .266 with 12 home runs.

Batista played in 161 games for the Orioles in 2002, batted .244 with 31 homers, and earned his second All-Star Game selection.

In 2003 Batista again played in 161 games. His production fell off slightly: .235, with 26 home runs. After the season he opted for free agency. He signed with the Montreal Expos for one year at $1.5 million. The Expos became his fifth big-league team in seven major-league seasons. For the Expos he batted .241, slugged 32 home runs and drove in 110 runs, seventh highest in the National League.

Hitting 89 home runs and driving in 296 runs over three seasons should have been enough for Batista to earn another major-league contract. Tampa Bay, Detroit, and Houston reportedly offered him deals. But none came close to the two-year, $15 million contract he signed with the Fukuoka Daiei Hawks of the Japan Pacific League. The deal also included a $5 million signing bonus. The Hawks, were looking to splurge on a young major-league talent, offered him well over the $1.5 million the Expos had paid him. Batista, now 31 years old, took the offer and crossed the Pacific to play Japanese baseball.

In Japan Batista played in 135 out of the season's 136 games, batted .263, and hit 27 home runs. Perhaps this should have been enough for him to deserve another shot in the JPL. But it was not to be. Possibly Batista was too laid-back in Japan and seemed lackadaisical. Perhaps, it was the adjustment to Japanese culture. He had some unusual behavior on the field in Japan. See, for instance, a video that turns up in a web search of "Tony Batista scares pitcher."[5] One Japanese beat writer dubbed Batista "Mr. Nonchalant."[6] But most likely it was the fact he was the highest-paid player on the team but didn't produce the highest numbers. Although Batista finished a league leader in several statistical categories, apparently his numbers didn't justify his salary and the Hawks wanted younger talent. Batista was 31. Rather than pay another $15 million, the Hawks bought out his contract for $4.5 million.

Photo courtesy of the National Baseball Hall of Fame

Two days after getting his release, on December 15, 2005, Batista inked another deal to return to the United States with a one-year, $1.25 million contract with the Minnesota Twins. His bat was expected to fill a power void in the Twins lineup and he would serve in a needed role at third base and designated hitter.

The Twins' hopes were not met. In 50 games, Batista batted just .236 with 5 home runs, and was released on June 14. Twins manager Ron Gardenhire said, "If you are not going to hit home runs, then you've got to be able to run. We were hoping that Tony would hit a few more home runs."[7]

Batista played winter ball in the Dominican Republic in the 2006-2007 season for the first time in the eight years since he adopted his trademark batting stance. Batista needed the winter league to help market himself for another big-league contract at the age of 32. He batted only .213 in 18 games, and signed a minor-league deal with the Washington Nationals with an invitation to spring training. Batista made the 2007 Nationals roster in spring training but had little power impact, hitting only two home runs in 80 games.

At the age of 34, Batista returned to play 16 games in the Dominican Winter League and again landed a minor-league deal with the Nationals. This time he didn't make the major-league, and played only 17 games at Triple-A Columbus. He played winter ball again, but was unable to attract even a minor-league contract.

According to Baseball-Reference.com, Batista made just shy of $40 million playing in the major leagues and Japan. He donated a large portion of his salary to charities and churches and saw himself as a Christian missionary.

When his team played on the road, Batista made it a practice to donate to local churches. He once asked his Kansas City taxi driver to take him to any church. The driver randomly selected Country Club Christian Church, where Batista asked to see the minister. The minster was tired after that Monday after officiating at three weddings and preaching three times the weekend before. Batista instructed her to open the Bible and turn to Malachi 3:10: "Bring ye all the tithes into the storehouse, that there may be meat in mine house, and prove me now herewith salt the Lord of Hosts. If I will not open you the windows of heaven, and pour you out a blessing, that there shall not be room enough to receive it." Batista then spoke a little bit in broken English and said, "I am convinced of this." He gave her a thick white envelope with the Fairmont Hotel logo. Batista left and said something about the taxicab still waiting outside. Inside the envelope was $16,400. The church finance director said later, "It revives your faith in people. I still think players are paid too much but there are ones who are blessed."[8]

Batista said to a reporter in 2006, "God uses me. Everywhere I go I talk about Him and the power he has." Batista was almost always available before and after game for an autograph.[9] But the memory of that awkward wide-open stance remains in the hearts of baseball fans.

SOURCES

The author consulted Tony Batista's player file at the National Baseball Hall of Fame Library, and relied upon Baseball-Reference.com.

NOTES

1. Gar Ryness and Dewart Caleb, *Batting Stance Guy: A Love Letter to Baseball* (New York: Simon and Schuster, 2010), 36-41.
2. Miguel Tejada, email correspondence with Julio Rodriguez, July 23, 2018.
3. Steve Riach, *Life Lessons From Baseball* (Colorado Springs: Honor Books, 2004), 13-17.
4. Riach.
5. "Throwback Sports Clip Of The Week: Tony Batista Scares The Hell Out Of Asian Pitcher!," YouTube.com, December 2, 2011. youtube.com/watch?v=lUiQlPzcm44.
6. Wayne Graczyk, "Batista's Number Didn't Justify His Massive Salary," *Japan Times*, December 18, 2005.
7. Jayson Williams, "Line Up Redo Puts Batista out, Bartlett In," *St. Paul Pioneer Press*, June 24, 2006.
8. Joe Capozzi, "Batista's Gift to Church Exemplifies Generosity," *Cleveland Plain Dealer*, August 5, 2002.
9. Jonathan Weeks, *Latino Stars in Major League Baseball: From Bobby Abreu to Carlos Zambrano* (New York: Rowman and Littlefield, 2017), 6-8.

GEORGE BELL

by Seth Moland-Kovash

Two firsts were combined into one event in 1987 as the first Most Valuable Player Award won by a member of a Canadian team also happened to be the first MVP won by a player of Dominican descent. The player in question, George Bell, played in 12 seasons from 1981 through 1993 for three major-league teams. That 1987 season was the peak offensive year for the right-handed left fielder and designated hitter, as he hit 47 home runs and edged out Detroit Tigers shortstop Alan Trammell for the honor.

Jorge Antonio Bell Mathey was born on October 21, 1959, in the Dominican Republic town of San Pedro de Macorís. This southeastern Dominican town has produced so many baseball players that it is sometimes called "the cradle of shortstops." This list of greats from San Pedro de Macorís include Bell's contemporaries Henry Rodríguez and Sammy Sosa, who would both figure in Bell's own transaction history.

Bell was originally signed as a 19-year-old by the Philadelphia Phillies in 1978. Two years later, the Toronto Blue Jays, at the urging of legendary scout Epy Guerrero, selected Bell from the Phillies in the 1980 Rule 5 draft. Bell would spend most of the remainder of his career with the Blue Jays, earning induction into the Blue Jays' Level of Excellence, an honor shared with only 10 others as of 2018.

The Blue Jays opened the 1981 campaign in Detroit against the Tigers on April 9 and Bell was there. With the Blue Jays trailing 5-2 in the top of the eighth inning, Bell was brought in to run for Toronto's cleanup hitter, John Mayberry. Three straight outs meant that Bell got no action as a runner, but he stayed in the game as a left fielder for the Tigers' half of the eighth inning. Only one ball was hit his way—a triple over his head and off the wall by Al Cowens.[1] After another fruitless pinch-running appearance, Bell was left on the bench for nearly two weeks. His first plate appearance came on April 21 at home against the Milwaukee Brewers. Bell entered the game in the seventh inning to play left field in a 6-0 losing cause. He batted in the bottom of the ninth inning with his team trailing 6-2 and facing Moose Haas and grounded out to shortstop. The next day Bell made his first start, in right field and batting third in a batting order that was struggling. The struggles would continue, as the Brewers took the game 8-1 and the Jays fell to 3-9. Bell began the game with two groundouts back to the pitcher but got his first major-league hit in the fifth inning with a double to right field off Mike Caldwell. He did not score.

Bell's rookie campaign was cut short when he ran into an outfield wall chasing a foul ball on June 9. He did not return until August 10 and finished his rookie campaign batting .233/.256/.350 in limited duty. Those numbers are not eye-catching but there were flashes of power and speed in his game even at 19 years old, and he garnered some American League Rookie of the Year votes.

Bell spent 1982 in Syracuse with the Blue Jays' Triple-A affiliate, but another injury-riddled year saw him get into only 37 games with 131 plate appearances. It was no surprise, therefore, when the Blue Jays had him start 1983 (still just his age 23 season) in Triple A. When he was called up, to start on July 12 in Kansas City, Bell made the most of his opportunity and hit a two-run home run and a double as the designated hitter. Other than a final abortive comeback attempt in 1993, Bell was done with the minor leagues for good.

The Blue Jays were hitting their stride in 1984, Bell's first full season in the major leagues. Behind the pitching of Dave Stieb and the veteran Doyle Alexander and the developing outfield trio of Bell, Lloyd Moseby, and Jesse Barfield, this year was the beginning of a period of winning baseball in Toronto. Bell was a big part of that success. The 1984 team under manager Bobby Cox finished a distant 15 games behind the Detroit Tigers in the AL East, but the signs of good things to come were developing. All three of those outfielders were 24 years old and coming into their own. Bell ended the season with a batting line of .292/.326/.498 and perhaps most importantly stayed on the field the whole season, playing in 159 games primarily as a corner outfielder. He finished the year with 26 home runs, a number that was very consistent throughout the remainder of his career, other than the one MVP year with 47. His consistent appearances in the lineup were also a feature of Bell's career right up until the very end as he avoided any long layoffs until the end of his career in 1993.

It was Bell's successful 1984 season, and the lack of recognition he felt about it, that began a reputation for being hostile (or at least uncooperative) to the media that hounded Bell for the rest of his career. He was often referred to as laconic, especially in comparison to his longtime and loquacious teammate Barfield.[2] In 1984 the Toronto sportswriters voted Dave Collins as the team MVP over Bell. During spring training in 1985, Bell declared that he was no longer speaking to newspaper reporters and accused them of racism in their selection.[3]

In 1985 the Blue Jays finally got over the hump and won the AL East with a record of 99-62, edging out the New York Yankees by two games. Bell was at the heart of the batting order, anywhere from third to fifth with the cleanup spot being his through the second half of the season. The Jays lost the ALCS to the Kansas City Royals in seven games. Bell did not have a home run during the series but did contribute three doubles to the cause.

The next year the Jays slid back a bit but Bell contributed in his incredibly consistent way, with a slash line of .309/.349/.532. He also began to get recognition as one of the game's best, finishing 1986 in fourth place in the MVP voting. But much more was to come in 1987. That season the Jays had the same outfield of Bell, Moseby, and Barfield while adding the young designated hitter Fred McGriff. Jimmy Key and Jim Clancy had come to join Stieb on the pitching staff. Things looked good. It was a tight race and only a season-ending sweep at the hands of the Tigers saw the Jays miss the playoffs again, finishing just two games behind the Tigers. But George Bell had his career year.

Bell led the league in only one offensive category, with his 134 runs batted in pacing the American League. He paired that with his career-best and club-record 47 home runs, bested only by Mark McGwire's 49. All these home runs came from Bell's 6-foot-1, 190-pound frame. The Most Valuable Player voting was tight (only 21 points) between Bell and Detroit's Trammell. Trammell won the division title on the field, but Bell won the respect of the writers for the way in which he helped his team throughout the year. Interviewed by telephone when the award was announced, Bell said, "I'm very happy. ... Because when you win the MVP everything shows that you've worked hard. That you're a winner. It's one of the greatest things that's (happened) to me in the last three years."[4]

Controversy stalked Bell in the 1988 season. Blue Jays manager Jimy Williams wanted to make him a designated hitter. This plan offended Bell's pride in his role as a major-league star. He felt it was an undue attack on his defensive abilities; it would have made him the youngest regular designated hitter in the American League. Things blew up in a spring-training game on March 17 when Bell refused to take the bat when he was due up. He was suspended for one day and fined $1,000 but the resentment lingered.[5] Bell "won" the argument as he played in only seven games as a designated hitter in 1988, and 149 in his preferred left field.

Jimy Williams was fired after a 12-24 start to the 1989 campaign and new manager Cito Gaston more regularly made the move of Bell to DH, saying, "People refuse to believe that George is a team player, but he is. George just wants to be respected and dealt with straight-up."[6] Bell's time at DH increased to only 19 games but the precedent had been set as the Blue Jays improved under Gaston to win the AL East before losing in the ALCS again, this time in five games to the Oakland Athletics.

Photo courtesy of the National Baseball Hall of Fame

The following season, 1990, was Bell's last before free agency. He had a solid and consistent year, with a line of .265/.303/.422, earning his second All-Star selection while contributing to the Blue Jays' 86-76 record as his designated-hitter role kept creeping up, with 36 appearances. Bell had seemingly adjusted and reconciled himself to his perceived lack of respect as one of baseball's best with his own confidence in his performance. He told USA Today's Chuck Johnson in June, "I don't think people compare me in the category of superstar. I think they compare me as a so-so player. Nobody gives me credit. But I go out there and play my game. I don't care."[7]

After the 1990 season Bell had his first chance at the free-agency market. He signed with the Chicago Cubs for a guaranteed three-year $9.8 million, going to the National

League, where the designated-hitter question would not be an issue. Bell joined Andre Dawson in the Cubs' outfield, so the Cubs now had both 1987 MVP winners. Bell was a Cub for just 1991, earning a National League All-Star selection with his .285/.323/.468 line and 25 home runs.

During 1992 spring training, Bell was traded across town to the Chicago White Sox and back to the American League. Coming the other way in the trade to the Cubs were pitcher Ken Patterson and a young Sammy Sosa. The White Sox saw Bell and his power as the key to getting them over the hump in the AL West. Bell was also much more amenable at this point in his career to a role that emphasized time at designated hitter with a bit of time in left field. He responded with a very solid 1992. The power was still there but the batting average began to slip, and the strikeout total began to rise, just slightly. Still, his 25 home runs and .255/.294/.418 line in 1992 were a solid contribution. The following year was more a disappointment for himself; he hit only 13 home runs, his fewest since 1983, and had a batting a line of .217/.243/.363. He missed 40 games in July and August after having surgery to repair torn cartilage in his right knee. When he returned in September, it was clear that something was still wrong. The White Sox did win the division in 1993 but Bell did not appear in the ALCS, which Chicago lost to the Blue Jays. Bell responded by making very harsh comments about manager Gene Lamont.[8] The White Sox responded by declining to pick up Bell's $3.3 million option for 1994 and released him on October 13.

Bell chose to retire at this point, returning to his native Dominican Republic. He has spent most of his time in retirement on his 37-foot boat and golfing, enjoying the sun and waters of his native land. He has also done some short-term coaching with the Dominican World Baseball Classic teams.[9] In 1996 he and former teammate Dave Stieb were the charter inductees to Toronto's Level of Excellence. Throughout the years, Bell spent time with the Blue Jays as a minor-league instructor and consultant. In 2013 he was inducted into the Canadian Baseball Hall of Fame. As of 2018, Bell's name was still high on leaderboards of Blue Jays hitters. He was fourth in runs batted in (740), fifth in hits (1,294), and sixth in home runs (202). His 47 home runs in 1987 rank second in single-season total for a Toronto slugger (José Bautista, 54 in 2010). He was one of only two Blue Jays to win the AL MVP award, being joined by Josh Donaldson in 2015.

SOURCES

In addition to the sources cited in the Notes, the author also used Baseball-Reference.com and Retrosheet.com.

NOTES

1. Dave Matthews, "Sparky Uneasy with Tiger Victory," *Lansing (Michigan) State Journal*, April 10, 1981: C-2.
2. For example, in a piece by Maury Allen, "Barfield, Bell Help Jays gel," *New York Post*, June 9, 1987.
3. Marty York, "Who's This Guy, George Bell?" *The Sporting News*, July 13, 1987: 16.
4. Jim Donaghy, "Bell Lures AL MVP Title Across Border," *Albany Times Union*, November 18, 1987: D-1.
5. Neil McCarl, "Blue Jays' DH Role: It's No Bell Prize," *Toronto Sun*, March 26, 1988: 22.
6. "Behind the Seams," *USA Today*, August 11, 1989: 6C.
7. Chuck Johnson, "Bell Confident He'll Eventually Earn Respect," *USA Today*, June 26, 1990.
8. Mike Shalin, "Benched Bell Trashes Lamont," *New York Post*, October 9, 1993.
9. Teresa Nickerson, "Interview of the Month," torontobluejays.com, February 6, 1997, retrieved November 1, 2018..

RAFAEL BELLIARD

by Joe Cox

On the night of September 26, 1997, the Atlanta Braves and New York Mets were playing out the dregs of the regular season before a small crowd at Shea Stadium. But if part of baseball's appeal is that any trip to the ballpark can yield historic accomplishments, the partisans of New York were in for a treat.

In the seventh inning, Atlanta shortstop Rafael Belliard turned on a fastball from Mets lefty Brian Bohanon and hooked it over the left-field wall for a game-tying home run. The Braves dugout exploded, with many of Atlanta's biggest stars grinning like Little Leaguers as Belliard circled the bases and returned to the dugout amid an atmosphere of pandemonium. The celebration seemed to be of the type reserved for a pennant clincher or a ninth-inning grand slam. It was a long time coming.

"I've been looking for that for 10 years," Belliard exclaimed after the game. "Finally, I get it tonight. I'm dreaming."[1]

Rafael Belliard, 5-foot-6 shortstop extraordinaire, had hit his only previous big-league home run on May 5, 1987. After 10½ years and 1,869 major-league at-bats, Belliard finally managed his second – and final – big-league home run.

Belliard, as much as anyone, typified the good field/no hit shortstops who proliferated in the big leagues during his reign from the early 1980s to the late 1990s. He earned his way into the major leagues with his foot speed and fielding prowess and stayed there despite his lack of skill on offense, particularly power.

Belliard may be best remembered today for his 10½-year homerless drought. But instead of being memorialized as a ballplayer for what his career didn't include, Belliard could as easily be remembered for his decade and a half in the major leagues, for his slick glove, solid bunting, and for being a part of a Braves team that allowed him to appear in four World Series, and even star in one.

And then every 10 years or so, he'd add a home run.

Rafael Leonidas Belliard Mattias was born on October 24, 1961, in Puerto Nuevo, Dominican Republic. Like many boys his age, Belliard spent a large part of his childhood refining his baseball skills, which in his case were largely defensive. "In the Dominican, we play all year long, no matter where," he reflected in 1991. "There you practiced every day like spring training. You have like one month off, then you're back in practice."[2]

Photo courtesy of the Pittsburgh Pirates

When Belliard was 17, he took a bus trip to Santo Domingo, where he tried out for a Dominican military team. When his slick fielding earned him a spot on the squad, his compensation was roughly $80 per month.[3] Belliard's big break likely was the 1979 Pan American Games, where his Dominican squad finished second, losing only to champion Cuba. Scouts may have watched the games to observe a lackluster 5-3 US squad, which failed to medal, but they couldn't fail to observe the pint-sized Dominican shortstop who not only caught everything hit to him, but managed to bat .375 in the eight games played.

Pittsburgh scout Pablo Cruz urged the Pirates to sign Belliard. When some questioned Cruz about the infielder's diminutive size, Cruz told them "not to worry about balls hit over his head, because there wouldn't be many hit through his legs."[4] Cruz also told other Pirates executives, "He has winning blood."[5]

Belliard signed with Pittsburgh in 1980, and that winning blood didn't manifest itself right away. In the summer of 1980, in 20 games split between the Gulf Coast League and the Pirates' South Atlantic League farm team in Shelby, he hit .182. He split time between second base, third base, and shortstop, and while his defensive skills were obvious, so were the limitations of his game. Few pegged Belliard as a long-term major leaguer.

The story essentially remained the same in 1981, when Pittsburgh made Belliard the everyday shortstop for the Class-A Alexandria Dukes. Belliard, who was just 19, played in 127 games and showed many of the skills that would define his career. He was part of 73 double plays at shortstop, which nearly led his league, had a dozen sacrifice bunts, and stole 42 bases. He also posted a batting line of .216/.264/.250 and fanned 92 times.

For many players, a promising career could have ended right there. But Belliard's destiny was shaped by the acts of the parent club, who were about to trade 1981 shortstop Tim Foli to the California Angels. Pittsburgh then planned to hand the everyday job to Dale Berra. The son of Yankee Hall of Famer Yogi Berra, Dale was a Pittsburgh first-round draft choice and had filled a utility role with the team for several seasons. He not only had the pedigree to be an everyday big leaguer, he had some of the necessary skills, but he struggled with consistency. In 1982 Berra would be the Pittsburgh shortstop, but he would need a backup, particularly somebody strong with the glove.

Meanwhile, Rafael Belliard spent most of the 1982 season with Double-A Buffalo. The starting job at shortstop there belonged to highly touted prospect Gregory Pastors. Pastors hit .193, and Belliard significantly outplayed him, batting .274 in 124 at-bats and posting a higher fielding percentage. Accordingly, on September 6, the Pirates called Belliard to the major leagues. He played in nine games, mostly as a pinch-runner and defensive replacement. He experienced his first major-league at-bat on September 25, pinch-hitting a single off Montreal's Scott Sanderson before stealing second base and scoring a run. Belliard ended the season 1-for-2 at the plate and handled four chances flawlessly in the field.

Belliard spent the next three seasons bouncing between the minor leagues, brief stints in Pittsburgh, and on one occasion, a lengthy trip to the disabled list. Most of 1983 was spent in Double-A Lynn (where he hit .262 in 431 at-bats). Most of 1984 was spent on the disabled list after Belliard fractured his left fibula on a bad landing from a difficult infield throw in Chicago. If there is any karma bounceback, surely it was 1985, when Belliard spent most of the season in Triple-A Hawaii (where he hit .246 in 341 at-bats). Altogether Belliard played in 41 big-league games from 1983 to 1985. He was 9-for-43 at the plate during those seasons.

Meanwhile, Pittsburgh had continued to rely on Dale Berra at shortstop, despite declining offensive returns and three consecutive 30-error seasons. Berra's performance issues may be somewhat explained by his appearance in the Pittsburgh Drug Trials of 1985. After the 1984 season, the Pirates dealt Berra to the Yankees, where his father was the manager. Among the players they gained in return was Tim Foli. A March 1985 item in *The Sporting News* indicated that Belliard might split time with Foli,[6] but the latter retired after hitting .189 in 37 at-bats in Pittsburgh.

The Pirates went with Sam Khalifa at shortstop in 1985. He promptly hit .238 and made 16 errors, and after Pittsburgh went 57-104, manager Chuck Tanner was sent packing, to be followed by a career minor leaguer named Jim Leyland. It was one of the most fortunate moments of Rafael Belliard's career.

In the spring of 1986, Belliard was trying to play his way into a crowded shortstop rotation in Pittsburgh. The Pirates returned starter Khalifa and veteran Johnnie LeMaster. But Belliard made his mark. The Pirates released LeMaster before Opening Day, with Leyland telling a reporter, "Belliard played his way on the club. He has more versatility than LeMaster."[7]

Belliard spent his first full season in the big leagues under Leyland, who valued both youth and defense. As Belliard continued to improve, Khalifa struggled, and was ultimately sent down to the minors. The Pirates signed veteran U L Washington, but gave the majority of time at shortstop to Belliard. Rafael even provided some offensive punch early in the season, going 15-for-33 during one streak, and hitting .248 in the first half of the season, with 23 RBIs and 10 stolen bases.

He played in 117 games in 1986, mostly at shortstop, although he occasionally filled in at second base. His defense continued to be a highlight, as he finished fourth in the NL in range factor per nine innings as a shortstop, and fifth in the league in total zone runs among shortstops. Offensively, Belliard's 11 sacrifices were seventh most in the National League. That said, his .233/.298/.262 offensive line ensured that Belliard would continue to split time with more offensively capable middle infielders.

The 1987 season was something of a step back for Belliard. In spring training, Pirates GM Syd Thrift told a reporter, "You really need two (shortstops)."[8] Concern over Belliard's physical durability and his shy, quiet nature were cited as evidence in favor of the Pirates' search for another shortstop.[9] For the first half of the season, the concerns seemed unfounded. Belliard launched his first career home run on May 5, a three-run blast off the Padres' Eric Show. While Belliard had some struggles, Leyland spoke out in his favor, telling reporters that while Belliard was "not a .300 hitter," he also was "not a .200 hitter, either."[10] Leyland drew parallels between Belliard's defensive skills and those of Baltimore shortstop Mark Belanger, ultimately telling the media, "If the lineup just does what they can do, we feel we can play Belliard at shortstop and not worry about it."[11] It didn't work out that way in 1987.

Belliard was hitting .187 on July 8, when he was demoted to Double-A Harrisburg. He hit .338 there, and was recalled by the Pirates on August 16. Belliard promptly went 6-for-10 before ending his season by breaking his leg on August 26 while completing a double play against the Reds. The brief hot streak did allow Belliard to finish the season at .207, but he played in only 81 games, batting 203 times to post his .207/.286/.271 offensive line.

Over the next three years in Pittsburgh, the same basic pattern followed. The Pirates – particularly Leyland – appreciated Belliard's smooth glove and versatility. (Belliard even played a few games at third base for the Pirates in 1989 and 1990.) However, he simply didn't hit enough to be more than a part-time player. In 1988 Belliard played in 122 games, but was part of a three-headed Pittsburgh shortstop group (along with Felix Fermin and Al Pedrique) that combined to have more errors (20) than RBIs (17). Belliard played less in 1989 (67 games, 154 at-bats) and 1990 (47 games, 54 at-bats). Pittsburgh was increasingly playing shortstop Jay Bell at the position, and in 1990 Belliard's future was again in jeopardy after he was left off the Pirates' postseason roster when the team reached the 1990 NLCS.

In December 1990, a free agent, Belliard signed a two-year, $800,000 contract with the last-place Atlanta Braves. Braves GM John Schuerholz acted on some rave reviews from those close to Belliard. Former Pirate Sid Bream, who would play with Belliard in Atlanta, told Schuerholz, "He's as good a shortstop as Ozzie Smith."[12]

Veteran manager Bobby Cox used Belliard in tandem with good-hit, no-field shortstop Jeff Blauser, and the young Atlanta pitching staff, which included John Smoltz, Tom Glavine, and Steve Avery, provided many leads that justified keeping the light-hitting Belliard in games for defensive purposes. But Cox saw Belliard as his everyday shortstop, and told Rafael so. "I told him I hadn't really done that," recalled Belliard.[13]

Belliard played in 149 games in 1991, and batted 353 times, both career highs. He didn't lack for production, batting a career-best .249 and having some genuinely impressive hot streaks at the plate. On May 7 and 8, in a home series against the Cardinals, Belliard had five hits, including three doubles and a triple, to go with eight RBIs in the two games. Meanwhile, Belliard continued to impress Cox with his glove work. Late in the season, the skipper said, "Defense is a main part of the reason we are where we are and those two guys on the left side of our infield [Belliard and third baseman Terry Pendleton] are as good as there is."[14]

When Atlanta played its way to a division title on the last weekend of the season, Belliard found himself taking on some familiar faces in his first playoff appearance. The Braves faced the Pirates in a seven-game NLCS, and Belliard started all seven games. He went 4-for-19 in the series, but also helped Braves pitchers rack up three shutouts over Pittsburgh, the final a 4-0 win in Game Seven.

From there, Belliard had a World Series to remember in the Braves' seven-game loss to the Twins. He again started every game, and went 6-for-16 at the plate, knocking in four runs. He also went errorless in 29 defensive chances, including four double plays, two of which helped preserve Game Seven as a scoreless tie until the 10th inning, when Minnesota broke the Braves' hearts. Despite the tough loss, Belliard had experienced his best season as a big leaguer and finished it with a superb World Series. "I knew I was playing for something important," Belliard said a quarter-century later, also admitting, "Hey, it did (surprise) me."[15]

In 1992 Belliard and the Braves played their way back to the Series again. This time, Rafael played in 144 games, earning 285 at-bats. But he hit only .211, and thus found himself filling in for defensive purposes by the time of the playoffs, batting once in the NLCS and contributing only a sacrifice bunt in the World Series against the Blue Jays. Still, observers cited Belliard for making "a sizeable contribution to the Braves' 1991 National League pennant" and being "just as important in 1992."[16]

From there, Belliard would serve Atlanta only as a reserve. Blauser had come into his own as an offensive threat, and while Rafael still appeared for defensive purposes at shortstop or occasionally at second base, he never again eclipsed 180 at-bats in a season.

The remaining highlight of Belliard's career was the 1995 season, when he did take those 180 at-bats, playing in 75 games for Atlanta, and finally winning the World Series that had eluded the squad. Belliard batted .222 in 1995, but Jeff Blauser was injured down the stretch run and Belliard again found himself an everyday shortstop in the World Series.

Belliard went 0-for-16 at the plate in the Series, but found ways to contribute, even during a hitting slump. His successful seventh-inning squeeze bunt in Game One was the winning margin of the Braves' 3-2 win over the Indians. He remained on the field to the end of the clinching Game Six, joining the dogpile on the pitching mound when Mark Wohlers retired the final batter of the Braves' title run.

From there, age and the continued improvement of other Braves shortstops spelled the gradual decline of Belliard's big-league career. He did manage his elusive second career home run in late 1997, but the following spring, after starting the season 5-for-20 and playing in seven of the Braves' first eight games, Belliard tore his left quadriceps muscle.[17] While he did rehabilitate himself from the injury, and the Braves had him on postseason standby if he was needed, Belliard never played in another major-league game after April 9, 1998.

In bits and pieces of 17 seasons in major-league baseball, Belliard finished his career as a .221 hitter. His 508 career hits included only two home runs, and he knocked in 142 total runs. Belliard's career OPS+ of 46 is a testimony to his struggles at bat, but he was a career .974 fielder at shortstop, and he ranks among the top 75 shortstops in total zone runs (since the stat can be tracked, which dates back to 1953).

Belliard transitioned from playing to coaching, spending several years with Atlanta as a roving minor-league instructor and then coaching for the Tigers.[18] During the offseason before 2013, Belliard was diagnosed with prostate cancer, but he underwent surgery with positive results.[19] In 2014 Belliard went to work for the Kansas City Royals, first as a special assistant to the general manager, and then, starting in 2015, as a roving infield coordinator. When not on the road, he lives in Boca Raton, Florida, with his wife of over three decades, Leonora. They have a son and two grandchildren.

While comic foibles of Belliard's decade-long chase after his second home run might be the biggest memory that casual fans have of his career, his four decades in Organized Baseball point to the incredible success of the undersized glove man. Perhaps instead of Belliard's inability to hit the long ball, future fans should know of his defensive skills, his positive attitude throughout his career's many twists and turns, and his surprising postseason heroics.

NOTES

1. Buster Olney, "It's No Small Feat as Braves' Belliard Hits a Rare Homer," *New York Times*, September 27, 1997.
2. C. Ron Allen, "Touching Bases: Series Star for Braves Offers to Help Abused and Abandoned Children's Home in Boca," *South Florida Sun Sentinel* (Fort Lauderdale), November 13, 1991.
3. Steve Wulf, "Standing Tall at Short," *Sports Illustrated*, February 9, 1987. Interestingly, *Sports Illustrated* said it was a Navy team, while the *Atlanta Journal-Constitution* referred to it as an Army squad in a September 16, 2016, profile of Belliard, which is cited below.
4. Charles Feeney, "Belliard Has the Right Bloodlines," *The Sporting News*, June 30, 1986: 21.
5. Feeney, "Belliard Has the Right Bloodlines."
6. Charles Feeney, "Foli May Share Short with Belliard," *The Sporting News*, March 25, 1985: 31.
7. Charles Feeney, "Pirates' Accent on Youth Added Khalifa, Belliard," *The Sporting News*, April 21, 1986: 26.
8. *The Sporting News*, February 16, 1987: 34.
9. *The Sporting News*, February 16, 1987: 34.
10. Bob Hertzel, "He's Still a Glove Man," *The Sporting News*, May 25, 1987: 15.
11. Hertzel, "He's Still a Glove Man."
12. Joel Bierig and Bruce Levine, "Brave New World," *The Sporting News*, May 27, 1991: 10.
13. I.J. Rosenberg, "Belliard Provided Defense, Clutch Play During Braves' Run," *Atlanta Journal-Constitution*, September 16, 2016.
14. Ross Newhan, "In Defense, Pendleton, Belliard are Fallible," *Los Angeles Times*, September 22, 1991.
15. Rosenberg, "Belliard Provided Defense."
16. Dave Nightengale, "Make a Deal, Face the Wheel," *The Sporting News*, November 23, 1992: 41.
17. *The Sporting News*, April 20, 1998: 38.
18. Rosenberg, "Belliard Provided Defense."
19. Jason Beck, "Following surgery, Belliard grateful for quick response," MLB.com, February 23, 2013, mlb.com/news/following-surgery-belliard-grateful-for-quick-response/c-41910186.

Pedro Borbon

by Jorge Iber

Given the offensive firepower of the Big Red Machine, it is quite easy to overlook the contributions of the pitching staff to the franchise's success and its two World Series banners in 1975 and 1976. Clearly, it was a run-scoring powerhouse that featured talents like Johnny Bench, Pete Rose, Joe Morgan, and Tony Pérez and often simply pummeled divisional, National League, and World Series opponents into submission. Still, it is also necessary to highlight the contributions of players like Don Gullett, Gary Nolan, Jack Billingham, Clay Carroll, Tom Hall, and others who served at the pleasure/behest of manager George "Sparky" Anderson (also known as Captain Hook), a man who never shied away from bringing in a reliever or juggling a starting rotation. One of the key members of this staff during the glory years of the 1970s, indeed one of the best relievers in all of baseball during this era, was a proud, intense, and very often temperamental Dominican named Pedro Borbón.

Pedro Borbón Rodriguez was born on December 2, 1946, in the town of Mao in what is now known as Valverde Province (it was part of Santiago Province until 1958), Dominican Republic. Sources on Borbón's life provide little information that details his schooling,

Photo courtesy of the National Baseball Hall of Fame

though some indicated that he never attended high school. Given the economic and social circumstances of Dominican society during this era, it is possible that Pedro received only a scant formal education. What he always possessed, however, was a fiery and competitive disposition, and this was manifested in part by his love for cockfighting from a young age. Borbón has also indicated that he did not play baseball in his youth until he was about 16. Given the ubiquity of the sport in the Dominican Republic, this tale seems a bit far-fetched (though very much in keeping with his character).

Borbón claimed that he initially played catcher until he was struck in the head by a bat as he reached for a pitch. This settled matters in his mind, and Pedro quickly made the switch to the mound, where he felt he would be safer (and could take greater advantage of his strong and resilient arm). In mid-October 1964, at the age of 17, he signed with the St. Louis Cardinals, and was shipped off to his first farm system assignment, in Cedar Rapids, Iowa (Midwest League), for the 1966 campaign.

Borbón spent three years in the Cardinals system and pitched quite well: 6-1, 1.96 for Cedar Rapids; 5-4, 2.29 for St. Petersburg (Florida State League), and 8-5, 2.34 for Modesto (California League). Used almost solely as a relief pitcher (just three starts in the three seasons), he had still not advanced beyond Single-A ball after his third season, 1968. When he was not placed on the Cardinals' 40-man roster after that season, he became eligible for the Rule 5 draft and was selected by the California Angels. In order to protect him, the Angels had to keep Borbón in the major leagues for the entire 1969 season.

Borbón made his major-league debut on April 9, 1969, against the Seattle Pilots, pitching three shutout innings in relief of starter Andy Messersmith and earning an impressive victory. But his promising start was an aberration, as he pitched in just 22 games for the Angels, and finished 2-3 with a 6.15 ERA. While the Angels believed a "sore arm" was to blame, he was included in a big trade they made in November with the Reds; Borbón moved to Cincinnati with pitchers Jim McGlothlin and Vern Geishert in exchange for outfielder Alex Johnson and infielder Chico Ruiz. The Reds needed starting pitching, and coveted the 26-year-old McGlothlin. Borbón was a minor part of the deal.[1]

Borbón did not make a positive first impression with his new ballclub, as he was involved in what Commissioner Bowie Kuhn considered an "inexcusable and intolerable" act during a game in the Dominican Winter League in December.[2] Borbón was fined severely by major-league baseball as a result of two confrontations with umpires. Initially, he was fined $50 and suspended for three Winter League games, but Kuhn felt this was not sufficient. In February 1970 the commissioner raised the fine to $500 and suspended Borbón (and Rico Carty as well) for the following winter season. This was the first of several incidents in which Borbón's fiery temper tarnished his reputation with his major-league colleagues and officials.[3]

During the 1970 summer season, the young Dominican fireballer spent most of his time with Indianapolis of the Triple-A American Association, where he finished 5-2 with a 3.30 ERA. He made it to Cincinnati for several weeks in midsummer, but had a 0-2 record and a 6.75 ERA. The Reds breezed to the division title and the National League pennant, but Borbón played no part in the postseason festivities. He was later granted permission to return to play in the Dominican Winter League, toiling on the mound for Licey.[4]

The 1972 campaign saw Borbón's breakthrough for the Reds, and he produced excellent and flexible relief work the entire season. In one two-week stretch starting in late June, during which the Reds won 13 of 14 games, Pedro made five relief appearances, for a total of 14⅓ innings, yielding only one run and six hits while earning four saves and one win. "He can throw, and throw and throw," Anderson crowed. "Even when I don't plan to use him, he wants to throw in the bullpen."⁵ Coach Ted Kluszewski considered Borbón to possess a "million-dollar arm."⁶ For the season, the young Dominican finished 8-3 with a 3.17 ERA in 62 games and 122 innings, while the Reds went all the way to the seventh game of the World Series before falling to the Oakland Athletics. Borbón pitched nine times in the postseason; his only poor performance was in Game Seven of the Series, as he gave up the deciding runs to the A's and took the loss.⁷

While 1973 was in many ways the best year of Borbón's career on the mound (11-4, 2.16 ERA in 80 games and 121 innings), it was also the year in which he became involved in a fracas that helped cement his reputation as a hot-tempered player, all too willing to be involved in fisticuffs. On October 8, with the Reds playing the Mets during Game Three of the NLCS, Pete Rose and New York shortstop Bud Harrelson became embroiled in a fight after Rose's hard slide into second base. As a result of the ensuing wrestling match, both benches cleared. At the end of the fracas Borbón retrieved what he believed to be was his cap from the Shea Stadium turf. When he realized it was actually a Mets hat, he took a bite out of the offending article. Similar incidents occurred later on in Borbón's career (a fistfight with teammate César Gerónimo in the Reds clubhouse, an altercation with Pirates pitcher Daryl Patterson in which Borbón bit his protagonist, and some run-ins at Cincinnati nightspots).⁸ Through it all, Borbón continued to pitch consistently excellent and durable baseball. In the 1973 NLCS, Borbón won Game One and saved Game Four, but the Reds fell to the Mets in five games.

The next four years were remarkably similar for Borbón. In fact, for the six-year period beginning in 1972, Borbón put up a 52-27 record, with a 3.06 ERA and 70 saves, averaging 71 appearances and 126 innings per season. Of course, the Reds were one of history's greatest teams in this period, winning four division titles and two World Series. In the victorious 1975 and 1976 postseasons, Borbón pitched in seven games. In his career he hurled in 20 postseason games, finishing with a win, three saves, and a 2.42 ERA.

Eventually the Reds dynasty faded away. The 31-year-old Borbón had an 8-2 record in 1978 but his 4.98 ERA was a better indicator of his struggles. After he started 2-2, 3.43 in 1979, on June 28 the Reds dealt their veteran reliever to the Giants in exchange for utilityman Hector Cruz. His first two appearances for San Francisco came against his old club—he earned a victory against the Reds on June 29 and picked up a save on July 1. Overall, however, the Reds were likely correct in their assessment that Borbón was no longer the pitcher he had been. He finished 4-3 for the Giants, but his ERA was 4.89. After he was released just before the 1980 season, Borbón signed with the Cardinals at the end of April but was let go after only 19 innings pitched with an ERA of 3.79, giving up a home run in each of his last three appearances. His final game in the major leagues was on May 25, 1980. The following spring, he was toiling for Monterrey in the Mexican League.⁹

Borbón was married to Griselda Ventura and they had three children, Pedro Jr., Harold, and Miguel. Pedro Jr. (born November 15, 1967, in Mao), followed in his father's footsteps and pitched in the major leagues between 1992 and 2003; the high point of his career came in 1995 when his Atlanta Braves won the World Series. When the young Pedro was a teen, his parents divorced and his relationship with his father became strained. "After the divorce, my dad was ... mentally messed up. He felt like a failure. So he kind of disappeared from my life," he told a reporter in 1995.¹⁰ Pedro Jr. eventually moved to New York City to live with relatives, and he became a standout pitcher at DeWitt Clinton High

School and later at Ranger Junior College in Ranger, Texas. Father and son did not see each other on a regular basis for many years, and the younger Borbón noted in a 1999 interview that the relationship was still a work in progress: "We talk every four or five months. There's a lot of fuel there. We don't want to put a match to it because it'll explode. So we talk like we just talked yesterday."[11]

Although Borbón's career was often marred by incidents of violence and poor judgment, his time in the Cincinnati bullpen was marked by much success as he became the "go-to" reliever for one of the best teams in baseball history. After retiring from the major leagues Borbón continued to pitch in various minor and semipro leagues in Latin America and the US. In 2011 he resided in Pharr, Texas, just across the border from Reynosa, Mexico, along with his second wife. The Reds in 2010 inducted him into their Hall of Fame in recognition of his contributions to the Big Red Machine.

Pedro Borbón died, at age 65, on June 4, 2012, at his home in Pharr. He had been battling cancer. Among the many tributes from former teammates, Tony Pérez recalled, "I always enjoyed his company on and off the field. He was a great guy."[12]

SOURCES

Bjarkman, Peter J. *Baseball's Great Dynasties: The Reds* (New York: Gallery Books, 1991).

Frost, Mark. *Game Six: Cincinnati, Boston, and the 1975 World Series: The Triumph of America's Pastime* (New York: Hyperion, 2009).

Hertzel, Bob. *The Big Red Machine* (Englewood Cliffs, New Jersey: Prentice Hall, Inc, 1976).

Lawson, Earl. *Cincinnati Seasons: My 34 Years with the Reds* (South Bend, Indiana: Diamond Communications, Inc., 1987).

McCoy, Hal. *The Relentless Reds* (Shelbyville, Kentucky: PressCo, 1976).

Posnanski, Joe. *The Machine: A Hot Team, A Legendary Season, and a Heart-Stopping World Series: The Story of the 1975 Cincinnati Reds* (New York: William Morrow, 2009).

Walker, Robert Harris. *Cincinnati and the Big Red Machine* (Bloomington, Indiana: Indiana University Press, 1988).

NOTES

1. Earl Lawson, "Shoppers and Swappers Check Maloney Showcase," *The Sporting News,* December 13, 1969: 38; "83 Percent Red Turnover in 3 Year Howsam Reign," *The Sporting News,* January 24, 1970: 41.

2. John Wiebusch, "What a Miracle This Is! Dead Angels Walk Again," *The Sporting News*, September 13, 1969: 19.

3. John Wiebusch, "Kuhn Fines Two for 'Inexcusable Conduct' in D.R.," *The Sporting News*, February 21, 1970: 47.

4. Miguel Frau, "Licey Romps to Caribbean Championship, *The Sporting News,* February 27, 1971: 31; "D.R. Data," *The Sporting News,* December 11, 1971: 55.

5. Earl Lawson, "Reds Forecast 150 Runs for Galloping Morgan," *The Sporting News,* July 1, 1972, 5

6. Earl Lawson, "Reds Forecast 150 Runs for Galloping Morgan."

7. Earl Lawson, "Reds Forecast 150 Runs for Galloping Morgan."

8. Earl Lawson, "Reds Copy A's Plan With Fist Fight," *The Sporting News,* August 16, 1975, 40; Earl Lawson, "Caught on the Fly" *The Sporting News*, December 31, 1977, 62; Jeff Meron, "Put Up Your Dukes," *ESPN Page 2,* http://espn.go.com/page2/s/list/basebrawl.html; Pedro Borbón Hall of Fame Directory page, http://mlb.mlb.com/cin/hof/directory.jsp?hof_id=111227.

9. Salo Otero, "Ex-Major Leaguers Hold On in Mexico," *Laredo Morning Times*, May 9, 1981: 41.

10. Stacy Y. China, "After Up and Down Times, Bronx's Borbón Jr. Up Again," *Newsday*, October 26, 1995: A74.

11. Karen Crouse, "Adversity Makes Borbón Better," *Daily News* (Los Angeles), July 27, 1999. https://www.thefreelibrary.com/ADVERSITY+MAKES+BORBON+BETTER.-a083618333on December 20, 2018.

12. "Pedro Borbón dead at 65," *Cincinnati News*, June 4, 2012.

RICO CARTY

by Wynn Montgomery

In 1964, a 24-year-old Dominican strongman named Ricardo Adolfo Jacobo (Rico) Carty burst into the major leagues like a tropical storm. After two hitless at-bats in 1963, Carty's batting average (.330) in his first full season was the second highest in the majors. Only Roberto Clemente hit better, and only a phenomenal year by Philadelphia's Richie Allen prevented Carty from being voted Rookie of the Year. He had exceeded the high expectations created by a stellar four-year minor-league apprenticeship and quickly became "one of the most popular players ever to wear a Milwaukee uniform."[1] After the Braves relocated, his popularity grew in Atlanta, where the left-field stands became known as "Carty's Corner."[2]

Lofty predictions regarding Carty's future did not materialize due to an unfortunate combination of illness, injuries, ineptitude on defense, and a reputation as a troublemaker. Concerns about Carty's prowess in the field plagued him throughout his seven seasons with the Braves. His 1973 move to the American League—which included an abbreviated appearance with the Oakland Athletics—coincided with the birth of the designated hitter, which most baseball people thought fit Rico like a glove, but Carty initially resisted.[3] Poor performance in his first year as a DH seemed to have ended his career, but a good season in the Mexican League earned Carty the chance to resurrect his career.

Rico Carty's baseball journey began in San Pedro de Macoris, Dominican Republic, where he was born on September 1, 1939, one of 16 children. His mother, Olivia, was a midwife; his father, Leopoldo, worked in the sugar mill and played club cricket.[4] Rico played pick-up baseball until he was 15, when he followed the example of four uncles and turned to boxing. He won his first 17 bouts (12 by KOs), but turned to baseball full-time after one embarrassing ring defeat.[5]

In 1959 Carty joined (as a catcher) the Dominican team that played in the Pan-Am Games in Chicago, and he attracted considerable attention. Eight major-league teams and four Dominican League clubs offered him contracts, and the naïve youngster signed them all. George Trautman, head of minor-league baseball at the time, resolved the resulting dispute in favor of Milwaukee.

Carty's professional baseball career began in 1960 with Davenport/Quad Cities in the Class-D Midwest League. He struggled both with the English language and with minor-league pitching, but moved up to Class-C Eau

Claire in 1961. In 1962, at Class-B Yakima, Carty showed the hitting skills that would ensure his future success. He also showed the penchant for injury that would limit that success. His .366 average was leading the Northwest League when he tripped over first base, pulling a leg muscle and ending his season. He lost the batting race but made the year-end league All-Star team and was the Topps Class-B All-Star catcher.

Carty started the 1963 season at Triple-A Toronto, where he was hailed as "the best catching prospect ... in 10 years."[6] Even so, he was sent down to Double-A Austin to be converted into an outfielder because the Braves had a bevy of young backstops. The only blemish on Rico's season, and perhaps another portent of the future, came when he decked a spectator for heckling him.

Despite his late arrival, Carty ended the season among Texas League leaders with a .327 average, 27 home runs, and 100 RBIs. He made his major-league debut on September 15, 1963, striking out as a pinch-hitter. The future looked bright for Carty, who was now being touted as "the best young hitting prospect in the [Braves] organization."[7] He had an outstanding 1963-64 season in the Dominican League and then married Gladys Ramírez de Jacobo. They would have six children, who produced 16 grandchildren.[8] One son, Rico Jr., played 16 games as a Seattle Mariner farmhand.

After Carty's fine winter season, Braves farm director John Mullen compared him to Orlando Cepeda,[9] and his Grapefruit League performance justified the praise. He hit .408 and led the team with 13 RBIs. Carty made the Braves' 1964 Opening Day roster, but did not play regularly at first as manager Bobby Bragan tried to balance playing time among his outfielders (Hank Aaron, Felipe Alou, Lee Maye, and Carty). When Alou was hurt in late June and Rico took over in left field,

Photo courtesy of the National Baseball Hall of Fame

the Braves won 16 of their next 23 games. In late August, he ended a rare batting slump in dramatic fashion, delivering two 5-for-5 days within a week. He led the Braves in batting (.330) and slugging (.554), and made Topps' Rookie All-Star Team.

In January Carty became the first Brave to sign his 1965 contract (for a salary of $17,500).[10] He had a strong season in winter ball and reported for spring training, where Bragan was determined to transform him into a first baseman. Rico never mastered the new role and injured his back while trying to do so. Carty's back ailment kept him out of the lineup often throughout that season; he never played more than a week at a time. He complained that Bragan often jerked him from the lineup late in games, undermining his confidence,[11] but Carty's fielding lapses often justified the manager's actions. Late in the season, a doctor discovered that Carty's right leg was slightly shorter than his left and prescribed a corrective shoe, quieting those who had accused the slugger of exaggerating his back pain.

While the 1965 season was disappointing, Carty hit when he played, compiling a .310 average in 83 games (all in left field). He also demonstrated his willingness to speak out when he thought he'd been wronged. Both traits continued throughout his career—as did frequent trade rumors, which began to circulate during that offseason.

Carty spent the winter of 1965-66 in a new environment, playing winter ball for the Aragua Tigers in the Venezuelan League. He wore his new orthopedic shoe and led the league with a .392 batting average and 13 home runs, a new season record. When he returned to the US, he was again headed for a different setting—the Braves' new home in Atlanta—and renewed enthusiasm about his potential to become "the next great hitter in the National League"[12] Even so, he was the Braves' fourth outfielder, behind Aaron, Alou, and Mack Jones.

On June 4, 1966, Carty was inserted into the lineup as the starting catcher, and the Braves promptly won seven consecutive games as Rico went 12-for-24. But after nine games, he was back in left field. Trade rumors continued, but Carty was in the lineup to stay. He played in 151 games, even filling in at first base and third base, and hit .326 (third in the NL). During the offseason, Carty was the Brave most sought after player in trade, but the team now saw him as "the next NL batting champ."[13]

Before returning to the Dominican League for winter ball, Rico signed his 1967 contract (in the $25,000 range). He had another good season with the Estrellas Orientales, but his temper flared again, garnering him a $50 fine for insulting an umpire, and his injury jinx reappeared as he was hurt in a car crash.

The 1967 season began with optimism in Atlanta. The team had finished fifth in 1966, but had compiled a winning record (33-18) after Billy Hitchcock replaced Carty's nemesis Bragan. Those hopes faded quickly, however, as both the Braves and Rico had dismal seasons. The Braves fell to seventh place, and Carty had his first sub-.300 season in the majors, although he was relatively injury-free. The low moment of the season came on June 18, when Carty engaged in a "brief but heated scuffle" with Hank Aaron.[14] At the time, details were scarce, but Aaron later said that he was angry because Carty had loafed on a ball into the outfield and had called him a "black slick."[15] At season's end, the Braves were actively seeking trades, and Carty was "among the most likely to go."[16]

Carty won the 1967-68 Dominican League batting title (.350) and led Estrellas to the regular-season title and the playoff championship. He reported for spring training down ten pounds to his "fighting weight" of 190 and downplayed teammate Clete Boyer's offseason criticism (echoing Aaron's) that Carty "doesn't give 100 percent."[17]

Three weeks into 1968 spring training, Carty's injury jinx struck with a vengeance. He was diagnosed with tuberculosis. While the disease was "not as serious as first suspected," Rico was lost to the Braves for the season.[18]

When he reported for spring training in 1969, a rejuvenated Carty tied for the team lead in batting (.333) during the spring, but a dislocated shoulder put him on the disabled list on Opening Day. He finally got into a game on May 2 as a pinch-hitter and responded with a game-tying sacrifice fly. In his first start, on May 18, he re-injured that troublesome shoulder and missed another two weeks.

Carty was in and out of the lineup for much of the season, but returned to spark the Braves in their stretch drive to the first NL

West division title. He had hits in 19 of the final 21 games (17 Atlanta wins), averaging .383 and driving in 22 runs. He drove home the game-winning run in the division-clinching game and finished the season with a team-leading .342 average in 104 games.

The Braves lost that first League Championship Series in three straight games to the New York Mets, but Carty played well in what would be his only postseason appearance, hitting .300 and compiling a .462 on-base percentage and a .500 slugging average, but with no RBIs. He finished a surprising second to Tommie Agee as the NL Comeback Player although, as Hank Aaron observed, Agee "only came back from a bad year [while] Rico came back off a hospital bed."[19]

Carty hit .333 in the Dominican League that winter. He was also fined $50 and suspended for three days for shoving an umpire. Major League Baseball later added a $500 fine for "inexcusable and intolerable" conduct.[20]

Carty opened the 1970 season even better than he had ended 1969. He would have been a shoo-in for All-Star selection by the fans, but his name wasn't on the ballot. The list of 48 candidates in each league had been compiled during spring training, and Carty wasn't included. The fan voting period began on May 16, the day that saw the end to Rico's 31-game hitting streak, a team record that lasted until 2011. More than 2 million fans voted, and Rico received 552,382 votes (67,000 more than Pete Rose) to join Hank Aaron and Willie Mays in the NL's starting outfield as the first "write-in" All-Star.

Carty injured his wrist just before the All-Star Game, but started the game, batting twice (a walk and a groundout) before being replaced. In the latter half of the season, he suffered other injuries (a pulled leg muscle and a chipped bone in his finger caused when he was hit by a pitch), but he led the NL in batting average (.366) and on-base percentage (.454).

In the midst of his best season ever, however, Rico was involved in another fight with a teammate – pitcher Ron Reed. Carty insisted afterward that "it was just a misunderstanding,"[21] but he was on the trading block despite having the highest career batting average among active players.[22] Sports columnist Dick Young suggested that Carty was an excellent choice for any team "looking for a big bat and willing to accept a big headache."[23]

On December 11, 1970, a different form of physical conflict took Carty off the market; he collided with Dominican League teammate Matty Alou and suffered a fractured knee and ligament damage. He was flown to Atlanta for surgery on what a team doctor called "as bad a knee injury as an athlete can have."[24] With his career in jeopardy, he returned home to recover – after signing a contract that included a raise over his 1970 salary of $45,000.

Carty reported for 1971 spring training with his leg in a brace, and he hobbled out of the dugout on Opening Day to a standing ovation. He took batting practice on July 18 and hit the first pitch he saw off the top of the fence in left field. He was scheduled to return to the lineup on August 5, when the first 15,000 fans would receive buttons that read "SMILE – the Beeg Boy's Back."[25]

But a blood clot in his damaged leg ended any hope of a comeback, and Carty missed his second full season in four years. His bad luck didn't end there, however. On August 24 he and his young brother-in-law were involved in a fight with two off-duty Atlanta policemen when Rico took umbrage at a racial slur. Atlanta Mayor Sam Massell labeled the incident "blatant brutality" and suspended the officers.[26]

Although Carty played only sporadically during spring training and seemed destined to start the 1972 season as a pinch-hitter, he received a $50,000 contract after a trial period imposed by the Braves because of concerns about his physical condition. He hit well when he played, but developed elbow tendinitis and went on the disabled list with a pulled hamstring. He played in only 86 games that season and hit just .277. Though his career batting average (.315) was still the highest among active players,[27] in October the Braves traded him to the Texas Rangers.

Neither the Atlanta press nor Braves fans were happy about the trade, but Rico said he was not surprised because he and new manager Eddie Mathews were not on good terms.[28] Rangers GM Joe Burke admitted that some would call the trade a gamble, but expressed confidence that Carty had matured and was eager to play.[29] New Rangers manager Whitey Herzog emphasized that he was looking for "ballplayers, not Boy Scouts" -- a description that certainly fit Rico Carty.[30] Then Carty suffered another Dominican League injury; a pitch from Pedro Borbón fractured his jaw.

There was good news, however. The American League had adopted the designated-hitter rule, and Herzog called Carty "the perfect man for such a role."[31] Rico did not agree. The man whose defensive skills had been described as "amusing at best"[32] and who had accumulated more outfield errors (40) than assists (31) wanted to play on defense.

During 1973 spring training, Rico took a parting shot at the Braves, again singling out Eddie Mathews for criticism.[33] Word leaked out that Carty had won a $20,000 judgment against the Braves, whom he accused of shortchanging him by not sharing the funds the team received (under an agreement between MLB and the Dominican League) after his 1971 knee injury.[34]

On the field things were not going well for Carty. By early June his .203 average had cost him the Rangers' DH job. He was back in left field and feuding with his manager.[35] When he was sidelined after breaking a small bone in his foot sliding into second base on July 19,

Rico's initial foray into the American League was over. He was hitting only .232 with three homers and 33 RBIs in 86 games for the Rangers when the Chicago Cubs acquired him on waivers on August 13.

Carty made his Cubs debut the following day, grounding out as a pinch-hitter in a loss to the Braves. The next day, he was batting cleanup and did so for most of his time with Chicago. His best day as a Cub came on August 28 in his first game as a visitor at Atlanta-Fulton County Stadium; he hit a two-run homer in his first at-bat and later singled to drive in two more runs in a 9-6 Cubs win. That was his only home run for the Cubs and half of his RBIs, and on September 11, after 22 games with the Wrigleyites, Carty was sold to the Oakland Athletics. He again demonstrated his willingness to attack local legends, blaming his demise in Chicago on Ron Santo, whom he called a "selfish ballplayer."[36] The more likely reason was his .214 batting average and .257 slugging percentage – both career lows.

The Athletics were leading their division by six games when they acquired Carty "for reasons unclear to outside observers," and they finished the season in the same position.[37] Rico appeared in seven of the Athletics' final 18 games, hitting .250 (2-for-8) and getting his only RBI with a solo home run. The A's went on to win the World Series, but Rico was not eligible for postseason play. When he was released on December 12, Rico complained that he had gotten only a termination telegram from the A's, who "didn't give me a Series share, a ring, a handshake – nothing at all."[38]

Everyone except Carty thought his career was over. He played winter ball in Mexico and then signed with Cordoba in the Mexican League, where his performance justified his self-confidence. He hit .354 (second in the league) with 11 home runs and 72 RBIs in 112 games,[39] and the Cleveland Indians, who were in a tight divisional pennant race, signed Rico to a $72,000 annual contract through the 1975 season. After 11 hitless at-bats, his first Tribe hit was a two-out, ninth-inning, game-tying RBI single. He then fought through a pulled hamstring to hit .363 in 33 games as a designated hitter and first baseman.

Carty was back with Cleveland in 1975, and the 35-year-old hit .308 and tied for the team lead in game-winning RBIs (9). He was even better in 1976, hitting above .400 until injuries once again shelved him. He played in a career-high 152 games, compiled a .310 batting average, and led the team with 83 RBIs. He had even become a fan of the DH rule, and Cleveland's baseball writers voted him Man of the Year.[40]

Despite this performance, the Indians did not protect Carty in the 1976 expansion draft. The Toronto Blue Jays made him their fifth pick but quickly traded him back to the Indians. In 1977 he was the highest-paid Indian, making an estimated $90,000, but he started slowly.[41] He was hitting .200, and the team was in the division cellar (4-9) when he accepted the Wahoo Club's 1976 Man of The Year award with "one of the strangest acceptance speeches in history," criticizing manager Frank Robinson, who shared the head table, for "lack of leadership."[42] Carty had taken his reputation for confrontation to a new level, and when Robby fined Rico for "insubordination" after a June 6 dugout clash, local writers speculated that Carty would soon be traded.[43]

Instead, less than two weeks later, Robinson was fired. Carty finished the season hitting "only" .280 while leading the team in RBIs (80). He signed on with Cleveland for 1978, but when the Tribe acquired Willie Horton, Carty became expendable and was traded to the Blue Jays during spring training.[44]

Carty had 19 RBIs in April for Toronto. His troublesome hamstring again put him out of action briefly, but in a seven-game August homestand, Rico hit three homers and drove in six runs, bringing his season totals to 20 and 68, new franchise records. That was his farewell performance for the Jays, who soon traded Carty to Oakland for Willie Horton, whose arrival in Cleveland had led to Rico's departure.

Carty quickly made the trade look extremely one-sided in favor of the A's. After going hitless in his first game, he went on a 15-game hitting streak — two short of the club record. He hit eight homers in his first 19 games with Oakland and continued to top Horton's Toronto performance in every important offensive category. Carty's 31 homers for the season were his career high and set a new record at the time for designated hitters.

Carty made it clear that he intended to test the free-agent market in 1979 and indicated that his next team would be his last. Even so, the Blue Jays reacquired Rico, believing they could sign him because they could play him every day.[45] When Carty was granted free agency, four teams sought him, but the Blue Jays signed him to a five-year partly-guaranteed contract for $1.1 million plus an immediate loan of $120,000 – not bad for a 39-year-old player with a history of frequent injuries.[46] Carty's 31-page contract was described as "probably the bulkiest in the history of baseball."[47]

After skipping winter ball, Carty pulled a calf muscle in spring training and hit under .200. The regular season saw no major improvements. In early June he was hitting only .250 and was the target of boos from Toronto fans. On July 1 he was benched after hitting only one homer in almost two months. Carty blamed his slump on a "freakish injury" – a swollen hand caused when he accidentally stabbed himself with a toothpick.[48] That 1979 season had few highlights for Rico, but on August 6 he hit his 200th career home run, becoming the oldest player (at 39 years, 339 days) to achieve that milestone. Overall, however, it was his worst season except for 1973, when he had shuttled among three teams. When Jays manager Roy Hartsfield was fired after that season, he observed that it had been "hard to live with Rico Carty's virtual lifetime deal."[49]

Hartsfield's successor did not have that challenge. Carty hit poorly in winter ball, where he was again hampered by a leg injury, and was still favoring his calf when spring training started. He was unconditionally released on March 29, 1980. His "lifetime" deal as a player had lasted one year, although he still worked for the Blue Jays as a Latin American scout.

Carty's major-league playing days were over, and his lifetime batting average had dropped to .299. Early visions of superstardom had not been realized, but, despite losing two entire seasons to illness and injury, he had played 13 seasons in the majors. He was big (6-feet-2) and slow, but he was a natural-born hitter. The flamboyant, self-described "Beeg Boy" made more comebacks than a boomerang, and few who saw him play will ever forget his aggressive right-handed swing and his trademark one-handed catches. He was a study in contrasts—known for his infectious grin and also for his fierce glare at the plate; popular because of his cheerful banter with fans yet branded a troublemaker. Carty argued that the latter reputation was unfounded, claiming he simply "stood up for his rights."[50] The record shows that he defended those rights frequently and that he was an equal-opportunity combatant, engaging in physical and/or verbal conflicts with teammates, managers, umpires, fans, local police, and at least one front office.

Rico Carty remained a hero in his homeland, where he lived as of 2014. During his playing days, he returned to the Dominican Republic almost every year to play winter ball, saying, "I owe my country a lot."[51] He retired as the Dominican League's all-time home run leader (59). That record was eclipsed, but Carty's legend survived. He didn't get to Cooperstown, but he is enshrined in two Halls of Fame, the ones honoring heroes of Caribbean Baseball (1996's inaugural class) and Latino Baseball (2011). He is an honorary general in the Dominican Army,[52] and he once thought he had been elected mayor of his hometown until a recount proved otherwise.[53]

Baseball gave Carty financial security,[54] and he stayed active in the game at home and elsewhere. In 1988 Rico led the Dominican team to a third-place finish in the first Men's Senior Baseball League World Series and won the home run contest in the 40-plus age bracket. League founder Steve Sigler said, "He's still an amazing hitter [at age 49], and he was the only one using a wooden bat."[55] He may have summarized Rico Carty's career: The "Beeg Boy" could hit … and he did things his way.

AUTHOR'S NOTE

I regret that this biography was completed without input from the subject. Extensive efforts to locate Rico Carty were fruitless. One representative of the Atlanta Braves said that Rico "has dropped off the map." Obviously, there is plenty of information on his career; I hope I have done him justice. If not, I'm sure he will let me know.

SOURCES

In addition to the sources cited in the Notes, the author consulted:

Kurlansky, Mark. *The Eastern Stars: How Baseball Changed the Dominican Town of San Pedro de Macoris* (New York: Riverhead Books, 2010).

Atlanta Braves Illustrated Yearbooks (1966-1972)

Chop Talk, the official monthly magazine of the Atlanta Braves

Milwaukee Braves Yearbook, 1964

Milwaukee Journal, Sarasota Herald-Tribune, Sports Illustrated, Baseball-Almanac.com, Baseballprospectus.com, Baseball-Reference.com, HardballTimes.com, MLBlogsNetwork (mlb.com), and Retrosheet.org.

NOTES

1. Bob Wolf, "Rookie Rico Set Off Tom-Tom Beating by Braves' Faithful," *The Sporting News,* July 25, 1964.
2. Wayne Minshew, "Friendly Rico Rates Tops on Tepee List," *The Sporting News*, July 12, 1969.
3. Randy Galloway, "Carty Shuns DH Job – I'm No Invalid," *The Sporting News*, March 24, 1973.
4. Rob Ruck, *Raceball: How the Major Leagues Colonized the Black and Latin Game* (Boston: Beacon Press: 2011). 202-204.
5. Mark Kurlansky, *The Eastern Stars: How Baseball Changed the Dominican Town of San Pedro de Macoris,*
6. "Leafs Rave Over Kid Carty," *The Sporting News*, April 20, 1963, 33.
7. Bob Wolf, "Braves Examine Hot-Shot Kids In 1964 Blue Print," *The Sporting News*, September 28, 1963.
8. Chris Boone, "Carty Still Loves the Braves," *ChopTalk*, April 26, 2006.
9. Bob Wolf, "Carty Rated Excellent Chance to Crash Braves Picket Party," *The Sporting News*, January 18, 1964.
10. Bob Wolf, "Braves Load Their Bench With Wallop in Oliver Bat," *The Sporting News*, January 16, 1965.
11. Bob Wolf, "Carty Lets Out Yelp In Bragan's Doghouse," *The Sporting News*, August 28, 1965.
12. Furman Bisher, "Ache-Free Carty May Put New Punch In Tepee Bats," *The Sporting News*, March 19, 1966.
13. " 'Everybody at Convention Eyed Carty,' Says McHale," *The Sporting News*, December 17, 1966, 30.
14. "Aaron-Carty Feud Explodes on Plane After No-Hitter," *The Sporting News*, July 1, 1967, 12.
15. Hank Aaron, with Lonnie Wheeler, *I Had a Hammer* (New York: Harper-Collins, 1991), 190.
16. Wayne Minshew, "Braves Cut Price Tags, Seek Deals," *The Sporting News*, October 7, 1967.
17. Jay Searcy, "Clete Takes Verbal Jab at Rico; 'He Loafs,' Claims Third Sacker," *The Sporting News*, February 24, 1968.
18. Wayne Minshew, "TB Kayoes Carty for Year," *The Sporting News*, April 13, 1968.
19. Wayne Minshew, "Same Old Rico – He's Hitting a Ton," *The Sporting News*, February 14, 1970.
20. *The Sporting News*, February 21, 1970: 49.
21. "Reed, Carty Have Fight Before Game," *Milwaukee Journal*, August 21, 1970.

22 Frank Eck, "Two-Year Tempo of .356 Lifts Carty to Lofty .321 for Career," *The Sporting News*, November 14, 1970.

23 Dick Young, "Young Ideas," *The Sporting News*, September 12, 1970.

24 Wayne Minshew, " 'With God's Help, I'll Be Back' – Carty," *The Sporting News*, January 30, 1971.

25 "Smile – That Beeg Boy's Coming Back to Braves," *The Sporting News*, August 7, 1971: 30.

26 "Carty Beaten; Atlanta Policemen Suspended," *Sarasota Herald-Tribune*, August 26, 1971.

27 Bob Fowler, "Killer, Oliva Express Doubt Over DH Rule," *The Sporting News*, February 3, 1973.

28 Wayne Minshew, "Braves Swapping of Carty Puts Mathews on Hot Seat," *The Sporting News*, November 18, 1972.

29 Merle Heryford, "Rangers Get Carty to Beef Up Attack," *The Sporting News*, November 11, 1972.

30 Randy Galloway, "Herzog Seeking 'Ballplayers, not Boy Scouts," *The Sporting News*, December 23, 1972.

31 Oscar Kahan, "DH's May Give Needed Hypo to AL," *The Sporting News*, January 27, 1973.

32 Peter Carry, "Player of the Week," *Sports Illustrated*, September 14, 1964

33 Wayne Minshew, "Carty Fires Volley at Mathews," *The Sporting News*, April 7, 1973.

34 Jerome Holtzman, "Reuschel Hungry for 20-Win Season," *The Sporting News*, May 19, 1973.

35 Merle Heryford, "Rico-Whitey Spat Ends in Truce," *The Sporting News*, June 23, 1973.

36 Ron Bergman, "A's Acorns," *The Sporting News*, October 6.

37 Ron Bergman, "A's Have a Credo: Do Jobs the Hard Way," *The Sporting News*, October 27, 1973.

38 *Sarasota Herald-Tribune*, August 25, 1974.

39 Cleveland Indians roster, *The Sporting News*, March 15, 1975.

40 On his sentiments regarding the DH rule, see Russell Schneider, "Carty's Ex-Bosses Wince – But Injuns Grin at Hot DH," *The Sporting News*, June 12, 1976.

41 Milton Richman, "Average Regular's Pay Rockets to $95,149," *The Sporting News*, April 23, 1976.

42 Russell Schneider, "Tepee Totters From Oral Blasts at Robinson," *The Sporting News*, May 14, 1977.

43 Russell Schneider, "Carty Exit Almost Certain After Hassle With Robby," *The Sporting News*, June 25, 1977.

44 Neil McCarl, "Jays Get Carty and Bosetti to Beef Up Anemic Attack," *The Sporting News*, April 1, 1978.

45 Neal McCarl, "Jays Miss Goal, Post 102 Losses," *The Sporting News*, October 21, 1978.

46 Murray Chass, "Ten Aging Free Agents Hit $15 Million Jackpot," *The Sporting News*, March 3, 1979.

47 Murray Chass, "Carty's Pact 31 Pages Long," *The Sporting News*, March 3, 1979.

48 Neil McCarl, "Howell Returns With Hot Bat and Tongue," *The Sporting News*, July 21, 1979.

49 Stan Isle, "Kroc Also Big in Milk – Milk of Human Kindness," *The Sporting News*, November 17, 1979.

50 Russell Schneider, "Rico's Bat a Bargain Buy for Indians," *The Sporting News*, September 14, 1974.

51 Rob Ruck, *The Tropic of Baseball: Baseball in the Dominican Republic* (Lincoln, Nebraska: Bison Books, 1999), 161.

52 Bruce Markusen, "Card Corner: Rico Carty," *Hardball Times*, October 8, 2010.

53 Bruce Markusen, "Cooperstown Confidential," MLBlogsNetwork, July 6, 2005 (mlb.com).

54 Rob Ruck, *The Tropic of Baseball,* 161.

55 Bob McCoy, "Keeping Score: Never Over the Hill," *The Sporting News*, November 21, 1988.

Luis Castillo

by Richard Bogovich

The 2017 All-Star Game was played in Miami, so it was natural for major media outlets to give some attention to the franchise hosting it. As one example, less than two weeks before the big event, Fox Sports reposted a FanSided article on the top five candidates among former Marlins to have their uniform numbers retired. On that short list was Luis Castillo.[1]

Luis Antonio Castillo Donato was born on September 12, 1975, in San Pedro de Macorís, Dominican Republic. His parents, Antonio and Faustina, raised Luis, his two brothers, and three sisters under incredibly humble conditions. Luis and his brothers were crammed into a small bedroom in a cement-block house. The family lived in the city's core, and its main baseball stadium happened to be just down the street. Luis's father first worked in a sugar mill but after losing that job resorted to selling fruit from the back of a pickup truck.[2]

Luis was 6 years old when he began playing baseball, but because he lived in a poorer area, some of his early experience was unusual. "Every boy in San Pedro de Macorís plays baseball in the front of his house with bottlecaps," reported Luis's brother Julio César, and they'd be struck with sticks instead of an actual bat.[3] As Luis and his friends grew older and took the game more seriously they had to be increasingly creative when it came to equipment. Instead of anything close to a conventional glove, Luis first used part of a plastic milk carton in the field. He would cut off some of it but keep the part with the handle and use it more like a scoop than a mitt.[4]

Luis didn't acquire an actual baseball glove, a used one, until he was around 12 years old. Instead of a real baseball, sometimes they made their own from rolled-up socks. When he was old enough to try out for organized teams he obtained a pair of spiked shoes, size 10½, but his feet were more than two sizes smaller so he stuffed the shoes with paper. He used a small workman's glove as a batting glove. He was able to improve it, he recalled, because he'd go "to the summer league games in the Dominican, and watch every game."[5] He'd also watch players afterward to see if they threw anything away. When one discarded a batting glove that surely was too large for Luis, he peeled off the Franklin logo and fastened it to his workman's glove. During winter league seasons he had opportunities to watch his favorite player, Alfredo Griffin, but reportedly didn't actually dream of becoming a major leaguer himself until about a year before he signed his first pro contract.[6]

Castillo's makeshift equipment has been credited with helping him build strength, speed, and skill. From swinging his first bat, an iron rod, he developed his wrists, and whenever he was able to use a real glove, it was so much easier to snag a drive than with a milk carton. Thus, when he was 11 he earned an opportunity to travel with a San Pedro team for a regional tournament in Puerto Rico. He could afford to go only because his mother awoke before dawn and made lunches that he took by bicycle six miles away, to sell to workers in the city's duty-free business park, where his sisters worked in grim sweatshops. Perhaps the most incredible aspect of Luis's youthful saga is that his bike had only one pedal and no brakes. All of the effort and struggle paid off: Luis's team won the tournament and he was the leading hitter. He was also grateful to his parents for guiding all six of their children away from lives plagued by crime and drugs. Baseball served as a good distraction. "I was being raised in a dangerous environment. I liked being in the streets and if I didn't respect my mom, I wouldn't be what I am," he said after his first season as a National League All-Star. "Thank God I listened to my mom and dad."[7]

For Luis's 14th birthday his mother gave him his first brand-new glove, a Juan Samuel model. Samuel was born in the same city and had been a major-league All-Star twice by then. "It was real expensive," Luis said. "I don't come from a family that has a lot of money, so my mom bought that for me and it was hard for me because I think that's money she can use to buy food for my family to eat."[8]

Nelson Rodríguez, founder of the youth league in which Luis honed his skills, would have considered Faustina naïve if she thought at the time that her son could play in the major leagues in the States. "No one imagined this, not even him," said Rodríguez, who coached Samuel and several other future major leaguers. "He was skinny and small ... very quiet. But with a great desire to get better."[9]

"I played baseball because I liked it," Castillo confirmed. "I didn't know I was going to be a professional player and be in the big leagues. I would play in the streets and people would be like, 'Hey, you're good.' I didn't know."[10]

According to the *2011 New York Mets Media Guide*, Luis graduated from the Colegio San Benito Abad high school in 1991,[11] though Kevin Baxter of the *Miami Herald* said that Castillo dropped out. Regardless, Luis's sister Maribel, a year old than him, told Baxter that schooling didn't seem the path to her brother's goals. "He was serious, but he was also restless," she recalled. "He never wanted to go to school ... because he wanted to play." Fortunately, a man named Virgilio Reyna decided to recommend Castillo to major-league scouts.[12]

According to the back of Castillo's 1995 Kane County Cougars baseball card, the scout who signed Castillo on August 19, 1992, a few weeks before his 17th birthday, was Julián Camilo ("Julio" in the *2011 New York Mets Media Guide*). The expansion Florida Marlins, who were preparing to debut in the National League in 1993, gave Castillo $2,800 to add him to their ranks. Impulsively, he bought a moped for his family as an alternative to shabby bicycles.[13] He tried to celebrate with some friends who must not have met with his mother's approval, but that evening didn't last as long as he'd planned. Faustina tracked the group down around midnight, lectured her son in front of the others, and then ordered him to walk back home with her.[14]

In 1993 Castillo didn't need to leave the island to begin his pro career. He was assigned to Florida's rookie-level team in the Dominican Summer League. His batting average was .282 and his on-base percentage was .368 in 69 games. He drove in 31 runs and scored 48. In 1994 he played in the States on another short-season, rookie-level team, the Gulf Coast League Marlins. His batting average dipped to .264 but he stole 31 bases in 57 games.[15]

For 1995 Castillo was assigned to the Class-A Kane County Cougars in Chicago's western suburbs. The Marlins' director of player development, John Boles, had great preseason expectations, calling Castillo the best prospect among second basemen he'd ever seen. At that point Castillo had reached his major-league height of 5-feet-11 but his weight was just 146 pounds.[16] He didn't disappoint, and was selected to the Midwest League all-star game played on June 20 in suburban Grand Rapids, Michigan.[17] During a stolen-base attempt a month later he slid head-first into the knees of Fort Wayne shortstop Mike Moriarty and both players ended up on the disabled list for the remainder of the season. Castillo sustained a serious shoulder injury and Moriarty suffered a torn anterior cruciate ligament. Castillo was hitting .326 at the time.[18]

At the start of the 1996 season, Castillo was ranked as the Marlins' number-two prospect by *Baseball America*. He started the season with the Double-A Sea Dogs in Portland, Maine. When John Boles would visit, he'd made a point of hitting groundballs to Castillo. "He didn't do it for anyone but me," Castillo noted. "He said, 'Luis, if I'm going to be a manager in the big leagues, you'll be with me right away.' I said, 'Thank you.' I never think he would manage in the big leagues."[19] Castillo was named to play in the Eastern League all-star game on July 8 in Trenton, and three days later Boles was named manager of the Marlins, to finish the season started by Rene Lachemann. Less than a month later, the Marlins brought up Castillo and pitcher Felix Heredia from Portland.

Late that same day, August 8, Luis Castillo made his major-league debut at home against the Mets as the starting second baseman and leadoff hitter. He was hitless in three plate appearances before being lifted for a pinch-hitter. He saved other milestones for maximum impact the next day. Again atop the lineup versus the Mets, he singled in the fourth inning for his first major-league hit. He scored his first run that inning, and it was his team's only one before extra innings. In the bottom of the 10th, Castillo faced Doug Henry with two outs and singled home Alex Arias from second base with the winning run. Castillo hit his first career home run before the month was over, on August 30 in Cincinnati off Mike Remlinger. All told, Castillo batted .317 in 109 games for Portland and .262 in 41 games for the Marlins.

Boles was replaced by Jim Leyland as manager of the Marlins for 1997 and Leyland chose Castillo to start at second base on Opening Day. By being paired regularly with shortstop Edgar Renteria, who was also 20 years old, Castillo became half of the youngest everyday middle-infield duo in the history of the National League.[20] His highlight-reel play of the season may have come on June 10 against the Giants, when teammate Kevin Brown took a no-hitter into the seventh inning. A wire-service account of the game said the best defensive play came that inning when J.T. Snow hit a grounder behind second base and Castillo made a backhand play in order to throw Snow out at first.[21] Overall, though, Castillo's season was an unsatisfactory one, and when his batting average was only at .240 in late July, he was sent down to Triple-A Charlotte. He hit very well there, .354 in 37 games, but was not brought back up to the majors and thus didn't play with the Marlins in the 1997 World Series. About five years later, Clark Spencer of the *Miami Herald* summed up what that October 26 was like for the Marlins' Opening Day second baseman: "With a heavy heart, Luis Castillo

Photo courtesy of the National Baseball Hall of Fame

clicked on a television that October night in 1997 and watched the Marlins win the World Series. There was his friend, Liván Hernández, hoisting the Series MVP trophy. Castillo had learned to drive using Hernández's Land-Rover when the two were roommates in Double A the season before," Spencer wrote. "There was his other friend, Edgar Rentería, delivering the winning hit in Game 7. He and Rentería had come up through the Marlins' farm system together."[22] At least it turned out that there was a silver lining. Though he hadn't played in the postseason, as an outcome of the Marlins' championship he received $70,000. "As soon as I got that money, I told my mama, we want to get you out," Castillo recalled. "So I bought her a house."[23]

Castillo's hot stint in Charlotte didn't earn him a trip back to the majors at the start of 1998. Even a 32-game hitting streak from May 24 to July 3 didn't earn him an immediate call-up by the Marlins. Still, when he had his on-base percentage at .403 in early August, with 74 runs scored in 100 games, Florida's management could ignore him no longer. However, after returning to the majors on August 4 he just barely hit above .200 the rest of the way.

Meanwhile, Jim Leyland had gone from winning the World Series to a record of 54-108. It wasn't his fault, because by the start of the 1998 season the ownership had traded Brown and 10 other key players, leaving their manager with the youngest squad in the majors. "Florida manager Jim Leyland must have felt like a daycare worker this year," quipped a Florida sportswriter. "The Marlins played a major-league record 27 rookies in 1998."[24] Leyland resigned on October 1.

The collective failure of the Marlins' younger position players in 1998 reopened a door for Castillo, and it was pushed wide open when John Boles was named to his second stint as the team's manager. Castillo spent all of 1999 with the Marlins, and was a major-league starting second baseman for the remainder of his professional career. Castillo rewarded Boles for his faith with a .302 batting average in 128 games, and his 50 steals ranked fourth in the National League. The South Florida Chapter of the Baseball Writers' Association of America named him the team's MVP for the season.[25]

Castillo proved in 2000 that the previous season was no fluke. He achieved the highest marks of his major-league career with 101 runs scored, a batting average of .334, an on-base percentage of .418, and 62 stolen bases. The latter figure was the best in the majors and thus netted him that year's Lou Brock Award. Interestingly, seven of those thefts came in a bunch. On May 17 against San Diego, Castillo set a club record and career high with four steals, and the next day he had three more. As a result, he fell one shy of the National League record for steals in consecutive games, which was set by Walt Wilmot of the Chicago Colts on August 6-7, 1894.[26]

Castillo's attitude pleased manager Boles. After one game that season Castillo walked into his manager's office and put a wad of cash on the desk for failing to bunt successfully. It was a payroll refund of sorts. "He was dead serious," Boles recalled. "He was so disgusted with himself."[27]

The 2001 season was Castillo's only mediocre year as a regular for the Marlins; he batted .263. Boles was fired on May 28, although the team's 22-26 record certainly wasn't atrocious. There's no indication that Castillo slumped afterward. Boles was replaced for the remainder of the season by Hall of Famer Tony Pérez, who'd been elected to Cooperstown the previous year.

It's entirely possible that Castillo was distracted by the fact that he and his wife, Angie, were expecting their first child, who arrived shortly after the season wrapped up. Luis Angelo Castillo was born on October 12, 2001. In any event, the new father performed very well for the Marlins during the first half of 2002, despite the fact that he didn't see Angie and the baby from the start of spring training until July 8. Castillo flew his wife and son in from the Dominican Republic for a very special occasion: He'd been named a National League All-Star for the first time, and the game was the next night.[28]

What really got Castillo noticed during the first half of 2002 was his 35-game hit streak, from May 8 through June 21. During that span he had 62 hits in 154 at-bats, a .403 clip. It was the longest streak since Paul Molitor of the Brewers had one of 39 games in 1987. That 1987 season Benito Santiago of the Padres had set the record for the longest streak by a Latino player at 34 games. At the time of Castillo's accomplishment, he tied the sixth longest streak in National League history and the 10th longest overall. As of 2018 he has been surpassed and tied by two Phillies: Jimmy Rollins hit in 38 straight games across the 2005 and 2006 seasons, and Chase Utley hit in 35 straight games in 2006.

Not surprisingly, media attention intensified across the hemisphere after Castillo's streak reached 30 games. When it reached 31, a Florida sportswriter (whose report was reprinted by a newspaper in Arizona) learned that people Castillo knew may have been bothering him more than random journalists. "The Florida Marlins second baseman normally is happy to hear from home, but lately each ring of the phone ratchets up the pressure a notch," wrote Brian Bandell. "'A lot of friends from the Dominican Republic call me,'" Castillo himself said. "'I don't like that.'"[29] That's not to say dealing with the reporters was easy, because Castillo still struggled with English when an interpreter wasn't available. On the day he extended his streak to its maximum, a *New York Times* reporter noted that Castillo had asked for guidance from teammate Mike Lowell, who was born in Puerto Rico of Cuban descent. "He asks me about the media and what to say," Lowell said. "I just tell him to say what you feel."[30]

Though Castillo wouldn't reunite with his wife and infant son for about two more weeks, on the night his streak reached 35 games he was able to celebrate with six relatives who attended that home game against the Tigers. Traveling together to the ballpark were a female cousin, two nephews, a brother-in-law, his sister Altagracia, and their mother, whose spirits weren't undercut by the knowledge that they reached their seats (29 rows behind home plate) about an inning *after* Castillo extended his streak with an infield single in the bottom of the third. The family members told a reporter that although he asked his family for prayers and took figurines reflecting their Catholicism to adorn his locker – behavior consistent with the anxiety hinted at by many of his comments in the media – they instead perceived signs, mostly in his body language, that he remained confident in his abilities. But the keen interest across the baseball world didn't mean much in that part of Florida, as only 5,865 fans were on hand.[31] The turnout the next day, a Saturday, jumped to 14,713 but they saw Castillo go hitless in four plate appearances.

The Marlins honored Castillo with a special night on July 3, and 11,785 fans turned out for it. The pregame festivities included a presentation by the Dominican Consulate. Castillo in turn took advantage of the opportunity to launch the Luis Castillo Gear for Kids Fund in conjunction with the Florida Marlins Community Foundation. He got the ball rolling with a $5,000 donation but fans were asked that night – and annually while he was a Marlin – to bring donations of new or used baseball equipment to be shipped to children in the Dominican Republic.[32]

Six days later was the All-Star Game in Milwaukee. The fans had voted José Vidro of the Expos as the starting National League's second baseman, and the NL manager, Bob Brenly of the Diamondbacks, had chosen Junior Spivey from his own team as a backup. Spivey replaced Vidro after three innings, and Castillo replaced Spivey after the seventh inning. As a result of the contest lasting 11 innings (at which point it was notoriously ended as a 7-7 tie) Castillo played four innings and batted twice. He flied out to center field both times. Defensively he logged three assists.

Castillo finished 2002 with a batting average of .305, and his 48 stolen bases won him his second Lou Brock Award. In addition, he was named team MVP for the second time by the South Florida Chapter of the BBWAA. On October 23 Castillo underwent arthroscopic surgery in his right hip to repair a torn labrum, but over the course of the next year there was ample reason to believe the procedure was successful.[33]

By the winter of 2002-2003 Castillo was a multimillionaire at 27. He had bought himself a Mercedes and wore expensive jewelry, but most of his earnings went toward relatives. His sister Maribel's family was occupying their childhood house by then, and he paid to have rooms added, a tile floor installed, and a second story built. He did likewise to the house next door, which was their brother Julio César's. He moved his parents and one grandmother to Santo Domingo, the capital and largest city, into a large two-story home in a middle-class neighborhood. He, Angie, and young Luis Angelo were living across town in a modest apartment near the city's country club.[34]

On several fronts Castillo was at least as good in 2003 as he was the prior season. He was selected as an All-Star for the second consecutive year, this time by Dusty Baker of the Giants. He did get to play in the game again, and again went hitless in two plate appearances. He improved on his 2002 batting average somewhat at .314, and reached a career high in base hits in the process, with 187. In light of his first "glove" as a youngster, in terms of individual achievements Castillo may have been most thrilled to receive his first Rawlings Gold Glove Award. He received votes for National League Most Valuable Player, and his total ranked 21st.

The main reason to believe that Castillo's hip surgery in October of 2002 had a lingering effect is that his stolen bases dropped from 48 in 2002 to 21 in 2003. He was caught stealing 19 times, so his success rate was barely above 50 percent. (He presumably made a necessary adjustment during 2004, when he again stole 21 bases but was caught just four times.)

On top of another admirable year individually, 2003 was the only time when Castillo played in the postseason as a Marlin. He was effective offensively in the National League Division Series against the Giants, whom the Marlins eliminated, three games to one. He batted .294 with three doubles and three walks. He didn't bat well against the Cubs in the National League Championship Series, but on October 14 he unwittingly helped perpetuate one of the strongest supposed curses in sports history. The Cubs led the best-of-seven series three games to two and were ahead 3-0 at home with one out in the eighth inning. Castillo lofted a pitch from Mark Prior toward elevated seats along the left-field line, where the ball was deflected away from a leaping Moisés Alou by fan Steve Bartman. Given a chance to extend his plate appearance, Castillo coaxed a walk from Prior. Castillo eventually ended the inning by batting again, that time popping out to second. Between his at-bats, the Marlins scored eight times and that was pretty much the ballgame. The next night they rallied from two runs down to win 9-6 and advance to the franchise's second World Series in its short existence.

Castillo's hitting against the Yankees was even worse than against the Cubs. After five games the Marlins led, three games to two. The two remaining games were scheduled for Yankee Stadium, and the sixth game was the 100th World Series contest played there. Andy Pettitte and Josh Beckett each pitched shutout ball through the first four innings. Pettitte retired the first two Marlins in the top of the fifth but gave up a single to Alex Gonzalez. Juan Pierre advanced Gonzalez to second with a hit. That brought up Castillo, who was hitless in his 14 previous at-bats. Castillo was a switch-hitter and thus batted right-handed against the lefty pitcher. Pettitte's first pitch was a called strike and Castillo swung at the second one without making contact. Castillo fouled off the next two pitches, and two more were outside the strike zone to even the count, 2-and-2. *New York Times* sportswriter Rafael Hermoso described well what happened next: "Castillo lined the seventh pitch to right field, sending Gonzalez, the Marlins' previous unexpected star, chugging around the bases. Gonzalez broke from second on contact and was going to test right fielder Karim Garcia's arm. The throw was on line. Gonzalez slid with his feet behind the plate. Catcher Jorge Posada took the throw in front of the plate and reached back with his glove. But Posada never made the tag as Gonzalez slid by the plate and dragged his left hand across the back of it. Umpire Tim Welke signaled that Gonzalez was safe, and the crowd grew quiet."[35]

The Marlins scored another run, on a sacrifice fly the next inning, and Beckett shut out the Yankees, so Castillo's timely hit was the game-winning RBI. He helped seal the deal with one out and a Yankee on first base in the bottom of the eighth inning when he fielded a grounder and tossed to Gonzalez to begin a double play.

Hermoso included quotes by Castillo about his decisive at-bat and his excitement for the Marlins as a whole, but the article led with a description of Castillo's body language toward the end of the game: "... Castillo could not contain himself. As Josh Beckett fired his final pitches to the Yankees, trying to finish them off in the ninth inning last night, Castillo was playing deep in the dirt infield, bouncing in place like a jumping jack. ... Finally Beckett tagged out Jorge Posada along the first-base line, and Castillo was freed."[36]

Castillo was a free agent after the World Series, and the Mets reportedly made a strong effort to sign him. Instead, at the beginning of December he and the Marlins agreed on a deal worth $16 million over three years, less than what the Mets offered.[37] Not surprisingly, his big purchase that offseason was a farm that his father, then 72 years old, had always fantasized about owning.[38]

That same offseason Castillo said he and fellow Dominican Moisés Alou teased each other good-naturedly about that infamous foul ball in the playoffs. "He said we were lucky," Castillo reported. "I told him, 'When you guys go to spring training, go early and put fans in the way and try to catch a fly ball, because maybe it can happen again.'"[39]

Castillo had another good year for the Marlins in 2004, with a .291 batting average. His high point for the season was likely on May 22 when he hit his only major-league grand slam, against Arizona's Steve Sparks. It was especially significant because Castillo averaged only three homers a season. He wasn't named an All-Star again in 2004, but he won his second consecutive Gold Glove.

In 2005 Castillo was named an All-Star again, this time by Tony La Russa of the Cardinals. He was much busier in that All-Star Game than in the other two. He replaced starting second baseman Jeff Kent in the bottom of the second inning and played the rest of the game; there was no other second baseman on the squad. In the top of the seventh inning, he got his first (and only) hit as an All-Star, a leadoff single against Kenny Rogers of the Rangers. Castillo scored when the next batter, Andruw Jones, homered. In the field he had two putouts and three assists, and helped turn a double play.

When the season ended Castillo's batting average stood at .301, the fifth time in his seven years as a Marlins regular that he hit at least that well. He hit .423 against left-handers, the highest average against them in the NL. On April 18 against Washington, Castillo walked four times, a career high that foreshadowed an impressive mark by season's end: He was the hardest man to strike out in the National League. He had one strikeout per 16.38 plate appearances.[40] Castillo continued to excel in the field as well, and was awarded his third consecutive Gold Glove.

At the end of the 2005 season, Castillo was 29 years old and had spent a decade playing for the Marlins. On December 2 the Marlins traded him to the Minnesota Twins for two pitching prospects, Scott Tyler and Travis Bowyer. Tyler never pitched above Triple A. Bowyer was in eight games for the Twins in 2005 but never pitched an official game for any Marlins minor-league team.

When Castillo was interviewed with his new team in mid-March, he seemed genuinely content that he was no longer a Marlin. Why? He had achieved the big goal he set early on: "I would take care of my family." And by 2006, he had. "Now everybody is happy in my family," he said. "When I go to the Dominican Republic, I feel happy. That's what I have been wanting to do. That's the dream I have. That's why I feel so good."[41]

In his new league, his stats for the season didn't look much different from his better ones with the Marlins. He hit .296, and his 25 stolen bases represented his highest total since 2002. The Twins won the Central Division so Castillo experienced the second (and final) postseason action of his career. The Twins were swept by the A's but Castillo fared better than he did in the 2003 playoffs against the Cubs and Yankees. His batting average in the three games was .273 (3-for-11) and his on-base percentage was .429.

On July 30, 2007, after 85 games, Castillo was batting .304 for the Twins. On that day they traded him to the Mets for outfield prospect Dustin Martin and catcher Drew Butera. Castillo hit .296 for the Mets and his combined batting average for the season was .301.

The 2008 season was a disappointing one for Castillo. He played only 87 games and his batting average plunged to .245. On July 3 he was placed on the 15-day disabled list with a strained left hip flexor, and didn't return to action until August 25.[42]

Castillo rebounded well in 2009. In 142 games he batted .302 and stole 20 bases. He and Angie celebrated the birth of their second child, daughter Adonai, on July 30. That day proved to be a lengthy one for her dad. He and Angie were up by 7:30 that morning, and the baby was born four minutes before noon. The Mets had a doubleheader against the Rockies, and Castillo felt he'd be letting down his teammates if he didn't play in one of the games. They won 7-0 without him, but lost the nightcap 4-2 with him in the lineup.[43]

"She wanted me to stay, but I told her the situation," Castillo said. "We had a lot of injuries, and if you can help them play better, you do it." George Vecsey of the *New York Times* hinted that another part of Castillo's motivation was to continue making amends for what Vecsey said "was probably the most egregious error in the history of the franchise, which is saying a lot. (This is coming from a writer who witnessed Marvelous Marv Throneberry.)"[44]

At Yankee Stadium on June 12, the Mets were ahead 8-7 going into the bottom of the ninth inning. With two outs, Derek Jeter was on second base and Mark Teixeira was on first. Alex Rodríguez hit a routine pop fly behind Castillo, who simply dropped it. Because Castillo was as surprised as everyone else, he threw to second in a vain attempt to get Rodríguez. Meanwhile Teixeira was closing in on home plate with the winning run.

"It would have been easy to hide," Vecsey wrote. "Luis Castillo could have taken the longest shower in the history of baseball – or skulked out into the night, unshowered."

He could have hidden, but he was very accountable," said Alex Cora, who was playing shortstop. "There were people ready to bury him, but he handled it the right way."[45]

Vecsey noted that Castillo intended to take a day off when his wife gave birth, but a rainout created the doubleheader that day. "Forty-five minutes after the delivery, he left for the ballpark and went hitless as the Mets lost, but the main thing was that he showed up," Vecsey concluded.[46]

In 2010 Castillo played in 86 games for the Mets and batted only .235. He was placed on the disabled list on June 4 with a bruised right heel. He was reinstated on July 19. It was his final season with the Mets, and as something of a last hurrah he stole home in Chicago as part of a double steal on September 4. He had only two hits in 15 at-bats in that month and October. On the last day of the season, October 3, against Washington, he popped out to shortstop as a pinch-hitter.[47] That was his final appearance in a professional game.

Castillo did report for spring training with the Mets in February 2011, but he frustrated Mets manager Terry Collins when he was expected to arrive early yet didn't. It turned out that his brother, Julio César, was undergoing a serious surgical procedure. "I asked him, 'Why didn't you tell me?,'" Collins said of Castillo. "It certainly would have changed the way I looked at things. I hope his brother's going to be OK." In any event, Collins confirmed that Castillo would compete with Daniel Murphy, Brad Emaus, and Justin Turner for the starting assignment at second base.[48] Turner won the starting job. The Mets released Castillo on March 18. Three days later the Phillies signed him to a minor-league deal.

Paul Hagen of the *Philadelphia Daily News* seemed to think that Castillo was worth giving a chance, and suggested that he was treated unfairly with New York. "For disgruntled customers in Queens to make Castillo the lightning rod for all their unhappiness about the ineffectiveness of Oliver Pérez, the injuries to Carlos Beltran and José Reyes, the Bernie Madoff scandal and every other ill that has befallen their favorite team is obviously silly," Hagen wrote.[49]

His colleague Sam Donnellon took a different view when Phillies manager Charlie Manuel expressed annoyance that Castillo was late arriving at their camp as well, writing that Castillo's reputation was that of "a well-paid, aging star showing signs of spoil in both his game and his attitude." The difference of opinion became moot on March 30, when the Phillies released Castillo.[50]

Castillo has maintained a low profile since 2011, but during the summer of 2019 he was rather suddenly implicated in Dominican drug trafficking. However, he was cleared of involvement after little more than a week.[51] As an example of him choosing the limelight after his retirement, for the 2017 All-Star Futures Game in Miami he was the bench coach for the World Team, managed by former teammate Edgar Renteria.[52] Later that year he was inducted into the Dominican Republic Sport Hall of Fame.[53] That 14-year-old kid in San Pedro de Macorís who could barely see himself as a major leaguer someday surely had no dreams of being honored at a ceremony like a hall of fame induction.

SOURCES

In addition to the sources cited in the Notes, the author relied on Baseball-Reference.com for baseball data.

NOTES

1. Phil Kimmel, foxsports.com/mlb/story/miami-marlins-whose-number-should-be-the-first-retired-040717, June 30, 2017.
2. Kevin Baxter, "Motherly Love," *Miami Herald*, February 23, 2003: 1C.
3. Dave George, "Family Late, But Happy," *Palm Beach Post* (West Palm Beach, Florida), June 22, 2002: 1C.
4. Mark Long, "From Milk Cartons to Majors," *Los Angeles Times*, June 11, 2000: D1.
5. La Velle E. Neal III, "Castillo Still Hungers to Win," *Minneapolis Star Tribune*, June 22, 2007: 1C.
6. Neal.
7. Baxter.
8. Joe Capozzi, "Castillo Gives Dreams to Dominican Kids," *Palm Beach Post*, August 14, 2005: 7B.
9. Baxter. Rodríguez also coached Luis Mercedes, Guillermo Mota, Manny Alexander, and José Cano as youngsters.
10. Neal.
11. *2011 New York Mets Media Guide*, 47.
12. Baxter.
13. Dave Hyde, "Luis' Heart 2nd to None," *South Florida Sun-Sentinel* (Fort Lauderdale), March 29, 2004: 13C. "He didn't drive a car until 19, when his good friend and then-agent Andy Mota rented one for him to try," Hyde added
14. Baxter.
15. *2011 New York Mets Media Guide*, 47.
16. Bryan Byrnes, "Young Cougars Don't Lack Talent," *Daily Herald* (Arlington Heights, Illinois), April 5, 1995: section 2, page 11.
17. *2011 New York Mets Media Guide*: 46. In contrast to his 1995 weight, on page 44 his weight was listed as 191 pounds.
18. Bryan Byrnes, "Kane County Experiencing Power Shortage in Dismal Second Half," *Daily Herald*, July 25, 1995: section 2, 2.
19. Neal.
20. *2011 New York Mets Media Guide*, 46.
21. "Marlins' Kevin Brown No-Hits San Francisco Giants," *Guantánamo Bay* (Cuba) *Gazette*, June 13, 1997: 11.
22. Clark Spencer, "Hitting It Big," *Miami Herald*, July 9, 2002: 1D.

23 Jim Souhan, "Hard Times Make Twins' Castillo Thankful," *Minneapolis Star Tribune,* March 19, 2006: 1C.

24 Ken McVay, "On Second Thought," *News Herald* (Panama City, Florida), October 2, 1998: 1B.

25 *2011 New York Mets Media Guide,* 46-47.

26 *2011 New York Mets Media Guide,* 47.

27 Neal.

28 Dave George, "Castillo Glad to Be Reunited with Wife, Son," *Palm Beach Post,* July 9, 2002: 3C. His son's date of birth is from the *2011 New York Mets Media Guide,* 44.

29 Brian Bandell, "The Buzz Grows as Castillo's Streak Hits 31," *Prescott* (Arizona) *Daily Courier,* June 18, 2002: 7A.

30 Charlie Nobles, "Castillo Keeps Hitting, Passing Hornsby's Run," *New York Times*, June 21, 2002: D5.

31 George, "Family Late, But Happy."

32 "South Florida Honors Luis Castillo," *Palm Beach Post*, July 3, 2002: 8C (a half-page ad). A Marlins press release dated September 23, 2003, posted at marlinsbaseball.com/topic/4451-marlins-press-release/, confirmed Castillo's initial monetary donation. The team's 2005 calendar, at miami.marlins.mlb.com/mia/community/calendar_archive_05.jsp, included the 4th Annual Luis' Gear for Kids Day on August 14.

33 *2011 New York Mets Media Guide,* 46-47.

34 Baxter. In this 2003 article Angie was referred to as Castillo's fiancée, but in Dave George's July 9, 2002, article she was called his wife, as she was in 2004 and 2009 articles cited herein.

35 Rafael Hermoso, "Castillo Rewards Marlins' Faith with Timely Hitting," *New York Times*, October 26, 2003: section 8, page 2.

36 Hermoso.

37 "D'backs Acquire Sexson in 9-Player Deal with Brewers," *Daily Herald* (Arlington Heights, Illinois), December 2, 2003: section 2, page 2.

38 Hyde.

39 "Castillo Trades Barbs with Chicago's Alou," *Johnstown* (Pennsylvania) *Tribune Democrat,* February 26, 2004: B4.

40 *2011 New York Mets Media Guide,* 45.

41 Souhan.

42 *2011 New York Mets Media Guide,* 45.

43 Michael Obernauer, "Oh Baby! Castillo Makes It to Flushing for Nightcap," *New York Daily News,* July 31, 2009: 75.

44 George Vecsey, "Yes, Luis Castillo Is Still with the Mets," *New York Times*, March 3, 2010: B13.

45 Vecsey.

46 Vecsey.

47 *2011 New York Mets Media Guide,* 44.

48 "Castillo Arrives in Mets' Camp," *Palm Beach Post*, February 21, 2011: 4C.

49 Paul Hagen, "Luis Castillo Gets Audition with Phillies Just in Case Scouts Are Wrong," *Philadelphia Daily News*, March 22, 2011: 48.

50 Sam Donnellon, "This Just in: Luis Castillo Is an Issue," *Philadelphia Daily News*, March 23, 2011: 71.

51 Colin Dwyer, "Ex-MLB Players Octavio Dotel, Luis Castillo Cleared Of Drug Ring Allegations," National Public Radio, August 30, 2019, https://www.npr.org/2019/08/30/755971282/ex-mlb-players-octavio-dotel-luis-castillo-cleared-of-drug-ring-allegations.

52 Jonathan Mayo, "Rosters Set for Futures Game," MLB.com, June 29, 2017; mlb.com/news/2017-mlb-futures-game-features-top-prospects/c-239464456.

53 "Inmortalizan a Varios al Pabellón de la Fama del Deporte Rep. Dom.," *El Nuevo Diario* (Santo Domingo, Dominican Republic), October 17, 2017: 31.

César Cedeño

by John DiFonzo

"At 22 Cedeño is as good or better than Willie was at the same age. I don't know whether he can keep this up for 20 years, and I'm not saying he will be better than Mays. No way anybody can be better than Mays. But I will say this kid has a chance to be as good. And that's saying a lot."

— Leo Durocher, May 1973[1]

Such praise may seem absurd, but consider that at age of 22, Cedeño completed his second straight year of batting .320, hitting 20-plus home runs and stealing 50-plus bases, demonstrating that rare combination of power and speed, the second player in history to reach those levels in home runs and stolen bases in the same season.[2] Cedeño could do it all – run, hit, hit with power, had a strong arm and made spectacular catches playing center field. So popular was Cedeño that the Astrodome was called "César's Palace."

César (C.C.) Cedeño (pronounced seh-DANE-yo) was born on February 25, 1951, in Santo Domingo, Dominican Republic to Diogenes and Juana (Encarnacion) Cedeño. By age 11 he was working in the same nail factory as his father. His father bought a grocery store and wanted César to help out and run errands instead of wasting his time playing baseball. Another article suggested that he wanted César to help his mother out around the house. César's mother was supportive of his ballplaying and bought him a glove and shoes without her husband's knowledge. As a 12-year-old, César practiced catching fly balls at night by throwing a ball in the air higher than the street light, then on its descent, tried to catch the ball while at the same time avoid getting hit by it. The neighbors thought he was crazy. When he was 14, César quit school to work full time at the nail factory. A year later he returned to Fidel Ferrer School.

The Dominican Republic was open territory and draft rules did not apply and players were signed as free agents. In the fall of 1967, Houston Astros scouts Pat Gillick and Tony Pacheco were searching the Dominican Republic for talent. Pacheco told how they discovered the 16-year-old Cedeño: "I was managing in the winter leagues and our game was rained out, but a local game was being played. We went to watch some other fellow, but the manager told us to look at Cedeño."[3] Gillick said, "We noticed this kid and liked the way he moved, his actions and his size. We saw him throw and then we saw him go up and get a hit and go up and get another hit. We decided we wanted to look at him. After the game, we arranged for him to go with us and some more players to San Pedro, about 60 miles away, for a workout Monday morning."[4] The location was arranged to avoid being noticed by other scouts. After the tryout Gillick decided he wanted to sign Cedeño and met with his father because Cedeño was a minor. Gillick discovered that the St. Louis Cardinals had offered Cedeño $1,000 to sign, but his father refused. Gillick offered up to $1,500, but the negotiations stalled. Then Gillick's friend on the island, Epy Guerrero, warned him that Cardinals scout Diómedes Olivo was on his way and would arrive in 15 minutes. Gillick then doubled his offer to $3,000 and Cedeño's father accepted. When Olivo arrived, Gillick held up the contract and said, "You're a few minutes too late."[5]

"When I was 15, I was still sitting on the bench in a Santo Domingo junior league," Cedeño said, "and we only played on Sundays. I probably hadn't played as many as 100 games when I was signed."[6] He was assigned to the Covington (Virginia) Astros of the rookie Appalachian League. "I worked hard to learn English. I watched TV—cowboy movies and cartoons. I learned English from the Flintstones," said Cedeño in an interview.[7] He batted .374 in 36 games and was promoted to the Cocoa Astros of the Class-A Florida State League, where he batted .256 in 69 games.

In 1969 Cedeño spent a full season playing for the Class-A Peninsula (Hampton, Virginia) Astros in the Carolina League. Tony Pacheco was his manager and corrected a flaw in Cedeño batting by getting him to bend his front knee when he swung his bat. Cedeño batted .274 with five home runs in 142 games and led the league in doubles with 32. That same season he played in the Winter Rookie Class in the Florida Instructional League North and batted .278 in 37 games and got rave reviews from scouts. Cedeño played well in winter league ball in the Dominican Republic, where Rico Carty helped him with his batting.

In 1970 Cedeño was impressive in spring training and started the season in Triple A with the Oklahoma City 89ers of the American Association. Some inside the organization felt the 19-year-old was ready to join the Astros, but others did not want to rush him. But Cedeño's progression was quicker than anyone in the organization could have imagined. He proved to be an excellent fielder, making catches in front and behind him. Cedeño had a strong arm, hit line drives, and had power to all fields. In 54 games he batted .373 with 14 home runs and 61 RBIs. Manager Hub Kittle encouraged Cedeño to be aggressive at the plate; he walked only eight times and struck out only 26 times in 247 at-bats. Kittle compared Cedeño to Felix Millan, star of the Atlanta Braves: "Sandy (nickname given by his teammates) has those same quick wrists and he's the same fiery competitor that Felix was when I had him at Yakima."[8]

Cedeño was called up on June 20, at 19 the youngest player in the National League. He debuted that night Atlanta, starting in center field and batting third. In his second at-bat, Cedeño singled off George Stone for his first major-league hit. He added another single and went 2-for-5. Cedeño struggled his first month in the majors and was dropped to seventh in the lineup. On August 14 he crashed into the center-field wall, sprained his ankle, and was out a week. Cedeño ended the season batting .310 with 7 home runs, 42 RBIs, and an OPS of .790. Manager Harry Walker said, "He has more natural ability than anyone in our organization. He can do everything – run, throw, hit, and catch the ball. He has fine natural instincts for the game. He has a lot to learn, but he learns quickly and you usually only have to tell him something once."[9] Roberto Clemente praised the rookie phenom: "One of the best-looking young players I've ever seen."[10] Although he played in only 90 games, he finished fourth in the National League Rookie of the Year voting.

In 1971 Cedeño started the season in right field. The reason was unclear. Some speculated that it was to take advantage of his strong arm; the other theory was that it was meant to motivate Jim Wynn by moving him back to center field. Cedeño started out slowly, batted .186 and struck out 32 times in 129 at-bats (24.81 percent) and on May 20 was removed from the starting lineup. He returned to the starting lineup on May 31 when Wynn had a sore wrist. He was 7-for-9 with two doubles, two home runs, and six RBIs in his next two games. Cedeño rebounded from a season low .180 batting average on May 30. He said, "I'm watching the ball now. I wasn't following the ball all the way. I was swinging hard and pulling my eye off the ball."[11] Despite the slow start, Cedeño led the National League with 40 doubles, batted .264 with 10 home runs, and led the team with 81 RBIs, but struck out 102 times.

In 1972 the 21-year old Cedeño blossomed and there was speculation that he would be the game's next superstar. He led the National League in batting through August,[12] until he was overtaken by the hot bat of Billy Williams and finished fourth with a .320 average. Cedeño tied for the league lead with 39 doubles, hit 22 home runs, stole 55 bases, drove in 82 runs, had a .385 on-base percentage and a .537 slugging percentage. He also lowered his strikeout total to 62. Cedeño was named to his first All-Star squad, won the first of his five consecutive Gold Gloves and finished sixth in the 1972 National League MVP balloting.

It was probably natural to compare Cedeño and Clemente because their styles were similar. Both players hit to all fields with some power, not primarily home-run hitters. Both had strong arms, but Clemente's

Photo courtesy of the National Baseball Hall of Fame

was considered the best of all time in 1972, and both were Latinos. Both players have been described as "playing all-out baseball, with not a little flamboyance, and both were accused of hot-dogging."[13] Maury Wills said in defense of Cedeño, "When a player like Cedeño is on the other side, he's a hot dog. When he is on your side, he plays hard and is colorful."[14] Harry Walker, who managed both Cedeño and Clemente, said, "Clemente and Cedeño are the two most exciting players in baseball today. Whether they are catching the ball, throwing it or running the bases, or batting, they do it all-out and with flair. When they are involved, you're always on edge expecting something to happen. They make things happen."[15] Said Clemente: "I don't think it's fair to him. When I came up, I did not like to be compared to other players."[16] "I don't want to be the second Clemente," said Cedeño. "I would rather be the first Cedeño."[17] When Hank Aaron was asked who was the last player to come into the league with as much ability as Cedeño, he simply replied: "Me."[18]

By 1973 Cedeño had established himself as one of the league's best players and was voted by the fans as an All-Star Game starter. His offensive production was comparable to his previous season: He batted .320 again, finishing second in the National League to Pete Rose. He hit 25 home runs and stole 56 bases. But his runs, hits, and RBIs were down and he struck out more. Cedeño played hard, diving for line drives and running into walls, but general manager Spec Richardson was questioning his toughness: "Cedeño got hurt and stayed hurt, he can't play with any pain."[19] Cedeño returned to the Dominican Republic to recuperate and play winter-league ball.

While there Cedeño injured his knee. He went to Houston to get it checked out and was advised to rest until spring training. Cedeño returned to the Dominican Republic. In the morning of December 11 at about 2:00 A.M., Cedeño and 19-year-old Altagracia de la Cruz checked into the Keko Motel, located in a poor section of Santo Domingo. The couple had been out drinking and Cedeño had ordered two beers. There were reports of an argument and loud noises coming from their room. A motel employee testified that a gunshot was fired about 10 minutes later. Cedeño called a motel employee and told him that "a woman has been killed," and then fled the scene in his sports car.[20] Cedeño said, "I went to my house, told my wife what happened, then went to the police. I was scared. I saw my baseball career was in danger."[21] Cedeño, accompanied by his father, turned himself into the police about eight hours later.

Cedeño was carrying a .38 caliber Smith & Wesson revolver, for which he had a permit. He told the police he had been robbed of $5,000 in jewelry and cash and needed the gun for his protection. Cedeño testified that de la Cruz asked to see the gun and when he refused, she tried to wrestle it away from him and the gun fired, resulting in her death. Cedeño was held in the local jail with three other men. The police conducted paraffin tests and concluded that only the victim had recently fired a gun. The police report stated, "It has not been possible to fix any blame on César Cedeño."[22]

Cedeño's fate was in the hands of the Dominican legal system and he was held in La Fe Precinct Jail. District Attorney Maximo Henriquez Saladin brought a charge of voluntary manslaughter, which in the United States was equivalent to second-degree murder. General manger Spec Richardson and Pat Gillick came down from Houston. Cedeño's American wife, Cora, who was at the couple's home in Santo Domingo at the time of the incident, visited him in jail every day and brought him food. De la Cruz's parents sued Cedeño for a reported $100,000 in damages on behalf of de la Cruz's 3-year-old daughter. (Cedeño was not the father.) Jim Wynn understood why Cedeño carried a gun: "I played one year over there and I think it's a fairly common thing. I know a lot of people do it. They have so much trouble down there and a lot of it has to do with changes in the government."[23]

On December 31, 1973, Magistrate Socrates Diaz Curiel reduced the charges against Cedeño to involuntary manslaughter and freed him on $10,00 bail after 20 days in jail. On January 15, 1974, Cedeño was found guilty of involuntary manslaughter. The conviction could have resulted into up to three years in prison, but Cedeño got off with only a $100 fine. A transcript of the court ruling said that Cedeño had been found responsible for acting "imprudently in allowing the victim to obtain the firearm he was carrying, and in handling it clumsily it discharged, causing her death."[24]

Cedeño settled the two civil cases against him. The Astros were criticized for only being concerned about the impact on the franchise and not showing any concern for the victim. Of the tragedy, Cedeño responded, "I am sorry about what happened. But this will help me grow up faster. I think this will help me be a better person."[25] He knew there would be backlash from the opposition's fans and players, but, "I think I can handle it. I've been thinking about it and I'm ready for anything. Since I've come into the league, they've yelled at me, called me hot dog. This is different, but I won't think about it."[26] Commissioner Bowie Kuhn did not suspend Cedeño, though he had the power to do so; he did not even comment on the matter.

Cedeño got off to a hot start in the 1974 season. By the All-Star break he was leading the National League in RBIs (75), second in home runs (19), third in stolen bases (36), tied for third in runs scored (62), and tied for fourth in hits (112).[27] Perhaps because of backlash by fans, Cedeño was not elected a starter in the All-Star Game but was chosen as a reserve. He did not place in the top six National League outfielders in the fan voting.[28] On July 17, there was a reminder of the offseason incident when teammate Bob Watson was awakened by a phone call in his Pittsburgh hotel room. A Latino-sounding voice said, "I'm going to shoot Cedeño just like he shot that girl."[29] A shaken-up Watson informed his manager and police were present that evening at Three Rivers Stadium as a precaution. The phone call occurred a day after a newspaper article criticized Cedeño's role in the fatal incident. Manager Preston Gomez told Cedeño, "This is something that you will have to live with the rest of your life."[30]

Cedeño went into a slump from August until the end of the season (.194, four home runs), which he blamed on a "bad loop" in his swing. For the season, Cedeño struck out a career-high 103 times and his batting average (.269) was his second worst. Despite the second-half swoon, Cedeño achieved career highs in home runs (26) and RBIs (102). It was his third straight season with more than 20 home runs and 50 stolen bases. At age 23, the young Dominican was still considered a budding superstar. The impact of the offseason tragedy and workload weighed on Cedeño. "I went through a lot of problems with the fans and such. I had a lot of people against me and it made it a little tougher to do my job. ... I haven't played that many games (160) since 1971. I think I can help the club more if I play 150 games and rest maybe 10 or 12 games."[31]

Cedeño's next three seasons, 1975-1977, were solid but for him unspectacular. He didn't have that breakout .350, 30 home runs, 120 RBIs season that was expected. He batted between .279 and .297 and hit fewer than 20 home runs each season. Cedeño was still spectacular in the field and stole more than 50 bases for the sixth consecutive year. He was still dogged by de la Cruz's death and by unreached potential. "No matter what I do, they think I had a bad year," he said.[32]

Of the fatal incident, Cedeño had two responses: "It never affected my playing" and "I'd rather not talk about it."[33] Fans heckled him with yells like "Who are you going to kill next?"[34] Rival players taunted Cedeño, calling him, "the fastest gun in the West."[35] Teammate Bob Watson thought the incident affected Cedeño. "He was so young, so proud, that I think he tried extra hard to prove to everyone that it never bothered him," said Watson. "He had a good season [1974], but he altered his swing trying to hit homers. After that, maybe pitchers adjusted, and he hasn't readjusted himself."[36]

Cedeño's injuries and aggressive style of play were taking its toll. He never fully recovered from injuring his right knee in winter ball in 1972 and it took him 20 to 30 minutes to get his problem ankles loose every day. In spring training in 1977 Cedeño tore ligaments in his finger when he ducked out of the way of a pitch thrown by a pitching machine. "He certainly never dogs it," said manager Bill Virdon. "In fact, I guess you could say he plays with reckless abandon."[37]

Cedeño hit a low point on June 22, 1977. He had gone 0-for-5 in a game in Montreal and 0-for-20 to lower his batting average to .179, and asked Virdon to take him out of the lineup. After a few days off, Cedeño was back in the lineup and batted .349 the rest of the season to raise his average to .279.

Cedeño was eligible for free agency after the 1978 season. The Astros did not want to lose their 27-year-old star and signed him to a record 10-year, $3.5 million contract.

On June 16, 1979, in the bottom of the fifth inning against the Chicago Cubs in the Astrodome, Cedeño tore the medial collateral ligament in his left knee sliding into second base while trying to take an extra base on an RBI single. The attending doctors performed two-hour surgery to repair the knee and were confident that Cedeño would play again. Dr. Harold Brelsford noted, "When we examined the knee under general anesthesia, we found previous ligament damage and were able to repair that, too. César has had trouble with that knee before. And it could be that next year his knee will be stronger than it was this year."[38] Cedeño was in a cast for six weeks and then had six weeks of rehab. He played in the last two games of the season.

Cedeño's daily offseason regimen included a two-mile run, 30 minutes of baseball running sprints, and a session with Nautilus weights. He was confident of a full recovery. "Some people have predicted I will lose three or four steps, I will prove them wrong," he said. "I think my best years are in the future. ... I don't think I've been physically sound for four years. I've had four operations, three on my hands. ... Some people don't realize that I have been taking shots for the past five years because I was having pains in my leg. Hopefully I won't ever have to complain again."[39]

The Astros were contenders in the NL West in 1979 and with the emergence of rookie Jeffrey Leonard, along with José Cruz and Terry Puhl, they had an abundance of outfielders. Cedeño, the five-time center-field Gold Glove winner, was moved to first base. He said, "Don't forget, I was signed as a first baseman and played more than 200 games at first base in the minors. I have always taken infield practice."[40] He played in 91 games at first base in 1979 and played well, but he was not the Cedeño of old. He was slowed down by the recovery from MCL surgery and was hospitalized for a week in August with hepatitis. Cedeño finished the season batting .262 and a then-career-low .374 slugging percentage.

In 1980, at age 29, Cedeño reclaimed his starting center-field position and had one of his best seasons. He tied for fourth in the National League in batting with a .309 average, and had 48 stolen bases and a career-high .389 on-base percentage. The Astros led the Los Angeles Dodgers by three games with the final three in Dodger Stadium. The Dodgers won all three to force a one-game tiebreaker. The Astros prevailed and won their first National League West title.

The Astros met the Philadelphia Phillies in the NLCS. Game Three was the first playoff game in Astrodome history. In the sixth inning Cedeño grounded into a double play, stepped on first base awkwardly and fractured his right ankle, ending his season. The Astros won the game in extra innings, 1-0, and took a two-games-to-one lead. The Astros had the Phillies on the brink of elimination in Games Four and Five, but the Phillies came back to win both in extra innings and take the series. Cedeño, meanwhile, began another lengthy rehabilitation.

In the strike-shortened 1981 split season, Cedeño played in 82 games—45 at first base and 34 in center field. His offensive production was down: a .271 batting average with 5 home runs and 12 stolen bases.

On September 8, in a game in Atlanta-Fulton County Stadium in front of only 2,800 fans, Cedeño struck out to end the first inning. He went after a fan in the stands who had been heckling him since the prior day's game, yelling "Killer, killer, killer." Cedeño said afterward, "If I had been alone, I probably would not have reacted that way. But my wife was with me on this trip. Cora has been subjected to the same language and treatment. She was near tears. I don't think any man would want his wife to hear him called that. At the time I went into the stands, I was pretty much emotionally involved. I didn't have any intention of hitting the man. I just wanted to see if he had the nerve to call me that to his face. He didn't. He was shaking."[41] Cedeño was fined $5,000, but was not suspended. The fan was ejected from the ballpark. Cedeño's agent argued for a policy to deal with abusive fans. No charges were pressed against either Cedeño or the fan.

The Astros won the second-half National League title and lost to the Dodgers inn five games in the Division Series. Cedeño batted only .214 in the series and did not play in the deciding game.

In the offseason, Cedeño, a player with trade-veto rights, approved a trade to the Cincinnati Reds for Ray Knight, a player he fought with during the 1979 season. A happy Cedeño said, "I believe I'll benefit from a change of scenery and believe my best years are still ahead of me."[42] The Reds planned to play him in center field after trading Ken Griffey Sr. earlier in the offseason, which pleased Cedeño, who grew reluctant to move from that position under Virdon. He felt his broken ankle was healed, saying, "During the past season, I played with only 17 percent flexibility in my ankle, and favoring the ankle caused me to have hamstring and back problems."[43] After a month of offseason rehab, Cedeño reported, "Already it's up to 80 percent flexibility, I'm ready to steal 50 bases for the Reds this season."[44] It was reported that Cedeño had a stormy relationship with Virdon and accused the club of not giving him enough time to recover from some of his injuries.[45] Houston teammates took jabs at Cedeño, claiming that he didn't play while hurt and left more than his share of runners on base.

In his three-plus seasons in Cincinnati, Cedeño stole only 57 bases, hit 30 home runs and batted .265. In 1983 he was moved to right field. In 1984 he played a utility role, splitting time at first base and all three outfield positions.

In August 1985 Cedeño was being used primarily as a pinch-hitter and was batting under .250. On the 27th St. Louis Cardinals lost their right-handed slugger, Jack Clark, to the disabled list. The Cardinals held a three-game lead in the National League East over the New York Mets, and Clark was one of their few players who could deliver a big hit. Cedeño was unhappy with his part-time role in Cincinnati, telling sportswriters, "I accepted the fact that I wasn't going to play much, but I don't think you would like it if they didn't let you write all the time either."[46] While the Cardinals were in town on August 28, Reds coach Jim Kaat suggested to manager Whitey Herzog that the Cardinals acquire Cedeño. A deal was struck the next day for the 34-year-old Cedeño in exchange for rookie-league outfielder Mark Jackson. Jackson never played above Class-A.

Cardinals general manager Dal Maxvill said, "Our thinking is (Cedeño) can help us in the stretch run. He is not going to be playing a great deal unless we have injuries, but it's nice to have someone on your bench that makes managers do something they may not want to do."⁴⁷ Cedeño was happy for the opportunity. "It's no secret that my contract is up in five or six weeks and there is no doubt in my mind that I can still be a regular player for somebody," he said. "I am happy to have an opportunity like this – to play with a contender – came around. I welcome whatever they want me to do. I'm thrilled an organization like the Cardinals had interest in me. It's a great feeling to be wanted."⁴⁸

Cedeño platooned at first base with veteran Mike Jorgensen and pinch-hit. On August 30 against the Astros, in his first appearance for the Cardinals, he hit a pinch-hit home run on the first pitch to him by Mike Scott. On September 6, Cedeño pinch-hit for Jorgensen and hit a grand slam off the Braves' Gene Garber to secure an 8-0 victory. Later the Cardinals and Mets, tied for first, squared off in a three-game series in Shea Stadium. The Mets took two of the three games. In the second game, Cedeño led off the 10th inning with a home run off Jesse Orosco that was the difference in a 1-0 game. The Cardinals left New York one game behind the Mets and Cedeño became the starting first baseman until Jack Clark returned. On September 15 against the Cubs, Cedeño went 5-for-5 with the game-winning hit, a home run in the seventh. In the division-clinching game, a 7-1 victory over the Cubs on October 5, Cedeño helped break open a tight game with a home run and two RBIs.

In 28 games, Cedeño batted .434 with 6 home runs, 19 RBIs, and a .750 slugging percentage. Herzog said, "If we hadn't got Cedeño, we would have been at least three games out of first, maybe more, going into this last week. If we didn't have him, a few lefties may have stopped us and that may have sent us into a slump. But he didn't let our morale go down."⁴⁹ Said Cedeño, "I always believed in my own ability. I knew I could still play and was trying to prove I could. I think I did. It was one of the most exciting months of my life."⁵⁰

The Cardinals defeated the Dodgers in the NLCS. In Game One of the World Series, against Kansas City, Cedeño doubled in the decisive run in the top of the fourth inning. As the Cardinals lost to the Royals in seven games, Cedeño played in five games and batted .133. Overall, in four postseason series, Cedeño played in 17 games, hitting .173 in 52 at-bats.

After the season Cedeño was a free agent and signed with the Toronto Blue Jays. After hitting .188 in nine exhibition games, he was released on April 3. But the Dodgers were in need of help after Pedro Guerrero suffered a knee injury and signed Cedeño to a one-year contract. He played in 37 games for the Dodgers, batting .231, and was released in early June. Cedeño finished out the season with Louisville, the Cardinals Triple-A affiliate.

Cedeño played in the Mexican League in 1988. In 1989, at the age of 38, he was invited to the Astros spring training as a nonroster player. He was released on March 28, closing the books on his major-league career. Later that year, Cedeño played in the inaugural season of the Senior Professional Baseball Association.

Cedeño had a temper that he could not control at times. A Houston reporter who regularly covered the team said, "César has a very bad temper. When he is going good, he can be the most cooperative guy around. But if he's going bad, or has an injury, then he's a difficult to get along with."⁵¹ Cedeño racked up fines and suspensions not already noted because of his temper. In 1971 he threw his helmet after striking out and accidentally hit teammate Wade Blasingame. The two argued, teammate Doug Rader joined in, and he and Cedeño started shoving each other. In 1972 Cedeño was fined $250 and suspended for three games for bumping umpire Frank Pulli. During spring training in 1975, Cedeño was fined $200 for smashing a glass water cooler after he popped out to the shortstop in an exhibition game in which he also homered and doubled. A piece of glass was lodged in a teammate's eye, but it was easily removed by the team doctor. During the 1975 season Cedeño was fined $250 and suspended for three games for bumping umpire Bruce Froemming. In 1978 he was fined $5,000 for injuring himself when he punched the plexiglass dugout roof, injuring his hand and requiring 17 stitches. In 1983 Cedeño was fined $100 and suspended for three days when he threw a temper tantrum because he was not selected by the manager to fly first class.

In the offseason Cedeño received treatment for stress management. He also had a history of off-field episodes. In 1985 he was charged with drunk driving when, after his car struck a tree, he refused to take a breath test, paid a $400 fine and $7,000 for property damage. Cedeño was put on probation. In 1987 he was charged with smashing a glass in a man's face in a Houston area nightclub after the man accidentally bumped into him. In 1988 Cedeño was arrested and charged with assault causing bodily injury and resisting arrest. The woman Cedeño had beaten was his girlfriend, Pam Lamon, with whom he had a four-month-old daughter. Cedeño was drunk and angry about custody of the child, took the child from Lamon and drove off. He was still married to Cora at the time. In 1992 Cedeño was arrested for assaulting Lamon who was four months pregnant with his child. He was also charged with resisting arrest. Lamon's victim's statement read, "César has a serious drinking problem and only becomes abusive when he drinks. I have begged him to get help, but he won't."[52]

Cedeño was a minor-league coach and hitting instructor for the Astros from 1990 to 1994 and 1997 to 2001. He was a coach in the Washington Nationals organization in 2009. In 2012 he returned to the Astros as the hitting coach for the Greenville Astros of the Appalachian League. In 2018 Cedeño was the hitting coach for the Astros team in the rookie Gulf Coast League.

SOURCES

In addition to the sources cited in the Notes, the author also consulted articles in *The Sporting News* as well as Retrosheet.org, Baseball-Reference.com, and the National Baseball Hall of Fame clipping file.

NOTES

1. Ron Fimrite, "Now Let Us Render Unto César," *Sports Illustrated*, May 21, 1973, si.com/vault/1973/05/21/618333/now-let-us-render-unto-cesar, accessed November 17, 2018.
2. Lou Brock was the first in 1967. Cedeño accomplished this feat three times, second behind Rickey Henderson, who did it four times. Cedeño is the only player to have three consecutive seasons of 20 home runs and 50 stolen base as of 2018.
3. Bob Moskowitz, "Teen-Ager Cedeño a Terror at Bat," *The Sporting News*, July 12, 1969: 49.
4. John Wilson, "César Cedeño … The Next Super Star," *The Sporting News*, August 19, 1972: 3.
5. John Wilson, "César Cedeño … The Next Super Star."
6. Harold Petersen, "Hail, César! And Hello," *Sports Illustrated*, August 2, 1972, si.com/vault/1972/08/07/614021/hail-cesar-and-hello, accessed November 23, 2018.
7. Petersen.
8. Bob Dellinger, "Astros Hail 89ers César as Minors' Top Prospect," *The Sporting News*, June 6, 1970: 33.
9. John Wilson, "Cedeño Dances While the Astros Fiddle," *The Sporting News*, September 12, 1970: 15.
10. Wilson, "Cedeño Dances While the Astros Fiddle."
11. John Wilson, "Astros' Cedeño Earns New Chance With a Hot Bat," *The Sporting News*, July 3, 1971: 12.
12. On August 31 Cedeño led Williams .342 to .340. Both were batting .340 on September 1. Williams passed Cedeño on September 2 and led him the remainder of the season.

13 Wilson, "César Cedeño … The Next Superstar?"
14 Wilson, "César Cedeño … The Next Superstar?"
15 Wilson, "César Cedeño … The Next Superstar?"
16 Wilson, "César Cedeño … The Next Superstar?"
17 Wilson, "César Cedeño … The Next Superstar?"
18 Wilson, "César Cedeño … The Next Superstar?"
19 Joe Heiling, "Faded Astros Face Pruning Job from Fed-Up G.M. Richardson," *The Sporting News*, September 22, 1973: 17.
20 "Prosecutor Recommends Cedeño's Full Acquittal," *New York Times*, January 15, 1974: 44.
21 "Cedeño Expects Reaction," *New York Times*, January 23, 1974: 25.
22 Joe Heiling, "Cedeño Tragedy Tosses a Cloud Over Astros," *The Sporting News*, December 29, 1973: 27.
23 Heiling, "Cedeño Tragedy Tosses a Cloud Over Astros."
24 "Cedeño Expects Reaction."
25 Joe Heiling, "César Set for Brickbats: 'I May Be a Better Player,'" *The Sporting News*, February 9, 1974: 33.
26 Heiling, "César Set for Brickbats. 'I May Be a Better Player'"
27 Larry Wigge, "Batting Averages, Including Games of July 24," *The Sporting News*, August 10, 1974: 39.
28 "Dodgers, Reds Place Three on Major All-Star Team," *The Sporting News*, July 27, 1974: 11.
29 Joe Heiling, "Cedeño's Life Periled by Pittsburg Caller," *The Sporting News*, August 3, 1974: 7.
30 Heiling, "Cedeño's Life Periled by Pittsburg Caller."
31 Joe Heiling, "Cedeño Aims to Be Astros' Leader," *The Sporting News*, October 26, 1974: 25.
32 Peter Gammons, "César's Salad Days Are Over/Supposed Superstar Cedeño of Houston Is Playing More Like a 'Could Have Been,'" *Sports Illustrated*, August 1, 1977.
33 Gammons.
34 Gammons.
35 Gammons.
36 Gammons.
37 Gammons.
38 Harry Shattuck, "Cedeño's Knee Injury Gives Astros Another Limp," *The Sporting News*, July 8, 1978: 16.
39 Harry Shattuck, " 'Best Years Ahead' Trumpets César of Astros," *The Sporting News*, March 10, 1979: 51.
40 Harry Shattuck, "Leonard Gets Help as Astros' Rookie Star," *The Sporting News*, June 23, 1979: 10. According to baseball-reference.com, the only minor-league games in which Cedeño played first base are the 97 games he played in 1969 between Peninsula Astros and Florida Instructional League Astros.
41 Harry Shattuck, "Cedeño Is Fined. Goes After Fan," *The Sporting News*, September 26, 1981: 23.
42 Earl Lawson, "Reds to Put Cedeño in Center Field, Ankle Healed," *The Sporting News*, January 2, 1982: 40.
43 Lawson.
44 Lawson.
45 Harry Shattuck, "Astros Very Cool to Scott Pay Bid," *The Sporting News*, January 9, 1982: 45.
46 Rick Hummel, "Price Is Right in Cedeño Deal," *The Sporting News*, September 16, 1985: 19.
47 Hummel.
48 Hummel.
49 Dave Nightingale, "Races to the Wire, Herzog Played His Cards Right Down the Stretch," *The Sporting News*, October 14, 1985: 17.
50 Jared Hoffman, "What a Move, When the Cardinals Acquired Aging César Cedeño for '85 Stretch Run, They Found the Ultimate Difference-Maker," *The Sporting News*, July 21, 1997: 47.
51 Abby Mendelson, "Whatever Happened to César Cedeño?," *Baseball Quarterly*, Winter 1978-1979: 46.
52 Henry Pierson, "Ex-Astro Charged With Attack on Pregnant Girlfriend, Cops," *Orlando Sentinel*, September 29, 1992. articles.orlandosentinel.com/1992-09-29/news/9209290123_1_astros-Cedeño-pregnant-girlfriend, accessed on November 23, 2018.

JOSÉ DELEON

by Richard Cuicchi

Once described as the "best losing pitcher in baseball,"[1] José DeLeon was an enigma for most of his major-league career. As a starting pitcher, he showed promise, including periods of brilliance, but he usually ended up frustrating his teams, which eventually gave up on him because he had a difficult time winning games.

The first eight seasons of DeLeon's major-league career were like a roller-coaster ride, intermixing near no-hitters and double-digit strikeout games with numerous losing streaks. His won-lost record was often plagued by a lack of run support and playing for losing teams, but he was also responsible at times for his own periods of mediocrity stemming from losses of self-confidence and difficulties in managing his pitch repertoire. Thus, his volatile career was difficult to assess from year to year and sometimes even within a season. He was labeled "certifiable ace" one year and "hard-luck loser" the next.

DeLeon was born on December 20, 1960, in Rancho Viejo, LaVega, Dominican Republic, the son of Elipidio DeLeon who was a catcher in the Dominican League. His father was one of nine brothers who once played together on a team managed by his grandfather. Two of the brothers went on to play professional

Photo courtesy of the Pittsburgh Pirates

baseball, which inspired young DeLeon to pursue baseball as a career.[2]

His father was unable to support six children working in the Dominican rice fields, so he got a job in a leather factory in New York City, and eventually sent for his family. They settled in Perth Amboy, New Jersey, across the Hudson River from New York City, in 1972 when DeLeon was nearly 12 years old.[3] His father took employment in an air-conditioning parts factory while his mother worked in a coat factory.[4]

In his sophomore season at Perth Amboy High School, DeLeon led the state in strikeouts, averaging two per inning, as he compiled a 10-3 record. However, he dropped out of school during his junior year to live with his grandmother in the Dominican Republic for a while.[5]

Pittsburgh Pirates general manager Harding Peterson, who grew up near Perth Amboy, had been told in 1977 by an acquaintance, Sam Marsicano, that DeLeon, then a high-school freshman, was a promising player. After DeLeon attended a workout in Pittsburgh, the Pirates began following his development in high school. Peterson learned that DeLeon wouldn't be eligible to play scholastic sports as a senior, and with special permission from the commissioner's office, he was eligible for the June 1979 draft.[6] "We took him in the third round. We didn't want to take a chance of drafting him lower and perhaps losing him," Peterson said.[7]

Making his professional debut with the rookie league Gulf Coast League Pirates in 1979, DeLeon demonstrated that he was pretty raw as a player, posting an ERA of 6.41 and WHIP of 1.932 in 59 innings pitched.

The 6-foot-3 right-hander showed a propensity for striking out batters and progressed to Triple-A Portland by 1982, but with a 1.706 WHIP, he was still not very efficient. However, things seemed to click for DeLeon in 1983 with Triple-A Hawaii, when he dramatically lowered his ERA to 3.04, averaged nine strikeouts per nine innings, sported a WHIP of 1.241, and won 11 games in 20 starts. His results produced a Pacific Coast League all-star team selection.[8]

DeLeon's performance with Hawaii earned him a call-up to the Pirates, who had won 10 of 11 games to secure sole possession of first place in the NL East Division on July 21. DeLeon made his major-league debut on July 23 against the San Francisco Giants, when he started and pitched into the ninth inning, allowing only two runs on four hits, striking out nine, and claiming the win.

DeLeon's next two outings were even better. He won a four-hit complete game against the San Diego Padres on July 27 in which the Padres didn't get their first hit until Alan Wiggins hit a single with one out in the seventh inning. Then DeLeon threw a nine-inning one-hitter in the second game of a doubleheader against the New York Mets on July 31. Hubie Brooks singled with one out in the ninth inning to break up DeLeon's no-hitter. In front of family and friends in Shea Stadium, DeLeon walked only three batters and whiffed 11. (The Mets won the game, 1-0, in the 12th inning.) Pirates manager Chuck Tanner, who couldn't recall a rookie pitcher coming so close to back-to-back no-hitters, said of DeLeon, "He could be the difference for us in the race."[9]

But Tanner's Pirates fell short of a division title, finishing second behind Philadelphia, which advanced to the World Series. DeLeon upheld his part by finishing the season with a 7-3 record, including another game (August 20) in which he got into the seventh inning before yielding a hit. He posted a 2.83 ERA and struck out 118 batters in 108 innings in 15 starts, earning him a few votes for the NL Rookie of the Year Award.

With his auspicious rookie season, expectations for DeLeon in 1984 were naturally high. Yet the baseball community was anxious to see whether DeLeon was just a flash in the pan.

The Pirates were a different team in 1984; they finished in last place (75-87) in the East Division. With DeLeon posting a 7-13 record, it would appear on the surface that he had a disastrous season himself. But his won-lost record was not the whole story. He flirted with four more no-hitters, including one in which he had a perfect game going into the seventh inning.[10] The Pirates lost three of those games. In 16 of his starts, the Pirates scored one run or less while he was in the game. (The Pirates ranked 10th out of 12 NL teams in runs scored for the season.) From July 17 through September 9, DeLeon suffered nine consecutive losing decisions in 11 starts, but only one time did he fail to get past the fifth inning. He finished with a respectable 3.74 ERA and 1.243 WHIP, when the league averages for those stats were 3.60 and 1.323.

DeLeon's performance was more suspicious in 1985, however. The Pirates were even worse in 1985, winning only 57 games and finishing 43½ games behind the St. Louis Cardinals in the division. DeLeon contributed to the Pirates' miserable season, finishing with one of the worst winning percentages (.095) for a starting pitcher in baseball's modern era. He won only two of 21 decisions.[11] He suffered through two significant losing streaks during the season: seven in a row at the start of the season (April 11 through May 27); and 11 losses to end the season (June 19 through October 4). Again, the Pirates were among the worst NL teams in runs scored. (The Pirates sent DeLeon to Hawaii in July and he was was 4-0 in five starts.)

According to Cardinals catcher Tony Peña, DeLeon's lack of confidence was a factor in his disastrous season. "It would get to his head. He would say, 'I'm going to pitch a good game, but I'm going to lose because we don't score any runs,'" Peña said. "He was pitching as well as he did the other years, but he got too frustrated, too confused. He thought he wasn't any good."[12]

In the offseason Pirates GM Syd Thrift attempted to boost DeLeon's outlook by giving him a substantial salary raise, from $27,500 to $160,000.[13] But still the Pirates demoted DeLeon to Hawaii to start the 1986 season. He went 5-8 in 14 starts and posted a 2.46 ERA in two stints with the Islanders. When he was called up to the Pirates, he was relegated to bullpen duty. After only nine appearances, in which his ERA was over 8.00, the Pirates gave up on DeLeon and traded him to the Chicago White Sox on July 23 for rookie Bobby Bonilla.

DeLeon pitched well for the White Sox in his 13 starts. His won-lost record (4-5) didn't accurately reflect his performance, as he recorded an impressive 2.96 ERA, and his opponents' slash line was .179/.296/.285. However, he had little overall impact with the White Sox, who finished in fifth place in the AL West Division.

Chicago was optimistic about DeLeon going into the 1987 season and slotted him in the rotation behind Rich Dotson and Brian Bannister. He logged his most starts (31), innings (206), and wins (11) to that point in his career, but his ERA jumped to 4.02 and he lost 12 games. He finished the season with six wins in seven decisions, as the White Sox ended in fifth place again. DeLeon's late-season improvement wasn't enough for the White Sox to retain him.

Over the winter, DeLeon became a target for acquisition by the St. Louis Cardinals, who sought to add depth to their rotation. After several months of trade talks, a deal was consummated in February 1988. The White Sox received pitcher Ricky Horton, outfielder Lance Johnson, and cash in exchange for DeLeon. St. Louis had just come off a pennant-winning season, so the move appeared to be a good one for DeLeon.

It turned out to be a solid year for DeLeon, but the Cardinals' fortunes took a nosedive in 1988 because of the loss of Jack Clark to free agency and injuries to the pitching staff. Danny Cox, Greg Mathews, and Joe

Magrane were unable to put in full seasons, and DeLeon became the workhorse of the staff with team-leading 34 starts and 225⅓ innings pitched. He struck out a career-high 208 batters (third in the NL), the most by a Cardinals pitcher since Bob Gibson's 208 in 1972. DeLeon led the staff with 13 wins and posted a 3.67 ERA. The Cardinals were never in contention for the division title and finished in fifth place, 25 games behind the division-leading New York Mets.

With his performance in 1988, it seemed that DeLeon was finally shedding the label of hard-luck pitcher, especially accomplishing what he did with a weak Cardinals team. He confirmed in 1989 that his previous season was no fluke. In his first eight games of the season, he posted a 6-2 record and a 2.90 ERA. DeLeon was being called a "certifiable ace."[14] On August 30 he had one of the best outings of career when he yielded only a single to Cincinnati in the fourth inning on his way to facing the minimum 33 batters in 11 shutout innings. He issued no walks and struck out eight in his no-decision game which the Cardinals lost in the 13th inning.

DeLeon and teammate Magrane (18-9, 2.91 ERA) created a formidable one-two punch in the Cardinals rotation. DeLeon posted career highs in wins (16), innings pitched (244⅔), WHIP (1.034), complete games (5), and shutouts (3), while posting a 3.05 ERA. Leading the NL in strikeouts (201), he was only the second Cardinals pitcher to post back-to-back 200-strikeout seasons.[15] The third-place finish by the Cardinals was only the second season DeLeon had played on a winning team to that point in his career.

Yet even during this career-best season, DeLeon couldn't avoid another significant losing streak. In a stretch of seven games from June 13 to July 16, he had six consecutive losing decisions and a 5.91 ERA in only 35 innings pitched. However, he bounced back after that disappointing stint by allowing only 51 hits in 98⅓ innings pitched from July 21 to September 18, as he picked up eight wins and posted a 2.01 ERA.

At the age of 29 it appeared that DeLeon had at last reached the potential envisioned for him as a Pirates rookie in 1983. He was drawing comparisons with Cardinals legend Bob Gibson as a strikeout artist. An article in the October 2, 1989, issue of *The Sporting News* was headlined "DeLeon Finally Has Arrived." His success was largely attributed to his "increased use of his fastball to complement his breaking pitches." Cardinals manager Whitey Herzog said that when DeLeon would get hit hard, he had a tendency to back off the use of his fastball.[16]

The Cardinals were so confident of DeLeon's performance that they signed him to a three-year, $6.5 million contract in January 1990.

But then DeLeon's career was torpedoed again with a dismal season in 1990. With the Cardinals regressing to a last-place finish in the NL East, DeLeon regressed with them. For the second time in six seasons, DeLeon absorbed 19 losses, the most in the league. His ERA increased by almost 1½ runs, and he lost seven consecutive games twice. He became the first pitcher since Phil Niekro to lead the league in losses twice.[17] If there was any consolation for DeLeon, it might be that teammate Magrane lost 17 games.

The Cardinals' offense didn't help DeLeon's confidence much, since they were second-to-last in the league in runs scored. During his last 17 starts of the 1990 season, the Cardinals scored a total of 36 runs. During that stretch DeLeon lost 14 games, won one, and had two no-decisions.

Before the 1991 season, Cardinals manager Joe Torre reflected on DeLeon's depressing 1990 season, saying, "DeLeon's performance paralleled, a little, what I saw when (Steve)

Carlton lost 19 games in 1970. He was afraid to throw his fastball. I think pitchers fall into that. When they start losing, they start to become defensive. Plus, with DeLeon, there was the confidence factor."[18]

DeLeon's performance rebounded in 1991, although his record didn't reflect it. He finished with a 5-9 record in 28 starts, but his 2.71 ERA was the sixth best in the National League. He gave up more than three earned runs in only three of his 28 starts, but he had the third-lowest run support (2.8 per 9 innings pitched) among National League starters.[19]

The 1992 season started out as a shaky one for DeLeon; he was 2-6 record with a 4.28 ERA in 12 starts. He was moved to the bullpen by the Cardinals on June 12. During the balance of his time with the Cardinals through August 27, he made 17 appearances, including three spot starts, and posted a 5.14 ERA. On August 5, in one of those starts against the Phillies, he and the bullpen failed to hold a three-run lead going into the sixth inning. The game was indicative of hard-luck circumstances DeLeon had experienced over the last three seasons when he recorded only eight wins in his last 60 starts.[20] The Cardinals released DeLeon on August 31, and he finished out the season with the Philadelphia Phillies who signed him on September 9.

There was some thought that Phillies pitching coach Johnny Podres, a change-up guru, could help DeLeon integrate an effective off-speed pitch into his repertoire.[21] However, DeLeon was unable to break into the starting rotation with a regular slot.

DeLeon wound up splitting the 1993 season between the Phillies and the Chicago White Sox, who acquired him for the second time in exchange for Bobby Thigpen on August 10. His primary role with both teams was as a reliever. He posted a respectable 2.98 ERA. In the only postseason experience of his career, DeLeon pitched twice in the American League Championship Series against Toronto, which won the series in six games.

DeLeon played the final two seasons of his career in relief roles with the White Sox and the Montreal Expos, who acquired him in a trade in August 1995 for pitcher Jeff Shaw. DeLeon was 34 years old when he retired.

DeLeon finished his 13-year career with an 86-119 won-lost record. That doesn't completely define his career. Of his 119 losses, 53 (45 percent) came during seven strings of consecutive losing decisions comprising six or more losses each. He was a victim of playing for losing teams that offered poor run support, while his career ERA was 3.76, with a career ERA+ of 102, indicating he was slightly above average in runs allowed. DeLeon showed flashes of brilliance with numerous no-hit bids and several high-strikeout seasons during his paradoxical career. But his two seasons of league-leading 19 losses overshadowed his high points, resulting in a career largely tainted by a losing reputation.

DeLeon and his wife, Natasha,[22] have three children: José Luis, Giancarlo, and Anthony.[23]

SOURCES

In addition to the sources cited in the Notes, the author also consulted the following:

1992 St. Louis Cardinals Media Guide.

1994 Chicago White Sox Media Guide.

Baseball-Reference.com.

NOTES

1. John Dewan and Don Zminda: *The Scouting Report: 1992* (New York: HarperCollins, 1992), 602.

2. Rick Hummel, "From Prospect to Suspect to Star," *The Sporting News*, May 22, 1989: 12.

3. Charles Feeney, "Rookie DeLeon Amazes Bucs," *The Sporting News*, August 15, 1983: 14.

4. Hummel.

5. Hummel.

6. Hummel.

7. Feeney.

8. *1986 Pittsburgh Pirates Media Guide*, 30.

9. Feeney.

10. The 1984 games in which DeLeon approached no-hitters were played on May 20, June 20, July 17, and August 24.

11. Only nine major-league pitchers have had a season winning percentage of .100 or lower since 1900 (20 or more starts).

12. James Kaufman and Alan Kaufman: *The Worst Baseball Pitchers of All Time* (New York: Carol Publishing Group, 1995), 156.

13. Ibid.

14. Peter Pascarelli, "Under Trying Circumstances, Reds Holding Up," *The Sporting News*, May 15, 1989: 14.

15. *1993 Philadelphia Phillies Media Guide*, 197.

16. Rick Hummel, "DeLeon Finally Has Arrived," *The Sporting News*, October 2, 1989: 16.

17. Seymour Siwoff, Steve Hirdt, Tom Hirdt, and Peter Hirdt, *The 1991 Elías Baseball Analyst* (New York: Simon & Schuster, 1991), 329.

18. "Coleman Is Seeking Aggressive Pitchers," *The Sporting News*, February 4, 1991: 39.

19. Baseball-Reference.com. baseball-reference.com/leagues/NL/1991-starter-pitching.shtml. Retrieved November 21, 2018.

20. "N.L. East: St. Louis Cardinals," *The Sporting News*, August 17, 1992: 31.

21. John Dewan and Don Zminda, *The Scouting Report: 1993* (New York: HarperCollins, 1993), 566.

22. *1986 Pittsburgh Pirates Media Guide*.

23. *1993 Philadelphia Phillies Media Guide*.

MIGUEL DILONÉ

by Seth Moland-Kovash

A right-handed-throwing, switch-hitting outfielder who had much more success from the left side because of his ability to "swing-and-run" and beat out slap base hits, Miguel Diloné was perhaps the quintessential journeyman. He played for seven teams (including two stints with the Pirates) over a 12-year career and had more than 400 plate appearances in only two of those years. While his career numbers, including a slash line of (.265/.315/.333) in 2,182 plate appearances during those 12 years would not stand out to anyone, there was one glorious summer when Diloné was third in batting average in the American League.

From the moment Diloné hit a baseball field in the United States, he was off and running. Born on November 1, 1954, in Santiago, Dominican Republic, he was signed as a 17-year-old by the Pittsburgh Pirates. In that 1972 season, Diloné came in third in stolen bases in the New York-Penn League as an outfielder for Niagara Falls. He stole 41 bases in 61 gamesd and was caught only 10 times. In 1973, Diloné was promoted to the Class-A Western Carolinas League and proceeded to set a league record with 95 stolen bases in 115 games. As a 19-year-old playing for Salem in the Carolina League, Diloné was having his best year yet in 1974. He was batting .333/.414/.444 with 85 stolen bases when he was called up to Pittsburgh for September. He was the youngest player in the National League at the time.

In the second game of a home doubleheader against the Philadelphia Phillies on September 2, 1974, Diloné came in to play center field in the ninth inning as part of a double-switch

Photo courtesy of the Pittsburgh Pirates

in an 11-1 Pirates victory. No plays were needed in center field that day. Diloné's first plate appearance came a few days later, on September 7 against the Montreal Expos. It was the bottom of the 12th inning in a 5-5 game with a runner on first base and two outs when manager Danny Murtaugh called on Diloné to hit for pitcher Ramon Hernandez. He worked a walk from pitcher Dale Murray. The Pirates' young slugger Dave Parker followed Diloné to the plate and drove in the winning run.

Throughout the rest of that season, Diloné continued to see time as a pinch-hitter and primarily as a pinch-runner. He got his first major-league stolen base on September 15 at Montreal. He scored his first run on September 23, in the top of the 10th inning of a 5-4 Pirates victory. Diloné's first run at the major leagues in 1974 ended with 12 games but only three plate appearances. He walked once and stole two bases, scoring three times and still looking for his first hit.

For his 20-year-old season in 1975, Diloné largely repeated 1974. He spent the bulk of the year in the minors again, but this time in Triple A at Charleston in the International League. He struggled much more at the plate, posting a slash line of .217/.291/.270 in 125 games. He was still a speedster but was kept to 48 stolen bases at this level. Once again he was a September call-up and saw time primarily as a pinch-runner. He got into 18 games, with six plate appearances. He scored eight runs and added two stolen bases, but still had no major-league hits. The 1976 season was a near-repeat performance statistically with the bulk of the year spent at Triple A (though he did manage a .336 batting average in 449 plate appearances) and a September call-up.

Diloné got his first starting assignment on September 28 against the Cubs. Starting in center field and leading off, he was 2-for-4. Diloné wasted no time, beating out a groundball to third base. He scored on a sacrifice fly by Richie Zisk. With his first two singles (he also beat out a groundball in the hole to shortstop in the third inning), Diloné showed off the "slap-and-run" style that characterized his hitting at its best. With 1977 a near repeat of the previous three years (substitute Columbus for Charleston as Pittsburgh moved their Triple-A affiliates and add an extended stay on the disabled list for a dislocated finger from a stolen-base attempt), Diloné spent the Septembers of four consecutive seasons with the Pirates. His cumulative line for his efforts was .145/.181/.145 in 75 plate appearances, with 21 stolen bases and 23 runs scored. The speed was real, but the Pirates felt they had seen enough.

On April 4, the eve of the 1978 season, the Pirates traded Diloné along with Elías Sosa and a player to be named later (Mike Edwards) to the Oakland Athletics. The A's sent the Pirates former Pittsburgh legend Manny Sanguillen so that he could finish his career as a Pirate after a brief sojourn in Oakland. Diloné spent only one year with Oakland, but the A's did give him the chance to spend the whole year in the major leagues, installing him as their regular left fielder. He stole 50 bases but still strugglde mightily at the plate. He hit .229/.294/.271 though he was able to get his first major-league home run.[1] In 1979 Diloné started out with Oakland but his struggles continued. He was batting .187/.237/.275 when he was sent down to Triple-A Ogden on June 24. Diloné was rescued from more time at Triple A when the Chicago Cubs purchased his contract from the A's on July 4. Used again primarily as a pinch-runner and defensive replacement with a few spot starts, he batted .306/.342/.306 with 15 stolen bases in 38 plate appearances.

The 1980 season began, as so many previous years had, with Diloné not making the team out of spring training and being sent to the minor leagues, Wichita of the American

Association in this case. He did not spend much time in Wichita, however, as the Cleveland Indians came calling and purchased his contract from the Cubs on May 7. He got a chance to play regularly in Cleveland in 1980 and made the most of it. Originally brought in as an injury replacement for center fielder Rick Manning, Diloné platooned in left field briefly with Joe Charboneau but quickly earned the starting job. He was frustrated with his reputation as a speedster who couldn't hit and felt it was due to his lack of consistent playing time. In an interview with the *Akron Beacon Journal* in August of 1980, he said, "People said I can't hit. They see my .214 batting average [his career mark heading into 1980]. But I never played regular. I only played eight games in a row once until this season."[2] Missing 25 games that season before the Indians acquired him, Diloné blew away his career marks with a line of .341/.375/.432 and added a team-record 61 stolen bases (third in the American League). His .341 mark was also third in the league – well behind AL leader George Brett's .390 but still very impressive.

It looked as though Diloné had perhaps finally found his spot. Maybe he was right and all it took was regular playing time for him to prove himself. He looked forward to the 1981 season as an opportunity to prove that 1980 was no fluke. During the 1980-1981 offseason, he did as he always did and returned to his native Dominican Republic to spend time with family and play more baseball. He was three days late in reporting to Arizona for his first spring training with the Indians because of some legal trouble back home. Diloné had been accused of statutory rape after a consensual sexual encounter with a young woman who said she was 17 years old. The case was adjudicated in the Dominican court system and it was determined that the young woman, at the urging of an unscrupulous attorney,

had falsified her birth certificate (she was actually 18) in an attempt to extort $5,000 from Diloné. The court proceedings obviously distracted Diloné and caused him to be late for spring training.[3]

When he was finally able to report to camp, Diloné was surprised (and offended) to learn that his starting job was in jeopardy even after his breakout performance in 1980. "From the day I came to camp," he said in broken English, "I was confused. First I couldn't get out of the [Dominican Republic] because I was accused of rape. Then I arrive late and I am told I have to fight for my job in left field. Why should I have to fight for a position after I bat .341 the season before? I don't understand that."[4] Diloné did not respond well to the challenge, as he acknowledged a year later – "Now I am prepared to fight [for my starting job]. Last spring I was not."[5] That strike-shortened 1981 season was a part-time season for Diloné and his numbers took a step back. In just 72 games and 289 plate appearances, he hit .290/.334/.346. His speed was still there, as he stole 29 bases in this limited time. Diloné beat out Charboneau for the starting job in 1982 and things looked hopeful for him – he was given regular playing time again. But he did not perform. His game slipped quickly. In 412 plate appearances (the second-most of his career, to 1980) he hit only .235 and stole only 33 bases, a rate far lower than he had previously been hitting.

Things went from bad to worse quickly in 1983. At age 28, Diloné should have been entering his prime, but the numbers did not bear that out. Through July 14, when the Indians demoted him to Triple-A Charleston, Diloné was batting only .191. Worse from a media perspective is that Diloné was being paid $225,000 to hit in Triple A, making him the most expensive minor leaguer the Indians had ever had. Cleveland's coaches thought the problem was one of approach – they believed that Diloné had stopped bunting for hits and was trying to hit for power, and it ruined his value. General manager Phil Seghi said, "He started swinging for the fence. Everything he hit was in the air. He quit bunting. Then the bottom fell out of his batting average."[6] So the Indians sent Diloné to Triple A hoping he could return to his old form. It would not happen again in Cleveland. On September 1 Diloné was traded as the player to be named later in an earlier deal in which the Indians received Rich Barnes from the Chicago White Sox. He played in only four games for the White Sox, going 0-for-3 with one stolen base and one run scored. Less than a week later, on September 7, Diloné was traded back to Pittsburgh along with minor leaguer Mike Maitland for Randy Niemann. Back with the Pirates, Diloné repeated his early-season pattern in Pittsburgh, appearing seven times but only as a pinch-runner.

A free agent for the second time, Diloné was signed this time by the Montreal Expos in January 1984 to a one-year deal. He played most of two seasons for the Expos as a 29- to 30-year-old. For a player whose game depended on speed, the decline came quickly. In shared playing time in 1984 and 1985 with Montreal, he had 280 plate appearances and hit .249/.312/.324 with 34 steals. The stolen-base numbers were starting to slip as well. On July 10, 1985, Diloné was released by the Expos. He signed as a free agent with the San Diego Padres two weeks later. After spending two weeks in Triple-A Las Vegas, Diloné joined the Padres. He ended his career as it always had been – not hitting much and for very little power but running when he was on base. His San Diego line in 27 games and 50 plate appearances, was 10 stolen bases and .217/.280/.261. That was the end of major-league baseball for Miguel Angel Diloné.

From the Dominican Republic to Pittsburgh to Oakland, Chicago (Cubs), Cleveland, back to Chicago (White Sox this time), back to Pittsburgh, to Montreal and San Diego over the course of 12 years, Diloné slapped and bunted his way on base and ran with the best of them. His career averages of .265/.315/.333 show a hitter whose batting average was close to average, but who hit for almost no power. His 267 stolen bases place him 207th all-time, but his rate was a bit better. He was more successful than his peers, so his career success rate of 77.39 percent bumps him up to 58th place.

During and after his major-league career, Diloné played in his native Dominican Republic for 22 seasons. He led the Dominican League in stolen bases for 10 of his first 12 years and as ofg 2019 still held the league's career stolen-base record.

In a freak accident on a foul tip during a practice, Diloné was struck in the face by a baseball and lost his left eye in 2009. He was coaching a 15-year-old prospect and giving him batting tips at the time.[7] As of 2019 he remained active in baseball in his hometown of Santiago and throughout the Dominican Republic.

SOURCES

In addition to the sources cited in the Notes, the author also used Baseball-Reference.com and Retrosheet.com

NOTES

1. This was a rare occurrence indeed, as he ended his career with only six home runs. This one came to lead off the bottom of the first inning for the A's against the Yankees' Don Gullett in a 6-4 A's victory.

2. Bob Nold, "There's No Doubt About His Speed …," *Akron Beacon Journal*, August 5, 1980: B1.

3. Sheldon Ocker, "Acceptable Excuses: Jail or Death," *Akron Beacon Journal*, March 5, 1981: B1.

4. Hal Lebowitz, "The Other Face of Senor Diloné," *Cleveland Plain Dealer*, March 22, 1982: 1-C.

5. Lebowitz.

6. Terry Pluto, "Diloné's Demise Is Hard to Figure Out," *Cleveland Plain Dealer*, July 16, 1983: 6-C.

7. "Miguel Diloné Loses an Eye in Baseball Accident," *Diario Libre*, March 17, 2009. Retrieved from web September 30, 2018.

Juan Encarnación

by Paul Hofmann

Signed as a lanky, 16-year-old amateur free agent by the Detroit Tigers in December 1992, Juan Encarnación was the embodiment of a five-tool, can't miss prospect. He could hit for average and power, run, play any of the three outfield positions with above-average range, and throw. He was blessed with all the tools for success. Tigers hitting coach Alan Trammell called Encarnación the most talented player he had seen in his 20-plus years with the Tigers organization.[1] Despite his immense natural talents, Encarnación's injury-plagued career fell short of expectations and will be remembered as one of unfulfilled potential that ended too early.

Juan De Dios Encarnación was born on March 8, 1976, in Las Matas de Farfán, Dominican Republic, the fourth of eight children born to Inocencio Encarnación and Eufacia Santiago, who were rice and vegetable farmers.[2] Growing up in the Pueblo Nuevo section of the city, Juan dreamed of growing up and becoming an engineer.[3] He was a shy kid who didn't speak very much, but was a solid student at Mercedes Maria Mateo High School, the same high school that produced major-league catcher Alberto Castillo. Juan was a pitcher for most of his youth, and only began playing the outfield and batting regularly about a month before he signed with Detroit.

Tigers scout Ramon Peña is credited with signing Encarnación after seeing him play in a local tournament. "I loved his bat speed and the way the ball jumped off his bat," Peña said.[4] He signed the young outfielder for $3,000. After signing, Encarnación recalled Peña telling his father, "The only thing I want from him, to close this deal, is for him to smile."[5] Juan did smile, and his career path changed from engineering to professional baseball player. Looking back on his choice to pursue a professional baseball career over continuing his education, Encarnación said his career was an education in itself: "Life in professional sports is like a university. You have to interact with people from different cultures, from different countries, and eventually, it has an effect on you."[6]

Encarnación arrived in the United States unable to speak English, and started his professional career at the age of 18 with the Bristol (Virginia) Tigers in 1994. In 54 games with the Appalachian League's rookie Bengals, the young Dominican demonstrated both his great potential and how much he had to learn. While he hit .249 with four home runs and a team-leading 31 RBIs, he also struck out 54 times in only 197 at-bats. After the rookie league season ended, Encarnación was promoted to the Fayetteville Generals of the low Class-A Sally League. In 24 games with the Generals, he hit a paltry .193 with one home run and four RBIs. He ended his first professional season by playing in three games with the Lakeland Tigers of the high Class-A Florida State League. For the year he hit a combined .234 with 5 home runs and 35 RBIs.

Encarnación spent the entire 1995 season with Fayetteville. He played in 124 games and finished with a .282 average, 16 home runs, and 72 RBIs. His offensive production slipped at Lakeland in 1996, when he hit .240 with 15 home runs and 58 RBIs. Despite his delayed progress, the Tigers remained confident that Encarnación was a key piece of the future. After all, at 20 years old he was still growing into his 6-foot-2 frame.

Encarnación had a breakout year in 1997 when he hit .323 with 26 home runs and 90 RBIs for the Jacksonville Suns of the Southern League. On July 21 he earned MVP honors in the Southern League All Star Game when the Double-A circuit's all-stars beat the Seattle Mariners, 9-3, at Raleigh, North Carolina. His season was rewarded with a call-up to the Tigers when rosters expanded in September.

On September 2, 1997, Encarnación made his major-league debut against the Atlanta Braves at Turner Field in Atlanta. The Tigers' starting right fielder went 0-for-3 against left-hander Denny Neagle, who tossed a four-hit shutout to earn his 19th victory of the season. The next day Encarnación got his first major-league hit and RBI when he laced a 1-and-2 pitch from right-hander Paul Byrd to right field for a single that plated Tony Clark.

Four games into his major-league career, Encarnación hit his first big-league home run, a two-run shot off Angels southpaw

Photo by Vincent Laforet/Allsport

Allen Watson that landed in Tiger Stadium's left-field grandstand. Two innings later, in his second at-bat of the game, his right hand was broken when Watson hit him with a pitch. Encarnación played through the injury for another seven games until he was shut down on September 14. The injury was a major setback for both the young outfielder and the organization. With the team well out of the pennant race, Tigers manager Buddy Bell and general manager Randy Smith had hoped to get a good look at Encarnación during the final month of the season.

The following spring, Encarnación's bid to make the Detroit roster ended prematurely when he fouled a ball off his left foot, breaking yet another bone. After missing the remainder of spring training and more than a month of the regular season, Encarnación had a four-game rehabilitation stint in Lakeland before joining the Tigers' top farm club, Toledo. In 92 games with the Mud Hens, Encarnación batted .287 with 8 home runs, 41 RBIs, and 24 stolen bases. On August 18 he joined the Tigers for the remainder of the season and started 39 of the final 40 games in the outfield. He was spectacular over the 40-game stretch. He hit .329, hammered 7 home runs, drove in 21 runs, and stole 7 bases. He made only one error, recorded four assists, and demonstrated that he was capable of being an everyday major-league outfielder. His performance validated all the reports of his tremendous talents and he appeared to be headed for stardom in Detroit.

Great expectations were placed on Encarnación as he entered his first full major-league season in 1999. Settling into his role as the Tigers' everyday left fielder, the 23-year-old picked up where he left off the previous fall with a 2-for-5 Opening Day performance that included a home run on the first pitch of the season from Texas Rangers right-hander Rick Helling. Encarnación's batting average hovered around .290 until mid-June before he tailed off and finished with a .255 average, 19 home runs, 74 RBIs, and a career-high 33 stolen bases. He missed the final week of the season when he suffered a fractured cheekbone after being hit by a pitch by Royals right-hander Blake Stein.

Encarnación's play during the 1999 season drew mixed reviews. He tormented Tigers fans and management alike with play that vacillated between the "blockheaded and brilliant."[7] This was particularly evident in the field, where he earned 10 outfield assists but also made nine errors, including two on May 23 when he dropped consecutive fly balls with runners on base. Nonetheless, club officials believed Encarnación was still learning the game and was poised to take that next step.

Encarnación moved to center field for the 2000 season and hit safely in 27 of the Tigers' first 30 games, including a career-high 19-game hitting streak from April 16 to May 7 in which he hit .346. He was batting .300 as late as July 13 before cooling off a bit to finish at .289 with 14 home runs and 72 RBIs. He followed this with a subpar 2001 season. As he split time between right field and center field, Encarnación's average dipped to .242 with only 12 home runs and 52 RBIs. When the Tigers unsuccessfully tried to trade the outfielder before the July 31 deadline, manager Phil Garner candidly disclosed that Encarnación would see little playing time the rest of the season.[8] The outfielder made only one start in September and ended his five-year career with the Tigers with a pinch-running appearance on September 10.

Encarnación's fall-off in home runs and RBI production were not the only reasons why the Tigers soured on their one-time top prospect. In fact, his decline in power numbers was easily explained by the team's move from hitter-friendly Tiger Stadium to the cavernous Comerica Park.[9] His stock plummeted with the Tigers because he had developed a reputation as a player who was difficult to coach, showed little patience and a lack of discipline at the plate, and had lapses of concentration on defense.[10] No longer part of the Tigers' rebuilding plans, Encarnación was dealt, along with right-handed pitching prospect Luis Pineda, to the Cincinnati Reds for outfielder-first baseman Dmitri Young.

The change of scenery seemed to reinvigorate the outfielder. Encarnación hit 16 home runs and drove in 51 runs for Cincinnati prior to the All-Star break. But still he was sent packing after just 83 games in a Reds uniform. On July 11, 2002, he was dealt to the Florida Marlins with utility infielder Wilton Guerrero, a fellow Dominican and the younger brother of Vladimir Guerrero, and left-handed pitcher

Ryan Snare. The Reds received right-hander Ryan Dempster. In 69 games with the Marlins, Encarnación added another 8 home runs and 34 RBIs to his season totals. Offensively, 2002 was one of his better seasons. He played in 152 games and hit .271 with 24 home runs and 85 RBIs.

The move to Miami seemed to be a perfect fit for Encarnación. He was closer to his native Dominican Republic and the city was steeped in Latin American culture. The Marlins were also a team on the rise. The team had a good mix of veterans, led by future Hall of Famer Ivan Rodriguez and All-Star second baseman Luis Castillo, and emerging stars like Miguel Cabrera. This, coupled with a solid pitching staff, had the Marlins positioned to contend for the NL East title. Encarnación was an integral piece of the puzzle, serving as the Marlins' everyday right fielder.

Encarnación played in a career-high 156 games during the 2003 season and hit .270 with 19 home runs and 94 RBIs, second on the team to third baseman Mike Lowell, who drove in 105 runs. His defensive contributions figured significantly in the Marlins' 91-71 finish, good enough for second place in the NL East. That season Encarnación became the first Marlins outfielder to post a 1.000 fielding percentage as the team earned a wild-card spot in the National League postseason. He would go on to play in 221 consecutive errorless games.

Encarnación struggled at the plate during the 2003 playoffs. In the Marlins' four-game Division Series victory over the San Francisco Giants, he went just 2-for-15, contributing a solo home run off Joe Nathan in Game Two. He hit another home run, a Game One solo shot off the Chicago Cubs' Carlos Zambrano, and went 3-for-12 as the Marlins beat the Cubs in seven games to advance to the World Series. As his postseason struggles continued, Encarnación was dropped in the batting order and increasingly relegated to pinch-hitting and defensive-replacement roles. In six appearances in the World Series against the New York Yankees, he went just 2-for-11 with five strikeouts and one RBI, a Game Six sacrifice fly that provided the Marlins with an insurance run in Josh Beckett's Series-clinching five-hit shutout.

On December 13, 2003, the World Series champion Marlins sent Encarnación to the Los Angeles Dodgers in exchange for minor-league outfielder Travis Ezi. The move allowed the Marlins to shed his $3.5 million-a-year salary, while Ezi never progressed beyond Double-A. The trade reunited Encarnación with childhood friend Odalis Pérez. He and Pérez grew up across the street from each other in Las Matas de Farfán.

Encarnación struggled with the Dodgers. In 86 games he was hitting just .236 with 13 home runs and 43 RBIs when he was traded back to the Marlins. The trade-deadline move packaged the outfielder with catcher Paul Lo Duca and pitcher Guillermo Mota in return for first baseman Hee-Seop Choi, left-handed pitching prospect Bill Murphy, and 2003 World Series hero Brad Penny. The return to Miami and his familiar right-field position with the Marlins did little to bring Encarnación out of his season-long slump. After the trade he hit only .238 with 3 home runs and 19 RBIs in 49 games with the Marlins.

The right fielder rebounded and enjoyed a consistent 2005 season. He started the season on a high note when slugged a first-inning, Opening Day grand slam off future Hall of Famer John Smoltz. Five days later he connected for another grand slam off the Washington Nationals' Antonio Osuna. In 141 games, Encarnación hit .287 with 16 home runs and 76 RBIs, solid numbers for an outfielder ready to test the free-agent market.

After the 2005 season Encarnación was named to the Dominican Republic's roster for the inaugural World Baseball Classic in 2006. He was the team's starting right fielder and went 2-for-4 with two runs scored in its opening-game victory over Venezuela. In five additional games Encarnación went 1-for-16 and did not appear in the team's 3-1 semifinal loss to Cuba. He finished the tournament with a .150 average, no home runs, and no RBIs as the Dominican Republic finished in fourth place.

When St. Louis right-fielder Larry Walker retired after the 2005 season, Cardinals general manager Walt Jocketty was in search of a right fielder who could be reliably productive, not necessarily spectacular.[11] Although he was no longer the five-tool prospect of a decade earlier, Encarnación was still a more than serviceable outfielder with upside potential. After all, he was a youthful veteran, only 29 years old, who had played in more than 1,000 big-league games and experienced what it took to win a World Series. On January 10, 2006, he agreed to a three-year, $15 million contract and joined a potent Cardinals lineup that included Albert Pujols, Jim Edmonds, and Scott Rolen.

Encarnación proved to be a good fit for the 2006 Cardinals. Despite being slowed by a sore left wrist during the second half of the season, he played in 153 games and finished the season with a .278 batting average, 25 doubles, 19 home runs, and 79 RBIs. His biggest contribution to the Cardinals' NL Central championship was his .310 batting average with runners in scoring position.[12]

With his wrist becoming progressively worse during the postseason, Encarnación again saw his playing time diminish during the playoffs. He went 4-for-14 in the NL Division Series against the San Diego Padres, including a Game Four triple that plated Pujols with the series-clinching run. He followed this with a 4-for-22 performance in the Championship Series against the New York Mets and failed to register a hit in nine plate appearances in the World Series against the Tigers. He finished the postseason 8-for-44 (.182).

As was the case after the Marlins' Series victory in 2003, Encarnación was noticeably absent from the Cardinals' World Series victory parade. Rumors circulated that he was unhappy with his reduced playing time during the Series, but Encarnación explained that he had to attend to a family issue back in the Dominican Republic. "I had to see my son," he said. "He had a little problem." Encarnación underscored the importance of family in his life when he went on to say, "I will do anything I can for my family."[13]

Hoping that rest would heal the ligaments in his wrist, Encarnación delayed having surgery until December, when it was clear that his wrist was not responding to rest. The delayed decision to surgically repair the damage cost the Cardinals right fielder the first six weeks of the 2007 season. After returning to the lineup on May 13, Encarnación struggled to find his timing and got off to a slow start. He gradually rediscovered his swing and on May 30 he started an 18-game hitting streak, the second longest of his career. During the streak he hit four home runs and drove in 13 runs. Encarnación continued to raise his average throughout July and into August. After a 0-for-3 performance against the Houston Astros on August 30, Encarnación's average stood at .283 with 9 home runs and 47 RBIs. No one could have foreseen this was the final game of his career.

The course of Encarnación's career and life were forever changed by a stray foul ball during the sixth inning of the Cardinals game against the Cincinnati Reds on August 31. Encarnación was in the on-deck circle waiting to pinch-hit for Randy Flores when teammate Aaron Miles fouled off an 0-and-1 pitch from Jon Coutlangus. The ball was on top of Encarnación before he had a chance to react and it hit him flush in the left eye.[14] He sustained multiple fractures to his left eye socket. Dr. George Paletta, the Cardinals' medical director, called it the "worst trauma I've seen."[15] He said Encarnación's eye socket was crushed on impact and that the optic nerve had sustained severe trauma. While Encarnación was able to walk off the field, the injury left his career in jeopardy.

The Cardinals outfielder missed the entire 2008 season and was granted free agency that November. However, no organization showed any interest in signing him with the hope that his eyesight would eventually improve over time; indeed, his eyesight never returned to normal. He finished his 11-year major-league career with a .270 batting average, 156 home runs, 667 RBIs, and 127 stolen bases. While those numbers may have fallen far short of the expectations placed on him after having the five-tool label stamped on him early in his professional career, Encarnación enjoyed a productive major-league career that saw him win two World Series championships. And yet, at 31 years old, his best baseball might still have been ahead of him.

Nearly seven years after Encarnación was injured, the Reds' Aroldis Chapman was hit in the head with a line drive. Cincinnati outfielder Ryan Ludwick was asked by reporters if that was the worst baseball injury he had seen. He replied, "It's a tie. I was in St. Louis when Juan Encarnación got hit in the on-deck circle." Ludwick recalled, "It was same reaction. It was shock on the field. I was instantly praying for the guy and hoping for the best."[16]

Looking back on the fateful night that ended his career, Encarnación claimed the injury had little impact on him psychologically. While recuperating, he realized, "God is the one who decides when things are over."[17] While his career was over, baseball provided him with a platform to fall back on that positioned him for the future.

As of 2019 Encarnación, who has four children, split time between his home in Green Cove Springs, Florida, and the Dominican Republic. Stateside he stayed busy with the Juan Encarnación Foundation, a nonprofit organization that assists people and other nonprofits to provide shelter, school supplies, clothes, and other daily necessities to those in need. In the Dominican Republic he and his family own a number of small family enterprises involved in construction and the exporting of fruits and vegetables to the United States. He became a social activist and an active supporter of the Modern Revolutionary Party, a social-democratic political party.

NOTES

1. Stephen Cannella, "Breaking Out Talented Tiger Juan Encarnación Needs Fewer Fractures and More Seasoning," *Sports Illustrated*, June 28, 1999: 74.

2. Circulo de Grandes – Juan Encarnación. Retrieved from youtube.com/watch?v=bq7nU8cGss0.

3. Encarnación's younger brother Nidio is a member of the Dominican Congress.

4. Canella.

5. Circulo de Grandes – Juan Encarnación.

6. Circulo de Grandes – Juan Encarnación.

7. Circulo de Grandes – Juan Encarnación.

8. "Detroit Tigers," *The Sporting News*, September 17, 2001: 54.

9. It wasn't until after the 2002 season that the Tigers decided to bring the fences in at Comerica Park.

10. Mark Schmetzer, "N.L. Central: Cincinnati Reds," *The Sporting News*, December 24, 2001: 57.

11. "Why Cardinals Were Impressed by Juan Encarnación," December 28, 2015. Retrosimba.com.

12. "Why Cardinals Were Impressed by Juan Encarnacion."

13. Matthew Leach, "Notes: Encarnación Discusses Injury," January 14, 2007. cardinals.com.

14. Matthew Leach, "Encarnacion Struck in Face by Foul Ball," September 1, 2007. mlb.com.

15. "Encarnación Likely Out for 2008 Season; MLB Future in Jeopardy," Associated Press, January 16, 2008. Retrieved from espn.com.

16. Trent Rosecrans, "Chapman Hit Reminiscent of Juan Encarnación," Cincinnati.com, March 20, 2014.

17. Circulo de Grandes – Juan Encarnación.

Tony Fernández

by Tom Hawthorn

Tony Fernández was all limbs. At shortstop, the gangly fielder scuttled after groundballs before pirouetting to make an underarm throw with a slight flick of the wrist. At the plate, he slashed at the ball before scurrying around the bases.

Tall and lean at 6-feet-2 and 165 pounds, the infielder enjoyed a 17-season major-league career. He played in the postseason for three different teams and won a World Series championship in 1993 with the Toronto Blue Jays, the team that originally signed the impoverished teenaged amateur from the Dominican Republic. Along the way, he earned four consecutive Gold Gloves as the best-fielding American League shortstop, so good a player that his acquisition by the New York Yankees in 1995 delayed the ascension of top prospect Derek Jeter.

Fernández combated stereotypes in all his baseball stops. Some reporters, unwilling to acknowledge he was being asked to field provocative questions in a second language, thought him sullen and diffident. As a devout Christian, he eschewed the late-night revelry others thought helped a team bond. Though lacking a formal education, he was a wise analyst of what it meant to play professional sports in a foreign land in a foreign language where his ethnicity meant something different than it did back at home.

"Latin players have been misunderstood, made out to be moody, hostile, lazy, erratic," Fernández said in 1992, by which time he was an established star. "We are an emotional people. But we are honest and sincere, and the difficulty of the change in cultures has just never ever been fully accepted and appreciated. Of course it all still hurts. But not as much as it used to."[1]

Octavio Antonio Fernández Castro was born in San Pedro de Macoris, Dominican Republic, on June 30, 1962, to the former Andrea Castro and José Fernández, a man of Haitian descent born as a Fernando who took as his surname Fernández. He supported as best he could a family of 11 children (seven boys, four girls) as a cane cutter in the sugar fields. Baby Octavio's hairless head was so outsized that his father dubbed him El Cabeza (The Head), a nickname that would stick through adolescence.

The boy's arrival came a year after the assassination of the brutal dictator Rafael Trujillo, the leader of a cult of personality, who was known as El Jefe (The Boss). Trujillo used baseball as a means of expressing his nation's — and, by his twisted measure, his own – glory.

In the 1950s the government built a trio of stadiums modeled on Miami Stadium, where the Brooklyn and Los Angeles Dodgers and, later, the Baltimore Orioles trained each spring. One was constructed in the capital of Santo Domingo, a larger one in Santiago, and the third in San Pedro de Macoris, about 50 miles east of the capital.

The Fernández family lived just beyond the right-field fence of Estadio Tetelo Vargas, named for a star of Negro League and Caribbean baseball. The surrounding Barrio Restauracíon was a tough district of dirt roads with single-story shacks and shanties boasting tin roofs and no running water.

Like most of the other boys in the neighborhood, Fernández spent all his free time around the park, which was home to the Estrellas Orientales (Eastern Stars). He was among the urchins who would climb trees for a better unpaid view of a game, quickly scrambling down to pursue any ball hit in their direction. The boys played *pelota* with whatever was at hand – broken broom handle, rolled-up socks covered in tape, the occasional stray baseball. Sometimes his mother asked the boy to skip pickup games to push the family's vegetable cart along the bumpy, dusty streets, a task for which his older brothers were too ashamed.

The boy also scrounged work at the stadium as a batboy, a groundskeeper, and as an all-around laborer, a skinny kid who could be pressed into service loading the team's bus. Of course he shagged fly balls and chased groundballs with the eagerness of a pup. Early on, he showed soft hands, perhaps because he was too poor to afford a leather glove, instead using scraps of cardboard or a flattened milk carton tied to his left hand. He showed an adroit sense of the game obvious to any learned eye who saw him field on the uneven diamonds of the Dominican. At the same time, he was hobbled by a bone chip in his right knee. The nagging injury put him

Photo courtesy of the National Baseball Hall of Fame

on the reject list for scouts and bird-dogs. The injured prospect was damaged goods, a *tullido*, a cripple, lame. His mother pestered a doctor in the capital who, after also being pressured and likely paid by one persistent scout, operated on the boy's knee. The family was so poor the boy shared a hospital bed with another lad as he recuperated for six weeks.

Two years later, his legs still not at full strength, the still-growing teenager – as lean as a stalk of sugar cane at an even 6-feet and, 140 pounds – boarded a bus to the capital for a tryout in front of the scout. Epifanio "Epy" Guerrero, whose big break was signing César Cedeño to Houston, had since opened an academy for prospects a few miles outside Santo Domingo. By then working for the Blue Jays, Guerrero signed the 17-year-old Fernández, who had been a student at Gaston Fernando de Ligne high school, on April 24, 1979. Only after the money for his signing bonus arrived and the boy dumped a large pile of pesos on his mother's bed did she fully appreciate that baseball was a profession and not just a pastime.

At 18, Fernández was assigned to the Kinston (North Carolina) Eagles of the Carolina League. The young infielder was promoted to the Triple-A Syracuse (New York) Chiefs late the following season. After nearly four full campaigns in the minors, he made his major-league debut with the Blue Jays in a game against the Detroit Tigers at Exhibition Stadium in Toronto on September 2, 1983. Manager Bobby Cox sent Fernández in as a pinch-runner for Cliff Johnson in the eighth inning of a tie game. The rookie advanced to a second a wild pitch, to third on a single by Ernie Whitt, and then scored on another wild pitch by Aurelio Lopez. The Jays went on to lose the game in extra innings.

Toronto management was grooming the rookie as a replacement at short for Alfredo Griffin, a fellow Dominican and a stellar fielder himself who would be traded to Oakland after the 1984 season.

The seven-year-old Blue Jays franchise enjoyed its first winning season in 1983. The new shortstop would be a key figure as the team became a contender through the decade with starters Dave Stieb and Jimmy Key, reliever Tom Henke, catcher Ernie Whitt, and an outfield of Lloyd Moseby, Jesse Barfield, and George Bell, yet another superb Dominican to be imported to Canada from Hispaniola. The lineup made the postseason in 1985 (losing the American League Championship Series to the Kansas City Royals in seven games) and 1989 (losing the ALCS to the Oakland A's in five games). The infamous Blue Jays' swoon of 1987 during which they lost the final seven games of the season to be passed in the standings by the Detroit Tigers was explained in part by injuries to Whitt and, especially, Fernández, who suffered a fractured olecranon bone at the tip of the elbow of his throwing arm when Bill Madlock of the Tigers took him out in a slide at second base on September 24.

In 1986 Fernández recorded 213 hits, the first Blue Jay to beat the 200-hit marker. That season he played in the first of five career All-Star Games (four with Toronto, one with the San Diego Padres) and won his first of the four consecutive Gold Gloves. "He makes the spectacular commonplace," said teammate Garth Iorg.[2] In 1989 he committed just six errors in 741 chances for a .992 fielding average.

After the 1990 season, during which he hit a league-leading 17 triples, Fernández was part of a blockbuster trade when he was dispatched with slugging first baseman Fred "Crime Dog" McGriff to San Diego for Roberto Alomar and Joe Carter.

Fernández played two seasons for the Padres before being traded to the New York Mets. After just 48 games, he was traded to the Blue Jays, who by then were defending world champions. When they repeated by defeating the Philadelphia Phillies in six games in the World Series, the returned shortstop played a key role, banging out seven hits (six singles and a double) in 21 at-bats. He knocked in nine runs in the Series, just one short of Ted Kluszewski's standard for a six-game Series.

As a free agent, Fernández signed with the Cincinnati Reds for 1994, before joining the Yankees the following season. For the Yankees, he played in 108 games and drove in 45 runs, hitting for a .245 batting average with a .322 on-base percentage. He missed the 1996 season as he recovered from a fractured right elbow incurred diving for a groundball in spring training. Fernández later signed as a free agent with the Cleveland Indians, returning to the postseason in 1997. Once again he was superb at the plate, touching Florida

Marlins pitchers for 8 hits in 17 at-bats. The shortstop's contribution to World Series lore came in the bottom of the 11th inning. With a runner on first and one out, Craig Counsell hit a potential inning-ending groundball to Fernández at second base. As the fielder moved to his left to field the ball, he raised his glove just enough to graze the three-hopper, which rolled slowly into right field. On NBC, Bob Costas shouted: "Fernández has it go through him!"[3] The runner, Bobby Bonilla, got to third base, only to later be thrown out at the plate by Fernández on a fielder's choice on Devon White's grounder. The Marlins went on to win the World Series on Édgar Rentería's liner up the middle, which pitcher Charles Nagy nearly snagged.

Fernández, a free agent, once again returned to the Blue Jays for two seasons at second and, mostly, third base. The infielder spent the 2000 season in Japan with the Seibu Lions before joining the Milwaukee Brewers at the start of the 2001 season. He was released after 28 games and the Blue Jays yet again picked him up and he saw action in 48 games before retiring as a player.

In 17 seasons, the infielder batted .288 with 2,276 hits, including 92 triples and 94 home runs. In 11 World Series games, he hit .395 with 13 runs batted in. He holds several Blue Jays club records (as of 2019), including hits (1,583), triples (72), and games played (1,450). Fernández was added to the Level of Excellence display at the Rogers Centre in Toronto on September 23, 2001. In 2007 he was inducted into the Pabellón de la Fama de Deporte Dominicana (Dominican Sports Hall of Fame) in Santo Domingo. The following year, he was named to the Canadian Baseball Hall of Fame at St. Marys, Ontario.

Over the years, Fernández's dedication to a stretching regimen and a willingness to try all manner of exercise gizmos earned him the locker-room nickname of Mr. Gadget.

The former player spent three years, from 2012 to 2014, as a special assistant to Texas Rangers general manager Jon Daniels.

Fernández became an ordained Pentecostal minister in 2003. Raised in a churchgoing household, he professed to be born again at a clubhouse chapel service at Fenway Park in 1984. "They think because I take things easy, I don't care about baseball anymore," he said a year after his revelation. "They take it all wrong. I am a better player because I am playing now for the glorification of God."[4]

Fernández and his wife, Clara, as of 2019 operated the Tony Fernández Foundation, a charitable organization to help underprivileged youth in his homeland. The nonprofit foundation has offices in Canada, the United States, and the Dominican Republic. The foundation has as its goal an ambitious plan to build a stadium, schools, a convention center, an orphanage, gymnasium, trade school, teen dorms, hotel, and a restaurant on a 500-acre spread outside San Pedro.

The couple's first of five children, Joel, was born July 18, 1985. He was followed by Jonathan, Abraham, Andres, and Jasmine. The first two boys and the first daughter were given names beginning with the letter J in homage to the Jays.

Late in 2017, Fernández announced on Twitter, using the handle @TonyCabezaFdez, which incorporates his childhood nickname, that he had been hospitalized after being diagnosed with polycystic kidney disease. He was released in time for Christmas.

Two years later, his health took a perilous turn. Diagnosed with pneumonia as well as kidney failure, he was put in an induced coma. He died on February 15, 2020, after suffering a stroke in a hospital in Weston, Florida.

SOURCES

In addition to the sources cited in the Notes, the author consulted Retrosheet.org, Baseball-Reference.com, and the following:

Bjarkman, Peter C. *Toronto Blue Jays* (London: Bison Books, 1990).

Blair, Jeff. *Full Count: Four Decades of Blue Jays Baseball* (Toronto: Random House Canada, 2013).

Kurlansky, Mark. *The Eastern Stars: How Baseball Changed the Dominican Town of San Pedro de Macoris* (New York: Riverhead Books, 2010).

Prats, Frank. "Estadios de Béisbol Dominocanos," *Bajotecho*, November 2008.

Turner, Dan. "Jays' Pennant Dance Has Latin Beat," *Ottawa Citizen*, September 27, 1985.

NOTES

1. Joe Sexton, "From Poverty to Pushcart to Pros," *New York Times*, December 6, 1992.

2. Jim Prime, *Tales from the Blue Jays Dugout* (New York: Sports Publishing, 2014).

3. Major League Baseball, "1997 WS Gm7: Fernandez Makes Error on Grounder," *YouTube.com*, October 2, 2013. youtube.com/watch?v=EpswMjFRZ-M.

4. Wayne Parrish, "Fernandez Gives the Credit to God for Improved Play," *Toronto Star*, June 24, 1985.

JULIO FRANCO

by Leslie Heaphy

Hailed as the next Robin Yount, Julio Franco debuted with the Cleveland Indians in 1983. Franco came to the Indians from the Philadelphia Phillies as part of a five-player deal for Von Hayes. Expected to be the Phillies' shortstop of the future, Franco had found himself without a regular chance to play when the Phillies signed Ivan DeJesus. That signing became good news for the Indians, who made Franco the must-have in the Hayes trade. For Franco his trip to Cleveland began one of the longest careers in baseball history, with comparisons to Chicago's Minnie Miñoso. What best sums up Franco's career and life is his comment when he returned to the game in 2015: "It feels outstanding, I miss it so much. The smell of the grass, the crack of the bat, and being around baseball again is outstanding."[1]

Franco began his major-league career at age 23 with his double-play combo partner, Manny Trillo, batting between him and Garry Maddox in the Phillies lineup. After coming to the United States from the Dominican Republic, Franco had to find a home and the Indians gave him his first shot at the majors. Phillies scout Quique Acevedo persuaded Franco's mother to let him come to America, signing for $4,000. (She was raising three boys alone after his father died in 1979 at age 38 and she wanted the best for her boys.) Born on August 23, 1958, in Hato Mayor del Rey, Julio Cesar Franco came to the United States for an opportunity that would never have happened in his hometown. He had been working in a factory after graduating from Divine Providence High School, just to get the chance to play on their baseball team.[2]

The Phillies sent Franco to their rookie-league team in Butte, Montana, in 1978. Franco batted .305 and earned a trip to Bend, Oregon, the following season where he earned league MVP honors playing for the Central Oregon Phillies in the Northwest League. From Oregon, Franco moved up to the Class-A Carolina League, hitting .321 with 99 RBIs to help Peninsula win the league championship. After Franco's success at Peninsula (Hampton, Virginia), he moved up to Double-A Reading and then on to Triple-A Oklahoma City in 1982. Franco hit well at every level, which led to an April call-up by the Phillies in 1982. In his first game, against St. Louis, Franco went 1-for-4. After playing in 16 games with the Phillies, Franco was traded in a five-player deal to Cleveland.[3] Cleveland announcer Nev Chandler said of the Indians' new shortstop: "Julio Franco's star burns the

Photo courtesy of the National Baseball Hall of Fame

brightest, as he's considered one of baseball's best prospects. Julio will be an Indians shortstop of the future."[4]

As a rookie with Cleveland, Franco displayed the characteristics that would follow him for his whole career. He could hit, he covered a lot of ground at short, and was a health nut and also a bit of a character. A sportswriter called him "a bit eccentric" because he owned a baby tiger named Jana as a pet for a while and also a wolf. He pretended at times not to speak English so he would not have to talk to reporters. Franco's errors at short were chalked up to immaturity and the fact that he actually got to so many more balls because of his range. What was not as forgivable was his lack of hard work or what some saw as a lack of serious commitment to the game. As an example, in 1985 Franco never showed up for one game and the club had no idea where he was. They sent a teammate to find him and he later claimed he was sick but the Indians fined him $2,300. In another 1986 game he came to the ballpark, dressed to play, and then simply left without explanation before the game. Even with all the ups and downs, Franco was runner-up for the American League Rookie of the Year Award, losing out to Ron Kittle of the Chicago White Sox. Franco hit .273 with 80 RBIs.[5]

Franco spent six seasons with the Indians, hitting over .300 in the last three and ending with a .295 average and 131 stolen bases. While he did not display a great deal of power, Franco knocked in a lot of runs, making sure his hits counted. He neither walked nor struck out much. While Franco continued to improve each season with the Indians, his personality and approach to the game did not always go over well. Manager Pat Corrales said of his mercurial shortstop, "Julio Franco is the kind of guy you want to kiss one time and kick the next."[6] The 1987 season was his best offensively even though he missed nearly a month after hyper-extending his elbow. The Indians moved Franco to second base in 1988, hoping his defense would prove less of a liability there. Franco won the Silver Slugger Award that season after hitting .303.[7]

But at the end of that 1988 season, Franco found himself on the move again when the Indians traded him to Texas for first baseman Pete O'Brien, second baseman Jerry Browne, and outfielder Oddibe McDowell. Franco proved that Texas made a good decision as he made *The Sporting News'* all-star team in 1989 at second base. Then in 1991 he won the batting title, hitting .341. Beating out Wade Boggs for the crown, Franco became the first Ranger to win a batting championship.

Even with his success in Texas, Franco found himself looking for a new team in 1994. He signed a one-year deal with the Chicago White Sox. Franco played in 112 games and hit .319.

Franco loved baseball so much that he found himself heading to Japan in 1995 after the strike in major-league baseball. Franco became the designated hitter and first baseman for the Chiba Lotte Marines, under manager Bobby Valentine.[8] He was offered $7 million for two years, and as he stated, "For $7 million, I'll play against Martians on Mars and use a green ball."[9] He helped lead the Marines to their best season and earned best first baseman honors. After one season in Japan, Franco returned to the United States, joining the Indians for the second time. Franco never thought he would return to Cleveland but he played for the Indians in 1996 and 1997, picking up his 2,000th hit off Oakland starter Willie Adams. Franco again played in 112 games in 1996, hitting an impressive .322 at age 37.

With his 2,000th hit, sportswriters began asking Franco if he was done or if he had goals he still wanted to achieve. Franco's response was simply that he wanted to play as long as he could. He would later amend that to state that he would play until he was 50. Keeping to his word, Franco signed with Milwaukee in 1997 and with the Tampa Bay Devil Rays in 1999. He played in only one major-league game that season and ended up with the Mexico City Tigers, batting .423 in 93 games. In 2000 he joined the South Korean Samsung Lions before returning to the United States in late 2001 with the Atlanta Braves, where he remained through the 2005 season.[10]

Franco continued to hit everywhere he went, regardless of his age. His success led to some questions about possible steroid use but nothing ever came of the conversation. Franco's longevity and strong play were easily credited to his work ethic and healthy living. Franco was incredibly strict about what he ate, with no fried foods and nothing that was not natural. Some of his daily shakes tasted terrible but Franco said that did not matter because they were good for him. A visitor to his Florida apartment once described a typical Franco breakfast of 14 egg whites followed by oatmeal, a banana, and grapefruit juice. His daily diet consisted of nearly 5,000 calories, designed to keep him playing for as long as he could and also to just keeping him alive. He developed three key rules to live his life by: "Eat well, work hard and get proper rest."[11] Franco never believed in going to the doctor, preferring instead to practice traditional Chinese medicine and using herbs, mushrooms, and tea from around the world.

Franco's hard work and longevity kept him with the Braves from 2002 through 2005 and then he signed a two-year deal with the New York Mets. After his time with the Mets, Franco signed back with Atlanta and then decided to announce his retirement at age 49 while he was playing for the Quintana Roo Tigers in Mexico, where he was hitting .250. Franco had previously stated he would know when the time was right and when the numbers told him it was time. Announcing his retirement was a sad day but he knew the decision was the right one to make.

As his career wound down, Franco achieved a number of firsts. He reached 2,500 hits with the Braves, and became the oldest player to hit a grand slam in an 8-4 win over the Phillies; he was 45. Franco was also the oldest player to hit a pinch-hit home run against the Padres, also at age 45. That home run was also the first pinch-hit home run of his career. The previous record had been set in 1907 by Deacon McGuire who was only 43.[12] Franco hit what turned out to be his last home run at age 48 in 2007, making him the oldest major leaguer to hit a home run. The home run came off future Hall of Famer Randy Johnson in a 5-3 Mets win. Tom Dunn, a fan from Stony Point, New York, returned the ball to him. In return Dunn was stunned to receive a signed bat for his kindness.[13] Franco also became the oldest player to hit two home runs in a game and the oldest to steal two bases in one game during his final stint with the Mets.[14]

After Franco officially retired, he could not stay away from the game. He tried golfing and scuba diving but nothing worked to fill the hole left by baseball. He stated, "I don't see myself out of baseball. I can go fishing, go play golf, or go to Starbucks but at the end of the day, I love baseball and this is what I want to do."[15] He came back to manage the Gulf Coast League Mets and then at age 55 he signed with the Fort Worth Cats in the Independent United League, giving him a career that spanned four decades. Franco went 6-for-27 for Fort Worth. Fort Worth manager Mike Marshall remarked, "Everyone loved watching him play. He had a real charisma on and off the field. We're excited and as far as my young guys … being able to learn and watch him handle himself on the field and off the field, I think it'll be a real bonus for our organization."[16] Franco admitted that the comeback was only partially about playing again. What really mattered to him was reminding people he was still around. Coming back opened up new possibilities for coaching or managing. Spending his time in the DR coaching his son was rewarding but not enough.[17]

At age 56 Franco signed in 2015 as player-manager of the Ishikawa Million Stars in Japan's six-team independent league. The Stars won three championships between 2007 and 2015. One of Franco's teammates on the Stars was female knuckleball pitcher Eri Yoshida. Not expecting to actually play, Franco found himself playing fairly regularly after an injury to a player. Of the team's first 14 games, Franco played in 10, hitting .333 with 4 RBIs. Franco told local reporters that he hoped to manage in Japan for a few years before returning to America to manage and then he hoped to find a front-office job. Franco tried to combine the best of the American game and the Japanese style, all in an effort to win every game.[18]

To keep that dream alive in 2016, Franco took a job as a batting coach for the Lotte Giants in South Korea. Franco was always willing to do whatever it took to play baseball.[19]

He based his dream of managing a major-league team on his desire to stay in the game and because he believed he had much to offer young players. He said, "I know it's hard to get there, but everybody who got there went the same road. It hasn't been easy for anybody. I think I can bring a lot to a club. I'll keep learning and one day I'll eventually get there and again I'll be a rookie, a rookie manager."[20] Franco said he loved teaching young players about the game, and wanted to give back for all those who helped him from the day he first came to America to play. Catcher Jack Daru of the Stars expressed the players' joy in having Franco as a manager: "He has a lot of knowledge and is very wise so we pick his brain a lot. He's given us a different insight into the game because he's played here and in the United States."[21]

Outside of baseball Franco has been married to Ivis Trueba since 1991. He is a self-described health nut and born-again Christian who became a US citizen in 1991. Baseball has been his whole life and focus since 1979 when he came to the United States. Franco came in with an unorthodox batting stance that earned him five Silver Slugger awards, three All-Star Game appearances and MVP of the 1990 All-Star Game. When you count all his seasons, in the majors and beyond, he is a member of the 4,000-hit club. His success at the plate kept him in the game longer than even he could have imagined, as he ended his career with a .298 batting average, 173 home runs and 1,194 RBIs in 2,527 games after 23 seasons. He played 15 seasons in the AL and eight in the NL. The only place he did not have success at the plate was in the postseason.

Franco played in nine division or championship series, totaling 31 games. He hit only .224 in 98 at-bats.

Franco is remembered for his unique batting stance and his hitting, as well as his love of the game.[22] Everywhere he played he became a fan favorite, Fort Worth Cats VP Scott Berry said, "To me, he exudes the love for the game."[23]

SOURCES

In addition to the sources cited in the Notes, the author relied on Baseball-Reference.com and MLB.com.

NOTES

1 "Julio Franco: Being Around Baseball Again Is Outstanding," The Jim Rome Show, jimrome.com, May 22, 2014.

2 Mark Hale, "Mets Go Old, Hook Franco, 47," *New York Post*, December 9, 2005; Julio Franco player file, National Baseball Hall of Fame, Cooperstown, New York; Michael Mooney, "At 57, Julio Franco Can't Quit Playing Baseball," ESPN.com, September 15, 2015.

3 Franco player file.

4 "Today in Tribe History," didthetribewinlastnight.com, February 12, 2009.

5 Franco player file; Mooney; *Albany Times Union*, May 27, 1983; Associated Press, "Indian Shortstop Julio Franco Misses the Game," *Los Angeles Times*, June 9, 1986.

6 Jason Lukehart, "Top 100 Indians: #60 Julio Franco," letsgotribe.com/top-100-indians/2013/3/4/4022630/top-100-indians-60-julio-franco; baseball-reference.com/players/f/francju01.shtml.

7 Lukehart; Zack Meisel, "Looking Back at the Career of Former Cleveland Indians Infielder Julio Franco," cleveland.com/tribe/index.ssf/2015/09/looking_back_at_the_career_of.html, September 16, 2015.

8 Murray Chass, *New York Times*, December 7, 1988, in Franco player file; *Dallas Morning News*, June 1, 1991.

9 Mooney.

10 George Vescey, "Sports of the Times; Julio Franco Made the Most of His Exile," *New York Times*, April 15. 2002; *Cleveland Plain Dealer*, June 12, 1996; *USA Today*, December 22, 1994; Lukehart.

11 Ben Shpigel, "Breakfast at Julio's," *New York Times*, March 1, 2006.

12 Franco File; *Philadelphia Inquirer*, August 21, 2005; *USA Today*, September 13, 2007.

13 Zach Braziller, "Julio Franco, 55, Proves It's Never Too Late for Baseball Comeback," *New York Post*, May 19, 2014.

14 Wayne Cavadi, "Julio Franco: The Ageless Wonder," baseballhotcorner.com, February 10, 2015.

15 Associated Press, "Julio Franco a Player-Manager in Japan: 'I Don't See Myself Out of Baseball,'" *USA Today Sports*, May 10, 2015.

16 Ryan Fagan, "Julio Franco Set for Return to Pro Baseball at 55 years old," sportingnews.com, May 17, 2014.

17 Steve Hummer, "Former Brave Julio Franco Still Defying Age," myajc.com, May 31, 2014.

18 Mooney.

19 ESPN.com, February 10, 2015; AP article.

20 Israel Fehr, "Julio Franco Is Still Playing Baseball at Age 56," sports.Yahoo.com, February 9, 2015.

21 "Julio Franco a Player-Manager."

22 Jun Hungo, "Julio Franco, 56 Years Old, Joins a Japan Team as Player-Manager," *Wall Street Journal*, February 9, 2015; Julio Franco, baseball-reference.com; Mike Axisa, "Julio Franco, 56, Joins Semi-Pro Team in Japan as Player-Manager," MLB.com, February 8, 2015.

23 Hummer.

DÁMASO GARCÍA

by Paul Goodson

Dámaso Domingo (Sanchez) García, an 11-year major leaguer (1978-1989), began his career with the New York Yankees, but the second baseman-shortstop is best known for his seven seasons with the Toronto Blue Jays. His playing days ended with brief stints in Atlanta and Montreal. His final appearance with the Expos came on September 12, 1989.

Garcia was born in Moca, Dominican Republic, on February 7, 1957, to Dámaso García Bautista, a farmer, and Juana Sanchez Nuñez, a housemaid. The elder Garcías met in college and later married in San Francisco de Macoris, Juana's hometown.[1]

Dámaso had an unusual path to the major leagues. He began playing soccer at age 7, became a local star, playing as central defender, and received a scholarship to play soccer for Pontificia Universidad Católica Madre y Maestra in Santiago (where he also participated in track and field, and studied mechanical engineering for two years.[2]) He was captain of the Dominican Republic national soccer team when New York Yankees scout Epy Guerrero signed him as an amateur free agent in March of 1975.[3] He had played baseball as a boy but had been away from the game for four years after his soccer coach

Photo courtesy of the National Baseball Hall of Fame

ordered him to not play baseball.[4]

Despite those four years away from the game, García found immediate success in the minors. His first assignment was to Oneonta of the Class-A New York-Penn League. He showed skill with the bat, hitting close to .300 before a late-season slump left him with a

.268 batting average.[5] His fielding was suspect (17 errors in 49 games) but quickly improved. He would become a solid defensive player in his major-league career with a lifetime .980 fielding average. Years later García reflected on the season spent at Oneonta as the key to his major-league career. Specifically he credited manager Mike Ferraro, saying, "I didn't know how to catch a ball, I didn't know how to turn a double play, I didn't know how to hit. I had to learn everything and I was trying to learn English at the same time. Everything was work, work, work. I owe it to Mike Ferraro. He had all the patience in the world with me."[6] Ferraro recalled, "We had extra workouts every afternoon in spring training. I had to show him how to use the four corners of the bag for different situations."[7] According to Ferraro, García possessed tremendous natural talent with a powerful arm and great range at second base.[8] Combining those in-born abilities with the hard work of 1975 helped him to blossom into a big-league talent.

García maintained an upward trajectory in the minors over the next three seasons. In 1976 he was moved from Low A (Oneonta) to High A (Fort Lauderdale). The following season was spent in West Haven of the Double-A Eastern League and in 1978 he manned second base for Triple-A Tacoma. A midseason injury to the Yankees' Willie Randolph brought García his first big-league appearances the same year. [9]

García's major-league debut came on June 24, 1978, in Detroit, when he was inserted at second base in the bottom of the eighth. The next day he got his first start and went 2-for-4 against the Tigers. He grounded out his first time up, but singled in the fifth against the Tigers' Steve Baker and again in the ninth against John Hiller. His first RBI came against the Boston Red Sox on June 27, on a sacrifice fly against Jim Wright. It was his only run batted in of the year. He batted just .195 in 18 games, but he had tasted the majors at last.

In 1979 the 6-foot-1, 165-pound right-handed batter was back at Triple-A (Columbus) except for a brief September call-up. With Randolph deeply entrenched at second, the Yankees used García in 10 games at shortstop and one at third base. It was clear that he was expendable to the team. In November 1979 he was part of a deal with the Blue Jays that sent him along with Paul Mirabella and Chris Chambliss to Toronto in exchange for Rick Cerone, Tom Underwood, and Ted Wilborn.[10]

With Toronto García flowered into a solid player. Even before spring training arrived the Blue Jays were confident that he would be their second baseman in 1980.[11] García demonstrated that the team had good reason for trusting in his abilities. In his first full major-league season he hit .278 in 140 games with 30 doubles and 13 stolen bases. He made 16 errors at second base, but was also involved in turning 112 double plays as he began his tandem with shortstop Alfredo Griffin (a pairing that would last until Tony Fernández took over at short in 1985). Toronto batting instructor Bobby Doerr (a fine second baseman in his own right) was impressed with García's talent: "He's going to be a good hitter. In the next three or four years, he's going to hit 15 to 18 home runs. He's got such a quick stroke."[12] (For the record, García never hit more than eight home runs in a season.) García's rookie year performance did not go unnoticed as he finished fourth in the American League Rookie of the Year voting and placed second behind Joe Charboneau for *The Sporting News* AL Rookie award.[13] He was also recognized by Topps, which named him as second baseman on its 1980 Rookie All-Star Team.[14]

García's 1981 campaign proved less successful, primarily due to injuries. He had a team-high 48 days out of the lineup during the strike-shortened season. His ailments included flu, a sore right knee, and a broken bone in his right hand after Ed Farmer hit him with a pitch.[15] His batting average dipped to .252 in just 64 games.

Undeterred by the rash of injuries in 1981 García returned in 1982 to have the finest season of his career. Manager Bobby Cox moved him to the leadoff spot in the lineup.[16] He responded with a slash line of .310/.338/.399, lashing 32 doubles and ranking second in the American League with 54 stolen bases (trailing only Rickey Henderson). García established team records with his 54 SBs, 185 hits, and 89 runs scored.[17] He earned a Silver Slugger Award for his efforts.[18] *The Sporting News* named him its American League All Star at second.[19]

García was frustrated with the business side of the game. Before the 1982 season began, he chose to forego use of an agent and negotiated a two-year contract for $300,000 with Toronto general manager Pat Gillick. However, when he reported to spring training he refused to sign the contract, and as a result the Jays renewed his contract for one year at $90,000.[20] After the season he went to arbitration, this time with agent William Goodstein representing him. García won the case and was awarded the $400,000 he asked for, but he was furious and asked to be traded after the Blue Jays argued that he was undeserving of that amount and countered with an offer of $300,000.[21] Gillick had this to say about the negotiations: "We presented the facts, we did not try to knock him down. We don't intend to trade the guy, and we are under no obligation to do so."[22]

Despite Gillick's statement denying a possible trade of García, he was the subject of regular trade rumors after the 1983 season. He was included in discussions with Seattle, Texas, the Chicago White Sox, St. Louis, and Montreal.[23] In the end none of those deals materialized and García was signed by Toronto to a five-year deal before the 1984 season began.[24]

García's performance remained solid before and after the negotiations and trade rumors. In 1983 he hit .307 and swiped 31 bases; he followed that with a .284 average and 46 steals in 1984. The Blue Jays were becoming contenders, and García was seen as the sparkplug for the Toronto offense. Teammate Dave Collins saw him as "our catalyst, he's a tremendous athlete."[25]

The Blue Jays finished in second place in the AL East in 1984 and improved in 1985 to win the division with a 99-62 record. In its first postseason appearance, Toronto fell in seven games to Kansas City in the 1985 American League Championship Series. García had seven hits in the series, including four doubles, and scored four runs. He was named to *The Sporting News* American League All-Star team.[26] García was selected as a reserve for the 1984 and 1985 All-Star Games.

The 1986 season began with a disgruntled García. In spring training new Blue Jays manager Jimy Williams announced that Lloyd Moseby would move to the leadoff spot with Dámaso dropped to the ninth spot.[27] This move infuriated García. Rather than thriving at the bottom of the order, he entered a prolonged slump to begin the season. After a loss in Oakland on May 14, García made perhaps the worst mistake of his career by burning his uniform. In 1987 he said, "My one regret is burning my uniform. I regret what I did and I will always regret it. I meant no harm."[28] His actions brought a rebuke in front of the entire team by manager Williams.

In August García and teammate Cliff Johnson got into two fights during batting practice before a game. García was upset that Johnson (who was on the disabled list) was allowed to take batting practice with the active roster players.[29] According to witnesses, García took the first swing but missed Johnson. Johnson then hit García in the side of the head and a wrestling match ensued. Teammates had to separate the two players.[30] García was banished to the clubhouse, but returned later to reignite the fisticuffs. Manager Jimy Williams and other players intervened to break up the second fight.[31]

After his tumultuous 1986 season it was no surprise that García found himself traded to Atlanta with Luis Leal in exchange for Craig McMurtry. Former Blue Jays manager Bobby Cox had moved to Atlanta as general manager and arranged the deal. He had succeeded in motivating the moody García in Toronto and it was hoped he could do the same with the Braves.[32]

As it turned out, a knee injury sidelined García for the entire 1987 season. He found this situation extremely frustrating: "I'm desperate to play, I'm desperate to get well and help this club. I want to play, but going crazy won't help."[33] He did return in 1988 but slumped badly, batting just .133 in 30 at-bats to start the season. Bobby Cox remained confident as he remembered the past streaky hitting of García. "He wouldn't hit, and then all of sudden there would be a four-hit game, a two-hit game, another four-hit game," Cox said. "That's why I'm not worried about it. He always comes out of it."[34] A little over a month later the still-slumping second baseman was released. Cox lamented, "We really thought Dámaso could help us. I don't know what happened, but somewhere Dámaso lost interest in playing. We just couldn't have that on the club."[35]

After being dropped by Atlanta, García signed with the Dodgers and was assigned to Triple-A Albuquerque. He played in just three games before reinjuring his knee.[36] Los Angeles quickly released him. Before the 1989 season he signed with Montreal. His performance was closer to his career norms as he appeared in 80 games and managed a .271 batting average. Late in the season the Expos, who were well out of playoff contention, benched García in order to give some younger players a look.[37] García's original club, the Yankees, gave him one last chance in 1990 but released him during spring training.[38] García reconciled himself that his career was in the past. "No one has called," he said a couple of months into the season. "But even if they did, I wouldn't play anymore. I've had enough."[39]

Knee injuries had hampered García's playing career, but a much worse health problem awaited him in retirement. In 1991 he began experiencing double vision, which led to discovery by doctors of a malignant brain tumor.[40] After he recovered from surgery and chemotherapy, he returned to Toronto in 1992 to toss the first pitch to former teammate Alfredo Griffin before Game One of the American League Championship Series.[41] As a result of the cancer surgery and treatment, García suffers from limited speech and motor skills.[42]

In 1985 it was discovered that García's 6-month-old son, Dámaso Alejandro, suffered from hemophilia. He had received top-notch care throughout his father's playing days. García's wife, Haydée, was astounded by the limited medical care available when they returned to the Dominican Republic after her husband's baseball career ended.[43] Dámaso and Haydée started an organization to provide workshops to Dominican families whose children have the condition. In 1998 they founded a baseball camp to raise awareness and funds for children with hemophilia.[44] In the years following other players have contributed to the effort, including Tony Fernández, Pedro Martínez, and Moises Alou.[45] In 2012 Haydée was recognized with the Novo Nordisk Haemophilia Foundation Community Award.[46]

SOURCES

In addition to the sources cited in the Notes, the author also consulted Baseball-Reference.com.

NOTES

1. Haydee Garcia, email correspondence with Bill Nowlin, July 11, 2017.
2. Ibid.
3. John Brockman, "Garcia Kicks Soccer Habit in FIL," *The Sporting News*, October 25, 1975: 23.
4. Brockman.
5. Brockman.
6. Joe Gergen, "From the Heart: Minor League Mentor Mike Ferraro Gets a Message from Garcia: Thank You!" *The Sporting News*, October 28, 1985: 11.
7. Gergen.
8. Gergen.
9. Phil Pepe, "Yankees Purify the Air – And Billy Breathes Easier," *The Sporting News*, July 15, 1978: 19.
10. Arlie Keller, "Chambliss May Be Dealt Again," *The Sporting News*, November 24, 1979: 57.
11. Neil MacCarl, "Blue Jays Ponder Howell's Role," *The Sporting News*, January 12, 1980: 41.
12. Neil MacCarl, "Blue Jays Got the Message to Garcia About Hitting," *The Sporting News*, May 31, 1980: 10.
13. Bob Sudyk, "Top 1980 Rookie Players: Joe Charboneau," *The Sporting News*, November 22, 1980: 42.
14. "A.L. Tops in Rookies," *The Sporting News*, December 13, 1980: 56.
15. Neil MacCarl, "Strike Didn't stop Jays from Hurting," *The Sporting News*, January 23, 1982: 46.
16. Neil MacCarl, "Jays' Garcia Earns Super Rating at 2B," *The Sporting News*, June 14, 1982: 27.
17. Neil MacCarl, "Jays Finish Strong, Best Record Ever," *The Sporting News*, October 18, 1982: 41.
18. Lowell Reidenbaugh, "The Silver Sluggers," *The Sporting News*, November 15, 1982: 50.
19. Ben Henkey, "In the A.L. Right Makes Might," *The Sporting News*, November 8, 1982: 28.
20. "Jays' Garcia Earns Super Rating at 2B."
21. Neil MacCarl, "Garcia Is Furious Despite Salary Win," *The Sporting News*, March 7, 1983: 35.
22. MacCarl, "Garcia Is Furious Despite Salary Win."
23. Peter Gammons, "Only Stupidity Could Deprive Aparicio," *The Sporting News*, November 28, 1983: 58.
24. Neil MacCarl, "Upshaw, Garcia Sign for Five Years," *The Sporting News*, February 27, 1984: 36.
25. Stan Isle, "Garcia Sparks Blue Jays," *The Sporting News*, June 18, 1984: 32.
26. "1985 TSN All-Star Squads," *The Sporting News*, October 28, 1985: 18.
27. Dave Nightengale, "Repeating: Why Is It So Difficult?" *The Sporting News*, April 1, 1986: 9.
28. "Blue Jays," *The Sporting News*, February 16, 1987: 31.
29. "Blue Jays," *The Sporting News*, August 18, 1986: 21.
30. "Blue Jays," *The Sporting News*, August 18, 1986: 21.
31. "Blue Jays," *The Sporting News*, August 18, 1986: 21.
32. Moss Klein, "Can New Blood Rid Angels of Old Curses?" *The Sporting News*, February 16, 1987: 30.
33. Gerry Fraley, "Braves Wait for García," *The Sporting News*, June 22, 1987: 16.
34. Gerry Fraley, "García, Braves Slump Together," *The Sporting News*, April 25, 1988: 16.
35. Gerry Fraley, "García's Disappointing Stay Ends," *The Sporting News*, May 30, 1988: 19.
36. Ian MacDonald, "García Opens Comeback with Early Heroics," *The Sporting News*, April 17, 1989: 22.
37. "Expos," *The Sporting News*, October 2, 1989: 18.
38. "Ex-Blue Jay García Happy Down on the Farm – His Own," *Chicago Tribune*, June 19, 1990.
39. "Ex-Blue Jay García Happy Down on the Farm – His Own."
40. Paul White, "García Still Making a Difference," *USA Today Baseball Weekly*, February 26, 2002: 4.
41. Tim Wendel, "García Comes Back to Throw First Pitch," *USA Today Baseball Weekly*, October 20, 1992.
42. "García Still Making a Difference."
43. Wendel.
44. Wendel.
45. Wendel.
46. "How Family History Led to Award-Winning Commitment," nnhf.org/news_and_events/nnhf_news/dominican_republic_award.html.

César Gerónimo

by Jorge Iber

Playing on a squad that featured such top-rank stars as Johnny Bench, Pete Rose, Joe Morgan, and Tony Pérez made it challenging for other players to gain notoriety in their own right. During the 1970s it was easy to overlook the contributions of "other" Reds who made up the roster of the Cincinnati's Big Red Machine. While César Gerónimo is sometimes slighted in the eyes of the media and public, his exceptional arm, glove, and range in center field, and his timely hitting, helped him play an essential role in bringing two World Series titles to the Queen City. Indeed, his career was marked by historic events: Gerónimo scored one of the most significant and controversial runs in World Series history in 1975 and holds one distinction (as a strikeout victim) unlikely ever to be repeated by a major-leaguer. Once he retired after the 1983 season, Gerónimo began contributing to the sport in another way: by improving the lot of Dominican youngsters who were pursuing their dreams (athletic, academic, and personal) against what were often overwhelming odds.

Cesar Francisco (Zorilla) Gerónimo was born on March 11, 1948, in the municipality of Santa Cruz de El Seibo, El Seibo Province, Dominican Republic. While it was quite

Photo courtesy of the National Baseball Hall of Fame

common for Dominican children of this era to not receive much formal schooling, Cesar's parents worked diligently so that their son would not only be properly educated, but would serve the Catholic Church as a priest. With this aim, Cesar was enrolled in the Santo Tomas de Aquino seminary at the age of 12 and remained there for five years. Eventually he withdrew and attended (and graduated from) high school. His father was quite happy, for he had wanted his son to pursue an athletic career. Throughout his time in these settings, there was one constant in Cesar's life: a love of baseball, and particularly the New York Yankees. "I liked it at seminary, but I really wanted to be a ballplayer and I knew if I went on to become a priest that would never happen," he once said.[1]

Neither the seminary nor his high school fielded a baseball team, so Cesar instead played basketball, soccer, and slow-pitch softball (on a club with his father). Gerónimo's success on this squad, predominantly because of his strong throwing arm, led to tryouts with the New York Mets and the Yankees, and the Yankees signed the 19-year-old prospect in 1967 as a pitcher-outfielder. (While blessed with phenomenal arm strength, he was awful at bat.) His first two teams were in rookie leagues: Oneonta in the New York-Pennsylvania League and Johnson City (Tennessee) of the Appalachian League. His lack of hitting was evident at both locales. Gerónimo played four games for Oneonta and hit a meager .100, followed by an even more anemic .071 in 19 games for Johnson City. The next season the Yankees moved him to Fort Lauderdale in the Florida State League hoping he would find something resembling a reasonable stroke. While there was some improvement, it was marginal (a .194 average in 109 games and 324 at-bats) and the notion of moving Gerónimo permanently to the mound gained acceptance.

At about this time Gerónimo came to the attention of Grady Hatton, a scout for the Houston Astros, who recommended the outfielder to his boss, assistant general manager John Mullen. Then, at the 1968 winter meetings, Howie Haak, a scout for the Pirates, raved to Mullen about Gerónimo's arm and bemoaned the fact that Pittsburgh did not have room on its roster for the young Dominican. The conversation clinched Mullen's interest, and the Astros invested $8,000 on the unproven prospect, selecting Gerónimo in the third round of the Rule 5 draft.[2]

The Astros, as required by the draft rules, kept Gerónimo on the major-league roster for the entire 1969 season, using him mainly as a late-inning defensive replacement and pinch-runner. Gerónimo got into only 28 games and had eight at-bats (two hits). For 1970, no longer required to keep him in the majors or risk losing him, the Astros assigned Gerónimo to their Columbus (Georgia) affiliate in the Double-A Southern League, where he hit a more respectable .269 in 74 games, and called him up for 47 games (37 at-bats) late in the season. Gerónimo played winter ball and continued to work on both his hitting and fielding. Heading into the 1971 season, the Astros felt he could be useful as a pinch-runner and pinch-hitter. And there were those who believed that "if he were a regular, he would be the best fielder on the team."[3] He justified the Astros' faith in his defensive prowess by launching a strike from the left-field corner of the Astrodome to nail Duke Sims of the Dodgers at third base on Opening Day. But at the plate, while he had a few good stretches, he hit only .220 in 94 games (82 at-bats). Once again, he headed off to play winter ball in hopes of continuing to improve all facets of his game.[4]

Gerónimo's statistics in Houston were certainly not dazzling, and he was now playing behind All-Star center fielder César Cedeño, but once again fate intervened to boost his career prospects. In late November 1971 the Cincinnati Reds negotiated a swap that sent first baseman Lee May, second baseman Tommy Helms, and utilityman Jimmy Stewart to the Astros in exchange for second baseman Joe Morgan, infielder Denis Menke, pitcher Jack Billingham, outfielder Ed Armbrister, and Gerónimo. For some, the young Gerónimo seemed little more than a throw-in.

Reds general manager Bob Howsam, however, argued that because the Reds had moved to the spacious Riverfront Stadium, it was necessary to have outfielders with speed who could cover more ground.

Finally given an opportunity to play semi-regularly, and helped by extensive work with batting instructor Ted Kluszewski, Gerónimo improved to .275 in 120 games (255 at-bats) in 1972, many as a late-innings replacement. With the fleet veteran Bobby Tolan returning from an injury and manning center field, Gerónimo mainly played right field that season. Once again, he played winter ball, and began the 1973 season as the Reds' center fielder, with the now struggling Tolan shifting to right. Gerónimo injured his shoulder while making a catch and then slumped badly to .210. There was some reason for hope, as he had raised his average from .149 in July, and hit over .300 in September. Anderson argued that Gerónimo was still an asset to the Reds. "If a guy can save you a couple of runs with his fielding and throwing, it is just as important as driving home a couple of runs."[5]

After that dismal campaign, Gerónimo again headed home to the Dominican Republic to play baseball, where he got some well-timed assistance from his manager, Tommy Lasorda. The work paid off, as Gerónimo hit .281 in 150 games for the Reds in 1974 and earned the first of what would be four consecutive Gold Glove Awards. On July 17 he became the 3,000th strikeout victim of Bob Gibson, a feat he oddly duplicated on July 4, 1980, when he was the 3,000th victim for Nolan Ryan. Given his seminary training, Gerónimo was very philosophical about this "feat": "I was just at the right place at the right time," he said.[6]

In 1975, in his second full season holding a regular position, Gerónimo hit .257 and led the NL in outfield putouts with 408. In the World Series against the Boston Red Sox, Gerónimo scored the winning run in Game Three, leading off the bottom of the 10th inning with a single, moving to third after a controversial collision between Boston catcher Carlton Fisk and pinch-hitter Ed Armbrister, and scoring on a single by Joe Morgan. For the Series, hit .280 (7-for-25) with two home runs, as the Reds won the classic in seven games.

Gerónimo had his best individual season in 1976 as he hit .307 with 11 triples, second in the league. The Reds again waltzed to the World Series and swept the Yankees. Gerónimo batted .308 while playing every inning for the second straight October.

Gerónimo hit .266 with a career-high ten home runs in 1977 and copped his fourth Gold Glove award, but the Reds were overtaken by the Dodgers in the NL West, and many of the team's regular players began to depart. Pérez had been traded after the 1976 season, and Rose and Morgan soon left for free agency. Gerónimo stayed with the Reds through the 1980 season, but his hitting fell to .226, .239, and .255, and he was a part-time player most of that time.

In January 1981 the Reds dealt Gerónimo to the Kansas City Royals for infielder German Barranca. Gerónimo played the final three years of his career mainly as a defensive replacement, compiling only 324 at-bats and hitting .244 He played his final game in the majors on August 28, 1983, against the Texas Rangers. The Royals released him after the season. In 1,522 major-league games he batted .258 with 51 home runs, and 392 RBIs.

Gerónimo was always known as a quiet and reserved individual, who brought much stability and class to the Reds' locker room. He and his wife, Elizabeth, were married in 1971 and had two children, Cesar Jr. (born December 19, 1972) and Giselle (born December 17, 1975).[7] Given his religious training, it is not surprising that Cesar got involved in causes linked to social justice after his departure from the majors. First, he was involved with the Federacion Nacional de Peloteros Profesionales, which represented the interests of Dominican ballplayers in their dealings with the teams on the island. Later, he worked at the training camp set up on the island by the Hiroshima Toyo Carp of the Japanese baseball league, a facility that Mark Kurlansky in his book *The Eastern Stars* called "one of the better appointed academies" on the island.

Gerónimo also was a founder and a board member of the Dominican Republic Sports and Education Academy, aimed at providing proper training, nutrition, and on-field instruction to young Dominican athletes, and working to make sure they are educated, have a working knowledge of English, and are given basic instruction in financial matters.[8]

In other words, César Gerónimo continued to do the same caliber of work that he performed with the Reds during the Machine's glory days. He was not about bringing great attention to himself. He merely did the best he could to make it possible for his team (and then his countrymen) to succeed in the often-difficult world of baseball. While he never became a Catholic priest, in many ways in recent years he was involved in a type of ministry that his Jesuit instructors at the Santo Tomas de Aquino seminary would certainly approve. The Cincinnati Reds inducted him into their Hall of Fame in 2008.[9]

SOURCES

Bjarkman, Peter C. *Baseball's Great Dynasties: The Reds* (New York: Gallery Books, 1991).

Frost, Mark. *Game Six: Cincinnati, Boston, and the 1975 World Series: The Triumph of America's Pastime* (New York: Hyperion, 2009).

Hertzel, Bob. *The Big Red Machine* (Englewood Cliffs, New Jersey: Prentice-Hall, Inc., 1976).

Lawson, Earl. *Cincinnati Seasons: My 34 Years with the Reds* (South Bend, Indiana: Diamond Communications, Inc., 1987).

McCoy, Hal. *The Relentless Reds* (Shelbyville, Kentucky: PressCo, 1976).

Posnanski, Joe. *The Machine: A Hot Team, A Legendary Season, and a Heart-Stopping World Series: The Story of the 1975 Cincinnati Reds* (New York: William Morrow, 2009).

Walker, Robert Harris. *Cincinnati and the Big Red Machine* (Bloomington, Indiana: Indiana University Press, 1988)

NOTES

1. Ritter Collett, *Men of the Machine: An Inside Look at Baseball's Team of the 1970s* (Dayton, Ohio: Landfall Press, 1977), 210.

2. Jim Ogle, "Inside Pitch: Light Hitting Gerónimo Provided Yank Surprises," April 10, 1971; part of the César Gerónimo file at National Baseball Hall of Fame Library and Stan Isle, "Hurlers Are Hottest Items in Majors' Draft," *The Sporting News,* December 14, 1968: 33-34.

3. *The Sporting News,* March 27, 1971: 39-40.

4. John Wilson, "Astros Toughen 6 Arms on Florida Pad," *The Sporting News*, November 15, 1969: 53; ; "Astros Beat War Drums for Gerónimo," *The Sporting News*, March 27, 1971: 39-40; "Dodgers Learn Gerónimo Boasts Rifle for an Arm," *The Sporting News*, April 17, 1971: 8; and "Farmhands Fuel Strongest Astro Drive of Season," *The Sporting News*, October 2, 1971: 22.

5. Earl Lawson, "Sure Hands Cesar Wins Cincy Salute," *The Sporting News*, April 15, 1972: 21 and 28.

6. Mark Purdy, "Mild Mannered Cesar Often Misunderstood During 9 Years As Red," *Cincinnati Enquirer*, January 18, 1981. Both items are from César Gerónimo file, Baseball Hall of Fame Library.

7. César Gerónimo pages, *1980 Cincinnati Reds Media Guide*, 36, 37.

8. "The Champs of '75," *Sports Illustrated*, July 31, 2000; Alan M. Klein, *Sugarball: The American Game, the Dominican Dream* (New Haven: Yale University Press, 1991), 41, 55. Mark Kurlansky, *The Eastern Stars: How Baseball Changed the Dominican Town of San Pedro de Macoris* (New York: Riverhead Books, 2010), 197. For more information on the Dominican Republic Sports and Education Academy (DRSEA), visit the organization's website at: www.drsea.org. Here, you can also download copies of their publication, "DRSEA Informer." For more information on the Hiroshima Toyo Carp, visit www.japanball.com/carp.htm.

9. Cincinnati Reds Hall of Fame, Member Directory; César Gerónimo, Class of 2008. http://mlb.mlb.com/cin/hof/hof/directory.jsp?hof_id=114723.

Alfredo Griffin

By Justin Krueger

Alfredo Claudino Griffin was a professional baseball player for 20 years, 18 of which were in the major leagues. He was a fan favorite for his outgoing personality and sure-handed glove in the middle infield. And he's the answer to two great trivia questions: (1) Who was on deck when Joe Carter hit the ninth-inning Game Six home run off Mitch Williams of the Philadelphia Phillies to win the 1993 World Series? (2) Who was the first player to have played on the losing end of three perfect games (Len Barker in 1981, Tom Browning in 1988, and Dennis Martínez in 1991)?

Griffin was born on October 6, 1957, in Santo Domingo, Dominican Republic. He was the youngest of three brothers. His father, Alberto Reed, in order to financially support the family worked on the docks of Santo Domingo during the day and at night was a musician at local clubs. Young Alfredo developed a love of music from his father and would often be found playing the conga at parties and fiestas as he grew older.[1] With civil unrest and the resulting turf wars arising from a coup d'etat in 1965, Alfredo's mother made the decision to take him and his two brothers away from the capital city and back to her family. His father stayed in Santo Domingo.[2]

Upon moving back to Consuelo at age 8, Alfredo eventually made his way to playing baseball for the local sugar mill, Ingenio Consuelo, at the behest of his uncle Clemente Hart who was a cricket player later-turned baseball player. Hart played baseball locally for the Estrellas Orientales, a Dominican Winter League team. The Consuelo sugar-mill team had several other future major leaguers on its roster, including Rafael Santana, Nelson Norman, Rafael Ramírez, and Julio Franco. Major league scouts were plentiful at its games.[3] Griffin was signed as a 15-year-old nondrafted free agent by the Cleveland Indians on August 22, 1973, by Cuban scout Reggie Otero. At the time, Griffin played second base. Otero believed that he possessed excellent range on the field, and suggested a move to shortstop.[4] With the signing Griffin became one of the growing number of players to sign professional contracts from San Pedro de Macoris, a port city on the country's southern coast. That area of the Dominican Republic in the late 1970s and early '80s became known as the City of Shortstops with the major-league success of players like Griffin, Pepe Frias, Rafael Ramírez, Julio Franco, and Tony Fernández.[5]

Not long after Griffin signed with the Indians he was in A-ball. He was batting exclusively right-handed. In 1975, upon the request of San José player-coach Gomer Hodge who "told me to take the next at-bat left-handed. I slapped the ball and almost beat it out."[6] It turned out his early season batting struggles that had seen his average dip to around .080 had opened a path to becoming a switch-hitter.[7] Over the next few years he continued to work on his switch-hitting with Indians minor-league instructor Tommy McCraw. McCraw told him to keep at it, hit the ball on the ground, and take advantage of his speed. Griffin ended his major-league career with 1,688 hits in 6,780 at-bats. While none of his offensive statistics are eye-popping, they are reflective of a player known mostly for his glove who played the field with enough consistency to enjoy a major-league career for nearly two decades.

His minor-league career started in 1974 with stops in rookie ball with the Gulf Coast League Indians and the High-A Reno Silver Sox. Griffin spent the entire 1975 season with the High-A San José Bees. Through his first three seasons in the minors he racked up 43 steals. Highlighting his penchant for aggressiveness on the basepaths, he was also caught stealing 25 times. Griffin took a significant step forward in 1976. While starting the season again at San José, he earned a call-up to Williamsport of the Double-A Eastern League. After spending about 60 games at San José and Williamsport he played in 22 games with the Triple-A Toledo Mud Hens before getting his first major-league call-up.

Upon his first major-league call-up Griffin noted, "No, I am not excited, I am not nervous, but I am very happy."[8] Griffin made his major-league debut on September 4, 1976, as a late-inning substitution. His first hit came on September 7. Upon entering the game in the sixth inning, Griffin hit a single to left field on the very first pitch he saw from Milwaukee Brewers starting pitcher Gary Beare. Beare happened to be making his major-league debut in what turned out to be a nine-inning complete-game 17-4 victory over the Cleveland Indians. He was 18 years old. Between then and his last major-league appearance, in October 1993 as a member of the World Series-winning Toronto Blue Jays, Griffin strung together an 18-year career. Thirteen of those seasons were as an everyday starter for the Indians, Oakland Athletics, Los Angeles Dodgers, and two stints with the Blue Jays.

After a few short stints in the majors with the Indians from 1976-1978 in which he appeared in 31 games total, Griffin was eventually traded to the Blue Jays along with Phil Lunsford in exchange for pitcher Victor Cruz prior to the start of the 1979 season. It was as a Blue Jay that Griffin cemented his status as a major-league shortstop. Jerry Howarth, longtime Blue Jays broadcaster, said, "The Jays couldn't have asked for a better player or role model. He was at the leading edge of an influx of talented Dominican Republic players for the shore of Lake Ontario. ... Alfredo was a big part of the success story of the Blue Jays."[9]

At 5-feet-11 and 165 pounds, Griffin was known more for his defensive ability than anything he had to offer offensively. His best offensive season was his 1979 American League Rookie of the Year campaign. He batted .287, had 179 hits, hit 10 triples, and scored 81 runs. He shared the award with Minnesota Twins third baseman John Castino. He had been named the AL Player of the Month for September after batting .347 with six doubles, four triples, six RBIs, and five stolen bases. That season Griffin turned 124 double plays, a Blue Jays team record that he surpassed the next season with 126 double plays. He also made a league-leading 36 errors. In 1979

Photo courtesy of the National Baseball Hall of Fame

Griffin was called a bright spot in the otherwise unremarkable three-year history of the Toronto Blue Jays.[10]

Griffin's early success in the major leagues was neither immediate nor without growing pains. Recalling his early struggles, he said:

"It was 1979. I was hitting about .170 after the first month. My confidence was shot. Our hitting coach [1986 Hall of Fame inductee] Bobby Doerr said, 'I'll help you, but you're about down to your last chance to stay in the majors.' So before our game in Texas that night, he worked with me on choking up on the bat, and relaxing a bit. Only trouble was, I did not speak English very well then. Or understand it. So he drew some pictures, and asked Rico Carty – one of our veteran Blue Jay players – to help out. Al Oliver, of the Rangers, was also with us. All three of them were very encouraging. ... I really appreciated their help. They not only improved my batting; they also built up my confidence."[11]

Griffin's value beyond his glove work was as a positive influence in the clubhouse. It was common for people to comment that Griffin was a positive influence on his teammates. A sentiment further echoed by A's front office adviser Bill Rigney, who said of Griffin: "His character? Top of the line."[12] This is high praise for a player who ended his career with a total WAR (wins above replacement) of 3.0, ranging from a career high of 3.4 in 1986 to a career low of -2.3 in 1990. By these analytical measures Griffin would be considered a replacement-level player. Not bad at all for a player able to carve out an 18-year major-league career.

During his first stint as a Blue Jay, Griffin played home games in the oft-windy and outdoor confines of Exhibition Stadium in Toronto. Recalling his early days in Toronto, Griffin said:

"Everybody said it was a bad place to play baseball. But I was a happy man to become a major-leaguer in Toronto playing at Exhibition Stadium every day. It gave me my future. It secured the future for my family. I made my living out of the place, so I've got nothing bad to say about the old place."[13]

Regardless of the playing conditions, Griffin had more than a few accomplishments during his first stint with the Blue Jays. He tied Willie Wilson of the Kansas City Royals for the American League lead in triples in 1980 with 15. He finished in the top 10 in the category four other times. It was also here that Griffin played in a personal best 414 consecutive games. Griffin played in all 162 regular-season games four times during his career. In 1984, he was an odd selection for the American League All-Star team. John Feinstein of the *Washington Post* explained:

"Major league baseball pays the expenses for each player here and for one guest. In most cases, players bring wives or girlfriends. Dámaso Garcia, the Toronto Blue Jays' second baseman, brought his shortstop, Alfredo Griffin. When the Tigers' Alan Trammell hurt his arm and could not play tonight, Manager Joe Altobelli named Griffin to the team, partly because he's a fine player, but mostly because he was here."[14]

Garcia's wife had decided not to attend, and so Griffin came as his guest. It seemed like a good idea. The Blue Jays were slated to start the second half of the season in Oakland right across the bay from where the All-Star Game was being played in San Francisco. Griffin entered the game as a replacement for Cal Ripken in the sixth inning. He had no at-bats; Don Mattingly pinch-hit for him in the ninth inning. It was Griffin's only All-Star Game appearance.

Even though Griffin was popular in the clubhouse and with Blue Jays fans, his days as the full-time shortstop for the Blue Jays were numbered. In 1983 he began to split time at shortstop with the up-and-coming wunderkind and fellow Dominican Tony Fernández. After two seasons, Fernandez took over as the full-time shortstop. Griffin was on this way out.

In December 1984 Griffin was traded to the Oakland Athletics with Dave Collins and cash for relief pitcher Bill Caudill. Griffin starred with the Athletics for three seasons (1985-1987). Athletics GM Sandy Alderson touted him as "the glue that held us together."[15] In his first season, he won his only Gold Glove. In his first two seasons he played in all 162 regular-season games. But by 1987, with the Athletics looking for playing time for Walt Weiss, their up-and-coming shortstop, Griffin was again on his way to another team. He was traded to the Los Angeles Dodgers in December 1987. He went to the Dodgers along with pitcher Jay Howell in a three-team trade that also involved the New York Mets. Hoping that Griffin would be a positive influence on Dominican infielders in the organization,

Dodgers GM Fred Claire cited Griffin's character as a needed positive. Dodgers manager Tommy Lasorda commented, "I haven't seen him that much but I hear he's a hell of a player. I looked over at his record and he's played all 162 four times and more than 140 the other two. That's something we haven't had."[16]

As luck would have it, Griffin's ability to avoid injury and be a stabilizing presence on the field did not initially work out well for the Dodgers. On May 21, less than two months into his first season with the Dodgers, Griffin was hit by a Dwight Gooden fastball and broke his right hand.[17] He missed the next 59 games. For the season, he ended up batting .199 in 95 games. With on-base and slugging percentages in the .250s he was a serious offensive liability. Still, Griffin played an integral role in the Dodgers' World Series victory over the Athletics as he started all five games at shortstop. He batted .188 with three singles. In an interview published in 2001, Griffin called the World series victory "the most special moment in my career."[18]

Even with the injury and offensive struggles of the previous year, Griffin signed a three-year contract extension with the Dodgers in January 1989, a signing that included the highest salary of his career: $1 million, in both 1989 and 1990.

A free agent after the 1991 season, Griffin returned to the Blue Jays for what were his last two major-league seasons. No longer a full-time shortstop, and quite possibly a greater offensive liability than ever, he nevertheless enjoyed enormous team success. Playing in only 109 games over the two years, Griffin tallied zero home runs, 10 doubles, and no triples over 245 at-bats. With only 13 RBIs to go along with an average barely above .220, Griffin was used sparingly. The Blue Jays won the World Series both seasons; Griffin appeared as a defensive replacement in both Series.

Griffin hit 24 major-league home runs; in eight seasons he had none. He hit a career-best four homers in three seasons. He hit 245 doubles and 78 triples. He drove in 527 runs with a career high of 64 in 1985. As a light-hitting infielder, Griffin never cracked a slugging percentage of .400 during a full season. His highest slugging percentage was .364 in 1979 and 1986. With a career slugging average of .319, he was never much of an offensive threat, a notion substantiated when considering his career batting average of .249 and on-base percentage of .285. Griffin struck out 664 times. His season high was 65. He drew 338 walks, with a high of 40 in 1979 and a low of 4 in 1984 (in 442 plate appearances).

Griffin made baserunning an adventurous endeavor. Having decent speed and a penchant for over-aggressive running on the basepaths led to plenty of good and bad decisions alike. A game in 1991 provides a clear illustration: Griffin walked and kept going after reaching first base. It did not work. He explained, "Man, I'm just playing baseball, trying to get something started."[19] Manager Tommy Lasorda commented, "It's a great play if you make it, even though I don't think I've ever seen anybody try it before."[20] In 1980 Griffin had 18 steals and was caught stealing 23 times. In three seasons he had stolen-base results under 50 percent. He had 192 stolen bases in the major leagues. But in a nod to his over-aggressiveness on the basepaths, he was caught stealing 134 times. Still, Griffin had decent speed. In eight seasons, he stole at least 10 bases, and in three others swiped at least 20. He had a career-high 33 stolen bases with the run-happy Oakland Athletics in 1986. His three seasons with the Athletics (1985-1987) resulted in his three highest single-season steal totals (24 in 1985, 33 in 1986, and 26 in 1987).

Griffin's fielding statistics are more impressive. He had a fielding percentage of .961 with 348 career errors, 340 of which were made when he was playing shortstop. Early on, he led the American League for four straight seasons (1979-1982) in errors by a shortstop with 36, 37, 31, and 26. He also led the National League as a member of the Dodgers in 1990 when he had 26 errors. Prone to off-balance and errant throws, especially at the start of his career, Griffin recalled, "Using two hands gave me problems, I'd put my right hand too close to the glove and sometime the ball would hit my bare hand. So, in my third year I switched to one hand (pickups)."[21]

With his playing career over, Griffin did not stay away from ballfields for long. In 2018 he completed his 19th season on the Los Angeles Angels coaching staff. He has served as both the first base coach (for 18 seasons) and infield coach (for one season). He worked as a roving minor-league instructor for the Blue Jays in 1995, and as their first-base coach in 1996 and 1997. He was a coach for the Dominican Republic team that won the 2013 World Baseball Classic. and was the general manager of the Estrellas Orientales (Eastern Stars) in the Dominican Republic Winter League, for whom he played for 12 major-league off seasons. The club has retired his number 4 jersey. Griffin was elected to the Dominican Sports Hall of Fame in 2002.

SOURCES

In addition to the sources cited in the Notes, the author consulted Griffin's clippings file from the National Baseball Hall of Fame, Baseball-Almanac.com, Baseball-Reference.com, Retrosheet.org, and theBaseballCube.com.

NOTES

1 Mark Kurlansky, *The Eastern Stars: How Baseball Changed the Dominican Town of San Pedro de Macoris* (New York: Riverhead Books, 2010), 99.

2 Kurlansky, 99.

3 Kurlansky, 99.

4 Kurlansky, 100.

5 Kurlansky, 97.

6 Associated Press, "Switch Hitting Takes a Special Skill," *Daily News Online* (Longview, Washington), June 2, 2018. Retrieved from tdn.com/sports/switch-hitting-takes-a-special-skill/article_c18ab4df-e8f4-55fa-a87b-3c918c90cf89.html.

7 "Switch Hitting Takes a Special Skill."

8 Russell Schneider, "Quick-Grower Griffin Brightens Indian Summer," *The Sporting News*, September 25, 1976: 12.

9 Jim Prime, *Tales from the Toronto Blue Jays Dugout: A Collection of the Greatest Blue Jays Stories Ever Told* (New York: Sports Publishing, 2014), 117.

10 United Press International, "Co-winners for AL Rookie Honors," *Salina Journal,* November 27, 1979.

11 Bob Bloss, *Rookies of the Year* (Philadelphia: Temple University Press, 2005), 135.

12 Ross Newhan, "Dodgers Pay a Big Price (Welch) to Improve: They Get a Shortstop and Two Relief Pitchers," *Los Angeles Times*, December 12, 1987. Retrieved from articles.latimes.com/1987-12-12/sports/sp-6647_1_relief-pitcher.

13 Richard Griffin, "Alfredo Griffin Takes a Trip Down Memory Lane," Toronto *Star,* June 3, 2009. Retrieved from thestar.com/life/travel/2009/06/03/alfredo_griffin_takes_a_trip_down_memory_lane.html.

14 John Feinstein, "Making the All-Star Team the Hard Way," *Washington Post*, July 10, 1984. Retrieved from espn.com/espn/page2/story?page=list/worstallstars.

15 Newhan.

16 Newhan,

17 Sam McManis, "Hit, Throw and Run: Guerrero Throws Bat at Pitcher; Dodgers Lose 5-2," *Los Angeles Times*, May 23, 1988. Retrieved from articles.latimes.com/1988-05-23/sports/sp-2199_1_dodgers-lose.

18 Rich Marazzi, "Alfredo Griffin: Dominican Dandy," *Sports Collectors Digest*, January 26, 2001: 70.

19 Bill Plaschke, "Baseball: Daily Report: Dodgers: Griffin Explains His Baserunning Ploy," *Los Angeles Times*, August 1, 1991. Retrieved from articles.latimes.com/1991-08-01/sports/sp-231_1_alfredo-griffin.

20 Plaschke.

21 Glenn Schwarz, "A's Expect Griffin to Cement the Infield," *San Francisco Examiner*, March 4, 1985: D1.

Pedro Guerrero

By Frank Morris

Godsends always arrive on schedule. But God sends great baseball hitters far less frequently than are promised by even the most clairvoyant of baseball prophets. SABR-sophist Bill James once proclaimed the Los Angeles Dodgers' Pedro Guerrero "the best hitter God had made in a long time."[1] It was the mid-1980s, and Guerrero was in the prime of his career. In little more than half a decade, he was a World Series MVP as a rookie, a perennial All-Star and MVP candidate and the highest-paid Dodger in franchise history. His 1985 season was a blue streak of record-setting at-bats. There was every reason to believe that Guerrero would have an epic career.

But fate would conspire to ensure that Guerrero never more than fleetingly achieved the greatness predicted by James. Guerrero's career ultimately proved a hero's (or anti-hero's) journey; a mythical story of a young island prodigy plucked from impoverished obscurity by supernatural aid, followed by an archetypal course of triumphs and temptations. An obligatory abyss prompted atonement and, most recently, divine resurrection.

Pedro Guerrero was born June 29, 1956, in San Pedro de Macoris, a dense provincial city on the east coast of the Dominican Republic. Before gaining international notoriety as the "Land of Shortstops" for its abundance of recent major league talent, the Caribbean nation had already produced a number of baseball stars including Juan Marichal, Ozzie Virgil, Rico Carty, the Alou brothers, and Guerrero's future major-league mentor, Manny Mota.

In the early 1970s, Guerrero's island community offered few prospects beyond a life of labor in the surrounding sugar cane fields. Guerrero was barely a teenager when he left school to help support his family cutting cane for the island's local rum industry. Though his earnings were less than $3 US a week, the strapping youth was as adept as most men at hewing, stripping, and heaving large bundles of cane stalks.

While the young teenage Pedro provided for his divorced mother and siblings by day, he enjoyed playing the drums during evenings and organized baseball on weekends. By age 16, Guerrero stood out amongst his peers in a local youth league, primarily at third base, littering the neighborhood with warped baseballs smashed over apartment buildings.

Word spread through the island's baseball circles of an extraordinary young talent amongst the *petromacorisanos* in San Pedro.

Latin scouting pioneer Reggie Otero, representing the Cleveland Indians, decided the teenager was worth a visit. Otero described his first impression of the Dominican prodigy: "He was five-feet-11, 157 pounds. I looked at the width of his shoulders, back and front, and knew that he would get heavier and stronger. He had lived off rice and beans." i

In late 1972, Otero offered Guerrero a pro contract, which included a $2,500 bonus to be paid out on New Year's Day of 1973.

Guerrero began his pro baseball career at age 17 with a season of rookie ball in the remote Gulf Coast League. Pedro eventually distanced himself from his rookie league peers, both athletically and geographically. In April 1974, the Indians, seeking pitching help, traded Guerrero to the Los Angeles Dodgers for minor leaguer left-handed pitcher Bruce Ellingsen.

Dodgers personnel director Al Campanis had inside information. Los Angeles had recently hired Reggie Otero, who recommended the acquisition of Guerrero.

Ellingsen proved a disastrous acquisition for the Indians, pitching in 16 major league games before leaving baseball altogether at age 25. Ellingsen's flame-out, contrasted with the distance and height of Gucrrero's career, ranks the trade as one of the most lopsided straight-up swaps in baseball history.

The Dodgers saw great promise in their new farmhand. Guerrero cut a striking figure, balancing upper body strength with quickness afoot. It wasn't long before the minor-league sensation was lauded as a five-tool prodigy who could hit for power and average in addition to fielding many positions.

Despite his early aptitude, the Dodgers were content to let Guerrero ripen in their cabbage patch of talented farm prospects. In any case, there was no vacancy in the L.A. infield for the foreseeable future. Shortstop Bill Russell and second baseman Davey Lopes formed one of baseball's best double-play combos, and perennial All-Stars Steve Garvey and Ron Cey were fixtures at first and third bases. The Dodgers were clearly the "haves" in the unlocked world of free-agent baseball. Los Angeles won three pennants between 1974 and 1978, receiving a steady supply of pitching talent from Triple-A Albuquerque and adding talent through trades and free agency.

While the Dodgers failed to capture a World Series title in 1977 and 1978 losses to the Yankees, Guerrero shined in the minors, hitting .300 or better in six seasons and being named to minor-league All-Star teams at both first and third base. In 1977, he was leading the Pacific Coast League at Triple-A Albuquerque with a .403 batting average when he fractured his left ankle in the field. The injury cost him a call-up to the majors.

Guerrero sought to overcome his first significant injury and dedicated himself to rigorous rehab. He reflected on the setback in a 1982 interview with *Sports Illustrated*: "Before, I wasn't interested in being a good base runner or working on my defense. All I worried about was my hitting. After I got hurt I had a lot of time to think. There was a lot more money in baseball than when I signed, and I was thinking that if I played better I could make good money someday."[2]

Guerrero's hard work finally earned him a call-up in late 1978. His first major league at-bat came in the fifth inning of a September blowout loss against Randy Jones and the San Diego Padres. Pedro was sent in to pinch-hit for former minor-league roommate and future nemesis Rick Sutcliffe, and promptly singled for the first of 1,618 hits he would garner in his big-league career. Exactly a year later he hit his first major-league home run off Padres pitcher Bob Owchinko, appearing in 25 games total in 1979.

Pedro made significant contributions to the parent club in 1980. He filled a valuable

Photo courtesy of The TOPPS Company

utility role over two stretches during the season, spelling an ailing Davey Lopes at second and a slumping Rudy Law in center. Overall, Guerrero played six different positions in 1980 and batted an impressive .322 with 7 homers and 31 RBI in 183 at-bats.

The talented tyro did everything he could to endear himself to management during these early years, proving himself an unselfish, jovial teammate who could deliver timely hits and field where needed. Off the field, Guerrero had bought himself a fun toy in the form of a new Ford Thunderbird, and was often seen with a gorgeous new lady-friend riding shotgun.[3] He was courting Denise, a young woman of Latin and European ancestry from New Mexico. In the beautiful young companion, Pedro had met his lifelong love. The couple would soon marry and move into a condominium in the Wilshire District of Los Angeles.

1981 started fortuitously for the deserving Dodger. Incumbent right fielder Reggie Smith was still rehabilitating from an arm injury suffered the year prior, leaving an open spot for Guerrero at the start of the season. Pedro made the most of the opportunity. His early numbers in 1981 were All-Star caliber. The Dodgers were atop their division and Guerrero's average well above .300 when a players' strike halted the season full stop in early June.

The season resumed in August, but two months were lost from the schedule. League officials considered alternative playoff formats after the long lay-off. Pennant races were replaced by a prosthetic playoff system pairing "first half" winners against "second half" winners in each division, infused with a pair of wild card teams and grafted over with a divisional playoff. The Dodgers would benefit from the lopsided logic, guaranteed a playoff spot for their first-half success. The second act would be a different story.

The All-Star Game was played in Cleveland on August 9 as an introduction to the re-start of the season. Guerrero's .325 first half batting average won him a spot on the NL roster, his first of five All Star nods. Pedro batted only .269 in the latter half of the split campaign as the Dodgers posted a mediocre 27-26 record the rest of the way.

Guerrero's slump continued into the postseason. The Dodgers were pushed to the brink in two consecutive playoff rounds against Houston and Montreal, but managed to overcome the deficits in each series. In the final game of the National League Championship Series against the Montreal Expos, Los Angeles' Rick Monday hit a miraculous ninth-inning home run in Montreal's Olympic Stadium to win the Dodgers the pennant.

Fittingly, the wealthy and powerful Dodgers met the wealthy and powerful New York Yankees in the World Series. It was their third fall classic matchup in five years, and the latest installment in a rivalry that dated back 40 years, across two coasts and two New York City boroughs.

The Yankees gained the early advantage while the Dodgers looked disoriented at the plate, dropping the first two games. In the third game, played at Dodger Stadium, Los Angeles squandered an early three-run lead as the Yankees scored four runs against rookie phenom Fernando Valenzuela. Yankees reliever George Frazier settled in nicely after entering in the third for starter Dave Righetti, snuffing a two-on, no-outs Dodger threat.

Guerrero came to bat in the fifth against Frazier with Garvey and Cey on base and no outs. In the third, Pedro had faced the same situation, fouling off two bunt attempts before striking out swinging on five pitches. The logical decision was to move the runners over once again. Dodger Manager Tommy Lasorda's instinct told him otherwise.

Expecting a sacrifice, Yankee third baseman Aurelio Rodriguez bit hard when Guerrero squared his stance. Pedro withdrew from the bunt and hacked a ground ball past the outstretched glove of the drawn-in Rodriguez. The hard grounder allowed Garvey to score and Cey to advance to third. Guerrero hustled to reach second base, and Cey scored the go-ahead run on a subsequent double play. The pair of runs was enough as Valenzuela held on to secure the 5-4 comeback win.

The Dodgers won a back-and-forth 8-7 battle to even the Series in Game Four, but were on the ropes again at home in Game Five. Ron Guidry baffled the Dodgers, cruising into the seventh with a two-hit shutout and nine strikeouts. After dispatching Dusty Baker on three pitches, a Louisiana Lightning strike was answered with a resounding peal of Blue Thunder as Guerrero smashed a home run to deep left field. Guerrero commented on his solo shot after the game: "I hit a slider… as soon as I hit it I knew it was gone."[4] Steve Yeager followed with another homer, and the back-to-back round-trippers were enough for a 2-1 win, Los Angeles' third in a row.

Guerrero had factored into three straight World Series wins, but his crowning performance sealed the series for the Dodgers.

Pedro bombed the Bronx in Game Six with five RBIs and eight total bases amassed on a triple, homer, and bases loaded single. His one-man show capped a 9-2 victory and gave the Dodgers their first World Series title in 16 years. Guerrero was named co-MVP of the Series along with teammates Ron Cey and Steve Yeager.

Despite his fall classic heroics, Dodger management was said to have entertained a deal in the offseason that would send Pedro to the Padres in exchange for their stellar shortstop, Ozzie Smith. Rumors subsided and Guerrero was still a Dodger for the start of the 1982 season. The Dodgers confirmed their confidence in their burgeoning star by awarding Guerrero Steve Garvey's long-time spot as Dodgers cleanup hitter. The former league MVP was bumped to third in the order. Pedro came through with a tremendous campaign. By season's end, Guerrero led the team in batting (.306), runs (86), home runs (32), runs batted in (98), slugging (.543) and became the first Dodger to hit 30 home runs and steal 20 bases in a season. He finished third in National League MVP voting behind Dale Murphy and Lonnie Smith. It would mark the first of four times Pedro would finish in the top four of MVP voting.

Despite his breakout totals in 1982, Guerrero and Dodgers floundered at season's end, losing eight straight games and coughing up a division title to Atlanta in ignominious fashion. The agonizing skid saw the Dodgers lose six of eight games by one run, three in extra innings. The season came down to a final four-game series against the Giants, in San Francisco, with the division title up for grabs. The Dodgers needed to win each game, but Guerrero was conspicuously absent for the full set. Rumors swirled about off-field excesses. Without clear explanation, a sore hand and hamstring were assumed the cause.

Still, Los Angeles won the first three without their cleanup hitter. In Game 162, Giants second baseman Joe Morgan broke a 2-2 seventh-inning tie with a three-run homer that won the game and kept the Dodgers out of the playoffs.

The colossal collapse was the death knell for the old Dodgers guard. Davey Lopes was already gone to Oakland. Ron Cey was next—feeling disrespected by Dodger brass, the third baseman went public with his sentiments and was soon traded to the Chicago Cubs. Steve Garvey also left, signing a handsome contract with division rival San Diego.

With these long-timers gone, the Dodgers turned to young talent: Steve Sax, Greg Brock, Mike Marshall, and Guerrero. Pedro, or "Petey" as he was affectionately called, was now a centerpiece of the team on and off the field, appearing in local advertisements and public service announcements recorded in both Spanish and English.

Guerrero took over at third base for the 1983 season. Offensively, he was rock-solid, batting .298, with 32 home runs, 103 RBIs, and 23 stolen bases. Defensively, he was a nightmare, amassing 30 errors. The miscues made Pedro furious, and his frustrations spilled over into conflict with opposing players.

One particular loss of temper nearly cost him his life. In a game against Houston, Guerrero led a mound charge at Astros pitcher Frank LaCorte who was thought to be throwing at teammate Ken Landreaux's head. "He's in trouble," warned Guerrero in a post-game interview "I never forget anything like that."[5]

Houston's Nolan Ryan would counter Guerrero's threat. In a subsequent contest, the Houston fireballer accidentally let one slip, beaning Guerrero in the head with a fastball that cracked his batting helmet. "I thought I was dead," said the head-hunted Dodger.[6] Guerrero had the helmet sent to the Astros clubhouse after the game for Ryan to sign.

Despite inconsistencies, the "Baby Blues" endured to win the division title that had eluded them the year prior, posting a 91-71 record. The Dodgers met the NL East champion Philadelphia Phillies in the best-of-five National League Championship Series. Guerrero was largely ineffectual. In Game Three, Pedro committed a mental mistake by throwing to first instead of home, allowing a Phillie run to cross the plate in a 7-2 Dodger loss. Guerrero told the press afterwards: "I can't look at the ball and the runner," said Guerrero. "I should get help from somebody."[7] The Baby Blues were put to bed for the winter by Steve Carlton in Game Four, 7-2.

In February of 1984, the Dodgers awarded their All-Star slugger with a princely 5-year, $7 million deal. It was the largest contract in franchise history. The kid from San Pedro de Macorís who dropped out of school to cut cane was now one of the richest athletes in America.

When spring training started in Vero Beach, Guerrero's closest friend on the team, Dusty Baker, was absent from the clubhouse. The veteran had been granted free agency and signed with the rival Giants at season's start. This left Guerrero as the only remaining regular from the 1981 Championship squad. Pedro was visibly distressed, arriving overweight and exhibiting lethargy in the field. Rumors swirled about the slugger's work ethic and off-season partying. In a miserable start to the regular season, Guerrero managed only three RBIs in his first 60 at-bats and ended April with a dismal .179 average. He was also on pace for another 30 errors.

With the team languishing, skipper Lasorda blasted his underperforming squad and benched Guerrero for two midseason games with a phantom knee injury. After the admonishment, Lasorda met with Guerrero and tried a bit of psychiatry on his flummoxed slugger. The manager posed an imagined scenario, asking Pedro to envision himself at third base with the game on the line in the ninth inning. Lasorda asked his player what would be going through his mind.

"God, please don't let him hit the ball to me," Guerrero replied.

The skipper asked what else he was thinking.

Guerrero added: "God, please don't let him hit the ball to Sax," referencing second baseman Steve Sax, another young Dodger with pronounced fielding issues.[8]

Pedro was soon relieved of third base duties and sent to the outfield. The move allowed Guerrero to relax and find his hitting mojo. Before the switch his average was .277; afterwards .336. Guerrero ended the season with a .303 average, but he had totaled only 16 homers and 72 RBIs. It was a hard campaign for the newly-minted millionaire after two straight seasons of 30 HRs and 100 RBIs. "If I'd known what would happen, I never would have signed for all that money," Guerrero said.[9]

The start of 1985 inexplicably had Guerrero back at third, again fielding feebly and hitting humbly. With his team a game below .500 on June 1, Lasorda freed Guerrero to left field. Like clockwork, his funk shook immediately upon hitting the outfield grass.

The shake-up would trigger an explosion of historic proportions. Pedro hit a June-record 15 home runs in one of the greatest slugging skeins by any player in baseball history. In his final at bat of June, Guerrero beat Atlanta with a two-run homer off Bruce Sutter to give a 4-3 win, his 15th of the month.

The offensive outburst made headlines across the country and landed Guerrero on the cover of *Sports Illustrated*. The accompanying article portrayed Guerrero at his personal and professional apex. "When I was playing third last year, I wasn't patient at the plate," Guerrero said. "This year I am." Hitting coach Manny Mota attested to his prodigy's mental sharpness. "He's a changed man. ... He's happy, and his mind's clear."[10]

Amazingly, Guerrero was even better in July, hitting .460 with .563 on-base and .794 slugging averages. On July 23, he started a streak of reaching base in 14 consecutive at-bats, a senior circuit record and just two shy of Ted Williams' major-league mark of 16 straight. The streak ended on the 27th, but over the four-day span Guerrero had put together a stretch of two singles, three doubles, two homers, six walks, and a hit by pitch.

The singular resurgence lifted the dithering Dodgers to a postseason berth, but Los Angeles eventually squandered a 2-0 NLCS advantage against the pennant-winning Saint Louis Cardinals. Guerrero was again kept under wraps by opposing pitching, hitting only .250 with no homers and four RBI in the series.

Guerrero's 1986 season ended before it began. On April 3, in the final spring training game a day before the season opener, Pedro caught his cleat in an aborted slide attempt. The result was a ruptured a patella tendon in his left knee. It was the third base-running injury of his career. Guerrero was lost until the final month of the season, and the Dodgers finished 23 games behind the division-winning Houston Astros.

Guerrero rebounded in 1987. He batted a career high .338, smacked 27 home runs and 89 RBIs to win major-league Comeback Player of the Year honors. Guerrero's batting average was the highest by a Dodger since Tommy

Davis hit .348 in 1962. But while locked-in at the plate, Pedro was becoming a destabilizing force in the clubhouse. He openly criticized teammate Mike Marshall for not playing through injury, resulting in a clubhouse scrap between the teammates. Despite making his fourth All-Star team, Guerrero complained about his lack of at-bats in the 1987 contest, blaming a conspiracy against the Dodgers franchise. "Everybody hates the Dodgers," stated the sour slugger.[11]

Los Angeles made a fateful roster move during the offseason by inking free agent Kirk Gibson from the Detroit Tigers. L.A.'s new number three hitter was in many ways a stark contrast to the long-time Dodger hitting behind him. Gibson was straight from central casting as the hardscrabble grunt who made up for awkward aesthetics with incomparable strop. Guerrero played the antagonist, implicit in incidents superfluous to winning baseball games.

As elder statesman in the clubhouse, Guerrero fanned an atmosphere of immaturity that immediately drew the consternation of Gibson. An anonymous jokester made Gibson the target of a spring-training joke by rubbing the inside of his cap with eye black. Gibson blew up, calling his teammates "clowns" and storming out of training facility. The wind-up smacked of Guerrero. Pedro denied involvement, but a line had been drawn. The Dodgers clubhouse faced a choice: Guerrero's grin or Gibson's glower.

Guerrero's once carefree aloofness was now shrouded by apathy. He'd made a habit of losing his cool in recent years, and blew his temper in a May contest against the Mets when David Cone hit him with an innocuous curveball. Pedro slung his bat back at the mound, aiming at the Mets' starter. The act led to a four-game suspension from National League President Bart Giamatti. Many, including unnamed Dodger teammates and recently suspended Pete Rose, thought the outburst deserved a more stern suspension.

Los Angeles remained in contention late into the summer of 1988. Clinging to a slim division lead with the trade deadline approaching, the Dodgers were at a precarious point between wait-and-see and all-in. The Dodgers had a particular need—left-handed pitching—a commodity the St. Louis Cardinals were willing to offer in the form of proven starter John Tudor, the league leader in ERA at the time. The Dodgers offered Guerrero in return for the crafty southpaw.

The deal was made official on August 16. It was a bitter turn for the longtime Dodger. Guerrero had gone from a streaking division leader to an out-of-contention St. Louis squad. While he waited out the last weeks of season at first base for St. Louis, the Dodgers lengthened their lead over the second-place Reds, finishing 94-67. With a balanced staff led by other-worldly ace Orel Hershiser and Gibson's work ethic pervading the clubhouse, the over-achieving Dodgers won the pennant in a hard-fought seven game series over the New York Mets. The team's success carried into the World Series. Aided by Gibson's miraculous walk-off home run in Game One, Los Angeles pulled off an amazing four games to one triumph over the powerhouse Oakland A's to win the 1988 World Series championship. Kirk Gibson was named National League Most Valuable Player at season's end.

Post-season gestures of appreciation by his former team only salted Guerrero's emotional wounds. The Dodgers sent Guerrero a framed collage depicting images of his Dodger years – which had shattered during delivery. Guerrero threw the gift in the trash.

The Dodgers also graciously offered Guerrero a 50% share of their World Series bonuses, though Pedro took offense along with the money. "What ticked me off is they gave John Tudor more than they gave me," said Guerrero about the 75% share given to Tudor. "I told (the Dodgers) if you want your money back, I'll give it back. I've got more than all you guys put together."[12]

Guerrero would make more disparaging comments about the Dodgers and his former teammates over the next year. Upon reuniting with Lasorda months later, Guerrero was repentant. "The problem with writers," Guerrero was reported as saying, "is they write what I say and not what I think."[13]

The Cardinals were not expected to contend in 1989. Instead, they surprised with a strong campaign that had them contending for a playoff spot before falling short in the season's final weeks.

Guerrero was instrumental in the team's success. Cardinal teammates expressed support for Guerrero as the league's most valuable player. "There's no one like Pete when it comes to a pennant race and clutch situations," said catcher Tony Peña. "He's put this team on his back and carried it all year."[14]

In total, the Cardinal first-baseman posted another All-Star season with a .311 average, 17 homers, a league-leading 42 doubles and a career-best 117 RBIs. Guerrero batted .400 with runners in scoring position over the year and finished third in NL MVP voting.

1990 was a disappointment for the aging slugger, whose 34th birthday on June 29 was spoiled by former teammate Fernando Valenzuela. The Dodger pitcher no-hit the Cardinals, with Guerrero grounding into a double-play to end the game.[15] There were more confrontations with opposing moundsmen and another stint on the disabled list with a lower back strain. Guerrero ended the season with only 13 home runs, 80 RBIs, and a .281 average, a 30-point drop-off from the previous year.

Guerrero's decline continued in 1991. An August collision with catcher Tom Pagnozzi on a foul ball resulted in a hairline fracture of Guerrero's right leg. Remarkably, Pedro remained in the game to drive in tying runs in both the ninth and the 12th innings, eventually scoring the winning run. Despite his valiant effort, Guerrero was placed on the disabled list. He was ineffective after a late-season comeback and finished with career lows in home runs and RBIs.

Things fell apart for Pedro Guerrero in 1992. In mid-April, teammate Todd Worrell took umbrage to Guerrero's post-game clubhouse invitation to a young Dominican from the opposing Cubs named Sammy Sosa. Cardinal teammates began shouting and Guerrero jumped over a table to throw a punch at Worrell. The pitcher caught the flailing slugger and deposited him into a locker before being pulled away.

Guerrero was contrite afterwards: "I shouldn't have brought him in," Guerrero said. "It was my mistake."[16]

The season ended badly for the former star. A shoulder injury limited him to 43 games in which he hit just .219 with one home run.

Guerrero was granted free agency in October of 1992. The next spring, Pedro split time with the Sioux Falls Canaries of the Northern League and the Charros de Jalisco of the Mexican League. He returned to the Canaries in 1994 and signed with the Double-A California Angels squad before retiring from the game for good in 1995.

Over his 15-year major-league career, Pedro Guerrero totaled 215 home runs, 898 RBIs, 1,615 hits, and an even .300 lifetime average. The five-time All-Star hit .300 seven times in 10 seasons with the Los Angeles Dodgers, and was a top vote-getter in four Most Valuable Player Awards.

There's no question Guerrero was the best hitter of his era, and in 1985 there was every reason to believe the star was trending towards a Hall of Fame career. His delay in the minors and nearly five seasons lost to injury made Pedro Guerrero a classic example of what might have been, with circumstance ultimately outweighing talent.

Instead of going quietly into retirement, Guerrero made headlines at the end of the decade in embarrassing fashion.

In 1999, Guerrero was implicated as the "money man" in a Drug Enforcement Administration investigation on a purchase of 15 kilograms of cocaine in Miami. Guerrero was released on $100,000 bail and pleaded not guilty in the criminal trial in June 2002.

Guerrero tapped top-shelf criminal defense lawyer Milton Hirsch as his counsel. Hirsch considered the evidence – Guerrero's voice on tape and several eyewitnesses, all of whom were undercover DEA agents. Plus, the ex-major leaguer had confessed to the crime. "But other than that, they had nothing," Hirsch said in a later interview.[17] It took only four hours for Hirsch to convince the jury his client was innocent of conspiracy charges.

Those closest to Guerrero were unequivocal in their support. They knew the former ballplayer as a loving family man, not the dim-witted patsy suggested by his defense. Guerrero had endeared himself to thousands of fans and his legacy in major league baseball was that of a kind, outgoing person who made mincemeat of major league pitching for 15 years and had his caprices like the rest of the world.

As far as the lordly talent Bill James ascribed to him early in his career, Guerrero has been honest about not meeting his full potential:

"I feel I did a good job in the time I played, but not as good as I was supposed to be if I lived the life I'm living now," Guerrero said. "I would have put up better numbers and been a better person. I'm not a bad guy. I used to come to the park with a hangover every day and I could still play like that. Can you imagine if I had been 100 percent sober all the time? It's too late now to think about. ... "[18]

Almost a decade after the trial, Pedro experienced a personal rebirth. The burn that guided him through years in the minors and a cruel succession of injuries had re-ignited. Spiritually revitalized, Guerrero set his sights on a familiar goal: getting back to professional baseball.

"I feel like a new man," Guerrero declared. "I know I did a lot of wrong things and especially when I was playing...I let down a lot of people. Now, I'm a new man. I go to church, I'm reading the Bible, I pray every day. The last three years, I quit drinking. That was my big problem. Now, I'm working with kids in the Dominican. I tell them to stay away from drugs and drinking. I'm 100 percent different."[19]

Guerrero found success as a manager, skippering the Tijuana Tuernos in the Mexican League in 2012 and the Vallejo Admirals of the 4-team Pacific Association of Professional Baseball Clubs in 2013. In 2014, Pedro was back on top again, leading the Rieleros de Frontera club of the Mexican minor leagues to the Liga del Norte championship.[20]

Pedro made headlines again in February 2015 after suffering a stroke in the Dominican Republic.[21] Just over two years later, on April 3, 2017, the 60-year old was hospitalized in New York after suffering a second stroke.[22] Doctors initially declared him brain dead, but a follow-up diagnosis confirmed him to be in a coma, though with little to no brain activity shown on CAT scans.[23] According to his wife, she was approached by doctors with a request to take him off life support and sign a document certifying his death. Unwilling to give up on her husband, she held hope for a miracle. "It was his second massive stroke," she said the day after he was admitted. "He's recovering, the doctor said he can improve."[24]

Her prayers were answered when, astonishingly, Guerrero woke from his coma two days later. In surprisingly high-spirits after his near-death experience, Pedro fielded calls from family and friends, including well-wishes from former Dominican Republic President Leonel Fernandez.

"This is a miracle," Pedro's wife said of her husband's recovery.[25]

Another testament to his indefatigable life force, the theme of resurrection has been an enduring one in the latter half of Pedro Guerrero's improbable journey.

NOTES

1. Bill James, *The Bill James Baseball Abstract 1986* (New York: Ballantine Books, 1986), 279.
2. Jim Kaplan, "A Bolt Out Of The Dodger Blue." *Sports Illustrated*, August 5, 1985. https://www.si.com/vault/1985/08/05/622521/a-bolt-out-of-the-dodger-blue
3. Jim Kaplan, "A Hit Every Place He Plays." *Sports Illustrated*, October 4, 1982.
4. Ron Fimrite, "The Series Was Up For Grabs." *Sports Illustrated*. November 2, 1981.
5. Herm Weiskopf, "Inside Pitch." *Sports Illustrated,* July 11, 1983.
6. Associated Press, *Santa Fe New Mexican*, September 16, 1983.
7. Ron Fimrite, "The Old And The Relentless Beat The Young And The Restless," *Sports Illustrated*. October 17, 1983.
8. "Baseball Anecdotes & Stories," Baseball Almanac, accessed October 18, 2012 at www.baseball-almanac.com/humor1.shtml.
9. Gordon Edes, "Hotter Than a Heat Wave in June," *Los Angeles Times*, June 30, 1985.
10. Kaplan, "A Bolt Out Of The Dodger Blue."
11. *St. Louis Post-Dispatch*, July 19, 1987: 60.
12. Bruce Anderson, "Share and Share Alike, Kind Of." *Sports Illustrated*, October 30, 1989. https://www.si.com/vault/1989/10/30/120883/share-and-share-alike-kind-of-baseballs-judgment-day-comes-when-teams-vote-how-to-allot-world-series-loot
13. Paul Sullivan, "National League: The Week In Review." *Chicago Tribune*, May 7, 1988.
14. Peter Gammons, "A Series To Shout About." *Sports Illustrated*, September 18, 1989.
15. Larry Stewart, "Guerrero in No Mood to Congratulate Friend: Cardinals: His double-play grounder in the ninth preserved no-hitter, spoiling his 34th birthday." *Los Angeles Times*, June 30, 1990.
16. Rick Hummel, "'Enemy in Clubhouse Causes Guerrero and Worrell to Clash," *St. Louis Post-Dispatch*, April 19, 1992.
17. Stan Sinberg, "When Milton Hirsch isn't churning out legal thrillers, he's championing the unjustly imprisoned," Super Lawyers, June 2008. https://www.superlawyers.com/florida/article/the-storyteller/9b7eb25f-4ef2-4278-97fd-466b29a3eb06.html

18. Ken Gurnick, "Guerrero Sincere He's Turned Life around." MLB.com, May 3, 2010. http://losangeles.dodgers.mlb.com/news/print.jsp?ymd=2010050&content_id=9764478

19. Tom Hoffarth, "Pedro Guerrero's latest comeback attempt." *Los Angeles Daily News*, May 3, 2010. http://www.insidesocal.com/tomhoffarth/2010/05/03/pedro-guerreros/

20. Matt O'Donnell, "Pedro Guerrero introduced as manager of Vallejo Admirals," *Vallejo Times-Herald*, April 13, 2013. http://www.timesheraldonline.com/article/zz/20130509/NEWS/130506824

21. Steve Dilbeck, "Ex-Dodger Pedro Guerrero recovering from apparent stroke," *Los Angeles Times*, February 16, 2015. http://www.latimes.com/sports/dodgers/dodgersnow/la-sp-dn-dodgers-pedro-guerrero-recovering-20150216-story.html

22. "Dodgers icon Pedro Guerrero in life-threatening condition after stroke," *Sports Illustrated*, April 4, 2017. https://www.si.com/mlb/2017/04/04/dodgers-pedro-guerrero-health-update-stroke

23. Associated Press, "Former Dodger Pedro Guerrero hospitalized after stroke," April 4, 2017.

24. Craig Calcaterra, "Pedro Guerrero out of coma, improving following stroke," NBCSports.com, April 6, 2017.

25. Darren Hartwell, "Ex-Dodgers Star Pedro Guerrero Wakes Up From Coma In 'Miracle' Recovery," NESN.com, April 5, 2017.

Vladimir Guerrero

By Cosme Vivanco

One of the most electrifying ballplayers of his generation secured his place in baseball history by following a simple rule: See the ball, hit the ball. Vladimir Guerrero was a force of nature. Watching Guerrero hit from the stands was one of the great pleasures a baseball fan can have on a beautiful summer day. While the home-run records were being shattered at an incredible pace, Guerrero set himself apart from the pack by defying the baseball gods. He was blessed with "five-tool" characteristics but played in an unconventional manner. Guerrero was gifted with a rocket of an arm, but you'd never knew if the ball was going to reach its destination. He displayed blazing speed on the basepaths. Guerrero swiped 40 bases in one year, but also got caught 20 times, leading the league in that category.

But it was the hitting that took your breath away.

The duel between a pitcher and a hitter is a complex struggle for ownership of home plate. If a pitch was delivered upstairs, or three feet outside, it didn't matter to Guerrero. He wanted to send it into a different galaxy regardless of its location. Pitching around Vladimir was futile. On the first pitch he hit .363 and slugged .660. On 3-and-1 counts, he hit .417. He slugged 126 home runs on the first pitch of an at-bat, more than Barry Bonds and Mark McGwire. "You know how you pitch around hitters sometimes," Cubs pitcher Kevin Tapani said. "He's impossible to pitch around. He can hit any pitch, and I would never ever throw him the same pitch twice in a row."[1]

In the era that belonged to home-run kings that destroyed the space/time continuum, Vladimir Guerrero's best years were played in front of anemic crowds in Montreal. Nevertheless, he was warmly regarded by many of his peers and fans.

Vladimir Alvino Guerrero was born on February 9, 1975, in the town of Nizao Bani in the Dominican Republic. When Vladimir's mother, Altagracia, was three months pregnant with him, his father disappeared. Along with four half-siblings, the family lived in harrowing conditions. The shack they stayed in had no running water or electricity. When a hurricane blew the roof off, all seven family members cramped together in one little room where they shared two beds. When Vladimir was 6, his mother left but didn't abandon him. Altagracia would illegally sneak into Colombia and Venezuela to work as a cook and a maid, sending her paychecks back home.[2]

With no running water, Guerrero drank from puddles. As a student, he missed so many classes while working in the fields harvesting vegetables that he dropped out of school altogether after the fifth grade. That lack of education and the language barrier was the primary reason why he rarely gave interviews to the press. While working with his grandfather tending cattle in the fields, Guerrero developed an incredible grip and strength in his upper body. "I had to bring in the cattle," he said. "The bulls were stubborn, and I had to pull them until they did what they were supposed to do." He pointed to his arms: "That's what made me strong up here."[3]

Nizao Bani was not known as a hotbed for great ballplayers, but baseball was an integral part of the community. A lemon or lime was rolled up in old socks. A guava tree limb was used for a bat, and milk cartons were used to make fielders' gloves. By the age of 5, Vladimir was already developing his skills as a great hitter and would share the field with much older kids. His talent as a low-ball hitter would emerge during a form of baseball that the children loved playing known as "La Placa." Home was a license plate, and the batter had to keep his bat touching the dish until the pitcher released his pitch.

As Vladimir honed his craft, his older brother, Wilton, established himself as the best ballplayer in Nizao Bani. Drawing similarities to All-Star shortstop Tony Fernández, Wilton Guerrero was a big-league prospect who signed a deal with the Los Angeles Dodgers. Wilton and Vladimir's brother, Eleazar, was another prospect but didn't make it out of the Dodgers' Dominican Academy. The youngest brother, Julio Cesar, signed a $750,000 bonus with the Boston Red Sox Class-A team, but eventually flamed out.

When Vladimir was 16, he went to Campo Las Palmas, the Dodgers' academy, for two four-week sessions. The opinion of Dodgers scouts was that he was a slow, fat player with a long swing. However, the sentiments echoed by many didn't deter Vladimir from fulfilling his destiny. "I knew I would be signed," he said. "There are so many teams. The Dodgers thought I had a long swing and I was slow, which I was because I was fat. I started to lose weight in the Dodgers' camp because I was practicing two times a day."[4]

The Texas Rangers also gave Vladimir a look but also passed on him.

Montreal Expos scout Fred Ferreira, a Latin America scout who was universally recognized by many as the "Shark of the Caribbean," offered Vladimir a tryout. With just a pair of mismatched spikes and a sock jammed into one that was too big, Guerrero hopped on the back of a friend's motorcycle and headed for the training camp. Although he pulled a muscle running to first base in his only at-bat, Vladimir so impressed Ferreira with his arm, decent speed, and his trim physique that he signed with the Montreal Expos on February 24, 1993, two weeks after his 17th birthday, for $2,000.

Now a member of the Expos farm system, Guerrero began to shoot up the ranks as quickly as possible. In 1994, he played in 37 games for the Expos' team in the Gulf Coast rookie league and batted .314 with 5 home runs and an OPS of .928. The next season he jumped to number 85 in *Baseball America's* top 100 prospects list by slugging 16 home runs and batting .333 for the Class-A Albany (Georgia) Polecats. Guerrero's raw talent and work ethic impressed Albany skipper Doug Sisson. "He worked hard, and he had an innocence to him," Sisson said. "He went out and played with a smile on his face. He never thought about messing up. When we're 6 years old, we're trying to just go out and do something great. He played like that. He just thought about how much fun he could have and how many great plays he could make."[5]

In 1996 Guerrero impressed Expos brass with a .360/.431/.618 performance that included 24 home runs and 96 RBIs in both Single-A and Double-A ball. On September 19, 1996, Guerrero made his major-league debut by going 1-for-5. His lone hit was a single off Atlanta Braves left-hander Steve Avery. Two days later, Guerrero hit his first major-league home run, off Mark Wohlers on a fastball that was low and away and just a few inches off the plate.

In 1997, Guerrero ranked number 2 in *Baseball America's* prospect list behind the Braves' Andruw Jones. In spring training, he won a spot as the Expos' starting right fielder, but in late March he broke a bone in his left foot when he fouled a ball off it, delaying his season debut. On May 3, he made his first appearance of the year, against the San Diego Padres. In two at-bats, he went hitless. The next day Guerrero hit his first home run of the 1997 season, in the fifth inning off Sterling Hitchcock as the Expos defeated San Diego, 9-3. Three days later, Guerrero had the best game of his young career as he hit a double and two singles, drove in one run and scored three in Montreal's 19-3 rout of the San Francisco Giants.

In a June 3 game against the host New York Mets, Guerrero displayed his defensive skills as he threw out catcher Todd Hundley trying to score on Carlos Baerga's double to the wall. Guerrero made the out from the warning track on a one-bounce strike. After the game Mets manager Bobby Valentine said, "That was an awesome throw. That guy doesn't need a cutoff or relay. He needs a bigger ballpark."[6]

After a second stint on the DL, Guerrero returned to action on June 21. He homered and had two hits in Montreal's 4-3 victory over the Florida Marlins. For the season he posted a .302/.350/483 line with 11 home runs and 40 RBIs, and finished sixth in the NL Rookie of the Year voting. He also tied for the league lead in errors by an outfielder with 12. Living in a different town with a different language presented some challenges. While getting accustomed to his new way of life, Guerrero brought his mother to Montreal to feed him. And when he brought leftovers to his teammates, the tradition continued all the way to his stint with the Los Angeles Angels.

Having manager Felipe Alou and reigning Cy Young Award winner Pedro Martínez as mentors helped Guerrero tremendously. Martínez gave Guerrero the address to his apartment in the event he got lost in the city.

The Expos knew they could not afford to pay Martínez what he could attract in free agency, and traded their All-Star pitcher to the Boston Red Sox. In the ruins of a 1998 season in which the Expos lost 97 games, Guerrero emerged to become the team's new star. He finished the campaign with a .324/.371/.589 line. He slugged 38 home runs, had 109 RBIs and 202 hits, and posted a WAR of 7.4. Guerrero finished 13th in the NL MVP voting. After the departure of Pedro Martínez, fans clamored for the Expos to not let this new budding superstar walk away. Before the end of the 1998 season, the Expos signed Guerrero through 2003 for $28 million. The magic continued in 1998, as Guerrero's brother Wilton joined the club in a seven-player-deal. The two brothers lived in apartment with their mother.

With a new deal that secured his stay in Montreal, Guerrero kicked off the 1999 season with a three-hit performance that included a home run in the top of the first off Pirates pitcher Francisco Cordova and four RBIs as the Expos won their Opening Day contest in Pittsburgh, 9-2. Wilton Guerrero contributed three hits as well. On July 27, Guerrero went 1-for-4 in a 4-2 loss against the Chicago Cubs but it was the start of the longest major-league hitting streak in 12 years. On August 10, Guerrero slugged two home runs and drove in four runs as the Expos topped the Dodgers, 6-4. On the 20th he homered and rapped two singles to help lead Montreal to a 5-3 win over the Cincinnati Reds. Then on the 23rd Guerrero hit two singles, sent a homer to right, and drove in three runs as the Expos beat the visiting St. Louis Cardinals, 11-7. His 31-game hitting streak came to a halt on August 27 as the Expos lost to the visiting Cincinnati Reds, 4-1. Guerrero went 0-for-2 with an intentional walk. "Maybe I had a pitch to hit in my first at-bat but after that, I never saw a good pitch," he said. "I was trying to hit the pitches, but only if they were strikes."[7]

In his next game Guerrero exacted his revenge with a two-out walk-off home run off Scott Williamson to give the Expos an 8-6 edge over the Cincinnati Reds.

In the next to last game of the 1999 season, Guerrero slugged two home runs and drove in six runs as the Expos defeated the Philadelphia Phillies, 13-3.

Guerrero completed his fourth season in the majors hitting .316/.378/.600 with 42 home runs, 131 RBIs, 193 hits, and a 4.4 WAR. He made his first All-Star Game appearance, finished 11th in the NL MVP voting and won his first Silver Slugger award.

Guerrero was quietly emerging as one of the more exciting superstars in major-league baseball. With all the endorsement opportunities at his disposal, he remained humble and committed to his Dominican roots. The Expos suggested that Guerrero take English lessons but there was no persistent need. His bat would do the talking for him.

The 2000 Montreal Expos finished the season in fourth place in the NL East with a 67-95 record. Guerrero slugged 44 home runs with a .345/.410/.664 line and finished with a WAR of 5.9. His most notable moment came on April 26 when he hit his 100th career home run, off the Colorado Rockies' Julian Tavarez.

In 2001 and 2002, Montreal won 151 games and lost 173. Major League Baseball proposed elimination of the franchise (along with that of the Minnesota Twins) as a ploy by the owners to put pressure on the players union during discussions for a new contract. MLB acquired ownership of the franchise before the 2002 season, with owner Jeffrey Loria being allowed to purchase the Florida Marlins. But the uncertainty shrouding the Expos' future didn't derail Guerrero's production on the field. He compiled a .322/.398/.580 line in those two seasons, including 73 home runs. He stepped up his running game and joined the 30/30 club (30 home runs/30 stolen bases) in both seasons, and was one homer short of making it 40/40 in 2002.

What Vladimir Guerrero was missing in his impressive résumé was a postseason appearance.

Under second-year manager Frank Robinson, the Expos contended for wild card in 2003, but for Guerrero the season was gearing toward disaster. After injuring his back during a game against the Florida Marlins in late May, the right fielder was in so much pain that he could barely get out of bed in his Miami hotel room. For the first time in six seasons, he had a stint on the disabled list with a herniated disk. "I thought his season was over, and I thought our season was over," said general manager Omar Minaya.[8] With Guerrero on the DL from early June until late July, the Expos limped to an 18-29 mark.

But from August 13 to August 28, Guerrero carried Expos to the thick of the wild-card race, batting .327/.407/.731 with 5 home runs and 14 RBIs. But even his hot bat wasn't enough to stop the team from fading down the stretch. Montreal finished the season in fourth place in the five-team NL East with an 83-79 mark. Despite his lengthy stint on the DL, Guerrero managed to squeeze in another

Photo courtesy of Dreamstime

productive season with a .330/.426/.586 and 25 home runs. In his most notable game, on September 14, he hit for the cycle and drove in three runs as the Expos defeated the visiting New York Mets, 7-3.

With all the ambiguity surrounding the Expos, it was certain that Guerrero wouldn't sign with the team once he decided to test the waters of free agency, even though the organization offered him a five-year, $75 million offer. (He rejected it.) Guerrero was pursued by the Orioles, the Mets, and the Dodgers. Baltimore offered him a six-year deal in the neighborhood of $78 million. The Anaheim Angels, under the new ownership of Arte Moreno, were making a splash in free agency in their attempts to repeat their postseason success of 2002. They signed pitchers Bartolo Colon and Kelvim Escobar. They also committed to outfielder José Guillén. Out of nowhere, Moreno landed the biggest fish in the free-agency pond, when he signed Guerrero to a five-year, $70 million deal that included a $5 million signing bonus. The Angels had a $15 million option for 2009 that included a $3 million buyout.

The New York Mets had offered Guerrero a deal worth five years and $71 million but with only three years and $30 million guaranteed. The Mets couldn't obtain insurance in the event of another back injury to Guerrero. Arte Moreno was willing to roll the dice.

At his unveiling as a new member of the Angels, Guerrero spoke to sportswriters in Spanish as he received his jersey number 27. Arte Moreno stepped up to the lectern to interpret. "He said, 'I am very happy to be here,'" Moreno said, "And I am very happy to be here, too."[9] Angels manager Mike Scioscia was also pleased. "We got the number one guy out there on top of everyone's list," Scioscia said.[10]

Guerrero's first April with the Angels was productive. He was .326/.374/.598 with 6 home runs and 15 RBIs as the Angels finished the month with a 13-10 record. But it was the month of September that paid huge dividends for the organization. On September 1, the Angels were three games behind the first-place Oakland Athletics. Guerrero kicked it into high gear, going .363/.424/.726 with 11 home runs and 25 RBIs as the Angels slid past the A's to win the AL West Division title. Guerrero would finally display his talents in baseball's biggest showcase, the postseason. In his first postseason game, against the Boston Red Sox, Guerrero went 0-for-5. With Anaheim down 6-2 in the top of the seventh inning of the deciding Game Three, Guerrero slugged a grand slam off Mike Timlin to tie the game and give the Angels new life just as he had in the month of September. But in the end, Red Sox DH David Ortiz blasted a two-run homer off Jarrod Washburn to complete a sweep of the Angels in the Division Series.

Although the Red Sox sent the Angels packing for the winter, the risk Arte Moreno took on Guerrero paid off. Throughout his career in Montreal, Guerrero played in relative obscurity. Now in a major market, with a playoff berth under his belt, Vladimir received the AL's Most Valuable Player Award. He Guerrero hit .337/.391/.598 with 39 homers, a league-leading 366 total bases, 126 RBIs, and a WAR of 5.6. It was the fifth time in baseball history that a player switched leagues and won the MVP in his first season with the new team.[11]

"Our expectations were high, and he met every one of them," said manager Scioscia. "He carried the team single-handedly [down the stretch]. All of major-league baseball had its eyes on Vlad, and he had an incredible season, and I think it speaks volumes about the talent he has."[12]

The next season, the Angels repeated as AL West champions. Guerrero's production took a bit of a dip; he finished .317/.394/.565 with 32 home runs and 108 RBIs. In the Division series against the New York Yankees, Guerrero hit .333 as the Angels beat the Yankees in five games. However, the story was much different in the ALCS as the Chicago White Sox held Guerrero in check with a minuscule batting average of .050, as the White Sox won their first pennant since 1959.

Between 2006 and 2008, Guerrero hit .319/.384/.541 and averaged 29 home runs. The Angels won consecutive division titles in 2007-08, but wound up losing to the Red Sox in the Division Series each year. Guerrero hit .360 in the seven postseason games against the Red Sox in 2007-08. In 2009, now used primarily as a DH, Guerrero had a lackluster season, playing in just 100 games (he went on the disabled list twice), hitting only 15 home runs and driving in 50 runs with a WAR of 0.7

The Los Angeles Angels once again won the division title and secured another date in the postseason with the Red Sox. This time, the Angels exacted their revenge by sweeping the Red Sox and punching their ticket to the ALCS against the Yankees. Guerrero batted .400 in the series against Red Sox, with two RBIs.

After dropping the first two games to the Yankees in New York, the Angels needed a win in Game Three. In the bottom of the sixth, with the Angels down 3-1, Guerrero slammed a two-run homer off Andy Pettitte to tie the game, and the Angels eventually won, 5-4 in 11 innings. In Game Five, with the Angels down to the Yankees three games to one and on the brink of elimination, Guerrero hit a single to center in the bottom of the seventh to the tie the game, 6-6. Kendrys Morales hit a go-ahead single to give the Angels new life with a 7-6 victory.

In the end, however, the Yankees proved to be too much as they won the ALCS in Game Six, 5-2, and went to the World Series. Just as he did in that blazing 2004 season, Guerrero stepped up and carried his team when they needed him the most in the ALCS. He batted .370, with 10 hits and 5 RBIs.

Injuries were starting to pile up on Guerrero. He partially separated his shoulder while diving head-first into home plate in 2005, and sat out three weeks. In 2008, he needed surgery to repair a torn meniscus in his right knee. The march of time couldn't be stopped. In an exhibition game against the Los Angeles Dodgers, Guerrero tore his right pectoral muscle while making a throw from right field to third.

After the 2009 campaign, Guerrero left the Angels for the hitters' paradise known as the Ballpark in Arlington. As a DH, he enjoyed a productive season with the Texas Rangers. He hit .300/.345/.496 with 29 home runs and helped the 2010 Rangers earn their first trip to the World Series. The Series was different for Guerrero. In his first at-bat in his first World Series appearance, he singled off San Francisco Giants pitcher Tim Lincecum in the top of the first to give the Rangers a 1-0 lead. But he went hitless in his next 13 at-bats. For the 2010 postseason, Guerrero went .220/.242/.271 with no homers. Father Time had caught up with him.

A free agent after the season, Guerrero signed with the Baltimore Orioles for 2011. It was a disappointing season. The 36-year-old finished .290/.317/.416 with just 13 homers. The Orioles let him go after the season, and as the 2012 season approached, Guerrero remained unsigned. On May 10, 2012, he signed a minor-league deal with the Toronto Blue Jays. In his first game for the Class-A Dunedin Blue Jays, he hit a home run. After 20 at-bats (four homers), he was promoted to the Triple-A Las Vegas 51s. He batted .303 but asked for and was granted his release on June 12.

After the minor-league stint, Guerrero returned home to the Dominican Republic to get another crack at baseball glory. On November 4, 2012, he signed with the winter-league Tigres del Licey. But after two weeks, Guerrero quit upon being informed by the club that he would be used primarily as a pinch-hitter.

Guerrero put together a video of him working out in hopes that a major-league club would give him an opportunity to continue his career. But the only club to offer a comeback shot was the Long Island Ducks of the independent Atlantic League. He declined their offer. On September 14, 2013, Guerrero announced his retirement during a radio interview in the Dominican Republic. Citing his family as his main priority, Guerrero said his biggest regret was not reaching the 500-home-run mark. He retired with a .318/.379/.553 line, 449 home runs, and 1,496 RBIs. He and Garry Templeton are the only major leaguers to have one-third of their walks be intentional.

In July 2015, Guerrero's son, Vladimir Jr., an infielder, signed a $3.9 million deal with the Toronto Blue Jays at the age of 16. That season was ranked as the top international free agent by *Baseball America*. In September 2017, ESPN named him the top prospect of the year.

In an interview in March 2009, Vladimir Guerrero disclosed that he was 34 years old, a year older than the record books said.[13]

In June 2012, after being hit with a paternity suit by a woman named Heidy Ogando, he was required to release the details of his finances and it was revealed that he had fathered eight children with five different women and paid $25,621 a month in child support. The report said that throughout his career he had accumulated more than $25 million in stocks and bonds.[14]

In January 2017, Guerrero missed election to the Hall of Fame by just 15 votes in his first year of eligibility. On January 24, 2018, the man who dazzled fans throughout his career with his unorthodox style earned entry into the Hall. With 92.9 percent of the vote, he joined Chipper Jones, Jim Thome, and Trevor Hoffman as the newest inductees elected by the members of the Baseball Writers Association of America (BBWAA). Jack Morris and Alan Trammell were selected as 2018 inductees by the veterans committee the previous month.

"I'm extremely proud of that and I'm humbled," Guerrero said through an interpreter. "There were so many great Dominican players before me, and I never thought I'd be the first position player to make it.

"I know there's a group coming that could give me some very good company from my country: Adrian Beltre, David Ortiz, Albert Pujols. ... I know I'll have some company very soon."[15]

Despite having his best years in an Expos uniform, it was announced that Guerrero would wear an Angels cap on his Hall of Fame plaque, the first player in the franchise's history to do so.

"I will forever be thankful to the Expos and to the beautiful people of the city of Montreal, sad that the team does not exist any more, and in a way it made the decision a little easier," Guerrero told the *Los Angeles Times*. "But with the Angels and how much Arte believed in me when he invested in me, the chance to win, the great memories with the playoffs, the fans, celebrating championships, that's what drove me to this decision."[16]

Guerrero will join pitchers Pedro Martínez and Juan Marichal as the third Hall of Famer to represent the Dominican Republic. When he returned to the island after the voting results were announced, he was greeted at the airport by music and dancers. His fellow countrymen paid their respects to the newest Hall of Famer by throwing a small parade in his honor.

"This award is for the entire Dominican Republic, it's for all of us," Guerrero said. "This is proof that you have to pursue your dreams. When I signed, a lot of people said I would last only three months and that I was going to be released. Today I can say I played in the big leagues for 16 years."[17]

SOURCES

In addition to the sources cited in the Notes, the author consulted Baseball-Reference.com and Retrosheet.org.

NOTES

1. Tom Verducci, "Expo 2000," *Sports Illustrated*, May 1, 2000: 44. si.com/vault/issue/704438/62/2.
2. Jay Jaffe, "JAWS and the 2017 Hall of Fame Ballot: Vladimir Guerrero," SI.com, December 13, 2017. si.com/mlb/2016/12/13/jaws-2017-hall-of-fame-ballot-vladimir-guerrero
3. Esmeralda Santiago, "The Quiet Warrior," *Sports Illustrated*, August 30, 2004: 74.
4. Santiago.
5. Mark Simon, "Legend of Vladimir Guerrero Goes Way Beyond His Numbers," ESPN.com. espn.com/blog/sweetspot/post/_/id/77157/legend-of-vladimir-guerrero-goes-way-beyond-his-numbers.
6. Simon.
7. "Guerrero's Hit Streak Comes to An End at 31," WashingtonPost.com. washingtonpost.com/archive/sports/1999/08/28/guerreros-hit-streak-comes-to-an-end-at-31/21cb30f4-a5a8-48a2-9e81-59bbe33416f4/?utm_term=.5c352856afdd.
8. Albert Chen, "The Last Run? Free-Agent-to-Be Vladimir Guerrero Has Kept Montreal in the Playoff Race," *Sports Illustrated*, September 8, 2003: 83.
9. Associated Press, "Slugger will receive $5 million signing bonus," ESPN.com, January 12, 2004. espn.com/mlb/news/story?id=1706614
10. Associated Press, "Slugger will receive $5 million signing bonus."
11. The other four were Frank Robinson (1966), Dick Allen (1972), Rollie Fingers (1981), and Kirk Gibson (1988).
12. Dave Sheinin, "Angels' Guerrero Named AL MVP," *Washington Post*, November 17, 2004: D06.
13. Tim Brown, "Angels' Guerrero Is A Year Older Than Listed," Yahoo! Sports, March 6, 2009. https://www.yahoo.com/news/angels-guerrero-older-listed-224800441--mlb.html?soc_src=mail&soc_trk=ma
14. Daily Mail Reporter, "Baseball Star Fathers EIGHT Children by FIVE Different Women… and They Cost Him $25,000 a Month," *Daily Mail* (United Kingdom), June 11, 2012. http://www.dailymail.co.uk/news/article-2157578/Major-League-Baseball-star-Vladimir-Guerrero-My-children-cost-25k-month--thats-cool.html#ixzz55x77u996

15 Bill Shaikin, "Vladimir Guerrero Elected to Baseball Hall of Fame Along With Chipper Jones, Jim Thome and Trevor Hoffman," *Los Angeles Times,* January 24, 2018. latimes.com/sports/mlb/la-sp-hall-of-fame-announcement-20180124-story.html.

16 Bill Shaikin, "Vladimir Guerrero Will Go Into Hall of Fame in an Angels Cap," *Los Angeles Times*, January 25, 2018. latimes.com/sports/mlb/la-sp-vladimir-guerrero-hall-20180125-story.html.

17 Daniel Kramer and Dionisio Soldevila, "Vlad Receives Hero's Welcome in Return to DR," MLB.com. mlb.com/news/vladimir-guerrero-gets-heros-welcome-in-dr/c-265477118.

JOSÉ GUILLÉN

By William H. Johnson

Throughout much of his major-league playing career, he appeared to be a polarizing fusion of skills. One was a rare talent for hitting baseballs. The other, at times, seemed like an unerring instinct for finding the midst of controversy, great or small. José Manuel Guillén, a right-handed-batting and -throwing outfielder who was capable enough with a bat to produce a .270 batting average, hit 214 home runs, and drive in 887 runs over the course of a 14-year major-league career, was so difficult at times that he bounced around nine different organizations during the span. His baseball career was marked by pronounced highs and a few distinct lows, the latter including implications of use of performance-enhancing drugs in the 2007 Mitchell Report.[1]

Guillén's baseball career, however, was never predestined to end in such relative ignominy. In fact, it is a testament to his abilities and drive that he reached such a professional height at all. Born in San Cristobal, Dominican Republic, on May 17, 1976, the boy quickly grew to love the baseball, as did so many of his contemporaries. By the age of 10, playing in undersized shoes on rocky, dirt fields, and against the objections of his father, who labored in a bottle-making factory in town, José grew fixated on the game. Erzo Guillén thought in practical terms, that the boy should learn to earn a realistic living on the island. His mother, Modesta, disagreed, and actually paid for his formal baseball league team uniform. The league had some equipment donated by some local scouts and "leftovers from the big leaguers who grew up there (DR) and never forgot it."[2] Guillén had no spikes, and did not even own a glove until Raul Mondesi gave him one when the boy was 15. "My mom bought me my first bat when I was 12. I was so proud."[3]

The boy had talent, but one unnamed Texas Rangers scout told him, "You're too skinny. You'll never make it."[4] Guillén got his measure of psychological revenge at age 18 (August 19, 1993), however, when he signed with the Pittsburgh Pirates for $2,000 and reported to their Gulf Coast League team for the 1994 season. By 1996, batting .322 for the Lynchburg Hillcats, he was named Most Valuable Player in the Carolina League, and on April 1, 1997, he made his major-league debut against the San Francisco Giants. Despite his 0-for-4 day at the plate, he went on to post a .267 batting average in 143 games. That performance earned him a spot on the 1997 Topps All-Star Rookie Team.

By mid-1999, though, Guillén's performance had declined to the point that the Pirates demoted him to Triple-A Nashville. Though he regained his stroke and batted .333 for more than a month in the Pacific Coast League, the Pirates still traded him and Jeff Sparks to the Tampa Bay Devil Rays for Joe Oliver and Humberto Cota. Over the next two years, Guillén never batted over .275, and on November 27, 2001, he was given his outright release.

Less than a month later, on December 18, the Arizona Diamondbacks signed Guillén for the 2002 campaign, but released him on July 22. The Rockies then signed Guillén, but then released him three days later, on August 1. From that figurative closed door came an open window in Cincinnati. The Reds signed him on August 20 and were rewarded in 2003 with Guillén's best performance to date. He slashed a line of .337/.385/.629 in 91 games that year. The Reds, not convinced that Guillén could sustain that pace, sold "high" and traded him to Oakland for three players, including future rotation anchor Aaron Harang.

In a new league and new city, Guillén continued to hit well and finished the year with 31 homers and a .311 batting average. These were the Oakland Athletics, renowned for low payroll and a collective willingness to take risks on younger players,[5] so rather than re-sign the outfielder to a long contract and elevated money, they cut salary by releasing him on October 30. The Anaheim Angels signed the free agent on December 20, 2003, and he repaid their faith by driving in 104 runs in 2004.

It was in Anaheim that the first controversy arose around Guillén. During the eighth inning of a late-season game against Oakland, Angels manager Mike Scioscia removed his outfielder for a pinch-runner. "Guillén walked off the field slowly, then flung his helmet toward the end of the dugout where Scioscia

Photo courtesy of the National Baseball Hall of Fame

was standing. He then walked to the opposite end of the dugout and, after entering it, he threw his glove against the dugout wall."[6] The next day, Sunday, the Angels suspended Guillén for the rest of the season. Interestingly, the incident wasn't the first outburst; the outfielder "went on a profanity-laced tirade after being beaned in a game at Toronto in May, complaining that his teammates weren't retaliating for him."[7] It was a difficult denouement to what had been Guillén's best season on the diamond.

The die was cast, though, and on November 19 the Angels traded Guillén to the Montreal Expos – in the process of becoming the Washington Nationals – for Maicer Izturis and Juan Rivera. The Nationals' arrival in Washington stirred tremendous excitement in the normally jaded city. A new ballpark on the Potomac River was in the works, but it wouldn't be ready for three years at the earliest. The team acquired Guillén's lower-cost bat[8] as part of a short-term effort to sustain fan enthusiasm during the transition. As had become his modus operandi, the outfielder responded well to the change of venue, playing in 148 games and slugging 24 home runs and 32 doubles.

Naturally there were squabbles. The most notable occurred during a three-game series in Anaheim, Guillén's first visit since his suspension the previous year. During the second game of the series, when managers Frank Robinson and Mike Scioscia engaged in an argument over a separate, on-field issue, Guillén could not contain himself. "Sitting in the visiting clubhouse Wednesday night … Guillén let loose on Scioscia. "I don't got truly no respect for him anymore because I'm still hurt from what happened last year. I don't want to make all these comments, but Mike Scioscia, to me, is like a piece of garbage. I don't really care. I don't care if I get in trouble. He can go to hell. We've got to move on. I don't got no respect for him. … I want to beat this team so bad. I can never get over about what happened last year. It's something I'm never going to forget. Any time I play that team, Mike Scioscia's managing, it's always going to be personal to me."[9]

Also in keeping with Guillén's history, the next year, 2006, saw a decline in his offensive output. This time, however, there was a medical reason. In July, after only 69 games, he was diagnosed with a torn ulnar collateral ligament (UCL) in his right elbow. Dr. James Andrews performed reconstructive surgery on the elbow on July 25, and sent Guillén to his home in Miami, Florida, for physical therapy.[10] For what was likely a combination of reasons, the Nationals did not re-sign Guillén, instead offering him salary arbitration, and he was granted free agency on October 30.

He was not out of work for long. Searching for a "corner outfielder with power," the Seattle Mariners signed Guillén on December 4.[11] Guillén signed for a personal high salary of $5 million, with a $9 million option for the next year. The newest Mariner, playing alongside quiet professionals like Ichiro Suzuki and Adrian Beltre, produced as expected, hitting .290 and driving in 99 runs. By this time, he'd also married his girlfriend, Yamel, also from the Dominican Republic and with whom he fathered sons José Jr. and José Manuel.

In what might have felt like an annual rite, Guillén was again designated a free agent on October 30, able to sell his services to the highest bidder. Complicating this, however, was the first hint of his involvement with performance-enhancing substances. On November 6, 2007, Mark Fainaru-Wada and Lance Williams, *San Francisco Chronicle* staff writers, broke a report that Guillén "ordered more than $19,000 worth of drugs from the (Palm Beach Rejuvenation Center) between May 2002 and June 2005."[12] ESPN's Jerry Crasnick followed this up by speculating about the potential effect of the accusations on Guillén's future. "Kansas City GM Dayton Moore was asked if the Royals might rethink their interest in the free-agent outfielder. No, Moore replied – sort of. And he was only comfortable addressing the topic in general terms. "Unfortunately, there was a period of time in baseball that we all know now that circumstances like this were occurring," Moore told the *Kansas City Star*. "I think you have to put it into perspective to that particular period of time even if it is a negative mark on the game."[13]

The Royals pressed forward, aware of the potential pitfall, and signed Guillén to a three-year contract worth $36 million. He was suspended for the first 15 days of the season for violating Major League Baseball's drug policy,[14] but that punishment was rescinded following agreement between the Players Association and MLB regarding changes to the entire drug-testing program. Despite the chaos, Guillén still managed 20 homers and 97 RBIs in his first year with the team. Not one to enjoy tranquility, he again made the news on August 26 when he got into a row with a fan at a game in Arlington, Texas. Guillén reportedly yelled profanities and made gestures at a fan who had been loudly accusing the player of lack of effort (even though Guillén had singled in his previous time at bat). After his teammates restrained him, and the fan was removed by security, the game resumed without incident.

That winter, Guillén played for the Dominican Republic in the 2009 World Baseball Classic, but managed only one hit in 12 at-bats. The normally strong Dominican team finished the tournament with a 1-2 record and an early return home. On July 22, 2009, Guillén tore a ligament in his right knee while tying on a shin guard preparing to come to bat against the Los Angeles Angels, and he missed the next 10 weeks, returning for games on September 1 and 2 to close out his season.

Guillén batted only .242 over those 81 games in 2009, and even though he got his 1,500th hit on May 21, 2010, the Royals sent him to the San Francisco Giants on August 12 for cash and a minor leaguer. Almost immediately after joining the team, Major League Baseball restricted him from postseason eligibility due to his appearance in the Mitchell Report.[15] Guillén's final game came on October 3, 2010, but the shadow of illegal drugs kept him from ever suiting up again.

The *New York Daily News* summarized the recurring case against Guillén:

"... José Guillén only put himself and his wife in a world of legal hurt when the Giants' outfielder allegedly arranged for a shipment of nearly 50 preloaded syringes of human growth hormone to be sent to his San Francisco address in September, while his team was clawing its way to a playoff berth. ... (DEA) agents, who were monitoring the activities of the suspected supplier, intercepted the package when it was sent to the Giants' outfielder to the attention of Yamel Guillén – José Guillén's wife, who also goes by Yamel Acevedo.

Federal agents contacted Major League Baseball's Department of Investigation about the shipment and the DOI, according to sources, continues to investigate the matter and whether anyone else in baseball might have been involved, especially since Guillén has a history of acquiring HGH and steroids. ... After the DEA tracked the September package, believed to have been sent from Miami through the San Francisco Airport, agents then arranged a controlled delivery to the home of Guillén, where Yamel Guillén signed for the package. Once she penned her signature, DEA agents identified themselves and Yamel Guillén consented to a search. She is believed to have left the country in recent weeks, returning to the Dominican Republic."[16]

On November 1, 2010, José Guillén again became a free agent, cut loose by the Giants, his 10th major-league organization. In 2012, Enrique Rojas of ESPNDeportes reported that Guillén was working out back at home in the Dominican Republic with the intention of making a comeback at age 36.[17] Rojas noted that Guillén had "apparently drawn interest from at least a couple teams," but the attempt never really gained momentum.

NOTES

1. George Mitchell, *Report to the Commissioner of Baseball of an Independent Investigation into the Illegal Use of Steroids and Other Performance Enhancing Substances by Players in Major League Baseball*, 2007.

2. Paul Daugherty, "Ode to an Act of Kindness," *Cincinnati Enquirer*, June 22, 2003 (online: reds.enquirer.com/2003/06/22/wwwred1doc22.html. Accessed October 1, 2017).

3. Daugherty.

4. Daugherty.

5. Michael Lewis, *Moneyball* (New York: W.W. Norton and Company, 2003).

6. Jim Mone, "Angels Suspend Guillén Without Pay for Rest of Season," *USA Today*, September 28, 2004 (online: usatoday30.usatoday.com/sports/baseball/al/angels/2004-09-26-Guillén-suspension_x.htm#).

7. Mone.

8. The league average was just under $2.7 million (cbssports.com/mlb/salaries/avgsalaries), while Guillén's contract was for only $3.5 million (baseball-reference.com/players/g/guilljo01.shtml).

9. Barry Svrluga, "Sparkling Debut for Nats' Drese," *Washington Post*, June 16, 2005 (online at washingtonpost.com/wp-dyn/content/article/2005/06/16/AR2005061600099.html).

10. "Nationals Right Fielder José Guillén Has Successful UCL Reconstruction Surgery on Right Elbow," online at washington.nationals.mlb.com/news/press_releases/press_release.jsp?ymd=20060725&content_id=1574471&vkey=pr_was&fext=.jsp&c_id=was.

11. Corey Brock, "Mariners Targeting Ex-Nat Guillén," MLB.com, December 2, 2006 (online at m.mariners.mlb.com/news/article/1749651//).

12. Mark Fainaru-Wada and Lance Williams, "Baseball's José Guillén, Matt Williams Bought Steroids From Clinic," *San Francisco Chronicle*, November 6, 2007 (online at sfgate.com/sports/article/Baseball-s-José-Guillén-Matt-Williams-bought-3234893.php).

13. Jerry Crasnick, "Clubs at Mercy of Circumstances Beyond Their Control," ESPN.com, November 23, 2007 (online at espn.com/mlb/hotstove07/columns/story?columnist=crasnick_jerry&id=3122788).

14. Dick Kaegel, "Royals Slugger Guillén Suspended," MLB.royals.com, December 6, 2007 (online at m.royals.mlb.com/news/article/2320510).

15. Michael Schmidt, "Giants' José Guillén Linked to Drug Investigation," *New York Times*, October 28, 2010 (online at nytimes.com/2010/10/29/sports/baseball/29guillen.html).

16. Teri Thompson, "Probe of Giants OF Guillen deepens," *New York Daily News*, November 14, 2010 (online at nydailynews.com/sports/baseball/dea-agents-intercepted-hgh-package-attention-giants-José-guillen-wife-source-article-1.451054).

17. "José Guillén," NBC Sports.com. https://www.nbcsports.com/edge/baseball/mlb/player/16320/José-guillen

CRISTIAN GUZMÁN

By Gregg Omoth

In 2001 the Minnesota Twins ran a series of commercials called "Get to Know 'Em," featuring their young players; one of these commercials highlighted Cristian Guzmán. The focus of the commercial was on his speed and used an image of a sports car and a speedometer to highlight that speed. Leading the AL in triples three times during his career, his ability to turn hits into the outfield into extra-base hits made him one of the most exciting players to watch during the early years of his career. His speed was his ticket to the big leagues before he rounded out his game to be an All-Star hitter and capable fielder. He dealt with a variety of injuries that affected his play in several seasons and eventually shortened his career.

Born Cristian Antonio Guzmán on March 21, 1978, in Santo Domingo, Dominican Republic, to Tilson and Nancy Guzmán, Cristian was one of 10 children – five girls and five boys. Unlike many youngsters in the Dominican Republic, he was not drawn to baseball at an early age. He spent most of his time working with his father on the family farm in Bani, growing tomatoes, yucca, and papaya. His favorite sport was basketball, and he occasionally skipped school to play pickup games. His friends liked baseball and soccer, so he decided to give baseball a chance, even though he thought it was boring.[1] He started playing baseball seriously at the age of 15 when a family friend, Emerson Garcia, was signed by the San Diego Padres. That signing opened Cristian's eyes to the opportunities baseball presented for a better life for his family and him.[2] He also had two uncles playing in the Phillies organization who encouraged him to pursue baseball.

New York Yankees scout Victor Mata signed Cristian as an amateur free agent on August 24, 1994. He remained in the Dominican Republic playing for the Yankees in the Dominican Summer League in 1995. In 1996 he was sent to the Yankees' Gulf Coast League team in Florida. There he showed some promise, hitting .294 in 42 games. In 1997 he split time between Greensboro and Tampa, establishing himself as a prospect.

The Yankees had an established shortstop, Derek Jeter, but needed a second baseman. The Minnesota Twins had a disgruntled second baseman and needed young talent throughout their organization. On February 6, 1998, the Yankees traded Guzmán to the Twins along with Brian Buchanan, Eric Milton, and Danny Mota for second baseman Chuck Knoblauch.

Guzmán's first year in the Twins organization was spent at New Britain in the Eastern League. He played well offensively but had 32 errors in the field and struck out over 100 times. In 1999 he went to spring training in a competition with Denny Hocking and Rule 5 pick Joey Espada for the Twins starting shortstop job. The Twins were a young team with little hope of competing, so the prospect of starting a raw shortstop with potential was an option. They believed Guzmán could make the plays on defense but were concerned with his ability to hit. The Twins made the decision to take a chance and go north with him as their starting shortstop. They had some additional concerns with Guzmán off the field – mainly his limited English skills. After four seasons in the minors he was able to understand English well but struggled speaking the language. The Twins arranged for him to take English-language classes and he lived with pitcher LaTroy Hawkins, who understood some Spanish but would only speak English to Guzmán.[3]

Guzmán's rookie season showed his promise and his limitations. On defense he showed the ability to make some of the tough plays but he struggled with some of the routine ones. In 1999 a strained right hamstring put Guzmán on disabled list at the end of May. In September he served a three-game suspension for charging the mound in an August 31 game against the Toronto Blue Jays. He was upset when a pitch from Paul Spoljaric was near his head. Guzmán tackled Spoljaric and gave him a black eye. His hitting developed over the year; at the beginning he struggled to make contact and when he did, it was often weak groundballs. With his speed, the Twins stressed the need to hit the ball on the ground. By the end of the season Guzmán was making better contact and started driving the ball more.

The 2000 season showed a vast improvement for Guzmán in all facets of the game. He set the Twins record for triples in a season with 20 – the highest single-season total in the AL since Willie Wilson hit 21 in 1985. He improved in every offensive category while playing in 156 games. Off the field he continued to take English lessons five days a week while the team was at home and was more comfortable with giving interviews in English. His parents moved to Minnesota to live with him during the season, making the transition easier.[4] The Twins were impressed with Guzmán's progress and signed him to a four-year, $9 million contract in August, allowing them to avoid three years of arbitration and give Guzmán some financial security. The Twins were looking to Guzmán as an important part of a young team that had a bright future.

On June 4, 2001, in a game against the Cleveland Indians, Guzmán provided an example of how his speed could impact a game. In the seventh inning he laid down a bunt that was fielded by the pitcher, Ricardo Rincon. Rincon threw wild to first and the ball rolled toward the right-field corner. By the time the ball was recovered and thrown in, Guzmán was sliding across home plate, scoring on a bunt single and a three-base error.

In July Guzmán played in his first All-Star Game, striking out in his only at-bat. But shortly after the All-Star break he went on the disabled list with a rotator-cuff injury. He missed 33 games and the Twins slumped, losing 25 of the games. His laid-back approach to rehabilitation frustrated the Twins and would lead to future problems. Playing in only 118 games in 2001, Guzmán still managed to lead the AL in triples with 14 and batted .302.

The 2002 season was a disappointment for Guzmán due to several nagging injuries, but he still set a career high in at-bats with 623. His overall play, however, was not up to the expectations set the previous two years. Guzmán's lackadaisical approach to rehabbing injuries once again put him at odds with

Photo courtesy of the Minnesota Twins

his manager, Ron Gardenhire. However, the Twins won the Central Division title and Guzmán made his first postseason appearance. He scored the winning run in a Game Five win over the Oakland A's in the Division Series. In the AL Championship Series, the Twins fell to the Anaheim Angels in five games. After the season, the Twins decided not to resign David Ortiz, one of Guzmán's closest friends on the team. A fellow Dominican, Ortiz was credited with helping keep Guzmán motivated on the field.[5]

In 2003, for the third time in four seasons Guzmán led the AL in triples, with 14. The Twins, though, were starting to lose their patience with him and started listening to trade offers at the winter meetings.

The 2004 season was one of Guzmán's more consistent seasons, second among AL shortstops in fielding percentage at .983. But after the season the Twins declined to pick up the fifth year on his contract, making him a free agent. The Twins were working on a limited budget and still had questions about Guzmán's commitment to improving his game. Free agent Guzmán signed a four-year deal worth $16.8 million with the Washington Nationals. One of the first big acquisitions for the Nationals, he was expected to anchor their infield.

Guzmán's first year in Washington was a struggle that found him hitting in all spots in the batting order trying to find a way to help the team. By August he was hitting only .190 and manager Frank Robinson was starting to pinch-hit for him and bench him on occasion. The fans were booing Guzmán, and he was losing his confidence. There was talk that the Nationals might release him and eat the remaining years of his contract. He managed to have a good September and raise his season-ending average to .219. This was Guzmán's worst year since his rookie season; the Nationals had had higher expectations for his production and defense.

Going into the 2006 season, the Nationals signed veteran shortstop Royce Clayton to provide some insurance at the position. Over the winter Guzmán lost some weight and had laser surgery on his eyes so that he would not have to wear contacts. He entered spring training with a positive outlook and expected to bounce back. In late March the Nationals placed him on the disabled list with a sore shoulder. After a couple of months of rest and rehab, it was announced on May 5 that Guzmán would have season-ending surgery to repair a torn labrum in his shoulder.[6]

Guzmán returned as the starting shortstop for the Nationals under new manager Manny Acta in 2007. With a healthy shoulder, he started the season strong, even after missing some games with a hamstring injury. In late June he was hitting .329 when in a game against Cleveland he slapped a tag on Josh Barfield attempting to steal second base. On the play Guzmán damaged ligaments in his thumb and had surgery the next day. The injury kept him out until late September, when he played in three games, ending another frustrating season for Guzmán and the Nationals. Just when the Washington fans were starting to warm to him, his season was lost and one started to hear suggestions that he bore the stigma of being injury-prone.

In 2008 Guzmán was back in the lineup as the starting shortstop and hitting leadoff. He was named to the All-Star Game for the second time in his career. He credited his success to better vision from the Lasik eye surgery in 2006.[7] His stellar play also earned him a two-year contract extension at $8 million a year in late July. Playing through a thumb injury, he went into a slump in August. Breaking out of the slump, he started hitting and on August 28 he hit for the cycle in a game against the Dodgers with a triple in the eighth inning. His solid play continued the rest of the year and he finish fourth in the NL in batting average at .316 and hits with 183.

Guzmán started the 2009 season by getting 17 hits in his first seven games before a hamstring injury forced him to go on the 15-day disabled list. Upon returning from the DL, he played well enough to be one of the five players up for the fan vote to make the NL All-Star team, eventually losing out to the Phillies' Shane Victorino. In August the Nationals placed Guzmán on waivers and the Red Sox claimed him, but they were unable to work out a deal to send him to Boston. A sore right shoulder limited Guzmán to pinch-hitting during the final two weeks of the season. During the offseason he had arthroscopic surgery on the shoulder.

The Nationals had concerns about Guzmán's durability going into the 2010 season, mainly due to his shoulder issues. They started discussing the possibility of playing him at second base, turning the shortstop job over to Ian Desmond. This would be a significant change for Guzmán, who had never played any position in the field except shortstop.

On July 31 the Nationals sent Guzmán and cash to the Texas Rangers for minor leaguers Tanner Roark and Ryan Tatusko. Initially Guzmán let the Nationals know that he was not going to accept the trade per his rights as a 10-year veteran with five years of service with one team. He eventually decided to accept the trade, realizing that his time in Washington was done. After getting only three hits in 34 at-bats, Guzmán went on the disabled list with a strained quadriceps in August. The Rangers decided not to re-sign him at the end of the season.

After Guzmán sat out the 2011 season with a shoulder injury, his former manager, Manny Acta, who was managing the Cleveland Indians, persuaded Guzmán to go to spring training with the Indians in 2012. He signed a minor-league contract with hopes of making the team as a utilityman. He started the spring strong, but a strained hamstring limited his opportunities late in the spring. At the end of spring training, the Indians released Guzmán.

Guzmán's career was one that started with a rapid rise to an All-Star shortstop at age 23 with a bright future. Injuries and questions about his desire led to a shortened career that did not live up to the early expectations. However, his speed led to his legacy as one of the best triples hitters of his generation. In retirement he spends his time with his wife and three children, while staying involved in baseball, working with young players in the Dominican Republic.[8]

SOURCES

In addition to the sources cited in the Notes, the author also consulted Baseball-Reference.com and Retrosheet.org.

NOTES

1 Gordon Wittenmyer, "Quick Study: Cristian Guzmán Has Gone From Novice to All-Star in Eight Years," *St. Paul Pioneer Press*, July 10, 2001: C1.

2 Jeff Perlman, "The Triple Threat: The Twins' Cristian Guzmán Has Made Three-Baggers His Specialty," *Sports Illustrated*, July 31, 2000.

3 LaVelle E. Neal III, "Everyone Is Pulling for Guzmán," *Minneapolis Star Tribune*, July 30, 1999: 16C.

4 Chip Scoggins, "Speaking of Success … Twins Shortstop Cristian Guzmán Is Becoming One of Baseball's Best Young Players, and He'll Soon Be Able to Tell Everyone About It," *Minneapolis Star Tribune*, July 23, 2000.

5 Tom Powers, "Twins Probably Will Be Fine," *St. Paul Pioneer Press*, December 21, 2004.

6 Steven Goff, "Guzmán Will Have Surgery, Is Out for Year," *Washington Post*, May 6, 2006.

7 Rich Campbell, "Nats Get Eyeful of Improved Guzmán a Better View of the Game: All-Star Cristian Guzmán Finally Playing Up to Nationals' Expectations," *Free Lance-Star* (Fredericksburg, Virginia), July 14, 2008.

8 Fox Sports North, "Catching Up with Former Twins All-Star Cristian Guzmán," foxsports.com/north/video/1292067395855, August 3, 2018.

RUDY HERNÁNDEZ

By Richard Bogovich

It may surprise you to learn that by 1960 just two players born in the Dominican Republic had played in the majors: Ozzie Virgil and Felipe Alou debuted in 1956 and 1958, respectively. In 1960 they were joined by Julian Javier in the season's second month. On July 3, 1960, Rudy Hernández became the first Dominican pitcher in the majors, a little more than two weeks before the famous Juan Marichal.

Rodolfo Alberto Hernández Fuentes was born on December 10, 1930,[1] in the city of Santiago de los Caballeros to Serafina Fuentes, a Puerto Rican, and Rubén Néstor Hernández Polanco. Rudy's father was from nearby Tamboril.[2] Rudy's siblings, Rubén and Lourdes, were born 13 months before and after him, respectively. One branch of Rudy's family tree has been traced back a few generations. A maternal great-grandmother, Barbara Fuentes, was a Puerto Rican slave freed no earlier than 1872. Rudy's parents were reportedly married in New York City in 1926,[3] though 1928 is indicated in the family's entry in the 1930 US census. On April 10, 1930, the family of three was residing at 1171 Elder Avenue in the Bronx. Living with them were the elder Rubén's brother, Amado, and 16-year-old brother-in-law, Paublo Villafane. Rubén was a

Photo courtesy of the National Baseball Hall of Fame

bookkeeper for a bank and Amado's job was cleaning for Interborough Rapid Transit, part of the New York City subway system.

The family returned to the Dominican Republic by the time Rudy was born. His parents eventually decided to raise their children in the United States. Serafina was adamant about not living in the Dominican Republic permanently so she returned to New York first and then her husband followed. Rudy was about 7 years old when the children moved to New York. His father later worked as an accountant for the Teamsters Union for many years.[4] A New York passenger list for the *S.S. Leif*, which departed from Puerto Plata, Dominican Republic, on April 21, 1939, included Rodolfo Alberto Hernández Fuentes, age 8, traveling with his sister and parents. Based primarily on New York City phone books, from at least 1945 to 1960 the family's residence was 803 West 180th Street in Manhattan.

Rudy had an uncle who was a military attaché at the Dominican embassy in Washington, Captain Juan Hernández. Rudy visited him often during the summer. After Hernández made his major-league debut in Washington's Griffith Stadium, he told a *Washington Post* reporter he'd been there before with his uncle, who last took him there when he was 9 years old. His uncle's chauffeur was a huge baseball fan and would take Rudy to watch the Senators play multiple afternoons in a row.[5]

Rudy attended Manhattan's High School of Commerce, and box scores in April of 1947 showed a Hernández in its baseball team's lineup at first base.[6] A year later he was one of 12 players featured in a team photo printed in the *New York Post*.[7] In his first year as their center fielder, he had a batting average of .348,[8] and the school later presented him an award named after Lou Gehrig, its most famous athletic alumnus.[9] In 1948 Commerce's baseball team finished second to Manhattan's George Washington High School. Hernández continued on the team in 1949 and had one of his better games in a 6-5 loss to Newtown High, when he had three hits in four at-bats and scored twice.[10]

As a high-school athlete Rudy may have been as highly regarded for basketball as for baseball. He reportedly turned down a four-year basketball scholarship offered by Seton Hall.[11] During the 1948-1949 school year Commerce's basketball team was in the playoffs of New York City's Public Schools Athletic League but lost in overtime on March 3, 1949, to Stuyvesant High. Naturally, media attention focused on the winning team. "Shoved into the background were the efforts of Rudy Hernández and Herman Taylor with 17 and 14 markers, respectively," wrote one reporter. "A story book one-hander from near mid-court by Hernández four seconds before the end of the regulation time had extended the game an extra session."[12]

Commerce's team fared better the next school year, and it became something of a local legend by the late 1950s as its stars made names for themselves elsewhere, including Taylor, who played with the Harlem Globetrotters. Also on the 1949-1950 Commerce team was Frank Kasprzak, whose Holy Cross team won the NIT championship in 1954. Joining them was freshman Tony Windis, who later averaged over 20 points per game as a star at the University of Wyoming and played for the Detroit Pistons in 1960. Commerce's team that season won 21 consecutive games on its way to winning the PSAL championship.[13] Hernández was in Commerce's lineup in November but wasn't when they completed their amazing run in March.[14] By the spring of 1950 he was signed to a contract by New York Giants scout Bubber Jonnard and was assigned to Class-D Oshkosh (Wisconsin State League).[15]

Opening Day for the Oshkosh Giants was May 4 in Appleton. At least one day before, Oshkosh manager Dave Garcia announced his starting lineup, and it included Hernández in center field.[16]

In his first official inning as a pro, Hernández was charged with a throwing error, but he made amends in the seventh inning. Appleton's Merle Barth had doubled, and he tagged up on a long fly to center field. Hernández nailed him with "a perfect throw," and the Appleton newspaper printed a photo of the double play as Oshkosh's third baseman was "waiting for Barth to come in." The game ended up being terminated after 13 innings, and the newspaper explained that tie wouldn't count in the standings but all individual statistics did count. Hernández went hitless but stole a base.[17]

The two teams were supposed to meet again the next day but three league games were called off because of high winds.[18] Thus, Hernández's first hits as a pro came at home on May 6, 1950, against the Green Bay Bluejays. In a 17-14 win he had two hits in five at-bats and scored three times.[19] Less than a week later, in an 8-1 victory over the same team, Hernández was the offensive star with four hits in five at-bats.[20] The next month he was in the spotlight for two "sensational" defensive plays against the Janesville Cubs. "He covered a wide area like a tent to rob Pete Nitrini of a hit with a diving, one-handed catch in the second inning and to take a blow labeled for extra bases away from Joe Yambor in the fourth," wrote the Janesville paper's sports editor. "Hernández raced to the fence in center-right to make an easy catch of Yambor's hard smack."[21]

Late in the season Hernández received a little media attention for an unusual reason. For Parker Pen Night in Janesville on August 17, a record crowd of almost 4,000 was entertained for an hour prior to the game. In addition to races and other contests involving players and umpires, there were musical performances. A quartet of Janesville Cubs performed two songs, as did "Rudy Hernández, fleet center fielder of Oshkosh."[22]

On September 2 the Oshkosh Giants clinched the pennant. "We won practically every honor that was possible to win that year," Hernández recalled three years later.[23] His batting average was just .241, but that figure excludes 10 playoff games in September. Oshkosh defeated Fond du Lac three games to one in the first round, and then Hernández became red-hot at the plate. He helped Oshkosh defeat Janesville in the finals, four games to two, with 8 hits in 18 at-bats, four runs scored, at least four walks, and an RBI, mostly batting eighth or seventh in the lineup.[24]

During the offseason Hernández played the first of many seasons in Puerto Rico's winter league, for the team in Ponce. Each team was required to have a minimum number of Puerto Ricans on its roster, and he counted as one because his mother was born there. His manager was Hall of Famer Rogers Hornsby, and he lived in the same building as future major leaguers Bill Skowron and Clint Courtney.[25]

For 1951 Hernández was promoted to Class-C St. Cloud (Northern League). His batting average improved to .262. "True, my hitting did pick up," he commented in 1953, "but I wasn't considered a notorious hitter by any stretch of the imagination." Nevertheless, his skill as a fielder was clear, and he shared the team's most valuable player honors.[26]

To start 1952 Hernández was promoted to Class-A Sioux City (Western League), where early on he was tried at second base.[27] Hernández wasn't hitting well after 20 games, and before mid-June he was with Class-B Sunbury (Interstate League). He broke his ankle sliding in a game on July 22 and was out for the rest of the season.[28]

Hernández spent all of 1953 with Class-B Gastonia (Tri-State League). At the beginning of the season he expressed concerns about plateauing. "I've been optioned out three times by the Giants," Hernández said, "and I believe it's time that I do something." He was still committed to reaching the majors. "That's simply why I've got to buckle down and make good here." He also appeared to confess some overconfidence back in 1950. "I didn't want to play Class D baseball, thought I knew all the angles," he said regarding his assignment in Oshkosh. "As a matter of fact, I frankly believed I was ready for Class B ball, and, maybe, even Class A ball my first year."[29]

Hernández performed very well early in the season for Gastonia. Team statistics in late May showed him with a batting average of .293 in 150 at-bats, and in mid-June two sportswriters with the *Asheville Citizen-Times* were advocating that he be named a league all-star.[30] But Hernández slumped considerably in June and his average slid to .254 by the time he was "returned" to the New York Giants organization before the end of July.[31] He then vanished from sports pages in August and September.

It was time to try a different approach, and that started in Puerto Rico's winter league. Hernández's first manager there, Rogers Hornsby, had pointed out a hitch in his swing, and at some point Hornsby recommended that he become a pitcher.[32] For the 1953-1954 season in Puerto Rico, Phillies right-hander Steve Ridzik likewise encouraged him to try pitching. The person who ultimately convinced Hernández was Roberto Clemente. Clemente's first season in Puerto Rico's winter league was 1952-53,[33] and he joked that because Hernández had struck him out, he could strike out anyone.[34]

As a new pitcher, for 1954 Hernández was sent back to Class-C Muskogee (Western Association). He won his first eight starts, and sportswriters throughout the league noticed. One paper in a banner headline trumpeted, "Undefeated Rudy Hernández to Pitch Against Joplin at Muskogee Tonight."[35] He ended the season with a record of 15-4. He allowed just 7.1 hits per nine innings, thanks partly to four three-hitters.[36] He also excelled at bat: .425 in 80 at-bats, and with five doubles, three triples, and five homers, his slugging average was .750.

In October *The Sporting News* reported that Hernández was to rejoin Class-A Sioux City in 1955.[37] But his progress toward the majors was delayed by military service, which kept him from pitching for Sioux City until 1957. He didn't play for any military team during his two years of active duty.[38]

Meanwhile, on September 23, 1956, Ozzie Virgil made his debut for the New York Giants and thus became the first Dominican-born player. "I knew it was a race to the line between Rudy and myself," Virgil said 50 years later. "I had no idea I would be the first Dominican. The Dominican Republic had much better players than I was. I made a big jump that year."[39]

Hernández was discharged in time to play in the 1956-57 Dominican winter league, for Escogido, along with Virgil and Felipe Alou.[40] In April *The Sporting News* reported that he was assigned to Class-A Sioux City.[41] He spent all of 1957 with Sioux City.

Early in the season Hernández made *The Sporting News* for his role in enforcing baseball's unwritten rules, against the Lincoln Chiefs on May 7. The weekly wrote: "In the seventh, after Harry Williams homered for the Chiefs, Hernández knocked down Roberto Sanchez, 5-6 Chief shortstop. With Hernández at bat in the eighth, [Art] Murray backed him out of the box with four inside pitches and the Soo hurler rushed to the mound, swinging his bat. Other players prevented a scrap, but when the game was over Murray hit Hernández with a flying tackle.[42]

Hernández's best pitching performance of the season probably came on June 28, when he defeated Topeka 2-1, allowing only two singles.[43] He won nine games and lost eight for the Soos, with a high earned-run average of 5.66. He started the 1958 season at Double A for the first time, Corpus Christi of the

Texas League. But after four starts, with an 0-3 record and an ERA above 8.00, he was sent back to Class-A, first Sioux City, then Springfield (Eastern League). His combined record with the three teams was a discouraging 0-9 with an ERA of 8.15. The Giants released him after the season.

In January of 1959 Hernández signed with the Miami Marlins, a Baltimore affiliate in the Triple-A International League.[44] In April, before the season began, Miami sent him to Double-A Chattanooga in the Washington Senators organization.[45]

Hernández spent all of 1959 with the Chattanooga Lookouts. After his ninth game he sat comfortably atop the Southern Association's ERA rankings at 2.21.[46] However, he bruised his hand in New Orleans during early June when he was one of about 10 Lookouts who climbed into the stands to scuffle with some abusive fans. On June 8 he overcame his sore hand against New Orleans to take a two-hitter up to the final out, and hung on to defeat them, 4-1.[47] After that he went seven weeks without a victory. On July 30 he finally won again, 5-1, in another rematch with New Orleans.[48] In the end his record was only 8-12 but his ERA was a respectable 3.42. It proved to be his last pro season as a starting pitcher.

For 1960, at long last Hernández made it to Triple A, with the Senators' American Association team in Charleston. In 31 appearances through June, all in relief, his ERA was 2.70. A potential setback then turned out surprisingly well: "Charleston Senators ace reliever Rudy Hernández has come up with a sore arm and is on his way to Washington, D.C., for treatment by the Washington Senators' club physician," the *Charleston Gazette* reported on July 2. "There's a chance, if Hernández' arm comes along okay, that Washington may keep him and add him to its major league roster."[49] That chance turned into reality, and on July 3, 1960, Rudy Hernández became the first Dominican-born pitcher in the major leagues.

That day the Senators hosted the Cleveland Indians for a doubleheader. In the first game Senators starter Bill Fischer gave up five runs in the first five innings. Manager Cookie Lavagetto summoned Hernández in the top of the sixth inning. The first Cleveland batter he faced was Chuck Tanner, who grounded out to second. He walked the third batter but struck out the fourth to end the inning. In the seventh inning he retired the Indians 1-2-3, all on fly outs to center field. In the eighth inning he gave up a single but for the second time faced only four batters. The Senators lost the game, but Hernández had a very good debut.

Less than a week later, on July 9, Hernández earned his first win in the majors, against Baltimore. The game was tied 2-2 in the bottom of the seventh when Senators starter Hal Woodeshick yielded singles to the first two Orioles. Hernández relieved and the first batter he faced sacrificed. The next batter was walked intentionally to load the bases with one out. Hernández coaxed Gene Woodling to pop out into foul territory, then struck out Gene Stephens looking to end the threat. The Senators followed with a five-run outburst, and Hernández had little difficulty in the final two innings.

Hernández notched his second victory against the White Sox at home on July 29, his third on August 8 in Kansas City, and his fourth on August 14 in Yankee Stadium, not far from where he grew up. In the latter contest, the Senators had already won the first game of a doubleheader. The Yankees tied the nightcap at 3-3 in the bottom of the ninth inning. Hernández pitched the 13th and 14th with leadoff baserunners getting nowhere in either inning. The Senators scored three in the top of the 15th, and Chuck Stobbs earned a save in the bottom half of the frame to end it. After six weeks, the rookie's record stood at four wins, no losses. Hernández suffered his only loss of the season at home to Chicago on August 30. He pitched in 21 games overall.

The Senators relocated to Minnesota and became the Twins in 1961, but a new Washington franchise was created as the American League expanded from eight teams to 10 (with the other new one being the Angels). The new Senators selected Hernández from the previous Senators in the expansion draft. Hernández, pitching for Ponce in Puerto Rico, said, "This is the best baseball news I ever have gotten in my life. It gives me confidence."[50] In mid-February of 1961 it was announced that he had agreed to terms with his new club.[51]

On April 10, 1961, Hernández experienced Opening Day on a major-league roster as the new Senators played their first official game, at home against the White Sox. He pitched in his final major-league game less than a month into the season. It was at home on May 4 versus the Tigers. The last batter he faced was Al Kaline, whom he threw out at first base on a grounder. It was his seventh appearance, and he ended it with a good 3.00 earned-run average, but he was a victim of unique circumstances. Each team had been allowed 28 players on its roster during the season's opening month, and Hernández was one of three players optioned to Triple A in order to reach the 25-player limit.[52]

For the remainder of 1961 through 1964 Hernández continued to pitch in the minor leagues, almost always at the Triple-A level, in several major-league farm systems. He continued to play in Caribbean winter leagues even longer.[53] After the 1964 season he retired as a player. He has two daughters, Maria Veronica "Vicky" Hernández and Jennifer Muñoz, though he never married.[54]

By 1971 Hernández was operating a bar in San Juan, Puerto Rico, called Rudy's 10th Inning Lounge.[55] After his site was sold, he opened another lounge, Rudy's on the Beach.

When an earthquake struck Nicaragua in late 1972 and Roberto Clemente coordinated humanitarian aid in Puerto Rico, Hernández had a modest role in the relief effort and thus was interviewed at length about Clemente's death on December 31, 1972, when a plane loaded with relief supplies crashed. "On the final morning of Roberto Clemente's life, Rudy Hernández was in his bar and suddenly remembered the 'mercy kettle,'" wrote sportswriter Jerry Izenberg, in the Newark Star-Ledger.

"It was a big iron pot and people were throwing money in it for the earthquake victims since the relief campaign began. They would have put money into any cause Roberto was behind," Hernández told Izenberg. "I called the house to find out what to do with it and [his wife] Vera told me he was asleep, but I remembered he wanted it to go to Nicaragua to show the people how much we cared."

"I told her I would send Manny (Sanguillen) to the airport with it," Hernández told Izenberg. "The day before, Roberto had stopped by the bar and I remember I urged him not to go because it would be New Year's Eve. But he said, 'If I don't, who will?'" Hernández also spoke at length at how Clemente's death devastated Puerto Ricans.[56]

A few years later Hernández shuttered Rudy's on the Beach and went to work for Puerto Rico's Department of Sports and Recreation. For more than 25 years he was a baseball instructor for youth of the inner city and housing projects in and around San Juan, and then retired there. Hernández has had other connections to baseball, including scouting for the Cubs and Orioles. He focused more on reporting than on trying to help sign players. When Orlando Cepeda started a baseball school in the late 1970s near San Juan, Hernández became one of the instructors.[57]

As an instructor Hernández could share life lessons with athletes he tutored. He could speak from personal experience about not being discouraged by setbacks. Perhaps more importantly, he could testify credibly about setting high goals while also not being reluctant to change your plans.

NOTES

1 Almost all sources instead identify 1931 as the year of Hernández's birth, although it is shown as 1933 on his 1961 Topps baseball card. When he re-entered the United States from the Dominican Republic on January 29, 1960, his year of birth on the passenger list was 1930 (with his longtime address of 803 W. 180th St., N.Y., confirming that it wasn't some other Rudy Hernández). His nephew Rubén Hernández provided to the author a photo of Rudy's current passport, which also shows 1930 as his year of birth.

2 Cuqui Córdova, "Béisbol de Ayer: Rudy Hernández," *Listín Diario* (Santo Domingo, Dominican Republic), July 5, 2008: listindiario.com/el-deporte/2008/07/05/64968/beisbol-de-ayer. Córdova devoted his weekly *Béisbol de Ayer* columns to different aspects of Hernández life during July and August of 2008.

3 Genealogy Report: Descendants of Maria Rosario, genealogy.com/ftm/u/h/l/Jaimee-E-Uhlenbrock-NY/GENE1-0004.html; details about "Rudi" and Serafina Fuentes are on the same web page, while details about Barbara Fuentes are on the second page. Jaimee Uhlenbrock, Professor Emerita of the State University of New York, New Paltz, in email to the author on July 9, 2018, noted that details on the home page, about Barbara Fuentes' mother were due for substantial revision and thus should be discounted.

4 Email to the author from Rubén Hernández, October 28, 2016.

5 Bob Addie, "Bob Addie's Column," *Washington Post*, July 5, 1960: A15; Bob Addie, "Pitcher Hernandez and Chauffeur Often Watched Senators Play Here," *Washington Post*, March 7, 1941: A16. Regarding Rudy's parents, Thomas E. Van Hyning (see Note 25) said, "His father was the son of [dictator Rafael] Trujillo's top general in the Dominican military." However, in email to the author on July 5, 2018, Rudy's nephew Rubén said that may be confusing Rudy's uncle Juan, the captain, with Rudy's paternal grandfather. Rubén added that Rudy's father also served in the Dominican military though with a rank likely no higher than master sergeant. He also noted that Rudy's aunt Margarita, wife of the aforementioned uncle Amado Hernández, was sister of a Dominican president, but that was Joaquín Balaguer and not Trujillo. Amado and Margarita had a daughter, also named Margarita, who served as secretary of state for her uncle Joaquín. She and cousin Rudy kept in touch often.

6. "Flushing Wins over Commerce by 9-0 Score," *Long Island Star-Journal*, April 9, 1947: 14; "Jamaica Leads in Short Game," *Long Island Star-Journal*, April 15, 1947: 12. The latter game was rained out about halfway through the fourth inning but the newspaper printed the stats anyway. In the earlier game Commerce managed only three hits, one of them by Hernández.

7. *New York Post*, April 22, 1948: 42.

8. Cuqui Córdova, "Béisbol de Ayer: Rudy Hernández," *Listín Diario* (Santo Domingo, Dominican Republic), July 12, 2008: listindiario.com/el-deporte/2008/7/12/65826/Beisbol-de-ayer.

9. Addie, "Pitcher Hernandez."

10. "Jamaica Plays Tie with Commerce," *Long Island Star-Journal*, March 29, 1949: 13; "Newtown Nine Scores, 6-5," *Long Island Star-Journal*, April 5, 1949: 13. It was in the former article that Commerce was referred to as "runner up last year to George Washington in Manhattan."

11. Ken Alexander, "Ken's Pen: Three Years under Giant Option[,] Rudy Figures This Is Do or Die," *Gastonia* (North Carolina) *Gazette*, May 2, 1953: 14.

12. "Bryant Five Bows in PSAL Playoffs," *Long Island Star-Journal*, March 4, 1949: 17.

13. "Easy-Going Cowboy Star Getting Raves," *Uniontown* (Pennsylvania) *Morning Herald*, January 30, 1958: 11. The article focused on Windis but noted his connection to Taylor, Kasprzak, "and Rudy Hernandez, who last year received $9,500 for signing to pitch for a New York Giant farm team."

14. "Cagers Warm Up as Football Fades," *Brooklyn Daily Eagle*, November 16, 1949: 27. The box score's lineup included Taylor, Hernández, and Kasprzak. Hernández wasn't in any of the Commerce lineups printed in the *New York Times* on March 3, March 14, and March 19. The same is true for "Commerce Five Wins School Final, 67-50," *New York Times*, March 24, 1950: 34.

15. Alexander: 14.

16. "Champion Oshkosh '9' Invades Goodland Field Thursday Night," *Appleton* (Wisconsin) *Post-Crescent*, May 3, 1950: 26.

17. Orv Wonser, "Only 863 See Papers, Giants in Thrilling 13-Inning 5-5 Tie," *Appleton Post-Crescent*, May 5, 1950: 17, 19.

18. "Friday Night's Results," *Appleton Post-Crescent*, May 6, 1950: 11.

19. "Bluejays Drop 2 to 1, 13-Inning Thriller on Error at Oshkosh; Lose Opener by 17 to 14," *Green Bay Press-Gazette*, May 8, 1950: 17. Garcia was the big star, setting a league record with nine RBIs.

20. "Appleton Hurler Fans 19 Fondy Batters; Papermakers Cop 14-3," *La Crosse* (Wisconsin) *Tribune*, May 13, 1950: 6.

21. George Raubacher, "Cubs' All-Star Hopes Given Boost by Fond du Lac," *Janesville* (Wisconsin) *Daily Gazette*, June 26, 1950: 12.

22. "Sports Hash," *Janesville Daily Gazette*, August 18, 1950: 10. Elsewhere on the page the paper said 3,996 were in attendance.

23. Alexander: 14. The only other Oshkosh player to reach the majors was pitcher Joe Margoneri, with the Giants in 1956 and 1957.

24. See box scores in *Janesville* (Wisconsin) *Daily Gazette*, September 11 through 16, 1950, on pages 11, 12, 10, 6, 11, and 10, respectively.

25. Thomas E. Van Hyning, *Puerto Rico's Winter League: A History of Major League Baseball's Launching Pad* (Jefferson, North Carolina: McFarland & Company, Inc., 1995), 121.

26. Alexander: 14.

27. Alex Stoddard, "Soos May Be in Thick of W.L. Race," *Beatrice* (Nebraska) *Daily Sun*, April 14, 1952: 3.

28. "Caldwell First to Post No. 15," *The Sporting News*, August 4, 1952: 34.

29. Alexander: 14.

30. "Report on Rockets," *Gastonia Gazette*, May 30, 1953: 12; Ken Alexander, "Ken's Pen," *Gastonia Gazette*, June 18, 1953: 22.

31. "Deals of the Week," *The Sporting News*, July 29, 1953: 31.

32. Van Hyning, 121.

33. Van Hyning, 53-55.

34. Email to the author from Rubén Hernández, October 28, 2016.

35. "Undefeated Rudy Hernandez to Pitch Against Joplin at Muskogee Tonight," *Joplin* (Missouri) *News Herald*, June 9, 1954: 2B.

36 "Chico Hernandez Stops Joplin on Three Hits as Giants Win, 12-2," *Joplin* (Missouri) *Globe*, April 27, 1954: 8; "Elks in Comeback after Three Losses," *Hutchinson* (Kansas) *News Herald*, June 10, 1954: 2; "Elks Lose to Iola Indians," *Hutchinson News Herald*, June 29, 1954: 2; "Elks in Split with Giants," *Hutchinson News Herald*, July 30, 1954: 2. Hernández homered in the first of these two games. In the first of these articles it was indeed implied that Rudy had been given the nickname "Chico."

37 "Deals of the Week," *The Sporting News*, October 20, 1954: 28.

38 Email to the author from Rubén Hernández, October 28, 2016.

39 "Virgil Celebrates 50th Anniversary" *Berkshire Eagle* (Pittsfield, Massachusetts), September 22, 2006: C2.

40 Joe King, "Stoneham Seeks Another White in Dominican Loop," *The Sporting News*, November 28, 1956: 21; Félix Acosta Núñez, "Lopat Takes Hill, Helps U.S. Stars Decision Natives," *The Sporting News*, January 9, 1957: 20.

41 "Deals of the Week," *The Sporting News*, April 24, 1957: 34.

42 "Three Hits, Seven RBIs," *The Sporting News*, May 15, 1957: 37.

43 "Sioux City Tops Topeka Twice," *Albuquerque Journal*, June 29, 1957: 15.

44 "Miami Goes South for More Talent," *Findlay* (Ohio) *Republican Courier*, January 29, 1959: 17. Proof that this wasn't some other player with the same name was provided by Luther Evans, "Marlins Deflated in Opener," *Miami Herald*, March 23, 1959: C1, when he was referred to as "Rudolph Albert Hernandez … former outfielder." See also Eddie Storin, "Indianapolis Mauls Marlins Again," *Miami Herald*, April 3, 1959: 2C. The latter reported on a game in which "Rudy Hernandez was fairly effective, limiting the American Association Indians to one run on one hit and three walks in two innings."

45 "Deals of the Week," *The Sporting News*, April 22, 1959: 28.

46 "Dixie Averages," *The Sporting News*, May 27, 1959: 35.

47 "Lookouts' Kaat Back in Form," *The Sporting News*, June 17, 1959: 33.

48 "Bradey Has 5.01 ERA, Wins 15," *The Sporting News*, August 12, 1959: 35.

49 "Sore Armed Hernandez Leaves Sens," *Charleston* (West Virginia) *Gazette*, July 2, 1960: 9.

50 "5 Drafted by Nats Pleased with Pick," *Findlay* (Ohio) *Republican Courier*, December 16, 1960: 25.

51 Bob Addie, "New Nats Will Start Wednesday," *Washington Post*, February 19, 1961: C1. Hernández became very fond of his new manager, Mickey Vernon, according to an email to the author from his nephew, Rubén Hernández, October 28, 2016.

52 Mike Rathet, "Major League Cutdown Time at Midnight," *Corpus Christi* (Texas) *Caller-Times*, May 10, 1961: 21.

53 For example, see Miguel J. Frau, "Pity Crabbers! Even Weather Adds to Woes," *The Sporting News*, November 20, 1965: 29.

54 Email to the author from Rubén Hernández, October 28, 2016.

55 Thomas E. Van Hyning, *The Santurce Crabbers: Sixty Seasons of Puerto Rican Winter League Baseball* (Jefferson, North Carolina: McFarland & Company, Inc., 1999), 118.

56 Jerry Izenberg, "It Was the Night the Happiness Died," *Newark Star-Ledger,* December 30, 2002: 39.

57 Email to the author from Rubén Hernández, October 28, 2016.

JULIÁN JAVIER

By Paul Geisler

Besides being a superb fielding but often light hitting second baseman with the St. Louis Cardinals for more than a decade, Julián Javier was a central figure in the history and development of baseball in the Dominican Republic.

Javier completed his playing days with a career .257 batting average. But in 19 World Series games, he batted .333 and belted a three-run home run in the 1967 Series. The bespectacled Javier also became one of the greatest defensive second basemen ever for the Cardinals, as well as one of the best bunters in baseball.

Manuel Julián Javier Liranzo, better known as simply Julián Javier, was born on August 9, 1936, in San Francisco de Macoris, Dominican Republic, which became his lifelong hometown. From 1960 to 1972, he played 12 seasons with the St. Louis Cardinals and one with the Cincinnati Reds. Tall and lanky at 6-feet-1 and 175 pounds, he batted and threw right-handed. A second baseman throughout his career, he won two World Series championships – 1964 and 1967 with the Cardinals– and played on two All-Star teams.

Son of a truck driver and the tallest of eight children, Julián developed his speedy running by racing other children to and from

Photo courtesy of the National Baseball Hall of Fame

school – that is, when he wasn't skipping school to listen to World Series broadcasts. In high school he played shortstop and batted cleanup, hitting .375. He learned to type nearly as fast as he could run, and considered a career in accounting or engineering. But when the Pittsburgh Pirates held a tryout in 1956 with 200 aspirants, scout Howie Haak persuaded Javier to set aside any other career choices and sign the only contract the Pirates offered that day, for only $500.[1]

Hampered by injuries, Javier's professional career started slowly. But after three seasons working his way up the Pirates' chain, he flourished at their Triple-A affiliate Columbus in 1959, leading the International League with 19 sacrifice hits and batting .274. The *Baseball Digest* scouting report on him for 1960 accurately described his coming major-league legacy: "Fastest man in league last year and has good range on grounders. Good arm and excellent hands. Fair hitter, but no power. Has good chance despite lack of power at plate."[2]

Javier wanted to succeed quickly and said, "I want to build a home and need the money,"[3] but the Pirates already had an all-star, golden glove second baseman in their lineup: future Hall-of-Famer Bill Mazeroski, who was four weeks younger than Javier.

Javier's big break came on May 28, 1960, when the Pirates traded him and pitcher Ed Bauta to the Cardinals for veteran pitcher Wilmer "Vinegar Bend" Mizell and pitcher Dick Gray. The swap helped both sides, as Mizell helped the Pirates become champions in 1960, while the Cardinals had found their starting second sacker for the next 12 seasons.

Javier made his major-league debut the day of the trade, and got two hits against the San Francisco Giants. The Cardinals kept the deal secret until they posted their lineup. Even broadcaster Harry Caray did not hear about it until he reached the ballpark. Cardinals general manager Bing Devine surprised most observers by giving up a veteran starting pitcher for an unproven minor-league prospect; however, Eddie Stanky, the Cardinals' director of player procurement, had insisted that Javier was one of the best he had seen.[4]

Julián, or Hoolie, as many called him by his rookie year, finished the season as the leadoff hitter. He batted only .237 and led the National League in errors with 24, but also led the league with 15 sacrifice hits, and in the field he showed good range and quickness, enough to be named to the Topps All-Rookie team.

A year later Javier continued to impress with his glove and sparked debates as to who was the fastest in the league, he or Vada Pinson. Commentators began to link him to great Cardinals second basemen Rogers Hornsby, Frank Frisch, and Red Schoendienst, all of whom won championships with the Redbirds.[5]

Javier returned to his home country during offseasons to hunt, work on his farm, and play winter ball. He got in trouble in early 1963 for participating in exhibition games not authorized by major-league teams and was fined $250 by Baseball Commissioner Ford Frick. Under their agreement with Frick, winter-league teams agreed not to sign any players from the US without their team's approval, and Latin players would play in their home countries only in regularly organized and pre-approved games.

Javier improved his batting average over 40 points to .279 in 1961, and hit .263 in both 1962 and 1963. He posted career highs in stolen bases (26) and runs scored (97) in 1962. He led the league in putouts by a second baseman two years in a row with 377 in 1963 and 360 in 1964.

In 1963, when Bill Mazeroski dropped off the All-Star roster due to an injury, Javier completed an all-Cardinals starting All-Star infield, with Bill White at first base, Dick Groat at shortstop, and Ken Boyer at third base. He also played in the 1968 All-Star Game.

Bothered by a sore back in 1964, Javier nonetheless managed to play in 155 games in the Cardinals' championship season, with 12 home runs and a career-high 65 RBIs. His batting average dropped to .241, and he once again led the league in errors with 27. A sore hip limited his World Series efforts to only the first game, in which he had no plate appearances, pinch-ran and scored a run, and played two innings in the field. Dal Maxvill played second base in place of Javier.

The injuries continued to limit Javier the next two seasons, and his offensive performance diminished to its lowest point with the Cardinals. He batted .227 in only 77 games in 1965, then .228 in 147 games in 1966. He faced losing his starting job to versatile utility fielder Jerry Buchek, who could play second, third, and short.

Javier started 1967 with some major changes. He added 10 pounds in weight, employed new wrap-around glasses, and picked up a heavier bat, going from a 31- to a 35-ounce one. During spring training bullpen coach Bob Milliken threw curve after curve to him, working to control Javier's tendency to bail out on tough right-handed pitchers. The changes paid early dividends as he opened the season with a seven-game hitting streak and a .407 average.

Manager Schoendienst noticed the obvious improvement, saying, "Hoolie's been watching the ball a lot better. I think his new glasses might be helping as much as anything. He's been taking the bad pitches he used to swing at, especially those balls outside."[6]

The good returns continued throughout the season, as Javier stayed healthy and produced one of his best offensive seasons, with a .281 average (.325 against left-handers) in 520 at-bats, and a career-high 14 homers. He finished ninth in voting for the National League Most Valuable Player award, as he helped propel the Cardinals into the postseason for the second time in four years.

In July 1967 a double play started by a little tap Javier hit back to the pitcher led to a spontaneous quip by Cardinals broadcaster Jack Buck. The 1-6-3 play went from pitcher John Boozer to shortstop Bobby Wine to first baseman Tony Taylor, but Buck reported, "That double play went from Boozer to Wine to Old Taylor."[7]

The Cardinals followed Bob Gibson's pitching to beat the Boston Red Sox in the first game of the 1967 World Series. In the second game, a 5-0 Cardinals loss, Javier broke up Jim Lonborg's no-hitter in the eighth inning with a double to the left-field corner with two outs. Lonborg went on to surrender only Javier's hit in a complete-game shutout.

After two more wins by each team, the World Series went to a Game Seven. In the sixth inning of that deciding game, Hoolie smashed a three-run home run off Lonborg and ensured Bob Gibson's third Series victory and St. Louis's second championship in four years. Javier's renewal from the beginning of the season carried through to the end, as he compiled a .360 batting average in the Series.

Javier returned to his native Dominican Republic a national hero. President Joaquín Balaguer conferred on him the Order of the Fathers of the Country, the country's highest decoration.[8] The Pittsburgh Pirates played an exhibition game against Dominican stars in Santa Domingo about a week after the Series ended, with natives Matty Alou and Manny Mota and Puerto Rico native Roberto Clemente, but the biggest welcome of the day went to the Cardinals' second sacker.[9]

The Cardinals won the pennant again in 1968 but Javier's batting average dropped 21 points, to .260. He played in the All-Star Game that season. Despite his .333 batting average in the 1968 World Series, the Cardinals lost in seven games to the Detroit Tigers.

Javier's average rebounded in 1969 to a personal best of .282, and he continued as a Cardinals starter through 1970. Early in the 1971 season, Javier returned to the Dominican Republic to be with his brother, Luis, who died while he was there. His playing time lessened considerably that season, as he started only

68 games at second base, yielding a major part of the playing time to Ted Sizemore.

Javier's orientation to professional baseball in the US did not include a full understanding of his obligations to the Internal Revenue Service. In October 1970 the IRS filed tax liens against him for as much as $84,320, covering tax years of 1961 and 1963 through 1969. His annual salary came to an estimated $50,000 at the time. When he received word of the proceedings, he had already returned home to the Dominican Republic. The unresolved debt jeopardized his return to the US to play in 1971.[10] Apparently he had received no advice, or perhaps misguided information, as he had filed no tax returns for several years. He thought the withholding from his paycheck satisfied his obligations.[11] He employed a lawyer, settled the debt for considerably less than the original claim, and arrived in Florida in 1971 in time for spring training.[12]

In March, 1972, the Cardinals traded the 35-year-old Javier to the Cincinnati Reds for pitcher Tony Cloninger. He became very much a part-time player, starting only 17 games for the World Series-bound Reds, now playing mostly third base and batting only .209. Still a contributor until the end, Javier started at second base in the final regular-season game of his career, on October 1. In his last regular-season at-bat, he bunted to help set up the only run of the game in a Reds 1-0 win over the Los Angeles Dodgers.

Javier played in his fourth World Series with the Reds that season. His sacrifice bunt in his very last plate appearance contributed to a run for the Reds in Game Four, as the Reds fell to the Oakland Athletics in seven games. The Reds released him two days after the Series ended.

Without a job in the big leagues, Javier headed home to the San Francisco de Macoris, where he began to organize a professional franchise to compete in the Dominican winter league. He took a turn at managing in 1974 with the Yucatan Leones of the Mexican League, then returned home to stay with family and to help further develop baseball in his home country. To give youngsters a good start in baseball, he founded the Dominican branch of the Khoury League, later renamed the Roberto Clemente League to honor the Pirates legend.

In 1975 Javier put together a summer league of four teams that competed in his home territory. He and his son Stan teamed to form the Gigantes del Cibao, which became one of the regular contenders in the Dominican winter league. He was chosen the all-time second baseman for the Aguilas Cibaeñas, and his number (25) was retired by the Dominican Winter Baseball League.

Julián Javier built has major-league career largely around his speed and slick glove. Multiple sources rated him as the widest-ranging second baseman in the league, largely due to his great speed and quickness. His especially long fingers reminded many of a concert pianist, yet he said, "They help me in typing."[13]

Gene Mauch called Javier "the greatest I ever saw on getting pop flies and as good as anyone on coming in on a ball." His middle-infield partner, Dal Maxvill, considered him one of the best ever, especially at going to his right. "I've never seen that play made by anyone else," Maxvill said. "I'm spoiled if he doesn't make it." On slow grounders, Maxvill said, "he goes in low, doesn't straighten out and fires the ball with something on it. I've seen him throw just this far [six inches] off the ground."[14]

Javier earned another nickname, the Phantom. Orlando Cepeda pointed out his smooth moves around second base: "Hoolie comes out of nowhere like a phantom." Maxvill said, "Hoolie's like a ghost out there. Runners try to nail him, but he gets the throw off so smoothly – and then he disappears."[15]

Javier combined his speed and stick skills to become rated one of the league's best bunters. He ranked first or second in sacrifice hits three out of his first four years with the Cardinals. He also produced the rare combination of a skillful short game and a surprising ability to hit the long ball, especially in clutch situations. His three home runs hit in 1-0 games place him in a tie with many others for sixth all-time, behind Ted Williams, who had five, and four others with four.[16]

Javier often surprised with his sudden displays of oomph, like the grand slam he hit in 1961 on his 25th birthday to beat the Pirates, 4-0. In May 1964 the Cardinals rode his three-run homer to victory over the Phillies, 3-2. That day he claimed he had stuffed himself with vitamins given to him by his brother, who was a doctor. Four days later he hit a grand slam and ended the week with 12 runs batted in.[17] In July 1969 he launched a ball to the roof of Connie Mack Stadium in Philadelphia, after which he said, "I didn't eat any breakfast, and all I ate before going to the park was a small salad. If I had eaten a big salad, I would have hit the ball over the roof and out of the park."[18]

Javier's batting average fluctuated greatly from year to year, partly due to injury but also because of other factors such as pitch selection. According to batting coach Dick Sisler, the better numbers seemed to come when he refused to swing at bad pitches, especially low and outside sliders and curves from right-handed pitchers.[19]

Sisler saw a major constant in Javier's statistics: He always hit much better against left-handers than against right-handers (.299 lifetime against lefties, .233 when facing righties). In three seasons (1965, 1968, and 1970) the gap amounted to more than 150 points in batting average against left-handers. The old stalwart Branch Rickey suggested once that Javier might become a really great hitter if he learned to switch-hit, but Javier continued to hit from one side of the plate.[20]

An incident in February 1964 in the Dominican Winter League involving Javier and umpire Emmett Ashford, then a nine-year veteran of the Pacific Coast League, played a major role in vaulting Ashford through the racial barrier to become the first African American umpire in the major leagues. With Javier at bat, Ashford called two strikes on him on low outside pitches, Javier's common nemesis at the plate. He protested the calls, saying, "Why you call the pitch on me? You know I don't like that pitch."

"Why the hell do you think he's throwing it?" answered the ump.

Javier shot back: "Oh, a comedian!" Ashford told Javier to get quiet and bat. As Javier stepped back in, he took a called third strike right down the middle of the plate. He turned in protest and landed a punch on Ashford's jaw.[21] The umpire responded with a couple of his own shots, using his mask and actually drawing blood. The fans "could have strung me up on the spot," remembered Ashford. "But they were with me, and I think that's what put me over the top."[22]

Javier received an indefinite suspension at first, but the Peñalty was quickly reduced to three days and a $50 fine because of the Dominican's popularity. Ashford's first reaction led him to resign from the Dominican league for the rest of the season. He finally relented when Javier apologized on the radio. Soon afterward, American League president Joe Cronin purchased Ashford's contract, apparently convinced that he knew how to face difficult situations. The popular Ashford then made history in his American League debut on Opening Day, 1966, in Washington.

Among his seven children, Javier's son Stan, named for Cardinals great Stan Musial, played major-league baseball for 18 seasons with eight different teams. Another son,

Julián J. Javier, developed a noted medical practice as a cardiologist in Naples, Florida. A third son, Manuel Julián Javier, became an engineer in Santiago, Dominican Republic.

Estadio Julián Javier, the stadium in San Francisco de Macoris, was built as a namesake tribute to one of the pioneer Dominican major leaguers. It became both the home of the Gigantes del Cibao, the baseball team he formed, and a crown to the popularity and success of Manuel Julián "Hoolie" Javier Liranzo.

SOURCES

In addition to the sources cited in the Notes, the author also consulted Ancestry.com, Baseball-Reference.com, and Retrosheet.org.

NOTES

1. Neal Russo, "Javier Something Special with Bat as Well as Glove," *The Sporting News*. September 2, 1967.
2. Herbert Simons, "Scouting Reports on 1960 Major League Rookies," *Baseball Digest*, March 1960.
3. Jack Herman, "Cards Find Comet in Swifty Javier," *The Sporting News*, June 15, 1960.
4. Jack Herman, "Redbirds Boost Firepower with Changed Lineup," *The Sporting News*, June 8, 1960.
5. ,Neal Russo, "Swift Keystoner Rated Key Man in Redbirds Future; Cuts Down on Strikeouts," *The Sporting News*, August 23, 1961.
6. Neal Russo, "Hoolie's Hot Bat Fuels Redbird Takeoff," *The Sporting News*, May 6, 1967.
7. "Boozer-Wine-Old Taylor Knocks Cards on Ears," *The Sporting News*, July 8, 1967.
8. , "Dominican Republic Gives Hero's Welcome to Javier," *The Sporting News*, November 4, 1967.
9. Fernando Viscioso, "Pirates Defeat Native Stars Before 19,152," *The Sporting News*, November 4, 1967.
10. Neal Russo, "$84,320 U.S. Tax Liens Brought Against Javier," *The Sporting News*, October 17, 1970.
11. Neal Russo, "Javier Figures in '71 Redbird Plans," *The Sporting News*. January 30, 1971.
12. "Bunts and Boots - Javier Tax Settlement," *The Sporting News*, April 3, 1971.
13. "Baseball's Week," *Sports Illustrated*, July 8, 1963.
14. Neal Russo, "Hoolie's Hot Bat Fuels Redbird Takeoff," *The Sporting News*, May 6, 1967.
15. Neal Russo, "Redbird Phantom Striking Dread in Hearts of Enemies," *The Sporting News*, August 23, 1969.
16. Lyle Spatz, ed. *The SABR Baseball List & Record Book* (New York: Scribner, 2007).
17. "Baseball's Week," *Sports Illustrated*, May 25, 1964.
18. "Baseball's Week," *Sports Illustrated*, July 21, 1969.
19. Russo, "Redbird Phantom."
20. Bob Broeg, "All-Star Team of Switch-Hitters," *The Sporting News*, February 17, 1979.
21. A. S. "Doc" Young, "Ashford Was One Ump with Box-Office Appeal," *The Sporting News*, December 26, 1970.
22. Joe Falls, "The Ump GETS This Decision," *Baseball Digest*, July 1966.

Stan Javier

By Richard Cuicchi

Stan Javier's baseball heritage included his former major-league father and a Hall of Fame teammate of his father's. One might think that situation would propel a youngster from the Dominican Republic to relentlessly pursue a major-league career for himself. Instead, baseball was viewed by Javier as just another sport he played while growing up, and even as he entered pro baseball as a 17-year-old, he still hadn't fully set his sights on reaching the big leagues.

Yet Javier did indeed reach the major leagues and played in 17 seasons with eight different teams. He spent the better part of his career fighting for a full-time job as an outfielder. Whether he played regularly or as a role player off the bench, he routinely demonstrated his value to the team with his solid defense, speed on the bases, ability to switch-hit, and versatility to play all outfield positions. He played on six postseason teams, including the 1989 World Series champion Oakland A's.

Born Stanley Julian Antonio Javier on January 9, 1964, in San Francisco de Macoris, Dominican Republic, he was the son of Julian and Ines (Negrin) Javier. The fourth of five children, he had a brother and three sisters.[1]

Julian Javier had just finished his fourth major-league season with the St. Louis Cardinals when Stan was born. Julian was the second baseman of the 1963 National League All-Star infield that also included Bill White, Dick Groat, and Ken Boyer. Stan was named after another of his father's famous teammates, Hall of Famer Stan Musial.[2]

The elder Javier in 1960 had been the third Dominican player to reach the major leagues, following Ozzie Virgil Sr. and Felipe Alou. Stan was among the first 92 players from the Dominican Republic to reach the majors during 1956 to 1984. By the end of the 2016 season, the number of Dominican players had mushroomed to a total of 669 major-league players from the tiny country.[3]

Organized amateur sports leagues were not prevalent during Javier's time growing up in the Dominican Republic. Youngsters played a lot of street ball, although he did play in the Roberto Clemente League, which was comparable to Little League in the United States. He played baseball at La Altagracia High School, but similarly the organization of high-school team sports was sporadic.[4]

Javier recalled that he didn't get much coaching in baseball skills from his father, since baseball was just another sport he played. He said, "As a youngster I didn't know I wanted to be a baseball player. I participated in whatever sport was in season, mostly unorganized. I probably played more basketball than baseball while growing up. It was kind of by accident that I landed in baseball."[5] (Javier's interests in basketball were resurrected after his baseball playing career ended.)

A natural right-handed hitter, Javier taught himself to switch-hit, because his opponents in pickup games insisted he hit left-handed so they wouldn't lose their ball on a small playing field. It was a skill that became a critical asset during his pro career. By the time he was 15 or 16 years old, he began to show promise as he faced tougher competition. He refined his game with coaching assistance from Jose Garcia, who had previously worked with professional players. However, since there weren't any pro scouts attending his games, Javier's father, by then retired as a player, decided to take him to Florida for spring training in 1981, and arranged tryouts with several major-league clubs.[6]

After the tryouts the New York Mets, Pittsburgh Pirates, and St. Louis Cardinals wanted to ink Javier to a contract. The Javiers agreed to sign with the Cardinals because of Julian's prior relationship with the club. The Cardinals signed 17-year-old Stan as a nondrafted free agent on March 26, 1981.[7]

Javier returned to the Dominican Republic to finish out his high-school year and then reported to Cardinals affiliate Johnson City in the Appalachian League. He wore uniform number 6, Stan Musial's number.[8] His two years with Johnson City were marked by .400-plus on-base percentages and few errors in the field. He was named to the league's postseason all-star team in 1982. Javier said of his time in the Cardinals system, "Coaches George Kissell and Johnny Lewis helped me tremendously during those first years. I had a good attitude, and I hit it off well with those guys."[9]

Despite his early success, Javier said, he was not yet thinking about playing in the major leagues. "When I was playing in the rookie league, I thought I was in a good place at the time. I was having fun playing ball. I wasn't worried about my future. As a kid, I had not talked with my dad about a baseball career, so there was no pressure from him to reach the majors."[10]

On December 14, 1982, Javier was traded by the Cardinals with Bobby Meacham to the New York Yankees for three minor-league pitchers. One story had it that the Yankees owed the Cardinals for giving up Willie McGee in a deal the year before. However, Cardinals GM Joe McDonald said the trade had nothing to do with the McGee trade.[11] On the other hand, *The Sporting News* in 1985 reported that the Javier-Meacham trade to the Yankees was indeed related to the McGee deal in 1981, as a condition for George Steinbrenner to back Cardinals owner August Busch's quest to fire Commissioner Bowie Kuhn.[12]

Javier spent the entire 1983 season with Greensboro of the Class-A South Atlantic League, where he began to acquire a label as a top organizational prospect by hitting .311, with 12 home runs, 77 RBIs, and 33 stolen bases. Greensboro manager Carlos Tosca was a big influence in his improvement in hitting. Javier was rewarded by being placed on the Yankees' 40-man roster for 1984.[13]

Along with Brian Dayett and Otis Nixon, Javier was considered among the best outfield prospects by the Yankees.[14] He broke spring-training camp with the Yankees in 1984 because outfielder Steve Kemp was injured. Javier wound up staying with the Yankees for the month of April because of injuries to Dave Winfield and Ken Griffey Sr. Of that brief stint with the Yankees, Javier recalled, "I was waiting to be sent down to the minors, but the Yankees kept me around to play defense when other players got hurt. At

Photo courtesy of the National Baseball Hall of Fame

one point, I requested to be sent to the minors so I could play every day. My teammate Lou Piniella said I was probably the only player to ever request a demotion."[15]

Javier made his major-league debut as a 20-year-old on April 15, 1984, against the Chicago White Sox when he replaced Dave Winfield in right field and went hitless in one at-bat. He played in seven games for the Yankees in April and spent the balance of the season between Double-A Nashville and Triple-A Columbus.

After the 1984 season, the Yankees reluctantly bundled Javier with several other prospects (Tim Birtsas, Jose Rijo, Eric Plunk) and Jay Howell in a trade with Oakland for Rickey Henderson, Bert Bradley, and cash. The deal was prompted by the A's lack of confidence that they could retain Henderson after the 1985 season. Their director of baseball administration, Walt Jocketty, insisted that Rijo and Javier be part of the deal and remained steadfast on this condition during negotiations.[16]

An analysis of the biggest deals in major-league history, in terms of the greatest swap of future major-league talent, ranked this trade among the top four when using the Win Shares metric. The trade was cited for being the model for deals involving prospects for superstars entering free agency.[17]

After being among the league leaders in stolen bases, walks, and runs scored with Double-A Huntsville in 1985, Javier played parts of the 1986 and 1987 seasons on the A's major-league roster. However, he hit poorly (.202 and .185) during both campaigns.

The A's decided not to retain center fielder Dwayne Murphy in 1988, instead using Javier and Luis Polonia in a platooning role. In his first full major-league season, Javier played in 125 games and batted .257, with 2 home runs and 33 RBIs. In his first 40 games, Javier had already achieved career highs in hits (43) and RBIs (18).[18] He was caught stealing only once in 21 attempts during the season, one of the highest percentages (95.2%) in a season for players with at least 20 stolen bases.[19]

With a team that included Mark McGwire, Jose Canseco, Don Baylor, Carney Lansford, Dave Henderson, and Walt Weiss, the A's swept the Boston Red Sox in the American League Championship Series, but then lost to the Los Angeles Dodgers in five games in the World Series. Javier batted .500 in the postseason, collecting three RBIs. He became the seventh second-generation player to play in a World Series.[20]

Oakland repeated as American League champion in 1989. Rickey Henderson was reacquired in June, but then Canseco went on the disabled list for a good part of the season, again allowing Javier more playing time. On August 5 in Seattle, he played his first game at second base, his father's old position, fielding three grounders and helping to turn a double play. Javier batted .248 in 112 games.

The A's swept the San Francisco Giants in the World Series, marked by the Bay Area earthquake, which interrupted the Series for 10 days between Games Two and Three. When many of the A's players were sending their families back home when the Series was suspended, Javier kept his family and relatives in the area. He said, "They're going back to Candlestick. They said they were coming here to see the World Series and they're going to see it."[21] Javier made just one Series appearance, as a Game Three defensive replacement for Jose Canseco.

Javier avoided arbitration with the A's in January 1990 by signing a one-year contract for $310,000, but on May 13 he was traded to the Dodgers for Willie Randolph. The A's outfield had become crowded, with Felix Jose replacing Javier as the platoon player for regulars Dave Henderson, Rickey Henderson, and Jose Canseco. Javier welcomed the trade at the time, saying, "It was fun playing for the A's in some points, I had fun winning a lot; but I wasn't playing much, so it was good to leave. I consider myself an everyday player. I couldn't get that chance in Oakland."[22]

With the Dodgers, Javier played with the confidence he gained while in Oakland. In his first six weeks, he was the team's hottest hitter, with a 12-game hitting streak in June. He finished the season with a .304 batting average in 104 games. He frequently filled in at center field for Kirk Gibson, who was dealing with leg problems after missing the first months of the season. The Dodgers finished second in the West Division.

Over the winter, the Dodgers added outfielders Darryl Strawberry and Brett Butler, who were slated for starting roles. Wanting to find a way to get into the starting lineup, Javier figured he could vie for a spot at third base, even though he had never played there.

Jeff Hamilton had been the Dodgers' third baseman in 1988-89, and surgery in 1990 kept him out most of the season. Javier prepared himself for the new position by taking groundballs during the winter in the Dominican Republic. When Dodgers manager Tommy Lasorda was asked about the prospect of Javier playing third base, he said, "Why not? He learns well. He wants to play. Let's see what happens." Lasorda acknowledged that Javier had been his best outfielder in 1990.[23]

Javier wound up playing mainly as the fourth outfielder in 121 games in 1991; his batting average dropped nearly 100 points, as he was troubled with a sore wrist for most of the season. Javier took his demotion in stride saying, "I know my job. I know I'm the fourth outfielder. I don't like it, but I'll make the best out of it and help out where I can."[24] At one point during the season, he was 0-for-24 in his pinch-hitting appearances. Javier had wrist surgery two days after the season ended.

Javier started the 1992 season with the Dodgers but shoulder and elbow injuries kept his playing time down. He managed only five starts during the Dodgers' first 73 games. Javier recalled about the season, "My aggressive style of play caused me to miss games. The Dodgers knew I could hit, but they ultimately felt I couldn't be counted on to be healthy."[25] Consequently, the Dodgers traded Javier to the Philadelphia Phillies on July 2. Javier moved into a starting role with the Phillies, seeing action in 74 games while batting .261 and stealing 17 bases. After the season he became a free agent, and signed with the California Angels for 1993, during which he batted .291 in 92 games. A free agent again after the season, Javier returned to the A's. With Dave Henderson now gone from the team, Javier was a starter for the A's in the strike-shortened 1994 season. He hit safely in his first 17 games. After hitting only 13 homers in his eight previous major-league seasons, he showed an unlikely power display when he hit 10 home runs while batting .272 and stealing 24 bases – his best season to that point.

Javier re-signed with the A's for the 1995 season and put together his second consecutive solid year as a starter. He batted .278 with 8 home runs and led the A's with 36 stolen bases. From May 31 to October 1, he had 28 consecutive steals, an A's record until Coco Crisp stole 36 straight in 2012.[26] He broke the American League record for most chances (334) without an error by an outfielder, previously held by Brian Downing (330) in 1982.[27]

When put in a regular outfield job, Javier was showing major-league front offices he was a valuable player to have around because of his versatility, his reliable glove, and his speed. His ability to switch-hit and bat in the leadoff position were additional pluses.

After the San Francisco Giants chose not to re-sign Deion Sanders following the 1995 season, Javier signed a two-year contract, turning down an offer from the Texas Rangers. He began 1996 as the Giants' regular center fielder, but a hamstring injury ended his season in mid-July.

The 1997 season brought new challenges for Javier when the Giants acquired Darryl Hamilton to play center field. Javier won out in a competition with outfielders Darrin Jackson and Marvin Benard for the fourth outfielder spot. When Hamilton missed games early in the season because of thumb and hamstring injuries, Javier ably filled in. Giants manager Dusty Baker later decided to platoon Javier in right field with Glenallen Hill, who had suffered lapses in hitting and defense.[28]

Never known for his propensity to hit home runs, Javier hit the first home run in the major leagues' first interleague game, on June 12, 1997.[29] In the top of the third inning, he hit his round-tripper off Texas Rangers pitcher Darren Oliver. It was only the 34th home run of his career. Throughout the season Javier batted in practically every position in the batting order and was frequently inserted for defensive purposes when he wasn't starting. Altogether, he appeared in 142 games and batted .286. The Giants finished first in the National League West Division, but lost to eventual World Series champion Florida Marlins in the Division Series.

The Giants liked Javier for his versatility and re-signed him as a free agent after the 1997 season. He started 1998 as their regular right fielder. With the Giants later acquiring veteran outfielders Joe Carter and Ellis Burks at the trade deadline and Benard's offensive breakout that season, Javier's opportunities for outfield starts during the last two months diminished. In any case, Javier got into 135 games and batted .290.

Javier was put on the trading block after the season, with the Giants using him as trade bait to acquire a pitcher. However, teams were unwilling to pick up his $1.7 million salary.[30] He started the 1999 season platooning with Benard in center field, but then emerged as the Giants' regular left fielder when Barry Bonds went on the disabled list for 10 weeks with an injured elbow. On August 31 Javier was finally dealt to the Houston Astros, who needed a short-term outfielder rental to help win their division.

The deal paid off for the Astros. Javier batted .328 in the final month, and Houston finished first in the NL Central Division. Javier started three of the four games in the Division Series, as the Astros lost to the Atlanta Braves. Javier said of his experience with the Astros, "I was a veteran bringing experience to the team. I had been hitting well with the Giants, and I carried over that momentum to the Astros. The Giants no longer had a need for me, so I understood the trade. The Astros played hard, and I liked playing for them. They liked that I could run, play defense, and get good at-bats. The "Killer B's" (Jeff Bagwell and Craig Biggio) were fun to play with."[31]

Over the winter Javier signed with the Seattle Mariners, his eighth major-league team. He was one of six free agents acquired by GM Pat Gillick that altered the makeup of their lineup and contributed to their being in contention most of the 2000 season.[32] Javier was one of seven Mariners outfielders whom manager Lou Piniella mixed and matched against opposing pitchers. By this time in his career, Javier had lost a few steps, but was still a consistent switch-hitter and played solid defense in all three outfield positions. He played in 105 games as the Mariners finished second in the West Division. They defeated the Chicago White Sox in the Division Series, but lost to the New York Yankees in the Championship Series. For the season, Javier batted .275, but he was ineffective in the postseason.

The Mariners picked up the option year of Javier's contract for 2001. A pinched tendon in his left knee limited his play, although he wound up hitting .292 in 89 games. The Mariners won 116 games to win the West Division. They defeated the Cleveland Indians in the Division Series before losing to the Yankees again in the Championship Series. In his sixth year on a postseason team, Javier contributed a home run in the ALCS.

During the offseason, Javier, then 37 years old, was faced with a difficult career decision: When is it time to get out of the game? He ultimately decided to retire. Of his rationale, he said, "[Mariners manager] Piniella liked the type of player I was. I liked being treated like a veteran. We were having fun, selling out the stadium every day. Safeco was a big stadium and I took advantage of it as a gap hitter and situational hitter; so it was perfect for me. However, it was becoming harder for me to be 100 percent every day. When I was hurt, I was miserable. I respected the game and when I felt like I couldn't be 100 percent, I felt it was time to leave. Plus, my children were getting older, and they had become an increasing priority for me. I could have signed for another year and been a 'lazy' player, but that was not the type of player or person I was."[33]

During his 17 major-league seasons, Javier batted .269 with 1,358 hits, 57 home runs, 503 RBIs, and 246 stolen bases. He is among the leaders in highest career stolen-base percentage (82.8 percent, minimum of 100 steals).[34]

Javier remained active in professional sport endeavors after his playing career. He was the general manager of the Dominican Republic team for the 2006 and 2009 World Baseball Classic tournaments and owned the Gigantes del Cibao baseball team in the Dominican Winter League. He was a special assistant with the Major League Baseball Players Association. As of 2018 he was vice president of the Toros del Este in the Dominican Winter League.[35]

Reverting to his passion for basketball as a youngster in the Dominican Republic, Javier founded Liga Nacional de Baloncesto (Dominican National Basketball League) and as of 2018 owned its team Indios de San Francisco de Macoris.[36]

Javier and his wife, Genoveva, have three children, Karla, Marcel, and Ines Marie.[37]

Javier wound up having a substantial major-league career like his father. Yet there was hardly a season that he didn't go into spring training battling multiple players for an outfield spot, sometimes even as a backup. He never put up big offensive numbers that made him a cinch for a starting role on any of his teams. Nevertheless he became a valuable member of some very good teams by making the most of his opportunities to get into the lineup due to his style of play.

SOURCES

In addition to the sources cited in the Notes, the author also consulted media and information guides of several major-league teams, and

Gardiner White, Sarah. *Like Father, Like Son: Baseball's Major League Families* (New York: Scholastic, Inc., 1993), 61-71.

Geisler, Paul Jr. SABR BioProject: Julian Javier, sabr.org/bioproj/person/b8bf06ec, accessed March 20, 2017.

Nothington, Tom. "Stan Javier Is Making People Believe Baseball Is His Game," *Yankees Magazine*, August 4, 1983: 29.

Pietrusza, David, Matthew Silverman, and Michael Gershman, eds. *Baseball: The Biographical Encyclopedia* (New York: Total Sports Illustrated, 2000), 554.

Spatz, Lyle. *Yankees Coming, Yankees Going: New York Yankee Player Transactions, 1903 Through 1999* (Jefferson, North Carolina: McFarland & Company, Inc., 2000), 233-234.

NOTES

1 Stan Javier, telephone interview with the author, February 13-14, 2017.

2 "Cards Sign Young Javier," *The Sporting News*, April 11, 1981: 46.

3 Baseball-Reference.com.

4 Javier interview.

5 Javier interview.

6 Javier interview.

7 Javier interview. Numerous publications have reported that Javier was 16 years old when he signed his first contract with the St. Louis Cardinals in 1981. Javier said he believes this mistake is likely attributed to his birthday being inadvertently transposed from January 9 to September 1, since the typical Dominican Republic format for dates at that time was dd/mm/yy.

8 "Another Stan the Man?" *The Sporting News*, August 16, 1982: 43.

9 Javier interview.

10 Javier interview.

11 Rick Hummel, "Cards Preparing for Arbitration," *The Sporting News*, January 24, 1983: 40.

12 Dave Nightingale, "Yankees Got More for McGee Via 'Trade,'" *The Sporting News*, December 2, 1985: 57.

13 " '84 Looks to be Exciting," *Yankees Magazine*, January 26, 1984: 19.

14 Moss Klein, "A.L. East Notebook," *The Sporting News*, February 6, 1984: 42.

15 Javier interview.

16 Moss Klein, "Risky Business Has A's Prospering," *The Sporting News*, June 9, 1986: 20.

17 Dave Studeman, "The Biggest Deals of All Time," *Hardball Times*, March 30, 2005, hardballtimes.com/the-biggest-deals-of-all-time/, accessed March 20, 2017.

18 "A.L. West Notebook," *The Sporting News*, June 20, 1988: 43.

19 Lyle Spatz, ed., *The SABR Baseball List & Record Book* (New York: Society for American Baseball Research, 2007), 336.

20 Stan Isle, "Pitching Coach No Longer a Yankee Barometer," The Sporting News, November 7, 1988: 7.

21 "A.L. West: Athletics," *The Sporting News*," November 6, 1989: 64.

22 Bill Plaschke, "For Dodgers, Rainout Beats Another Loss," *Los Angeles Times*, May 14, 1990: C1, C15.

23 "Javier to Pursue Third-Base Job," *The Sporting News*, February 4, 1991: 39.

24 "Baseball: N.L. West," *The Sporting News*, July 1, 1991: 17.

25 Javier interview.

26 "Crisp's Club Record Steals Streak Ends at 36," June 21, 2012, m.mlb.com/news/article/33705134//, accessed March 20, 2017.

27 Pedro Gomez, "A.L. West," *The Sporting News*, October 9, 1995: 50.

28 Henry Schulman, "N.L. West," *The Sporting News*, June 9, 1997: 43.

29 "Interleague History," mlb.mlb.com/mlb/history/interleague/, accessed March 20, 2017.

30 "American League: Toronto," *The Sporting News*, March, 22, 1999: 35.

31 Javier interview.

32 "Baseball: Seattle," *The Sporting News*, October 9, 2000: 20.

33 Javier interview.

34 Spatz, 335.

35 Javier interview.

36 Javier interview.

37 Javier interview.

JOSÉ LIMA

By Rory Costello

Flamboyance, like flakiness, is in short supply in 21st-century major league baseball. José Lima, the Dominican who pitched for five teams in the majors from 1994 to 2006, was one of the last distinct "characters." Zany and irrepressible, extreme and exasperating, Lima was a born showman who loved being the center of attention. He was a recording artist who wrote songs and performed with his own bands; he once sang the national anthem before a game at Dodger Stadium. He happily mingled with fans, especially children. He even posted to Dominican Internet baseball forums.[1]

Lima's big-league record was marked by surprising peaks; the righty won 21 games in 1999 and came back in 2003-04 after many thought he was washed up. There were also deep chasms, as his overall record was 89-102 with a 5.26 ERA. Yet his love for the game led him to keep going in Mexico, Korea and independent leagues as late as 2009. The next year, he died of a heart attack at the untimely age of 37. His memory lives on in his exuberant rally cry: "It's Lima Time!"

José Desiderio Rodríguez Lima was born on September 30, 1972. U.S. baseball references give his birthplace as Santiago (Santiago de los Caballeros, in full), the second-largest city in the Dominican Republic. This appears to be imprecise, for Santiago is also the name of a province in the Cibao region. Various Dominican sources, including a feature from October 2010, have shown his exact birthplace as Salaya, part of Sabana Iglesia, a municipal area in Santiago province.[2]

Additional information on Lima's family background comes courtesy of a 1999 feature in *Sports Illustrated* by Kostya Kennedy. "The oldest of seven children, he grew up in a three-room house on a fertile plot of land outside the city of Santiago. His father, Francisco Rodríguez, was a catcher for 12 years on a touring Dominican amateur team and supported his wife, Nurys Lima, and his seven children by working for the local lottery system and running out roosters for cockfights."[3] Like the Alou brothers, the most prominent Dominican example, Lima became known in the U.S. by the maternal half of his double Spanish surname. The same is true of his younger brother Joel (born 1989), also a pitcher, who turned pro in the Dodgers system in 2008.

Kennedy continued, "The Limas [sic] never lacked for food – they kept farm animals and cultivated mangoes and plantains – but José began supplementing his family's income at age 11 by singing in nightclubs. At 13 he entered a competition at a festival and sang before a gathering of thousands. He belted out a song from the Villa-Lobos operetta *Magdalena*, outperforming nine other vocalists to win. His success prompted José to attend music classes. He became so intent on a singing career that he might never have played baseball beyond the sandlots."[4] During his playing days, he had groups called Banda Mambo – "Mambo" was one of his nicknames – and *La Fuga* (The Escape). He cut at least four albums.[5]

"When he turned 15, however, Francisco asked him to give ball playing a serious effort, and José joined a team in the Dominican youth league. He pitched (going 9-0), played centerfield and was named his league's MVP."[6] On July 5, 1989, Ramón Peña of the Detroit Tigers signed 16-year-old Lima out of Las Charcas High School for a mere $2,000.[7]

Lima's statistics in his first five years of minor-league ball (1990-94) were not eye-catching. He never had a winning record – in fact, he was 24-45 with a 4.03 ERA overall. Yet he showed a live arm, striking out nearly eight batters for every nine innings pitched. His minor-league baseball cards, which show a skinny teen (6'2" and 170 pounds), mention that he already relied on a circle change-up too.

Lima moved up the ladder steadily, making it to the majors for the first time early in the 1994 season. He got into three games in April and May. That August, while the majors were on strike, he threw a no-hitter for the Triple-A Toledo Mud Hens. He struck out 13 Pawtucket Red Sox while walking just one in front of Tigers manager Sparky Anderson and GM Joe Klein.[8]

Lima was up and down between Detroit and the minors in 1995 and 1996. He got 15 starts in 1995 but served mainly as a reliever in '96, starting just four times in 39 games.

Photo courtesy of the Kansas City Royals

His overall record was not impressive: 8-15 with a 5.90 ERA. In December 1996, the Tigers sent him to the Houston Astros as part of a nine-player trade.

The Astros continued to use Lima out of the bullpen in 1997, and again the results were weak (1-6, 5.28 in 52 games). He pitched one inning in relief as the Atlanta Braves swept Houston in the NL Division Series. In 1998, however, he suddenly blossomed after joining the rotation. The Astros were dealing with injuries to other starters, and Lima virtually demanded of manager Larry Dierker and pitching coach Vern Ruhle that they use him.[9] He started strongly and didn't look back, going 16-8 in 33 starts, and his 3.70 ERA was below the league average. Sharp control – just 32 walks in 233⅓ innings – was a big part of his success. He was not in the playoff rotation, though, because the Astros had acquired Randy Johnson at the end of July.

The 1999 season was by far Lima's best. He was 21-10 with a 3.58 ERA; he finished second in the National League in wins behind teammate Mike Hampton and third in the majors behind countryman Pedro Martínez. Again his location was outstanding, with 44 walks in 246⅓ innings. He was named to the All-Star Game for the only time in his career, pitching one scoreless inning, and came in fourth in the Cy Young Award voting. Looking back at the trade after he was named to an All-Star team for the only time in his career, he was thankful. "Detroit saved my life," Lima remarked, eyes flashing. "I came from hell to heaven. I'm on a winning ballclub."[10]

Kostya Kennedy described Lima vividly that June. "He takes the field with stirrups that extend to the top of his calves and begins a game-long dance that evolves pitch by pitch. He flaps his elbows, squeezes his fist, points, shrugs, grimaces, nods, jumps, kicks and writhes. He swivels his torso after one pitch and gyrates his hips after the next. After a big strikeout he busts a move that would make John Travolta proud, mock-shooting his victim with his forefinger and thumb."[11] Opponents often didn't take kindly to Lima's histrionics, but those who joined him as teammates saw what was in his heart.

Houston won the National League's Central Division for the third straight year, but Lima lost his only start as Atlanta again defeated the Astros in the first round of the playoffs. Nonetheless, in January 2000, Lima signed a three-year contract for $18.75 million. To put it mildly, owner Drayton McLane and the team didn't get their money's worth. The Astros moved from the pitcher-friendly Astrodome to Enron Field (as it was originally known before the massive corporate fraud was revealed in late 2001). Lima had a year that can only be described as dreadful: 7-16, 6.65 ERA, and a league-leading 48 home runs allowed in 196⅓ innings. The *Hamilton* (Ontario) *Spectator* summed it up neatly, "Lima is a flyball pitcher who is being killed by Enron's 315-foot left-field wall that draws baseballs like a neon light at night draws bugs."[12]

Things were pretty much the same over the 2001 and 2002 seasons. In aggregate, Lima was 10-18, 6.19, giving up 47 homers in 234 innings. In June 2001, Houston traded him back to Detroit for Dave Mlicki. The Tigers didn't even keep him around for the full year in 2002, releasing him in early September.

Lima went to indie ball for the first time in 2003, and he did a fine job for the Newark Bears, going 6-1, 2.33 in eight starts. In his tribute to Lima, Joe Posnanski of *Sports Illustrated* wrote, "The Royals' grand old scout Art Stewart had heard through his inexhaustible grapevine that Lima was throwing a decent fastball." This was important because there had come to be little difference between his fastball and change-up.[13]

In early June, Kansas City bought his contract, and because they were desperate for pitching, they sent him into action straight away. After a no-decision, he won seven straight starts before a groin injury threw him off stride; he finished with marks of 8-3, 4.91 in 14 starts. "He danced and sang and said the craziest things," Posnanski added. "His teammates absolutely loved him and were entirely annoyed by him in equal measure. Reporters hovered around him because he was always good for something."[14]

After Lima died, Joe Torre, who saw him as Yankees manager, said, "He was a showman, a hot dog. But he'd win games; and I think a lot of times, it wasn't his ability but his ability to will himself to do it. In talking himself into it, I think he sort of intimidated some of the opposition too."[15]

The Royals wanted Lima back, and he wanted to stay, but they couldn't come to terms. "Bob Dutton of the *Kansas City Star* report[ed] that Lima thinks he is entitled to more than the $500,000 plus incentives the team is offering him and he may look elsewhere for employment."[16] Other teams weren't exactly lining up; he signed a minor-league contract in late January 2004 with the Los Angeles Dodgers. The nonroster invitee did quite well with L.A. that year: 13-5, 4.07 in 36 games (24 starts). But as Jon SooHoo of ESPN wrote, "Lima only found his way onto the Dodger roster the way fringe players often do, thanks in part to the misfortune of others. If Paul Shuey hadn't ruptured a tendon in his thumb at the end of March 2004, Dodger fans might never have heard of 'Lima Time.'"[17]

SooHoo added, "It was almost as much of a miracle that Lima stayed on the roster. His ERA on May 9, after nine appearances, was 7.91. But then Lima began having those 'Lima Time' moments. And although bad outings would crop up here and there, he became something of an unlikely hero."[18] Before the turnaround, he also made the papers by singing "The Star-Spangled Banner" ahead of a start against the Chicago Cubs on May 13. The *Los Angeles Times* and *La Opinión*, the city's leading Spanish-language newspaper, both showed a photo of him at the mike, accompanied by his 5-year-old son José Jr. and remarkably buxom blonde wife Melissa.[19]

Lima's finest hour in the majors came on October 9, 2004. The Dodgers trailed the St. Louis Cardinals in the NL Division Series, two games to none, and manager Jim Tracy turned to Lima in Game Three. He responded with a five-hit shutout, allowing just one walk while striking out four. Alex Cora, who played second behind Lima at Dodger Stadium that evening, said, "I still remember 50,000 people going 'Lima, Lima' in the ninth inning."[20]

The Cardinals knocked the Dodgers out the next day on their way to the World Series, but that was still the club's first postseason win since they knocked off Oakland to win it all in 1988. Lima had only one other shutout in the majors; it came in 1998 with Houston.

Near the end of October, Lima became a free agent again. Jon SooHoo wrote, "Not surprisingly, the popular feeling in town was that the Dodgers had to bring Lima back – how could they not? But ... it was almost inevitable that Lima would not return. Based on the rules that existed at the time, the Dodgers were actually operating at a disadvantage compared with the other 29 teams in baseball in that they had to offer him salary arbitration or forfeit the right to negotiate with him on the open market. Essentially, the system at the time required the Dodgers pay Lima more than any other team had to. And given that Lima's performance was so fluky, it just didn't make sense for them to do so."[21]

On Christmas Day 2004, he returned to the Royals on a one-year contract. Kansas City GM Allard Baird said, "He's a proven guy that can give you innings and wants the ball in big situations, so we're glad to have him."[22] Lima was the Opening Day starter for K.C. in 2005, and he couldn't wait for the career-first opportunity. As Bob Dutton wrote, "Spend any time around José Lima, and it quickly becomes apparent he is never at a loss for words. Anytime, anywhere, any subject. Without even asking, he is always ready with an answer, a comment or, on occasion, just noise. These words, delivered from the heart and off the cuff, are seldom slowed by the hesitation required for reflection."[23]

Unfortunately, the $2.5 million investment was disastrous once again. Granted, Kansas City finished with a 56-106 record that year, but Lima's winning percentage (5-16, .238) was well below the club's. He didn't win his first game until June 15 and gave up 31 homers in 168⅔ innings, which led to a 6.99 ERA. Yet, as ever, he was optimistic. In late September, Bob Dutton noted, "Even now, as he approaches his final start in a miserable season, Royals veteran José Lima still envisions the best of times."[24]

It was little surprise that the Royals did not renew Lima's contract. But another organization was still willing to give him a chance: the New York Mets, who signed him to a minor-league deal in February 2006. Arriving at spring training, "he wore a silver three-piece suit, a black fedora and large diamond earrings. He happily posed for photographers and he was hardly about to dwell on his less than stellar statistics of the previous season. He had another number in mind, announcing that he owned more than 2,000 suits. 'I've never worn the same one twice,' he said. 'I give the old ones to my brothers. They wear the same size that I do.'"[25]

Lima's record in his first six starts at Triple-A Norfolk was unremarkable (3-2, 5.10), but New York called him up in May after Brian Bannister and John Maine got hurt.[26] Manager Willie Randolph said of Lima – sporting bleached-blond hair, which he also braided into cornrows—"He'll help us as needed. Lima's been in the league. You hope he'll come in, locate his pitches, and work a little Lima magic."[27]

The hope was misplaced. He got three consecutive starts – all remarkably similar, all losses. Nonetheless, "he still carried his trademark enthusiasm and energy to the ballpark every day."[28] After accepting a reassignment to Norfolk, Lima got one last chance on July 7, at Shea Stadium against the Florida Marlins. He gave up just one run through three innings, but during the fourth the roof caved in. Even after opposing pitcher Dontrelle Willis smacked a grand-slam homer, Randolph kept Lima in, but the hook came after one more base hit.

After finishing the season in Norfolk (7-8, 3.92), Lima Time came to Mexico. He had a nice year with the Saltillo Saraperos in 2007, leading the staff with a 13-4, 3.60 record in 22 starts and representing the Northern division in the Mexican All-Star Game.[29] Even after he faded from the major-league scene, Lima and his doings were still visible in the Dominican press.

He then went to the Korea Baseball Organization in 2008, pitching for the Kia Tigers.[30] "Lima played as a Tiger for seven months from the beginning of the 2008 season, before being ousted in the middle of the season for underperforming. He was 3-6 with a 4.89 ERA in his 14 appearances."[31] He returned to the Atlantic League, going 5-5, 4.98 in 11 starts for the Camden Riversharks.

Lima spent his final pro summer in the Golden Baseball League in 2009, posting totals of 6-7, 3.95 in 16 starts, first for the Long Beach Armada and then the Edmonton Capitals. He never lost hope of making it back to The Show. "We're all here for the same thing," he told the *Los Angeles Times* while pitching for Long Beach (one teammate was another pitcher who died too soon, Hideki Irabu). "If you work hard and stay focused, no reason you can't get picked up by some major league team. I'm not giving up, man. Trust me, I'll be back. It'll be Lima Time again."[32]

Lima's last professional action came in Dominican winter ball. He played off and on there for 14 seasons, starting in 1991-92 with his local team, Águilas Cibaeñas. He spent several winters with the Escogido Leones before coming back to the Águilas in 2004. Overall, he posted a record of 32-26, 3.12 in the Dominican League. Although he was just 1-4 with a 6.39 ERA in the winter of 2009-10, he still planned to play again, even though he did not sign with any club for the summer of 2010.[33]

Lima's personal life was complicated. By one 2012 account, he had at least six children by six different women.[34] Dominican sources say that he had two official marriages. His first wife was named Betzabel Osirys Knotts; they were married on October 15, 1994 and divorced on October 6, 1997. The second was Melissa (maiden name Langholz), though unconfirmed reports also describe her as a common-law wife. She was the mother of his son José Jr.; after Lima died, she got married to Roberto Clemente, Jr.

From his relationship with Dominican model Dalla Leclerc, Lima had a daughter named Kammiell. Names are available – though not specifics about mothers – for two other children, Elijah José and Brianna. For roughly a year before he died, Lima was in a relationship with Dorca Astacio, though they were apparently not married.[35] It's also of some note that in the early 1990s, Dorca, whose maiden name was García Thomas, was married to another Dominican big-leaguer, pitcher Pedro Astacio.[36]

Lima's relationships tended to overlap, going off and on while he played the field. In 2004, he had to pay $475,000 to a woman who filed a lawsuit against him because of unhappy consequences from their 2003 encounter.[37]

Lima and Dorca made their home in Pasadena, California. He continued to enjoy going to Dodger Stadium; during the month of May 2010 alone, he went several times. On Friday, May 21, he "sat in the front row of the field level behind home plate and received a loud ovation when he was introduced between innings."[38]

Lima went out dancing on Saturday night, but the following morning, he took ill. Dorca told ESPN's Spanish-language site, ESPNdeportes.com, "José was complaining while sleeping and I just thought he was having a nightmare. . . I called the paramedics, but they couldn't help him. It was a massive attack." She added, "He was a man full of life, without apparent physical problems and with many plans and projects on his agenda."[39]

Luchy Guerra, longtime coordinator of Latin American affairs for the Dodgers, was the first person Dorca contacted. He said, "When I arrived at the house, I couldn't believe that it was possibly true. I didn't believe it until I saw him lifeless. We had dinner Saturday night and all he could talk about was his new baseball academy for kids and what he could do with it."[40] In addition to the planned academy in the L.A. area, he had one in mind for Dominican children in the town of Jinamagao. He was also thinking about getting into broadcasting.[41]

Lima's body was brought first to New York City, where a wake was held in the Corona section of Queens that drew such Latino big-leaguers as David Ortiz, Robinson Canó, and Tony Peña.[42] The following day in the Dominican Republic, thousands of fans attended his funeral in Estadio Cibao, home of the Águilas.[43] He was buried in the cemetery in Salaya/Las Charcas.[44]

In September, the Los Angeles Department of Coroners released the autopsy report, which did not state conclusively that heart failure was the cause of death – "likely" was the word used – but noted some risk factors for fatal cardiac arrhythmia. The report also revealed no trace of illegal substances in his system. "Now José will be able to rest in peace," Dorca told ESPNdeportes.com. "Those of us who loved José have not only suffered his death, but also the quick judgments lashed out by many people about the supposed reasons for his death."[45]

A myriad of articles attest to José Lima's gregarious nature, infectious energy, high spirits, and funny antics. It's impossible to capture them all here, so two last simple quotes will suffice. Catcher Brad Ausmus, who handled Lima with the Tigers and Astros, said, "You come to realize that the energy you see on the mound isn't a false persona, that's José Lima."[46] The other came from Josh Rawitch, a public relations man for the Dodgers: "I don't know if Lima had any regrets but of this much I'm certain – he lived every day of his 37-plus years to the fullest. In fact, I'd venture to guess that he put 100 years of life into his 37 years on Earth."[47]

SOURCES

In addition to the sources cited in the Notes, the author also consulted Baseball-Reference.com, Retrosheet.org, and www.checkoutmycards.com.

OTHER REMEMBRANCES OF JOSÉ LIMA NOT USED IN THIS BIOGRAPHY

Borelli, Steven. "To many, 'Lima time' meant approachable, outrageous and fun." *USA Today*, May 24, 2010 (http://content.usatoday.com/communities/dailypitch/post/2010/05/to-many-lima-time-meant-approachable-outrageous-and-fun/1)

Brown, Tim. "Lima's legacy lives on." Yahoo! Sports, May 23, 2010 (http://sports.yahoo.com/mlb/news?slug=ti-lima052310)

Drellich, Evan. "Dodgers recall Lima's infectious personality." MLB.com, May 23, 2010 (http://mlb.mlb.com/news/article.jsp?ymd=20100523&content_id=10373838&vkey=news_la&fext=.jsp&c_id=la&partnerId=rss_la)

Jackson, Tony. "Lima 'loved being a Dodger.'" ESPNLosAngeles.com, May 23, 2010 (http://sports.espn.go.com/los-angeles/mlb/news/story?id=5212721)

Justice, Richard. "Lima holds special place in hearts of Astros fans." *Houston Chronicle*, May 24, 2010 (http://www.chron.com/sports/justice/article/Justice-Lima-holds-special-place-in-hearts-of-1695838.php)

Mellinger, Sam. "Lima's time was filled with joy." *Kansas City Star*, May 23, 2010. (No longer available online)

NOTES

1 As observed by Rory Costello in November 2005 while researching Midre Cummings, who also played for Águilas Cibaeñas in the Dominican League during the 2005-06 season. Lima's post is not presently visible, but the memorable part was that he wrote, "¡Sí, soy yo, Lima!" ("Yes, it's me, Lima!")

2 "Recordando a José Lima," De La Zona Oriental.net, October 23, 2010 (http://www.delazonaoriental.net/2010/10/23/recordando-a-José-lima/)

3 Kostya Kennedy, "The Mambo King," *Sports Illustrated*, June 14, 1999 (http://sportsillustrated.cnn.com/vault/article/magazine/MAG1016148/index.htm)

4 Kennedy, "The Mambo King."

5 *Press-Enterprise* (Riverside, California), May 13, 2004.

6 Kennedy, "The Mambo King."

7 "Baseball Notebook." *Detroit News*, August 1, 1999. This Ramón Peña, who has signed dozens of major-leaguers over the years, is not to be confused with the brother of longtime major-league catcher Tony Peña. That Ramón Peña appeared in eight games as a reliever for the Tigers in 1989.

8 Clyde Hughes, "Hens' Lima tosses no-hitter," *Toledo Blade*, August 18, 1994: 29.

9 Kennedy, "The Mambo King."

10 "Ex-Tiger Lima relishes All-Star attention," *Detroit News*, July 13, 1999.

11 Kennedy, "The Mambo King."

12 "Last night in baseball," *The Spectator* (Hamilton, Ontario), June 23, 2000: E2.

13 Joe Posnanski, "Lima Time ended too soon, but the show, as always, must go on," *Sports Illustrated* website, May 24, 2010 (http://sportsillustrated.cnn.com/2010/writers/joe_posnanski/05/24/José.lima/index.html).

14 Posnanski.

15 Keith Thursby, "José Lima dies at 37; pitcher helped Dodgers reach 2004 playoffs," *Los Angeles Times*, May 24, 2010.

16 Jim Baker, "Peep Show." ESPN.com, November 26, 2003. (http://proxy.espn.go.com/insider/story?id=1671664&campaign=INOS05&source=INgspider).

17 Jon SooHoo, "Remembering José Lima: Time ticks away so fast," ESPN.com (http://espn.go.com/blog/los-angeles/dodger-thoughts/post/_/id/5139/lima).

18 SooHoo.

19 *La Opinión* (Los Angeles, California), May 14, 2004: 10C.

20 Ian Begley, "Mets' [José] Reyes on Lima: 'A great guy'," ESPNNewYork.com, May 24, 2010 (http://sports.espn.go.com/new-york/mlb/news/story?id=5213357).

21 SooHoo, "Remembering José Lima: Time ticks away so fast"

22 Wire service reports, December 27, 2004.

23 Bob Dutton, "Lima can't wait," *Kansas City Star*, April 4, 2005: C1.

24 Bob Dutton, "Lima shoots for big finish," *Kansas City Star*, September 28, 2005: D5.

25 Richard Goldstein, "José Lima, Colorful and Popular Pitcher, Dies at 37," *New York Times*, May 23, 2010.

26 Marty Noble, "Notes: Lima set to start," MLB.com, May 6, 2006. (http://mlb.mlb.com/news/article.jsp?ymd=20060506&content_id=1440365&vkey=news_mlb&fext=.jsp&c_id=mlb)

27 "Hurting Mets turn to 'Lima magic'," *Chicago Tribune*, May 7, 2006: 16.

28 Begley, "Mets' Reyes on Lima: 'A great guy.'"

29 "José Lima convocado al Juego de Estrellas," *Listín Diario* (Santo Domingo, Dominican Republic), May 26, 2007.

30 James Jahnke, "What's 'Lima Time' in Korean?" *Detroit Free Press*, January 12, 2008: B2.

31 Yi Whan woo, "Pitcher José Lima dies," *Korea Times*, May 24, 2010.

32 Kurt Streeter, "José Lima hopes his time will come again," *Los Angeles Times*, June 14, 2009.

33 Enrique Rojas, "RD dedicará temporada a José Lima," ESPNDeportes.com, August 3, 2010 (http://espndeportes.espn.go.com/news/story?id=1072414&s=bei&type=story).

34 Candice M. Giove, "Former Mets pitcher Lima's legacy includes 6 kids with 6 moms," *New York Post*, June 3, 2012.

35 Kennedy, "The Mambo King." "Recordando a José Lima." Felix Pérez, "Esposa de José Lima es oriunda de Gaspar Hernández," *La Perla de la Costa Norte* (Gaspar Hernández, Dominican Republic), May 25, 2010 (http://www.laperladelacostanorte.com/2010/05/esposa-de-José-lima-es-oriunda-de.html). Giove, "Former Mets pitcher Lima's legacy includes 6 kids with 6 moms."

36 Pérez, "Esposa de José Lima es oriunda de Gaspar Hernández." "Astacio y su esposa reciben a la cigüeña," *La Opinión*, September 28, 1994: 5C.

37 Robert Crowe, "Herpes victim wins $475,000 from ex-Astro Lima," *Houston Chronicle*, December 2, 2004.

38 Thursby, "José Lima dies at 37; pitcher helped Dodgers reach 2004 playoffs."

39 Enrique Rojas, "Muere a los 37 años lanzador José Lima," ESPNdeportes.com, May 24, 2010. (http://espndeportes.espn.go.com/news/story?id=1026715&s=bei&type=story)

40 Rojas.

41 "Recordando a José Lima."

42 Associated Press, "Ortiz, Cano among mourners at José Lima's wake," May 28, 2010. (http://aol.sportingnews.com/mlb/story/2010-05-28/ortiz-cano-among-mourners-José-limas-wake)

43 Marcelo Peralta, "Miles despide a José Lima en el Estadio Cibao," *El Nuevo Diario* (Santo Domingo, Dominican Republic), May 30, 2010.

44 Cornelio Batista, "José Lima recibió ayer su último adiós en el cementerio de Las Charcas, lugar donde nació," *Diario Libre* (Santo Domingo, Dominican Republic), May 31, 2012. (http://www.diariolibre.com/deportes/2010/05/31/i247482_index.html)

45 Enrique Rojas, "José Lima likely died of heart failure," ESPNdeportes.com, September 9, 2010. (http://sports.espn.go.com/mlb/news/story?id=5550824)

46 Thursby, "José Lima dies at 37; pitcher helped Dodgers reach 2004 playoffs."

47 Josh Rawitch, "Lima Time in Heaven," Inside the Dodgers blog, May 23, 2010, (http://insidethedodgers.mlblogs.com/2010/05/23/lima-time-in-heaven/)

JULIO LUGO

By Justin Krueger

At 6-feet-1-inch and weighing 165 pounds, Julio Lugo was built for the infield. He was tall, slender, and fast. He played for seven major-league teams: the Houston Astros, Tampa Devil Rays, Los Angeles Dodgers, Boston Red Sox, St. Louis Cardinals, Baltimore Orioles, and Atlanta Braves.

Julio Cesar Lugo was born on November 16, 1975, in Barahona, Dominican Republic, an eco-tourism destination, fishing center, and port city located in the southwest of the country. It sits approximately 100 miles west of the capital city of Santo Domingo. The town lies off the beaten track from more tourist-popular destinations, and is considered one of the poorest communities in the country.[1] Lugo recalled playing ball when "there were rocks and sticks [for balls and bats] and cartons of milk [for gloves]. ... It was rough."[2] When he was 13 years old his family moved to Sunset Park in Brooklyn, New York. It was here that he became a New York Mets fan. His favorite player was Howard Johnson. After the move to New York, Lugo's mother often worked multiple jobs, usually in a factory or an office building. Sixteen-hour workdays were not uncommon for her in order for the family to be able to make ends meet.

A graduate of Fort Hamilton High School in Brooklyn, Lugo received a scholarship to play college baseball 1,400 miles away in small-town Oklahoma. Beginning in August 1993, he attended Connors State College, a public junior college of about 2,000 students in Warner, Oklahoma, a town of 1,500 in the eastern part of the state. He played for the Cowboys of Connors State for two seasons, and earned a first-team National Junior College Athletic Association All-American selection. In the 1994 amateur draft, Lugo was picked in the 43rd round by the Houston Astros, and signed with the Astros after his graduation in 1995. When he made his major-league debut in 2000, he was the lowest drafted Astros player to make it to the majors with the team.

After four years in the minor leagues, Lugo had worked his way up to become a top-quality infield prospect in the Astros farm system. *Baseball America* considered him the team's seventh-best prospect in 1999 and the sixth in 2000.

Lugo began his professional career in 1995 as a 19-year-old member of the Low-A Auburn Astros in the New York-Penn League. He spent time at second base, shortstop, and the outfield. In 59 games he batted .291, had 16 RBIs, stole 17 bases, and made 12 errors.

Photo courtesy of the Boston Red Sox

With the Class-A Quad Cities River Bandits (Midwest League) in 1996, Lugo batted .295 and made 29 errors in 122 games. He spent 1997 and 1998 with the High-A Kissimmee Cobras (Florida State League). In 1997 he batted .267 and made 41 errors in 124 games; and in 1998 he batted .303 and made 42 errors.

Despite his difficulty fielding, Lugo advanced out of Class A and spent the 1999 season with the Double-A Jackson Generals (Texas League). He made 29 errors in 115 games, but hit .319 with 10 home runs and made the Texas League All-Star team. He started the 2000 season with Triple-A New Orleans but was called up to the Astros in mid-April. During his time in the minor leagues Lugo mostly played shortstop, but also had spent time at second base, third base, and the outfield. Over his 5½ years in the minors, Lugo was adept on the basepaths: He stole 164 bases and was caught stealing 62 times; he swiped a career-high 51 bases in 1998 with Kissimmee. Showcasing his speed, Lugo hit 14 triples during both his seasons with Kissimmee.

Lugo made his major-league debut, as a pinch-runner for Tony Eusebio in the eighth inning, on April 15, 2000, and played in his last major-league game on August 23, 2011, with the Atlanta Braves. His first hit came in his third game, on April 19 in Los Angeles, and his first run batted in followed a week later on April 26, in Houston against the Chicago Cubs. For the season (116 games) he batted .283 (and had an on-base percentage of .346) with 40 RBIs and 78 runs scored. In 60 games at shortstop, he made 12 errors, a .951 fielding percentage.

In 2001 Lugo settled in as the Astros regular shortstop, batting .263 in 140 games. In August 2002 his season was cut short at 88 games when a pitch from Cubs pitcher Kerry Wood broke his left forearm. Before the 2003 season Lugo won his arbitration case with the Astros for $1.575 million. He had earned $325,000 in 2002.

Early into his fourth season with the Astros, in May 2003, Lugo was abruptly designated for assignment by the Astros. Many believed this was in direct response to his arrest on a charge of misdemeanor assault for allegedly hitting his wife in the face and smashing her head on the car. On the next day he was designated for assignment by the Astros. GM Gerry Hunsicker said:

"The fact of the matter is that a lot of things went into this decision. For a number of days now, all of us in the baseball side have been discussing ways that we can help this club get out of its slump. ... Certainly, Julio shouldn't be singled out as the reason this ballclub is where it is. But anybody that's been involved in our club know that the shortstop position has been under some scrutiny. Many of us felt like a change there, if we had an option, could possibly be one of the ways we could improve our club."[3]

At the time of his designation, the Astros had scuttled to an 11-15 record in the first month of the season. Hunsicker added:

"We felt it was in Julio's best interest and in the best interest of the organization to put this situation behind us as quickly as possible and let Julio get on with his career elsewhere."[4]

With the decision made, Adam Everett regained his spot as the Astros' starting shortstop. Lugo, however, was not out of work long. He was picked up by the Tampa Bay Devil Rays a week later. Lou Piniella, manager of the Devil Rays, commented, "Everybody makes mistakes. ... You learn from mistakes and you go forward. At the same time, we're looking to improve our baseball team."[5] It was believed that Lugo would add a stabilizing force at the top of the lineup and in the middle infield.

In July of 2003, Lugo was acquitted of assault by a Houston jury. During the trial, his wife, Mabely, changed her initial statements and testified that Lugo had not intentionally hurt her and that it was she who had provoked the argument between them. After barely 30 minutes of deliberation, the jury returned a not-guilty verdict, providing vindication for Lugo, who said that the whole ordeal had been little more than a misunderstanding of events. Trial prosecutor Catherine Evans said afterward, "How sad it is to hear a woman say over and over, 'I hit myself against the truck. ... I provoked him. ... It was my fault.'"[6] Some of the jurors asked Lugo for his autograph after the trial ended.

After Lugo's first season on the Devil Rays, their general manager, Chuck LaMar, commented, "Julio did a fine job for us in 2003. He provided us with more run production than we've had from that position in the past and his defense improved as the season wore on."[7] Lugo had driven in 53 runs and scored 58. Of his 17 errors in 117 games for the Devil Rays, only one came in the last 34 games of the season. It appeared that the change in scenery was a positive experience for Lugo. At the end of the season, the Devil Rays and Lugo went to salary arbitration, resulting in a $3.35 million salary for 2005.

Lugo ended up starring with the Devil Rays from May 2003 to July 2006, during which he had some of his best offensive statistics. He achieved career highs with 41 doubles and 75 RBIs in 2004, and 6 triples, 61 walks, and 182 hits in 2005. A good clubhouse presence, Lugo hoped his efforts would lead to a long-term contract. The Devil Rays were offering around $8 million a year for four years; however, Lugo was looking for upward of $10 million a year over the four years.

By the end of July, the 2006 season was turning out to be a career year offensively for Lugo. He was batting .308 and slugging .498, had swiped 18 stolen bases, and hit 12 home runs. The offensive statistics combined with his quality defensive range made Lugo a valuable trade piece for the small-market Devil Rays. At the trade deadline in 2006 he was dealt to the Los Angeles Dodgers for power-hitting prospect Joel Guzman and minor-league outfielder Sergio Pedroza. He was replaced on the Devil Rays by rookie Ben Zobrist.

On hearing the news of his trade, Lugo said, "I was very surprised. I didn't think anything was going to get done. I thought it was going to come down to the last minute. I didn't think certainly it would be the last, last minute. ... I love it here [Tampa Bay]. I really want to say that. I tried to get something done but it's a business. ... I'm not disappointed because I know both sides tried."[8]

Major offensive struggles were a cornerstone of Lugo's time with the Dodgers: In 49 games he batted only .219, with no home runs and only 10 RBIs. Defensively, Lugo was used in a utility role; he spent time playing third base, second base, and the outfield.

After that rough finish to the 2006 season, Lugo went on the free-agent market. In December 2006 he signed a four-year, $36 million contract with the Boston Red Sox. It was hoped that Lugo could slot into the leadoff position and provide improved offense at the shortstop position. Best laid plans and all: His tenure in Boston did not go accordingly. In contrast to slick-fielding Alex Gonzalez, the previous Red Sox shortstop, Lugo was prone to clumps of bad plays usually as a result of errant throws from not properly setting his feet before releasing the ball. Lugo himself noted, "I know I'm an aggressive shortstop. I'm going to take chances that other shortstops don't take. That's just the way I am. That's my game."9

Lugo's aggressiveness on defense and his streaky fielding did not endear him to Red Sox Nation, and fans were prone to boo him.

In 2007 Lugo's offensive struggles continued from the end of the previous year. From mid-June to early July, he went on a 0-for-31 streak that dropped his batting average to .189. After a 14-game hit streak in mid-July, Lugo got his batting average up to .226.

Despite the struggles of his first year in Boston a personal highlight of the season came in late September 2007. Lugo got to face off against his younger brother Ruddy, a relief pitcher for the Oakland Athletics. He drew a walk. Afterward, Lugo commented that while the experience was a dream come true, "It's weird to face him. We never faced each other ever."10

Overall, in his first season with the Red Sox, Lugo provided adequate offensive numbers even though his batting average of .237 was less than in previous years. He still had 36 doubles, 8 home runs, and 73 RBIs. And he stole 33 bases in 39 attempts.

During the 2007 postseason, Lugo batted .300 with one stolen base in the ALDS against the Los Angeles Angels, .200 with two RBIs in the ALCS against Cleveland, and then hit .385 (walking three times to achieve a .500 on-base percentage) in his only World Series, as the Red Sox swept the Colorado Rockies.

Lugo had seen postseason play twice before, going 0-for-8 in the 2001 NLDS for Houston, and 1-for-4 with a double in the 2006 NLDS for the Dodgers.

The 2008 season proved to be difficult. Lugo played in only 82 games, spending time on the disabled list for a strained left quad. He batted .268, over 30 points higher than the previous season, but had only one home run and drove in only 22 runs. In 2009 his offensive struggles continued. He began sharing playing time with infielder Nick Green. In 37 games, Lugo had only one home run, 8 RBIs, and three stolen bases. His batting average had once again climbed and it was sitting at .284 in July. However, in an attempt to dump the struggling Lugo's salary, the Red Sox sent him and cash to the St. Louis Cardinals for outfielder Chris Duncan before the trade deadline. Arriving in Boston 2½ years earlier, Lugo was believed to be the long-term solution at shortstop. But his time in Boston did not meet expectations. In 51 games for the Cardinals, Lugo batted .277. The switch to a part-time utility role was an adjustment for Lugo as he was used to being an everyday player.

Just before the start of the 2010 season, the Cardinals traded Lugo to the Baltimore Orioles for cash or a player to be named later. The move was an insurance move for the Orioles in case their second baseman, Brian Roberts, who was recuperating from a herniated disc, was not ready to start the season. Lugo ended up playing 93 games. He had no home runs and 20 RBIs, and for the first time in his career he was thrown out stealing (7 times) more often than he was successful (5 SB's).

Released by the Orioles after the season, Lugo signed a minor-league contract with the Atlanta Braves in late May of 2011. Hoping that the signing would be a harbinger for continued success at the major-league level, Lugo commented, "I am very optimistic and happy, playing baseball is what I like to do best."[11] After starting the season with the Triple-A Gwinnett Braves, Lugo was called up to the major leagues one last time and played the final 22 games of his major-league career before being released on September 2. He batted only .136 with 3 RBIs. A highlight of his time in Atlanta came when he scored the winning run against the Pittsburgh Pirates on a controversial call in the bottom of the 19th inning. The Braves won 4-3, but umpire Jerry Meals and MLB later admitted that the call was blown. Lugo finished his career with a .967 fielding percentage.

A minor-league deal with the Cleveland Indians fell through in 2012. In 2013 Lugo played with the Peoria Explorers of the Freedom Pro Baseball League, an independent organization based in Arizona. In 27 games he batted .326. (The league folded before the 2014 season.) During the winter of 2013 Lugo played with Leones del Escogido of the Dominican Republic Winter League. In the 2013 Caribbean Series, Leones attained the best record of the tournament at 5-2, but lost the championship game to Mexico 4-3 in 18 innings.

Noting that the end of his playing career was imminent, Lugo expressed his desire to spend more time with his kids and to play a more involved role in his construction business down in the Dominican, "I played good and had a good career…and I just think it's the right time now."[12]

Lugo played in 1,352 major-league games over his 12-year career. He was a full-time starter for seven seasons. His career batting average of .269 included a high of .295 in 2005. Lugo had 198 stolen bases in 267 attempts, a stolen-base percentage of slightly above 74 percent.

Lugo made a triumphant return to Fenway Park in May 2018. He was playing in the first Red Sox alumni game held in 25 years. In the four-inning affair, Lugo plated the only runs of the game with a two-run home run off his friend, Hall of Fame pitcher Pedro Martínez. "It was awesome," Lugo commented of the homer.[13] At least for a moment, Lugo's lackluster time in Boston was overshadowed.

In August 2018 Lugo was inducted into the All American Amateur Baseball Association (AAABA) Hall of Fame in Johnstown, Pennsylvania. He was the MVP of the tournament in 1994 (before the Astros drafted him) as his Brooklyn team won the championship against Altoona. In the tournament he batted .464 (13-for-28). Reflecting on the tournament after his induction, Lugo noted, "The AAABA opened the door for me" into professional baseball.[14] A door that led to a career in the major leagues.

Lugo died of an apparent heart attack on November 15, 2021 as he was leaving a Santo Domingo gym in his native Dominican Republic after a morning workout. His death came one day before his 46th birthday.

SOURCES

In addition to the sources cited in Notes, the author used information from Lugo's National Baseball Hall of Fame clippings file, as well as Baseball-Almanac.com, Baseball-Reference.com, and theBaseballCube.com.

NOTES

1. Mark Kurlansky, *The Eastern Stars: How Baseball Changed the Dominican Town of San Pedro de Macoris* (New York: Riverhead Books, 2010), 210.

2. Michael Morrissey, "Longshot Lugo Making Most of Chance," *New York Post*, May 3, 2001. Retrieved from nypost.com/2001/05/03/longshot-lugo-making-most-of-chance/.

3. José de Jesus Ortiz, "Incident Disturbs Teammates," *Houston Chronicle*, May 2, 2003.

4. Michael A. Lutz, "Houston Shortstop Julio Lugo Arrested," *Beaumont Enterprise*, May 2, 2003. Retrieved from beaumontenterprise.com/news/article/Houston-shortstop-Julio-Lugo-arrested-758340.php.

5. Martin Fennelly, "Black Eye Doesn't Look Good on Rays," *Tampa Tribune*, May 17, 2003.

6. Jeffrey Gilbert, "Jurors Acquit Ex-Astro Lugo in Assault Trial," *Houston Chronicle*, July 17, 2003.

7. Marc Topkin, "Lugo Retained, Perhaps at 2B," *St. Petersburg Times*, October 30, 2003.

8. Marc Topkin, "Lugo Trade Saga Ends Way Out West," *St. Petersburg Times*, August 1, 2006.

9. Nick Cafardo, "Detractors Having a Field Day with Lugo," *Boston Globe*, April 18, 2008. Retrieved from archive.boston.com/sports/baseball/redsox/articles/2008/04/18/detractors_having_a_field_day_with_lugo/.

10. Mike Petraglia, "Brothers Lugo Realize a Family Dream," MLB.com, September 26, 2007.

11. Enrique Rojas, "Julio Lugo Agrees to Deal with Braves," ESPN.com, May 23, 2011. Retrieved from espn.com/mlb/news/story?id=6580979

12. Alden Gonzalez, "Lugo Will Likely Retire Following Caribbean Series," MLB.com, February 4, 2013. Retrieved from Julio Lugo's Hall of Fame clippings file.

13. Ken Powtak, "Julio Lugo on His Homer off Pedro Martínez: 'It Was Awesome,'" *Boston Globe*, May 27, 2018. Retrieved from boston.com/sports/boston-red-sox/2018/05/27/red-sox-alumni-game-pedro-Martínez-julio-lugo

14. Mike Mastovich, "AAABA 'Opened the Door' for Hall of Famer Julio Lugo," *Tribune-Democrat* (Johnstown, Pennsylvania), July 9, 2018. Retrieved from tribdem.com/sports/aaaba-opened-the-door-for-hall-of-famer-julio-lugo/article_f81f833a-8326-11e8-a5d8-9f13449373fb.html.

Juan Marichal

By Jan Finkel

This guy is a natural. He's got ideas about what he wants to do and does it. He amazes me.

— Carl Hubbell

No pitcher has made such magnificent use of his God-given equipment.

— Branch Rickey

If you placed all the pitchers in the history of the game behind a transparent curtain, where only a silhouette was visible, Juan's motion would be the easiest to identify. He brought to the mound beauty, individuality and class.

— Bob Stevens in *Baseball's Greatest Quotes* (1982)

Except for Sandy Koufax, who was otherworldly, Juan Marichal was the best pitcher—certainly the best right-hander—of the 1960s. His 191 wins exceeds Bob Gibson's second-place 164 by a huge margin. Indeed, he won more games than Gibson in each season of the decade. He's the only pitcher of the decade with more complete games (197) than wins. His 2.57 ERA is bettered only by Koufax's 2.36 and Hoyt Wilhelm's 2.16, but Wilhelm pitched only 1,103 1/3 innings. He's third in innings pitched behind Don Drysdale and Jim Bunning. His 45 shutouts lead the decade by four over Gibson. His 3.66 strikeouts-to-walks ratio is topped only by Koufax's 3.73.

He's arguably the National League's greatest All-Star Game pitcher, appearing in eight games, winning two while losing none, hurling 18 innings and giving up seven hits and two walks while striking out 12 and surrendering two runs (one earned) for a minuscule ERA of 0.50.

On July 2, 1963, he pitched a complete game, 16-inning 1-0 win over the great Warren Spahn.

And yet ...

He never won the Cy Young Award.

He had to wait until his third year of eligibility before election to the Hall of Fame.

All some people want to remember him for is one horrendous day.

Marichal (pronounced mah-ree-CHAHL[1]) finished with an impressive statistical line: 243 wins against 142 losses, an ERA of 2.89, 244 complete games (more than half of his starts), 52 shutouts, a strikeout-to-walk ratio of better than 3-to-1. He led the league in wins twice, in shutouts twice, in complete games twice, in innings pitched twice, in winning percentage once. It's a brilliant résumé, yet

Photo courtesy of the National Baseball Hall of Fame

he never quite gets the recognition he richly deserves. Why?

It's not a lack of skill. He had five pitches (slider, fastball, change, curve, and screwball) in his arsenal and could throw most of them for strikes over the top, three-quarters, or sidearm. Pete Rose, who saw more pitchers than any man in history, said Marichal was the best *pitcher* he encountered. (Rose actually did well against Marichal, with a .341 average, .400 on-base percentage, and .512 slugging percentage, with a tally of 42 hits in 123 AB that included 7 doubles, a triple, and 4 homers.[2]) It's not a matter of style. Marichal's high kick was unmistakable. So what is it?

Three possibilities emerge. First, through no fault of his own, Marichal didn't get to perform extensively on the World Series stage. Koufax and Gibson did. Second, and again through no fault of his, Marichal at 6'0" and 185 pounds didn't exude the athletic power of Koufax and Gibson. Koufax and Gibson looked like people who could and did overpower a hitter with the fastball or freeze him with the curve. Marichal didn't look overpowering. He looked like a finesse pitcher and usually worked that way, but he could blow away any hitter if he had to. Finally, his physical appearance and body chemistry may have had an effect. Former basketball players Koufax (6'2"-210) and Gibson (6'1"-195) cut imposing figures and looked like men working hard; in the dog days of July and August, as the game went along, fans could see Koufax and Gibson's beards getting darker and their jerseys getting wetter and wetter. Not so with Marichal. He didn't sweat. From the first pitch to the ninth inning he looked like a man freshly showered and shaved in a new suit and ready for dinner with a lovely lady. To make things worse, he always seemed to be smiling--one of his nicknames was Laughing Boy--no matter what the situation, the look of a man who's saying, "I'm going to win, we both know it, and there's nothing you can do about it." Scout Dewey Griggs saw this trait early in Marichal's career: "Never seems to exert himself," before concluding, "very good live fast ball... should go all the way."[3] Koufax and Gibson blew hitters away. They seemed to say, "Here it is, what are you gonna do about it?" Marichal toyed with them, embarrassed them.

Natividad Sánchez and Francisco Marichal had had Gonzalo, Rafael, and María before Juan Antonio was born October 20, 1937, in Laguna Verde, Monte Cristi, a province in the northwestern part of the Dominican Republic. Life was hard for most people in the poor farming village, and the Marichals were no exception, living in a palm bark shack without electricity. However, farming ensured their having food. Francisco died when Juan was three, leaving the family in even worse straits. Juan tended the family's horses, goats, and donkeys, and spent his free time fishing and swimming in the Yaque del Norte River.

When Juan was ten, tragedy nearly struck – he fell unconscious and lay in a coma for nine days. Poor digestion was the culprit, but treating it effectively in such a remote area was difficult. There seemed little hope for the boy, but a local doctor suggested giving him steam baths, and he regained consciousness.

Gonzalo, a solid baseball player, saw Juan's interest and taught his little brother the fundamentals of the game. It wasn't long before Juan was playing ball on weekends with Gonzalo and his friends. The boys had no equipment and little or no money, but they were creative. They would pay a shoemaker a peso to sew thick cloth around golf balls they'd found to make them the right size. Bats? Difficult, but not impossible. They fashioned them from the branches of a local hardwood tree. Gloves were a little easier; they made them from canvas tarp. Among the fledgling ballplayers in the area were brothers Felipe, Mateo, and Jesús Rojas (they used the surname Alou in the United States), who all enjoyed fine major league careers, all of them at one time or another with the San Francisco Giants. Marichal and the Alous have been close friends ever since.

Although "Manito" knew by age 6 that he wanted to be a ballplayer in the United States, he received no encouragement from his mother, who wanted him to get an education. Since there were no players from the Dominican Republic in the majors in the early 1940s, Juan's dreams seemed pretty far-fetched, so at age eleven he spent a short time cutting sugar cane for J. W. Tatem Shipping.

Marichal started out as a shortstop. Yet even though the Dominican Republic is known for producing shortstops, he wasn't destined to be one of them. Before he was ten years old, inspired by Bombo Ramos, a star on the Dominican national team who came from Monte Cristi, Marichal switched to pitching, imitating Ramos' sidearm delivery.[4]

Marichal left high school after the eleventh grade (something he later regretted) and spent a year in Santo Domingo. There his brother Gonzalo taught Juan to drive a truck and found a spot for him on the Esso Company team. Once he turned 16, Marichal came back home and joined a summer league in Monte Cristi to play for a team with the unlikely name Las Flores (flowers), sponsored by the Bermúdez Rum Company. He then signed on with the Grenada Company team (the Dominican subsidiary of United Fruit).

His big break wasn't far off.

Ramfis Trujillo, son of Dominican strongman Rafael Leónidas Trujillo, was a major sponsor of the Dominican Air Force team, known as Aviación Militar Dominicana. Ramfis saw Marichal pitch a 2-1 victory in Monte Cristi, and almost immediately Juan Marichal was enlisted (drafted) into the Air Force. Resistance to the "draft" wasn't an option – Ramfis and the Generalissimo's brother, Petán Trujillo, took their baseball seriously.[5] Marichal neither flew nor maintained aircraft nor took part in the defense of his country.

No conventional airman, Marichal pitched, developing the pinpoint control that was one of his trademarks. Progressing rapidly, he was signed as an amateur free agent by the New York Giants before the 1957 season. Ultimately, in 1958 he was signed for a $500 bonus by Giants scouts Horacio "Rabbit" Martínez, Frank "Chick" Genovese, and Alex Pómpez. He made his professional debut during the winter of 1957-58 with the Escogido Leones of the Dominican League, which had a working agreement with the Giants.

The young man breezed through the minor leagues. Starting in 1958 with Michigan City (Indiana) in the Class-D Midwest League, Marichal went 21-8 with a 1.87 ERA, pacing the league in wins, ERA, and innings pitched (245) and was among the league leaders with 24 complete games and 246 strikeouts. He followed that up in 1959 with Springfield (Massachusetts) in the Class-A Eastern League, topping the charts with 18 wins (against 13 losses), 8 shutouts, 208 strikeouts, and 271 innings pitched, throwing in a 2.39 ERA as a bonus. Through most of the season he still threw sidearm exclusively, but manager Andy Gilbert, fearing that he would injure his arm and explaining that he could throw a wider variety of pitches with greater velocity, convinced Marichal to take up an overhand motion. The result was the high-kicking, ball-concealing motion by which any knowledgeable fan can identify him. Promoted to Tacoma in the Triple-A Pacific Coast League in 1960, he won 11 games, lost five, and posted a 3.11 ERA. The Giants brought him up to the parent club in July.

Marichal resolved any questions about his readiness for the big leagues in his debut on July 19. All he did was shut out the Phillies, giving up one hit (a pinch-hit single to Clay Dalrymple in the eighth inning) while walking one and striking out 12. Proving that his debut was no fluke, four days later he put down the eventual World Series champion Pirates and Harvey Haddix, 3-1, on four hits, four walks, and six strikeouts. The Braves became his next victim, on July 28; he pitched 10 innings, surrendering two runs, a walk, seven hits while striking out six--to defeat Warren Spahn, 3-2. It added up to three wins and three complete games in nine days. He cooled off a bit from that point, finishing the season 6-2 with an ERA of 2.66 and six complete games.

Becoming a mainstay on the Giants wasn't the only thing on Marichal's mind, not with trouble back home. Trujillo was assassinated by his own armed forces on May 30, 1961, throwing the Dominican Republic into chaos. Meanwhile, Marichal had become engaged to Alma Rosa Carvajal, a neighbor of the Rojas Alou brothers. With turmoil in the Dominican deepening, Marichal asked Giants manager Alvin Dark during spring training in 1962 for a few days off to go home. Dark consented. Marichal went home, returned with Alma, and they were married on March 28. The Marichals have six children (Rosie, Elsie, Yvette, Ursula Raquel, Charlene, and Juan Antonio), 13 grandchildren, and one great-grandchild, and celebrated their golden anniversary in 2012.

Marichal leveled off a little but developed his craft over the next two seasons, posting a 13-10 mark with a 3.89 ERA in 1961. By 1962 he'd become a very good pitcher, going 18-11 for a power-laden Giants team that won 103 games that edged the hated Dodgers 2-1 in a three-game tie-breaker series and headed to the World Series against the mighty veteran Yankees. Marichal's 18 wins were good for third on the team behind Jack Sanford (24-7) and Billy O'Dell (19-14) and ahead of Billy Pierce (16-6), but his 3.36 ERA led the staff. As a bonus he pitched scoreless fourth and fifth innings of the first of two All-Star Games that year and was the winning pitcher in the National League's 3-1 victory.

Because of several rainouts in San Francisco, the seven-game Series, which the Yankees won, ran from October 4 to October 16. Marichal started Game Four at Yankee Stadium and was moving along with a 2-0 lead for four innings, giving up just two hits and two walks while striking out four. Striking out while trying to bunt off Whitey Ford in the top of the fifth inning, he injured his hand and was finished for the Series.

The Giants were a solid team, usually in contention through the sixties and early seventies, so no one would have guessed that they wouldn't appear in another World Series until 1989. World Series disappointment aside, Juan Marichal became a great pitcher in 1963 and remained one through 1969.

The 1963 season didn't start auspiciously for Marichal on April 10, as he lasted two

Photo courtesy of the National Baseball Hall of Fame

innings in Houston, giving up eight hits and four earned runs. Things didn't improve four days later as he lost to the Cubs in Chicago. Returning home, he righted himself and beat the Cubs, 5-1, on the 19th. From that point on he was practically invincible, finishing the season 25-8 (the first of three times he won at least 25 games) with a 2.41 ERA. For good measure he led the league with 321⅓ innings pitched. Along the way he got his revenge against Houston on June 15, throwing a no-hitter for a 1-0 win. Oddly enough, he abandoned his high kick for that one game.

On July 2 he defeated Warren Spahn 1-0 in 16 innings in what Jim Kaplan has called the greatest game ever pitched.[6] It was everything a game should be, a testament to the skill, courage, pride, and honor of two marvelous pitchers—perfect theater featuring the aging veteran (Spahn was 42 and had 338 career victories at the time) and the upcoming youth. Spahn and Marichal were mirror images of each other, with their high kicks and pitching hands almost touching the ground during their windups. Spahn had been pitching more with his head than his arm for a number of years; finessing his way through the powerful San Francisco lineup, letting them hit the ball, he gave up nine hits while striking out just two and walking one. Marichal took a different approach; in a year in which he struck out a career-high 248, he gave up eight hits, punched out 10 batters, and walked four. Neither pitcher backed off. Age wasn't about to be bested by youth, youth wasn't giving in against age. The game ended as it had to when Willie Mays homered with one out in the 16th inning. It illustrated what might be the central point about baseball, noted so beautifully by Bart Giamatti: "It breaks your heart. It is designed to break your heart."[7]

Koufax, like Marichal having his first great season, won 25 games, lost five, led the league with 11 shutouts, 306 strikeouts, and a 1.88 ERA. Following up, he was MVP of the World Series, throwing two complete-game victories as the Dodgers swept the Yankees. For his efforts he received the Cy Young Award (only one was presented from 1956 to 1966) and the National League Most Valuable Player award.

Marichal had another fine season in 1964, going 21-8 with a 2.48 ERA and a league-best 22 complete games. Gibson's final numbers were 19-12 and 3.01, but he took MVP honors in the World Series with two complete-game wins over the Yankees. The Cy Young Award went to Dean Chance of the Angels, who accompanied his 20-9 mark with a 1.65 ERA.

On paper the 1965 season looks like another typical Juan Marichal performance. A 22-13 mark with a 2.13 ERA is impressive, especially when it's accompanied by 24 complete games and a league-leading 10 shutouts.

All of that, and much more, came crashing down on August 22.

It was a long-anticipated Sunday game with the Dodgers in Candlestick Park with a lot riding on the outcome and the two best pitchers in the game facing off—Koufax for the Dodgers and Marichal for the Giants. The close pennant race notwithstanding, the two teams that had left Brooklyn and New York eight years before had carried their mutual hatred to their new homes in California.

Neither pitcher was particularly sharp. The Dodgers touched Marichal for single runs in the first and second innings; the Giants got one back in their half of the second. Both pitchers had been working inside, not hesitating to push hitters off the plate. When Marichal came to bat with one out in the third, Dodger catcher Johnny Roseboro told Koufax to retaliate. Koufax buzzed Marichal twice, provoking no reaction. But then Roseboro threw the ball back to Koufax very close to Marichal's ear. Marichal exploded, attacking Roseboro with his bat, hefting it over his head like an executioner in olden times to bring it crashing down on Roseboro's skull, opening a two-inch gash on the catcher's forehead. One of the worst brawls in Dodgers-Giants history ensued. When peace—such as it was—was restored, Marichal was ejected, and Koufax, badly shaken, got the second out of the inning, walked Jim Davenport and Willie McCovey, and served up a three-run homer to Willie Mays. The Giants won, 4-3, but Marichal drew a fine of $1750 (the highest in National League history up to that time) and a nine-day suspension. Many observers thought the numbers should have been reversed. The Giants also paid, finishing second on the season, two games behind the Dodgers.

The game has been rehashed many times, becoming something of a morality play. In 2011 Roger Guenveur Smith wrote and performed a one-man play called *Juan and John*. Roseboro forgave Marichal and supported him for the Hall of Fame, and the families remain close to this day.

Koufax was Koufax in 1965: 26-8, 2.04 ERA, a then-record 382 strikeouts (since broken by Nolan Ryan in 1973 with 383), 2-1 despite a 0.38 ERA in the World Series, a second World Series MVP award, a second Cy Young Award. As if that weren't enough, he pitched a perfect game (his fourth no-hitter) at Dodger Stadium on September 9, beating the Cubs and a luckless Bob Hendley, who gave up one hit, by a score of 1-0.

Tony Blengino argues in *Baseball's New Top 100* that Marichal's best season came in 1966.[8] Determining Marichal's greatest season is difficult since, like Warren Spahn, he had so many outstanding ones. A 25-6 mark combined with a 2.23 ERA, league-leading figures in winning percentage (.806), WHIP (.859), hits and walks per nine innings (6.7 and 1.1, respectively), throwing in 25 complete games is certainly impressive. Unfortunately for Marichal, Koufax exceeded him with league-bests 27 wins, 1.73 ERA, 323 innings pitched, 27 complete games, 317 strikeouts, and 5 shutouts. His 27 wins are the twentieth-century National League record for a southpaw, equaled by Steve Carlton in 1972. To the surprise of no one, he notched his third Cy Young Award. The surprise was his announcement of his retirement at age 30, making his the greatest final season any pitcher ever had.

The 1967 season is a mystery. Marichal was having his usual fine year for the first half. He was 12-7 with a 2.29 ERA and started the All-Star Game on July 11. He had pitched a complete-game win over the Dodgers on the 8th and made his usual start on the 14th, getting roughed up in five innings against Houston and taking the loss. He took another pounding and loss in Pittsburgh on the 18th and followed that on the 22nd with another short outing (5⅓ innings, two hits, two runs, one earned, for no decision) in Chicago. He appeared to be in a two-week slump, but back home in San Francisco and with an extra day or two of rest he beat the Phillies in a complete game and four days later did the same to the Pirates. On August 4, however, he pulled a hamstring running in the outfield at Shea Stadium. He didn't pitch again until August 25, against the Braves, lasting only 4⅔ innings and suffering the loss. That was his last game of the season, giving him a final mark of 14-10, 2.76, nowhere near the high standard he had enjoyed. Teammate Mike McCormick (22-10) took home the Cy Young Award.

In St. Louis meanwhile, Bob Gibson settled for a 13-7, 2.98 mark, his season shortened on July 15 when Roberto Clemente's line drive single back at the box broke his leg; ever the warrior, Gibson faced three more batters before leaving the game. At full strength for the World Series, he destroyed the Impossible Dream Red Sox with three complete-game wins and an ERA of 1.00 and was voted MVP of the Series. Two pitchers suffering sub-par, shortened seasons were gearing for the epic season that was on the horizon.

The 1968 season has been called The Year of the Pitcher with good reason. It seemed that most hitters left their bats in the rack, as averages slid to a depth not seen since the Deadball days of 1901 through 1919. Carl Yastrzemski led the American League with a .301 batting average, an all-time low for a batting champion. Every pitcher looked to be having a career year on his way to the Hall of Fame. Three pitchers stood out. Denny McLain of the Tigers went 31-6, the first pitcher to win 30 games since Dizzy Dean turned the trick in 1934; nobody's done it since. In the National League were Juan Marichal and Bob Gibson.

Marichal won a league-high 26 games against just 9 losses, posting a 2.43 ERA and leading the league with 30 complete games and 325⅔ innings pitched; in most seasons a pitcher with those numbers would run away with the Cy Young Award, but 1968 was extraordinary. Gibson posted a fine 22-9 mark, but his 1.12 ERA is the lowest since the Deadball Era, and his 13 shutouts (tied with Jack Coombs's mark in 1910) rank second to Grover Cleveland Alexander's major-league record 16, set in 1916. In addition, the Cardinals went to the World Series, where Gibson pitched valiantly, setting a Series record with 17 strikeouts in Game One and taking down McLain twice before being betrayed by his defense against Mickey Lolich in Game Seven. For his record-setting efforts, Gibson walked away with the Cy Young and Most Valuable Player awards for the National League.

Hitters in both leagues came back a bit in 1969, and although they dropped off a little, Marichal, Gibson, and McLain all had excellent seasons. Marichal went 21-11 and led the league with 8 shutouts and a 2.10 ERA. There was a new gun in town, though. Tom Seaver won 25 games while putting the hitherto hapless and hopeless New York Mets on his shoulders and carrying them to a three-game sweep of the Braves for the NL championship and a five-game World Series shocker over the powerful Baltimore Orioles. He won the Cy Young Award.

Marichal's 1970 season was a disaster. It started during spring training with a severe allergic reaction to penicillin. He lost weight over a few weeks and never completely regained his strength. The short-term effect was a 12-10 mark, an ugly 4.12 ERA, and a seriously diminished fastball. The only bright spot was picking up his 200th career win on August 28, a 5-1 complete game over the Pirates in Candlestick Park. The long-term effect was worse: chronic arthritis and severe back pain.

Left with pinpoint control and guile, Marichal put together his last good season in 1971, an 18-11 mark with a 2.94 ERA. He pitched the Giants' division-clinching win, beating the Padres 5-1 in San Diego on the last day of the season. Finally back in the postseason, he pitched well in Game Three but lost a 2-1, eight-inning complete game to the eventual World Series champion Pirates; home runs by Richie Hebner and Bob Robertson defeated him.

As often happens with finesse pitchers, the decline--as it had come with Warren Spahn--came swiftly, steeply, and suddenly for Juan Marichal. He started the 1972 season on April 15 with eight innings of shutout ball in a win at Houston. He then lost seven starts in a row; on May 17 he was 1-7 despite an ERA of 2.83. The nightmare ended on September 19 with loss number 16 and only six wins and a not-bad ERA of 3.71. Following a back operation, life got no better in 1973 even with an apparent improvement to 11-15, but his ERA was 3.82.

Having seen enough, the Giants sold Marichal to the Red Sox on December 7. The 36-year-old veteran returned to winter ball for the first time in six years, posting a 5-5, 2.12 record for Escogido. During his eight seasons with the Leones, "El Monstruo de Laguna Verde" won 36 and lost 22. (Political turmoil interrupted the Dominican League's operations in 1961-62 and wiped out the 1962-63 and 1965-66 seasons.[9]) He is the league's all-time leader in ERA with a 1.87 mark in 557⅓ innings.

In 1974, Marichal scratched his way to a 5-1 slate, but an ERA of 4.87, with the Sox, who released him on October 24. On the Ides of March 1975, Juan Marichal signed on as a free agent with the hated Dodgers. He started two games, lasting six innings and giving up nine runs. It was all over on April 16.

Then came five years of waiting. Marichal and Bob Gibson became eligible for the Hall of Fame in 1981. Despite their similar statistics, Gibson got in on his first try while Marichal obtained only 233 of the 301 votes he needed. In 1982, with Hank Aaron and Frank Robinson receiving their due, he came up a heartbreaking seven votes short of the 312 required. John Roseboro publicly announced that all was forgiven and urged the writers to vote for his friend, and on January 12, 1983, Juan Marichal was finally elected to the Hall of Fame, the first native of the Dominican Republic so honored.[10]

Marichal has stayed in baseball and sports in general since retiring as a player. He directed the Oakland Athletics' program in the Dominican Republic from the late 1980s to the mid-1990s; the program sent a number of players to the majors, most prominently 2002 American League MVP Miguel Tejada. Working as a broadcaster for Spanish radio in 1990, he watched his then-son-in-law José Rijo earn World Series MVP honors as Rijo helped pitch the Cincinnati Reds to a four-game sweep of the Athletics. From 1996 to 2000 he served in the cabinet of Dominican Republic President Leonel Fernández as his country's Minister of Sports and Physical Education. He still analyzes games for ESPN Deportes.

Despite the honors, there has been one moment of controversy. He and Pedro Martínez were filmed at a cockfight in the Dominican Republic in 2008. A segment of the American public got upset, but the practice is legal in the Dominican Republic, and Marichal and Martínez were there purely as spectators.

Marichal has a farm in the Dominican Republic and travels frequently to and from the United States. "I have 48 head of cattle and a lot of chickens," he told Stuart Miller. "I travel a lot, but when I'm here in the Dominican Republic, I come almost every afternoon. I really enjoy spending time with the animals and talking to my workers. It's very relaxing."[11]

Juan Marichal is a man respected and admired by all who know him. He's invariably kind to people who are in no position to do him any favors. Gabriel Schechter, a former research associate at the Hall of Fame, describes a telling incident. Schechter was working in the Giamatti Library when he heard that Marichal was in the gallery with some friends. He went out to introduce himself to the Hall of Famer. "Marichal," says Schechter, "introduced me to his friends and for ten minutes acted like *I* was the Hall of Famer in the group!" Another time Schechter and a friend decided to put together two theoretical teams of living Hall of Famers, good guys and not-so-good guys. Marichal was the easy choice for pitcher with the good guys.

Marichal sums up his goal in his autobiography: "Before I die, I will be happy if people say of me that I did something good for other people. … I want to be remembered more for helping people than for what I did in baseball."[12] He's achieved his goal.

ACKNOWLEDGMENTS

I am grateful to Mark Armour for his superb editing, to Rory Costello for providing me with additional material and straightening me out on Spanish names, to Rob Ruck for help with the timeline, to Carl Riechers for rigorous fact-checking, and to Bill Nowlin for supplemental editing and formatting. They made my work better.

SOURCES

In addition to the sources cited in the Notes, the author also consulted:

Bjarkman, Peter C. "Dandy, Sandy, and the Summer of '65," *Elysian Fields Quarterly*, Winter 1998, 47, 49-55, 57-59.

Boyle, Robert H. "The Latins Storm Las Grandes Ligas," *Sports Illustrated*, August 9, 1965: 24-26, 29-30.

Burgos Jr., Adrian. *Playing America's Game: Baseball, Latinos, and the Color Line* (Berkeley, Los Angeles, and London: University of California Press, 2007).

James, Bill, and Rob Neyer. *The Neyer/James Guide to Pitchers: A Historical Compendium of Pitching, Pitchers, and Pitches* (New York: Simon & Schuster, 2004).

Kaplan, Jim. *The Greatest Game Ever Pitched: Juan Marichal, Warren Spahn, and the Pitching Duel of the Century* (Chicago: Triumph Books, 2011).

Klein, Dave. *Bob Gibson, Juan Marichal, Vida Blue, Hoyt Wilhelm*. Great Pitchers Series 2. (New York: Grosset & Dunlap, 1972).

Lugo, Carlos J. Prospectus Q & A with Juan Marichal, April 5, 2005.

www.baseballprospectus.com/article.php?articleid=3905

Mandel, Mike, ed. "Juan Marichal," *San Francisco Greats* (San Francisco: Mike Mandel, 1979), 130-36).

Marichal, Juan, with Charles Einstein. *A Pitcher's Story* (Garden City, New York: Doubleday, 1967).

Ruck, Rob. *The Tropic of Baseball* (Westport, Connecticut: Meckler Publishing, 1991).

Wendel, Tim, and José Luis Villegas. *Far from Home: Latino Baseball Players in America* (Washington, DC: National Geographic, 2008).

Wendel, Tim. *The New Face of Baseball: The One-Hundred-Year Rise and Triumph of Latinos in America's Favorite Sport* (New York: HarperCollins, 2003).

This list is a sampling of the material available on Marichal. Marichal's file from the Giamatti Library at the Baseball Hall of Fame was particularly helpful. Baseball-reference.com and retrosheet.org were invaluable for statistics and play-by-play accounts of games. Paper of Record provided access to *The Sporting News*. The Baseball Index (TBI) was indispensable for source material. Marichal's record with Escogido comes from www.lasemanadeportiva.com.

NOTES

1. The tendency in the U.S. is to pronounce the last syllable as if it were "shall" – how it would sound in French – and to put the accent on the first syllable. In Spanish, however, the "ch" digraph is always pronounced as it is in the English word "change" – and unless an accent mark indicates otherwise, the stress falls on the last syllable of words ending in 'l'. The 1971 edition of *The Sporting News Baseball Register* got it exactly right.

2. The most successful hitter against Marichal was Dick Allen: 39 for 105 (.371) with eight homers. Joe Torre – 35 for 100 (.350), also with eight homers – was close behind. Ken Boyer and Hank Aaron also hit eight homers off Marichal.

3. John Odell, "The Hall of Fame Looks at Baseball Scouts," in Jim Sandoval and Bill Nowlin, eds., *Can He Play? A Look At Baseball Scouts And Their Profession* (Phoenix: Society for American Baseball Research: 2011), vi. E-Book.

4. Ramos died in the 1948 plane crash that is Dominican baseball's greatest tragedy.

5. Rafael Trujillo was mainly interested in baseball as a populist tool. He was an aficionado of horse racing.

6. For a full discussion and fascinating details about the duel between Spahn and Marichal, see Kaplan's excellent *The Greatest Game Ever Pitched: Juan Marichal, Warren Spahn, and the Pitching Duel of the Century* (Chicago: Triumph Books, 2011). Other worthy candidates for greatest game exist: Addie Joss's perfect game, 1-0 win over Ed Walsh during the thick of a pennant race on October 2, 1908; Joe Wood's 1-0 triumph over Walter Johnson on September 6, 1912 (one of the scores of 1-0 games Johnson won and lost over his career); Babe Ruth's 13-inning 1-0 defeat of Johnson on August 15, 1916; Fred Toney's 1-0, 10-inning no-hitter over Jim Vaughn (who threw a no-hitter through nine innings) on May 2, 1917; Leon Cadore and Joe Oeschger's 26-inning 1-1 standoff on May 1, 1920, tops everything for sheer endurance; Carl Hubbell's 18-inning, 12-strikeout, 0-walk, 1-0 defeat of the Cardinals' Tex Carleton and Jesse Haines on July 2, 1933; Harvey Haddix's 12 perfect innings against Milwaukee and Lew Burdette on May 26, 1959, an effort that resulted in a 1-0 loss in the 13th inning; and Sandy Koufax's 1-0 perfect game of September 9, 1965, over the Cubs' Bob Hendley, who allowed only one hit.

7. "The Green Fields of the Mind," *Yale Alumni Magazine*, November 1977; reprinted in Paul Dickson, ed., *Baseball's Greatest Quotations* (New York: HarperCollins, 1991), 155-56.

8. Tony Blengino, "Juan Marichal–1966," in John Benson and Tony Blengino, eds., *Baseball's New Top 100: The Best Individual Seasons of All Time* (Wilton, Connecticut: Diamond Library, 2001), 182-85.

9. It does not appear that Marichal ever played in any other winter leagues. The Oriente Indios of Venezuela made a pitch for him in January 1962, after the Dominican League's season had ended prematurely, but he did not join that club. During the winter of 1965-66, the Federation of Dominican Players formed a circuit of three teams known by colors – but Marichal stayed in shape by scuba diving for abalone in the Pacific Ocean.

10. Questions exist about why Marichal had to wait to gain election to the Hall of Fame. Conventional thinking indicates that a group of voters chose to punish him for the Roseboro incident. However, there is some reason to believe that Marichal was forgiven fairly soon after because less than one year later, on June 10, 1966, *Time* published a long, laudatory cover article by Charles Parmiter and Richard Saltonstall Jr. bearing the title "The Dandy Dominican." The cover featured a nine-part sequence of photos of Marichal's distinctive high-kick delivery and read "The Best Right Arm in Baseball." The authors cover much ground and mention but do not dwell on the Roseboro incident.

11. Stuart Miller, "30 Seconds With Juan Marichal," *New York Times* Baseball Blog, Interview of May 7, 2011. bats.blogs.nytimes.com/2011/05/07/30seconds-with-juan-marichal/

12. Juan Marichal with Lew Freeman, *Juan Marichal: My Journey from the Dominican Republic to Cooperstown* (Minneapolis: MVP Books, 2011), 243.

HORACIO MARTÍNEZ

By Rory Costello

Horacio "Rabbit" Martínez (1912-1992) was the prototype for the long line of shortstops from the Dominican Republic: slick-fielding, quick, and a threat on the basepaths. He had an outstanding career in the Negro Leagues with the New York Cubans (1935-36, 1939-47). Though professional ball was largely absent in his homeland while Martínez was active, he still played there, as well as Cuba, Venezuela, and Puerto Rico. Toward the end of his career, he was also a player-manager in Panama.

Martínez got his nickname from his speed.[1] He could hop like a rabbit too, as noted Pittsburgh photographer Charles "Teenie" Harris showed. At 5-feet-9 and 155 pounds, he was a classic light-hitting glove man. Yet even though he was not a powerful batter, his superb defense brought him to the Negro Leagues' East-West All-Star Game five times: 1940, 1941, 1943, 1944, and 1945. In that showcase, among a host of the greatest players from that or any era, he batted .545 (6-for-11). [2]

Had Martínez's African descent been a little less obvious, he might have been able to perform in the majors. In *Cuban Star*, a full biography of Hall of Famer and Cubans owner Alex Pómpez, author Adrián Burgos, Jr. gave insight into Rabbit's situation. "As a reflection of the capricious policing of baseball's racial divide, thirteen Latinos would perform in both the black baseball circuit and the major leagues during this Jim Crow era [1902-1945]... the key to this group's participation in the segregated majors was the public portrayal of them as not being U.S.-born blacks.

"Horacio Martínez... felt the impact of this truth. In 1943, sportswriters offered his name as a potential barrier breaker in the majors. The *Daily Worker* writer Nat Low cited the Brooklyn Dodgers as a possible destination, given its 'weakness' at shortstop. Mistakenly referring to Martínez as 'first, last, and always a Cuban, the *Norfolk Journal and Guide* writer Lem Graves noted that there were 'plenty of Cubans playing big league baseball, no fairer than Martínez.' The problem, as was the case with dozens of other Latino players, was Martínez's hair. That was what Pómpez informed the sportswriter, admitting to previous opportunities to sell Martínez to the Washington Senators or other clubs 'if 'Rabbit' had possessed the slick hair.'"[3]

Although his playing days came too early, Martínez's legacy to the big leagues as a scout is extremely significant. Alex Pómpez went to work for the New York Giants in 1950, after

Unattributed photo, n.d.

folding his Cubans team. He hired Martínez as a bird dog, and Rabbit eventually became the Giants' head scout in Latin America after Pómpez died in 1974. His signal accomplishment was helping to bring in the first wave of Dominican major-leaguers—men like the Alou brothers, Juan Marichal, and Manny Mota.

Horacio Antonio Martínez Estrella was born on October 20, 1912 in Santiago, the second-largest city in the Dominican Republic. His parents were Antonio "Toño" Martínez and Ana Rita Estrella. As is true of many ballplayers (not least Dominicans), there has been uncertainty about both the year and place of his birth. Some sources show 1915, and there are suggestions that the place was San Pedro de Macorís, the city that has provided many Dominican shortstops, or Santo Domingo.

However, the Hall of Fame of Dominican Sports (which inducted Martínez in 1970 as part of its fourth class) shows the 1912 date and Santiago.

The Martínez family had four boys and five girls. All of Horacio's brothers – Toñito, Aquiles, and Julio – also became prominent baseball players in their homeland.[4] In his late teens, Horacio became part of the team called General Trujillo, after the Dominican president/dictator, who had taken power in 1930. The squad traveled through the Caribbean and Central America during 1931 and 1932. In 1933 and '34, Martínez was shortstop for the Licey Tigres. Licey (main color: blue) and the Escogido Leones (red) are the two longest-running and best-known Dominican teams. At that time, though, the nation did not have a professional league.

Martínez married Idalia Tejeda Burgos from Santo Domingo in March 1935. The couple eventually had three children: Horacio Augusto, Roberto Pedro Antonio and Mirtha Altagracia. Shortly after his marriage, Horacio and another outstanding Dominican, catcher Enrique "El Mariscal" Lantigua, joined the New York Cubans. They were the third and third fourth of their countrymen to play in the Negro Leagues, after pitcher Pedro Alejandro San (who debuted with Pómpez's Cuban Stars in 1926) and Juan "Tetelo" Vargas, who is regarded as the most notable early Dominican player. Among the other first-rate players on the 1935 Cubans were Hall of Famer Martín Dihigo, Alejandro Oms, Luis E. Tiant, and Manuel "Cocaína" García.

In the winter of 1935-36, Martínez played pro ball in Cuba for the first time. He joined Santa Clara, featuring player-manager Martín Dihigo – but had to play second base, because the shortstop was another Hall of Famer, Willie Wells.[5] Rabbit spent all or parts of seven winters in Cuba from 1935 through 1944, not including 1938-39 and 1939-40. He hit .258

with one homer and 92 RBIs in 978 at-bats, mainly for Santa Clara and Habana (he also played briefly for Almendares).

In 1936, spring training for the Cincinnati Reds featured a voyage to Puerto Rico. Toward the end of the trip, the Reds split their squad, sending a group of 16 players to Ciudad Trujillo (as Santo Domingo was known from 1936 to 1961) to play Dominican teams on March 3 and 4.[6] The Reds swept Escogido and Licey, 7-1 and 4-2. Martínez – listed in the U.S. box score as "Horacio" – played for Licey. He was 2-for-4, though he also committed two errors.[7]

The New York Cubans did not operate during the 1937 or 1938 seasons. Special prosecutor Thomas Dewey had Alex Pómpez in his sights for involvement with the numbers racket in New York, and Pómpez hid out in Mexico for a portion of this time. His players, Martínez among them, looked mainly to Latin America for employment.

As has often been chronicled, 1937 was a remarkable year in Dominican baseball. The 1991 book by Rob Ruck, *The Tropic of Baseball*, gives an account featuring firsthand memories from people who were there. Rafael Trujillo was not a baseball fan (though his son Ramfis was); he really loved horse racing. Yet the Generalissimo was not happy because the 1936 championship had gone to San Pedro de Macorís, and the people around him were typically seeking greater glory for the dictator. Furthermore, baseball was a populist tool in Trujillo's hands – the 1937 professional season was dedicated to his re-election.

Thus, Ciudad Trujillo assembled a powerhouse. Licey, for whom Martínez had played in 1936, and Escogido were combined. Furthermore, the best Negro Leaguers of the day were lured to come down and play. The Dragons' list of luminaries included Satchel Paige, Josh Gibson, "Cool Papa" Bell, and more. Many of the Negro Leaguers actually came down relatively late in the series, which ran from March to July; they displaced Dominicans and Cubans. The proportion of native players in the league that year wound up being low – but Martínez was there throughout, playing for Santiago.[8]

The dean of Dominican baseball writers, Emilio "Cuqui" Córdova, focused exclusively on the events of the 1937 season in the 17th book of his series *Historia del Béisbol Dominicano*.[9] An earlier installment was devoted to Horacio Martínez, though unfortunately that fuller biography was not available as a source for this story.[10]

After the excesses of 1937, official pro baseball went on hiatus in the Dominican Republic for 14 years. Nonetheless, following the collapse, Martínez played for Licey when that club reformed.[11] During this time, he also played in his homeland against visiting teams (from Puerto Rico, for example) and in the Inter-Antillean Series with Cuba and Puerto Rico. Also, during the years that there was no professional league play, baseball remained the sport of choice for Dominicans. Contests continued in the nation and Martínez was a frequent participant.

He also ventured elsewhere in Latin America. A book called *Historia del Béisbol en el Zulia*, which focuses on the game in Venezuela's westernmost state, notes that he and Cuban shortstop Silvio García came down in 1937 to play with the Pastora club.[12] Rabbit remained with Pastora in 1938, taking part in a memorable 20-inning game on June 5. The winning pitcher, fellow Dominican Andrés Julio Báez, went all the way in the six-hour, twenty-minute battle and scored the game's only run.[13] Báez was known as "Grillo B" – he was the middle brother of three "Crickets" who are all in the Hall of Fame of Dominican Sports.

Martínez also played 11 games for Vargas in Venezuela in 1938, going 9 for 49 (.184) with one RBI. Furthermore, he reinforced the Ponce Leones in Puerto Rico's inaugural season of winter baseball, 1938-39. Until 1941, that circuit did not have full professional status – it was known as *La Liga de Béisbol Semiprofesional de Puerto Rico* (LBSPR).[14] Although Martínez's name does not appear in *Enciclopedia Béisbol Ponce Leones, 1938-1987* by Rafael Costas, Puerto Rican League historian Jorge Colón Delgado has confirmed that Rabbit was there (statistics remain under investigation).[15]

Alex Pómpez was back in baseball in 1939, and so were his New York Cubans. Martínez rejoined the roster. In June and July 1939, however, a series took place in Ciudad Trujillo between the Dominican Republic (represented by Licey and Escogido) and Puerto Rico (represented by the Ponce Leones). "Licey walked away with the championship trophy and Horacio Martínez was the top hitter in the competition."[16] This followed an earlier series in Puerto Rico, which featured Licey against Ponce and San Juan.[17]

Here and there Martínez attracted attention from the mainstream U.S. press. In July 1942, ahead of a doubleheader against the semipro Brooklyn Bushwicks at Dexter Park, the *New York Times* singled him out for praise, saying, "The Cuban Stars have been traveling at a fast pace since Horacio Martínez took the shortstop role a month ago."[18] The previous day, the *Brooklyn Eagle* had explained that Martínez joined the club late because he could not get transportation north for six weeks.[19]

Perhaps the real reason was the same as what took place in 1943, when Martínez also reported late to the Cubans. As the *New York Post* wrote that May, Rabbit had ignored Alex Pómpez's cables because he had been making good money at home in the Dominican Republic – but changed his mind, allegedly because he had been hitting Trujillo's favorite pitcher too well.[20]

In July 1943, the Cubans headed upstate to play the Niagara Falls Days at Hyde Park Stadium (later renamed for local hero Sal Maglie). The *Niagara Falls Gazette* wrote, "Horacio Martínez, at shortstop, continues to show why he is rated without a peer at that position. Speedy and sure, Martínez has come up from the Dominicans of Cuba [sic] rated by far the best shortstop from that island since the great Checon [sic], although many critics maintain he is the equal of the latter."[21] The doubly confused comparison was with Pelayo Chacón, the Cuban who had also been a long-time star in the Negro Leagues, and whose son Elio became a major-leaguer.

A day previously, the *Gazette* had written that Martínez, "sensational shortstop," along with Dave "Impo" Barnhill and Roy Campanella (misspelled as "Campinello"), had been in line for a 1942 tryout with the Pittsburgh Pirates that never materialized.[22] Neil Lanctot's biography of Campanella details how Pirates owner William Benswanger initially encouraged the notion, then backed down – but this account does not mention Martínez as one of the candidates.

Stanley Glenn, a star catcher who broke into the Negro Leagues with the Philadelphia Stars in 1944, told author Brent Kelley that he viewed Martínez as a Hall of Fame player. "He was a better hitter than [Phil] Rizzuto; he was also a better fielder. He could pick it, my friend."[23] Another Negro League chronicler, William McNeil, wrote, "Martínez was a defensive wizard of the caliber of Ozzie Smith. He had speed, grace, exceptional intuition, a sure glove, and a rocket for an arm. He was generally recognized as the best shortstop in the Negro Leagues during the late '30s and early '40s."[24]

Glenn was giving Rabbit too much credit with the stick. William McNeil also wrote, "The chink in Martínez's armor that kept him from becoming an all-time great was his weak bat. During his Negro League career his average hovered around the .230 mark."[25] Negro League records are patchy, but the general indication is in keeping with the more complete Cuban data. Rabbit compensated to some degree, however, with "small ball" skills. In his *Biographical Encyclopedia of the Negro Baseball Leagues*, James A. Riley wrote that Martínez was "a good bunter, fast on the bases, and good on either end of the hit-and-run play... Always a hustler."

Martínez was also a leader. At some point he became a manager; possibly the first time he did so was during the Inter-Antillean Centennial Series of 1944. This tournament commemorated the 100th anniversary of the Dominican Republic's independence from Haiti. Rabbit and Manuel Henríquez co-managed the home team, which upset Cuba – only the third time Cuba had lost an international competition in 20 years.[26] Martínez also managed his national team during the Amateur World Series of 1944, but the seventh edition of this tournament was marred by various protests. One of them came from Martínez in a loss to Cuba; he objected to the improper use of pinch-hitters.[27]

In the winter of 1945-46, Venezuela established its main professional baseball league. Martínez came down to play for Patriotas de Venezuela, going 14 for 52 (.269) in 13 games with no homers and seven RBIs.[28] That winter he also served as a player-manager in Panama. According to Dominican sources, the team was Colón; if so, that club was in the Canal Zone League, and boasted Cardinals center fielder Terry Moore. On January 3, 1946, however, the Panama Professional League began play with 28 players imported from Mexico, the U.S., and Cuba. This four-team circuit, which the *Sporting News* compared to Class-B ball, could have been the one Martínez joined.[29]

As Rabbit's career with the New York Cubans wound down in 1946 and 1947, Alex Pómpez brought in a variety of notable players. One of them was Orestes Miñoso, later known as "Minnie," who played third base in 1946. The shortstop that year was Silvio García, who pushed Martínez over to second base. García jumped to the Mexican League that summer, however, as Jorge Pasquel was luring many players south of the border with bigger money in his bid for major-league status.

Rabbit returned to the Panama Professional League in the winter of 1946-47 to play for Cadena Panameña de Radiodifusión. In 1947, with much of the luster gone from the Mexican scene, Silvio García came back to New York. There is no conclusive evidence that Martínez ever played in Mexico himself.[30] However, he concluded his U.S. career with a championship, as the Cubans (Negro National League) defeated the Cleveland Buckeyes (Negro American League) in the Negro World Series. What may well have been his final games as a pro came with Panama's Cervecería Nacional in 1947-48.

On Sunday, January 11, 1948, Dominican baseball suffered its greatest tragedy – an event that affected Horacio Martínez directly. A twin-engine plane flying from Barahona (in the southwestern part of the republic) to Santiago (in the central Cibao region) crashed into the Río Verde mountains. Except for catcher Enrique Lantigua, who had a premonition and drove instead, the entire Santiago club perished. That included Toñito and Aquiles Martínez, the former a popular catcher and the latter a fine-fielding second baseman. Julio Martínez, the club's teenaged mascot, also escaped because his own team had scheduled a game.[31]

The 1949 edition of the annals of the University of Santo Domingo showed that Martínez was employed there as a sports instructor (i.e., baseball coach). He eventually became the university's athletic director, occupying that job while he was scouting for the Giants. Felipe Alou, a pre-med student, was his cleanup hitter in 1955.

On December 28, 1956, Martínez managed his homeland's team against a squad of U.S. players in the Dominican League's All-Star game. The Dominican fans, who selected both teams, extended a special invitation to Eddie Lopat to come out of retirement and pitch. Lopat hurled the first two innings and got the win; Bill Mazeroski had the game's only homer. The *yanquis* were managed by John "Red" Davis, a minor-league skipper for the Giants who was then also managing Escogido (a sign of the ties between Horace Stoneham's franchise and the Dominican Republic).[32]

Martínez was a coach for Escogido; he also managed Licey for three games in 1951, the first season of the current Dominican League. In addition, he continued to manage the Dominican national team in amateur competition. One example was the 1959 Pan-American Games, held in Chicago.[33] Although the Dominicans finished eighth with a record of 2-3, a powerful young man named Rico Carty (who turned 20 during the tournament) made a strong impression on U.S. scouts. He was spotted by Milwaukee Braves scout Ted McGrew and soon thereafter went on to become another early Dominican big-league star.

Although Martínez did not sign Carty, he did land quite a few other players for the Giants besides the Alous and Manny Mota. Among the men who made it to the majors were José Vidal and Freddie Velázquez (who signed in 1958), Ricardo Joséph (1959), Pepe Frías (1966), Rafael Robles (1967), and Elías Sosa (1968). Sosa was the only one of them who played for the Giants, though. Perhaps for that reason, over time the franchise's interest in Dominican talent waned. Yet the great players whom Martínez signed felt immense loyalty and respect toward him. In July 1993, Juan Marichal described the poignant end of Rabbit's scouting career to authors Marcos Bretón and José Luis Villegas.

"When other scouts were earning twenty-five thousand and thirty thousand dollars a year, Horacio was only earning nine thousand dollars. So when the Giants were looking to liquidate some of their scouting positions, they were going to retire Horacio at half his salary. I was out of the organization but the Giants asked my opinion and I told them they should retire Horacio at his full salary because he didn't even earn a third of what other scouts were earning. And so they did, but [before that] when the Giants offered me a job [in the late 1970s] they were going to release him but I didn't permit that. For me, Horacio was like a father and I wasn't going to take his job away from him. He was the best scout they ever had."[34]

In later life, Martínez suffered from Parkinson's disease. Rob Ruck offered a moving depiction in *The Tropic of Baseball*. "Horacio Martínez, 77, is confined to a wheelchair in his Santo Domingo home. . .the once-graceful shortstop now can hardly speak. While struggling to describe his career to me on an earlier trip, Horacio Martínez's eyes had filled with tears, brought on by frustration. I make the mistake of telling Julio about his brother's efforts and the *Aguilas* coach excuses himself. He walks down the first base line into the right field corner where he sheds tears of his own."[35]

Horacio Martínez died on April 14, 1992. The following year, a powerful testament to his importance came from another of the most eminent Dominican baseball figures, Felipe Alou. Alou told Marcos Bretón and José Luis Villegas how much Martínez meant to him personally.

"There are American black players who have been elevated to the Hall of Fame, who have been recovered from the forgotten, and that work has been done by Americans. But we don't have and will never have that kind of representation to promote a Horacio Martínez. He wasn't just some scout. He was a great athlete and he spoke a great deal to me before I left to play in the United States. This was back in the 1950s when there was so much racism in the United States, but I came here aware of all those things because I had a great teacher. I was his first player signed to make it to the big leagues and for me, it was like I was on a mission."[36]

Alou expanded on this theme with Rob Ruck. When he was in his first pro season with the Giants, and encountered racism on a long bus trip in the Deep South, young Felipe was tempted to quit and go back home. Instead, "I thought about Horacio Martínez, not so much my mom and dad. I didn't want to let him down and I stayed."[37] Alou in turn then became an inspiration to many Dominicans.

Echoing Marichal and Alou, Manny Mota offered his own personal tribute in 2012. In a firm and even tone, he emphasized, "Mr. Horacio Martínez was without a doubt one of the greatest players in the history of the Dominican Republic. Besides being a great player, he was like a father to me. I've got a great deal of respect and admiration for him."[38]

In 2005, Martínez became one of 94 preliminary candidates named by the Hall of Fame's Special Committee on the Negro Leagues. The process had changed since Felipe Alou had talked about it in 1993 – there was at least some Latino representation among the wealth of prominent figures. The screening committee also included an expert on Latin America in Adrián Burgos. In 2012, Burgos discussed what happened with Martínez's candidacy.

"The five members of the nominating committee[39] voted on narrowing down the list. Each nominee had to meet the three-quarters of the vote threshold that the Hall requires for induction; 39 made that cut. The lack of stats and more than some testimonials from a few Negro Leaguers hurt Horacio's chances. For certain, we knew he was a fantastic fielder, but there was no Gold Glove award or a poll of the greatest fielders of the Negro Leagues. That also limited his chances."[40]

A few years after the Special Committee election, however, the Latino Baseball Hall of Fame (*El Salón de la Fama del Béisbol Latino*) was formed to recognize great Hispanic players. As part of its second class, announced in October 2010 and inducted in 2011, Horacio Martínez was named by the Hall's Veterans Committee. This institution is located in the Dominican Republic, and Martínez became the fourth Dominican honored. He followed Tetelo Vargas – and his two special protégés, Felipe Alou and Juan Marichal. Yet, as this kind, modest man said in 1975, "I have no complaints about life and although I have no money, it is my personal satisfaction of having always been an honest person."[41]

Special thanks to Peggy Fukunaga for contributing insights from her research on Dominican baseball, and to Rob Ruck for the Introduction and his advice. Continued thanks also to Manny Mota and José Mota, Adam Chodzko, Media Relations, Los Angeles Angels of Anaheim; SABR members Alfonso Tusa, Jorge Colón Delgado, and Adrián Burgos; Jesús Alberto Rubio.

SOURCES

Books:

Figueredo, Jorge S. *Cuban Baseball: A Statistical History, 1878-1961* (Jefferson, North Carolina: McFarland & Co., 2003).

Riley, James A. *The Biographical Encyclopedia of the Negro Baseball Leagues* (New York: Carroll & Graf Publishers, Inc., 1994).

Gutiérrez, Daniel, Efraim Álvarez, and Daniel Gutiérrez, Jr. *La Enciclopedia del Béisbol en Venezuela* (Caracas, Venezuela: Editorial Norma, 2007).

Internet resources:

Pabellón de la Fama del Deporte Dominicano (http://www.pabellondelafamadeportedom.com)

Edwin "Kako" Vázquez, "Horacio Martínez de Santiago Rep Dom," 1-800-BEISBOL (http://www.1800beisbol.com/baseball/Deportes/Beisbol_Dominicano/Horacio_Martínez_de_Santiago_Rep_Dom/)

www.licey.com

NOTES

1. Marcos Bretón and José Luis Villegas, *Away Games: The Life and Times of a Latin Baseball Player*, New York, New York: Simon & Schuster, 1999, 51. Some sources indicate that he was also called "Millito," but this may well be confusion with another player of the era named Luis Emilio Martínez.

2. Larry Lester, *Black Baseball's National Showcase* (Lincoln, Nebraska: University of Nebraska Press, 2001).

3. Adrian Burgos, Jr., *Cuban Star: How One Negro-League Owner Changed the Face of Baseball* (New York, New York: Hill and Wang, 2011), 159-160.

4. Rob Ruck, *Raceball: How the Major Leagues Colonized the Black and Latin Game* (Boston, Massachusetts: Beacon Press, 2011), 65.

5. Roberto González Echevarría, *The Pride of Havana* (New York, New York: Oxford University Press, 1999), 274.

6. "Red Rookie Trying to Emulate [Augie] Galan," *The Sporting News*, March 5, 1936: 6.

7. *The Sporting News*, March 12, 1936: 10.

8. Rob Ruck, *The Tropic of Baseball* (Westport, Connecticut: Meckler Publishing, 1991), Chapter 3.

9. Ubi Rivas, "Libro de Cuqui Córdova narra la calidad del torneo de 1937," *Hoy* (Santo Domingo, Dominican Republic), October 24, 2009.

10. Cuqui Córdova, *Horacio Martínez: El Rabbit* (Santo Domingo, Dominican Republic: Revista Historia del Béisbol, 2004).

11. At some point in his career, he also played one season for Escogido.

12. Luis Verde, *Historia del Béisbol en el Zulia* (Maracaibo, Venezuela: Editorial Maracaibo, S.R.L.), 1999.

13. Cuqui Córdova, " 'Grillo B' ganó un juego de 20 innings en Venezuela (05.06.1938), venciendo al zurdo cubano Lázaro Salazar 1 x 0," *Listín Diario* (Santo Domingo, Dominican Republic), March 30, 2010.

14. Thomas E. Van Hyning, *Puerto Rico's Winter League* (Jefferson, North Carolina: McFarland & Co., 1995), 9.

15. Cuqui Córdova's book also cites Puerto Rican sources, and Thomas Van Hyning also mentions in passing that Puerto Rican fans got to see Martínez.

16. William McNeil, *Black Baseball Out of Season* (Jefferson, North Carolina: McFarland & Co., 2007), 147.

17. 1939 newspaper reports in the Dominican newspaper *La Opinión*, as researched by Peggy Fukunaga.

18. "Bushwicks Meet Cubans," *New York Times*, July 19, 1942.

19 "Dimout Law Again Saves Bushwicks," *Brooklyn Eagle*, July 18, 1942: 10.

20 Stanley Frank, "Negro Ball Teams Carry On Despite All Difficulties," *New York Post*, May 29, 1943: 34.

21 "Barley Definitely Slated to Pitch for Days Against Cubans Wednesday," *Niagara Falls Gazette*, July 13, 1943: 13.

22 "New York Cubans Have Strong Team Here for Game Here Wednesday with Days," *Niagara Falls Gazette*, July 12, 1943: 11.

23 Brent Kelley, *Voices from the Negro Leagues* (Jefferson, North Carolina: McFarland & Co., 1998), 155.

24 William McNeil, *Baseball's Other All-Stars* (Jefferson, North Carolina: McFarland & Co., 2000), 174.

25 McNeil, 174.

26 Cuqui Córdova, "Serie Interantillana Centenario 1944," *Listín Diario*, December 17, 2011.

27 Rafael V. Peña, *El Big Show Desde New York* blog, November 14 and November 21, 2011 (http://www.radiario.com/index.php?option=com_content&view=article&id=368:radiario)

28 *The Biographical Encyclopedia of the Negro Baseball Leagues* incorrectly states that Martínez was player-manager for Caracas.

29 "Panama Pro Loop Begins Play," *The Sporting News*, January 10, 1946: 16.

30 *The Biographical Encyclopedia of the Negro Baseball Leagues* also states that Martínez played winter ball in Mexico (La Liga de la Costa del Pacífico began play in the 1945-46 season). However, leading Mexican baseball researcher Jesús Rubio could not find any evidence of it. There is no entry for Martínez either in the reference on Mexican summer ball, *La Enciclopedia del Béisbol Mexicano*, though there are gaps in that volume (for example, Hall of Famer Willard Brown).

31 Rafael V. Peña, "La Tragedia de Río Verde 1948," *El Día* (Santo Domingo, Dominican Republic), January 11, 2011. Ruck, *The Tropic of Baseball*, 102.

32 Feliz Acosta Núñez, "Lopat Takes Hill, Helps U.S. Stars Decision Natives," *The Sporting News*, January 9, 1957: 20.

33 Ruck, *Raceball*, 205.

34 Bretón and Villegas, 52.

35 Ruck, *The Tropic of Baseball*, 103.

36 Bretón and Villegas, 51-52.

37 Ruck, *Raceball*, 150.

38 Manny Mota, telephone interview with Rory Costello, May 21, 2012.

39 Rob Ruck was on the full 12-member voting committee.

40 Adrián Burgos, e-mail to Rory Costello, April 11, 2012.

41 Arturo Industrioso, *El Caribe* (Santo Domingo, Dominican Republic), June 21, 1975.

Pedro Martínez

By Norm King

Fred Claire wasn't a politician. However, like many politicians, the erstwhile executive vice president of the Los Angeles Dodgers said one thing when he was talking about Pedro Martínez in 1992, ended up doing the opposite, and regretted his action.

"I won't trade Pedro Martínez, I don't care who they offer," said Claire.[1]

Well, he did trade Martínez, and lost the services of one of the best pitchers of the last 50 years, a three-time Cy Young Award-winning pitcher with a career 219-100 record and a lifetime 2.93 ERA. More on the trade later.

Pedro Jaime Martínez was born October 25, 1971, in Manoguayabo, Distrito Nacional, Dominican Republic, the fifth of six children born to Paolino and Leopoldina Martínez. Manoguayabo was a poverty-ridden town nine miles from the country's capital of Santo Domingo, and the family lived in a tin-roofed hovel with dirt floors. Paolino supported the family by working as a janitor and performing odd jobs, while Leopoldina took in laundry. The Martínez children grew up poor, but they were well dressed for school and they took their education seriously.

They also took baseball seriously...very seriously. Pedro, along with his older brother Ramon, had pitching in their genes thanks to Paolino, who was a top-flight pitcher during the 1950s (he played with future big leaguers Felipe and Matty Alou, both of whom said he was good enough to play in the majors) with a mean sinkerball.

"I was too poor to leave the country," Paolino says. "When the Giants invited me for a tryout, I didn't have cleats. So I couldn't go to the tryout."[2]

Nonetheless, the young Martínez boys grew up playing baseball, using tree branches or other sticks they could find to fashion bats. For balls they would re-enact the French Revolution with their sisters' dolls. "When my sisters came home from school, they'd find [the dolls] with no head and they would go, 'Mommy! Mommy!'" he said.[3]

In addition to having his father as a pitching role model, Pedro looked up to his brother Ramon both on and off the field. Almost four years older than Pedro, Ramon became de facto head of the household when Paolino and Leopoldina divorced when he was 13, showing a maturity and leadership that influences Pedro to this day.

"What I know of baseball, and life off the field, I owe to Ramon," said Martínez. "Everything I am I learned from Ramon."[4]

Ramon pitched for the Dominican Republic team during the 1984 Olympics in Los Angeles at age 17, and was signed as a free agent by Los Angeles Dodgers scout Raphael "Ralph" Avila on September 1 of that year. The Dodgers sent him to their baseball academy back in the Dominican Republic to begin his professional career.

In the grand tradition of annoying little brothers everywhere, 13-year-old Pedro tagged along when Ramon went to the academy. Avila eventually noticed him tossing a ball around and decided to put the radar gun to his fastball – it clocked in at 80 miles per hour. Wisely, Avila told Pedro to keep on pitching. Pedro did just that, and in 1988, Avila signed Pedro, now 16, to get him into the Dodger fold before he could turn professional. Pedro continued pitching locally in 1988-89 with the Dodgers' Dominican Summer League affiliate, going a combined 12-3 over the two seasons.

Finally, in 1990 at age 18, he began his climb through the Dodgers' minor-league system with Great Falls of the rookie-level Pioneer League. His season was a harbinger of things to come, as he went 8-3 with a 3.62 ERA. His victory total was the highest on the team, as was his walk total of 40 in 77 innings.

His performance earned him a trip through the southwest United States in 1991. He started off in Bakersfield of the Class-A California League, where he won all eight of his decisions with a 2.05 ERA. Since it was clear that he was too good for that level, he then moved to San Antonio of the Double-A Texas League, and while his record there was only 7-5, he had a sparkling 1.76 ERA, prompting the parent club to move him yet again, this time to the Albuquerque Dukes of the Triple-A Pacific Coast League. Martínez struggled at this level, only going 3-3 with a 3.66 ERA.

Overall, Martínez went 18-8 with a 2.28 ERA and 192 strikeouts and 66 walks in 177⅓ innings pitched, becoming the first player to go through three levels in the Dodgers' system in one season, since brother Ramon did it three years earlier. *The Sporting News* named him its minor league player of the year.

"Although Pedro stands just 5-9 and weighs about 160 pounds, his fastball has been clocked at 90 mph," wrote Mike Eisenbath. "He also has a wicked changeup that seems to be a family gift."[5]

It was in spring training 1992 that Claire uttered his fateful words. Martínez was doing well at Dodgertown, the team's spring training facility in Florida at the time, and his reputation was growing to the extent that other teams asked about him. At the time, he wasn't going anywhere except Albuquerque, because the Dodgers felt that another year of seasoning at Triple A was in order for the 20-year-old.

In 1992, Martínez went 7-6 with a 3.81 ERA, but with 124 strikeouts in 125⅓ innings pitched and only 57 walks. His overall season earned him a September call-up and his first major-league start, a 3-1 complete game loss at Cincinnati.

Pedro had a good spring training in 1993 but was sent down again to Albuquerque just before the season began, but after pitching only three innings in one game with the Dukes, he returned to the Dodgers on April 9 after reliever Todd Worrell was placed on the 15-day disabled list.

He got into his first Dodger game that year, coming on for brother Ramon, who had only given up one run in six innings to the Atlanta Braves, but was down 1-0. Pedro gave up two more runs in 1⅔ innings. The final score was 3-0. Pedro and Ramon became the first brothers to pitch in the same game for the same team since Rick and Mickey Mahler did it in 1979 for, as it happens, the Braves.

His next appearance, and first loss of the season, came the following night in the Dodgers' opener home against St. Louis. Gerald Perry of the Cardinals arrived at the ballpark less than hour before game time because he thought it was a night game. Martínez wished he had stayed away because Perry hit a three-run homer off him in the seventh inning to erase a 7-5 Dodgers lead. The final score was 9-7 St. Louis.

Although the season didn't start the way he would have wanted, Pedro righted his pitching ship and went on to have a very good rookie year. He appeared in 65 games, all but two of them in relief, and finished with a 10-5 record and a fine 2.61 ERA. Perhaps his most impressive statistic was his 119 strikeouts in 107 innings pitched.

Good rookie season notwithstanding, Claire did indeed hear a trade offer that he couldn't refuse, and in November sent Martínez to the Montreal Expos in exchange for speedy second baseman Delino DeShields. For the Expos it was a cost-cutting move, as DeShields made $1,537,500 in 1993 and was eligible for arbitration. Martínez, on the other hand, had made $114,000 the previous season and couldn't go for arbitration for another two years.

The Dodgers had used Martínez almost exclusively in relief because they didn't think he had the size and strength to pitch deep into ballgames. The Expos saw him as a starting pitcher despite weighing less than 160 pounds, and put him into the starting rotation with Ken Hill, Jeff Fassero, Butch Henry, and Kirk Rueter.

It is well known among baseball aficionados that the 1994 Montreal Expos had the best record in baseball at 74-40 when their season and a possible World Series appearance were derailed by a players' strike. The pitching staff had the lowest ERA in the National League (3.56), and Martínez was a major contributor

Photo courtesy of the National Baseball Hall of Fame

to the team's success. He went 11-5 with a 3.42 ERA and 142 strikeouts in 144⅔ innings.

He also became known as a headhunter for his tendency to pitch high and inside, and acquired the nickname "Senor Plunk" from the Montreal media. He led the league in hit batsmen with 11, got thrown out of 12 games and got into three fights. That first fight occurred on April 13, when Reggie Sanders charged the mound after being hit on the elbow by a Martínez pitch with one out in the eighth inning. Even Sanders' teammates thought it highly unlikely that Martínez tried to deliberately to hit him at that point because Martínez was pitching a perfect game at the time.

"That's the way you've got to pitch," said Reds catcher Brian Dorsett, who broke up the no-hitter in the ninth by hitting a single with nobody out in the top of the ninth. "You've got to bust them in and keep them honest."[6]

"He's not trying to hit anyone," said Expos pitching coach Joe Kerrigan. "He isn't a malicious kid."[7]

An Expos fire sale saw the Expos lose Hill, Larry Walker, Marquis Grissom, and John Wetteland prior to the 1995 season. What had been a powerhouse the year before was an also-ran team that finished last in the National League East Division with a 66-78 record. Nonetheless, Martínez continued improving, going 14-10 with a 3.51 ERA and 174 K's in 194⅔ innings. He hit 11 batters again, but that represented an improvement because he pitched 30 more innings than he had the previous year, and left him in third place among league leaders behind Mark Leiter of the Giants with 17 and Darryl Kile of Houston with 12.

The highlight of Martínez' 1995 season, and perhaps of his career, came on June 3 against the Padres in San Diego. That night Martínez became only the second pitcher in history to take a perfect game into extra innings. Harvey Haddix went 12 perfect innings for the Pirates against the Braves in 1959 before losing his no-hitter and the game in the 13th. Pedro was perfect through nine, but the score was still 0-0. The Expos scored once in the top of the 10th, but Martínez gave up a double in the bottom of the tenth to leadoff hitter Bip Roberts. Closer Mel Rojas relieved him and got the next three hitters to preserve the win.

The Expos bounced back in 1996 with an 88-74 record, missing out on the National League wild card by two games. On the surface, it looks as if Martínez' season wasn't quite as good as the year before; he went 13-10, with the highest ERA of his career to date, 3.70. His won-loss record was hampered by the fact that the Expos only scored 22 runs in the ten losses. Nonetheless, he got his first All-Star nod and gave up two hits in one inning of work as the National League shut out the American League, 6-0, in Philadelphia.

Any questions about Martínez' abilities were answered in 1997. In the same season that DeShields left the Dodgers after three unspectacular seasons (.241 batting average and .326 on-base percentage from 1994-96), Martínez went 17-8, led the league with a 1.90 ERA, 305 strikeouts, and 13 complete games. He also struck out two American League hitters in one inning of work at the All-Star Game. He became the first and only Cy Young Award winner in Expos history, receiving 25 of 28 first-place votes (Greg Maddux got the other three). For Martínez, the award was more than a mere personal accolade, as he became the first Dominican pitcher to win it. Not only was he proud of that, he felt that fellow Dominican Juan Marichal should have won it at least once during his great career. He even gave his award to Marichal at a banquet after the season ended. Marichal, though deeply touched by the gesture, returned it back to Martínez.

From an Expos standpoint, the first Cy Young Award in the team's history was worth celebrating only because it increased Martínez' trade value. Pedro was one year away from free agency and Expos management wanted to trade him while they could still get something for him. Eventually they sent him to the Boston Red Sox for Carl Pavano and Tony Armas. After the trade, Martínez signed a six-year contract with the Red Sox worth $75 million, making him the highest-paid pitcher in baseball at the time.

The 1997 Red Sox under Jimy Williams finished fourth in the American League East Division with a 78-84 record. With Martínez in the rotation in 1998, Williams suddenly became a much better manager, piloting the Red Sox to a 92-70 record, good enough for second place in the division and the wild card playoff spot. Pedro had another magnificent

Photo courtesy of the National Baseball Hall of Fame

season, going 19-7 with a 2.89 ERA and 251 strikeouts. He was an All-Star for the third straight season -- for the American League this time -- but didn't appear in the game. He finished second in the Cy Young voting behind Roger Clemens of the Toronto Blue Jays.

Martínez also got his first taste of post-season action, as he took the mound in Game One of the American League Division Series against the Cleveland Indians. Pedro pitched seven strong innings, giving up three runs, striking out eight and not giving up any walks as the Red Sox won easily, 11-3. It was his only appearance of the series, as the Indians went on to win the next three and move on to the American League Championship Series.

Martínez had a season for the ages in 1999. He won the pitcher's triple crown, leading the league in wins (23 against four losses), ERA (2.07), and strikeouts (313). He not only started and won the All-Star Game for the American League at Fenway Park, but he did it in style, striking out five of the six batters he faced in two innings' work. He was also chosen the game's MVP.

The Red Sox again made the playoffs as the wild card in a rematch from 1998 against the Indians. Martínez started Game One and pitched four scoreless innings before leaving with a strained back muscle. Cleveland scored in the bottom of the ninth to win it, 3-2. Boston won two of the next three to knot the series at two going into Game Five. Meanwhile, the knot in Martínez' back disappeared.

Bret Saberhagen started the decider for Boston and was replaced by Derek Lowe in the second inning. After three innings, the score was 8-7 Cleveland. The Red Sox tied it in the top of the fourth; then on came Martínez in the bottom of the inning. What happened next became part of Red Sox lore.

For the next five innings, Martínez completely silenced the Indian bats. He threw 97 pitches, allowed no runs and no hits, walked three and struck out eight. In the meantime, the Sox scored four more runs to take a 12-8 lead. Martínez showed a sense of style by striking out Omar Vizquel to end the game and the series.

Martínez was the only bright spot in the ALCS against the Yankees, which the Bombers won in five games. Roger Clemens was now with the Yankees, and what was hyped as a big showdown between Pedro and Clemens in Game Three at Fenway ended up as games that are hyped as big showdowns often do. The Sox hammered Clemens for five runs in two innings and won going away, 13-1. Martínez pitched seven scoreless innings for the win.

While the Y2K scare was nothing more than hype in the hi-tech industry, Martínez' year 2000 deserved all the publicity it got. He won his second consecutive Cy Young Award by unanimous vote with an 18-6 record, and he led the American League in ERA (1.74), shutouts (4), and strikeouts (284). His season was especially impressive because it came at the height of the steroid era, when the overall American League ERA that year was 4.91. He held opponents to the lowest on-base percentage against (.213) in 100 years.[8] The Red Sox finished second yet again in their division, but did not make the playoffs.

The 2001 season was an odyssey of frustration and disappointment for Martínez as he contended with major injury for the first time in his career. He missed two months after with a minor rotator cuff tear, and did not pitch the rest of the season after a September 7 3-2 loss to the Yankees. He also got into a dispute with general manager Dan Duquette, who said in early September that Martínez was healthy enough to pitch. "I think Dan knows as much about medicine as I do, maybe less," said Martínez. "That's why I'm surprised he said I'm healthy."[9]

For the year, Martínez was 7-3 in 18 starts with a respectable 2.69 ERA in 116⅔ innings pitched.

Pedro bounced back in 2002 with a vengeance. He reached the 20-win plateau for the second time (20-4), won the ERA and strikeout titles (2.26 ERA, 239 K's) and was voted to the All-Star team, although he didn't play in the game (the infamous 7-7 tie in Milwaukee). He also finished second in the Cy Young Award voting to Oakland's Barry Zito.

Pedro's 2003 season will be remembered for two controversial incidents he was involved in during that year's ALCS against the Yankees.

Martínez had a 14-4 record that season and won the ERA title again with a 2.22 average. Red Sox manager Grady Little started limiting the number of innings Martínez worked and gave him an extra day's rest whenever he could. The Red Sox finished 95-67 and earned them their first playoff berth since 1999. After defeating the A's in the ALDS, the Sox hooked up in a memorable series that was a slugfest in more ways than one.

Martínez got his first start in Game Three with the ALCS tied at one game apiece. The Yankees had just gone ahead, 3-2, in the fourth when Martínez hit right fielder Karim Garcia with a pitch. No fight erupted, but it charged up an already electric atmosphere, and the benches emptied in the bottom of the inning when Clemens threw at Manny Ramírez.

Baseball brawls generally involve players from both teams running on the field and shouting "Oh yeah?" at each other. For some reason, the Yankees' 72-year-old bench coach Don Zimmer decided to take a run at Martínez, who wasn't in a very good mood himself after blowing a lead in the top of the inning. Martínez threw Zimmer to the ground, and while no one was injured, the game did suffer a black eye. Zimmer later admitted the encounter was his fault.

Although Martínez lost that game, the Red Sox hung in and forced a Game Seven. Little went with his ace, which was a good idea, at least for most of the game. Going into the eighth, the Red Sox led 5-2. With one out and a run in, and Hideki Matsui coming up, Little went to the mound and asked Martínez if he had anything left. Martínez said he did, but it turned out he was wrong.

"Little went to the mound, spoke to Martínez and patted him with encouragement, but then turned and stepped back to the dugout, not knowing that he was about to join Bill Buckner in Red Sox lore," wrote Buster Olney.[10]

Matsui hit a ground-rule double, which left runners at second and third. Yankee catcher Jorge Posada then got a bloop hit that drove in two runs and tied the game. Aaron Boone hit the series-winning homer off reliever Tim Wakefield in the 11th.

Since it's easier to replace managers than star pitchers, Little was fired after the 2003 season and Martínez stayed in the rotation. He wasn't quite as dominant in 2004, for even though he had a 16-9 record, his ERA was an un-Pedro-like 3.90. The Red Sox made the playoffs again in what proved to be an historic season for the team.

The Yankees and Red Sox met again in the ALCS. Martínez lost Game Two, going six innings in a 3-1 defeat. The Yankees wore out home plate with all the times they crossed the plate in a Game Three 19-8 battering, giving them a 3-0 series lead. But then the Yankees forgot they had to win four games.

The Sox stayed alive by winning Game Four, 6-4, in 12 innings. Pedro pitched Game Five and allowed four runs, leaving after six innings down 4-2. The Sox tied it in the eighth and won it in the 14th to make the series 3-2. After Curt Schilling's courageous outing in Game Six, the Sox completed the comeback in Game Seven. Martínez pitched the seventh inning and allowed two runs on three hits, but the Red Sox won the game easily 10-3.

After such an inspired comeback by the Sox, the World Series was anti-climactic, as they easily disposed of the St. Louis Cardinals in four straight games. After a mediocre ALCS, Martínez was excellent in his only World Series start, pitching seven shutout innings in Game Three and getting the win in a 3-1 Red Sox victory.

In the joyous victors' clubhouse at Busch Stadium, Martínez took a moment to remind fans of the departing Montreal Expos how important the city was to him by sharing the Red Sox victory with them.

"I'm glad I got it [the World Series win] and I would like to share it with the people of Montreal that are not going to have a team anymore," he said in an interview. "My heart and my ring is [sic] with them, too."[11]

Winning isn't everything in sports, nor is it the only thing. Professional sports is a business and like any businessman, Martínez took the opportunity to shop his wares to the highest bidder once he became a free agent after the 2004 season. That bidder turned out to be the New York Mets, who signed Martínez to a four-year, $53 million deal in December 2004 that included a $3 million signing bonus. The Red Sox worried how long his shoulder might hold up and had offered $40.5 million over three years. In addition to the salary, Martínez' contract included incentive clauses for winning the Cy Young Award and being named to the All-Star team as well as a luxury suite at Shea Stadium.

Martínez proved to be worth the price to the Mets, at least for the first year. He was 15-8 in 2005 and made the All-Star team. On a personal level, Pedro married his sweetheart Carolina Cruz that year, whom he met through his Pedro Martínez and Brothers Foundation in 1998 when she was a sophomore at Boston College. She was able to attend the university on a scholarship provided through the foundation.

In 2006 he made the All-Star team again, but only went 9-8 with an astronomical 4.48 ERA as injuries to his hip, calf, and toe limited him to 23 starts. He underwent major surgery for a torn rotator cuff that October, and missed the Mets' postseason, which saw them come within one game of going to the World Series. While the operation may have relieved pain, it cost him velocity on his fastball. It took 11 months for Martínez to recover, and he didn't make his first start of the 2007 season until September 3 against the Reds in Cincinnati. That was a milestone game for Martínez, as he became only the 15th pitcher to record 3,000 strikeouts when he got Aaron Harang on an 87 mile-per-hour fastball. For the season, Martínez went 3-1 in five starts with a 2.57 ERA.

The decline continued in an injury-filled 2008, as Martínez had the worst season of his career, a 5-6 won-lost record with a 5.61 ERA for a team that went 89-73. The Mets missed the playoffs by one game and there's no doubt having Pedro pitching at top capacity would have vaulted them over the Brewers and into the wild card.

The *annus horribilis* that was 2008 also included great personal sadness for Martínez, as his father died of brain cancer in July at the age of 78.

When the 2009 season began, Martínez could relate to the proverbial teenage girl waiting for the phone to ring on a Saturday night. Martínez was a free agent, but the 37-year-old's age and mediocre statistics did not attract teams. Finally, the Philadelphia Phillies, who were hoping to repeat as World Series champions, signed Pedro to a one-year $1 million contract on July 15. They hoped he could provide them with some quality starts and help them overcome injuries to their pitching staff. After three starts in the minors, he returned to the majors on August 12 at Wrigley Field and was the winner in a 12-5 Phils victory over the Cubs. He went five innings, gave up three earned runs, and struck out five.

Martínez contributed to the Phillies winning the National League East Division by compiling a 5-1 record with a 3.63 ERA in nine starts. He didn't play in the NLDS against the Colorado Rockies, which the Phillies won in four games. He pitched magnificently in Game Two of the NLCS against the Dodgers, going seven scoreless innings and leaving with a 1-0 lead. The bullpen couldn't hold on and the Phillies lost, 3-1. It was the team's only loss in the series, which they won in five games.

Then came the World Series against his old rival from the Red Sox days, the hated Yankees. Pedro started Game Two and gave up three runs in six-plus innings. Yankee starter A. J. Burnett was almost unhittable that night and the Yankees won, 3-1.

In what turned out to be the last game of his career, Martínez started Game Six with the Phillies down three games to two. He just didn't have it that night, giving up four runs in four innings as the Bombers won the game, 7-3, and the Series.

Overall, Martínez had a decent season, but something was missing and he knew that the time had come to hang up the spikes.

"You find yourself alone, ironing your clothes again and you find yourself moving your car and parking and driving by yourself home late at night after being on the road," said Martínez in an interview. "After achieving what I achieved in baseball, I felt like if I was going to go through all of that just to achieve a little bit more, I would rather not."[12]

Retirement has been good for Martínez, who is both a deeply religious man and a proud Dominican who has not forgotten his roots despite the millions he earned playing baseball. He and Carolina run the foundation, which is headquartered in Santo Domingo. His foundation has built a three-story school, and a facility that offers kids the chance to learn computers, English, and music as well as how to battle domestic violence and teen-age pregnancy.

He received a unique honor in 2011, when the Smithsonian Institution's National Portrait Gallery unveiled a painting of him done by Susan Miller-Havens.

He has also re-established ties with the Red Sox by becoming a special assistant to general manager Ben Cherington in January 2013. He celebrated another World Series win with the team that same season.

Martínez received a player's ultimate accolade on January 6, 2015 when he was elected to the Baseball Hall of Fame in his first year of eligibility. His name appeared on 91.1 percent of the ballots from the Baseball Writers Association of America.

Not bad for a kid who had to tear off dolls' heads to play the game he loved.

SOURCES

In addition to the sources cited in the Notes, the author also consulted:

http://www.mlbtraderumors.com

http://www.jockbio.com

http://www.baseball-reference.com/

http://www.nytimes.com/

http://dev.baseballlibrary.com/ballplayers

http://www.boston.com/sports/baseball/redsox/articles/2003/10/08/thrills_were_in_season/

http://www.hardballtimes.com

http://ftw.usatoday.com

http://www.nydailynews.com/

http://mlb.com

http://www.playerwives.com/mlb/boston-red-sox/pedro-Martínezs-wife-carolina-cruz-de-Martínez/

NOTES

1. "Pedro Martínez turning some heads in Dodgers' camp," *Ocala* (Florida) *Star Banner*, March 2, 1992.

2. Peter Gammons, Clemson Smith Muniz, "Pedro Martínez could throw Boston its best party in a long, long time," *ESPN Mobile Web Archive*, July 10, 2012 (note that this date refers to when the archived article was put on the ESPN website. It was probably written soon after Martínez was traded to the Red Sox in late 1997.)

3. Mike Shalin, *Pedro Martínez: Throwing Strikes* (Sports Publishing LLC, 1999), 21.

4. Shalin, 23.

5. Mike Eisenbath, "Minor League Player of the Year," *The Sporting News*, October 28, 1991.

6. Tim Kurkjian, "An Inside Job," *Sports Illustrated*, April 25, 1994.

7. Tim Kurjkjian, "Baseball," *Sports Illustrated*, May 16, 1994.

8. Statistics provided by the book *Red Sox Threads*, by Bill Nowlin published by Rounder Books.

9. Howard Ulman, "Martínez Criticizes Duquette," *Pittsburgh Post-Gazette*, September 5, 2001.

10. Buster Olney, "Boone's Blast, Rivera's Arm Lift Yankees," *ESPN the Magazine*, October 2003.

11. Television interview, *Reseau des sports* October 27, 2004. http://www.youtube.com/watch?v=RUXq77VXgvU

12. Sean Deveney, "Happily retired Pedro Martínez reflects on time with Red Sox," *sportingnews.com*, April 20, 2012.

RAMON MARTÍNEZ

By Gregory H. Wolf

Photo courtesy of the National Baseball Hall of Fame

Pedro Martínez, the Hall of Famer with three Cy Young Awards, is the most famous pitcher in the family, but older brother Ramon Martínez was outstanding in his own right. "What I know of baseball, and life off the field, I owe to Ramon," said Pedro. "Everything I am I learned from Ramon."[1] Three years after debuting with the Los Angeles Dodgers, Ramon won 20 games and tied a franchise record with 18 strikeouts in 1990. In the course of his injury-plagued career, he also hurled a no-hitter en route to a 135-88 record in parts of 14 seasons.

Ramon Jaime Martínez was born on March 22, 1968, in Manoguayabo, an impoverished town about nine miles west of Santo Domingo, the capital of the Dominican Republic. He was the first of six children born to Paolino, a janitor at a local school, and Leopoldina Martínez, who took in laundry and found piecemeal work. They raised their family in a humble abode with a corrugated tin roof and without an indoor bathroom. For generations on the small island nation, baseball had served as escape, albeit temporary, from the realities of poverty and hunger, and that was no different for the Martínez family. Paolino, a former pitcher who turned down a big-league tryout in the 1950s because he couldn't afford a plane ticket to the United States, raised his children to love the sport as much as he did. By his early teens, Ramon seemed like a natural, the star of his local squad, Los Bravos, which played 51 weeks a year, pausing only at Christmas. The lanky right-hander modeled his pitching after his idol, Mario Soto, the star Dominican hurler for the Cincinnati Reds.

At the age of 15, the 6-foot-3, rail-thin, 130-pound Ramon caught the attention of Ralph Avila, the legendary Dodgers scout and the most influential and best-connected baseball insider on the island. Martínez quit high school after his sophomore year to move into Avila's baseball academy, a showcase for big-league prospects. Defying expectations, Ramon was on the international stage in the summer of 1984 as a member of the Dominican national baseball team, which Avila also directed. Baseball was an exhibition sport at the Summer Olympics, held in Los Angeles. The youngest player on any of the participating teams, the 16-year-old Martínez took the mound at Dodger Stadium in front of dozens of major-league scouts and hurled three scoreless innings against Taiwan, sealing his fate. Soon thereafter Martínez tried out for the Dodgers, who signed him on September 1, 1984, on the recommendation of team scouts Avila and Eleodora Arias.

Martínez's professional career commenced in 1985 with the Dodgers' Rookie-level club in the Gulf Coast League. The following season, he struggled on the field (4-8, 4.75 ERA) with Class-A Bakersfield in the California League, and away from the park. Almost 4,000 miles from home, he was homesick and lost weight, which affected his strength and stamina. In the offseason, the Dodgers tried to "fatten" his now 6-foot-4 frame to 160 pounds. That winter Martínez donned the uniform of the Tigres de Licey, the capital city's famed team in the Dominican winter league, making seven relief appearances. He returned stateside in 1987 and set the Class-A Florida State League on fire (16-5, 2.17), earning all-star honors with Vero Beach. The unequivocal gem of the Dodgers farm system, Martínez was in high demand at baseball's winter meetings in 1987, but had acquired the "untouchable" tag from VP Fred Claire.

Added to the Dodgers' 40-man roster, Martínez participated in spring training in 1988, drawing rave reviews from everyone who saw him pitch. He's "further developed than any 19-year-old I've ever seen, including Dwight Gooden," cooed Karl Kuehl, the Dodgers director of player development.[2] With just 51 starts in the minor leagues, Martínez began the season with Double-A San Antonio (Texas League) and progressed to Triple-A Albuquerque (Pacific Coast League). With a combined 13-6 slate (2.58 ERA), it was only a matter of time before he was returned to the city where he first made headlines.

Martínez's boyhood dream was realized when the Dodgers summoned him to replace 43-year-old Don Sutton in August 1988. In his debut on August 13, the second youngest player in baseball (behind Roberto Alomar of the San Diego Padres) held the San Francisco Giants to four hits and a run in 7 2/3 innings at Dodger Stadium, yet emerged with a no-decision. "Ramonamania" was in full throttle when he picked up his first victory, tossing seven innings and yielding one unearned run to the Montreal Expos at Olympic Stadium to lower his ERA to 1.73 after four starts. "This guy's got his head in the game," commented catcher Mike Scioscia, and isn't afraid to make pitches."[3] Skipper Tom Lasorda praised Martínez's maturity and mused, "[H]e doesn't get rattled easily."[4] Martínez yielded more earned runs (10) than innings pitched (9 2/3) over the last month of the season and was not on the postseason roster for the NL West champs.

In preparation for another spring training with the Dodgers, Martínez pitched once again for Licey, posting a 9-2 record with a sub-2.00 ERA in about 100 innings (including postseason).[5] He was assigned to Albuquerque to start the 1989 campaign in order to work on developing a curveball to augment his overpowering mid-90s fastball and deceptive changeup. With an 8-1 record and averaging more than a strikeout an inning for the Dukes,

Martínez was called up to fill a temporary hole in the Dodgers staff. In the first game of a doubleheader against the Braves in Atlanta on June 5, Martínez dazzled everyone, tossing a six-hit shutout and fanning nine. Immediately after the game, VP Claire announced that Martínez would be returning to Albuquerque immediately. Though dejected and hurt by his demotion, Martínez blanked Vancouver on four hits in his next start, in the PCL. He was recalled after the All-Star break and finished with a 6-4 record (3.19 ERA). The Tinseltown press had a field day with Martínez's lanky body, describing him as the "physical antithesis to Fernando Valenzuela ... even skinnier than Orel Hershiser[,]"[6] and "built like an exclamation point";[7] however, the hurler was no china doll. He tossed 143 pitches in shutting out the Braves in Los Angeles and whiffing 12 on September 15.

"This year I'm here to stay," promised the 22-year-old Martínez in 1990 as the Dodgers kicked off the centennial anniversary of their franchise. "My goal is to win 15 games. But I think I can be a 20-game winner in the major leagues."[8] Martínez was right – on both accounts. Bill Plaschke, sportswriter for the *Los Angeles Times*, described the season as Martínez's "climb toward stardom."[9] Named the club's fourth starter, behind Valenzuela, Mike Morgan, and Tim Belcher, Martínez's national coming-of-age party took place on June 4 in Chavez Ravine when he blanked the visiting Braves on three hits and tied the club record of 18 strikeouts held by the immortal Sandy Koufax despite developing a blister on the middle finger of his right hand. The Braves hitters, quipped Plaschke, swung like "punch-drunk boxers [who] could barely lay a bat" on Martínez's offerings.[10] That victory was the first in a remarkable stretch of five starts during which he won four times, produced a 1.10 ERA and fanned 52 in 41 innings while averaging 130 pitches per outing to earn the NL Pitcher of the Month Award.[11] In his only All-Star Game appearance, he tossed one hitless inning, walking two and striking out one. The Dodgers made a late-season challenge to the Cincinnati Reds in the NL West, ultimately finishing in second place, and Martínez closed out the season on a strong note. When the club needed him most, Martínez won all four of his decisions by complete game in the last month of the season. In his final appearance, he tossed a five-hitter against the Padres to become the second youngest Dodger to reach the 20-win plateau, following only 21-year-old Ralph Branca in 1947. Martínez led the majors in complete games (12), ranked third in the NL in innings (234 2/3), tied for second in strikeouts (223 with Dwight Gooden of the New York Mets), and finished a distant second to Pittsburgh's Doug Drabek (22-6) in the Cy Young Award.

Despite missing the first 11 days of camp in a contract dispute, Martínez picked up in 1991 where he had left off the previous season. He concluded April with consecutive five-hit shutouts, the first two of seven consecutive victories. "He's one of the unique pitchers in baseball," gushed Lasorda. "He don't throw no [sic] forkballs. He doesn't throw no cut [sic] fastball. He comes out and throws hard. He just plays old-fashioned hardball."[12] Still essentially a fastball/changeup pitcher, Martínez was "smarter," opined Plaschke. "He no longer thinks he has to overpower every hitter to retire them."[13] Named to his second consecutive All-Star squad, Martínez won his league-leading 12th game on July 7, but the victory proved costly. His strained his left hip and missed the midsummer classic (and was replaced by teammate Mike Morgan). Seemingly headed toward another 20-win campaign, Martínez improved his record to 14-5 and lowered his ERA to 2.25 with a complete-game six-hitter against the Mets on July 30 to maintain the Dodgers' 4½-game lead in the West. Looking fatigued, Martínez lost his next three starts (15 earned runs in 17²/₃ innings), then suffered a bruised right bicep on a line drive by the Padres Jack Howell on August 20. That injury proved to have lasting consequences on Martínez's season, and perhaps career. An MRI revealed no structural damage and Martínez did not miss a start, but he was obviously not the same pitcher thereafter, leading Plaschke to ask, "What's wrong with Martínez?"[14] Robbed of his fastball and requiring cortisone injections to reduce the inflammation in his arm, Martínez tossed seven scoreless frames against the Braves on September 22 to keep the Dodgers in first place; however, he also strained his right hip. He lost his last two starts as the Dodgers fell out of first place in the final week of the season. Martínez's numbers looked good on paper (17-13, 3.27 ERA in 220¹/₃ innings), but his injury-induced collapse over the final two months (3-8, 5.50 ERA) and his decreased strikeout total (150) had the Dodgers concerned.

Martínez's excitement of having his brother Pedro in camp in 1992 (Pedro had been signed by the Dodgers in 1989) was tempered by chronic pain in his left hip, probably the result of overcompensating for his injured arm. The now 24-year-old hurler struggled in spring training and was shelled on Opening Day (seven hits and three runs in 2²/₃ innings) and didn't notch his first win until a month into the season. Naïvely convinced that Martínez would tell them if he was injured, team brass blamed his poor mechanics for his lack of effectiveness and control problems and not his ailing hip, which required several examinations by team physician Frank Jobe.[15] While the Dodgers plummeted to their first last-place finish in the NL West and their most losses (99) since 1908 (when the team was known as the Brooklyn Superbas), Martínez was shut down for the rest of the season after his third consecutive loss, on August 25.

Diagnosed with tennis elbow, Martínez (8-11, 4.00 ERA in 150²/₃ innings) began to hear the rumblings that he might be washed up after five seasons, plagued by hip and arm woes.[16]

A bright spot in Ramon's offseason was his marriage to Doris Altgracia Abria Leonardo in January 1993. They welcomed two daughters into the world, Doranni and Kisha.

Martínez's health was the Dodgers' biggest question mark heading into the 1993 season. With graybeards Hershiser (34), Tom Candiotti (35), and Kevin Gross (32) in the rotation, the club needed its young gun to bounce back to have a chance at the division crown. Playing through nagging pain in his left hip, Martínez won two of five decisions in April, acquiring the "tough-luck moniker" as the Dodgers were shut out twice in his losses. He kept that sobriquet the entire campaign as the offensively challenged Dodgers finished 12th of 14 teams in runs scored after ranking dead last the season before. Six days after tossing a three-hit shutout against the Rockies on May 23, Martínez fired a four-hitter to beat the Pirates and extend the Dodgers' winning streak to 11 games, their longest since 1976. While the Dodgers hovered around .500 all season, Martínez staked his claim as staff ace by blanking the Cardinals on four hits on August 22 to improve his record to 9-8 and lower his ERA to 2.87 But a combination of arm fatigue and hip pain played havoc with Martínez's effectiveness and control in his last seven starts, during which he won just once and posted a 6.19 ERA. Despite his pedestrian record (10-12), Martínez joined Hershiser, Candiotti, and Gross as a member of the 200-plus-inning club and produced a sturdy ERA (3.44, well below the 4.18 league average), but also paced the circuit in walks (104).

Spring training was bittersweet for Martínez in 1994. His brother Pedro, who had emerged as a reliable reliever in his rookie season, had been traded to the Montreal Expos for Delino DeShields in the offseason. Ramon made a statement in his season debut, fanning 10, the first time he reached double digits in strikeouts since August 9, 1990, and surrendered just one run to the Florida Marlins on April 7, but was collared with the 1-0 loss, By the end of the month, Martínez sported a 5.23 ERA, prompting discussion that he should be removed from the starting rotation. He found his groove in May and began June with two consecutive shutouts as part of 20 consecutive scoreless innings. In the latter of those victories, he was drilled on the wrist by a liner from the Marlins' Jerry Browne in the sixth inning and finished with a three-hitter. "[S]ome of his pitches are unhittable," declared pitching coach Ron Perranoski.[17] Martínez had been working diligently with the former reliever to improve his mechanics and to develop a more compact delivery that exerted less pressure on his arm and hip. Though subsequent X-rays of the pitcher's wrist were negative, the Dodgers nonetheless held their collective breath. If anything, Martínez was streaky: an ace when he could control his fastball or likely to be shelled if he couldn't. As talk of a players strike heated up, so did Martínez. He won his last four starts, culminating in a seven-hit shutout against the Reds in Cincinnati on August 11, four days after the birth of his first child, to keep the Dodgers (58-56) in first place. In what must have been an eerie feeling in the clubhouse prior to that game, the Dodgers representative to the players union, Brett Butler, led discussions about what the players would need to do after the game when major-league baseball's first work stoppage since 1981 was set to begin. Martínez (12-7, 3.97 finished sixth in the NL in both wins and innings (170 2/3) and re-established himself as one of the league's premier hurlers.

Los Angeles sportswriter Jim Murray once described Martínez as perpetually "overlooked" and "never the glamour pitcher of the staff."[18] He spanned the era of Dodgers icons Valenzuela and Hershiser to Hideo Nomo, the celebrated Japanese phenom who debuted in 1995. The lack of media attention, even in Los Angeles, enabled Martínez to focus on pitching. Free from chronic hip pain for the first time since in four years, he began the 1995 campaign by winning four of his first five starts, including Opening Day. On May 5 he became an answer to a trivia question by becoming the first visiting pitcher to beat the Colorado Rockies in their new ballpark, Coors Field. The next time he faced the Rockies, he was booed by his hometown fans when he was yanked after yielding eight earned runs in 4 2/3 innings on July 2. He atoned for his three consecutive poor starts in Dodger Stadium, long considered one of the best pitcher's parks in the majors, by tossing a no-hitter against the Florida Marlins on July 14, fanning eight and allowing only one walk. Bob Nightengale reported that Martínez abandoned his changeup and occasional curveball after the third inning, firing only fastballs the rest of the game.[19] Just 27 years old but the longest-tenured hurler on the staff, Martínez with his low-key, good-spirited personality helped deflate the pressure building in the Dodgers' season-long pennant chase. "[E]very time the Dodgers looked as if they were in a panic," opined Murray, "trying to look over both shoulders at once, Martínez calmed them down."[20] Martínez went 9-1 after the All-Star break, helping the Dodgers take the division crown in the last week of the season by one game over the Rockies. In what proved to be his last full injury-free season, Martínez (17-7, 3.66 ERA) finished third in the circuit in victories and innings (206 1/3). Pitching on seven days' rest, Martínez was shelled in Game One of the NLCS, surrendering seven runs in 4 1/3 innings in the team's disappointing three-game sweep by the Reds.

A highly-sought free agent in the offseason, Martínez became the highest-paid pitcher in Dodgers history when he signed a three-year deal for a reported $15 million. After winning on Opening Day, Martínez suffered a severely torn right groin muscle in his next start when he slipped in the batter's box. Sidelined for five weeks, he reasserted himself as the Dodgers' stopper in a tense season that saw Lasorda retire due to health problems, replaced by coach Bill Russell. "As a rookie," said Martínez of his injury-induced transformation as a pitcher, "I was just trying to blow the fastball by everybody. Now I realize to win, you don't have to do that."[21] On August 12 he notched his 100th career victory, and wouldn't lose again for the rest of the season as the Dodgers battled the upstart Padres for the division crown. In one of baseball's most anticipated matchups, Ramon faced his brother Pedro on August 29 in Montreal. The game unfolded as a classic pitchers' duel. Pedro went the distance, fanning a then career-high 12 and yielding just six hits; however, Ramon emerged victorious, holding the Expos to three hits over eight innings in a tense 2-1 win. Martínez won four straight starts in September, including an overpowering six-hit shutout (the last of 20 in his career) with 12 punchouts over the Padres on September 19 and then held the Giants to two hits over seven innings on August 24 to give the Dodgers a 1½-game lead. Needing only one win in the final four games to claim the crown, the Dodgers lost all four to finish in second place, but secured the wild-card spot as a consolation prize. The Dodgers were swept again in the NLCS, but that was no fault of Martínez, who tossed three-hit, one-run ball over eight innings in a Game One matchup with the Braves' Cy Young Award winner John Smoltz in an eventual 2-1 loss in 10 innings.

A fierce competitor who played through pain and never used it as an excuse for poor performances, Martínez battled through an up-and-down campaign in 1997. After a rough outing on June 14, he was diagnosed with a small tear in his left rotator cuff. Opting for rest instead of potentially career-ending surgery, Martínez returned nine weeks later and was bombed for six runs in three innings against the Mets on August 20. Fortunately for him, that game was rained out and the statistics deleted. With the Dodgers holding a one-game lead in the divisional race, Martínez got a second chance in the first game of a doubleheader on August 25. He held the Pirates to five hits and one earned run in five innings to emerge victorious en route to winning his first three starts after his long layoff and giving the Dodgers momentum for the stretch run. But the team lost 12 of its final 19 to fall out of first and missed the wild-card berth, too.

The Dodgers were optimistic that Martínez's late-season success would transfer into the 1998 campaign; however, the hurler's importance was not confined to the diamond. Los Angeles sportswriter Ross Newhan described him as one of the leaders in a diverse clubhouse and a role model for not just pitchers, but all of the Latinos on the club.[22] Only 30 years old, Martínez was the grizzled veteran, whose drive to compete in his 11th season despite injuries inspired his team. He was known as a tireless worker and physical-fitness nut who ran more than rookies. In his second start of the season, he flirted with a no-hitter for 7 1/3 innings and departed after eight innings of one-run ball against the Reds. In May he won all four decisions, including a two-hitter against the Diamondbacks. Through it all, his shoulder ached. On June 14, the exact date as the previous year, pain forced Martínez to retire early from a start. An MRI revealed more extensive damage to his rotator cuff, as well as cartilage damage, ending a feel-good comeback (7-3, 2.83) and placing his career in jeopardy.

Martínez underwent rotator cuff surgery in late June 1997. He played three more seasons, but was no longer the same pitcher. Granted free agency in the offseason, Martínez had few suitors. On March 11, 1999, he signed a two-year pact with the Boston Red Sox in order to have a chance to pitch alongside his brother, who had been traded to the Red Sox the previous year. After an extensive rehab in the minors, Ramon surprised everyone as a September call-up, winning his last two decisions, yielding a combined six hits and one run in 13 innings. With the wild-card Red Sox on verge of being swept in the ALDS, Martínez tossed 5⅔ gritty innings, yielding two runs, but did not factor into the decision in the Red Sox' eventual victory. The Red Sox took the next two games to advance to the ALCS, where they lost in five games to the New York Yankees. Martínez was collared with the loss in Game Two, surrendering three runs in 6⅔ innings. Martínez's second season in Boston was an extended nightmare. Often the beneficiary of Boston's potent offense, he went 10-8, but posted a 6.13 ERA and averaged less than five innings per start.

A free agent once again, Martínez inked an incentive-laden contract with the Dodgers, but was released during spring training in 2001. Subsequently signing with the Pirates, Martínez was granted his unconditional release after four starts, thus bringing his big-league career to an end after 11 seasons. Despite his injuries, Martínez retired with the second-most wins for a pitcher from the Dominican Republic, trailing only Juan Marichal (243). Pedro passed brother Ramon's win total in 2002 en route to 219 in his career. Ramon logged 1,895 ⅔ innings with a 3.67 ERA, completed 37 games, and tossed 20 shutouts. He was especially tough on Ozzie Smith (2-for-25, .080), Jay Bell (3-for-37, .081), and Ryne Sandberg (7-for-40, .175); but struggled against Roberto Alomar (13-for-29, .448), Mark Grace (20-for-46, .435), and Will Clark (19-for-46, .413).

Martínez remained close to baseball after his active playing days. Involved initially in a number of pitching academies in the Dominican Republic, he was named a special-assignment pitching instructor for the Dodgers in 2010, assigned to work with Latino pitchers. He served in that capacity for five years, also adding the title of senior adviser. In 2015 he took a similar job with the Baltimore Orioles, where he was reunited with pitching coach Dave Wallace whom he had considered one of the most influential coaches in his development as a pitcher. As of 2017, Martínez still held that position.

SOURCES

In addition to the sources cited in the Notes, the author also accessed Retrosheet.org, Baseball-Reference.com, the SABR Minor Leagues Database, accessed online at Baseball-Reference.com, SABR.org, and *The Sporting News* archive via Paper of Record.

NOTES

1. Mike Shalin, *Pedro Martínez: Throwing* Strikes (Champaign, Illinois: Sports Publishing LLC, 1999), 21.
2. Stan Isle, "Giants Clark Will Not Make Comparison," *The Sporting News*, April 11, 1988: 6.
3. Sam McManis, "Dodgers Rookie Martínez Gets First Win at Last, 2-1," *Los Angeles Times*, August 30, 1988: III, 1.
4. Sam McManis, "Dodgers Win, but Martínez Is Still Looking for His First," *Los Angeles Times*, August 19, 1988: III, 8.
5. Ramon Martínez page, Winter Ball Data. (winterballdata.com/).
6. Sam McManis, "A Dandy Dominican," *Los Angeles Times*, February 26, 1988: III, 10.
7. Mike Downey, "Dodgers Have Their Splendid Splinter," *Los Angeles Times*, September 23, 1991: III, 17.
8. Bill Plaschke, "Martínez, Dodger Fans Have Ball in 2-0 Victory," *Los Angeles Times*, April 23, 1990: III, 10.
9. Bill Plaschke, "Game of Catch Is Won by Martínez, Dodgers, 5-2," *Los Angeles Times*, June 17, 1990: III, 1.
10. Bill Plaschke, "Martínez Strikes It Rich," *Los Angeles Times*, June 5, 1990: III, 1. Martínez had a chance for the record with four outs to go, but recorded those outs on a popup and three groundouts, including a leaping stop by first baseman Mickey Hatcher.
11. Martínez's pitch totals were 127, 123, 148, 117, and 134. Baseball-Reference does not provide a pitch total for the fourth game; however, the *Los Angeles Times* did. Bill Plaschke, "Atlanta Tires of Martínez in 5-2 Dodgers Win," *Los Angeles Times*, June 26, 1990: III, 1.
12. Alan Drooz, "Dodgers, Martínez Make Win Over Phils Look Easy," *Los Angeles Times*, May 4, 1991: III, 1.
13. Bill Plaschke, "American League to See a Smarter Martínez," *Los Angeles Times*, July 7, 1991: III, 1.
14. Bill Plaschke, "Atlanta Answer Is Grand, Leaving Dodgers Slammed," *Los Angeles Times*, September 16, 1991: III, 1.
15. "Baseball Daily Report," *Los Angeles Times*, March 25, 1992: III, 4.
16. Steve Dilbeck, "Dodgers: Success Very Questionable," *San Bernardino County* (California) *Sun*, April 4, 1993: C1.
17. Maryann Hudson, "No Bullpen – Dodgers' Martínez Does It Alone," *Los Angeles Times*, June 9, 1994: A9.
18. Jim Murray, "Just Give Him the Ball, Please," *Los Angeles Times*, October 1, 1995: III, 1.
19. Bob Nightengale, Martínez Basks in His Glory," *Los Angeles Times*, July 16, 1995: III, 6.
20. Murray.
21. Steve Springer, "Martínez Reflects After 100th Victory," *Los Angeles Times*, August 13, 1996: III, 5.
22. Ross Newhan, "Dodgers Hoping $36 Million Buys Some Leadership," *Los Angeles Times*, February 1, 1998: III, 13.

JOSÉ MESA

By Joséph Wancho

"What have you done for me lately?" is a common refrain heard among fans of all sports. Diehard and casual fans are known to be a fickle bunch. Any time a player has an outstanding performance in one game, he or she is the toast of the town. The next day they falter and they are a bum. It is unfortunate that in many instances the boos are louder and last longer than the cheers. Except for the elite athlete, no player is exempt from getting "the business" or the "Bronx cheer" from the public.

On October 15, 1997, the Cleveland Indians were at Camden Yards to face the Baltimore Orioles in Game Six of the American League Championship Series. A pitcher's duel between the Indians' Charles Nagy and the Orioles' Mike Mussina was a delight. Both pitchers went deep into the game (Nagy 7 1/3 innings and Mussina eight) without surrendering a run. The bullpens were equally stingy until the top of the 11th inning, when the Tribe's Tony Fernández walloped a two-out home run to give Cleveland the slimmest of margins, 1-0.

Indians manager Mike Hargrove called on José Mesa to close out the O's and send Cleveland to its second World Series in three years. Mesa allowed a two-out single to Brady Anderson, and then struck out Roberto Alomar for the third out. It was the second save of the series for Mesa, who had lost his role as closer to Mike Jackson during the season.

Eleven days later, on October 26, Mesa was called on again by Hargrove in Game Seven of the World Series to close out the Florida Marlins in the ninth inning. If he was successful, it would be Cleveland's first World Series championship since 1948.

The Indians led 2-1 as Mesa trudged to the mound. But Moises Alou led off with a single to center field. Mesa struck out Bobby Bonilla, but Charles Johnson followed with a single to right field. Craig Counsell's sacrifice fly scored Alou to pull the Marlins even with Cleveland. The Marlins eventually won the game, 3-2 in 11 innings, and their first World Series championship.

Just as a team that wins has many contributors, the same is true when it loses. However, in the competitive world of professional sports, where winning is the only thing that matters, fingers seemingly must be pointed at the reason for a team falling short of the ultimate goal. Unfortunately, those fingers pointed at Mesa then, and to this day. For a closer the pendulum has big swings: lights out today, bum tomorrow.

But Mesa rose above that, became a successful closer for Philadelphia and enjoyed a 19-year major-league career. He reinvented his game to become one of the greatest relief pitchers of his time. As of 2018 Mesa ranked in the top 20 in career saves with 321.

José Ramon Mesa was born on May 22, 1966, in Pueblo Viejo, Azua, in the Dominican Republic. He was the 12th of 15 children born to Narciso and Maria Mesa. The Mesa family resided on a farm where they grew potatoes, green peppers, watermelons, and a surplus of coconut and banana trees. All of the Mesa children put in time working on the farm. Narciso left and started another family that produced nine more children. Narciso died suddenly in 1976 of a stroke.

At age 15, Mesa went to a tryout given by the Toronto Blue Jays. His main position was outfielder; he had never tried pitching. "I was a center fielder, with a little pop in my bat," said Mesa. "(Blue Jays scout Epy Guerrero) timed me in 7.4 seconds in the 60-yard dash, which meant I was probably too slow to play the outfield. But he still had me throw from the outfield."[1]

Mesa showed off his greatest asset for Guerrero, his powerful right arm. Even though Mesa had never pitched, Guerrero had him throw off a mound. After a few hours, Guerrero signed the teenager to a contract for $3,000. "I was the man of the family, and I had to get a job to help support my mother," said Mesa. "When I signed and went over to the States to play, I'd send money back to her every two weeks."[2] When Mesa left home, he had completed only the seventh grade in school.

Mesa reported to Rookie League ball in the Gulf Coast League in 1982. He pitched well, posting a 6-4 record with a 2.70 ERA. He led the league in shutouts with three.

However, Mesa never pitched higher than Double A for Toronto. On September 4, 1987, he was the "player-to-be-named-later" to complete a deal in which Baltimore sent pitcher Mike Flanagan to Toronto for pitcher Oswaldo Peraza and, subsequently, Mesa.

In spite of his relative inexperience pitching at higher levels, the Orioles activated Mesa immediately and he made his major-league debut on September 10, 1987, at Boston. Mesa gave a decent accounting of himself; he went six innings and surrendered three earned runs while striking out four batters. He won his first major-league game on September 30 at Detroit. The win dampened the Tigers' efforts to catch Toronto for the AL East crown. "I was just going after them," said Mesa. "I didn't care who they were."[3] Mesa, who worked 8 2/3 innings, threw 150 pitches and struck out four.

Baltimore returned Mesa to the minors for more seasoning. Unfortunately for Mesa, both the 1988 and 1989 seasons were cut short due to surgery on his right elbow both years. He pitched in only 21 games over those two seasons between Double-A Hagerstown and Triple-A Rochester. Mesa returned to Baltimore late in the 1990 season. He won three games in a row to post a 3-2 record with a 3.86 ERA.

Mesa received his first extended playing time in the big leagues with the Orioles in 1991. The Orioles as a franchise were in a bit of a free-fall from the winning teams that they usually fielded. From 1986 to 1991 their average record was 71-91. Mesa posted a 6-11 record in 1991 with a 5.97 ERA. He totaled 64 strikeouts against 62 walks in 123 2/3 innings pitched. Incredibly, Mesa was tied for third on the staff with the six wins, as Bob Milacki led the way with 10 victories.

Although he did not give up a run in spring training in 1992, his performance did not transfer over to the regular season. In 12 starts he was 3-8 with a 5.19 ERA. He whiffed 22 batters, but he also issued 27 free passes.

That was the book on Mesa. He could throw 95 mph, but he lacked control. Baltimore traded Mesa to Cleveland on July 14, 1992, for minor-league outfielder Kyle Washington. "He pitched well against us last year," said Hargrove. "He throws hard and he's had control problems. But when he's thrown strikes, he's been effective."[4]

Mesa became the answer to a trivia question on September 9, 1992, when he gave up Robin Yount's 3,000th career hit at County Stadium. Yount had also gotten his 1,000th and 2,000th career hits off Cleveland pitching. "I saw that and said, 'Well, maybe the guy's going to get No. 3,000 off Cleveland too,'" said Mesa. "And he did."[5]

The 1993 season was shrouded in black. It was bound to be an emotional season for many as the Indians were playing their last season at Cleveland Stadium. Although a brand new, open-air, baseball-only ballpark awaited them in 1994, there were many who had wonderful memories of the lakefront stadium.

But that all took a backseat on March 22, 1993, when Steve Olin, Tim Crews, and Bob Ojeda were involved in a boating accident on Little Lake Nellie near the team's spring training facility in Winter Haven, Florida. The trio ran head-first into an extended dock. Olin died instantly and Crews the next day. Ojeda recovered to pitch later that year.

The impact of that accident shadowed the team all season. Mesa, however, had a breakout year of sorts. Although his record was 10-12, he led the club in wins, complete games (3) and strikeouts (118). He was learning to pitch and not just throw hard. His strikeouts to walks (118/62) indicated he was making great progress. After one of those complete games, a 6-2 victory over Kansas City on May 12, Cleveland pitching coach Rick Adair gave a hint to Mesa's success. "When (Mesa) is pitching well, he is not overthrowing the ball, which he started to do at the end," said Adair.

"I just told him to stay within himself, to not overthrow the ball. When he's throwing the ball right, he's got three good pitches which he did tonight."[6]

The 1994 season breathed fresh air into the Indians franchise. The Tribe was in their new digs at Jacobs Field and they were suddenly the hottest ticket in town. Dennis Martínez, Tony Peña, and Eddie Murray signed as free agents in the offseason and Jack Morris came aboard just before the season started. Omar Vizquel came over in a trade with Seattle. These five players provided instant credibility and veteran leadership to an otherwise young team that already had talented players Jim Thome, Albert Belle, Manny Ramírez, Carlos Baerga, Kenny Lofton, Charlie Nagy, and Sandy Alomar Jr.

The Indians' new pitching coach in 1994, Phil Regan, talked to Mesa about moving to the bullpen. He had one of the key attributes to being a successful closer, a fastball that had been clocked at 98 mph. "I told him I didn't know that I could do the job," said Mesa.[7]

The coaches brought him along slowly, using him initially as a middle reliever, then a set-up man, and then a closer. At the last step, closer, he had problems. Mesa failed to protect four of six closer opportunities. "I wasn't prepared," said Mesa. "I didn't understand the job."[8]

However, Mesa finished the season with a 7-6 record, a 3.82 ERA, and two saves. He continued to master control of the strike zone, posting 63 strikeouts against 26 walks.

The 1994 season had brought a new alignment of the divisions in the major leagues. The Indians were now in the AL Central, and finished the season one game behind the White Sox. The season ended prematurely due to a players strike on August 12. The work stoppage canceled the entire postseason and delayed the start of the 1995 season until April 25, 1995.

Mesa's finest year in the big leagues was in 1995. He was successful in 46 of 48 save opportunities as he blew batters away with his blazing fastball. His 46 saves are a franchise record. "I love to watch those batters swing and miss against José," said catcher Peña. "Some of them say, 'Oh, my God.' I just tell them 'You better start your swing early.'"[9]

At one point in the season, Mesa converted 38 save opportunities in a row. He was selected to his first All-Star Game, pitching a scoreless inning at the Ballpark at Arlington. "He's been our MVP," said Paul Sorrento. "What he's done is unbelievable – 38 in a row and 44 out of 46. When he comes in, you know the game is over."[10] Mesa was the AL Rolaids Relief Man of the Year and was named AL Fireman of the Year by *The Sporting News*.

Cleveland won the Central Division in 1995 by 30 games over Kansas City, The Indians returned to the postseason for the first time since 1954. Mesa recorded a save in both the ALCS and the World Series, although the Indians fell to the Atlanta Braves in six games.

It would seem near-impossible to duplicate such a great season, but Mesa came close in 1996. He converted 39 of 44 opportunities for Cleveland. The Indians returned to the postseason, but were bounced by Baltimore in the ALDS. In Game Four, Mesa gave up a run to the Orioles that knotted the score at 3-3. He gave up the winning run. Mesa had pitched 3⅔ innings, the most he had pitched in two seasons. "It was very obvious how much the situation had to do with us sending José back out there," said Hargrove. "We haven't done that in two years. But he was very strong the inning before. We went to him and asked him if he could still pitch and he said 'yes.'"[11]

José Mesa had a tumultuous year in 1997 on and off the baseball field. It actually began on December 22, 1996, when he was arrested for gross sexual imposition in a suburban motel just west of Cleveland. A charge of

Photo courtesy of the National Baseball Hall of Fame

concealing a loaded handgun was added later when the weapon was found in the console of Mesa's vehicle at the time of his arrest.

Mesa was free on $10,000 bond and reported to spring training in Winter Haven with the rest of the Indians. However, the whole ordeal was on his mind, and his ERA in spring training was 6.93. He still had the power in his right arm, but the old bugaboo of location crept up again.

A court date was set for March 31, just two days before the start of the 1997 season. Defense attorney Gerald Messerman did not even put on a defense. The jury deliberated for eight hours before coming back with a verdict of acquittal. The credibility of Mesa's accusers was called into question. "Regardless of whether a crime occurred or not, the bottom line was that there wasn't enough evidence to convict beyond a reasonable doubt," said juror Bruce Pixler.[12]

After the verdict came down, a tearful and grateful Mesa said, "It's been tough. I was nervous, but I knew God was with me. And with God I can do the next thing: to win the World Series."[13]

The concealed-gun charge, which was tried separately, was also dismissed. The judge ruled that the police officers had seized it unlawfully.

Mesa lost his closer's role to Mike Jackson, and he was constantly taunted in his own ballpark with shouts of "Rapist!" He was a free man in the eyes of the legal system, but not in the court of public opinion. In his first 19 appearances, his record was 0-3 with a 7.45 ERA. "José had to handle a crisis in his life a lot bigger than baseball," said Hargrove. "An experience like that shakes you right to your core, and when he returned, he didn't have the same confident attitude."[14]

Mesa eventually regained his status as closer and saved 16 of 21 games in 1997. But it is the Game Seven loss in the World Series that proved to be his legacy in Cleveland. "I just didn't do my job," said Mesa. "It hurts a lot to think we were just two outs away."[15]

Mesa never recovered from his 1997 season. After he went 3-4 with a 5.17 ERA in 1998, he was included in a five-player deal that sent him to San Francisco on July 23, 1998.

Mesa signed in the offseason with Seattle. He converted 33 of 38 saves for Seattle in 1999. But his control problems were once again an issue, as he walked 40 batters while striking out 42. He was moved out of the Seattle closer role in 2000 in favor of Kazuchiro Sasaki. He appeared in 66 games as the Mariners finished second to Oakland by a half-game in the AL West. Seattle swept Chicago in the ALDS, and Mesa was credited with the win in Game One. But the Mariners were eliminated in six games by the Yankees in the ALCS.

After the season Mesa opted for free agency and signed with Philadelphia, a reported two-year deal for $6.8 million. He showed he was worth the money, saving 87 games over two seasons. In 2001 the Phillies finished two games behind Atlanta in the NL East. Philadelphia sprinted out to a 34-18 record in April and May and enjoyed an eight-game lead over Atlanta. But the Phillies couldn't hold the lead, playing under .500 the rest of the season. The one bright spot was Mesa, who converted 42 of 46 save opportunities. "When we signed him there were a lot of snickers in baseball – 'How can you give this guy this kind of money?,'" said Phillies manager Larry Bowa. "But he's definitely been tremendous. I have no idea where we'd be without this guy. People will say all this stuff about his character. But all I can say is that in two years, he's a solid citizen."[16]

Mesa showed 2001 was no fluke by racking up 45 saves in 2002, fourth in the NL. However, he tied for the league lead in blown saves with nine. Nonetheless, the 45 saves were the most by a Phillies reliever since Mitch Williams saved 43 games in 1993. In 2003 Mesa converted 24 of 28 save opportunities. He left the Phillies after the 2003 season, ranking number one in franchise history with 112 saves. He was eventually surpassed by Jonathan Papelbon, in 2015.

In April 2002 Mesa's former teammate Omar Vizquel published an autobiography, *Omar!: My Life On and Off the Field*. Chapter One focused on Game Seven of the 1997 World Series. It said, "The eyes of the world were focused on every move we made. Unfortunately, José's own eyes were vacant. Nobody home. You could almost see right through him. Not long after I looked into his vacant eyes, he blew the save and the Marlins tied the game."[17]

"If I face him, I'll hit him," said Mesa. "I won't try to hit him in the head, but I'll hit him. And if he charges me I'll kill him."[18] Mesa responded by hitting Vizquel with a pitch on June 12, 2002, at Cleveland. He beaned Vizquel three times after the book was published. The last occurrence came on April 22. 2006. Mesa was pitching for Colorado and Vizquel was with the Giants. Mesa drew a four-game suspension for his actions.

Mesa moved on to Pittsburgh in 2004, and pitched for the Pirates in 2004 and 2005. He showed that he could still hum the old pea across the plate, saving 70 games for the Pirates. He later pitched for Colorado (2006), Detroit, and Philadelphia (2007). On July 26, 2007, Mesa pitched in his 1,000th game. He became only the 11th major-league pitcher to reach that plateau.

José Mesa retired after the 2007 season. In 19 seasons his career record was 80-109 with a 4.36 ERA. He struck out 1,038 batters and walked 651. As of 2021, Mesa ranks 21st all-time with 31 saves.

Mesa and his wife, Mirla, settled in the Atlanta area. They have five children and grandchildren. Mesa helps coach their little-league teams. He keeps a close eye on José Jr., a pitcher in the New York Yankees farm system, who was named the Pinstripes Prospect Comeback Player of the Year in 2017.

On June 19, 2016, the Cleveland Cavaliers defeated the Golden State Warriors for the franchise's first world championship. It also ended the 52-year drought since the last time a professional Cleveland team won a world title. Shortly after the game ended, José Mesa Jr, tweeted "There you go Cleveland now leave the past in the past and build on this!"[19] It was his way of saying, get off his dad's back and stop blaming him for the city's failure to win.

As of 2021, Mesa Jr. was pitching in the Miami Marlins system.

NOTES

1. Paul Hoynes, "Rise and Sign," *Cleveland Plain Dealer*, July 16, 1995: 1-D.
2. Hoynes, "Rise and Sign": 16-D.
3. Tim Kurkjian, "Mesa Defies Logic and Tigers, Gives Orioles 7-3 Win," *Baltimore Sun*, October 1, 1987: F-1.
4. Paul Hoynes, "Indians Reneging on Changes," *Cleveland Plain Dealer*, July 17, 1992: 1-E.
5. Rick Braun, "Mesa Enjoys Making History," *Milwaukee Sentinel*, September 10, 1992: 1B.
6. Russell Schneider, "Mesa Perfect Cure for What Ails Tribe," *Cleveland Plain Dealer*, May 13, 1993: 4F.
7. Jerome Holtzman, "There's No Mess When Cleveland Calls In Mesa," *Chicago Tribune*, September 21, 1995: 4-10.
8. Holtzman.
9. Hoynes, "Rise and Sign": 16-D.
10. Holtzman, "There's No Mess When Cleveland Calls in Mesa."
11. Paul Hoynes, "A Dream Slips Away; Indians Eliminated by Orioles", *Cleveland Plain Dealer*, October 6, 1996: 1-D.
12. James F. McCarty and James Ewinger, "Mesa Found Not Guilty: Indians Star Says Justice System, God On His Side," *Cleveland Plain Dealer*, April 11, 1997: 1-A.
13. McCarty and Ewinger.
14. Tim Crothers, "Trial and Errors," *Sports Illustrated*, January 18, 1998: 57.
15. Crothers.
16. Claire Smith, "Veteran Mesa Has Steadied the Phillies," *Philadelphia Inquirer*, July 23, 2001: E5.
17. Omar Vizquel with Bob Dyer, *Omar!: My Life On and Off the Field* (Cleveland: Gray and Company Publishing, 2002), 1.
18. "Mesa Being Investigated by Commissioner's Office," ESPN.com, March 12, 2003, Player's File, Baseball Hall of Fame.
19. José Mesa Jr., Twitter.com, June 19, 2016, accessed online at https://twitter.com/JoeTable/status/744728829000884225, July 19, 2018

Raúl Mondesí

By J.W. Stewart

Raúl Ramón Mondesí possessed a wide array of skills making him a sought-after player early in his career despite a questionable temperament. A powerful arm in right field, he struck fear in baserunners. The might of his swing pushed runners home and balls over the fence. Most surprising given his 5-foot-11 and roughly 220-pound physique, he was an agile and daring baserunner and basestealer. His natural talents and ardent work ethic made him a threat in all phases of the game, yet his disposition and periodic inability to work with managers led to a career that fell far short of the expectations early in his career.

Born in San Cristobal, Dominican Republic, on March 12, 1971, Raúl and his five siblings were raised by his mother after his father, Ramon, died when Raul was very young. His mother, Martina, worked at a laundry and managed to support the family.[1] Mondesí first found his way to professional baseball in 1988 at age 16. The young talent tried out for the Oakland Athletics at their Dominican facility; however, the team passed on him, declaring him too small for the majors.[2] Instead, Pablo Guerrero and Ralph Avila, scouts for the Dodgers, discovered Mondesí when a neighbor arranged an invite the next year to the Dodgers' development camp. Avila heard Mondesí before seeing him; the sound of the ball striking Mondesí's bat immediately caught his attention. After watching the work out, Avila ordered his people to sign Mondesí right away. With his signature and a $4,000 signing bonus, Mondesí became part of the Dodgers organization. Despite his natural talent, the future star's experience with baseball was from the streets of his barrio and makeshift equipment. The Dodgers organization placed him in their Dominican summer league for two years to develop his skills and baseball knowledge.[3]

In 1990 the Dodgers organization assigned Mondesí to the Great Falls Dodgers in the rookie Pioneer League. In 44 games, he had 53 hits with 31 RBIs, 30 stolen bases, and a slugging percentage of .543. Mondesí clearly had developed the abilities Avila found lacking in 1987. The next year Mondesí found himself with the Class-A Bakersfield Dodgers, but his skills quickly pushed him up to the Double-A San Antonio Missions and then the Triple-A Albuquerque Dukes for the last two games of the season. He ended his first full year in the minor leagues with a .277 batting average and 39 RBIs. His 1991 stats, however, also revealed a recurring problem for Mondesí:

pitch selectivity. He struck out 69 times with only 13 walks.

During Mondesí's 1992 season with the Albuquerque Dukes, he exhibited another element that characterized his career: fits of emotional outburst. Toward the end of the 1992 season, the Dodgers promoted Mondesí's teammate Tom Goodwin to the majors. Mondesí, with marginally better stats, believed the Dodgers owed him the promotion. The Dukes left for a road trip soon after, and an angry Mondesí purposely missed the team plane. Normally this kind of stunt resulted in a fine; however, the Dodgers decided a demotion would be more instructive. Mondesí was sent back down to Double-A San Antonio for the last 18 games of the season.[4]

With the beginning of the 1993 season, Mondesí was back with the Albuquerque Dukes. Through 110 games, he hit .280 with 65 RBIs. Then in July, the Dodgers called Mondesí up to the majors. As he adjusted to the big leagues, his batting average actually rose, to .291 in the 42 games left in the season. After the season, Mondesí went home to the Dominican Republic to play for the Tigres del Licey club during the winter. The Tigres won the Caribbean World Series and Mondesí batted .450 during the Series.[5]

With the start of the 1994 season, there was significant anticipation about Mondesí's performance. Papers predicted that he could win Rookie of the Year, an award his new teammate Mike Piazza won the year before.[6] The only question for the Dodgers was whether Mondesí or Cory Snyder would man right field. Despite Snyder's veteran status, observers cited Mondesí's speed and powerful bat and predicted that he would easily earn the spot.[7] He did.

Mondesí spent most of the 1994 season in right field, With 16 assists, he quickly earned a reputation for turning doubles into singles and making runners who challenged his

Photo courtesy of the National Baseball Hall of Fame

arm regret it. By April, coaches were already mentioning Mondesí and Roberto Clemente in the same breath. With almost seven weeks of the season canceled by the players strike, Mondesí ended with a .306 batting average, 56 RBIs, and 16 stolen bases. His only downside, according to Dodgers manager Tommy Lasorda was his terrible walk-to-strikeout ratio.[8] Yet, his strong hitting and impressive fielding made him the unanimous choice among voters for National League Rookie of the Year.

Mondesí's 1995 season was just as productive as his rookie year with increases in home run, RBIs, and stolen bases. His performance in right field continued to be a serious threat in the league, leading to a Gold Glove Award at the close of the season. Mondesí's 1995 stats are all the more impressive because he played the last part of the season with torn cartilage in his knee. The Dodgers made it to the postseason, Mondesí went 2-for-9 as they were swept by the Reds in three games. At the end of October, Mondesí had arthroscopic surgery on his knee to fix the cartilage issue.[9] By January, he was back playing in the Dominican League.[10]

In the spring of 1996, Mondesí reported his knee felt great and signed a two-year contract with the Dodgers for $3.65 million. Despite the celebratory feel of the beginning of his third season with the Dodgers, Mondesí's batting average took a serious dive over a two-week period that included 24 consecutive at-bats without a hit. On May 5 he was hitting only .192.[11] The reason for the slump was trademark Mondesí: He was swinging at anything and everything. Lasorda and Mondesí agreed on the diagnosis and the treatment, intensive work with the hitting coach. At the end of April, he hit two singles and a three-run home run, and drove in five runs in a game. By June, he had worked his average back up to .258. Despite the rough start to the season, Mondesí finished the season batting .297, with 88 RBIs and the Dodgers' record for most extra-base hits, 71. The Dodgers just barely missed the postseason.

Mondesí spent three more seasons with the Dodgers. For a time, he became more selective in his pitching and toed the line with new manager Bill Russell. In addition to his superstitious routines of glove placement between innings, Mondesí also began wearing his pants rolled up to his socks after a successful experiment led to six hits in two days.[12] The 1997 season proved to be his best offensive year, as he batted .310 with a good deal more walks and fewer strikeouts. The Dodgers re-signed him in 1998 to a four-year deal with a guaranteed $36 million.[13] The 1998 season, however, brought repeated injuries, an unwanted move to center field, and a drunk-driving arrest.[14]

In 1999 Mondesí was back in right field but his placement in the lineup became a new point of contention. The team moved him from third to fifth in the batting order, and he became more vocal about his frustration. Even with 99 RBIs by the end of the season, his average had slipped to the lowest point of his career so far, .253. During a July 29 game, Mondesí sat in the bullpen while the team batted. In May left fielder Gary Sheffield publicly defended Mondesí, but in August he demanded a trade unless the team dealt with Mondesí's disruptions.[15] After being benched for showing up late to an August 10 game, Mondesí engaged in a "profanity laced tirade" against manager Davey Johnson and general manager Kevin Malone and declared that he "no longer considers himself a member of the Dodgers." Even after an apology, the team had little choice but to trade him.[16]

By November, Mondesí was off to Toronto along with pitcher Pedro Borbón in exchange for right fielder Shawn Green and a minor-league second baseman.[17] With a new home and a new, four-year, $45 million contract, Mondesí seemed to be back in old form during the 2000 season. Impressed with his fielding and daring speed around the bases, Toronto also found him to be a positive influence in the clubhouse.[18] Despite his rediscovered attitude and work ethic, his lack of ball selectivity returned, resulting in a noticeable decline in his productivity in the third spot of the batting order.[19]

Mondesí started the 2001 season by becoming the first Toronto Blue Jays player to steal home. In a game against the New York Yankees on April 17, he edged his way down the third-base line, and with pitcher Randy Keisler's windup, he sprinted home on a high and outside pitch. Catcher Jorge Posada did not come close to tagging him out.[20] The rest of the season, though, offered little more for Mondesí. His batting average slipped to .252 in a serious late-season slump. Needing to reduce their payroll and begin a rebuilding process, the Blue Jays looked for a buyer for Mondesí's expensive contract.[21]

Mondesí returned to Toronto for the 2002 season even as the team was still shopping the 31-year-old right fielder. The Yankees took Mondesí in July, giving up a minor-league pitcher and paying the rest of his 2002 salary and $7 million of the $13 million owed him for 2003.[22] Immediately, Yankees manager Joe Torre made it known to the public and Mondesí that he expected discipline and a team-first attitude.[23] Again, his comments to the papers toed the line, and he appeared to be fitting into the system. He hit his first home run for the Yankees three days after the trade, but in August he had his first run-in with Torre's expectations. After a home run against the Tampa Bay Rays, Mondesí jogged to first base with bat in hand and then casually flipped it in front of the Rays dugout. Torre was not amused and reprimanded the hitter.[24]

After the 2002 season, the Pirates offered a trade for Mondesí but owner George Steinbrenner refused, saying the Pirates wanted New York to pay too much of Mondesí's salary. The team asked him to lose weight over the summer, and Jorge Posada worked with him on his grip to improve his hitting.[25] Observers and the team, however, were still concerned about his lack of discipline at the plate. Their concerns were warranted. On July 11 Mondesí had just one hit in his last 24 at-bats. Torre benched him.[26] Later in July, Torre pinch-hit for the struggling hitter. Infuriated, Mondesí left the field, showered, and went home. The next day Torre expelled him for the stunt. Mondesí, through his agent, demanded that the Yankees trade him. Within a few days, on July 29, he was off to the Arizona Diamondbacks for the rest of 2003.[27]

After the 2003 season, Mondesí entered free agency; however, his declining production and reputation as difficult left him with few options. The Pirates, who had tried to purchase his contract the previous winter, signed him in February of 2004 for $1.15 million, just 12 percent of his 2003 career-high salary.[28] The 2004 season continued to bring problems for Mondesí. Former major leaguer Mario Guerrero sued Mondesí and several other players claiming that they owed him a portion of their salary for connecting them with major-league teams. According to Guerrero, Mondesí had promised him 1 percent of his salary.

A court in the Dominican Republic, found for Mario Guerrero and ordered Mondesi to pay $1 million. Out of concern for his family and to appeal the court decision, Mondesí asked for a leave of absence from the Pirates. He had put up stellar numbers for the Pirates before the court case became an issue. The distraction pushed him into a serious slump, so the team agreed to some time off.[29] However, Mondesí did not return for a three-game series in San Diego as promised. He felt unable to return and the team could not afford an absentee player, so the Pirates terminated his contract.[30]

A week later Mondesí signed a contract with the first-place Anaheim Angels. After only eight games, a tear to his right quadricep ended his time with the team. While on the disabled list, Mondesí missed multiple rehabilitation appointments. The Angels terminated his contract at the end of July.[31]

Mondesí returned to baseball in 2005 slimmer and without the distractions of lawsuits and issues at home. The Atlanta Braves and Mondesí agreed to a $1 million contract that included performance bonuses if he reclaimed his old power at the plate. The comeback lasted only two months. The team designated him for assignment on June 1, his playing limited because of a sore knee. Mondesí's baseball career was over.[32]

Throughout his career, Mondesí demonstrated a profound dedication to the Dominican Republic and especially to San Cristobal. After Hurricane Georges struck the island in 1998, Mondesí arranged for the first humanitarian aid to reach his hometown.[33] Between his commitment to his home and the Dominican Republic's fondness for celebrity political candidates, Mondesí's entry into Dominican politics was hardly surprising. First as a member of the legislature and then as mayor of San Cristobal from 2010 to 2016, Mondesí spoke often of helping the poor of his city and country. Another expected cause for the new politician was supporting and investing in athletic facilities for youngsters. In 2014 he spearheaded a major renovation of Radhames Park, which included facilities for various sports.[34]

Despite some successes as mayor, continual complaints of mismanagement plagued Mondesí's term. After he left office in 2016, the new mayor ordered an audit of the city's finances. Shortly after, Mondesí was convicted of various crimes relating to mismanagement of city funds and corruption. The court sentenced him to eight years in prison and a fine of about $1.25 million. Mondesí's defenders claimed he was a victim of corrupt courts and a political system seeking to discredit him.[35]

Mondesí ended his career with a lifetime average of .273 with his best year coming in 1997, when he hit .310 with a slugging percentage of .541. His on-base percentage always lagged due to the rarity of his walks. Only in his last year with Los Angeles and his second year with Toronto did Mondesí exhibit selectivity in his pitches, walking 71 and 73 times respectively. Every other year, his strikeouts tempered his ability to hit and steal bases. His value in right field is seen more in the impressions of fellow players and writers than in the stats. Sportswriters attributed his falling assist numbers to batters' fear of his arm and choosing not to challenge him.

Mondesí's two sons also entered professional baseball. Raul Mondesí Jr. played for a few years in the minors. Adalberto Mondesí began his career in 2012 and rose through the Kansas City Royals organization. He made his debut with the Royals during Game Three of the 2015 World Series against the New York Mets, striking out in his only at-bat. He had played with the Royals in 2016, 2017, and 2018.

For Mondesí's teammates and managers, his slugging and amazing fielding were the product of a serious work ethic, natural talent, and a passion for the game. However, that same passion ensured a serious amount of discord between Mondesí and his teams when he hit a slump. His inability to control his worst instincts led to numerous moves and poor relations with those meant to support him, likely erasing some of the greatness Ralph Avila saw in the summer of 1988.

SOURCES

In addition to the sources cited in the Notes, the author also made use of Baseball-Reference.com.

NOTES

1. Johnette Howard, "The Next Clemente?" *Sports Illustrated*, May 29, 1995: 38.
2. "Playing Hardball," *The Sporting News*, June 23, 1997: 38.
3. Johnette Howard, "The Next Clemente?"
4. Howard.
5. Gordon Verrell, "Los Angeles Dodgers," *The Sporting News*, February 21, 1994: 23.
6. Steve Dilbeck, "Taking Care," *San Bernardino County Sun*, April 3, 1994: C4.
7. Gordon Verrell, "Los Angeles Dodgers," *The Sporting News*, March 7, 1994: 26.
8. Gordon Verrell, "Los Angeles Dodgers," *The Sporting News*, July 18, 1994: 23.
9. Gordon Verrell, "Los Angeles Dodgers," *The Sporting News*, October 23, 1995: 19.
10. Gordon Verrell, "Los Angeles Dodgers," *The Sporting News*, January 29, 1996: 42.
11. Gordon Verrell, "Los Angeles Dodgers," *The Sporting News*, May 13, 1996: 27.
12. Steve Springer, "Club's Pitch," *The Sporting News*, August 11, 1997: 25.
13. "Inside Dish," *The Sporting News*, February 9, 1998: 53.
14. "Mondesí Back in the Lineup After DUI," *Daily Herald* (Chicago), June 15, 1998: 2.
15. Jason Reid, "Getting Mondesí Stirred Up," *The Sporting News*, May 10, 1999: 32; Jason Reid, "Positively Negative," *The Sporting* News, August 23, 1999: 72.
16. Reid.
17. "Mondesí Traded for Blue Jays' Green," *Paris* (Texas) *News*, November 9, 1999: 10A.
18. Tom Maloney, "Toronto," *The Sporting News*, September 18, 2000: 62.
19. Tom Maloney, "Toronto," *The Sporting News*, June 5, 2000: 41.
20. Tom Maloney, "Toronto," *The Sporting News*, April 30, 2001: 19.
21. Tom Maloney, "A.L. East," *The Sporting News*, December 17, 2001: 18.
22. Jack Curry, "Yanks Acquire Mondesí in Bid to Boost Offense," *New York Times*, July 2, 2002: D1.
23. Liz Robbins, "Mondesí Is Forced to Follow New Rules," *New York Times*, July 3, 2002: D3.
24. Ken Davidoff, "New York Yankees," *The Sporting News*, August 5, 2002: 23.
25. Tyler Kepner, "Fit and Feisty, Mondesí Predicts Big Year Ahead," *New York Times,* February 22, 2003: D3; Charles Nobles, "Mondesí Ready to Shift Hands, Not Teams," *New York Times*, March 14, 2003: D4.
26. Tyler Kepner, "Told to Take a Seat, Mondesí Is Down and Up," *New York Times,* July 11, 2003: D3.
27. Bill Finley, "Yankees Criticize Mondesí's Early Exit," *New York Times,* July 31, 2003: D3.
28. "Majors," *Gettysburg Times*, February 24, 2004: A1.
29. Jeffrey Cohan, "Mondesí Still Stuck in Courtroom Mess," *Pittsburgh Post-Gazette*, May 16, 2004: A1.
30. Alan Robinson, "Pirates Cut Ties with Mondesí," *Indiana* (Pennsylvania) *Gazette,* May 20, 2004: 17.
31. "Baseball Buzz," *Toronto* Star, July 31, 2004: C5.
32. "End of the Line for Braves' Mondesí," *Toronto Star*, June 1, 2005: C8.
33. Roberto Valenzuela, "Mondesí no sabe defenderse de una injusticia," *Diario Digital RD*, October 2, 2017. diariodigital.com.do/2017/10/02/mondesi-no-sabe-defenderse-una-injusticia.html.
34. "Inician trabajos de remodelacion del Parque Radhames," *Diario Digital RD*, August 5, 2014. diariodigital.com.do/2014/08/05/inician-trabajos-de-remodelacion-del-parque-radhames.html.
35. Roberto Valenzuela, "Mondesí no sabe defenderse de una injusticia," *Diario Digital RD*, October 2, 2017. diariodigital.com.do/2017/10/02/mondesi-no-sabe-defenderse-una-injusticia.html.

Manny Mota

By Rory Costello

Manny Mota never seemed to age. "He's scary," said Steve Garvey, his teammate with the Los Angeles Dodgers. "I wish just one spring he would show up with one gray hair."[1] That was in June 1979, a couple of months before the Dominican set the career record for pinch hits. Mota wound up with 150 of them, a mark that stood until Lenny Harris surpassed it in 2001. Mota was a superb contact hitter with a .304 lifetime average. Writers and announcers loved to come up with analogies about how he could deliver at any time under any conditions. The pithiest might have been from Jim Murray of the *Los Angeles Times*: "He could get wood on a bullet."[2]

The outfielder also played 20 seasons in the Dominican Winter League, tied for the most in the league's history – it would have been more except for political turmoil in his homeland. He is the all-time leader there in batting average at .333. He was also a successful manager at home. If Tom Lasorda hadn't been so entrenched with the Dodgers, and if Mota weren't such a loyal organization man, it would have been interesting to see what this quiet, humble, and remarkably gracious man could have done as a big-league skipper.

Manuel Rafael Mota Gerónimo was the sixth of eight children in a blended family.

Photo courtesy of the National Baseball Hall of Fame

His mother, Fredesvinda Gerónimo, had four children with her first husband, a man named Peña. Manny's half-brothers and half-sisters were named Darío, Odilia, Luisa, and Adriana. Fredesvinda then had four children with Andrés Mota: another boy named Andrés, then two more girls after Manny named Bárbara and Joséfina.

Andrés Mota, a soldier in the Dominican Army, died when Manny was between six and seven years old, before the lad could establish any lasting memories of his father. However, Andrés bestowed a nickname upon his son by which people still know him at home, though not in the U.S. – *El Chory*. It means something like Shorty or Pee Wee; as Mota explained in 2011, "I used to play with older guys, taller and bigger than me."[3]

After Andrés died, Fredesvinda opened a grocery store to support her children. She also made candy, which Manny helped sell.[4] "She try to raise me the right way," he said in 1969. "And I go to play ball at the Catholic school three blocks from our house and I listen to the priests."[5] That school was Escuela Salesiana de Artes y Oficios, now known as Colegio Don Bosco. The Salesian Society's primary mission is the Christian education of the young, especially of the poorer classes. This cause resonated with Mota, whose abiding religious faith and empathy toward poor children inspired him to do many good works.

"I didn't have any particular heroes when I was growing up," Mota told *American Chronicle* in 2006, "but my baseball idol was always Jackie Robinson." Although an underprivileged youth, Mota liked to play baseball whenever he could and "just have a good time with it."[6]

As of 1956, Mota was playing for the Dominican Air Force team, which is where he believes scouts first noticed him.[7] The club was sponsored by Ramfis Trujillo, son of Dominican dictator Rafael Trujillo. Several other future big-leaguers were also on the roster, including Juan Marichal and Mateo Rojas (known in the U.S. as Matty Alou), who would be Mota's teammates in San Francisco.[8] He said in 2011 that the other main benefit he derived from playing with Aviación Militar was military discipline.

On February 21, 1957, the New York Giants signed Mota, who had turned 19 three days before. The Giants were early to recognize the wealth of talent in Latin America, starting in Puerto Rico and then branching out into the Dominican Republic. One of their scouts was Alex Pómpez, who had owned the New York Cubans of the Negro Leagues. Horacio Martínez, who had played shortstop for Pómpez, was a coach with the Escogido Leones in the Dominican League. In 1956, Escogido club president Paco Martínez Alba – Rafael Trujillo's brother-in-law – formed a working agreement with the Giants. Thereafter, several men from the Giants chain – Red Davis, Frank Genovese, and Salty Parker – managed Escogido.[9] Along with Pómpez and Martínez, Mota also cited Genovese as one of the scouts who signed him. The bonus was a mere $400.[10]

In the minors, Mota played first base and second base in addition to the outfield. His first pro season, with Michigan City, Indiana of the Midwest League (then Class D), was strong: a .314 average with 7 homers and 91 RBIs. Mota's first experience in the Dominican League came in the winter of 1957-58. He joined Escogido, one of the two teams still boasting the greatest local tradition. The other is the Licey Tigres. Escogido wears red and Licey wears blue, and though this rivalry is not deadly like Bloods vs. Crips, it has always been intense. As it turned out, though, most of Mota's Dominican career came with Licey.

In 1958, Mota had another good year with Danville (Virginia) in the Class-B Carolina League (.301-8-55), despite the hurt feelings he endured facing segregation in the South. He later told author Bruce Adelson, "At least in '57 you could ride the bus as a human, everybody together, no matter the color of your skin. You couldn't do that in Danville." But that passage opened, "My goal was to play baseball; I wasn't going to let anything stop me from playing in the major leagues."[11]

Mota jumped to Triple-A Phoenix to start the 1959 season. That proved to be too much too soon, and so in late May he was optioned to Springfield in the Class-A Eastern League (.314-3-28). A normal progression resumed after that: Double A in 1960 (.307-4-79 for Rio Grande Valley in the Texas League) and Triple A in 1961 (.289-3-43 for Tacoma in the Pacific Coast League).

In 1960-61, he won his first of three batting titles at home, with a mark of .344 for Licey. However, following the assassination of Trujillo on May 30, 1961, the atmosphere in the country remained extremely tense. A nationwide strike and street fighting crippled attendance, and the Dominican League halted the 1961-62 season after the games of December 3.[12] Although various Dominican players continued their season in other leagues, such as in Puerto Rico, Mota stayed at home for the rest of that winter.

By the end of the 2018 season, over 700 men from the Dominican Republic had played in the major leagues. The tenth of them was Mota, who made the Giants roster after a good showing in spring training 1962. As UPI noted, likely unaware that his Dominican season had been truncated, the "slight 160-pound outfielder. . .may be far ahead of the others because he played winter ball."[13] His big-league debut did not come until the season's seventh game; his first hit came in his first start, at old Crosley Field in Cincinnati. It was a grounder off Jim Brosnan that just trickled through the right side of the infield.[14]

Mota endured the indignity of being called "Mickey" at times in the U.S. newspapers early that season. He appeared in 47 games with San Francisco through the end of July, starting 12 times and going just 13 for 74 (.176). There was little playing time for the outfield reserves, as Willie Mays played in all 162 games that year, fellow Dominican Felipe Alou played 154, and Harvey Kuenn played 130. Mota was a utilityman, appearing on occasion at third base and second base. The Giants sent him back down to Double A, where he hit .349 in 30 games for El Paso. He was not around for the World Series as the Giants lost in seven games to the Yankees.

On November 30, 1962, San Francisco traded Mota and Dick LeMay to the Houston Colt .45s for Joey Amalfitano. Near the end of the year, *The Sporting News* described Mota as "an outstanding speedster who has shown exceptional ability in spring training but has never been able to crack the Giant outfield, understandable when [considering] his competition."[15] That group also included Matty and Jesús Alou, plus Willie McCovey, who played a good bit of outfield in those years.

Dominican League play remained suspended altogether in 1962-63. Thanks to the connections of Licey executive Ernesto "Monchín" Pichardo, Mota went to Venezuela that winter, batting .308 in 120 at-bats in 31 games. When his club, Oriente, folded in January, he signed with San Juan of the Puerto Rican League.[16]

On a personal note, Mota also married Margarita Matos on February 16, 1963, shortly after the winter season ended. As Margarita recalled in 1990, she "watched a teen-age Manny walk past her house in Santo Domingo for five years before he began courting her. 'We lived in the same neighborhood, but he would never talk to me,' Margarita said. 'I think he was afraid of my mother, and it wasn't until she died that he approached me.'"[17] The best man at their wedding was Felipe Alou, who was an admired mentor to Mota.[18]

After his return to the U.S., the Colts sent him to the Pittsburgh Pirates not long before the 1963 season started (receiving Howie Goss and $50,000 in cash in return). Mota spent the first half of the 1963 season with Triple-A

Columbus, batting .293-5-20 in 75 games. In mid-July, the Pirates called him up, and he never played again in the minors.

On October 12, 1963, Mota participated in the one and only Latin American players' game, the last baseball game ever held at the Polo Grounds. He drove in two runs as the National League's Hispanic players won, 5-2. He then went on to win another Dominican batting title (.379).

Back in Pittsburgh in 1964, Mota really benefited from the support of the great Roberto Clemente. As David Maraniss wrote in his biography of Clemente, the star right fielder "identified with the struggle and became Mota's closest friend and adviser on the Pirates. At the stadium every day before games, they could be seen working on hitting, bunting, fielding, and throwing. 'He's always been a good hitter,' Clemente said of Mota at midseason, pushing his cause to skeptical Pirates beat writers. 'He can hit big league pitching if given the chance.'"[19]

Manager Danny Murtaugh used Mota in 115 games and gave him 271 at-bats that summer (.277-5-32). He even pressed Mota into service as a catcher on July 13 at Forbes Field. After doubling to open the eighth inning, starter Jim Pagliaroni left for pinch-runner Orlando Macfarlane, the backup catcher. Third-stringer Smoky Burgess – whose career-pinch-hitting mark Mota would later break – then struck out batting for Roy Face. But when Macfarlane had to leave the game with a minor injury in the 10th inning, Mota moved from left field to behind the plate. It was a rough experience, as he committed two passed balls, the second of which helped the Cardinals to score the winning run in the 12th.

After the 1964 season, Danny Murtaugh stepped down for health reasons and Harry Walker became Pittsburgh's new manager. Although the way Walker taught hitting wasn't for everyone, Mota was just the kind of slashing hitter that "The Hat" loved. "I paid attention to Harry and I learned," Mota said in 1969. "He convinced me that if you hit the ball in the air, it will usually be caught. I now hit the ball down and to all fields. He taught this old dog new tricks."[20]

Mota won his third Dominican batting crown (.364) in the winter of 1964-65. Even so, he played just a little more for the Pirates in 1965 than he did in '64, with an almost identical batting line (.279-4-29). He had to recover from an icy 5-for-54 start; he had been worrying about his family's safety because the Dominican political situation had flared up again. Pittsburgh's general manager, Joe L. Brown, got the Peace Corps' director of Latin American programs to see that Mota's family was okay and to bring them Stateside.[21] Months later, things weren't fully back to normal; the winter league proper did not operate in 1965-66. Instead, there was a three-team circuit formed by the Federation of Dominican Players. The teams represented colors rather than cities: the Blues, Yellows, and Reds. Mota was with the Blues.[22]

In 1966, Mota batted .332 for the Pirates while platooning with Matty Alou, another Harry Walker-type hitter. In a feature article about the pair that June, Pittsburgh beat writer Les Biederman said, "Mota is a standout every time he plays. Apparently he's destined to be one of those super-subs you read about in baseball and he could play regularly on many teams in the majors right now. There are few things Mota can't do. He can run, he can hit the ball, he seldom strikes out, he's a Grade A base-runner and he can go get 'em in the outfield. Mota is one of the best bunters in the game. He loves to bunt with two strikes, too."[23]

It's interesting to note that Biederman added, "Since Alou starts most of the games, Mota comes in handy as a pinch-hitter. The first eight times he was sent up, he came through with five hits."[24] While he was with the Pirates, Mota also had his own superstition; if he got a base hit, he would take a bath at exactly 3 P.M. the next day and also eat at the same time. "Clemente thought I was crazy," he said in 1974.[25] In 2011, though, Mota underscored the importance of a regular routine, calling it the main reason why he remained so fit during his playing career and beyond. "You have to discipline yourself and your body," he said. "You have to eat properly, work out, and rest as much as you can."

Mota continued to get 300 or so at-bats for the Bucs in 1967 and 1968, batting .321 and .281. In between those two seasons, he got his first experience as a manager, posting a 13-14 record with Licey after taking over in midseason for Hal Smith.[26] There was still tension in the Dominican, as soldiers were posted at Santo Domingo's Estadio Quisqueya to frisk people for weapons.[27]

Les Biederman focused on Mota in several more features during the rest of his time in Pittsburgh. The headlines called him "A Mighty Handy Guy with Bat in His Hands" and "The Guy the Bucs Couldn't Do Without." Yet ultimately, the Pirates decided that he was expendable. For one thing, "they put his name on the 'Ghoul Pool' sheet, a list of players available to restock a major league team which, God forbid, gets wiped out in an airplane crash."[28] Then Pittsburgh made Mota available in the expansion draft in October 1968, and the Montreal Expos made him their second pick. He spent less than half a season there, though – the Expos traded him to Los Angeles on June 11, 1969. Maury Wills also returned to the Dodgers in the deal, while Ron Fairly and Paul Popovich went to Montreal. Except for winter ball, Mota has remained in Dodger blue ever since.

Mota pointed to July 7-8, 1969, as his hottest burst in the majors. In three games against Atlanta, he peppered the Braves pitchers with 10 singles and a double in 14 at-bats. In 2006, he recalled, "I was really confident and focused. I was in a groove, swinging the bat and putting the ball in play. You have to know your strengths and abilities. I was not a long ball hitter."[29]

In the winter of 1969-70, again playing with Licey, Mota took over for Fred Hatfield as manager for the Dominican playoffs. The Tigres won the championship and thus joined in the revival of the Caribbean Series, which returned in February 1970 after a hiatus of nine years. The Dominicans finished behind Puerto Rico and Venezuela with a 1-7 record.

The Dodgers gave Mota a chance to play more against righties in 1970, and he hit .305 in a career-high 417 at-bats. A sad note to the season came on May 17, when a line drive off Mota's bat struck a 14-year-old fan named Alan Fish in the head. The youth died five days later. In 2008, Mota – known for his great love of children – said, "It's very difficult. . . It brings up bad memories. I felt guilty because I hit the foul ball. And a young boy lost his life."[30]

That winter, however, the Dominicans went 6-0 in the Caribbean Series under player-manager Mota, who had again taken over for Fred Hatfield late in the season. Mota went 11 for 19 (.579) and was named MVP of the series. In 2011, however, he remained remarkably humble about this accomplishment, deflecting the credit to others. "I was in the right place at the right time," he said. "I did my part and tried to help the team. I could not have done it without my family, teammates, and the fans, our tenth man. I had the Lord's blessing." Nonetheless, he still took clear pride in having helped to bring this title to his homeland.

Mota was the Dodgers' fourth outfielder in 1971, as rookie Bill Buckner played his first full season in the majors. Even though Frank Robinson arrived in L.A. in 1972, Mota was once again the primary left fielder on the strength of his .323 average. One moment that showed his style was a steal of home against Scipio Spinks of St. Louis. The daring sixth-inning play broke a scoreless tie, and the Dodgers went on to win 2-1. After the game, Mota said, "If you don't try it, you'll never make it."[31]

Just nine days before that play, Mota enjoyed what he termed a giant experience in his life. As he walked onto the field at Dodger Stadium for practice, he spied a white-haired Jackie Robinson sitting alone in the stands. The Dodgers were retiring Robinson's #42 that day, along with Roy Campanella's #39 and Sandy Koufax's #32. Mota expressed his gratitude for what Robinson had done on behalf of African-Americans, Hispanics, and mankind in general. Robinson, who died that October, thanked Mota in return with a handshake and a smile.[32]

In 1973, despite being a reserve once again, Mota made the All-Star team for the only time in his career. Manager Sparky Anderson of Cincinnati named him to the NL squad, saying, "We can do a lot of things with the guys on this team. Manny Mota is the best right-handed pinch-hitter in baseball."[33] At Royals Stadium in Kansas City, Mota grounded into a force play as a pinch-hitter in the eighth inning and then played the bottom of the eighth in left.

From 1974 onward, Mota was almost exclusively a pinch-hitter – a luxury unheard of today in an era of 12- and 13-man pitching staffs. He appeared in the field in just 17 games from 1974 through 1979. When manager Walter Alston informed him of his role in the spring of 1974, Mota "took the news calmly. 'We have so much young talent and these young players have to play. This club is very deep. The manager thinks I can contribute to this club and so do I. I like my job. I like to do things that help my team win games.'"[34]

During these six seasons, Mota was 76 for 243 (.313) as a pinch-hitter, with one homer and 51 RBIs. As early as March 1976, the L.A. press recognized that he was taking aim at Smoky Burgess' career mark of 144.[35] That June, when Mota was on the verge of getting his 100th pinch hit, Jim Murray wrote a vivid feature story about him. Among the key points: Mota's success stemmed from his mental approach and powers of concentration, as well as his conditioning.[36] Whereas Burgess was described as "a walking laundry bag" or "a beachball with arms," Mota's weight scarcely varied throughout his career. Manager Tom Lasorda joked in 1978 that Manny was "a waiter at the Last Supper" and "older than dirt." He added, "Mota should be made a saint. He might hit until he's 60." Said Mota, "I just try to concentrate on what I can do to help the team."[37]

In this period, the Dodgers won three pennants: 1974, 1977, and 1978. Mota was 3 for 5 with two doubles in the National League playoffs. One of those doubles came in Game Three of the 1977 NLCS, which Mota called in 2006 "the game I'll never forget."[38] With the Dodgers down 5-3 in the top of the ninth at Veterans Stadium in Philadelphia, 41-year-old Vic Davalillo beat out a drag bunt. Mota, with two strikes, then doubled to left. The ball went over the head and off the glove of Greg "The Bull" Luzinski, never a nimble flychaser (he normally came out for defensive replacement Jerry Martin in such situations). The Dodgers went on to win 6-5, advancing to the World Series. Davey Lopes, who was in the on-deck circle when Mota delivered, said, "When he turned around and smiled the way he did, I knew he was going to hit one for us."[39]

Unfortunately, Mota did not make a mark in World Series competition. He did not appear in 1974, was 0 for 3 in 1977, and drew a walk the only time he came to the plate in '78.

Yet for Mota, one of his biggest thrills came not in the postseason but in exhibition play. On March 19-20, 1977, the Dodgers played two games against the New York Mets in the Dominican Republic. In the second, before 10,000 delighted fans at Estadio Quisqueya and an international TV audience, Mota connected for a two-run homer off Mets ace Tom Seaver to cap a 4-0 victory. In 1991, he said, "I'll never forget that because it was one of the greatest feelings I ever had as a pinch hitter, coming in front of my home people. The fans went wild and I can't describe just how I felt to come through in front of the fans all over Latin America, the Dominican Republic, and back in L.A."[40]

In October 1979, President Jimmy Carter invited Mota to the White House to congratulate him on setting the career mark for pinch hits (#145 had come at Dodger Stadium on September 2 off Lynn McGlothen of the Cubs). Mota gave the grinning chief executive various souvenirs, including a Dodgers jacket with PRESIDENT CARTER on the back. He also asked for the U.S. to buy more Dominican sugar.[41]

Mota announced his retirement after the '79 season, but he was reactivated in both 1980 and 1982. During the 1980 pennant race, he went 3 for 7 as a pinch-hitter. His last base hit came on October 5 – the last game of the regular season – off Houston's Joe Sambito. It was an RBI single in the seventh inning, bringing the Dodgers within a run at 3-2 in a game that they would eventually win 4-3. That game left L.A. and Houston tied for the lead in the NL West at 92-70. However, the Astros won the one-game playoff the following day.

Mota's final action as a player in the Dominican league came in the winter of 1980-81. However, at the age of 44 on September 1, 1982, he came to the plate one final time in the majors. It was just his kind of situation: in the bottom of the 13th inning at Dodger Stadium, with L.A. behind 6-5, Steve Garvey was on second with one out. However, Jim Kaat – who was then 43 years old himself – got Mota to ground out to second. He later recalled it as one of the saddest days of his life because his mother (whom he had brought to Los Angeles to live her final days) died in the hospital before he could see her for the final time.[42]

Mota's 150 pinch hits came in 500 at-bats, for an even .300 average. By comparison, Lenny Harris got his 212 pinch hits in 804 at-bats (.264). The man who ranked second as of 2018, Mark Sweeney, was 175 for 679 (.258). At that time, 18 players had 100 or more career base hits in this role. Only two others were even over .280: Steve Braun and Burgess (both .283).[43]

Mota continued to serve the Dodgers organization in various capacities, notably as hitting coach from 1980 through 1989. Starting in 1999, he assisted and communicated with the Dodgers' Latin American players while also coordinating all aspects of opponent charting. He also worked on Spanish-language pregame and postgame broadcasts. In 2007, Major League Baseball cracked down on the number of coaches that a club could have on the bench. This meant that for a while (until there was a change in the coaching staff) Mota could not go on the road with the team.

The 2012 season marked Mota's 33nd as a coach, the longest tenure in Dodgers history. Only Nick Altrock (42 consecutive seasons from 1912 to 1953 with the Washington Senators) had a longer run with one club. Old Number 11 still looked almost as fit as ever in uniform. The Dodgers shifted Mota's role in the organization in 2013, expanding his role on Spanish-language broadcasts. They also assigned him new duties as a minor-league hitting instructor and in making community appearances. Mota accepted the change gracefully.[44]

In 2016, however, Dodgers manager Dave Roberts decided to bring Mota back to work with hitting coach Turner Ward and assistant Tim Hyers during pregame activities at home. Roberts, who knew Mota from his time playing for Los Angeles (2002-04), said, "I just feel that he brings a lot to the table, as far as the trust that the players have with him."[45] To this day, hitters at many levels also benefit from using the Manny Mota Grip Stick, a pine tar substitute that has been on the market since at least 1991.[46]

Mota managed for all or part of 16 seasons in winter ball, 12 in the Dominican Republic. He won back-to-back championships with Licey in 1982-83 and 1983-84. In the subsequent Caribbean Series, the Dominicans finished third (at 3-3) and last (1-4), respectively. Those were his only two full seasons running the Tigres; the following year, he moved on to Caimanes del Sur. He was Manager of the Year, and then became skipper of Escogido, with which the Dodgers had formed a working agreement. Considering the deep ties Mota had helped establish between Licey and L.A., this was akin to a coup d'état. He served with the Leones until partway through the 1987-88 season, when he took a front-office position and gave way to Phil Regan in the dugout.

In 1992, Mota returned to managing with Mexicali in the Mexican Pacific League, where he spent three winter seasons and part of a fourth. The Águilas had actually approached him the year before, but since the Dodgers were in a tight playoff race with Atlanta, he declined. In 1993, speaking with *La Opinión*, a Spanish-language newspaper in L.A., Mota did admit that someday in the not-too-distant future he hoped to get an opportunity as a big-league manager, as his role model Felipe Alou had.[47]

The closest he came was in 1996 – from July 29 onward, after Tommy Lasorda retired for health reasons, Mota was Bill Russell's bench coach. In fact, Russell was ejected in the ninth inning against St. Louis on September 13, so one may infer that Mota ran the club for the brief remainder of the game.[48] However, Mike Scioscia replaced him as bench coach starting in 1997. The Dodgers did interview Mota for the managing job after Davey Johnson was fired in 2000. That winter also featured his last duties as skipper to date, as he returned to Licey and replaced Grady Little in midseason.

Manny and Margarita Mota had six sons: José, Andrés, Domingo, Manuel Jr., Rafael, and Antonio. Andrés, known as Andy in the U.S., and José became major leaguers in the 1990s; Manuel Jr. (aka Gary), Domingo, and Tony were pro ballplayers too. After he quit playing, José went into a successful career broadcasting the game. The Motas also had two daughters (Cecilia and María de Lourdes, or Lulu).[49]

Their love of children inspired Manny and Margarita to form the Manny Mota Foundation. It all started in 1967 with just a large cooking pot for rice to feed hungry children in their native land. Starting in 1992, their humanitarian support extended to the greater Los Angeles area. Baseball clinics are just one of many of the Foundation's programs. Perhaps the most ambitious undertaking, though, is the multi-function *Campo de Sueños* (Field of Dreams) complex, for which the Dominican government donated 15 acres in 1995. Campo de Sueños is also the name of the foundation's annual dinner and auction in Los Angeles. When the foundation's website was still operating, there was a message from Manny and Margarita, which opened, "Helping the disadvantaged improve their lives is an extremely rewarding experience. For the past three decades we have been blessed with the opportunity to help others in many different ways."

Manny Mota's message as a human remained remarkably consistent. In 2011, he said, "I am very grateful to the people of my country and of the United States for giving me this chance. My wife and family have inspired me. I am blessed." He echoed closely what he said in 1979. "I like to live a friendly life. I like to be friendly to everybody because I think that's the way human beings can get to know each other better. To me it doesn't make any difference in the race of people or if he's a kid or an adult. I try to respect all people because I would like all people to respect me. That's the way I grew up and that's the way I'm going to die."[50]

Grateful acknowledgment to Manny Mota for his memories (telephone interview, February 11, 2011) and to José Mota for the introduction. Special thanks in turn to Jennifer Hoyer (Media Relations, Los Angeles Angels of Anaheim) for the introduction to José Mota.

This biography was originally published in February 2011. It was updated and expanded in December 2018.

MANNY MOTA ON THE ART OF PINCH-HITTING

"Pinch hitting is more mental than physical. You have to put all the preparation and positive thinking into one at-bat."

"I loved the pressure, hitting in the clutch with a man in scoring position and the game on the line. I had confidence in that situation." [51]

"When you're a pinch hitter, the first thing to keep in mind is that you're up there to swing the bat. Go down swinging if you have to, but remember the worst thing that can happen to a pinch hitter is to get called out on strikes. Nobody can fault you as a pinch hitter if you're aggressive, if you bear down, swing the bat, and make good contact." [52]

"Concentration is the key. . .You have to swing at good pitches and you have to know the pitchers." [53]

SOURCES

In addition to the sources cited in the Notes, the author also consulted:

www.Baseball-Reference.com

www.MannyMotaFoundation.org (site is no longer in operation)

www.licey.com

www.purapelota.com (Venezuelan statistics)

Bjarkman, Peter C. *Diamonds Around the Globe: The Encyclopedia of International Baseball* (Westport, Connecticut: Greenwood Press, 2005).

Bjarkman, Peter C. *Baseball with a Latin Beat* (Jefferson, North Carolina: McFarland & Co., 1994).

NOTES

1 Bud Tucker, "Manny Mota Always Ready," *Pittsburgh Press-Courier*, June 16, 1979: 15.

2 Jim Murray, "Nobody Knows Manny – Except the Pitchers," *Los Angeles Times*, September 22, 1971.

3 Telephone interview, Rory Costello with Manny Mota, February 11, 2011. Unless otherwise indicated, all quotes from Mota come from this interview.

4 Cary Osborne, "'The utilityman in this organization,'" Dodger Insider blog, June 8, 2018 (https://dodgers.mlblogs.com/the-utilityman-in-this-organization-2b159cfc45f1).

5 Roy McHugh, "Manny's World," *Pittsburgh Press*, July 30, 1969: B-1.

6 Christina Hamlett, "Going to Bat for the Kids: Manny Mota's Real Life," *American Chronicle*, October 11, 2006.

7 David Laurila, "Prospectus Q&A: Manny Mota," *Baseball Prospectus* website, July 6, 2010.

8 Rob Ruck, *The Tropic of Baseball* (Westport, Connecticut: Meckler Publishing, 1991), 70.

9 Jack McDonald, "Giants Reap Bumper Crop from Seeds Planted in Caribbean," *The Sporting News*, November 5, 1958: 7.

10 Maria E. Pérez, "Manny Mota: 'Yo soy un hijo de Don Bosco,'" *El Caribe* (Santo Domingo, Dominican Republic), March 15, 2018 (https://www.elcaribe.com.do/2018/03/15/gente/10-momentos/manny-mota-yo-soy-un-hijo-de-don-bosco/).

11 Bruce Adelson, *Brushing Back Jim Crow* (Charlottesville, Virginia: University of Virginia Press, 1999), 234.

12 "Political Turmoil Forces Dominican League to Fold," *The Sporting News*, December 13, 1961: 34.

13 Fred Down, United Press International, *Bridgeport Post*, March 14, 1962: 43.

14 Al Doyle, "Manny Mota: The Game I'll Never Forget," *Baseball Digest*, May 2006: 70.

15 Clark Nealon, "Colts Sound Call for Picket Race – Hardy Top Entry," *The Sporting News*, December 29, 1962: 28.

16 Eduardo Moncada, "Oriente Folds; Forfeits Games Left in Season," *The Sporting News*, January 26, 1963: 32.

17 Steve Henson, "Growing Up True Blue: Oldest Four Sons of Dodgers' Mota Make Baseball Their Chosen Field," *Los Angeles Times*, August 12, 1990.

18 Pérez, "Manny Mota: 'Yo soy un hijo de Don Bosco.'"

19 David Maraniss, *Clemente* (New York: Simon & Schuster, 2006), 171-172.

20 James Collins, "Mota Was More Than A 'Throw-In'," *Baseball Digest*, November 1969: 58.

21 Robert F. Buckhorn, United Press International, "Pirates to Peace Corps DP Helps Mota End Slump," *Daily Courier* (Connellsville, Pennsylvania), May 27, 1965: 9.

22 J. A. Sabino, "Olivo and Rivas Show Top Form in Mound Bows," *The Sporting News*, December 6, 1965: 36.

23 Les Biederman, "If You Could Buy Stock in Matty and Manny, Price Would Soar," *The Sporting News*, June 4, 1966: 15.

24 Biederman, "If You Could Buy Stock in Matty and Manny, Price Would Soar."

25 Bill Shirley, "Baseball Superstitions Are Still With Us," *Baseball Digest*, December 1974: 80.

26 Fernando Vicioso, "Fuentes Ties Two Records In One Game," *The Sporting News*, December 30, 1967: 47. The Hal Smith whom Mota succeeded was Harold Raymond Smith, not Harold Wayne Smith. "Smith, Former Bucco Aid, Joins Red Coaching Staff," *The Sporting News*, December 2, 1967: 47.

27 Russell Schneider, "Fans Are Frisked at Dominican Loop Games," *The Sporting News*, December 2, 1967: 53.

28 Jim O'Brien, "Manny Mota: Baseball's Premier Pinch-Hitter," *Baseball Digest*, September 1979: 88.

29 Doyle.

30 Kevin Baxter, "Foul Play," *Los Angeles Times*, June 17, 2008.

31 Ken Rappoport, Associated Press, "Aaron Pops, Mets Plop," *Courier-News* (Bridgewater, New Jersey), June 14, 1972: 45.

32 Luis Rodríguez Mayoral, "Manny Mota: Incredible in the Pinch," LaVidaBaseball.com, June 5, 2018 (https://www.lavidabaseball.com/mayoral-manny-mota/).

33 Bob Smizik, "All-Star Game: Showcase or Battleground?" *Pittsburgh Press*, July 24, 1973: 23.

34 United Press International, "Mota: Tough in the Pinch,"- *Palm Beach Post*, August 3, 1974: 54.

35 Retrosheet statistics now credit Burgess with 145.

36 Jim Murray, "Mota Is Highest Paid Player In Sport At 5 Grand Per Hit," *Los Angeles Times*, June 12, 1976.

37 United Press International, "Mota Sparks Dodgers," *Daily Chronicle* (De Kalb, Illinois), May 23, 1978: 11.

38 Doyle.

39 United Press International, "KC's McRae in Spotlight Again, LA Wins," *Waukesha* (Wisconsin) *Daily Freeman*, October 8, 1977: 14.

40 "Dodgers Zero in on Seaver, Mets," *St. Petersburg Times*, March 21, 1977. Manny Mota, as told to George Vass, in "The Game I'll Never Forget," *Baseball Digest*, April 1991: 79.

41 Associated Press, October 10, 1979.

42 Osborne, "'The utilityman in this organization.'"

43 Analysis based on Retrosheet statistics, which differ slightly from other counts.

44 Bill Shaikin, "Dodgers' Manny Mota Enters a New Mode," *Los Angeles Times*, April 22, 2013.

45 Hoornstra, J.P. "Manny Mota has a locker in the Dodger Stadium coaches' room again." *Los Angeles Daily News*, April 15, 2016.

46 Matt Winkeljohn, "On-deck Circle Sn Island of Calm," *Atlanta Constitution*, August 11, 1991: 51.

47 Manolo Hernández Douen, "Mota feliz con su cargo como manager de Mexicali," *La Opinión* (Los Angeles, California), August 14, 1993: B1.

48 Chris Baker, "Dodgers Lose a Game of Tag," *Los Angeles Times*, September 14, 1996.

49 Fernando Dominguez, "In Manny Mota's Family, Hope Running High for More Major-Leaguers," *Los Angeles Times*, February 13, 1992.

50 United Press International, "Mota: Pinch Hitter with a Philosophy," *Opelousas* (Louisiana) *Daily World*, July 16, 1978: 16.

51 Doyle.

52 Vass, 78.

53 George Vass, "These Are the Game's Five Greatest Pinch Hitters!" *Baseball Digest*, January 1977: 83.

DIÓMEDES OLIVO

By Rory Costello

In Homer's *Iliad*, Diómedes was one of the strongest Greek warriors. He was also the youngest – unlike his namesake, Dominican pitcher Diómedes Olivo. Olivo made his big-league debut with the 1960 Pirates at the age of 41. As of 2018, he was still the second-oldest "rookie" in major-league history, behind only Satchel Paige. Like Paige, Olivo had already been a durable star pitcher for many years. And as both Roberto Clemente and Danny Murtaugh are said to have remarked, the man may have been in his 40s, but his arm was 20.[1]

"Guayubín" (as Olivo was called, for his hometown) earned elite status among his nation's hurlers during the 1950s. He didn't even turn pro until his late 20s, but after he did, he pitched in at least six other nations: Puerto Rico, Mexico, Cuba, Venezuela, Nicaragua, and Colombia. His pro career – both summer and winter – spanned from 1947 to 1964.

In the majors the lefty's lifetime record was just 5-6, with a 3.10 ERA in 85 games (1960; 1962-63). During the 1962 season, at the age of 43, Olivo was a revelation to Stateside fans. His fastball was still lively, and "the way that guy throws a curve is murder," said one unnamed player.[2] Although Pittsburgh called Olivo up too late for him to be eligible for the 1960 World Series, he joined Virgil Trucks in throwing batting practice for the team during the Series.[3]

Diómedes Antonio Olivo Maldonado was born on January 22, 1919 (but rumors persisted that he was actually older). His parents were Arcadio Emilio Olivo Báez and Juana Ramona Maldonado Mejía. "Mamá Juana," as she was known, died in 1983 at the remarkable age of 103. She had five other children besides Diómedes: sons Arcadio, César Blas, and Federico; daughters Zena and Lucrecia. Federico – known as Chichí (or Chi-Chi in the US) – was also a star pitcher at home who had a short major-league career (1961; 1964-66).

Guayubín (full name San Lorenzo de Guayubín) is the second largest city in Monte Cristi Province, in the northwestern corner of the Dominican Republic. For this reason, Olivo earned another nickname, La Montaña Noroestana: The Northwestern Mountain. Emilio "Cuqui" Córdova, the dean of Dominican baseball writers, made that the subtitle of his short book about Olivo, which became the definitive biography in 2006.

Arcadio Olivo was a cattle rancher. During spring training in 1960, Diómedes recalled through interpreter Román Mejías, "When I put the cows away, I go into town to play. I start when I am 5 or 10 with pickup teams at home in Guayubín."[4] Olivo never picked up more than a smattering of English, relying on teammates such as Mejías, Clemente, Julián Javier, and Al McBean to get his message across. What didn't need translation, though, was his lively, cheery personality.

In 1990 a Dominican named Dr. José de Jiménez contributed a short but incisive overview of Olivo's life and career to SABR's *Baseball Research Journal*. He wrote, "By 1940 or so the owner of a baseball team in Puerto Plata, a neighboring province, was interested in his services. Since no one knew him in Puerto Plata, the comments among fans and sportswriters included: 'A great pitcher from Guayubín was signed;' 'The pitcher from Guayubín has arrived.' From that moment on he was baptized as Guayubín Olivo."

In 2010 Dominican sportswriter Rafael Peña chronicled Olivo's early years in Dominican ball, noting that he first played in the nation's capital, Santo Domingo, in 1944.[5] That year Olivo was named to the Dominican national team that went to Caracas, Venezuela, for the seventh Amateur World Series. Two years later the Dominicans went to Barranquilla, Colombia, for the Central American and Caribbean Games. Olivo's standout performance included a 13-inning win over Colombia, in which he allowed just one run on four hits.[6]

Professional baseball had been on hiatus in the Dominican Republic since 1937, and it did not resume until the summer of 1951 – yet there was still an active club scene. On September 28, 1947, Olivo pitched a no-hitter for Escogido against archrival Licey, the team for which he would later play 11 seasons. That winter he joined Aguadilla of the Puerto Rican Winter League, serving as both pitcher and outfielder. He was a robust man (6-feet-1, 195 pounds) who always took great pride in his hitting.

Olivo said in 1960 that he turned down an opportunity to join the Chicago White Sox in 1948 because he didn't speak English and didn't want to come to the United States and play in the minor leagues.[7] Pittsburgh sportswriter and broadcaster Myron Cope expanded on this theme in a feature for *Sports Illustrated* in the summer of 1962. "Back home in Guayubín… Olivo owns 500 acres of pasture, 50 cows and 200 acres on which he plans to build a small housing development. He labored hard over the decades, milking cows and pitching baseballs, and though he received occasional feelers from big-league clubs, he turned them down. For one thing, he had no taste for working his way up through the minors; then, too, he feared being shipped to a segregated southern town and felt his ignorance of English would make life doubly hard."[8] Olivo was a coffee-colored man who was termed a "Negro" by US standards.

Instead, his travels took him to Colombia during the summer of 1948, when pro baseball began in that nation. He joined Tejedores (Weavers) de Filtta, an industrial team sponsored by a woolen mill in Barranquilla. In his debut, on June 27, he took a perfect game into the ninth but finished with a two-hitter.[9] Colombian baseball historian Raúl Porto said Olivo went back to Filtta in both 1949 and 1950. He was a league all-star in both '48 and '49, leading the circuit in strikeouts both years. In 1949, the Tejedores were league champion.

Olivo also played ball in Venezuela during this period. One glimpse comes from May 1950, when the lefty was with Gavilanes, one of three teams in La Liga Occidental, in the western state of Zulia. The Sparrowhawks had a rivalry with Pastora, another team based in the oil city of Maracaibo.[10] Negro Leaguers like Max Manning and Terris McDuffie (the latter Olivo's teammate) were also in the league.[11] Sandalio "Sandy" Consuegra, then a Washington Senators farmhand, had also signed with Gavilanes the previous winter. The Cuban spent his $3,000 signing bonus, though, and when he asked Senators owner Clark Griffith to refund it in the spring, Griffith sent Consuegra back to Havana, delaying his big-league debut.[12]

Olivo remained in Puerto Rico for six more winters. In the 1950-51 season, Aguadilla sold him to San Juan after he suffered seven straight defeats.[13] This was a good break because the Senadores were a winning ballclub and the Tiburones (Sharks) were not – in fact, San Juan absorbed Aguadilla for the 1951-52 season. That team won the Puerto Rican championship and went to the Caribbean Series as a result. The tournament was held in Panama City (it is not certain whether Olivo ever played in the Panamanian winter league). The Dominican relieved in two games for Puerto Rico, which went winless, and became the first man from his country to pitch in the Caribbean Series.[14]

Olivo was among the league leaders in wins (9) and ERA (2.07) for San Juan in 1952-53. That season he conceived a child with a Puerto Rican woman named Crucita Rondón. The boy, Gilberto Rondón, was born on November 18, 1953, in the Bronx, New York. Gil inherited a bit of his father's talent, as he pitched 19 games for the Astros in 1976 and four for the White Sox in 1979. In later years he became a pitching coach, and one of his stops was with the Nicaraguan national team. He told Nicaraguan baseball historian Tito Rondón (they jokingly called each other "cousin"), "My mom had a thing for ballplayers, and one day she saw Guayubín Olivo, and decided she had to have him, and I was born!" However, Olivo married his wife, Olga Chávez Gómez, in 1953.[15] They had three children: Pedro, Olga (known as Titi), and Guillermo.

When pro ball returned to the Dominican Republic in the summer of 1951, Olivo came back home and joined the Licey Tigres. He won the Triple Crown of pitching that year, going 10-5 (in a 54-game schedule), striking out 65, and posting a 1.90 ERA in 128 innings. The 1951 season was tarnished, however, by an out-of-character incident on July 22. Olivo, after arguing a ball-and-strike call with umpire Willis Thompson, threw a ball at the ump's head, knocking him cold. He was ejected from the stadium and went to jail overnight. Originally, the star pitcher was going to be suspended for the season, but after Licey lobbied intensely, and Olivo himself wrote a public letter of apology in the magazine *La Nación*, the punishment was reduced to just six games.[16]

Olivo led the Dominican league in ERA again in both 1952 and 1954. Highlights of the 1954 season included breaking up Negro Leaguer Johnny Wright's no-hit bid on May 22. His ninth-inning pinch single made a winner of Ewell Blackwell, who was still hanging on (The Whip's major-league career ended in 1955). One week later Olivo threw a no-hitter of his own over Escogido, which had Hall of Famer Ray Dandridge and another powerful Negro Leaguer, Bob Thurman (who joined the Cincinnati Reds the next year).

After the 1954-55 season ended in Puerto Rico, Olivo came back home to face Japan's leading team, the Yomiuri Giants, as part of the Giants' Caribbean tour. The Dominicans took four of five games, losing only the opener as Olivo allowed the two tying runs in the ninth inning and five more in the 10th.[17]

Shortly thereafter, Olivo played in the US minors for the first time. The absence of Dominican summer ball was clearly a factor. Havana of the International League signed him, as owner Bobby Maduro stocked his team with players who had performed all around the Caribbean.[18] However, Olivo pitched just 13 innings in seven games for the Sugar Kings before going to the Mexican League. "My finger is smashed in a car door one day," he recalled in 1960. "It grow big, but they pitch me. Then they sell me to Mexico City."[19]

Olivo spent 1955 through 1958 with the Mexico City Diablos Rojos, with an aggregate record of 34-21. His 15-8, 2.65 performance helped the Red Devils win the league championship in 1956. However, he pitched just five games in Mexico in 1957. The Nicaraguan League (which played in the summers in 1956 and 1957) lured him and Cuban teammate Vicente López away.[20] Tito Rondón and his fellow local historian Carlos Mena recalled how Olivo was part of a group called The Lost Squadron that was supposed to reinforce the Bóer club but took weeks to arrive. When they finally did, it inspired Nicaraguan poet Óscar Pérez Valdivia to write verses in their honor. Olivo pitched very well for the Indios, going 8-5, 2.16 in 23 games (16 starts). It was too late for Bóer, though, which lost the championship to León (there were no playoffs). López and Olivo then went back to Mexico.[21]

Olivo continued to pitch at home after the Dominican season switched to the winter. Myron Cope's *Sports Illustrated* story opened with a recollection from a teammate. "In 1959 Dick Stuart, the Pittsburgh Pirates' nonconformist first baseman, returned from the Dominican Republic Winter League and described to Pirate brass an elderly left-handed pitcher he had seen there. 'I told them I'd been hitting against this guy for three years down there and I got two hits off him,' says Stuart. 'I told them, 'Sign this guy!' But you know how it is with me. Anything Stuart says around here, they say forget it.'"[22]

Olivo joined the Poza Rica Petroleros in Mexico for the summer of 1959, which was one of his best as a pro. He was 21-8 with a 3.02 ERA, helping the Petroleros become the league's champion by leading the league in victories and in strikeouts, with 233 in 247 innings. He set a league record by striking out 16 in a seven-inning game (the opener of

Photo courtesy of the Pittsburgh Pirates

a doubleheader).[23] He followed up with a typically capable winter for the Tigres (7-6, 2.33).

Howie Haak, the trailblazing scout who opened up all of Latin America, "prevailed upon General Manager Joe L. Brown to take the gamble" in signing Olivo.[24] Myron Cope wrote, "Even after the Pirates persuaded Diómedes to sign a contract... he failed to report to spring training. The Pirates finally sent a wire: REPORT TO TRAINING CAMP AT ONCE. The other day Diómedes explained through an interpreter that it was the wire that convinced him he was wanted in the U.S."[25]

Olivo was impressive in camp, surprising many with his hard stuff and "no trick deliveries."[26] Yet at the beginning of the 1960 season, Pittsburgh decided to keep righty Paul Giel instead. They returned Olivo to Poza Rica, which in turn sold his contract to the Pirates' top farm club, Columbus in the International League. He pitched well (7-9, 2.88 in 42 games, including 12 starts), and so Pittsburgh called the 41-year-old vet up that September. He made his big-league debut on

September 5 – becoming the sixth player (and third pitcher) from the Dominican Republic in The Show.

Olivo pitched in four games for the Pirates that month, with three of those appearances being mop-up duty. His most significant outing came on September 27 at Forbes Field, in a 16-inning win over Cincinnati. He pitched the 10th through the 13th innings, striking out six of the 19 men the Bucs' pitchers fanned that night.

Although Olivo's visa was due to expire on October 1, it was extended so he could be on hand for the 1960 World Series.[27] After the Pirates defeated the Yankees, the team awarded him a very modest $250 in cash for his September and postseason batting-practice services (Virgil Trucks, who joined the team in August, got $500). That winter Olivo again won the Triple Crown of pitching for Licey. He had 10 victories (against six losses), struck out 160 men – a league record that still stood as of 2018 – in 142 innings, and posted a 1.58 ERA.

Despite this performance, Olivo found himself back at Columbus in 1961. The Pirates had traded for another veteran lefty, Bobby Shantz, the previous December; Olivo was one of the last three men manager Murtaugh cut in spring training. He pitched very well in Triple-A, though, going 11-7 with a 2.01 ERA and 20 saves in 66 games. The Jets won the regular-season pennant (though they were knocked out in the playoffs) and manager Larry Shepard was still talking about the veteran's importance to the club nearly four years later.[28] The IL Writers' Association voted Olivo as the league's most valuable pitcher.

Dominican dictator Rafael Trujillo was assassinated on May 30, 1961, and the atmosphere in the country remained extremely tense. A nationwide strike and street fighting crippled attendance, and the Dominican League halted the 1961-62 season after the games of December 3.[29] Olivo then spent another short stretch in Puerto Rico with San Juan.

Before the 1962 season *Baseball Digest* issued this scouting report on Olivo: "Superb relief pitcher – perhaps the best in International League. Baffling prospect: Some say he's as old as 45 – but still pitches with great effectiveness." Danny Murtaugh kept Olivo with the Pirates that year, and he got his first big-league win at Wrigley Field on April 16. He thrived on frequent work, appearing 62 times, and formed an effective lefty-righty tandem with Elroy Face. He went 5-1 with a 2.77 ERA, also picking up seven saves. Murtaugh frequently used Olivo in a way that would become much more common in the future: as a lefty specialist to get one or two outs. Yet he could also pitch in long relief and got one start, in the season finale.

Dominican League play remained suspended altogether in 1962-63, but exhibition games were still taking place, and Olivo participated.[30] He also tended to his farm, although that December cattle rustlers made off with seven of his steers![31] Meanwhile, on November 19 the Pirates traded him to the St. Louis Cardinals along with Dick Groat for pitcher Don Cardwell and infielder Julio Gotay. Olivo started the 1963 season with St. Louis, but things did not go well, as he went 0-5 with a 5.40 ERA in 19 appearances. Manager Johnny Keane also used the vet in a specialist role, giving him just 13⅓ innings total. One of those outings came against the New York Mets at the Polo Grounds on June 7. Ron Taylor had weakened in the ninth inning, putting two runners on. Duke Snider was coming to the plate, and another lefty, Ed Kranepool, was on deck. The Mets won, 3-2, as the Duke hit a three-run homer to end the game.

Keane gave Olivo just two more chances to pitch before the Cardinals sent the 44-year-old down to Triple-A Atlanta in early July. There he enjoyed a late-career highlight, throwing a seven-inning no-hitter on July 22 in the opener of a doubleheader against Toronto. It could have been a perfect game except that he walked Bubba Morton on four pitches with two out in the seventh. Not only that, Olivo singled and scored the game's only run in the third inning.

Olivo wrapped up his pro career with one final season in Dominican winter ball. He was 9-3, 2.37 in 18 games for Licey. In 2006 his son Guillermo said, "The saddest day of my father's life was when he played his last game with Licey in 1964. He always felt most comfortable when they called on him to pitch with this team."[32] Olivo's totals with Licey from 1951 through 1964 were 86-46, 2.11 in 198 games and 1,166 1/3 innings pitched. That ERA is second only to Juan Marichal's 1.87 in league history, but Olivo pitched nearly twice as many innings. The Dominican League named its equivalent of the Cy Young Award for him.

After retiring as a player, Olivo spent seven years scouting for the Cardinals and then one more with the Mets in 1971. He signed at least one major leaguer, Pedro Borbón, Sr.[33] He most likely also signed his nephew, Milcíades "Mike" Olivo, who played pro ball from 1964 through 1975, getting as high as Triple-A for a few years. Mike and Chichí Olivo were both part of the Licey team that won the 1971 Caribbean Series for the Dominican Republic, led by player-manager Manny Mota. Forty years later, Mota and Diómedes Olivo remained Licey's two leading idols.

As of 1977, Olivo was undersecretary of state for sports in the Dominican Republic.[34] In an odd coincidence, he and his brother Chichí died less than two weeks apart. José de Jiménez wrote, "On February 15, 1977, at 57 [sic] years of age, [Diómedes] Olivo looked young and strong. That afternoon he went to play softball and early in the evening, reading some comments about the death of his brother Chi-Chi... Olivo suffered a sudden heart attack, dying a few minutes later.

"His death was a national catastrophe, the whole country was mourning, there was no music anywhere, the sky was cloudy.... The president of the Dominican Republic, Dr. Joaquín Balaguer, sent a telegram of condolence to his widow. To be frank: we all cried."

In the spring of 1960 Julián Javier (then a Pirates farmhand) discussed Olivo's stature in the Dominican Republic. Javier said, "His name means something down there like [Willie] Mays and [Mickey] Mantle mean in the United States. If we had Hall of Fame in Dominican, Olivo would be in it."[35] The Dominican Sporting Hall of Fame was established in 1967, and in 1973 it inducted Guayubín Olivo. Judging by the number of stories that are still written about him, his legend at home has not lost any luster since.

Special thanks to Eddy Olivo Cruz for providing the family tree compiled by his second cousin, Emilio Olivo (nephew of Diómedes Olivo). Continued thanks to Raúl Porto (Colombian information) and to SABR member Tito Rondón.

SOURCES

In addition to the sources cited in the Notes, the author consulted Baseball-Reference.com, Retrosheet.org, http://www.pabellondelafamadeportedom.com, and the following:

Córdova, Cuqui. *Guayubín Olivo: La Montaña Noroestana*. Issue 5 of *Historia del Béisbol Dominicano* (Santo Domingo: Revista Historia del Béisbol, 2006).

De Jiménez, José. "The Great Dominican, Diómedes Olivo." *Baseball Research Journal*, Volume 20. Society for American Baseball Research: 1990: 91-92.

Crescioni Benítez, José A. *El Béisbol Profesional Boricua* (San Juan, Puerto Rico: Aurora Comunicación Integral, Inc., 1997).

Bjarkman, Peter C. *Baseball with a Latin Beat* (Jefferson, North Carolina: McFarland & Co., 1994).

Bjarkman, Peter C. *Diamonds Around the Globe: The Encyclopedia of International Baseball* (Westport, Connecticut: Greenwood Press, 2005).

NOTES

1. "Pirate Profiles," *Evening Standard* (Uniontown, Pennsylvania), April 3, 1962: 20.
2. United Press International, "Buc Rookie's Oral English Sparse, but His Baseball 'English' Is Most Fluent," *Daily Courier* (Connellsville, Pennsylvania), July 7, 1962: 7.
3. Lester J. Biederman, "Olivo, Trucks New York-Bound, Too," *Pittsburgh Press*, October 6, 1960.
4. Associated Press, "Old Buc Rookie Has Been Around," *Evening Sun* (Hanover, Pennsylvania), April 1, 1960: 16.
5. Rafael V. Peña. "Guayubín Olivo." Blog of Asociación de Cronistas Deportivas de Santo Domingo – Filial Nueva York, May 14, 2010. (http://acdny.blogspot.com/2010/05/guayubin-olivo.html)
6. Cuqui Córdova, "La crónica de los martes," *Listín Diario* (Santo Domingo, Dominican Republic), December 9, 2008.
7. Red Smith, "Can Youthful Pirates Grow Up in 1960?", *New York Herald Tribune*, August 7, 1960.
8. Myron Cope, "An Elderly Diómedes In The Big Show," *Sports Illustrated*, July 16, 1962.
9. Córdova.
10. Alexis Salas H. *Los Eternos Rivales: 1908-1988* (Caracas, Venezuela: Seguros Caracas, 1988, 112).
11. "Sulia [sic] State League Opens," *The Sporting News*, April 19, 1950: 18.
12. *The Sporting News*, April 19, 1950: 52. Jack Hand, Associated Press, "Cuban Talent Pays Off For Senators," *Danville* (Virginia) *Bee*, June 22, 1950: 22.
13. Santiago Llorens, "Yankee Rookie Tops Star Poll in Puerto Rico," *The Sporting News*, January 3, 1951: 25.
14. Bienvenido Rojas, "Serie del Caribe: Olivo, primer criollo en lanzar," *Diario Libre* (Santo Domingo, Dominican Republic), January 26, 2007.
15. Bob Broeg, "He Comes on Strong," *Baseball Digest*, July 1963: 32.
16. Rafael Baldayac, "José Offerman revive caso Guayubín Olivo," *La Información* (Santiago, Dominican Republic), January 28, 2010.
17. Robert K. Fitts. *Wally Yonamine* (Lincoln, Nebraska: University of Nebraska Press, 2008), 183.
18. Pedro Galiana, "Cubans Rolling on Warm-Up in Winter Loops," *The Sporting News*, May 4, 1955: 29.
19. "Sportswriters Chat with Olivo via Mejias," *Pittsburgh Post-Gazette*, April 2, 1960: 15.

20 Miguel A. Calzadilla, "Trautman Probes Reports of Raids," *The Sporting News*, May 1, 1957: 36.

21 Miguel A. Calzadilla, "Sultans Renew Cincy Pact," *The Sporting News*, August 21, 1957: 46.

22 Cope.

23 "Ramon Lopez in Whiff Show," *The Sporting News*, June 6, 1964: 35.

24 Harry Keck, "How Old Is Olivo? 'About 42,' He Says," *The Sporting News*, May 23, 1962: 17.

25 Cope, op. cit.

26 Les Biederman, "Olivo, Pirates' 40-Year-Old Rookie, Dominican Hill Ace," *The Sporting News*, March 23, 1960: 15.

27 "Spanish Rolls, Pirate Olivo To See Series," *Pittsburgh Press*, September 6, 1960.

28 "Sam Jones to Lead Pennant Push by Jets, Shepard Says," *The Sporting News*, May 1, 1965: 35.

29 "Political Turmoil Forces Dominican League to Fold," *The Sporting News*, December 13, 1961: 34.

30 Associated Press, "Alou Fined for Winter Activities," *Baltimore Sun*, February 5, 1963: 17.

31 Associated Press, "Olivo Is Victim," *Journal Times* (Racine, Wisconsin), December 19, 1962: 29.

32 Nathaneal Pérez Neró, "El Licey bautiza 'dogout' con el nombre de Guayubín Olivo," *Diario Libre* (Santo Domingo, Dominican Republic), December 12, 2006.

33 Questionnaire received by Rod Nelson of SABR's Scouts Committee. Caveat: in retrospect, Nelson has not been able to confirm the other two names listed on the questionnaire, Larry Dick and Monchín Pichardo, as being Cardinals scouts. However, Pichardo became president and general manager of Licey in 1963-64, and Borbón Sr. spent his entire Dominican career with Licey.

34 "Obituaries," *The Sporting News*, March 5, 1977: 54.

35 Biederman, "Olivo, Pirates' 40-Year-Old Rookie, Dominican Hill Ace."

David Ortiz

By Bill Nowlin

"He's a superhero without a cape. That's the way we see him."

— Alex Cora[1]

Several of the biggest base hits in Boston baseball history came off the bat of "Big Papi," David Ortiz. He sports three world championship rings and then wrapped up his career with one of the best final seasons any player has ever enjoyed. Within months of leaving the game, he was honored by the Red Sox, who retired his jersey number 34. He had already become an instant icon in Red Sox Nation.

Had he done no more than lead the 2004 team to triumph over the Yankees and then the Cardinals, he would still go down in team history for his key role in helping them win their first World Series in 86 years. But he came up big again in 2007 and was overpowering in 2013.

Ortiz hit 541 home runs in the course of his major-league career, and 632 doubles. The only two batters before him to hit 500 homers and 600 doubles were Hank Aaron and Barry Bonds.

And Ortiz was, as a *New York Times* subhead once said, "a maestro in the statistics-defying art of clutch hitting."[2]

The toast of the town in Boston, David Americo Ortiz Arias came from the humblest of backgrounds. He was born in Santo Domingo, Dominican Republic, on November 18, 1975, but from around the age of 14 grew up in the community of Haina, on the southern coast just west of the capital. The city of around 84,000 people has been dubbed the Dominican Chernobyl and is considered to be one of the most polluted cities in the world. "According to the United Nations, the population of Haina is considered to have the highest level of lead contamination in the world, and its entire population carries indications of lead poisoning."[3] The problem almost certainly emanated from the Baterías Meteoro battery plant, a now-closed automobile battery recycling smelter. David Ortiz himself said, "Piles of batteries, some as high as three-story buildings, could be found in the city. That alone put our lives in danger. ... [B]attery acid and lead would seep into the soil."[4]

As if that weren't enough, the city was plagued with "Shootings. Stabbings. Drugs. Gangs. ...We were poor and our neighborhood was teeming with violence and crime." One day on his way to the bodega, young David saw a man murdered right in front of him.[5] Had it not been for the values instilled in him by his parents, Enrique and Angela, he might have grown up to a different life entirely – or lost his own life at an early age. Enrique worked at automotive repair, "from parts to repairs to sales," though he rarely had more than a moped himself. Angela originally worked as a secretary for the Department of Agriculture in Santo Domingo, but she "was always taking on jobs to pick up extra money. She would sometimes travel to other parts of the Caribbean, as far away as Curaçao and St. Thomas, to buy clothes and sell them to tourists at local hotels."[6] They worked hard, sacrificing to help provide for David and his younger sister, Albania.

David had talent at sports, basketball as well as baseball, with his father pushing hard for him to pursue baseball. David spent a lot of time at the Florida Marlins facility but elbow inflammation cropped up and they let it be known he wasn't being seen as a prospect. A *buscón*[7] named Hector "Machepa" Alvarez took David under his wing and a week and a half after David turned 17, he signed with the Seattle Mariners for $7,500 to $10,000.[8] He was sent to play rookie ball in Peoria, Arizona, in the summer of 1994. His salary was $59 per week.[9] He was far from home, in an alien environment, and he struggled. Had it not been for his sense of obligation to his parents and a competitive fire within himself, he might not have persevered. That first summer he played in 53 games and batted .246. In the summer of 1995, however, he bumped his average up to .332.

Ortiz was left-handed and grew to stand 6-feet-3 to 6-feet-4, listed at 230 pounds.

In his third year, Ortiz was assigned to the Class-A (Midwest League) Wisconsin Timber Rattlers in Appleton, Wisconsin. There he had five roommates, all Dominican, living in a two-bedroom home. (Until he made the majors, David always played professionally as David Arias, not David Ortiz.) That summer of 1996 saw him begin to hit for power as well as average, with 18 homers and 93 RBIs (both leading the team by a considerable margin), and a .322 batting average. Primarily a first baseman, he was now making $400 a week. He was voted the best defensive first baseman in the league.[10]

He also met a young woman from Kaukauna, Wisconsin, named Tiffany Brick. She was a photography student in Madison, and a fast-pitch softball player who had been voted "Most Athletic Girl" in her high school. They hit it off immediately and within two weeks, he says, the word "marriage" first came up.[11]

The Timber Rattlers made the 1996 league playoffs, but lost out in the final round.

On September 13 that year, Ortiz became the player to be named later in a trade with the Minnesota Twins, completing a deal made on August 29, when the Mariners acquired Dave Hollins in what may well have been a cost-cutting move for the Twins.

Ortiz played for four teams in 1997. First he was sent to Fort Myers to play in the Twins Class-A Florida State League team there. He hit .331 in 61 games, earning him a promotion to Double-A ball (with the Eastern League's New Britain Rock Cats in New Britain, Connecticut). There he hit 14 homers (.322 BA) in 69 games. He was promoted to Salt Lake City of the Triple-A Pacific Coast League and appeared in 10 games there, then became a September call-up to the Twins.

Ortiz's first two major-league at-bats came as a pinch-hitter during interleague play at Chicago's Wrigley Field. On September 2 he hit a fly ball out to deep left-center field. On September 3 he doubled to deep right-center for his first major-league base hit. He was 2-for-5 with his first run batted in on September 8 and, by season's end, had made a bit of a mark with just one home run, but with 16 hits in 49 at-bats (.327).

As a youngster, the first player who had made an impression on him, watching the 1991 World Series on a simple TV in the Dominican Republic, was Kirby Puckett. As soon as he was able, Ortiz took the number 34 in tribute to Puckett. But the Twins were no longer the team that had inspired him back in 1991. Not since 1992 had they won as many as half their games; they played in the uninspiring Metrodome, and they were near the bottom of the league in terms of attendance. Ortiz also had a difficult relationship with manager Tom Kelly.[12]

Through the first games of the 1998 season, Ortiz was hitting over .300 with 20 RBIs, and second on the Twins in slugging, but a broken right wrist saw him unable to play from May 9 to July 9, and hampered his power numbers for the year. (Interestingly, he'd stayed in the game after breaking his wrist, and even homered later in the game.)[13] He hit .360 in 18 September games, finishing with a .277 batting average. For the year, he drove in 46 runs despite missing two months; no one else on the Twins drove in more than 77.

In 1999, although the Twins were clearly in need of a big bat, Ortiz was one of the first players cut in spring training and he spent most of the year back in Salt Lake City. He put up some big numbers there, batting .315 with 30 homers and 110 RBIs. When called up in September, however, he was playing with a torn ACL and proved a very disappointing 0-for-20 at the plate, with 12 strikeouts.

There followed something of a journeyman season in the year 2000. Ortiz appeared in 130 big-league games, mostly as a DH, batting .282, and driving in 63 runs. His RBI total placed him fifth on the Twins; he ranked third in slugging percentage.

In 2001 he appeared in only 89 games, almost all as the DH. Another wrist fracture sidelined him for 2½ months. Though he hit

Photo courtesy of the Boston Red Sox

18 homers in the end (from August 9 through August 12, he homered in four consecutive games), he hit for only a .234 average, driving in 48 runs. He'd started off really hot, with 15 RBIs in his first 16 games, and was hitting .311 at the time of the injury. He clearly never fully recovered that season. He had shown plate discipline; in both the 2000 and 2001 seasons, he drew enough walks to add another 82 points to his on-base percentage. The Twins payroll in 2001 was the lowest in the majors when the season began.[14]

On New Year's Day 2002, tragedy struck; Ortiz's mother, Angela Rosa Arias, was killed in an automobile accident. Those who have watched David Ortiz hit home runs over the years will recall that, ever after, when he crossed the plate he would point heavenward to share the moment with his beloved mother.

The year 2002 was Ortiz's first exclusively in the major leagues, and he appeared in 125 games. (A mid-April surgery to remove bone chips in his knee cost him almost a month on the DL.) Ortiz hit .272, with 20 homers and 75 RBIs, totals that would have both been higher had he not missed so many games. Even then, he ranked third on the Twins in the latter two statistics. He appeared in 15 games at first base, but was typically the DH. The Twins made the postseason and Ortiz's ninth-inning double drove in the game-winner in the final Division Series game against the Athletics. The Twins lost the ALCS in five games to Anaheim; Ortiz hit .313 but drove in only a pair of runs.

Still skimping on payroll, the Twins weren't prepared to pony up the money needed to sign Ortiz to a new contract and they didn't want to go to arbitration with him, which might have forced them to pay him double the $900,000 or $950,000 he was being paid.[15] They tried to trade him, but every team in baseball passed, and so they simply released him on December 16, 2002.[16] Hard as it may be to believe today, the man who soon became perhaps the best DH in history and one of the most fearsome clutch hitters in postseason play was simply released. He was a man without a team. Notably, though, Tiffany Ortiz's response was, "Good. Now we can apply for a job in Boston."[17]

And Red Sox pitching ace Pedro Martínez (who was dining in the same restaurant in Santo Domingo the evening Ortiz got the word that he had been released) got to work, peppering the Red Sox front office with phone calls and telling them they simply had to sign David Ortiz. They did, with new Boston GM Theo Epstein offering a one-year deal for $1.25 million. It wasn't a big commitment at the time, and the pursuit of Ortiz barely made the Boston papers. The team had Shea Hillenbrand, and was engaged in negotiations to sign Kevin Millar and Jeremy Giambi.

But Ortiz put on something of a show in Dominican Winter League ball, batting .351 with 23 RBIs in 20 games.[18] The Dominican team won the Caribbean Series, and Ortiz was named MVP.[19]

The signing itself was famously dubbed an example of the Red Sox "shopping at Wal-Mart."[20]

Indeed, Epstein had proven a thrifty shopper, spending $5.3 million and landing David Ortiz, Kevin Millar, and Bill Mueller.[21] Millar fired up the ballclub with his "Cowboy Up!" movement in 2003 and his "Don't Let Us Win Tonight!" mantra in 2004. Mueller hit .326, good enough to win the American League batting title in 2003. And Ortiz, well, within three years he was being compared to Babe Ruth and described as "one of the all-time baseball bargains."[22]

Ortiz was expected to contend for the first-base slot. Epstein sent scout Dave Jauss to look him over and said, "He showed good hands and feet around the bag. Jauss gave a really good report. We're comfortable with him defensively, and more than comfortable with him offensively."[23]

It wasn't that Epstein needed Pedro Martínez and Manny Ramírez to speak up for Ortiz; he had already been tracking him back when Epstein was working for the Padres.[24]

Ortiz was given the locker next to Manny Ramírez. In both his autobiographies, Ortiz talked about the wholly different approach to the game (and the different atmosphere) he felt he encountered in the Red Sox organization and clubhouse. "I felt like I just got out of jail, bro," he wrote. I felt like I could hit the way I wanted to hit."[25]

Ortiz got off to a slow start with the 2003 Red Sox, hitting only one homer in April and batting just .200 as of May 1. He homered only once in May, but brought his batting average up to .272. Ortiz was still being passed over for others, until Pedro Martínez took the unusual step of telling Red Sox manager Grady Little that he wanted Ortiz in the lineup whenever he was pitching. Hillenbrand had been traded, and Giambi suffered numerous injuries and, ultimately, shoulder surgery. The job fell to Ortiz by default.

It was during this first season with the Red Sox that Ortiz acquired the nickname "Big Papi," bestowed on him by Red Sox broadcaster Jerry Remy.[26]

He homered only twice in June. But he added eight in July as he started to get on a roll. He hit two home runs in a July 4 game at Yankee Stadium and then two more in the next day's game as well, the first visiting player to ever do so.[27]

His first game-winning hit for the Red Sox was a pinch-hit single in the bottom of the ninth on July 26 against the Yankees. That one at-bat was described at length and in context by Jackie MacMullan of the *Boston Globe*.[28] From July 27 through August 7, 12 consecutive base hits were all extra-base hits (five doubles, two triples, and five homers). There were several games in which he seemed to make all the difference, such as a 5-4 win in 10 innings in Chicago, when Ortiz drove in four of the runs, including the game-winner.

By the end of the season, one which saw the Sox reach the playoffs, Ortiz had 31 homers and 101 RBIs. His .592 slugging percentage was tops on the team. He ranked fifth in league MVP voting.

Boston dropped the first two games of the 2003 ALDS to Oakland, but then took the next two. Ortiz hadn't had a base hit until the bottom of the eighth in Game Four, but he doubled and drove in two runs, winning the game for the Red Sox, 5-4, and sending the Series to Game Five, where the Red Sox prevailed. In the American League Championship Series against the archrival Yankees, Ortiz hit a two-run homer to kick off Game One. The next runs he drove in were in Game Six, his two-run single in the third making the score 4-1, his three RBIs in the game proving the margin in Boston's 9-6 win.

Ortiz's solo homer in the top of the eighth in Game Seven extended the Red Sox lead to 5-2 and it looked like a trip to the World Series was in the cards ... until Grady Little asked Pedro Martínez, to return to the mound and pitch another inning – only to see Pedro cough up three runs, see the game become tied, and watch the Red Sox lose it in the 11th. Any trip to the World Series would have to wait until 2004.

Ortiz said the 2003-04 offseason was full of sleepless nights for him. "The Game 7 loss to the Yankees had torn me up, knowing that we were just five outs away from going to the World Series. Anytime I got close to contentment, I'd feel the sting of that loss."[29]

He worked hard and came back better than ever. In 2004, now secure as a starter (34 games at first base, 115 as DH), he put up bigger numbers than ever: 41 homers (second in the league only to teammate Manny Ramírez's 43), 139 RBIs, a .301 batting average. Ortiz and Ramírez were a potent combination in Boston's batting order. Six times that season, they went back-to-back; on August 22 in the eighth inning of a game at Comiskey Park, they homered on consecutive pitches –first Manny off Freddy Garcia, and then Ortiz off reliever Dámaso Marte. Two teammates both hitting 40 homers, driving in 100 runs, and hitting for at least a .300 average had been done only eight other times since Babe Ruth and Lou Gehrig did it in 1931.

Ortiz was rewarded by being named to the American League All-Star squad for the first of 10 times. He homered in the All-Star Game. In May he had been signed to a new two-year contract with a team option for 2006.

The Red Sox finished second to the Yankees in the AL East. As the wild-card team, they took the first two games from Anaheim in the ALDS. In the bottom of the 10th in Game Three, after the Angels had overcome a 6-1 deficit to tie the game, Ortiz came up with two outs and homered to the opposite field off Jarrod Washburn to advance the Sox to the ALCS – where they faced the Yankees again. In the ALDS, Ortiz was 6-for-11 with four RBIs and five walks.

He drove in two runs in Game One against the Yankees, but the Red Sox lost the first three games, Game Three an embarrassing 19-8 beatdown in Boston. The story of Game Four and all that followed has been told at great length elsewhere.[30] The game went into the bottom of the ninth with the Yankees leading, 4-3. Two of the three Red Sox runs had been knocked in by Ortiz in the fifth. With Mariano Rivera on the mound, Kevin Millar walked, pinch-runner Dave Roberts stole second, and Bill Mueller drove Roberts in to tie the game. With the bases loaded, Ortiz popped up to second and the game went into extra innings. But Rivera wasn't going to be around if Ortiz got up again and, he said, "I liked my percentages against anyone who wasn't him."[31]

In the bottom of the 12th inning, with the score still tied, Ortiz got another opportunity. Paul Quantrill was pitching and Manny Ramírez singled to left field. Ortiz, as a DH not needing to play the field, studied Quantrill on video, and he was ready. He homered into the right-field stands, winning the game 6-4 and sparing the Red Sox the ignominy of being swept. And "David Ortiz became the only player in baseball history to hit two walk-off home runs in the same postseason" while the Red Sox became the first team since the 1910 Chicago Cubs to be the only team down three games to none and win Game Four in extra innings.[32]

No team had ever come back after losing the first three and won it all, but simply the reprieve of taking Game Four offered some salve to Red Sox fans.

Next up was Game Five. The fourth game had ended after midnight, in the early hours of October 18. The fourth game started that evening. Ortiz drove in the first run of the game, in the first inning. The Yankees took a 4-2 lead into the eighth, and Ortiz homered to make it 4-3, then watched a Jason Varitek sacrifice fly off Rivera tie the game. Ortiz led off the bottom of the 10th and struck out. Facing reliever Esteban Loaiza in the 12th, he walked but was caught stealing.[33] The game went into the 14th inning, Loaiza still on the mound. He alternated strikeout, walk, strikeout, walk, then faced Ortiz again. It was a 10-pitch at-bat. On that final pitch, Ortiz singled to center, driving in Johnny Damon, and for the second time on the same calendar date, he'd given the Red Sox a sudden-death, extra-inning walk-off win.

Suddenly this was a different Series entirely. Both teams went back to Yankee Stadium for Game Six. With four runs in the fourth, three on Mark Bellhorn's three-run homer, the Red Sox took that one, setting up another Game Seven.

One could well say the Red Sox were giddy with success with the Yankees uptight and maybe panicked. Ortiz hit a two-run homer in the top of the first. Damon drove in six runs. The Red Sox won it easily, 10-3. Ortiz had driven in 11 runs in the ALCS and was named MVP. In back-to-back ALCS against New York in 2003 and 2004, he had homered five times and driven in 17 runs.

After winning four in a row to overtake the Yankees, the Red Sox won the next four games, too, sweeping the St. Louis Cardinals in the 2004 World Series. For the first time in 86 years, the Red Sox were world champions.

Ortiz had driven in four runs, all in Game One, the first three coming on a three-run homer in the first inning.

And everyone knew he had come through in the clutch when the Red Sox were in the depths.

In the summer of 2005, Mariano Rivera stated what had become evident. Ortiz had developed as a hitter. "He used to have holes on the inside. You'd go outside. Holes? Now they're not there anymore."[34] Ortiz's work with video became legendary, it being written, "David Ortiz of the Red Sox does not look like a computer nerd, but he is. Ortiz is a slave to the laptop, hunkering over it several times a day, especially during games, to analyze at-bats. He wants to see how pitchers approached him, how he reacted and whether they had a counter-response."[35]

With Ortiz as a designated hitter, the Red Sox were always faced with a choice when playing in a National League ballpark, for interleague play or in the World Series: Do they play him at first base and thus keep him in the lineup, or do they opt for a perhaps improved defense by using their regular first baseman, whoever he may be at the time? The decision was easier because Ortiz was a very good fielder, with decent range. Over the course of his 20 seasons in the big leagues, he handled 2,169 chances with only 22 errors – a .990 fielding percentage. He also recorded 164 assists, a particular one a highlight indicating good situational awareness. It came in Game Three of the 2004 World Series, the first game in St. Louis. It was only the second game Ortiz had started at first base since July 22, and it had rained earlier in the day so he had been unable to take infield practice. But when the moment came, he was ready. In the bottom of the third inning, with the score 1-0 in Boston's favor, Cardinals starting pitcher Jeff Suppan led off and singled. After Edgar Renteria doubled to right field, the Cardinals had runners on second and third with nobody out. Larry Walker grounded to second base, and Mark Bellhorn threw to first base to get Walker. Ortiz recorded the out, but alertly had his eye on Suppan, who had indecisively headed toward home but then decided to retreat to third, only to be caught when Ortiz took a couple of steps toward third and fired the ball across the infield for a double play. The Cardinals failed to score in the inning.

Although the team enjoyed no postseason success in 2005, David Ortiz had a very good regular season. He led the majors in runs batted in, with 148. He upped his home run total to 47 but again finished second. He hit an even .300 and walked 102 times, just barely edging his OPS over a magic mark – to 1.001. His best single day was probably an August 12 game against the White Sox; he was 4-for-5 with two homers and drove in six runs. The Red Sox won, 9-8. After a game on September 6, when a solo Ortiz home run beat the Angels in the bottom of the ninth, 3-2, Red Sox ownership presented him with a plaque they had prepared and held for the right moment, proclaiming him the "Greatest Clutch Hitter in the History of the Boston Red Sox."[36] They couldn't have known how much history was yet to be written.

The Red Sox did make the postseason, but it was the White Sox' turn to break an even lengthier curse than the Red Sox had suffered. They swept Boston in three games in the Division Series; Ortiz hit .333 with one homer. The White Sox beat Houston and won their first World Series since 1917.

Early in 2006, Ortiz played for the Dominican Republic team in the World Baseball Classic. He hit three home runs (and walked once with the bases loaded) but Japan won the tournament and four players either matched or exceeded Ortiz's three homers.[37] In April he agreed to a four-year extension of his contract with the Red Sox, for an amount thought to be $52 million.[38]

In 2006 Ortiz had 31 home runs before the All-Star break. He set a franchise record with

54 home runs, this time leading the league. (Jimmie Foxx had held the Red Sox record, with 50 homers in 1938.) Ortiz's 137 RBIs also led the American League, as did his 355 total bases. It was a year that Boston finished third, however, and out of the postseason.

And speaking of clutch performances, in just the four-year stretch from 2003 through 2006, Ortiz had 15 "walk-offs" – two in 2003, five in 2004, three in 2005, and five in 2006.

The Red Sox had finished in second place eight years in a row, 1998 through 2005, and then third in 2006. In 2007 they were in first place from April 18 on and never once relinquished the spot.

The team won another world championship in 2007, again by a sweep (this time over the Colorado Rockies). Ortiz hit a career-high .332 batting average, and his .445 on-base percentage led the league. He homered 35 times and drove in 117 runs. His 1.066 OPS was the highest of his career; this was the third year in a row he topped 1.000.

After homering and driving in two runs to help beat the Angels 4-0 in Game One of the Division Series, the Angels walked him four times in Game Two. He homered again in Game Three, and Boston swept that series with Ortiz batting .714. It took the full seven games to beat Cleveland in the ALCS. Ortiz contributed three RBIs and seven runs scored; he hit .292. In the World Series, he drove in four runs and scored four. He was 5-for-15 with three doubles.

An amusing story surfaced in April 2008. It turns out that Gino Castignoli, a member of the construction crew building the new Yankee Stadium, had buried a Red Sox jersey bearing Ortiz's number 34 in concrete. When the story emerged, the team ordered jackhammers to work to remove the offending jersey.[39] (The jersey was later placed on auction on eBay to raise money for the Jimmy Fund, and fetched $175,110.)[40]

The next two times the Red Sox reached the postseason, Ortiz was unable to match his high standards of production. In 2008 he had a difficult year; playing in only 109 games, he hit .264 with 23 homers and 89 RBIs. He became an American citizen in June, but a serious left wrist injury on Memorial Day weekend made an already difficult season (due to a slow start) even more so. The team beat the Angels in four Division Series games with just one RBI from Ortiz, an insurance run on a single in Game One. They were down one game to three to Tampa Bay in the Championship Series with Ortiz even driving in one run, and with manager Joe Maddon employing a fairly dramatic defensive shift when Ortiz came to bat. Game Five was at Fenway Park, and when the Red Sox came up to bat in the bottom of the seventh, they were losing 7-0 and on the brink of elimination. After Dustin Pedroia drove in one run, Ortiz hit a three-run homer and put them back in the game. They scored three more runs in the eighth to tie it, and J.D. Drew won the game with a two-out RBI single in the bottom of the ninth. Ortiz knocked in the fourth run of a 4-2 win in Game Six, but the Rays prevailed in Game Seven. Ortiz had hit just .154 in the ALCS.

Shifting against Ortiz was often effective, though he had a significant number of opposite-field hits and was even known to lay down a successful bunt toward third base on occasion.

In the midst of the 2009 season, a story in the *New York Times* reported that both Ortiz and Manny Ramírez had turned up in 2003 on a list of players who had tested positive for steroids. That year was the first year of testing for steroids, and all tests were meant to be anonymous.[41] Ortiz vehemently denied ever knowingly taking any substances that might have resulted in a positive test, and said he believed that all players should be tested. If anyone was found guilty, he suggested a

Peñalty greater than any ever employed: "Ban them for the whole year."[42]

Ortiz has reportedly never been informed as to the substance for which he reportedly tested positive, and thus remains in the dark. Given that it was the first year of testing, the tests may also have been faulty. The same article said that Barry Bonds had not tested positive, but a later retest did show the presence of steroids. Years later, Commissioner Rob Manfred announced on October 2, 2016, that there were "legitimate scientific questions about whether or not those were truly positives," acknowledging that the tests were flawed, and that it was "entirely possible" that, in reality, Ortiz had not truly tested positive.[43] In the 13 seasons after 2003, and the 7½ seasons after the *Times* article, Ortiz was tested numerous times and no positive test ever occurred.

The Angels swept the Division Series in 2009. Ortiz was 1-for-12 (.083) with a single. During the regular season, he'd suffered a very slow start and at one point did not homer for 149 at-bats. He came to feel he might have been over-thinking his approach to batting and decided to "act like I was in Little League" – just to play to have fun, and unclutter his mind.[44] In the end, he hit for a .238 average but he had found his stroke and done damage: he drove in 99 runs. He homered 28 times.

The Red Sox didn't see the postseason again until 2013.

Ortiz's batting average picked up in 2010 and 2011 (.270 and .309). He'd had a very slow start in 2010 (.143 at the end of April, with one homer, and not passing .200 until May 14) and some became alarmed, thinking age had caught up with him. By the end of the season, though, he had 32 homers and had driven in 102 runs – numbers most players would give anything to attain. The team finished in third place.

In 2011 the Sox finished third again. Ortiz hit steadily throughout the season, falling four RBIs short of the 100 mark, homering 29 times.

In 2012, signed to just a one-year deal, he had a very strong first half, but a severely strained right Achilles tendon saw him only appear in one game after July 16. He played in only 90 games, though he drove in 60 runs, homered 23 more times, and hit .318. Under manager Bobby Valentine, the Red Sox finished in last place. Though not something we want to dwell on here, Ortiz absolutely shredded Valentine in his book *Papi: My Story*.

The year 2013 was a magical year, though it started with the horrible tragedy of the Boston Marathon bombing. It was April 15 – Patriots Day – and the Red Sox, per local tradition, started the game at 11:05 A.M., timed to end around the time the first runners of the Boston Marathon crossed the finish line, just two subway stops from Fenway Park. Ortiz was not in the game, but he was at the ballpark. He was still rehabbing from the Achilles problem, and didn't play his first game until April 20. The Patriots Day game ended at 2:08, and the team dressed to head for the charter going to Cleveland for the next day's game. At 2:40, two bombs exploded 12 seconds apart and three young people were killed, including 8-year-old Martin Richard. Dozens were injured and the city was under a "shelter in place" situation later in the week after the bombers killed an M.I.T. police officer and drove off without being caught. Ortiz was in Greater Boston all the time, and lived through what area residents experienced.

The team seemed to draw on the sense of togetherness, embodied in the "Boston Strong" movement, and in a powerful speech before the next Fenway game, an unfiltered Ortiz said, "This is our fucking city. And nobody is going to dictate our freedom. Stay strong."

Ortiz opened his season with a 2-for-4 game, kicking off a 15-game hitting streak. After the first nine games, at the end of April,

Former Boston Red Sox pitcher Pedro Martinez (right) and former Boston Red Sox left fielder Manny Ramirez pose for a selfie photograph with the 2004 World Series trophy, along with David Ortiz of the Boston Red Sox during Ortiz's honorary retirement ceremony in his final regular season game at Fenway Park against the Toronto Blue Jays on October 2, 2016.

Photo by Billie Weiss / Courtesy of the Boston Red Sox

he had 15 RBIs and was batting .500. He rarely missed a game after he got started, appearing in 137 games and batting .309, with 103 RBIs and 30 homers. The Red Sox rocketed from worst to first, from a 69-93 record in 2012 to 97-65. They beat Tampa Bay and then Detroit, and played the St. Louis Cardinals in the World Series. One of the most celebrated home runs of his career came in Game Two of the ALCS. The Tigers had won the first game, 1-0, and were leading 5-1 heading into the bottom of the eighth inning in Game Two.

Three and a half months earlier, on June 23, Joaquin Benoit had struck out Ortiz in the ninth inning of a game in Detroit. Ortiz filed the pitch away in his mind and was waiting for another chance to attack it. With Boston baserunners loading the bases, manager Jim Leyland called on Benoit to pitch to Ortiz. Big Papi was waiting.[45] Swinging at Benoit's first pitch, Ortiz hit a grand slam into the Red Sox bullpen to tie it. The Sox won it in the ninth. Clutch? No fan would say otherwise.[46]

There was no certainty the Red Sox would win the World Series. The Cardinals were up two games to one, and the score was 1-1 at the midpoint of Game Four. "We were playing like zombies," Ortiz said later. "Quiet, no emotion, a little stiff."[47] So he called a quick meeting right then and there in the dugout and basically gave them a pep talk, telling them how rare it was to get to the World Series, that they were better than St. Louis, and it was time to get going. A Jonny Gomes three-run homer in the top of the sixth followed, and the team never looked back.

Ortiz hit a spectacular .688 in the World Series (11-for-16), with eight bases on balls giving him a .760 on-base percentage. It was the highest batting average in World Series history. He drove in six runs and scored seven (two on his own home runs). The Red Sox won it in six games, and Ortiz collected his third world championship ring in 10 years (2004, 2007, and 2013). He was named Series MVP.

And after the Series, owner John W. Henry called on Ortiz, offering him a contract that in effect offered him a player option for as long as he wanted – a contract for the life of his playing career.[48]

In each of his next three seasons – his last three as a ballplayer – Ortiz drove in more than 100 runs, each season knocking in more runs than the season before. In 2014 he had 35 homers and drove in 104 runs. In 2015 he had 37 homers and drove in 108 runs. And in his final season – 2016, having announced his retirement before the season began – he had perhaps the best year any player has ever had in his final season. Playing in 151 games, he hit for a .315 batting average, led the major leagues with 48 home runs, led the American League with 127 RBIs (tied with Edwin Encarnacion), and led all of baseball in slugging (.620) and OPS (1.021).

It would have been nice to say Ortiz went out with another ring, but the Cleveland Indians swept the Red Sox in the ALDS. Ortiz was 1-for-9, the one hit a double. After the season, Ortiz was recognized for the second time with baseball's Hank Aaron Award (the first time had been in 2005). He won his seventh Silver Slugger Award.

Retirement awaited, though Ortiz was often seen around Boston during 2017. David and Tiffany Ortiz continued to maintain their principal residence in Massachusetts, with their three children, Jessica, Alexandra, and D'Angelo. There had been a time early in 2013 when the couple had separated, but in time they reconciled. Tiffany later told him, "As clutch as you were on the field, you did that and more to win me back and put our family back together again."[49]

For David, his number 34 was retired during the summer. He had a street named after him, as was the bridge that spans the Mass Pike as people leave Kenmore Square to go to Fenway Park. And he became Dr. David Ortiz when Boston University bestowed an honorary degree on him in May 2017.

Ortiz was active in charitable endeavors, and also saw his second autobiography published. Following a very moving visit to a Dominican hospital in February 2005 where he encountered children recovering from heart surgery, he established the David Ortiz Children's Fund in 2007 and partnered with Massachusetts General Hospital and CEDIMAT, the first Diagnostics and Advanced Medicine center in the Dominican Republic. The Fund sponsors an annual golf tournament in La Romana, DR, and has raised more than $2 million. It reckons to have "saved over 500 lives in the Dominican Republic" and helped others in New England.[50]

For his career as a whole, Ortiz hit better against right-handed pitchers, batting .294 for his career against them as opposed to .268 against lefties. He faced more right-handers, of course, but hit 421 homers off them as opposed to 120 off left-handers. Against Blue Jays pitching, he homered 62 times; against the Orioles, 55 times, and against both the Rays and the Yankees, 53. As the season progressed, he seemed to hit more home runs. In May: 79. In June, he hit 86. In July: 95. In August: 105. And in September/Octobe r, he hit 102. More of his home runs were hit on the road (300) than at home (241). Conversely, he drove in more runs at home (953) than away (815).

On September 13, 2017, the Red Sox announced a mutual long-term commitment between the ballclub and Ortiz: "In his new role, Ortiz will act as a mentor for current players, participate in recruitment efforts, make a variety of special appearances for the club, and work in a business development capacity for Fenway Sports Management and its partners."[51]

David Ortiz was shot in the back on June 9, 2019, while seated outdoors at the Dial Bar and Lounge in Santo Domingo. Within the first 10 days after the shooting, 11 suspects were arrested with several more still at large, but on June 19, prosecutors announced that Ortiz had not been the intended target of a contract killing, but that the gunman had been after another man who was seated near Ortiz. Many Dominicans were skeptical.[52] In the meantime, reportedly suffering injuries to both intestines, his gall bladder, and liver, he had been brought to Boston for medical treatment, where he underwent multiple surgeries over a period of more than a month at Massachusetts General Hospital. He was released from the hospital on July 26.

On September 9, before the Monday evening game against the Yankees, David Ortiz bounded up the steps of the Red Sox dugout and out onto the field to throw out the game's ceremonial first pitch. He spoke a few words, thanking the fans in Boston for their support and thanking a couple of the Yankees for making the time to come visit him. He had his big smile, was full of energy, and sat in seats next to the dugout for most of the game – at one point giving the jersey he had worn to a youngster seated several rows behind him. Big Papi was back.[53]

A POSTSCRIPT ON WALK-OFFS

Following up on walk-offs, the number any player can have is limited by the fact that you can have only one in a home game. David Ortiz had 20 in regular-season play. Two players had more – Frank Robinson (26) and Dusty Baker (21). No player in history had ever had more than two walk-offs in the postseason – but David Ortiz hit three of them in 2004.

DAVID ORTIZ WALK-OFF HITS

For the Twins:

April 4, 2000 – tie-breaking single in the ninth

July 31, 2002 – single in 10th

September 25, 2002 – home run in the 12th

For the Red Sox:

July 26, 2003 – single off the Wall in the ninth, against the Yankees

September 23, 2003 – HR in the 10th

April 11, 2004 – HR in the 12th

June 11, 2004 – single in the ninth

October 8, 2004 – HR in bottom of the 10th to clinch a win in the ALCS against the Angels

October 17, 2004 – home run in the 12th to win Game Four of the ALCS against the Yankees

October 18, 2004 – single in the 14th to win Game Five of the ALCS against the Yankees

June 2, 2005 – Three-run HR in the ninth to come from behind and beat the O's

September 6, 2005 – HR in the ninth

September 29, 2005 – single in the ninth

June 11, 2006 – Three-run HR in the ninth to overcome a 4-2 deficit

June 24, 2006 – two-run homer in the 10th

June 26, 2006 – single in the 12th

July 29, 2006 – single in the ninth

July 31, 2006 – three-run homer in ninth to overcome two-run deficit

September 12, 2007 – two-run homer in the ninth to overcome one-run deficit

August 26, 2009 – tie-breaking solo homer in the ninth

July 31, 2010 – three-run double in the ninth to overcome two-run deficit

June 6, 2013 – three-run tie-breaking homer in ninth

May 14, 2016 – double in the 11th

SOURCES

In addition to the sources noted in this biography, the author also accessed the *Encyclopedia of Minor League Baseball*, Retrosheet.org, and Baseball-Reference.com.

NOTES

1. Peter Abraham, "Ortiz Was All That Mattered at Fenway," *Boston Globe*, June 10, 2019: C4.
2. Jack Curry, "An Island of Calm in a Sea of Doubt: Ortiz's Clutch Hitting Keeps Red Sox Moored Despite Struggles," *New York Times*, September 17, 2005: D1.
3. worstpolluted.org/projects_reports/display/50.
4. David Ortiz, with Michael Holley, *Papi: My Story* (Boston: Houghton Mifflin Harcourt, 2017), 2.
5. *Papi: My Story*, 2-3.
6. *Papi: My Story*, 9, 125. David's father's name was Americo Enrique Ortiz and he had wanted to be a ballplayer himself. That aspiration was one of the reasons he worked closely with David, and encouraged him every step of the way. See David Ortiz, with Tony Massarotti, *Big Papi: My Story of Big Dreams and Big Hits* (New York: St. Martin's, 2007), 20-23.
7. A buscón in the Dominican Republic is a free-lance scout and agent. The word is Spanish for searcher.
8. In *Big Papi*, he said it was $7,500. In *Papi: My Story*, he said it was $10,000.
9. *Papi: My Story*, 13.
10. David Ortiz, with Tony Massarotti, *Big Papi*, 69.
11. *Papi: My Story*, 18.
12. In both of his autobiographies, Ortiz expresses his dissatisfaction with Kelly.
13. Gordon Edes, "Sox Officially Bring in Ortiz," *Boston Globe*, January 23, 2003: E3. Also see *Big Papi*, 95-96.
14. Murray Chass, "Surprising Twins Give Foes a Run for Their Money," *New York Times*, April 24, 2001: D1.
15. Bob Hohler, "Epstein Negotiating for Millar," *Boston Globe*, January 18, 2003: F3.
16. See, in particular, *Big Papi*, 191-192. The Associated Press said Ortiz was "released … before the draft to make room for shortstop José Morban." See, for instance, AP, "Anderson Released by Pirates," *Augusta* (Georgia) *Chronicle*, December 17, 2002: C4.
17. *Papi: My Story*, 38. David and Tiffany had sealed their longstanding relationship with marriage on November 16.
18. Bob Hohler, "Epstein Negotiating for Millar."
19. Joe Burris, "Opportunity Knocks for Sox' Ortiz," *Boston Globe*, June 12, 2003: C8.
20. Gordon Edes, "Sox Officially Bring in Ortiz."
21. Tyler Kepner, "Red Sox Trying to Picture the Parade," *New York Times*, February 8, 2004: SP1.
22. Harvey Araton, "New Babe in Boston Has Torre Looking for the Right Move," *New York Times*, October 1, 2005: D1.
23. Araton.
24. Gordon Edes, "Smashing Success," *Boston Globe*, September 12, 2003: E1.
25. *Big Papi*, 128.
26. Ricky Doyle, "Where Did David Ortiz's 'Big Papi' Nickname With Red Sox Come From?' NESN.com, October 3, 2016. See nesn.com/2016/10/where-did-david-ortizs-big-papi-nickname-with-red-sox-come-from/.
27. The last Yankee to do so was Roger Maris in 1961, hitting two homers in each game of the July 25, 1961 doubleheader. Gloria Rodriguez, "After a Boom, the Red Sox Go Bust," *New York Times*, July 7, 2003: D3.
28. Jackie MacMullan, "Ortiz's Bat Does Talking in the Ninth," *Boston Globe*, July 27, 2003: D1.
29. *Papi: My Story*, 62.
30. The author's admittedly biased preference is the oral history of the season as told by 59 players, coaches, support staff, and others in Allan Wood & Bill Nowlin, *Don't Let Us Win Tonight: An Oral History of the 2004 Boston Red Sox's Impossible Playoff Run* (Chicago: Triumph Books, 2014).
31. *Papi: My Story*, 80.
32. *Don't Let Us Win Tonight*, 137.

33. Ortiz did steal 17 bases in his regular-season career. He was caught nine times.
34. Jack Curry, "Big Guy, Big Numbers, Big Smile," *New York Times*, July 14, 2005: D1.
35. One of the better articles on Ortiz's work with video is Jack Curry, "A Scientific Hitter in the Computer Age," *New York Times*, October 12, 2007: D1.
36. Chris Snow, "A Blast, Like the Past," *Boston Globe*, September 7, 2005: F1.
37. Seung-Yeop Lee, KOR – 5; Adrian Beltre, DOM – 4; Derrek Lee, USA – 3; Hitoshi Tamura, JPN – 3; and David Ortiz, DOM – 3.
38. Associated Press, "Ortiz Agrees to Four-Year Extension," *Register-Star* (Rockford, Illinois), April 11, 2006: 27.
39. Karen Matthews, Associated Press, "Sox Shirt Found in Yanks' New Stadium," *Daily Northwestern* (Evanston, Illinois), April 14, 2008: 15.
40. Joshua Robinson, "Ortiz Jersey Cemented at the New Yankee Stadium Brings $175,110," *New York Times*, April 5, 2008: D3.
41. Michael S. Schmidt, "Stars of Red Sox Title Years Are Linked to Doping," *New York Times*, July 30, 2009: A1.
42. Schmidt.
43. Alex Speier, "Commissioner: 'Entirely Possible' Ortiz Did Not Test Positive in 2003," *Boston Globe*, October 2, 2016.
44. Jack Curry, "To Enjoy the Game Again, Ortiz Tries Playing It as if He Were a Boy," *New York Times*, September 26, 2009: D5.
45. See Ortiz's description in *Papi: My Story*, 195, 200.
46. Benjamin Hoffman of the *New York Times*, however, wrote an article entitled "Ortiz's Consistency Comes Across as Clutch." See the newspaper on October 15, 2013: B12. The eighth-inning homer saw Tigers right fielder Torii Hunter make a valiant effort to catch the ball before it landed in Boston's bullpen. He fell into the pen, both legs upraised behind him, forming something of a "V" while City of Boston policeman Steve Horgan, stationed in the bullpen, raised both of his arms in a celebratory "V" – creating an iconic image captured by *Boston Globe* photographer Stan Grossfeld. See, for instance, sports.yahoo.com/blogs/mlb-big-league-stew/boston-cop-fenway-bullpen-celebrates-david-ortiz-grand-132350182--mlb.html.
47. *Papi: My Story*, 204.
48. *Papi: My Story*, 207. Henry told Ortiz it was "a contract that allows you to play as long as you want to."
49. *Papi: My Story*, 205.
50. davidortizchildrensfund.org/.
51. Media release, Boston Red Sox, September 13, 2017. The actual description of his duties was vague in the extreme, so much so that Craig Calcaterra ran a piece headlined, "David Ortiz Will Be Doing … Um, Stuff and Things for the Red Sox." See nbcsports.com/2017/09/13/david-ortiz-will-be-doing-um-stuff-and-things-for-the-red-sox/. Chances were thought to be his work would be in a "player development consultant" role, along the lines of Carl Yastrzemski and Dwight Evans, but with Ortiz perhaps more active.
52. Danny McDonald, David Abel, and Aimee Ortiz, "David Ortiz Was Not Intended Target in Shooting, Officials Say," *Boston Globe*, June 20, 2019: A1. See also David Abel, "Many Are Skeptical of Mistaken-Identity Explanation," *Boston Globe*, June 20, 2019: A8. A detailed summary of the story, informed by a visit to the Dominican Republic, is Danny Gold, "David and the D.R.," *Sports Illustrated*, July 29 - August 5, 2019.
53. In his first comments to an English language publication, he talked about the experience to the *Boston Globe*. See Bob Hohler, "Near Death, Ortiz Pushed Through Despair," *Boston Globe*, September 15, 2019: 1, C9.

ALEJANDRO PEÑA

By Alan Cohen

"In a year that has been so improbable, the impossible has happened!"

— Vin Scully, October 15, 1988[1]

Alejandro Peña appeared in three World Series during his 15-season major-league career, but his first appearance was the kind of thing that you can only dream about. He was called in from the Los Angeles Dodgers bullpen in Game One of the 1988 World Series. His team was trailing the Oakland A's 4-3 at the Dodgers' ballpark. He pitched two scoreless innings, striking out three and allowing one hit, a harmless infield single with two outs in the ninth inning by Stan Javier. Peña was due up fourth in the ninth inning and it was determined that he would be removed for a pinch-hitter. With two outs, A's reliever Dennis Eckersley walked pinch-hitter Mike Davis as Dave Anderson, the apparent pinch-hitter for Peña, looked on from the on-deck circle.[2] But as Davis headed to first base, Kirk Gibson grabbed a bat and Anderson returned to the dugout. "Gibson, half man, half beast, whose arrival as a free agent in February had so dramatically transformed the Dodgers, now limped toward the plate to face Eckersley," an eyewitness wrote.[3] Peña was in the clubhouse when Gibson's iconic two-run pinch-hit homer on a 3-and-2 slider gave the Dodgers the lead in the World Series and Alejandro Peña had his first and only World Series win.

Photo courtesy of the National Baseball Hall of Fame

Alejandro Peña Vasquez was born on June 25, 1959, in the peasant village of Cambioso, Puerto Plata, Dominican Republic. As a boy, he worked with his father, also Alejandro, building dirt ovens near their home. It was hard work, and on Sunday, when they paused from work, young Alejandro would play baseball. One of seven children (five boys and two girls), he played third base as a youngster, and it wasn't until he was 15 that he played in any semblance of an organized league.

The timeline is unclear as to how Peña evolved from a scrawny third baseman to a hard-throwing pitcher, but Antonio Taveras, Alex Taveras, and Ralph Avila were involved in changing the direction of Peña's life. The first time he showed up for a Dodgers tryout on the island, he showed a strong arm and Avila told him that "his only chance, in my opinion, to sign a contract was to become a pitcher."[4] Alex Taveras, a Dodgers infielder who lived in the Dominican Republic, concurred that Peña would not make it as a third baseman.

Five months later, Peña had established himself as a pitcher and was playing semipro ball on Hispaniola, the island that the Dominican Republic shares with Haiti. Antonio Taveras, Alex's father, was a scout for the Dodgers, and he advised Avila that it was time to take another look at Peña. Avila picks up the story at this point: "The next night the son of a gun struck out 15 batters, strictly with fastballs. I knew if I didn't sign him, someone else would do it."[5] Peña signed with Avila as a free agent in 1978 for $4,000 and a $500 monthly stipend.

Peña was with Clinton in the Midwest League in 1979, going 3-3 with a 4.18 ERA. In 1980 he went 10-3 for Vero Beach in the Florida State League. He was promoted to Triple A during the 1981 season. At the time he was called up, he had a league-leading 22 saves with a 1.61 ERA for Albuquerque. His presence had positioned them to win the Pacific Coast League championship at the end of the season. They won the Southern Division by 25 games and defeated Tacoma in the postseason series for the league championship.

Peña was called up by the Dodgers on August 12, 1981, shortly after the end of the players strike. The 6-foot-1, 205-pound right-hander traveled to Atlanta and made his major-league debut the following evening, pitching a scoreless ninth inning against the Braves in a game the Dodgers lost 9-1. The following day, he picked up his first major-league save, pitching the final four innings against the Braves in a 5-0 Dodgers win. It was his longest outing of the 1981 season to date. (His longest outing with Albuquerque had been 2⅓ innings.)[6] At Pittsburgh on August 25, Peña entered the game after the Pirates had tied the score in the bottom of the ninth inning. There were two outs and the winning run was on second base. He induced Tony Peña to hit a comebacker for the inning's third out and the game went into extra innings. There was no scoring in the 10th inning as Peña retired the side in order. He picked up his first career win when the Dodgers broke through for two 11th-inning runs and Tom Niedenfuer came on for the save, pitching the bottom of the 11th inning.

Peña appeared in 14 games in 1981, had a 1-1 record, and was credited with two saves. His ERA was 2.84. The Dodgers advanced to the World Series, defeating the Expos in the League Championship Series. Peña appeared twice during the five games against Montreal, pitching 2⅓ scoreless innings. He did not play in the World Series win over the Yankees after being diagnosed early in the Series with a bleeding ulcer. He had collapsed after the second game and was admitted to a Los Angeles area hospital for observation.

Tellie (short for Telesila) Ceballos was a telephone operator in Los Angeles in 1981. She had been born on August 13, 1958 and came to the United States when she was 12 years old. She met Peña shortly after the World Series, and the two went out on a dinner date. They married in 1983. They have two children, Alejandro Jr. (born June 16, 1984) and Arianna Cristina (born October 19, 1989). As of 2015 their son was a doctor in Phoenix, and their daughter, an aspiring musician, lived in Georgia.[7]

Even with love in his life, Peña was the quiet man in the clubhouse because he had trouble leaning English. Although there were several Spanish-speaking players on the team. Peña, coming from a peasant village, had far less sophistication than his Latin comrades.

In 1982 Peña was off to a good start with the Dodgers, with a 1.29 ERA in his first 13 appearances, but he then ran into some difficulties. By July 15 he was 0-2, and his ERA had soared to 4.54. He was sent back to Albuquerque, where he did not fare much better, for the balance of the season.

In the offseason between 1982 and 1983, Peña pitched for Licey in the Dominican Winter League, and was managed by Dodgers coach Manny Mota. Peña sought the opportunity to pitch as a starter and Mota gave him the chance. Peña recorded four shutouts and found his way into the Dodgers rotation in 1983.

Peña spent two years in the rotation. In 1983 he pitched in 34 games, 26 as a starter. Most of his eight relief appearances came early in the season. Through June 12, despite missing two weeks with migraine headaches, he had relieved on eight occasions and started five times. At the time, he sported a 5-1 record and a 2.32 ERA. Three of those first five wins had been as a starter, including his first shutout, on May 24 at Philadelphia. That shutout came on the heels of shutouts by Bob Welch and Fernando Valenzuela, and represented the first time that the Dodger staff had pitched three consecutive shutouts since 1966 when Claude Osteen, Don Drysdale (with relief help from Phil Regan), and Sandy Koufax pitched successive shutouts from September 9 through September 11 while leading the Dodgers to the pennant. For the season, Peña went 12-9 with a 2.75 ERA. The Dodgers won the NL West and Peña pitched once in the League Championship Series against the Phillies, an ineffective relief stint in which he allowed two runs in 2⅔ innings. The Dodgers lost the best-of-five series in four games.

In 1984 Peña had his best season and narrowly missed being selected for the All-Star team, as teammate Fernando Valenzuela was chosen by manager Paul Owens. At the break, he was 10-4 with a 2.40 ERA and three shutouts. But the impact of a career-high 199⅓ innings took a toll and in early August he began to experience pain in his throwing shoulder. The pain subsided and on August 12 he defeated the Giants, 5-4, in 10 innings. However, the pain returned, and he pitched only three times the rest of the season. His season ended with a 12-6 record and a league-leading 2.48 ERA. He had hurled eight complete games and led the league with four shutouts.

The situation was made worse by Peña's language issues. In interviews with the media, he had to use the services of interpreter Jaime Jarrin. He was unable to properly communicate his condition to the Dodgers' medical personnel, and surgery was delayed. Peña would be essentially on the shelf for two seasons. It was hoped that rest during the offseason would help with the shoulder pain, but surgery proved necessary. Dr. Frank Jobe performed shoulder surgery (an arthroscopy) the following February.[8] Peña was on the DL for virtually the entire 1985 season, making only two late-season relief appearances.

Peña was restricted to bullpen activity early in 1986, making nine unproductive appearances. In July he returned to the starting rotation. He picked up his first victory since 1984 on July 7, when he allowed two hits in five innings as the Dodgers defeated the Cardinals, 1-0. It was his only win of the season. He pitched in 24 games in 1986 (10 as a starter) and went 1-2 with one save and a 4.89 ERA.

The man who started each of his 28 appearances in 1984 would evolve into a relief pitcher over the next three seasons and would be relieving exclusively starting in 1988, when he appeared in a career-high 60 games. Speaking of his new role, he said, "I like this role. I like the pressure and the close situations of this game. It looks like this motivates me more than starting did. I believe I've become a good short man. I hope other people believe it too."9 Although his won-lost record was only 6-7, he had 12 saves and struck out 83 batters in 94⅓ innings. The Dodgers won the NL West and Peña returned to the postseason for his third appearance. He had a win and a save against the Mets in the NLCS.

In Game Two, the Mets rallied in the ninth inning, had reduced the deficit to three runs and had two runners on base with one out when Peña was summoned. He secured the victory by getting Gary Carter on a fly ball to right field. In Game Three he was part of an eighth-inning bullpen implosion, yielding a double to Wally Backman as New York scored five runs against four Dodgers relievers and took a 2-1 lead in the best-of-seven series. In Game Four at New York, Peña entered the game in the ninth inning with the score tied 4-4. He pitched three scoreless innings, not allowing a hit, before being removed for a pinch-hitter. He wound up getting the win when Kirk Gibson homered in the top of the 12th inning.

After Kirk Gibson launched his game-winning homer in Game One of the World Series, the Dodgers defeated the A's in five games.

Peña was in peak form and his fastball was being clocked in the mid-90s. However, the speed of his fastball was in stark contrast to his pace of play. He was slow, methodical, patient, and deliberate on the mound for his entire career and was not about to change. "I've been that way my whole career. Why change it now?" he said. "I've been successful, so why would I want to make a change? If I can get a hitter out with this style, why would I want to pitch fast?"10

The Dodgers failed to repeat in 1989. Peña was 4-3 with a 2.13 ERA in 53 games, but only five saves as the Dodgers handed the closer role to Jay Howell. Los Angeles finished in fourth place with a 77-83 record and there were changes to be made. At the end of the season, Peña was traded to the Mets along with outfielder/first baseman Mike Marshall for infielder Juan Samuel. In his nine years with the Dodgers, Peña had gone 38-38 with 32 saves and a 2.92 ERA.

He arrived in New York as the Mets were beginning to look less like the championship squad they had been when they won the World Series in 1986 and a divisional championship in 1988 before falling to the Dodgers in the NLCS.

During the 1990 season, Peña went 3-3 with five saves and a 3.20 ERA. The Mets were treading water in the early part of the season. Bud Harrelson had replaced Davey Johnson as manager on May 29, and on June 4, after they lost five of six, the Mets' record stood at 21-26. Then they turned their season around. Between June 5 and August 3, they won 40 of 55 games to take over the division lead. During that stretch Peña was credited with a win, a save, and four holds. But after Labor Day, the Mets could not maintain their momentum and finished in second place, four games behind the Pirates.

Peña started the 1991 season with the Mets but was dealt to the Atlanta Braves on August 28. By then the Mets had fallen from contention and were in fourth place, 13½ games behind the division leaders. Peña had an excellent season with the Mets, going 6-1 with four saves and a 2.71 ERA. However, they realized that their chances at re-signing Peña, who was to become a free agent at season's end, were nominal and they obtained Joe Roa and Tony Castillo from Atlanta. The Braves, meanwhile, needed bullpen assistance, as their ace reliever, Juan Berenguer, had been injured. As Atlanta sportswriter Mark Bradley noted, Peña went from a capsized ship to a luxury liner.[11] He had a phenomenal five-week stretch run with the Braves, going 2-0 and saving 11 games in 15 appearances. From September 3 through October 4, he appeared in 14 games, all of which were won by Atlanta.

One of those saves was against the Padres on September 11. In that game, he came on in the ninth inning with the Braves leading 1-0. The Padres had gone hitless in eight innings against Kent Mercker and Mark Wohlers. Peña quickly got the first two batters, but Darrin Jackson hit a Baltimore chop to the left side of the infield that third baseman Terry Pendleton lost in the lights. The ball bounced off shortstop Rafael Belliard's glove and Jackson reached safely. The official scorer Mark Frederickson ruled the play an error by Pendleton. The no-hitter remained intact, and when the next batter, Tony Gwynn, skied to left fielder Otis Nixon, Peña had completed the combined no-hitter.[12]

The Braves, who had finished in last place the prior season, went 21-8 during Peña's hot streak and won the NL West by one game. On October 5, the day after Peña's last save of the season (and third in as many days), his services weren't needed as John Smoltz pitched a complete-game win over Houston, clinching the division title for the Braves. In the League Championship Series, they defeated the Pittsburgh Pirates in seven games. Peña recorded saves in three of the wins. He appeared in four games, was not scored upon, didn't allow any inherited runners to score, and yielded only one hit in 4⅓ innings. In Game Three, he entered the game in the bottom of the eighth inning. The Braves led 7-3, but the Bucs had loaded the bases with one out off Mike Stanton and Wohlers. Orlando Merced fouled out on a 3-and-1 fastball and got Jay Bell struck out looking. Peña had a 1-2-3 ninth for the save and Atlanta moved ahead in the series, two games to one.

In Game Six, with the Braves down 3-2 in the series, Peña came on to pitch the ninth inning at Pittsburgh with Atlanta leading 1-0. The Bucs' Gary Varsho opened the bottom of the ninth with a single to center field. He was bunted to second. With two out and Andy Van Slyke at the plate, Peña hurled a wild pitch and the potential tying run was at third base. The count went to 1-and-2 on Van Slyke and a classic pitcher-batter duel followed. The Pirates center fielder fouled off four consecutive pitches, the last three of which were hard-hit balls. During the first seven pitches of the at-bat, Peña had thrown a variety of pitches. Van Slyke said, "He threw a slider, a fastball, a forkball."[13] Braves catcher Greg Olson, who had driven in the only run of the game with a double in the top of the ninth, thought it was time for something different and called for a changeup. Van Slyke was frozen at the plate and looked at strike three. After the game, Van Slyke said, "I didn't even know he had that pitch."[14] The changeup had been in Peña's arsenal since early in 1984 when he had learned the pitch from coach Silvano Quesada while pitching for Licey in the Dominican Winter League, and perfected the pitch under the tutelage of Dodgers pitching coach Ron Perranoski.[15]

The Braves lost the World Series to the Twins in seven games. In Game Seven at the noisy Metrodome, Peña entered the scoreless battle in the bottom of the ninth inning. The first two batters in the inning had singled off

Mike Stanton. Peña came in and put out the fire. The game advanced to extra innings. In the bottom of the 10th, the Twins loaded the bases on a double, a sacrifice, and two intentional walks. As reported by *Sports Illustrated*'s Steve Rushin, pinch-hitter Gene Larkin "slapped the first pitch he got from Alejandro Peña to left center, over the head of Brian Hunter, who, like the rest of the Atlanta outfield, was playing only 30 yards in back of the infield in an effort to prevent Minnesota's Dan Gladden from doing precisely what he did: bound home from third base in the bottom of the 10th, through a cross-current of crazed, dazed teammates, who were leaping from the third base dugout and onto the field."[16]

Peña re-signed with the Braves after the season for $2.65 million, a substantial increase over the $1 million he was paid in 1991. Although Cleveland had made a two-year offer, Peña chose to sign a one-year deal with the Braves "because it's the most fun he ever had," according to his agent, Tom Reich.[17]

But the promise of the last five weeks of 1991 did not extend into 1992. Not right away, anyway. Although Peña had three saves in April, his May performance was horrific. In seven appearances that month, his 0-3 record included a blown save, and his ERA was 9.72. On May 16, after a poor performance, the crowd turned angry as Peña left the mound, and when he returned to the parking lot, he found that his car had been vandalized by someone using a key to scratch off some of the paint. He was no longer his team's closer. He was placed on the DL (eventually it was determined that his problems were in part due to bronchitis, strep throat, and a sinus infection). Once Peña returned from the DL, pitching coach Leo Mazzone detected a flaw in his delivery having to do with the release point.[18] And slowly Peña turned things around.

Healthy and delivering the ball like the Peña of old, Alexandro returned to form, and on July 8, with the Braves in danger of losing their fourth consecutive game, was given the ball in the ninth inning against the Mets in Atlanta. The "forgotten closer" entered the game with the bases loaded and none out. The Braves were leading 2-1. Peña got Howard Johnson on a popup and induced Willie Randolph to hit into a double play.[19] The save was his fourth of the season and first since April 28. From June 18, when he returned from the DL, through the end of the season, Peña saved 12 games and had a 2.30 ERA. From July 8 success through July 25, the Braves went on a tear. They won 13 games in a row to surge from six games behind the division lead to two games in front of the pack. Peña's only win of the season and eight of his saves came during the first 12 games of the streak, and he was credited with a hold in the Braves' 13th consecutive win.

The Braves once again finished first and faced the Pirates in the NLCS. But Peña's season was over. Experiencing elbow pain (tendinitis), he had spent time in late August and early September on the DL. The pain reached its threshold, surprisingly enough, after one of his best efforts. At Pittsburgh on August 17, he pitched the bottom of the 10th inning to save a 5-4 win. The last batter was Barry Bonds. As manager Bobby Cox recalled, "First pitch: fastball, whoosh! Second pitch: another fastball – and it was harder than the first. Third pitch: fastball again, and I swear it had more velocity than either of the first two. I'm just gaping at Peña. As for Bonds (who took the pitch for strike three), his eyes were bulging out; they were bigger than billiard balls. So, we all run out to the mound to shake Alejandro's hand, and just as I'm reaching for him, he says, 'Don't do it. My arm is killing me.'"[20] Peña was placed on the DL, and his September work had been limited to three nonsave appearances.

Toward the end of the season, Peña's wife, Tellie, organized an auction event where the wives of the Braves players raised money for victims of Hurricane Andrew by auctioning off broken bats, autographed jerseys and other items.[21] For Peña, the season would end on a sour note. On September 30, with the division championship already clinched, the Braves asked Peña to pitch the eighth inning against the Giants with the Braves trailing 1-0. Although he completed the inning, retiring three of the four batters he faced, he was in pain.[22] Peña was not used in the NLCS and was left off the roster when the Braves lost to the Blue Jays in the World Series.

A free agent once again, Peña signed with the Pirates during the offseason, but did not play in 1993. On March 26 he underwent surgery to rebuild a ligament in his pitching elbow. The procedure involved removing a ligament from his right wrist and reattaching it in his elbow. His contract with the Pirates was restructured into a two-year deal, and he returned to the mound in 1994. When his contract was restructured, Peña showed great class. He could have just made his salary, more than $1 million, for 1993 and moved on. He chose to return his signing bonus of $500,000 and signed a two-year deal calling for $175,000 in 1993 and $1.35 million in 1994. In describing the contract, he said, "I could live with myself better. I didn't feel right taking the money and not doing anything for the team. I didn't want to take the money and then go play for somebody else."[23]

Sidelined by bleeding ulcers at the beginning of the 1994 season, Peña started the season on the DL. He returned to the mound in May and was named the Pirates closer in June, after a great four-inning stint on May 26 when he came on the 10th inning and allowed no hits as the Pirates won in 13 innings. He had a brilliant month with seven saves, but his season ended on June 28. He was in immense pain after throwing the final pitch in his seventh save of the season, and an examination indicated that he had ligament damage in his elbow. He was finished for the season and the Pirates released him on June 30.[24]

Peña pitched for three major-league teams in 1995. He started the season with the Red Sox and was pitching well in his first 10 appearances with a save, a hold, and a 2.70 ERA. But then he hit a bad spell. He was scored on in six of his last seven appearances with Boston and his ERA ballooned to 7.40. The Red Sox released him on June 13. Two weeks later, he signed with the Charlotte Knights, the Triple-A affiliate of the Florida Marlins and pitched in nine games, saving five and posting a 0.96 ERA. The Marlins called him up on July 29.

With the help of a sinker developed under the tutelage of Marlins pitching coach Larry Rothschild during August was credited with six holds and two wins in 13 games. His ERA was 1.50 and he struck out 21 batters in 18 innings. At month's end he was traded back to the Braves for Chris Seelbach.

The Braves were a virtual cinch for a playoff berth, leading the NL East by 14½ games when Peña arrived. He was given the number 26 that he had worn in 1991 and became the set-up man for closer Mark Wohlers. He shored up the pitching-rich Braves, getting into 14 games. He was credited with three holds and struck out 18 batters in 13 innings.

In the best-of-five Division Series against Colorado, Peña was credited with wins in the first two games. In each instance, he gave up a run-scoring double after entering the game, only to see his teammates rally to win after he became the pitcher of record. In Game Four, he took over for Greg Maddux in the eighth inning with the Braves leading by six runs. Dante Bichette greeted him with a single and then Peña retired the next six batters and was mobbed at the mound after he struck out John Vander Wal for the final out of the game and series. In the NLCS against Cincinnati, Peña pitched in three of the four games as the Braves swept the Reds. He pitched the eighth inning in Games One, Two, and Four and was not scored upon.

"Oh yeah, I thought I'd be here again. I never give up on myself. I thought I had a couple of good years left even after Boston let me go this year."

– Alejandro Peña, October 22, 1995 on the eve of Game Seven of the 1995 World Series.[25]

In the World Series against Cleveland, Peña entered Game Two in the seventh inning. The Braves led 4-3 and there were runners at the corners with two outs. Albert Belle came to the plate. Eddie Murray lurked in the on-deck circle. Peña remarked about facing Belle. "Early this season, when I was with Boston, he hit a homer off me (on a fastball). This was revenge. I started him with a slider and then got him with three straight fastballs."[26] He got Belle out on a popup that catcher Javy Lopez caught behind home plate.

In the eighth inning Peña got two outs before walking Jim Thome, and Bobby Cox brought in Mark Wohlers, who got credit for the save. Peña was credited with a hold, and the Braves led the series, 2 games to none. The third game of the Series went into extra innings, and Peña came in to pitch the 11th. After successes in each of his first seven postseason appearances in 1995, Peña had a bad outing, yielding a leadoff double to Carlos Baerga and a game-winning single to Eddie Murray. He wasn't expecting to pitch that night as he had strained his lower back in pregame warmups. After the game, he admitted, "I couldn't follow through, but I had to pitch." (The Braves had already gone through four relievers)."[27] It was Peña's last appearance in the Series. The Braves won in six games, and Peña had gone 2-1 with a 1.29 ERA in eight 1995 postseason outings.

Peña was once again a free agent after the 1995 season. After signing a minor-league contract with the Marlins in December 1995, he had an excellent spring training and made the major-league roster. But after pitching in four April games, he was placed on the disabled list on the 17th with a strained rotator cuff. Dr. James Andrews performed surgery on June 18, but Peña never pitched again professionally.

For his 15-year major-league career, Peña was 56-52 with a 3.11 ERA. As a starter he had seven shutouts, and as a reliever he had 74 saves.

After he retired from baseball Peña paid serious attention to his golf game at his home in Georgia and stayed out of the game for more than 10 years. He was the pitching coach for the Dominican Summer League Dodgers from 2010 through 2013.

This biography first appeared in the 2020 SABR book, *Braves Win! Braves Win! Braves Win! The 1995 World Champion Atlanta Braves.*

SOURCES

In addition to the sources cited in the Notes, the author used Baseball-Reference.com. and Peña's file at the National Baseball Hall of Fame and Museum.

NOTES

1. Orel Hershiser (with Jerry B. Jenkins), *Out of the Blue* (Brentwood, Tennessee: Wolgemuth and Hyatt Publishers, 1989), 188.

2. Larry Schwartz, "Hollywood Ending for L.A., Gibson's HR Wins in Ninth," *Bergen Record* (Hackensack, New Jersey), October 16, 1988: S01.

3. Peter Gammons, "The Home Run," *Sports Illustrated*, October 24, 1988.

4. Gordon Edes, "Alejandro's Pain Is Real," *Los Angeles Times*, March 5, 1986: Sports-1.

5. Edes.

6. Gordon Verrell, "Dodgers: Kiddies in Pen," *The Sporting News*, September 5, 1981: 47.

7. I.J. Rosenberg, "Whatever Happened to Alejandro Peña?" *Atlanta Journal Constitution*, May 2, 2015.

8. Verrell, "Fastball No Longer in Peña's Arsenal," *The Sporting News*, March 11, 1985: 32.

9. Terry Johnson, "No Stopping Him: To Dodgers' Relief, Peña Back in Form," *Daily Breeze* (Torrance, California), April 25, 1989: D3.

10. Johnson.

11. Mark Bradley, "Peña Feels Lucky to Be a Brave," *Atlanta Journal*, August 30, 1991: H2.

12. Bob Nightingale, "A No-Hitter by Decision in Baseball: Mercker, Wohlers, Pena get Help from Scorer's Controversial Ruling as the Braves Beat the Padres, 1-0," *Los Angeles Times*, September 12, 1991: 1.

13. Joe Sexton, "Baseball: Peña Strikes a Big Blow," *New York Times*, October 17, 1991: B15.

14. Murray Chass, "Baseball: No Runs, No Pennant: Braves Force Game Seven," *New York Times*, October 17, 1991: B13.

15. Terry Johnson, "Peña Gets Results with New Pitch," *Daily Breeze* (Torrance, California), April 30, 1984: D1.

16. Steve Rushin, "A Series to Savor," *Sports Illustrated*, November 4, 1991.

17. Associated Press, "Atlanta Keeps Peña," *Augusta* (Georgia) *Chronicle*, December 20, 1991: 1B.

18. I.J. Rosenberg, "The Fire Burns Again: To Braves' Relief, Alejandro Peña has Regained His Health and Fastball to Fuel 11-Game Win Streak," *Atlanta Constitution*, July 24, 1992: E1.

19. Rosenberg, "Mets Fall 2-1, as Peña Saves Glavine's 13th," *Atlanta Constitution*, July 9, 1992: D1.

20. Dave Nightingale, "Hurtin' and Uncertain," *The Sporting News*, October 5, 1992: 10.

21. Susannah Vesey, "What Am I Bid?" *Atlanta Constitution*, September 25, 1992: G2.

22. Aileen Voisin, "Baseball: The Braves 1992 NL West Division Champions: Peña Feels Pain in His Elbow While Pitching Scoreless 8th," *Atlanta Constitution*, October 1, 1992: E8.

23. John Mehno, "Giving Something Back," *The Sporting News*, March 21, 1994: 16.

24. Ron Cook, "Peña's Release a Sad Farewell," *Pittsburgh Post-Gazette*, July 1, 1994: C1.

25. Lyle Spencer, "Peña Still has Shades of '88 Series in Him," *Riverside* (California) *Press-Enterprise*, October 23, 1995: D01.

26. Scott Tolley, "Indians Get Home Cooking," *Palm Beach* (Florida) *Post*, October 23, 1995: 3C.

27. Mike Berardino, "'Hired Guns' Shine at Just the Right Time in Braves Title Run," *Augusta* (Georgia) *Chronicle*, October 30, 1995: 4C.

Tony Peña

By Blake W. Sherry

In Tribe folklore, Tony Peña will always bring back moments of elation and unbound hope for a world championship after he crushed an early-morning pitch toward left field for a walk-off homer in the 13th inning of Game One of the 1995 American League Division Series. For the Indians, it was their first postseason since 1954, and left Indian fans dreaming, "Would this be the Indians' year?"

Antonio Francisco (Padilla) Peña was born on June 4, 1957, in Monte Cristi, Dominican Republic. He was born into a family of hard-working parents. His father, Octaviano, was a farmer, and his mother, Rosalia, a teacher for more than 30 years. Tony was raised with three brothers and a sister. While his father worked long hours, it was his mother who took it upon herself to teach Tony the finer points of baseball. Tony once said it was his mother who was the star of the family. "She was a real all-star," he said his rookie year. "She played softball and she pitched and hit better than most men."[1] Rosalia was strict with the family getting their education, insisting that Tony and his brothers keep up with their studies and not just play baseball. If he or any of his siblings had an exam the next day, studying had to come first.

Tony Peña was signed as an amateur free agent in July of 1975 by the Pittsburgh Pirates. Originally signed as an outfielder, he switched to catcher in his second year in the minors. He made his way through the Pirates farm system with stops with their Gulf Coast Rookie League team, Salem (Class A), Charleston (Class A), Shreveport (Double-A), Buffalo (Double-A), and Portland (Triple-A) before getting a call-up to the Pirates when rosters expanded on September 1, 1980. In eight games he hit a robust .429 (9-for-21).

Peña made the Pirates roster in 1981 but was initially stuck behind the strong backstop platoon of Steve Nicosia and Ed Ott. That had taken the Bucs to the 1979 world championship. However, it was not long before Peña became the starting catcher. His strong end-of-season showing in 1980 allowed the Pirates to trade Ott to the California Angels in April of 1981. At that point manager Chuck Tanner insisted that he now had two starting catchers in Peña and Nicosia.

After seeing action in just 66 games in that strike-shortened season of 1981, Peña emerged as the starting catcher toward the end of the season. One of the attributes of his game that fans noticed early in his career was his love for the game, not unlike the

Photo courtesy of the National Baseball Hall of Fame

joy of one of his Pirates predecessors, the perpetually smiling Manny Sanguillen. Said Peña, "I would love this game even if I wasn't getting paid to play."² Tanner saw even bigger things coming, stating, "It's just a matter of time before Peña is recognized as one of the outstanding catchers."³ Tanner was not alone in his observations; Atlanta manager Bobby Cox said that Peña "looks like an excellent prospect."⁴ Peña's .300 batting average and excellent defense garnered him a sixth-place finish in the Rookie of the Year voting. He was named Topps Rookie All-Star catcher and was selected to the UPI Rookie All-Star Team. Peña's hard work and desire to get better would serve him well. At year end, he said, "I will be better next year because of the experience I got this year," adding, "I made some mistakes. Chuck talked to me about them."⁵

As the Pirates' starting catcher in 1982, Peña began to hit his stride. In July he was named to the NL All-Star team. He batted .296 and hit 11 home runs in his first full year as a starter. He would subsequently be named to four more All-Star teams in his career. He had arrived.

In 1983 Peña established himself as one of the stars of the game. He was awarded his first Gold Glove while hitting a full-season career high .301. He added some power to go with the high average with a career-high 15 home runs and 70 runs batted in. Over the next three years, Peña was a fixture for the Bucs, becoming known for his low crouch behind the plate with one leg fully extended. Pittsburgh fans also loved his exuberance for the game, and he was a crowd favorite during his stay.

The 1983 season was a good one for the Pirates as well. They were tied for first place as late as September 17 with the Phillies. But the Bucs faded the last two weeks of that season, and then entered a down phase for the franchise that lasted nearly through the end of the decade. A miserable team in 1985 went 57-104 and failed to draw even 750,000 fans for the season. During that period it took a major push lead by Mayor Richard Caliguiri to put together a consortium of local businesses just to keep the Pirates in town.⁶

As the Pirates struggled in the mid-'80s to field a competitive team and to stay in Pittsburgh, Peña's ability to maintain his zest for the game was challenged. With three consecutive last-place finishes, the game was not as much fun. The 1985 season was the low point of his career. "It was no fun – no fun at all," he said. "There were the drug trials, the club was up for sale and we were losing, losing, losing. I am not a loser."⁷ A number of major leaguers, including several Pirates, but not Peña, were called before a Pittsburgh grand jury investigating cocaine use. As someone who had not taken drugs, Peña resented the guilt by association that all the Pirates endured. "The world thought that Pittsburgh was on trial," he said. "Everywhere anyone went, they heard about ball players and drugs, and heard about Pittsburgh. It was unfair. It was not right. Pittsburgh is a good town."[8] It wasn't until 1988 that the Pirates started to win back their fans.

In 1986, Peña's last with the Pirates, he hit a respectable .288 and made the All-Star team for the third consecutive year, but the team lost 98 games. Offensively, Peña's Pirates years were among the most productive of his career. His consistency on defense supported by his three Gold Gloves, four All-Star Game appearances, and a .286 composite batting average during his seven seasons in Pittsburgh garnered him consideration for the All-Time Pirate lineup. The baseball.about.com website ranked Peña in the top four Pirate catchers of all time by MLB expert Scott Kendrick.[9]

On April 1, 1987, Peña was part of a blockbuster trade that brought the Pirates two key players for their string of NL East crowns in the early '90s, and led Peña to his first World Series appearance. He was traded to the St. Louis Cardinals for pitcher Mike Dunne, catcher Mike LaValliere, and future All-Star and Gold Glove outfielder Andy Van Slyke. Given Peña's popularity, it was a surprise to Pirate fans, but gave reason for excitement to the Cardinals and their fans. Said Cardinals general manager Dal Maxvill, "We are getting one of the premier players of the game, as evidenced by what we had to give up to acquire him."[10]

Peña, however, was emotionally hurt by the trade. "I cried for a week,' Peña said. "The trade hurt me psychologically. I lost my stroke."[11]

Peña spent the next three years with the Cardinals and ended up being one of the key ingredients for their run at a championship in 1987. Getting his first taste of postseason baseball that season, he hit .381 in the NLCS as the Cardinals topped the San Francisco Giants in seven games and then hit a strong .409 in a losing cause in the World Series, won by the Minnesota Twins in seven games.

A year after the trade, on April 21, 1988, Peña got some personal satisfaction during an early-season return to Pittsburgh. He went 3-for-4, with two home runs and three runs scored in a 9-3 Cardinals victory over the Bucs. "It was nice to be back in my old ballpark," said Peña. "I've tried to put the trade behind me, and I just want to forget about that and do my job."[12] He played two more years in St. Louis and made another All-Star Game appearance in 1989.

Peña left St. Louis as a free agent after the 1989 season and signed with the Boston Red Sox. He spent the 1990 through 1993 seasons with the Red Sox. His leadership abilities again emerged in the Red Sox clubhouse, all while adapting to the American League. Similar to his stays in Pittsburgh and St. Louis, Peña displayed excellent defense and pitching staff management, which was exactly what Red Sox general manager Lou Gorman was expecting. Peña said Gorman told him, "I want you to catch, call the game and throw people out. That's what I need."[13] Peña made good on those expectations, winning a fourth Gold Glove in 1991. (He became only the second catcher to win a Gold Glove in each league; Bob Boone was the first.)

Red Sox pitching coach Bill Fischer went even farther with his praise, ranking him above Hall of Famer Johnny Bench, whom he watched for five years in Cincinnati as a coach. "I think Peña's the best catcher I've ever seen," Fischer said. "Bench made a lot more noise with his bat, but as far as catching goes I think Peña's better. He's so important to the pitching staff because of the way he handles a game and the way he keeps them loose."[14]

Photo courtesy of the National Baseball Hall of Fame

Yet, a humble Peña shies away from such praise. "I don't think I can take much credit," he said, They (the pitchers) threw the ball and made the pitches. They had the success. My job is to help the pitcher as much as I can. If something goes wrong, my job is to fix it. I keep full concentration on the game."[15]

Peña paid special attention to Latin players on the Red Sox, like Carlos Quintana and Ivan Calderon, to encourage them to assimilate into the team. In addition, he assisted the Latin community. (As an example, he took part in an event in the heavily Latino city of Lawrence to raise money to help immigrant Hispanic families.[16])

On February 7, 1994, the 37-year-old Peña signed a free-agent contract with the Cleveland Indians as a backup to Sandy Alomar Jr. It was the first time Peña signed as a non-starter. Worried about the Indians backup, General Manager John Hart approached Peña while in the Dominican Republic that winter. He gave a Tribe hat to Peña and asked him to think about being the backup catcher in Cleveland. A few days later, Peña called Hart and told him, "I'm wearing my Indians hat,"[17] and that's how Hart knew he had him in the fold. In a part-time role, he provided both spark and veteran leadership to help manage the pitching staff for the Indians. Peña spent the next three seasons as part of the Tribe.

The 1995 season started with Alomar on the disabled list, so Peña found himself back in the starting lineup. The Indians got off to the best start in baseball, going 41-17. With Peña catching, the pitching staff had the lowest ERA in the league through July 1. Peña played the whole first half of the season and ended up playing more than half the games that season as the Indians won their Central Division going away, winning 100 of their 144 games in a strike-shortened season. They won the division by a whopping 30 games.

Peña was one of the key ingredients to the success. Peña hit .262. As a catcher he was noted for his quick, productive mound visits with pitchers when he felt they weren't focused enough. "Tony has a master's degree in the game'" said Indians pitching coach Jeff Newman. "He gets the performance he should out of a pitcher. If a pitcher doesn't anything on a certain day, there is nothing a catcher can do. But if the pitcher has good stuff, a good catcher can make him put it in certain spots by calling the right pitch at the right time. Not every catcher can do that, but we have two who can."[18] Returning from the disabled list, Alomar was back behind the plate for the playoffs.

It was vindication for Peña. "I know there was a lot of doubt about me," Peña said. "They didn't know if I could catch every day. But I caught every day in winter ball in the Dominican to get ready for the season. I've done it every year I've played in the big leagues." He added that he feels 'the human body is like a car. If you drive your car every day for six months, and then shut it down for six months, it will break down when you start it up again. That's why I never take time off.[19]

With Alomar back, Peña played little in the postseason. But on October 3, he made it count. Peña's bottom-of-the-13th inning walk-off homer in Game One of the American League Division Series against the Red Sox gave early momentum to the Indians. The home run came off Boston's reliever Zane Smith some six hours after the game was supposed to start. It was the Indians' first postseason victory since their championship in 1948, a drought of 47 years. Of his blast, Peña said, "I wasn't sure if I was supposed to take or not. But when he [Red Sox pitcher Zane Smith] threw the pitch, it was too good to let go by."[20]

The Indians went on to beat Boston in the ALDS, and then Seattle in the AL Championship Series, before succumbing to the Atlanta Braves in six games in the World Series. Peña played in four games in the ALCS but in only two games of the World Series. Despite the Indians' loss of the World Series, Peña's ALDS home run continues to be cited as one of the most memorable moments in Indians history. The website didthetribewinlastnight.com described the home run as "the biggest moment in the biggest year in franchise history."[21]

Peña played in 67 games with the Indians in 1996. A free agent after the season, he signed with the Chicago White Sox in January 1997. He played in just 31 games with White Sox before being traded to the Houston Astros on August 15. He played in nine games with the Astros and, now 40 years old, was released after the season.

Peña spent that winter as a player/manager for the Aguilas Cibaenas in the Dominican League. As the season wore on, he played himself less and less despite getting some key hits early on. He retired as a player at the end of that season and began focusing on managing and coaching.

Julio Rodriguez contributes a memory of Peña's final time at the plate. "His last at-bat came in the final game of the playoff for the championship of the 1999-2000 season of the Dominican Winter League and 43 years old Tony Peña, was the manager-player of the

Cibaeñas Eagles. The game was tied in the bottom of the ninth inning and the potentially winning run for the Eagles was at third base with one out. Peña decided he would pinch-hit. The count went to 0-2. Watching in the stands, I thought, 'Oh, he will strike out.' But on the next pitch he hit a fly ball deep enough to center field for the winning run to score. That was a very appropriate finish for the career of the best catcher in Dominican baseball history."[22]

Peña spent the next several years as a minor-league manager before positioning himself as a major-league coach and ultimately a major-league manager. He managed the White Sox' Arizona Fall League team in 1998. He then took over as the manager of the New Orleans Zephyrs in the Pacific Coast League for the Houston Astros organization. There he won a PCL East title in 2001, before becoming a bench coach for the Astros in 2002.

Early in the 2002 season, on May 15, Peña was hired to manage the Kansas City Royals after the dismissal of Tony Muser. He became only the third Dominican to manage a major-league team. On June 25, as he and manager Luis Pujols of the Detroit Tigers exchanged lineup cards, they became the first Dominicans to do so in the major leagues. As fate had it, Felipe Alou, the first Dominican manager, was also there. He was a bench coach for the Tigers. Dominican Republic President Hipolito Mejia was also present for a special presentation from Commissioner Bud Selig. It was not the first time Peña and Pujols, also a former catcher, had been managerial opponents; they previously managed against each other in the Dominican Winter League.

In 2003, Peña's first full major-league season as a manager, he experienced initial success for the Royals as they finished above .500 for the first time since the strike-shortened season of 1994. He had restored enthusiasm and accountability to the budget-constrained team. He was an easy choice for American League Manager of the Year by *The Sporting News* and the Baseball Writers Association of America, getting 24 of the 28 first-place votes and becoming only the fifth manager to win the award in his first full season.

The Royals could not capture the magic again in 2004 and lost 104 games. After another slow start to the 2005 season (8-25), Peña resigned on May 10. After the final 3-1 loss to the Blue Jays, he said, "I can't take it anymore. We are not playing well. It's tough going to the ballpark and lose game after game. I haven't been eating. I haven't been sleeping."[23]

In November of 2005, Peña was hired by the New York Yankees as a first-base coach, a position he held until he became the bench coach in 2009. He also served as the team's catching instructor. In 2015 Peña returned to the role of first-base coach and was still currently in that role during there during the 2017 postseason run for the Yankees.

On February 11, 2012, in a ceremony in La Romana, Dominican Republic, Peña was inducted into the Latino Baseball Hall of Fame.

In March of 2013, Peña managed the championship Dominican Republic team in the World Baseball Classic. The team went an unprecedented 8-0, winning the final game 3-0 over Puerto Rico. The team was led offensively by the tournament's MVP, Robinson Cano. Pitcher Fernando Rodney had seven saves for the Dominicans. He managed the defending Champions again in 2017, but was eliminated in the second round of pool play winning one and losing two games.

Peña has a number of notable accomplishments as a player. As of the start of the 2015 season, he was sixth among major-league catchers with 1,950 games behind the plate, eighth in career putouts (11,212), and sixth in career double plays turned by a catcher (156). He had numerous seasons ranking in the Top 10 for Defensive WAR (wins above replacement).

Peña married the girl down the street, Amaris, who lived just three houses down from his. They had three children together: sons Tony Jr. and Francisco Antonio, and a daughter, Jennifer Amaris. Tony Jr. was signed as an amateur free agent shortstop by the Atlanta Braves in 1999. He made his major-league debut in 2006 and had a four-year major-league career. Francisco Antonio, has been in the minor leagues since 2007, and as of 2015 was playing in the Royals' farm system. Peña daughter, Jennifer Amaris, won the Miss Dominican Republic-USA beauty pageant in 2007.

One of Tony's younger brothers, Ramon, also played major-league baseball. He appeared in eight games as a relief pitcher for the Detroit Tigers in 1989. He registered no decisions and had a 6.00 ERA in 18 innings pitched.

NOTES

1. Charley Feeney, "Tanner Rates Peña All-Star of the Future," *The Sporting News*, October 17, 1981: 31.
2. Charley Feeney, "Bucs Given Strong Charge By 'Dominican Connection'," *The Sporting News*, June 20, 1981: 31.
3. Feeney, "Tanner Rates Peña All-Star of the Future."
4. Feeney, "Bucs Given Strong Charge By 'Dominican Connection'."
5. Feeney, "Tanner Rates Peña All-Star of the Future."
6. Ron Cook, "A Terrible Time of Trial and Error," *Pittsburgh Post-Gazette*, September 29, 2000: CC-3.
7. Charley Feeney, "Peña Wiser After Nightmare of '85," *The Sporting News*, March 10, 1986: 39.
8. Feeney, "Peña Wiser After Nightmare of '85."
9. Scott Kendrick, "Pittsburgh Pirates All Time Lineup," About.baseball.com, March 27, 2017. Retrieved December 5, 2017
10. "Pirates Deal Peña to Cardinals," *New York Post*, April 4, 1987. Player file Baseball Hall of Fame
11. Paul Hoynes, "What a Catch," *Plain Dealer*, July 2, 1995, 11-D.
12. "Peña Finally Gets Back at Pirates," *Los Angeles Times*, April 22, 1988: part 3-7.
13. Robyn Norwood, "This Free Agent Was a Catch for the Red Sox," *Los Angeles Times*, August 9, 1990: C6.
14. Joe Giuliotti, "Red Sox catch Peña Fever," *Boston Herald*, April 11, 1991: R27.
15. Sean McAdam, "A Good Guy to Have," *Providence Journal*, May 15, 1991.
16. Paul Lafond, "Sox' Tony Peña: I really like to help kids who are needy'," *Lawrence Eagle-Tribune*, June 29, 1990: 25-27.
17. Hoynes.
18. Hoynes.
19. Hoynes.
20. Jim Ingraham, "Picture-Perfect Play," *Morning Journal* (Lorain, Ohio), March 4, 1996: B1
21. Steve Eby, "The Greatest Summer Ever: Tony Peña," Didthetribewinlastnight.com, June 20, 2015. Retrieved December 5, 2017
22. E-mail from Julio Rodriguez on January 9, 2021.
23. Bob Dutton, "Royals Manager Tony Peña Resigns," KansasCity.com, May 11, 2005. Retrieved December 5, 2017

NEIFI PÉREZ

By Ralph Carhart

When Neifi Pérez signed his first major-league contract, on November 9, 1992, his employer had yet to engage in a single professional baseball game. Denver had been awarded a major-league baseball team in June of 1991, and the newly minted Colorado Rockies had already participated in the amateur draft of 1992. However, it wasn't until the days approaching the expansion draft in mid-November that they signed their first amateur free agent, 19-year-old Pérez. Born on June 2, 1973, in the municipality of Villa Mella, in the Santo Domingo Norte section of the Dominican Republic, Pérez would become a hero in the DR and a legend in Caribbean Series history. But like too many other players of his era, the extreme measures he took during his career ultimately cost him.

From the beginning, it was clear that the versatile, agile Pérez could cover ground in the field. Primarily a shortstop, Pérez could also play second base. The larger question was how well he would hit. With the power surge of the 1990s, baseball had evolved past the good-field/no-hit shortstop mold that had been the norm in the previous decades. Faced with these expectations, Pérez acquitted himself well enough in his first professional season, in 1993, with the Bend (Oregon) Rockies of the Northwest League. His numbers weren't memorable; he batted an ordinary .260 in low-A ball. But he led the team in hits and stolen bases. He also led the team in games played, a trademark statistic of Pérez's early career.

The following year saw a promotion to high-A, to the Central Valley Rockies of the California League. His batting average fell to .239, but his consistency continued, as he once again led his teammates in games played. Pérez was getting more comfortable on the basepaths as well, allowing him to transform his natural speed into triples, in which he also led the club. Unfortunately for Pérez, as he slowly began to develop his offensive game, he started to struggle on the field. He made 39 errors that season. He was, however, responsible for a California League milestone, the first unassisted triple play in the 53-year history of the league.[1] On May 9, in a game against the Bakersfield Dodgers, with Mike Kinney on second base and Matt Schwenke on first, Miguel Cairo hit a line drive right at Pérez. The runners already in motion, Pérez was able to snatch the ball out of the air, step on second base, and tag the oncoming Schwenke for the third out.

His rise through the ranks continued when he was sent to the Double-A New Haven Ravens at the start of 1995. The organization continued to work with him on his hitting, with occasional signs of hope. Pérez was underperforming at the plate when New Haven manager Paul Zuvella approached him before a mid-July game and challenged him to take his offense to a "higher level."[2] Pérez responded with a five-RBI night, including a two-run triple and three-run home run. He also cut his error total in half from the previous year. By season's end, he had made it all the way to the Rockies' Triple-A squad, the Colorado Springs Sky Sox.

Pérez began the 1996 campaign in Colorado Springs, and it was over the course of that season that the Colorado press finally began to call him the "Rockies' future shortstop." He had an electric year, hitting .316 with 12 triples, trailing only future major-league standout Bobby Abreu for the league lead in three-baggers. By the end of June there were rumors of his promotion. Still, he struggled on the field, particularly when it came to making hurried throws to first base on balls hit deep in the hole. He acknowledged that he had "to make better decisions. I have to learn when to keep the ball and not force a play."[3] He was tapped for the Triple-A All-Star game, where he scored the tying run on Brook Fordyce's eighth-inning home run, giving the National League future stars a 2-1 victory over their American League counterparts.[4]

Despite Pérez's success, the Rockies were committed to their current shortstop, Walt Weiss. It was not until the rosters expanded at the end of August that Pérez was called up. He quickly made his debut on August 31, a start in which he played the whole game. He manned second base, giving regular Eric Young the night off, and made three assists and one putout. At the plate he went 0-for-4 with a strikeout. He got his first hit on September

Photo courtesy of the Kansas City Royals

12, a night on which he went 2-for-4 and got his first two big-league RBIs. Pérez had a few more starts before the season ended, and filled in for late-innings defense for Weiss a handful of times. For his part, Weiss led the league in errors at shortstop with 30. Pérez's brief audition was impressive enough that the starting shortstop for the 1997 season was an uncertainty in the Rockies organization. Weiss himself told the media that he expected to be traded.[5]

Weiss was mistaken. When the Rockies played the Cincinnati Reds on Opening Day 1997, Weiss was the shortstop and remained so through most of the team's first 100 games. Pérez remained in Colorado Springs, where he tore up the league. By the end of June, halfway through the season, he was hitting .363 with eight home runs, already a career high. He became quite vocal that he felt he belonged in the majors, giving a hotheaded newspaper interview in which he said, "Everything I can learn in Triple-A, I've learned already. My time is over here. I hope they move me up ... before my patience is over and I do something crazy."[6]

The Rockies clearly agreed with their presumptuous young infielder. He was back in the majors within a week of that interview. At first he filled in around the infield, playing shortstop, second base, and third base. Weiss was having an adequate season, but a groin injury in late July put him on the disabled list and opened the door for Pérez to regularly play his natural position.[7] He excelled during Weiss's absence, hitting .333 with three home runs over 20 games. When Weiss returned, Rockies manager Don Baylor had no intention of pulling Pérez out of the lineup.

Instead, the Rockies traded regular second baseman Eric Young to the Los Angeles Dodgers and shifted Pérez to the right side of the infield, where he played for the remainder of the season. He was sharp at second base, to the tune of a .992 fielding percentage, and he finished the season with an outstanding rookie-year batting average of .291. Despite playing in only 83 games, half the season, he led the team in triples. He even got a vote for the Rookie of the Year Award, which went to Phillies standout Scott Rolen. That offseason the Rockies committed to their "shortstop of the future," as Weiss exited via free agency when he refused the Rockies' request that he move to second base to make room for Pérez.[8]

Pérez returned home to the Dominican Republic that winter to play for his national team in the Caribbean Series. The previous year the Dominican Republic had won its sixth Series championship since the tournament was revived in 1970, after a 10-year hiatus following the end of the Cuban Winter League in 1961. Pérez, who normally played for the Leones del Escogido in the Dominican Winter League, was invited to join league champion Aguilas Cibaeñas for the four-team tournament. Facing Mexico, Puerto Rico, and Venezuela, Pérez led Aguilas to the Dominican Republic's second straight title. Over the tournament, he batted .478 with five RBIs and six doubles. He hit a two-run home run in the Series finale, securing the victory over Venezuela. He was named the Caribbean Series MVP.[9]

Fresh off this achievement and tapped as the starting shortstop for the Rockies in 1998, Pérez appeared to have a very bright future. In spring training manager Baylor compared him to Luis Aparicio. Pérez, who just eight months previously was loudly touting his skills, had learned a modicum of humility in the ensuing time. He waved off the comparison, stating, "I want to wait and see what happens. ... I'm just going to play like I play."[10] Partnered with new second baseman Mike Lansing, acquired from the Montreal Expos, Pérez led the league in 1998 in double plays turned at shortstop with 127, over 30 more than runners-up Edgar Renteria and Chris Gomez.

His versatility in the field was tested in a June 7 game against the Anaheim Angels. An injury and lineup machinations left the Rockies without a catcher in a game they had tied 5-5 with two runs in the top of the ninth. Pérez was plugged in behind the plate and ultimately figured in the final score. He failed to handle a wild pitch by Jerry DiPoto and Angels slugger Jim Edmonds barreled in with the winning run before Pérez could corral the ball. It was Neifi's lone professional appearance as catcher.

His success at the plate fell a bit from his freshman year, as his batting average dipped by .017. He also seemed to be struggling to harness his inherent speed. He stole only five bases and hit one less triple than in the year before, when he had played only half a season. He did lead the league at putting bunts into play, with 67, but he struggled to turn those into hits. On the plus side, his 22 sacrifices were tops in the majors and he managed the statistical quirk of hitting for the cycle on July 25, despite not being a home-run hitter. He was also an injury-free presence in the lineup, appearing in all 162 games of a generally disappointing Colorado season. The Rockies finished in fourth place, 21 games behind the division champion San Diego Padres.

Pérez and the Rockies did have the pleasure of playing spoiler when, on the last day of the season, they defeated the San Francisco Giants, robbing them of the wild card. The Giants led 7-0 in the fifth, but the Rockies fought back and it was Pérez, with a ninth-inning leadoff home run, just his ninth of the year, that put the nail in the Giants' coffin.[11] The loss forced a one-game tiebreaker game against the Cubs, a contest the Giants lost.

Pérez returned to the Dominican League and the Caribbean Series during the 1999 offseason and made history. He led Escogido to the regular-season Dominican championship with a dramatic three-run home run in the bottom of the ninth of the final game of the season. Los Leones lost the best-of-nine championship series to Los Tigres del Licey, and it was they who secured a trip to Puerto Rico where they would represent the Dominican Republic in the Caribbean Series.[12] Once again, Pérez was asked to join the national team for the tournament, and once again he led the Dominican Republic to victory, its record third in a row. Playing alongside the likes of David Ortiz and Adrian Beltré, both likely Cooperstown-bound, it was Pérez who walked away with his second MVP trophy, hitting safely in all six games (12 hits) in the tournament.

Over the next two seasons Pérez continued to improve in Colorado, on the field and at the plate. He led the majors in at-bats and triples in 1999 and saw his batting average climb both of those seasons, reaching .287 in 2000. He won his lone Gold Glove that year, when he led all National League shortstops in assists, putouts, and double plays. His dWar (defensive wins above replacement) of 2.1 was third in the National League. The new century also marked arbitration for Pérez and his salary skyrocketed from $400,000 in 1999 to $3.5 million for the 2001 season. He had become one of the premier names in baseball.

The Rockies, however, remained mired in mediocrity. Pérez and his hefty new contract had become attractive trade bait,[13] and on July 25 he was included in a three-way trade that sent slugger Jermaine Dye to the Oakland A's while Pérez himself became a member of the Kansas City Royals. Pérez struggled adjusting at the plate in the new league and hit only .241 in 49 games played for the Royals. He also saw his team's fortunes fall; the Royals were even worse than the Rockies, finishing the year in last place at 65-97.

Pérez continued to participate in the winter leagues and perhaps it was this constant play that led to a decline at the plate in 2002. Or perhaps it was because Pérez aged two years overnight. Neifi was one of the players named in a minor scandal that offseason when it was revealed that a number of Dominicans had been lying about their ages. Increased scrutiny of birth documentation, a side effect of the terrorist attacks on September 11, revealed Pérez to be 28 instead of 26, as he had stated on his employment records.[14] Whatever the reason, he hit a paltry .236 and, perhaps most telling of his decline, only four triples in 145 games. The Royals lost 100 games that season, and with its conclusion, Pérez was put on waivers.

He was claimed by the San Francisco Giants, who a month later released him before signing him again on December 31. The move was a cost-cutting measure on their part as he signed for the bargain-basement price of $1.5 million, $2.5 million less than his salary the previous year with the Royals. With the Giants, Pérez saw his time more evenly split between shortstop and second base. He played in 120 games, filling in for regular shortstop Rich Aurilia and second baseman Ray Durham, who was twice on the disabled list that year, including missing almost the entire month of August.

The Giants also marked the first time in Pérez's major-league career that he was playing on a winner. The 2002 Giants were National League champions and Pérez came to camp in 2003 optimistic about being a part of a successful squad. The Giants did not disappoint, winning 100 games in 2003 (only one year after Pérez had lost 100 with the Royals). The Giants, with Barry Bonds at the ready, were heavily favored to beat the wild-card Florida Marlins in the Division Series. The Marlins shocked the baseball world by not only winning the pennant, but the World Series, defeating the New York Yankees in six games.

Pérez, relegated to his part-time role, made only four plate appearances in the postseason. He had one hit, a double to lead off the ninth inning of the fourth and final game of the Division Series. J.T. Snow knocked him in with a single, bringing the Giants to within one run of tying the game. After that, Marlins closer Ugueth Urbina slammed the door, ending the Series and the Giants' 2003 campaign.

When the Giants declined to sign Aurilia for the 2004 season, Pérez found himself once again elevated to being an everyday player as he took over starting shortstop duties. Things started well as he had a huge day at the plate on just the second day of the season, going 4-for-4 with two doubles and four RBIs, lifting the Giants to a 7-5 victory over the Houston Astros. The next three months, however, saw a steady and precipitous decline for Pérez. By mid-August he was hitting just .232. San Francisco was also floundering, 7½ games back and in third place. The Giants released Pérez on August 17 in order to bring up pitcher Kevin Correia from Triple A. In the words of Giants manager Felipe Alou, "(Pérez) showed up every day and didn't complain. ... We just felt we needed to add an arm."[15] Two days later, Pérez was signed by the Chicago Cubs.

Pérez began his tenure with Chicago in Iowa, playing for the Triple-A Cubs. His first visit to the minors since 1997 did not go well; he batted only .206 in 10 games. Chicago, chasing the resurgent Giants for the wild card, had a five-day layoff at the beginning of September when their series against the Marlins was postponed because of Hurricane Frances. When they returned to action on September 6, Pérez was on the roster, despite his poor minor-league showing. He made 67 plate appearances with the Cubs in that final month of the season and had one of the longest stretches of offensive excellence in his career, batting .371 during the pennant chase. Unfortunately for the Cubs, the Astros went 28-7 over their last 35 games, dashing Chicago's wild-card dreams.

When the 2005 season began, the Cubs were a team with an infield in flux, a fact that was exacerbated when star shortstop Nomar Garciaparra severely injured his groin in April. They attempted to address this issue by having Pérez bounce between playing shortstop and second base. By this point in his career, however, Pérez no longer had the infield versatility he once had. This became painfully obvious in a May 15 game against the Washington Nationals. In addition to an ugly 0-for-5 at the plate, Pérez had two errors in the same inning while playing second. Pérez tried to stay upbeat, stating, "It's the hardest day in baseball that you don't want to see, but you have to go through. ... But you have to forget about today and come back tomorrow."[16] The Cubs, for their part, seemed to have learned their lesson. While Pérez would fill in occasionally at second and third base over the remainder of the year, after that game he rarely played any position other than shortstop.

Pérez had such a successful season that when Garciaparra returned in early August, Cubs manager Dusty Baker lamented the loss of Pérez in the lineup. "I think he's proven he's more than just a utility guy. ... Am I supposed to bench Neifi now? This guy saved us."[17] Baker kept him in the lineup and Pérez responded, batting .299 over the last two months. The Cubs, however, had a terrible August, which all but eliminated them from postseason contention. While Pérez finished the year with his highest batting average since 2001, he went home at season's end still longing for a chance at playoff glory.

The Cubs' fortunes did not improve in 2006 and by midseason fans were screaming for Baker's ouster.[18] This was in no small part due to his dedication to Pérez. While Pérez was having another average season, the Cubs had a number of young players waiting in the wings. Fans were desperate for Baker to stop batting Pérez second in the lineup. Pérez not only had a substandard average for the lineup spot, but was also staying true to his career form and rarely collecting bases on balls. By mid-August, Pérez had a .266 on-base percentage.

On August 20 both Cubs fans and Pérez got their wish when he was traded from fifth-place Chicago to the first-place Detroit Tigers. The Tigers had lost their regular second baseman, Placido Polanco, to a shoulder injury and Detroit GM Dave Dombrowski traded minor-league catcher Chris Robinson for Pérez in the hopes that a steady veteran presence would help his team over the season's final weeks. Tigers manager Jim Leyland, who had managed Pérez with the Rockies in 2000, was excited about the new acquisition, stating, "He fits right in our mold. He's a wild-swinging son of a gun."[19] Pérez, who must have been looking forward to playing for a pennant contender, may have felt a little cursed. The Tigers, who had been in first place since May 16, had a miserable September, including losing their last five games. Detroit was 5½ games up when Pérez joined the team and after their loss on the final day of the season they only qualified for the wild card.

The Tigers rebounded in the postseason, making it to the World Series. Unfortunately for Pérez, Polanco was back in the lineup by the last week of September and Pérez spent most of the postseason watching from the bench. He made his first appearance, and his first-ever start in a playoff game, on October 11 in the American League Championship Series. Tigers first baseman Sean Casey injured his left calf in the first game of the ALCS[20] against the Oakland Athletics, and Leyland had to shuffle his infield, putting regular shortstop Carlos Guillen at first and plugging in Pérez to fill his vacated position. Pérez barely figured in the final result, an 8-5 Detroit victory in which he went 0-for-4 with a sacrifice hit. In the field he handled one chance and made one assist. His contribution to the 2006 American League pennant winners was effectively done that night. Pérez served as a late-inning replacement in Games One and Three of the World Series (the Tigers lost to the St. Louis Cardinals in five games), but he never came to bat in the postseason again in his career.

Although he had a guaranteed contract, 2007 was far from a sure thing for Pérez going into spring training. He ended up beating out Chris Shelton and Ramon Santiago for the final roster spot,[21] but his stay in Detroit, and the major leagues was almost complete.

Already mired in a miserable season, hitting just .172, Pérez on July 6 became the first player Peñalized for testing positive for a stimulant under Major League Baseball's new drug program. The program gave players a free pass when they failed the first test, only mandating counseling, which meant that Pérez's failed test was his second. He denied the allegations, stating, "I say to my fans that I am not stupid. I know the difference between good and bad and there are things to be known going forward, but my lawyer has advised me not to talk for now."[22]

Whatever defense he was going to provide went unheard when on August 3, while still serving his first suspension, Pérez failed his third test for stimulants and was handed an additional 80-game ban. The Peñalty would have extended beyond the 2007 season and leaked into 2008, but when Pérez was made a free agent at the end of the season, no team claimed him. Already an offensive liability, he was now also damaged goods. No player had ever been punished twice for violating the drug program and it spelled the end of Pérez's major-league career.

In 2008-09 Pérez once again returned to the Dominican Winter League, playing for his old team, Escogido. His championship days wreathed in Caribbean Series glory were over. He batted a meager .179 in 25 games that year and this time, when Aguilas represented the Dominican Republic in the tournament, Pérez was not asked to join them. He did have one more moment of glory when in 2012 he was named to the Caribbean Baseball Hall of Fame alongside his countryman Joaquín Andújar. He received the mandatory votes from a pool of 200 journalists, radio and TV broadcasters, and historians from Mexico, Puerto Rico, Venezuela, and the Dominican Republic. To celebrate the accomplishment, he was asked to throw out the first pitch of the Caribbean Series game between Mexico's Ciudad Obregon Yaquis and his beloved Leones, in Escogido's home ballpark before thousands of admiring hometown fans.[23] It was a crowning moment in a career that knew the ultimate pride of national victory and the ultimate shame of expulsion from the pinnacle of his sport.

NOTES

1 "Shortstop Turns Triple Play," *Santa Maria* (California) *Times*, May 11, 1994: B-3.

2 Cheryl Rosenberg, "Pérez Has Five RBI as Ravens Defeat Navigators, 9-4," *Hartford Courant*, July 13, 1995: C3.

3 "Rockies Future Shortstop Waits Patiently," *Casper* (Wyoming) *Star-Tribune*, June 30, 1996: D5.

4 "NL edges AL in AAA All-Star Game," *Bloomington* (Illinois) *Pantagraph*, July 11, 1996: B2.

5 Bruce Pascoe, "Shortstop for Rockies Is Status Quo," *Arizona Daily Star* (Tucson), February 22, 1997: C-5.

6 John Mossman, "The Future is Now: Pérez in Majors," *Casper Star-Tribune*, June 19, 1997: D1.

7 "Notes," *The Journal News* (White Plains, New York), July 29, 1997: 6D.

8 Kevin Clerici, "Pérez Ready for His New Role as Colorado's Starting Shortstop," *Arizona Daily Star*, February 23, 1998: C1.

9 "Domincan Roars Through Caribbean Series," *San Francisco Examiner*, February 10, 1998: B-7.

10 John Mossman, "Pérez Gets Rave Reviews," *Casper Star-Tribune*, February 24, 1998: D-1.

11 John Mossman, "Giant High Turns into Low," *Boston Globe*, September 28, 1998: D6.

12 Tracy Ringolsby, "Neifi Just Loves the Game," *Casper Star-Tribune*, February 9, 1999: D-1.

13 "Athletics Acquire Dye, Royals Get Pérez in Three-Team Deal," *Florida Today* (Cocoa, Florida), July 26, 2001: 2D.

14 Phil Rogers, "More Dominican-Born Players Admit Ages," *St. Louis Post-Dispatch*, March 3, 2002: D1.

15 "Giants Release Pérez," *Honolulu Star-Bulletin*, August 14, 2004: B7.

16 Howard Fendrich, "A Day to Forget for the Cubs," *Munster* (Indiana) *Times*, May 16, 2005: C3.

17 David Brown, "Garciaparra's Return Likely to Affect Pérez," *Northwest Herald* (Woodstock, Illinois), July 27, 2005: 5B.

18 David Haugh, "Blogosphere Therapy," *Chicago Tribune*, July 7, 2006: 4-7.

19 John Paul Morosi, "Trade With Cubs Brings Help at 2B," *Detroit Free Press*, August 21, 2006: D1.

20 "Rookies to Take Mound for Game 1," *Palm Beach West Post*, October 21, 2006: 9C.

21 "The Next Step," *Lansing* (Michigan) *State Journal*, April 1, 2007: 6C.

22 Larry Lage, "Tigers' Pérez Hit with 25-Game Suspension," *Daily Journal* (Vineland, New Jersey), July 7, 2007: C2.

23 Javier Maymi, "Francisco Liriano Lifts Escogido Leones," ESPN.com, February 5, 2012. espn.com/mlb/story/_/id/7544803/caribbean-series-francisco-liriano-andy-dirks-lift-dominican-republic-escogido-leones.

LUIS POLONIA

By John Struth

Luis Polonia, best known in his native Dominican Republic as the "atomic ant," had a nomadic career, playing for six teams in his 12 major-league seasons. He was a .293 career hitter, and played for four World Series teams, including the champion 1995 Atlanta Braves and 2000 New York Yankees.[1] He made a name for himself in Latin America, eventually being elected to the Caribbean Baseball Hall of Fame. His career was not without controversy both on and off the field. A visceral man, he could be happy one moment and testy or bitter the next. One thing he did not lack, however, was confidence.

Polonia was born on December 10, 1963, in Santiago, Dominican Republic. His father, Luciano, was a physician. Before Luciano went into medicine, he played "alongside Juan Marichal, Julian Javier and the Alou brothers. But Luciano Polonia is 5'4", and never got a chance to leave the Dominican Republic."[2] Luis had at least three siblings – Umberto, Francisco, and José.[3] In January 1984 Luis was signed as an amateur free agent by Juan Marichal, who was then scouting for the Oakland Athletics. He was discovered playing in the Dominican League, where he had distinguished himself at an early age.

Polonia began his professional career in 1984, playing with the Madison Muskies of the Class-A Midwest League. He batted .307, stole 55 bases, set the team mark with 10 triples, and scored 103 runs in 135 games played. He was a fan favorite in Madison, and was named the team's most valuable player by both the club and the fans.[4]

Polonia moved up to Huntsville, the A's Double-A affiliate, in 1985, and in 1986 played for Tacoma, their Triple-A team. He hit .289 for Huntsville and .301 for Tacoma. Beginning the 1987 season in Tacoma, Polonia was batting .321 after 14 games, with 18 runs scored, when he had sufficiently impressed the A's to be called up to Oakland after an on-field collision between Mike Davis and Dwayne Murphy sidelined Murphy.

Shortly after his call-up, Polonia hit his first major-league home run and first triple in a game against the Boston Red Sox on April 28. He was very excited about his first major-league home run. As for the triple, he said, "I was going for the triple, I hate doubles."[5]

Polonia continued to impress his teammates and manager Tony LaRussa into early June. Mike Davis said, "Some kind of way we have to keep Luis in this lineup. To me he's the igniter of our ball club right now."[6]

Photo by Focus on Sport/Getty Images

In August Polonia ended a prolonged slump with a double, triple, sacrifice fly, and three RBIs against the Seattle Mariners. Perhaps what ignited his turnaround was that before the game he got into a scuffle with teammate José Canseco. What began as a shouting match soon turned to a shoving match. Reggie Jackson and hitting coach Bob Watson stepped in between the two before the fight escalated. Polonia said, "Sometimes when you joke around with somebody, you take the joke. But if you don't feel good, you don't take it. ... I'm not afraid of nobody. I'm not going to hurt José, but I could find a lot of ways to do it. I'm not afraid."[7] Polonia ultimately acquitted himself well in his rookie campaign. He hit a solid .287, stole 27 bases, and scored 78 runs in 125 games played. The A's finished the season at .500 but had a nucleus of young players and veteran leadership that promised good things to come.

The 1988 campaign began with Polonia anticipating a full season with the A's. They had other plans and he was assigned to Tacoma. For a 24-year-old, with one partial year of big-league experience under his belt, he made waves by asking for a trade. "Right now, that's my wish. I'm tired of coming down to the minors every year and waiting for someone to get hurt," he said. "What should I expect? They signed three guys. Who got the worst part? Luis Polonia. I always get the worst part."[8]

He did eventually get a call-up and spent the second half of the season with the A's. What was apparent throughout the season was that Polonia did not fit into the A's plans as more than a fourth outfielder. And he was an outfielder with a liability: a poor fielder. In fact, after he cost the A's a game in the World Series with two misplays, the *Los Angeles Times* wrote of him: "The misadventures of Oakland's Luis Polonia in the outfield Tuesday night recalled this line from the Times staffer Mike Penner: 'He was best described last season by a teammate who provided a scouting report in the form of a Jeopardy question. A. Catch-22. Q. What do you get when you hit 100 fly balls to Luis Polonia?'"[9] Despite that sentiment, in 84 games and 288 at-bats, Polonia hit .292 scored 51 runs, and stole 24 bases. But between his complaining about going down to the minors and poor fielding, his stay with the A's was on shaky ground.

Polonia began the 1989 season with Oakland but was traded to the New York Yankees on June 21. He began his season slowly and by late April was hitting .214. By the time the trade was consummated, Polonia's average had risen to .286 in 59 games. He was traded, along with Eric Plunk and Greg Cadaret, for Rickey Henderson. Polonia was excited to be a Yankee, in part because of the large Dominican presence in the city. For the Yankees he batted .313 in 66 games.

One event in Milwaukee changed Polonia's fortunes with the team. On August 17 he was arrested and charged with sexually assaulting an underage girl. The next day Polonia pleaded no contest, avoiding a felony charge. He was freed and ordered to return for sentencing after the season. On October 2 Polonia was sentenced to 60 days and fined $1,500. He was also ordered "to make a $10,000 contribution to Sinai Samaritan Medical Center's sexual assault treatment center in Milwaukee."[10]

Polonia began 1990 as a Yankee. But he was on tenuous footing due largely to the Milwaukee incident. After only 11 games played he was traded on April 29 to the California Angels. "On the surface, it was merely an exchange of a hit man for a guy [Claudell Washington] with pop, a case of both the Yankees and Angels filling vital needs," a New York sportswriter wrote. "That's the obvious reason for the trade. The underlying implications are more intriguing. Polonia became persona non grata after he pleaded guilty to having sex with a minor. ... Polonia, on the other hand, never fit in. He was a lead off hitter, but the Yankees already had a good one in Steve Sax. And he was a defensive liability. Then the Milwaukee incident made him vulnerable."[11]

For Polonia the trade to the Angels was a boon: Through 1993 he was an everyday player. It probably helped that he and manager Doug Rader seemed to hit off. What he could not shake was the backlash that persisted from his sexual-assault conviction.

Two separate incidents, the first during the 1990 season and the second in 1991, illustrate Polonia's difficulties with fans. In July the *Los Angeles Times* reported, "The Alameda County district attorney will decide today whether claims by an 18-year-old spectator that he was struck by Angel outfielder Luis Polonia Thursday at the Oakland Coliseum warrant the filing of charges. ... Polonia allegedly slapped or pushed a fan after batting practice Thursday, when he heard the youngster shout insults. ... Polonia allegedly reached over the railing and made contact with the boy."[12]

In May the *Arkansas Gazette* (Little Rock) reported, "This season Polonia, a California Angels outfielder and Angel Manager Doug Rader got into a screaming match with [Jim] Northrup because Northrup called Polonia, 'Luis Lockup.' ... Polonia told Rader he was threatened and Rader attempted, unsuccessfully to have Northrup ejected. ... 'Luis Polonia was in a rage because I called him "Luis Lockup." Okay, now he was guilty. What kind of example is that?'" Northrup said.[13]

Not all was bad for Polonia, however. He quickly found a home with his new team, and on August 29 got a break that turned him from a platoon player to an everyday player. Against the Texas Rangers, with the score tied in the seventh inning. Jack Howell had reached second base and Texas manager Bobby Valentine had Dick Schofield intentionally walked. Rangers southpaw John Barfield was on the mound.

"Luis Polonia looked to his left, but no one stirred," wrote the *Los Angeles Times*. "... Polonia looked to his right. Still no one moved. He looked to his manager, Doug Rader, and Polonia heard the words he never thought he would hear."

Polonia reported that Rader told him, "Get ready to hit against the left-hander... Go out there," adding, "that was the best thing he could do for me."[14] Polonia singled in Howell. That opened the floodgates, and before the inning was over the Angels scored seven times.

Two weeks earlier Polonia had exacted some revenge on the Yankees, when he struck an inside-the-park grand slam against them on August 14. Reflecting on the game, he said, "I got my heart broken by the Yankees and A's. I get on fire every time I face them. I feel like I want to do so much. My heart is burning. ... It was the Yankees who got burned Tuesday night."[15]

Polonia finished the season batting .336 with the Angels. He played in 109 games. He also worked his way into everyday status moving into the new season. Polonia averaged 150 games played over the next three seasons. He averaged about 50 stolen bases a season and 80 runs scored. However, his batting averages dropped each season from .296 to .286 to .271. Entering free agency, Polonia signed with Yankees.

Polonia had always maintained that he wanted to return to New York. But by 1995 his role had changed and he found playing time diminished. Polonia and Yankees manager Buck Showalter did not see eye to eye.

Polonia batted a solid .311 in 95 games in 1994. He was a positive contributor to the Yankees' season. His teammates appreciated him and didn't mind poking fun at him either: "The Yankees hung a bat wrapped in tinfoil in their clubhouse yesterday to commemorate Luis Polonia's home run Tuesday night. They called it the Silver Slugger Award. It was Polonia's first home run in 650 at-bats."[16] The Yankees were in first place when the players strike ended the season in August. As he cleaned out his locker, Polonia said, "A weird day. ... I'm going to stay five, six days. Something might happen."[17] As the article added: "It didn't."

Right from the start of the 1995 season, Polonia and Showalter were at odds. This had carried over from the previous year when Polonia was benched four consecutive games against left-handed starters in July. Showalter was upfront with Polonia, telling him he would see limited playing time against southpaws. But Polonia didn't take that well. "I'm not happy. I know he's experimenting, but I don't like the idea. I don't like playing ball, hitting eighth or ninth. I think I did excellent last year. ... I was having fun. ... Imagine me hitting only against right-handers and hitting eighth."[18]

Polonia poked the wrong bear. With less playing time, he became more anxious. Not a recipe for success! In June he said, "I don't want to be traded but if it comes to the point where I'm the one who will be sitting, they should be reasonable and let me go somewhere where I can play."[19]

Reasonable the Yankees were, shipping Polonia off to Atlanta on August 11. The Braves acquired him to help the team in their stretch drive. Polonia played sparingly, getting in 28 games. In the playoffs and World Series, he contributed to the Braves championship run. In Game One of the Division Series between the Braves and Colorado Rockies, Polonia drove in David Justice on a slow roller that tied a tight ballgame in the sixth inning. A sacrifice by Polonia in Game One of the National League Championship Series with Cincinnati set up the winning run in the 11th inning. In the World Series against the Cleveland Indians, Polonia played the field in Games Three through Five, and was 4-for-14 with a home run and 4 RBIs.

With free agency looming, Polonia signed a nonguaranteed contract with the Seattle Mariners over the winter. He was released during spring training. On April 19 he signed with the Baltimore Orioles and was assigned to their Triple-A affiliate in Rochester. After 13 games he was called up to Baltimore.

Polonia's play did not impress the Orioles. On June 19 he made a baserunning blunder that seemed to seal his ultimate fate. Wrote the *Baltimore Sun*: "... (T)he biggest offender in this game of Stupid Oriole Tricks was Luis Polonia, who got picked off second while dustin' and adjustin' his uniform pants. ... 'He wasn't even looking at the pitcher or shortstop,' [manager] Davey Johnson said, "He was looking at the ground. Then the guy turned around. We're just not paying attention. That was just a vapor lock."[20]

The Orioles designated Polonia for assignment on August 2. In 58 games played, he had hit .240. On his way out the door, an obviously bitter Polonia took a parting shot. Buster Olney reported, "Polonia sharply criticized the way the Orioles play, saying that while they have the talent to win, they won't unless they approach the game more unselfishly." Olney went on, quoting Polonia, "People on the Orioles are always worrying about what other people do, criticizing, instead of just going out and playing the game right."[21]

"Players are critical? 'Players and coaches,' he said."[22]

Two weeks later, on August 17, Polonia again signed with the Braves. Perhaps they were hoping that he would repeat his previous success. During the remainder of the season he was used sparingly. In 31 at-bats he hit .419. He also didn't see much playing time in the postseason, going hitless in 10 at-bats and drawing a walk. But he was asked to contribute to the Braves in a unique way. "Polonia is the only Brave who has played for the Yankees, who has a feel for the dynamics of Yankee Stadium, who has some idea what it is like to play before the most rabid and volatile fans around. ... Polonia said the biggest topic of conversation would be the dimensions of the playing field."[23]

Perhaps it helped Atlanta. They won the first two games of the World Series, played in New York, before succumbing to the Yankees, four games to two.

When the season ended, Polonia had no contract. In March 1997 he signed with the Tampa Bay Devil Rays. They assigned him to the Mexico City Tigres. He hit .377 in 110 games, scored 105 runs, and stole 48 bases. That led to an invitation to spring training. However, Tampa Bay did not sign Polonia and he returned to Mexico City for the 1998 campaign. He had another stellar season, hitting .381.

On December 18, 1998, Polonia signed a minor-league contract with the Detroit Tigers. He was assigned to Toledo, their Triple-A affiliate, to start the season. After 42 games, he was called up. By mid-June Tigers manager Larry Parrish had said that Polonia had won the leadoff job. For Polonia, Detroit represented a triumph of perseverance. He said, "When you hang in there, God always gives you a chance. He gave me two bad years, maybe to see how I could take it. I always kept my faith."[24]

Used almost exclusively as a designated hitter, Polonia played in 87 games. He hit .324, and added some pop, hitting 21 doubles, 8 triples, and 10 home runs. His .526 slugging percentage was 100 points over any other season in his career. This earned him a return for the 2000 season.

Opening Day. Comerica Park. Luis Polonia, leading off for the Tigers, tripled. He then was singled in, scoring the first run in the ballpark's history. It could be argued that it was the highlight of his Detroit season in 2000. Though he continued to hit well, the Tigers were interested in seeing some of their younger prospects at the major-league level. As the trade deadline approached, they had another incentive to move on from Polonia. With just 52 more at-bats, he would be guaranteed a contract for 2001. Unable to trade him by the deadline, they released Polonia on July 31. In 80 games, he had hit .273.

Polonia didn't have to wait long before the Yankees came calling. He signed on for a third stint with them on August 3. Joe Torre said of the signing, "We're at a point now where we have to look at the little things that help you win a game here, there. ... I've always liked him as a hitter. He's got some speed. That makes up for problems he has defensively. And he works hard."[25]

In 37 games Polonia hit .286. His primary role was to spell David Justice in the field, allowing Justice to DH as the season wore along. Seeing limited play in the postseason, he did have one notable appearance in the World Series. In Game One his single helped the Yankees overcome a one-run deficit in the ninth inning. The Yankees went on to win the game in extra innings. They also went on to win the World Series, defeating the New York Mets. This was Polonia's swan song. After the Series he was made a free agent and never returned to the major leagues.

Polonia was not finished with baseball. He returned to play with the Mexico City Tigres for the 2001 and 2002 seasons. He also continued playing winter ball with the Dominican Republic. That led to continued appearances in the Caribbean Series, which the Dominican team won with regularity. In total Polonia made 14 appearances in that series. He also represented the Dominican Republic in the World Baseball Classic. In 2006, at age 42, he replaced an injured Vladimir Guerrero in the WBC.

Polonia also opened a baseball academy in the Dominican Republic. In 2016 he was named to the Caribbean Baseball Hall of Fame He finished his playing career in 2010.

Polonia had three children. One son, Rodney, was signed by the Pirates organization. His two other children went into careers as entertainers: Albert is a rap artist, Bianca an entertainer and singer. Luis also acted in the 2018 film *Jugando a' Bailar*. Surprisingly, he plays a baseball player.

Polonia ultimately had a long and fruitful career. He played in 1,379 games and batted .293. He played an important role on two pennant-winning teams, the 1988 A's and 1994 Yankees, who didn't play postseason baseball because of a labor dispute. He played in four World Series with the: A's, Braves (twice), and Yankees.

Perhaps he overvalued his own contributions. Certainly he felt he was an everyday player. With the exception of the California Angels, not one team he played for felt the same way. His strengths were that he could hit, he had speed, and from accounts, he was a good teammate.

His weaknesses were that he was a one-dimensional singles hitter. He was a poor baserunner, and while he stole 321 bases in the major leagues, he was thrown out 145 times, leading the league in that category three times. He was also a poor fielder. His career Wins Above Replacement score (WAR) stands at 9.0.

But Polonia really stands out for his tenacity. He never stopped believing in himself. It would have been easy to give up his dream after spending two years in Mexico City, but he picked himself up and refused to let his dream die away. Twice, in mid- and late career, he signed minor-league contracts, and then earned a spot on a major-league roster. So it can be said of him, he had a good career.

SOURCES

In addition to the sources cited in the Notes, the author also consulted:

Baseball-Reference.com/bullpen/Caribbean_Baseball_Hall_of_Fame#2011.

Baseball-Reference.com/players/p/polonlu01.shtml.

NOTES

1. Polonia also played in the 1988 World Series with the Oakland Athletics and in the 1996 Series with the Braves.

2. Robyn Norwood, "Polonia Aims to Give Angels a Quick Start," *Los Angeles Times*, March 3, 1992: 222.

3. Mark Kriegel, "Bronx Beams as Luis Makes Turn for Home," *New York Daily News*, April 4, 1994: 52.

4. "Polonia's First Season a Most Valuable One," *Wisconsin State Journal* (Madison), September 12, 1984: 23.

5. Frank Blackman, "Polonia Just Having Fun," *San Francisco Examiner*, April 29, 1987: 58.

6. Frank Blackman, "Polonia Has Made His Mark: A's Must Find Him a Spot," *San Francisco Examiner*, June 2, 1987: 53.

7. Frank Blackman, "Pugnacious Polonia Beats Up Mariners," *San Francisco Examiner*, August 11, 1987: 51, 55.

8. Frank Blackman, "Majors: Polonia Wants Trade," *San Francisco Examiner*, April 11, 1988: 56.

9. "Boston Masterpieces Hang in the Garden," *Los Angeles Times,* October 20, 1988: 183.

10. Michael Kay, "Luis Gets Sixty Days," *New York Daily News*, October 3, 1989: 68.

11. Phil Pepe, "Luis Swapped for Claudell," *New York Daily News*, April 30, 1990: 43.

12. Helene Elliott, "Bay Area District Attorney Mulls Charges Against Angels' Polonia," *Los Angeles Times*, July 27, 1990: 50.

13. Ken Boatmen, "Players See, Know Their Enemies," *Arkansas Gazette* (Little Rock), May 29, 1991: 42.

14. Helene Elliott, "Angels Let Polonia Hit, and Hit He Does," *Los Angeles Times*, August 30, 1990: 54.

15. Helene Elliott, "An Inside Job for Polonia," *Los Angeles Times*, August 15, 1990: 114, 118.

16. Jeff Bradley, "Flashes," *New York Daily News*, June 30, 1994: 78.

17. Jeff Bradley, "Short Year," *New York Daily News*, August 12, 1994: 23.

18. Jeff Bradley, "Buck Tinkering Peeves Polonia," *New York Daily News*, April 18, 1995: 44.

19. Tom Pedulla, "Ripken, Orioles Pound Yankees," *Journal News* (White Plains, New York), June 20, 1995: 25.

20. Ken Rosenthal, "It Might Be Difficult to Seek Shelter, When You're Not in the Storm," *Baltimore Sun*, June 20, 1996: 173.

21. Buster Olney, "Polonia, Heading Toward Exit, Takes a Shot," *Baltimore Sun*, August 3, 1996: 31.

22. Olney.

23. Curtis Bunn, "Polonia Spreading The News About Playing in New York," *Atlanta Constitution*, October 19, 1996: C11.

24. John Lowe, "Polonia's Arrival a Top Surprise," *Detroit Free Press*, June 10, 1999: 49.

25. Ronald Blum, "Yanks Re-Sign Luis Polonia," *Ithaca Journal*, August 4, 2000: 17.

Manny Ramírez

By Bill Nowlin

"Manny being Manny" – the simple phrase seemed to instinctively capture the essence of his baseball persona. He was one of the greatest right-handed hitters of the past 50 years. As of 2015, he ranked ninth all-time in career slugging percentage (.5854), has 555 major-league home runs (placing him number 14 – and he's got another 29 postseason home runs – more than any other player), and is number 32 in career on-base percentage (.4106). He won the American League batting crown in 2002 and was World Series MVP for the Boston Red Sox in 2004. He's a 12-time All-Star, with nine Silver Slugger awards, and he's third all-time in grand slams.

And yet his judgment was questionable. He was suspended for 50 games for testing positive for banned substances in 2009, and when he tested positive again in 2011, he retired rather than take the prescribed 100-game suspension.[1]

He's been called a hitting savant. And with his "fielding miscues, baggy uniforms, flowing dreadlocks, big hits, and tired anecdotes, the public is left with caricatures of Manny as a carefree goofball and spoiled superstar."[2] He earned over $200 million as a major leaguer. Yet biographers Rhodes and Boburg also write that, however inscrutable he may be, he "defines himself by what he is least known as—a dedicated athlete, a well-regarded teammate, and a beloved father, husband, and son."[3]

Ramírez was also beloved by fans entranced by his hitting and his charisma at the three main stops on his career route– Cleveland, Boston, and Los Angeles. Each time, he burned bridges behind him, leaving fans disappointed, or worse, though one wouldn't know that from the statistical record alone.

Named after his father (and a statesman of ancient Athens) as Manuel Aristides Ramírez, he was born on May 30, 1972, in Santo Domingo. His high school, though, was George Washington High School in New York City. An outfielder throughout his career, he was a first-round pick of the Cleveland Indians (the 13th pick overall) in the 1991 draft.

Manny moved to New York when he was 13. His mother, Onelcida, had worked a desk job at a dermatological institute in the Dominican Republic but in New York had to take a job as a seamstress in a sewing factory. Father Aristides had worked as an ambulance driver and then, after marriage, driving tank trucks. In New York he was a factory worker and sometimes in and out of work. Manny was the

Photo courtesy of the Boston Red Sox

only son in what seemed a matriarchal family, with his mother and his grandmother Pura; he had three older sisters. They moved into an apartment building in a Washington Heights neighborhood that was heavy with drug dealers and murders.[4] But Manny himself had started playing baseball at age 5, playing with the proverbial stick and bottlecap in the DR – and even announcing at 7 his ambition to play professionally. In New York he found Highbridge Park near the apartment and signed up for Little League under coach Carlos "Macaco" Ferreira. Bizarrely, Manny kept baseball separate from family and not even his sisters or mother knew he was ultimately named New York City Public High School Player of the Year, his sister Evelyn admitting, "When we found out that Manny was drafted, we had no idea. I mean, nobody knew about it. Somebody called us and told us to turn on the television ... the six o'clock news. We knew he loved to play baseball, but we had no idea."[5]

Manny was active in Brooklyn's Youth Service League ball from the age of 14, and played here and there in the various boroughs, not always letting school get in the way of baseball. He was often the first on the field and the last to leave. It is likely that school attendance being a prerequisite for sticking on the high-school team helped get him through school. He may also have been cut a little slack; "maybe that was when he began to realize that for a gifted athlete like him, the rules did not apply."[6]

Manny's lack of English-language skills left him unsure of himself in situations where conversation was called for, but his work ethic showed from an early age in punishing workouts, waking as early at 5 A.M. on a regular basis to get in his running – and quite often running up hills in the city, tugging a 20-pound tire behind him secured by a rope around his waist. Even years later, teammates on, say, the Boston Red Sox, mentioned that no one worked harder in the weight room and with training than Manny Ramírez. Under the baggy uniforms was a sculpted body that might have been featured in a fitness magazine; as a major leaguer, he was listed as an even 6 feet tall and 225 pounds.

Once on the Washington High team under coach Steve Mandl, Manny truly excelled. As early as age 17, he made the first of two trips to New Mexico with the Youth Service League to play in the Connie Mack World Series.[7] He hit for a .630 batting average in his junior year and was named to the All-City team. In his senior year, he surpassed that, batting .650. He was named New York City Player of the Year.

Needless to say, scouts began to pay attention – even if it meant making the trip into neighborhoods one could understatedly deem dodgy. Cleveland Indians scout Joe DeLucca followed Ramírez carefully, but also at a bit of a distance so the other scouts wouldn't see how interested he was. He wanted to make Manny a first-round pick, but there were 12 other teams picking first. Indians scout George Lauzerique told DeLucca, "No Latin-American immigrant kid has even been drafted in the first round," but that didn't faze DeLucca, who stuck to his guns.[8] The Indians selected Ramírez in the June 1991 draft, and signed him with a $250,000 bonus.

The Indians had Ramírez attend a two-week minicamp and then go to Burlington, North Carolina, for rookie ball in the Appalachian League. He did well – hitting .326 with 19 homers and more than one RBI a game – 63 RBIs in 59 games.

Ramírez's 1992 season was a tougher one. The Indians asked him to play winter ball in the Dominican Republic, but he quit after 15 days and returned to New York. Playing for the Kinston Indians, in the high Class-A Carolina League, he got off to a very slow start, but he started to hit in June and the beginning of July – when he broke the hamate bone in his left hand, costing him the rest of the season. He hit just .278 in 81 games.

In 1993 Ramírez was assigned to the Canton-Akron Indians (Double-A Eastern League), got into 89 games (.340, 17 HR, 79 RBIs) and got himself called up to Triple-A, to the Charlotte Knights (International League). He played in another 40 games and drove in 36 runs, with a .317 average – and also got himself called up to the major leagues, to Cleveland. He was later named *Baseball America*'s Minor League Player of the Year.

When he got the call, Ramírez asked Charlotte manager Charlie Manuel, "Can you come with me?"[9] The sentiment was emblematic of his attachment to certain mentors along the way. Needless to say, Manuel couldn't drop everything – he had the Knights on the way to the league pennant. Ramírez joined the Indians in Minneapolis on September 2 and was 0-for-4, though three of the balls were well-hit fly balls. The very next day, they played at Yankee Stadium, with lots of Manny's family and friends at the game. He hit a ground-rule double to left field his first time up, flied out in the fourth, hit a two-run homer to left in the sixth off Melido Pérez, and then hit another one – also to left – off Paul Gibson. Two homers, three RBIs, and a 7-3 Cleveland victory.

It was quite a splash but Ramírez struggled from that point on, getting only six more hits in 45 at-bats, with two more runs batted in and no more extra-base hits of any kind. With one exception, he DH'd, and pinch-hit in four games – and, perhaps a little oddly, pinch-ran in five. He ended the season, after appearing in 22 games, batting .170.

The Indians, once again, asked Ramírez to play winter ball. It was another fiasco; he even took one of the team buses and drove off, AWOL for the day. He wasn't welcomed back.[10]

The 1994 season ended with a players' strike. The Indians played 113 games, and Ramírez appeared in 91 of them. It was his official rookie year, and he came in second in Rookie of the Year voting, though compared to the rest of his stats, it was one of his least productive years. He did drive in 60 runs.

The Indians opened the 1995 season in Texas. The team went on to Detroit, and after they left, there was a typical Manny moment – he'd left his paycheck in a boot underneath his locker. It had to be shipped onward to him. Ramírez himself hit 11 homers in just the month of May. (He was named AL Player of the Month.) He made the All-Star team for the first time, drove in 107 runs (helped by 31 homers), and helped the Indians reach the World Series. He hit only .222 in the Series itself (with a .364 on-base percentage), with one homer, but there was only one Indian who hit higher – Albert Belle with .235. The Cleveland offense was clearly lacking – 19 runs in six games, losing to the Atlanta Braves.

Ramírez's early career was replete with a number of fielding and baserunning lapses. He was cut slack, of course, given his hitting – in 1996 he drove in 112 runs, with 33 homers. He hit for a higher average in 1997 (.328) but his RBIs declined to 88. Matt Williams, Jim Thome, and David Justice each drove in just over 100. The Indians made the postseason again, and went all the way to the World Series once more, playing the Florida Marlins. At one point or another, the Indians held a lead in each of the seven games, but in the end they lost four. Ramírez contributed some key hits in the first couple of rounds, but was 4-for-26 (.154) in the World Series. Average alone was deceptive; he drove in six runs in the seven games.

Occasional lapses aside, Ramírez had a strong and accurate arm. Twice he led the AL in assists from his position: 1996 as a rightfielder, with 19, and in 2005 as a left-fielder, with 17.

There was a time when Manny paid an unannounced visit to his old high school, and wandered into the gym where coach Steve Mandl was talking to the baseball team. Asked if he wanted to say anything to the team about hitting, Manny said, as simply as possible, "See the ball. Hit the ball."[11]

With 45 homers and 145 RBIs in 1998, Ramírez had an exceptionally productive season, despite a batting average six points under .300. At one point in September, he homered in four at-bats in a row and eight times in a five-game stretch. It was the second year he made the All-Star team, and the first year in what became a string of 11 consecutive annual All-Star selections. The Indians beat Boston in the ALDS but lost to the Yankees in the ALCS. Ramírez hit two homers in each round, batting .357 and .333 respectively.

There were thoughts, though, that Ramírez's fielding may have cost the Indians the chance to get to another World Series. It was Game Six, at Yankee Stadium, and the Indians had just scored five runs in the top of the fifth to pull to within a run of New York. (Thome hit a grand slam, but Ramírez had struck out with the bases loaded.) In the bottom of the sixth, Derek Jeter tripled to right field to drive in two big insurance runs – but the ball was a catchable one. A *New York Times* article was headlined: "Ramírez: Big Bat, Blunders." Ramírez had leapt to catch the ball, only to have it land at his feet. He wasn't charged with an error, but he had clearly erred in anticipating the ball's trajectory.

Ramírez drove in 20 more runs (to a total of 165, tied for 14th all-time for single-season RBIs) in 1999. He hit .333 (with a .442 on-base percentage) and scored 131 runs. He homered 44 times. For the fifth year in a row, the Indians made the postseason, but this time lost to the Red Sox in the Division Series. Ramírez got just one base hit in 18 at-bats (.056), but he did draw four bases on balls and scored all five times he got on base. Ramírez placed third in the MVP voting, the highest he ever ranked. (It was a ranking he tied in 2004.)

The year 2000 was Manny's contract year in Cleveland and he got off to a great start, but he was on the disabled list with a serious hamstring injury from May 29 to July 13, missing 39 games. Despite missing a quarter of the season, he still had 122 RBIs and 38 homers. He hit .351 and led the league in slugging (.697) and OPS (1.154). There was no doubt Ramírez was due for a big contract.

Red Sox GM Dan Duquette won the bidding war. Ramírez was a huge fan favorite in Cleveland and the Indians kept upping their offer, but he signed with the Red Sox for a reported $160 million/eight-year deal.[12] Manny had one final condition before signing: that the Red Sox hire Cleveland clubhouse man Frank Mancini, to accompany him to Boston.[13] It was reminiscent of him wanting Charlie Manuel to come with him from Charlotte. It also didn't happen.

Some wondered if Ramírez could handle the intensity of the Boston market. Rhodes and Boburg quoted Macaco as saying that "Manny's lack of anonymity at shopping malls was one of his primary dissatisfactions with life in Boston." Bizarre as that may seem, "Manny always wants to go to shopping malls. Sometimes we'll go two or three times a day." And it wasn't necessarily to buy anything.[14] He just liked going to malls, but quite naturally didn't want to be relentlessly fawned over and followed by fans.

Ramírez was the Red Sox DH into June, when he began to play left field. In late August he reverted to DH. (He was DH for 87 games and left fielder for 55.) He had a career high in strikeouts, with 147, but still achieved a .405 on-base percentage (hitting .306), and drove in 125 runs, 37 more than anyone else on the Red Sox. He had 41 homers, 14 more than Trot Nixon's second-place 27.

Ramírez lost more than a full month in 2002 due to a broken left index finger, fractured on a head-first slide into home plate on May 11 (he was out), and not returning until June 25. In 120 games, he drove in 107 runs, with 33 homers. His .349 average (.450 OBP) won the American League batting title.

It was back to the playoffs in 2003, the first full year under new ownership. Ramírez played in a career-high 154 games, and led the league in on-base percentage (.427). He hit .325, just one point behind the AL batting champion, teammate Bill Mueller. He hit 37 homers, drove in 104 runs (one behind teammate Nomar Garciaparra), and scored 117 runs. Too often, there seemed to be a discordant note. In late August the Yankees came to Boston for what was really a key series. Manny was excused from the game due to throat inflammation – but was discovered in the Ritz-Carlton bar with Enrique Wilson of the Yankees, which didn't go over well with the Red Sox fan base. Neither Ramírez nor David Ortiz hit that well in the Division Series, but the team pulled through and Manny's three-run homer in Game Five made all the difference in the 4-3 win.

Ramírez homered twice and drove in four runs in the ALCS against the Yankees, a series that went to seven games and seemed to be in Boston's hands until manager Grady Little (who'd been the bench coach on the Indians in Manny's last years there) put Pedro Martínez back into the game when he seemed so obviously out of gas. The Yankees rallied and tied the game, then won it on Aaron Boone's home run leading off the bottom of the 11th. Little was fired, and Terry Francona hired as manager for 2004.

Ramírez had more than once expressed a wish to get out of Boston. At the end of October the Red Sox placed him on waivers – they could have called him back if any team had claimed him, but none did. There was, after all, close to $100 million remaining on his contract. Perhaps the Red Sox did it just to make a point with Manny about what a good deal he had – so good no other team was willing to pay the freight to get him.

There was also discussion about trading Ramírez, as part of two trades that would have brought Alex Rodriguez from the Rangers for Manny and Jon Lester, and sent Garciaparra to the White Sox for Magglio Ordonez. A-Rod wanted to come to Boston and was willing to take a $25 million pay cut to do so, but the Players Association refused to sign off on such a hefty cut.

Early in 2004 Ramírez became an American citizen and, when he took his position before the game on May 11, he ran out to left field carrying a miniature American flag. He then handed it off to a spectator. He later joked, "Now they can't kick me out of the country." Before his first at-bat, the team played the song "Proud to Be an American" on the sound system.[15]

317

Manny Ramírez was World Series MVP in 2004, the Red Sox this time rolling over Anaheim in the Division Series (he had seven RBIs in three games) and then losing the first three games of the ALCS to the Yankees, only to come back and win an unprecedented final four in a row. Oddly, Ramírez didn't have even one RBI in the ALCS, though he hit .300 and scored three times.

Facing the St. Louis Cardinals in the World Series, Ramírez looked like a stumblebum in left field, committing two errors in Game One. He overran a ball in the top of the eighth, allowing one run to score, and then made an awkward slide to try to catch a ball on the very next play, letting it get past him as another run – the tying run – scored, costing the Red Sox the lead. He was 3-for-5 in the game with two RBIs.

In Game Three, he homered in the first inning and drove in another run later in the game, a 4-1 Red Sox win. Derek Lowe shut out St. Louis in Game Four and the Red Sox swept the Series. It was their first World Series win in 86 years. Any number of Red Sox players might have been voted MVP, but Ramírez (1-for-4 in Game Four, without either an RBI or run scored) got the nod, perhaps in recognition of his having had at least one base hit in every one of the 14 playoff games in which the Red Sox had played.

The Ramírez work ethic was noted earlier. Billy Broadbent, the Red Sox video coordinator, said Manny put in as much time with video as any other player or more, and he added a few twists to his study. Preparing for whomever he might face, if it was a pitcher against whom he'd not previously batted, he'd call up at at-bats of another right-handed slugger, like Miguel Tejada, and look to see how the pitcher had worked Tejada. "It's something he came up with all on his own," said Broadbent. "It's nothing we suggested. He came up to these determinations on his own. He was one of the hardest workers that you'd ever want to see."[16]

Ramírez may have seemed oblivious at times, or just downright goofy, but there were perhaps two unexpected aspects to the approach he took to hitting. First of all, the way he slipped into a kind of zen mode helped to create an almost preternatural focus, slowing down time and allowing all that he had learned to be brought to the fore. He could tune out distractions. Simply put, in the words of Jim Thome, "He's good at not letting things get to him."[17] He was perhaps like the "absent-minded professor, whose mind is so specialized and consumed by his craft that he is as helpless as a lamb outside the lab."[18] There was also craftiness in the way he would try to set up pitchers. Allard Baird reportedly told columnist Joe Posnanski that he believed "Manny will swing and miss at a pitch in April so that the pitcher will throw him the same pitch in September."[19] Alex Rodriguez told the *New York Times*, "When it comes to his craft, his art, his skill, he's as smart as anyone in the American League. And he takes it as seriously as anyone in the game."[20] If he was a savant, he was a studious savant. That doesn't mean he wasn't also a little flaky and a little naïve.

Ramírez never once hit over .300 in 2005, and was as low as .224 more than a quarter of the way through the season (on May 27, after game number 47). One month later, on June 26, he was leading the American League in RBIs (with 66) and he finished the season with career highs in homers (45, matching his 1998 season in Cleveland) and drove in 144 runs, just four behind the league leader, David Ortiz. This was the season when Manny stepped inside the Green Monster during a conference on the mound and didn't come out until after the first pitch after play resumed. He was also marching to his own drummer, when he insisted on taking a scheduled day off despite teammate Trot Nixon having suffered an oblique strain in late July. There was tension in the Red Sox clubhouse, which had a player apparently unwilling to set his personal wishes aside to help out his team in a pennant race. There was a stronger sense of him quitting on the team in 2006, when he reported himself unable to play because of patellar tendinitis and he missed 22 games from late August into September. He still drove in 102 runs but the Red Sox failed to make the postseason (they'd gotten into the ALDS in 2005, but were swept in three games, Ramírez hitting .300).

In 2007 the Red Sox won the World Series again. Ramírez started slow, got hot for a stretch, and then suffered his own oblique strain. His power numbers were down on the year, with only 20 homers and 88 RBIs (the first time he'd been below 100 in a decade, since 1997), but come the playoffs, he contributed. In Game Two of the Division Series, when Angels manager Mike Scioscia had Ortiz walked to get to Ramírez with two outs in the bottom of the ninth, it may have triggered something in Ramírez – he hit a walkoff three-run homer. His fourth-inning homer in Game Three was literally the game-winner, giving Boston a 2-1 edge in a game they won, 9-1.

In the 2007 ALCS, Ramírez was facing his former team, the Indians. He drove in 10 runs, with two more homers and a .409 average. The Red Sox swept the Rockies in the World Series; he hit .250 and drove in two runs, but all in all, he was .348 with 16 RBIs in the 14 postseason games.

The last guaranteed year of Ramírez's Red Sox contract was 2008. It was the year he joined the 500-HR club, homering off Chad Bradford in Baltimore on May 31. June was a tough month for Manny's reputation in Boston. First he got into a fight with Kevin Youkilis in the Red Sox dugout during a game. Then, on June 28, he got in an argument over complimentary tickets with traveling secretary Jack McCormick and shoved the 64-year-old man to the ground.[21] There were a couple of game-play situations where Ramírez seemed not to be giving his all. There were thoughts he was provoking the team into trading him. On July 31, at the trading deadline, two deals were done: Ramírez's contract was transferred to the Los Angeles Dodgers, who agreed to pick up the money remaining on his contract (the Red Sox freed him from the two option years), and Boston acquired left fielder Jason Bay from Pittsburgh to take his place.

If he'd been dogging it, it wasn't entirely self-evident; Ramírez had hit .347 during July. But he'd worn out his welcome in Boston. Once he hit Los Angeles, he became an instant sensation and he reveled in the "Mannywood" moniker given him. In 53 games, he drove in 53 runs, and he hit for a .396 average. The Dodgers won the NLDS (Manny hit .500 with two homers), but lost the NLCS in five games (Manny hit two more homers and drove in seven runs, batting .533).

Come 2009, however, Manny's hitting came back to earth – he was 37 years old, and hit .290 in 104 games, with 63 RBIs. He likely would have played more games, but he tested positive for a banned substance and was suspended for 50 games during the season, from May 7 through July 2.[22]

In 2010 Ramírez got off to a good start with the Dodgers, and was batting .322 through the end of June. But he played in only two games in July and, after a month, returned to play in five late-August games. The Dodgers placed him on waivers and he was selected by the Chicago White Sox on August 30. For the White Sox, he played in 24 September games but hit for only a .261 average, with just one home run and only two RBIs in 24 games. The White Sox chose not to try to re-sign him. At the end of January the Tampa Bay Rays signed Ramírez on perhaps something of a flyer but he again tested positive for a performance-enhancing drug and thus faced a 100-game suspension. He played in five games (batting .059) but then announced his retirement.[23]

After the 2011 season was over, however, Ramírez struck a deal under which he would accept a 50-game suspension and be permitted to return. He signed with the Oakland Athletics for 2012. He played in 17 games, batting .302 without a home run, for Oakland's Triple-A club in Sacramento, but never played for Oakland itself. The Athletics released him in June.

Ramírez played in Taiwan for the EDA Rhinos, but left at the midpoint of the season. His agent, Barry Praver, said, "The reason he decided not to return for the second half was to free himself to be available to play in the United States. This whole thing with Manny in Taiwan was a phenomenon. He invigorated the league. Attendance went through the roof. It was a very positive experience for both sides."[24]

The Texas Rangers signed Ramírez to a minor-league deal in July 2013, but six weeks later, after he hit .259 for Triple-A Round Rock in 30 games, they released him.

Near the end of May 2014, Ramírez signed with the Chicago Cubs and he was again asked to play in Triple-A, this time for the Iowa Cubs as a player/coach. He claimed he was a new man, that he and his wife, Juliana, had been in church for almost four years. "Now, I realize that I behaved bad in Boston," he said. The *Boston Globe*'s Christopher L. Gasper wrote, "Manny being Manny means something entirely different now if you are to believe Ramírez, who will turn 42 on Friday. Chastened by time, the diminishing of his skills, and his newfound faith, he has finally found a manager he likes – God."[25] Of course, time will tell. The Cubs' president of baseball operations, Theo Epstein, hoped he would become a mentor for Cubs prospects. He played in 24 games and hit .222 with three home runs.

NOTES

1. The 2009 drug was human chorionic gonadotropin, a fertility drug for women. See *New York Times*, May 10, 2009.
2. The best source for much more information about Manny Ramírez and the primary source for this biography is Jean Rhodes and Shawn Boburg, *Becoming Manny: Inside the Life of Baseball's Most Enigmatic Slugger* (New York: Scribner, 2009). The quotation noted here is from page 3.
3. Rhodes and Boburg, 5.
4. The "Ramírez family settled in one of New York City's most dangerous and drug-infested neighborhoods (between 1987 and 1991 there were 462 homicides, 58 percent of them drug-related, in Washington Heights' police precinct)." Rhodes and Boburg, 49.
5. Rhodes and Boburg, 9, 10.
6. Sara Rimer, *New York Times*, April 26, 2011. Rimer's lengthy profile of Ramírez, someone she had met and observed since his high school years is recommended to readers.
7. Rhodes and Boburg, 84, 85, 96.
8. Rhodes and Boburg, 111, 118.
9. Rhodes and Boburg, 147.
10. Rhodes and Boburg, 152, 153.
11. Rimer, *New York Times*.
12. *New York Times*, December 12, 2000.
13. Rhodes and Boburg, 193.
14. Rhodes and Boburg, 128, 143.
15. *Boston Globe*, May 12, 2004.
16. Author interview with Billy Broadbent on June 28, 2013.
17. *New York Times*, July 22, 1999.
18. Rhodes and Boburg, 290.
19. Rhodes and Boburg, 292.
20. *New York Times*, April 17, 2008.
21. It wasn't the first time Ramírez had struck a team employee. In 1998 he slapped Cleveland clubhouse assistant Tom Foster. See *New York Times*, March 30, 1998.
22. For a full report on the suspension, see the May 8, 2009, *New York Times*.
23. *New York Times*, April 9, 2011.
24. "Manny Ramírez Leaving Taiwan," ESPN.com, June 19, 2013. espn.go.com/mlb/story/_/id/9403816/manny-Ramirez-parts-ways-eda-rhinos-taiwan-league. Posted June 20, 2013.
25. *Boston Globe*, May 29, 2014.

RAFAEL RAMÍREZ

By Josh Sullivan

In March 1993 Rafael Ramírez was trying to secure a bench spot on the rebuilding Oakland Athletics. He was among the first cuts, nursing a sore arm and having been outplayed by another veteran, Dale Sveum.[1] The 35-year-old shortstop's career was effectively over. He spent 13 big-league seasons fielding grounders on two of the most inhospitable surfaces in the major leagues, the rocky terrain of Atlanta's Fulton County Stadium and the concrete-like turf of the Houston Astrodome. Both surfaces were different in their makeup, but they were similar in their mistreatment of infielders. In Atlanta, bad hops ricocheted off small pebbles and rocks, while in Houston, seams turned otherwise fieldable groundouts into errant singles. Yet Ramírez was undaunted in his service at the position, even through the constant scrutiny and criticism he faced. He was error-prone, but that rarely kept him out of the lineup. What kept him penciled in was his ability at the plate and his desire to do better every night.

Rafael Emilio Ramírez Peguero was born in San Pedro de Macorís, Dominican Republic, in 1958. He came from a well-to-do family and graduated from Liceo Gaston Fernando Deligne high school in 1977.[2] What his homeland lacked monetarily it made up for in shortstops and was known as "La Tierra de los Torpederos"[3] or land of the shortstops. Ramírez was one of many youths who escaped the poverty-stricken region for the diamonds of the United States during the 1970s and '80s. However, Ramírez was not a shortstop at first.

After signing with the Braves as an undrafted free agent in 1976, Ramírez played the outfield for several games with Bradenton of the rookie Gulf Coast League. Skipper Pedro Gonzalez, the man responsible for signing the outfielder, made a move that would forever change the youngster's career. The Braves had languished in last place for most of the 1970s after a 1969 season that saw them appear in the first-ever National League Championship Series. One of the gaping holes in the Braves' lineup was at shortstop. Several players, including Sonny Jackson and Pepe Frias, had tried to nail down the position. With maverick new owner Ted Turner at the helm, the expectations were high that the team was going to win ... and soon. If it was to do so, a new shortstop was in order.

It was apparent early on that the transition would be a difficult one. Even at his normal position, Ramírez made three errors in 11 games before his move to the infield. After being moved to shortstop, he made 29 errors in 30 games. At the plate, he didn't fare much better, batting a paltry .177. Still, he was only 19 years old. In 1978 Ramírez split time between Class-A Greenwood and Double-A Savannah, where the errors continued. The shortstop spent all of 1979 at Savannah, and though his batting average plummeted to .207, just above the Mendoza line, his fielding continued to improve. As the 1970s closed, a major-league opportunity seemed to be on the horizon for the budding shortstop.

In 1980 the Braves entered spring training with high hopes. Ted Turner had promised to bring a winner to Atlanta. "I don't want to see any more headlines calling Atlanta 'Loserville, USA,'" he announced.[4] The club featured young sluggers Dale Murphy and Bob Horner, with veteran knuckleballer Phil Niekro anchoring the rotation. To add playoff experience, the team acquired first baseman Chris Chambliss from Toronto along with slick-fielding shortstop Luis Gomez. Though there were other challengers for the position, Gomez proved to be Ramírez's greatest obstacle. The prospect was the last cut of the spring.[5] Skipper Bobby Cox's choice was difficult, but he knew that Atlanta needed a steady anchor for a position that for a decade had been a problem to fill.

By August the manager's patience had waned, and the time had come to bring up Ramírez.[6] Gomez was fielding well, but his offense was lagging. The heir-apparent was batting .281 with five homers at Richmond. The incumbent, though not pleased to be benched, saw the writing on the wall. Said Gomez, "When I came to the Braves, I was really excited because I saw no shortstop in the organization ready to play. Then I saw Raffy in the spring, and I knew immediately that he was going to be the man for the future. You can't mistake talent. I realize my role will be as a utilityman in the future." Losing his job to a "macorisano" was nothing new

Photo courtesy of the National Baseball Hall of Fame

to Gomez. Several years before, he had lost his starting job in Toronto to another native of San Pedro de Macoris, the newly acquired Alfredo Griffin; Griffin went on to win the Rookie of the Year Award.[7]

On August 4, 1980, Ramírez debuted as a pinch-runner late in a game at home versus Los Angeles. The next day he started at shortstop and went hitless in three at-bats, though he and Glenn Hubbard combined for a double play, the first of many to come for one of the most underrated double-play combos of the time. In that game, Ramírez also made his first error, on a grounder off the bat of Ron Cey. On August 6 Ramírez's fielding woes caused controversy. With one out in the top of the ninth, Dodgers Bill Russell and Dusty Baker hit back-to-back singles. Steve Garvey then hit a grounder to second. Hubbard fielded the ball and relayed it to Ramírez covering the bag. The rookie failed to touch the base before relaying to first. Garvey was called out at first, but second-base umpire Jerry Dale called Baker safe at second. This incensed Bobby Cox, who charged Dale to argue the runner was out. During the argument, tobacco juice made its way from the manager's mouth to the umpire's left eye. Dale claimed Cox spit on him; the manager had no comment. Regardless, Baker was still safe and no error was charged to Ramírez; the Braves lost 6-2. Of the misplay, Dale commented, "Ramírez must have thought he was still in the International League where they have two umpires and you don't have to hit the bag. We have four umpires and you have to hit the bag."[8] On August 9 Ramírez picked up his first hit, an RBI single off Bob Knepper in the second, the first of his four hits in the game. Little did Ramírez and the Braves know that their savior at shortstop had been found, though it would not be an easy ride.

Ramirez batted .267 in 1980 as the Braves improved over the final weeks of the season.[9] He made 11 errors in 46 games and helped turn 25 double plays. Things were looking up in Atlanta. However, a strike-shortened 1981 season dashed the hopes for the club. Ramírez struggled both in the field and at the plate. His batting average dipped to .218, and he led the league with 30 errors. After a dismal season, Cox was fired and, under new skipper Joe Torre, Ramírez's job seemed in jeopardy.[10] But Torre brought with him a can-do attitude and a whole new set of coaches. One of them was Dal Maxvill, a former infielder with plenty to teach the young shortstop.[11] Ramírez would need his help if he was going to remain in the big leagues.

Perhaps unsurprisingly, following the 1981 quagmire of a season, the Braves seemed ready to return to the drawing board once again at short. The team explored the option of signing veteran Mark Belanger. As well, Joe Torre pointed to backup Jerry Royster as a possible option should Ramírez struggle. "Ramírez is our shortstop, but if Royster were to have a good spring and look like the better player for the job, then naturally he'd win the position," said Torre.[12] Ultimately the club stuck with the incumbent. General manager John Mullen announced, "Shortstop is no longer a priority." However, an endorsement from Ted Turner helped even more. "We all like him. ... Everybody says he's going to be a great player," chimed in the owner.[13]

Maxvill, a 14-year big leaguer, quickly noticed a few things about his new pupil. "He had all the skills. He had a great arm, great hands, good range, very good temperament. The only things he lacked was experience and experience under pressure, and he's getting that now," the coach said.[14] His tutelage of Ramírez paid big dividends in 1982. Though he led the league with 38 errors, Ramírez led NL shortstops in putouts (300) and in double plays (130). His batting average also returned from the grave, rising 60 points to .278. The youngster's play in the field began to draw comparisons to that of perennial All-Star Dave Concepción of Cincinnati.[15] With comparisons like that, the pressure Maxvill mentioned was coming at Ramírez like a screaming line drive.

The Braves got off to a quick start in 1982. Ted Turner had dubbed the club "America's Team"[16] before the season and predicted the team would finish first in the West.[17] Taking their boss's prediction seriously, the team won a record 13 games in a row to start the season. Ramírez batted .333 with a homer and nine RBIs over the stretch and made only two errors while assisting in 11 double plays. Shockwaves moved throughout the National League regarding the upstart Braves. Commenting on the ever-growing crowds at Atlanta-Fulton County Stadium, Bob Horner quipped, "Usually, when there's excitement in a game we played, it was the other team doing something special."[18] Torre commented of the team's reversal of fortune from the previous season's misery, "They're the same faces, but not the same players. I think that the time comes when, with experience, some guys begin to reach their potential. I think that's what is happening here."[19] Still, the skipper kept it all in perspective, remarking, "Baseball is a long season. What I'm trying to do is keep the idea of a streak down with the players and keep the idea of playing good baseball up."[20] The Braves would need to follow that sage advice if they were to survive the season and take the division, for they soon learned that the baseball gods giveth and they taketh away.

After the win streak, the Braves suffered five straight losses and began a roller-coaster ride that saw them in first for most of the season. By July 29 "America's Team" was standing high atop the division, nine games ahead of second-place San Diego. Ramírez was batting .267 and he and Glenn Hubbard led the league in double plays. "Last year I tried too hard," said Ramírez. "Now I'm more comfortable. This is a good team. We'll go easy to the World Series if we keep playing like we've been playing."[21] But on July 30, the bottom began to fall out.

From July 30 to August 18 the team went 2-19, including an 11-game losing streak, and fell from first place. Ramírez batted .205 over 19 games of that 21-game drubbing. Now the Braves were four games behind Los Angeles. Suddenly, the media began to change its tune. "Are Torre's Braves Folding Their Tent?" read a headline in the *New York Times*.[22] Sportswriter Mike Davis was even crueler:"That's right – alert the paramedics. Fire up the respirator. Get this team some oxygen! The Braves are swallowing harder than a high school freshman on his first date. They've had their tickets punched – one way to Gag City. It's chokin' time in Georgia." Davis took a shot at Ramírez. "Their lineup does include some legitimate young talent, like Murphy and Horner and Glenn Hubbard. But it also includes people named Rafael Ramírez and Rufino Linares."[23] It was getting ugly.

However, all was not lost. The Braves reeled off six straight victories after the miserable run and found themselves in a tie for first. They battled the Dodgers the rest of the season, finally clinching the division on the last day, thanks to a Dodgers loss at San Francisco. For his part, Ramírez hit .333 with six homers following the 2-19 slide. Though criticism would accompany the shortstop throughout his career, early on the protestations had little effect on Ramírez for one simple reason: language. Early in 1982 the Dominican quipped, "I see the newspapers last year, but not understand everything."[24] There were few complaints now; the Braves were in the playoffs.

The NLCS opponent for Atlanta was the St. Louis Cardinals. The experts were quick to point out the superiority of St. Louis shortstop Ozzie Smith over Ramírez. The Braves shortstop had only eight errors fewer than the entire Cardinal infield. Smith's fielding percentage was .984 vs. Ramírez's .956. Though Smith may have been the superior fielder, Ramírez led at the plate. For the season, he hit outhit Smith .278 to .248 and had eight more home runs (10 vs. 2). For the September playoff run, Ramírez turned up the production by batting .324; Smith managed only a .152 average in 46 at-bats. But the postseason is the start of a new season; everyone begins anew.

In Game One, the Cardinals' Bob Forsch held the Braves to three hits in a 7-0 win. Ramírez was hitless. The Braves picked up their first runs of the series in Game Two, on Ramírez's single that turned into a "home run." With two out and Bruce Benedict on second, the shortstop singled up the middle. The hit easily scored the runner from second.

The ball rolled under center fielder Willie McGee's glove to the wall, allowing Ramírez to motor around the bases on what was ruled a three-base error.[25] But the Cardinals came from behind to beat the Braves 4-3. In Game Three, the Cardinals scored four times in the second and never looked back. Ramírez led off the game with a single, but that was his only hit in three at-bats. In the field he made his only error of the series. The Braves lost, 6-2. Atlanta's magical season had come to an end but had most certainly proved to be something to build upon.

In 1983 the Braves spent 83 days in first place, but where you are on the last day of the season is what counts. At the finish line on October 2 Atlanta was in second place, three games behind the Dodgers. It was a disappointing finish. But Ramírez's star rose to new heights. He flirted with .300 and finished the season batting .297. Ramírez also finished 16th in the MVP voting (Ozzie Smith finished 21st); the winner was fellow Brave Dale Murphy. Once again, Ramírez led the league in errors with 39, but he led National League shortstops with 116 double plays. The Ramírez/Hubbard tandem had formed a smooth double-play combination that closed up the once porous Atlanta middle infield. Joe Torre mused, "Mentally these two are quite a bit alike. They want to be in the lineup every day. You try to give them a night off once in a while and they'll invent reasons why they should be playing. You hear people say that this player gives 110 percent. I'm not sure I know what that means, except that nobody on the Braves plays harder than these guys."[26] Hubbard said, "It means a lot to me to lead the league in double plays, because last year they didn't even rank us in the top 20." Commenting on his tag-team partner, Hubbard added, "I said all along that, once Rafael got comfortable, he'd do a great job and I think that day's coming."[27]

The 1984 season brought yet another bit of luster to Ramírez's star. The shortstop was selected as a backup on the National League All-Star team. He was the first Braves shortstop to be selected since Johnny Logan in 1959, the first for the club in Atlanta. He joined teammates Dale Murphy and Claudell Washington on the roster, though he did not get in the game. It was the only selection of his career.

At the plate and in the field, the 1984 season was not as productive for the shortstop. His average dropped 31 points to .266. He made only 30 errors, but still led the league at his position. He led NL shortstops with 251 putouts and 94 double plays. At his highest point he batted .325 midway through the season. In the second half he slumped, batting .220. The Braves finished in second place, 12 games behind the eventual National League champion San Diego Padres. Joe Torre, one of Ramírez's biggest supporters, was fired as manager. Torre lamented, "Probably the worst thing that happened to me was winning the first year we were here because you got people's mouths watering for what's next, and we really never got to that plateau."[28] Eddie Haas became Ramírez's third big-league skipper.

The year 1985 saw the continued deflation of "America's Team" and the rise of a new threat to Ramírez's job security. The Braves won just 66 games and went through two managers, Haas and Bobby Wine. They finished in fifth place, 29 games out of first. Though Ramírez had agreed to a five-year contract in early January,[29] spring was not easy. In spring training Paul Zuvella competed with Ramírez for the shortstop job, finishing with a higher batting average and six fewer errors.[30] Ramírez won out in the end, but it seemed this foreshadowed things to come. Another shortstop, Andrés Thomas, was waiting in the wings. Thomas debuted as a September call-up on September 3 and saw his first game on defense replacing Ramírez in the ninth inning of a game on September 10. Suddenly it seemed like the odds were building against Ramírez.

Another of Ramírez's supporters was fired after the 1985 season, general manager John Mullen. His replacement was Bobby Cox. One of the first moves made by the new GM was the hiring of field manager Chuck Tanner. Tanner had led the Pittsburgh Pirates "We Are Family" squad to a World Series title in 1979. The veteran skipper came to an Atlanta team at a crossroads. Tanner liked the lineup, but the pitching rotation seemed suspect.[31] The Braves hovered around .500 for most of the season until a rash of losses in July sent the team into a tailspin. By season's end, the Braves were in last place. Ramírez's average dropped to .240. He played 57 games at third base as Thomas saw more action at shortstop. Ramírez made 21 errors in 86 games at shortstop while Thomas made 19 in 97 contests. Thomas outhit Ramírez, batting .267. With 1987 on the horizon, Ramírez could only ponder what might happen to his playing time in Atlanta.

Ramírez went to 1987 spring training with hopes of maintaining his starting job. Andrés Thomas was nursing a bad shoulder. Ramírez could hear the rumblings about his future, including trade rumors. But the veteran could not focus on any of that. He had to focus on maintaining his job. "They are talking about using Andrés, doing this and doing that," said the shortstop. "But I have to forget all that talk. I know I can do the job. But if I think about it, it will hurt me."[32] Ramírez was not ready to play utility or be a backup. "They're moving me around too much," he continued. "I don't play relaxed anymore. I want to play all year at one spot, like before."[33] Never a pessimist, Chuck Tanner commented on Ramírez's situation, saying, "He's going to be given every opportunity this spring. We think he just has a world of talent."[34] As the Braves broke camp, however, Ramírez found himself in the dugout watching Thomas play the position he had manned since August of 1980.

Early in the 1987 season, Ramírez found himself platooning with Graig Nettles and Ken Oberkfell at third base. But on April 19 Thomas injured his ankle while sliding into a base.[35] The injury forced Tanner to use Ramírez at short. Still, the former starter was not happy. "I don't want to play like this, because I don't want anybody to get hurt," he said.[36] Though the veteran was still demanding a trade, his optimist skipper Tanner said, "We're fortunate to have Ramírez. He'll do a great job for us."[37] Upon Thomas's return, both shortstops seemed to flip-flop starting assignments and trips to the disabled list; Thomas had shoulder and ankle issues while Ramírez was nursing knee problems.[38] This routine lasted until early August, when the Braves called up yet another shortstop, Jeff Blauser. Thomas was batting .231 with 20 errors and Ramírez .267 with nine errors in 38 games at the time of Blauser's arrival. With both Ramírez and Thomas battling injuries, it appeared that neither would have a starting job leading into the next season.

In December of 1987, after spending the entire season hoping for a trade, Ramírez was finally granted his wish. The Braves shipped the 28-year-old veteran to the Houston Astros for prospects Ed Whited and Mike Stoker. Atlanta manager Chuck Tanner finally admitted the obvious, stating after the trade, "We decided to go in a different direction in this organization. We're going with our younger players from our farm system."[39] The Astros, on the other hand, wanted to win right now. Ramírez was very pleased with his new situation. "I wanted to be traded," he said. "… I just don't like to sit. I think I'm a better player when I'm in there every day."[40] Ramírez was now healthy and the distraction of the young pups trying to invade his food bowl was now a thing of the past.

His arrival to Houston brought a sense of optimism. The veteran felt his fielding would improve. "I don't like to make excuses for my play, but fielding on AstroTurf should help," he said. "The ball will come fast, but there won't be the bad hops I took in Atlanta."[41] Defensively things improved. Ramírez made 23 errors, six fewer than the league leaders, Cincinnati's Barry Larkin and his old Atlanta teammate, Andrés Thomas. He batted .276. He had several big hits, including his first career grand slam in late May at Wrigley Field in Chicago. Ramírez claimed the wind was blowing out and that he was only looking to hit a fly ball. Cubs skipper Don Zimmer thought the ball left the yard rather quickly. "I blinked and the ball was gone," he said.[42] The shot was off Mike Capel and helped the Astros to a 7-1 victory.[43] The Astros finished in fifth place, just two games over .500, but 27 games ahead of the Braves, who lost 106 games; Chuck Tanner was replaced 39 games into Atlanta's rebuilding season. Hal Lanier was replaced as Astros skipper by Art Howe after the season.

In his second season in Houston, Ramírez's average fell once again, but that did not stop him from connecting for some big hits. Strange game-winning RBIs seemed to be his forte for the year. On June 4 came one of the most welcome RBIs of the season and possibly his career. The Dodgers came to Houston for a four-game series. The Saturday game began at 7:35 P.M. The starters were Bob Knepper for Houston and Tim Leary for Los Angeles. After six innings, the score was tied, 4-4. Suddenly, the bats shut off and no one scored for another 16 innings. Strangeness ensued with pitchers playing in the field, fielders pitching, pitchers pinch-hitting, and future Hall of Fame first baseman Eddie Murray playing third. Orel Hershiser and Jim Clancy, usually starters, each appeared in relief and combined for 12 innings of shutout baseball. The Astros used 21 players while the Dodgers played 23. In the bottom of the 22nd, third baseman Jeff Hamilton took the hill to face an exhausted Astros lineup. Bill Doran singled. One out later, Terry Puhl was walked intentionally. Hamilton struck out Ken Caminiti. Rafael Ramírez was next up. On an 0-and-2 count, Ramírez rifled a single over a leaping Fernando Valenzuela at first and into right field, scoring Doran and giving the Astros a 5-4 victory. The game officially ended at 2:50 A.M. Sunday. "I only like to play nine innings. Enough is enough," Ramírez said.[44] Another strange game-winning RBI came in August at the Astrodome. Cubs skipper Don Zimmer ordered an intentional walk with two outs in the ninth to get to Ramírez. One of the knocks against Ramírez had been that he was undisciplined at the plate. With the bases loaded, Cubs pitcher Jeff Pico walked Ramírez on five pitches, giving the Astros a 6-5 win. Ramírez said of Zimmer, "He does some strange things. He knows I'm a free swinger, but I had in mind to be patient and only swing on a 3-and-2 count."[45] Who needs walk-off singles and homers when you can walk with the bases full?

At shortstop, everything returned to normal in 1989. By the All-Star break, Ramírez led the league with 21 errors, almost equaling his total for the previous season.[46] Of his struggles, he noted, "When I first started professionally, I could catch and I couldn't hit. Now I can hit and I can't catch."[47] Ramírez settled down during the second half of the season, finishing the year with 30 errors, but again leading NL shortstops.

In November Ramírez signed a two-year deal to remain the Astros starter at short. "His signing provides us a continuation of service of one of the best offensive shortstops in the National League," said Astros GM Bill

Wood.⁴⁸ However, there was an interesting clause in his new contract: a "weight bonus." Though not a new idea to contracts, this weight clause had an interesting caveat. Ramírez would be weighed daily starting in spring training. If he averaged 187 pounds at the end of each month, the Astros would pay him an additional $12,500. This gave him the chance to make an additional $87,500 for the season on top of his $1.1 million salary.⁴⁹ Not only would staying trim help Ramírez to be more effective in the field, but it would also give him more in the bank.

Ramírez played 132 games in 1990. But he was now 31 and battling injury and weight problems. The Astros began to field trade offers and were looking at younger options at short, including Orlando Miller, Dave Hajek, Eric Yelding, and Andujar Cedeño. Their first-round pick that year was also a shortstop, Tom Nevers, who referred to Ramírez as "elderly." "That's the one thing I was hoping for was to go to a team with an elderly shortstop and not too many people coming up in the farm system," Nevers said.⁵⁰ It appeared that Ramírez was on his way out. As to the weight clause, he did not hit the mark at any point during the season, missing it by three pounds for the year.⁵¹

In 1991 Ramírez was still in an Astros' uniform, platooning and coming off the bench. He played behind Eric Yelding and saw action at various positions, including his first career start at second base, on May 28 at LA. He played in just over 100 games, but started only 45 times. To the Astros' chagrin, neither Yelding nor Ramírez fared well in the field. In fact, on May 25 at home against San Diego, both made errors that cost the Astros a win. Padres infielder José Mota singled and reached third when Yelding misplayed the ball in right field. Ramírez, who had replaced Yelding at shortstop in the eighth, then fielded a grounder from Bip Roberts and threw it into the dirt at first, allowing Mota to score what proved to be the game winner. Though the Astros had been optimistic in their seasonal outlook, the team was not contending and began looking to cut payroll. They fielded offers once again for the veteran shortstop. As summer approached, the Dodgers expressed interest as did Oakland, looking for a replacement for the injured Walt Weiss.⁵² However, Ramírez stayed put.

In 1992 the downhill slide continued. Ramírez signed a minor-league deal to stay with the club.⁵³ The starting shortstop was now Andujar Cedeño as the Astros, reminiscent of the 1970s Braves, continued the shortstop carousel. But by mid-April, with the free-swinging Cedeño coming up empty at the plate, Houston put Ramírez back into the starting role.⁵⁴ The veteran made sporadic starts throughout the season, save for some time he spent on the disabled list in June. In all, the Astros used six different shortstops in 1992, including Ramírez, Cedeño, Yelding, rookie Juan Guerrero, and veterans Casey Candaele and Ernie Riles. Desperate, the Astros even considered moving number-one draft pick Phil Nevin to shortstop, testing him at the position during a practice session in early September.⁵⁵ Ramírez started his final game at shortstop on August 22 at Philadelphia. He had one hit in five at-bats and scored twice; he made no errors. On September 29 the Astros were trailing 5-4 and facing Padres closer Randy Myers at home. Ramírez led off the bottom of the ninth with a pinch-single. After a sacrifice by Craig Biggio and a walk to Steve Finley, Luis Gonzalez smacked a walk-off double to left-center to give the Astros a win. It was the final hit of Ramírez's big-league career. In late October he elected free agency, joining Oakland the following spring, but did not make the team.

Rafael Ramírez collected 1,432 hits for his career and batted .261. He made 290 errors at shortstop. Though perhaps not Hall of Fame worthy, Ramírez certainly made the most of his 13-year career. Now an ex-major leaguer, he returned to San Pedro de Macoris. His son, Edgar Ramírez, was signed as a 16-year-old infielder by the Tampa Bay Devil Rays in 1996 and played through 1999, but never made the big leagues. He died at the age of 28 near San Pedro de Macoris.[56]

As a fielder, Ramírez was error-prone, but he was always ready for the next chance, never wanting to sit the bench. As a hitter, Ramírez was a leader at his position in a time when shortstops were known only for their fielding. He ignored the criticism of the media and performed his duties every game, even when it wasn't pretty or the playing field that friendly. What manager wouldn't want a player like Rafael Ramírez?

SOURCES

In addition to the sources cited in the notes, the author consulted the Rafael Ramírez player file and questionnaire at the National Baseball Hall of Fame, the online SABR Encyclopedia, Retrosheet.org, Baseball-Reference.com, MLB.com, and Newspapers.com.

NOTES

1. McClatchy News Service, "A's Notebook: Tigers Nibble About Rickey," *Santa Cruz Sentinel*, March 15, 1993: B-4.

2. Steve Wulf, "Standing Tall at Short," *Sports Illustrated*, si.com/vault/1987/02/09/114833/standing-tall-at-short-with-more-than-70-shortstops-in-organized-baseball-the-tiny-impoverished-dominican-republic-has-emerged-as-the-worlds-leading-exporter-of-mediocampistas, accessed May 31, 2018.

3. Enrique Rojas, "Buena cosecha de paracortos dominicanos," *Plainview* (Texas) *Daily Herald*, November 24, 2004. myplainview.com/news/article/Buena-cosecha-de-paracortos-dominicanos-8951737.php , accessed May 31, 2018.

4. Joyce Leviton, "Skipper Ted Turner Buys the Braves and Promises to Turn Atlanta into Winnersville, U.S.A.," *People*, February 2, 1976. people.com/archive/skipper-ted-turner-buys-the-braves-and-promises-to-turn-atlanta-into-winnersville-u-s-a-vol-5-no-4/, accessed May 29, 2018.

5. "Watch These 13 Rookies," *Democrat and Chronicle* (Rochester, New York), April 13, 1980: 6E.

6. United Press International, "Atlanta Moves Up Ramírez," *Hartford Courant*, August 5, 1980: 83.

7. Ken Picking, "Braves Bench SS Gomez, Promote Ramírez," Unattributed August 23, 1980, clipping in Ramírez's Hall of Fame player file.

8. Mike Littwin, "Dodgers Get a Call – and a 6-2 Victory," *Los Angeles Times*, August 7, 1980: 39.

9. Associated Press, "Cox's Move Looks Good Now," *Herald and Review* (Decatur, Illinois), August 20, 1980: 21.

10. See AP, "Braves Finally Sign Torre," *The Day* (New London, Connecticut), October 24, 1981: 24, and an unattributed, undated article titled "Braves Give Up on Ramírez Deal," from Ramírez's Hall of Fame player file.

11. Lee Whitney, "Have You Noticed Rafael Ramírez?" *Braves Banner*, October 11, 1983.

12. "Braves Give Up on Ramírez Deal."

13. "Braves Give Up on Ramírez Deal."

14. Whitney, "Have You Noticed Rafael Ramírez?"

15. Kent Hannon, "Are Torre's Braves Folding Their Tent?" *New York Times*, August 8, 1982.

16. Jason Foster, "The Untold Story of 'It's a Long Way to October,' a groundbreaking, forgotten baseball documentary," *The Sporting News*, May 2, 2017. sportingnews.com/mlb/news/its-a-long-way-to-october-atlanta-braves-documentary-video-1982-wtbs-glenn-diamond-joe-torre/yaabhb6wm7h91kirw1ijy0wm9, accessed June 2, 2018.

17 AP, "Atlanta's Turner Ready to Fly Pennant," *Galveston Daily News*, March 12, 1982: 17.

18 Ira Berkow, "Braves Win 12th Straight to Set Record," *New York Times*, April 21, 1982.

19 Berkow.

20 Berkow.

21 George Maselli, "Absurd: Who Would've Thought the Braves Would Be in 1st?," *Tallahassee Democrat*, July 12, 1982: 15.

22 Kent Hannon, "Are Torre's Braves Folding Their Tent?"

23 Mike Davis, "Braves' New World Is Coming Apart," *San Bernardino County Sun*, August 7, 1982: 33.

24 AP, "Baseball Tidbits: Quotes," *Quad-City Times* (Davenport, Iowa), March 9, 1982: 16.

25 Bob Fowler, "Brewers Force Final Game – Cards Win: Oberkfell's Single in 9th Turns Back Atlanta, 4-3," *Orlando Sentinel*, October 10, 1982: D1.

26 Phil Elderkin, "Hubbard and Ramírez Give Braves Solid Infield Tandem," *Christian Science Monitor*, June 21, 1983.

27 Mark Whicker, "Playing Well Is Mounds of Fun for Hubbard," *Philadelphia Daily News*, September 1, 1982: 74.

28 AP, "Braves Fire Manager Torre," *Washington Post*, October 2, 1984. washingtonpost.com/archive/sports/1984/10/02/braves-fire-manager-torre/03373120-47fc-4b18-8598-3ff312b281fc/?utm_term=.86fe389a26a9, accessed May 29, 2018.

29 AP, "A.M. Sportwatch: Braves Sign Ramírez," *Arizona Daily Star* (Tucson, Arizona), January 17, 1985: 9.

30 "Play Ball: Mahler Gets Call in Braves' Opener," *Anniston Star* (Anniston, Alabama), April 9, 1985: 11.

31 David Moffitt, "Brave Hopes Hurt Again by Pitching," *Tennessean* (Nashville, Tennessee), February 18, 1986: 37.

32 Joe Santoro, "All Ramírez Wants Is a Fair Chance," *News-Press* (Fort Myers, Florida), March 20, 1987: 37.

33 Santoro.

34 Santoro.

35 Gerry Fraley, "Rafael Wants Out, But…," unidentified article in the Ramírez Hall of Fame player file.

36 Fraley.

37 Fraley.

38 "Braves Ship Ramírez to Astros," unattributed article in the Ramírez Hall of Fame player file.

39 "Braves Ship Ramírez to Astros."

40 Neil Hohlfield, "…While New Astro Ramírez Soars," unidentified article in the Ramírez Hall of Fame player file.

41 Frank Carroll, "Astrodome New Home to Ramírez: Ex-Brave Looks to Mend Erring Ways in Houston," *Orlando Sentinel*, February 26, 1988: 36.

42 AP, "Ramírez Slam Humbles Cubs," *Herald and Review* (Decatur, Illinois), May 29, 1988: 11.

43 "Ramírez Slam Humbles Cubs."

44 Paul Hagen "In Orderly Fashion: Expos' Rodgers Goes Alphabetically to Bullpen," *Philadelphia Daily News*, June 9, 1989: 121.

45 AP, "'Percentage Baseball' Costs Cubs, Aids Astros," *Lincoln* (Nebraska) *Star,* August 19, 1989: 9.

46 AP, "The Inside Pitch: National League: Rose Offers Interesting Insight Into Baseball's Top Performers," *Press and Sun-Bulletin* (Binghamton, New York), July 11, 1989: 20.

47 Wire Services, "N.L. Notebook: Houston Astros." *South Florida Sun Sentinel* (Fort Lauderdale, Florida), July 16, 1989: 36.

48 AP, "Astros Agree to Terms with Rafael Ramírez," *Galveston Daily News*, November 16, 1989: 20.

49 Sun News Services, "Kaleidoscope: Calorie Counter Will Be Cash Counter," *San Bernardino County Sun*, November 19, 1989: 27.

50 Dave Dye, "Brewers' Dalton Hasn't Mastered the Art of the Deal: Draft Story II," *Detroit Free Press*, June 10, 1990: 44.

51 Tennessean News Services, "Sports A.M.: Sanderson, Yanks at Standstill," *Tennessean*, December 30, 1990: 22.

52 "Dodgers Notes," *San Bernardino County Sun*, and Paul Hagen, "Tonight: Phillies vs Houston Astros." *Philadelphia Daily News,* June 12, 1991: 84.

53 "Dodgers Notes," "Tonight: Phillies vs Houston Astros," and "Briefly: Baseball," *Clarion-Ledger* (Jackson, Mississippi), January 9, 1992: 24.

54 Rick Hummel, "Baseball Notebook: Free Agents Are Costing Cubs Plenty," *St. Louis Post-Dispatch,* April 19, 1992: 20.

55 Ray Finocchiaro, "NL Notebook: No. 1 Pick Green's Future May Hinge on Shoulder Surgery," *News Journal* (Wilmington, Delaware), September 13, 1992: 64.

56 "Scorecard: Obituaries," unidentified article from Ramírez Hall of Fame player file.

JOSÉ RIJO

By Charles F. Faber

Few, if any, baseball players have ever had as many peaks and valleys in their careers or in their lives as José Rijo. Raised in poverty in the Dominican Republic, he signed a contract with the New York Yankees at age 15. After three years in the minor leagues, he made it to the majors at the age of 18. Battling injuries, he was unable to win consistently and was traded twice in four years. He married the daughter of his country's most celebrated pitcher, and sued her for divorce. Although he missed part of the 1990 season due to injuries, he recovered in time to help pitch the Cincinnati Reds to a world championship, and was named the Most Valuable Player of the 1990 World Series. He became a hero to his countrymen. In 1995 Rijo was sidelined with a serious elbow injury and was out of baseball for five years. In 2001 he attempted a comeback, but was again struck by injuries. He twice won an award for exemplary conduct on and off the field. He won the Tony Conigliaro Award for his spirit, determination, and courage in overcoming adversity. After retiring as a player he became an assistant to the general manager of the Washington Nationals. He was fired amid allegations of improprieties in a baseball academy he operated in the Dominican Republic. His academy was closed. He was investigated for his association with a person accused of drug trafficking and money laundering. He was not found guilty of any wrongdoing. As of 2015 Rijo was once again helping young Dominicans with baseball aspirations. Once again he is a hero in his native land.

José Antonio Rijo Abreu was born on May 13, 1965, in the municipality of San Cristobal, in San Cristobal Province, Dominican Republic, on the Caribbean coast about 20 miles east of Santo Domingo in the sugar-cane producing area of the island. He was the son of Glady Abreu, a nurse, and Reynardo Rijo, a taxi driver, the 10th of the elder Rijo's 13 children. José's father left the family when the boy was 4 years old. José then shared cramped quarters in an aluminum-roofed four-bedroom house with his mother, grandparents, aunts, uncles, and many of his brothers, sisters, and half-siblings. "We were so poor," José said, "I had to play ball in a friend's shoes, which were too small. The shoes were so tight and worn out I had blisters on each of my toes."[1] He didn't see his father again for 19 years.[2]

Very little is known about José's early childhood. He was called Chago in his homeland, but the nickname never caught on in the United States. Like many Dominican boys he probably learned baseball in the streets

Photo courtesy of the National Baseball Hall of Fame

of his impoverished hometown. His first baseball may have been homemade, with a small pebble in the center and strips of cloth wound tightly around the core. Bats may have been broomsticks or tree branches. When he was 12 José was playing on an organized club equipped with real balls and real bats. He was very good, a *jugador de beisbol estrella* (star baseball player).

After Jackie Robinson broke the color barrier, the Dominican Republic became a prime source of major-league baseball players. By the time José was a teenager, scouts were flocking to the Dominican Republic in search of talented players. On August 1, 1980, scout Willie Calvino signed 15-year-old José Rijo to a contract with the New York Yankees for $3,500. The youngster quit school in the ninth grade. "I signed because I hated school, and my family needed the money," he explained. "I knew leaving school was a big gamble. If I didn't succeed in baseball, I didn't know what I would do."[3]

Rijo never said so publicly, but it must have been quite a thrill for a poor 15-year-old Dominican boy to sign a contract with the New York Yankees, who often were regarded as the most prominent baseball club in the entire world.

Major League Baseball now prohibits the signing of Caribbean players under the age of 16, but that rule was not in effect in 1980. Anyway, Rijo turned 16 before he started his professional career in 1981 in the Yankees farm system at $600 per month. In his first year, he was used sparingly for the Yankees team in the Rookie-level Gulf Coast League, winning three and losing the same number. In 1982 he was promoted to Paintsville, Kentucky, in the Advanced Rookie Appalachian League, where he posted an 8-4 record. Rijo later said that he had had pain in his elbow ever since he was 17 years old. An x-ray taken of his elbow in 1982 showed a bone abnormality, possibly a bone spur. But he kept pitching. Sometimes the pain got worse; sometimes it got better.

In 1983 Rijo was assigned to the Fort Lauderdale Yankees of the Class-A Florida State League. He was a skinny 18-year-old who still didn't speak English. He resolved to try to learn three English words every day.[4] He found lodging in a street near the beach that was home to drug users and hoods. Homesick, he spent most of his money on phone calls back to his family in the Dominican. Luckily, he heard about a local family that was known to take in an occasional Latin player. John Cummings was a computer programmer and his wife had come from Mexico. They weren't eager to take in another ballplayer. Caring for players was very demanding on their schedule. They had to take them to and from the ballpark, but they decided to take José in. "He was just like our baby," Cummings said. "He was the only one we got really close to, to the point where he was like a member of the family. He was one of those guys you could never stay mad at. He did what he did because he didn't want anything to mess up his chance at a career in baseball. When he came back for spring training in '84 … there was a major-league rule that players had to stay at the team hotel. Rijo refused to, because he wanted to stay with us."[5]

Rijo had his best minor-league season in 1983, going 15-5 with an ERA of 1.68 for Fort Lauderdale before being promoted to the Nashville Sounds of the Double-A Southern League (3-2). He led the Florida State League in wins, complete games, and earned-run average. He was named the league's Most Valuable Player. This performance earned Rijo a promotion to "The Show." At age 18 he was on top of the baseball world.

In 1984 Rijo won the James P. Dawson Award as the best rookie in the Yankees' spring-training camp. He achieved his goal of reaching the major leagues. George Steinbrenner, owner of the Yankees, hoped Rijo could compete with Dwight Gooden, the sensational teenage pitcher of the New York Mets, for the affection of Gotham's fans. On April 5, 1984, the 6-foot-1, 200-pound right-hander made his major-league debut. Rijo entered the game against Kansas City at the Royals Stadium in the third inning, with two on, two out, and the Yankees trailing, 14-0. He struck out Greg Pryor, the very first major-league hitter he ever faced. He finished the game, giving up only one earned run on four hits and two walks, while striking out five in 5 1/3 innings. It appeared to be an excellent start to a stellar major-league career. However, Rijo's high hopes for a great rookie season soon came crashing down. He won only two games and lost eight that year. He could not match the flamboyant Gooden either on the mound or in the hearts of fandom. On December 5, 1984, he was traded along with Tim Birtsas, Jay Howell, Stan Javier, and Eric Plunk to the Oakland Athletics for Bert Bradley, Rickey Henderson, and cash.

Rijo was pleased about the trade. "I think I had the Yankees mixed up in my head last year," he said. "I had a lot of pitching coaches in New York. One told me to do things one way. One told me to do things that way, and I was kind of confused. … I'm really happy to be here. I hope I play here the rest of my life. There is less pressure here. It is a better place for a young player to play."[6]

Rijo was disgruntled with the way the Yankees handled him. "I came in as a reliever," he said. "Then two days later they told me I was going to be a starter. People don't know about that feeling."[7]

When Rijo reported to the A's he was tired from playing winter ball. He told teammate Jay Howell that his arm and shoulder were bothering him and that made him throw everything up. He had no breaking ball. He claimed that he had lost it in New York when they were flip-flopping him between starting and relieving.[8]

Rijo's stay in Oakland was marked by injuries. In 1985 he split the season between Oakland and the Tacoma Tigers, the A's farm club in the Triple-A Pacific Coast League. While in Tacoma he developed a changeup to go with his fastball and slider. In 1986 he was brought back up to Oakland. During spring training he missed a couple of days of practice because he had an infection on his right toe. Manager Jackie Moore blamed the infection on Rijo trying to be trendy and not wearing socks.[9]

In the spring of 1986 Rijo was still chafing from comparisons with Gooden. He told Bay Area sportswriter Lowell Cohn that he could have matched Gooden's 24 victories the previous season if he had been given the chance. Was Rijo a cocky kid who should shut up until he gets a respectable season under his belt? Cohn wrote that Rijo knew he had a rare talent, was not bragging but only stating what he believed to be facts. "When you talk to him, he is pleasant enough. He tends to wear loud clothes like flaming red slacks with white shoes and no socks, but he speaks softly, shakes hands with reporters, innocently admits to counting his strikeouts as the game goes along."[10] Cohn concluded that Rijo's apparent arrogance was not a character flaw, but a prerequisite to greatness. In order to be successful, Cohn wrote, a pitcher must believe in his abilities, must cultivate the sin of pride.[11]

When he was healthy Rijo showed flashes of brilliance. On April 19, 1986, he struck out 16 Seattle Mariners at the Kingdome for a club record. Five days later, in a game at the Oakland-Alameda County Stadium against the same Mariners, he pitched a two-hitter while striking out 14. Once again he appeared on the brink of stardom. He was on top of the world. But once again the euphoria didn't last.

Shortly after his outstanding performance against Seattle, Rijo developed a problem with his left leg. At times he had no feeling in the leg. Unable to throw his fastball, he had to rely on his slider. In June he told a writer for the *Kansas City Times,* "Last night was bad, I couldn't get any sleep. I've got to forget about my leg, but it's a little tough. Right now I'm just running around. I haven't thrown a good fastball yet. I don't feel it yet. ... My leg is dancing all over the place when I plant it. I have no control."[12]

The A's tried Rijo in the bullpen, but that didn't work. They moved him back into the rotation, to no avail. He won nine games for the A's in 1986, and only two in 1987. Before the '87 season was over, he was sent back down to Tacoma.

During the season Rijo was dating Rosie Marichal, a student at San Francisco State University and the daughter of Hall of Fame pitcher Juan Marichal, the most celebrated pitcher ever to come out of the Dominican Republic. Marichal did not know the two were dating, and when the couple announced wedding plans he was furious. "Maybe because he knows how ballplayers are, the lifestyle of the guys," Rijo said. "I don't blame him. I had the reputation of going out a lot. ... The hunt was on every day."[13] Rosie and José were married in September. It was José's second marriage. Very little is known about his marriage to Alma Rijo, his first wife.

On December 8, 1987, Rijo was traded along with pitcher Tim Birtsas to the Cincinnati Reds for aging slugger Dave Parker. In three years with the A's he had won only 17 games.

Rijo began his Cincinnati career as a middle reliever. His first appearance for the Reds came on Opening Day. He pitched the sixth and seventh innings at Riverfront Stadium as the Reds downed the St. Louis Cardinals, 5-4. His next appearance came in the 16th inning of a game in Cincinnati five days later. He was hit hard, gave up five runs, and was charged with the loss as the Reds fell, 8-3, to Houston. It was the only game Rijo was to lose in relief all season. Over the next several weeks he was dominant in the sixth, seventh, and eighth innings. He credited his success to manager Pete Rose's faith in his judgment. "At Oakland I wasn't smart enough to call my own pitches. They called all of them. I went through hell but I learned," he said.[14]

By early June Rijo had won six games against only one loss. He was happy as a reliever. However, the Reds traded away starting pitcher Dennis Rasmussen on June 8, and they needed another starter. That very night Rose pressed Rijo to fill that role. In his first start he defeated the San Diego Padres,

7-1, giving up only one run on two hits in six innings and striking out eight Padres. Instead of basking in his success, Rijo was conflicted. "I consider myself a relief pitcher, and I don't want to ruin it by starting over. Tonight I help the team as best I can. Now I hope I can go back to my bullpen. I hope somebody else can do the starts."[15]

Rose responded by saying, "He wants to go back to the bullpen? Tell him he can go back to the bullpen – until Tuesday night against Houston, his next start. ... I have him penciled in for 21 more starts between now and the end of the season. He's a real horse, and he going to win a lot of games – as a starter."[16] As it turned out, Rijo made 19 starts and won 7 of 14 decisions as a starter, giving him a 13-8 record for the year. In August he experienced pain and weakness in his shoulder and was placed on the 21-day disabled list on August 18, the first of 10 times he was put on the DL during his career in Cincinnati. He was reinstated on September 8 and pitched well the remainder of the season.

The Reds were counting on Rijo to be one of their top pitchers and perhaps help them win a pennant in 1989. After finishing second in the National League West for four consecutive seasons, the Reds had reasonable expectations for a championship in '89. They got off to a great start, leading the division in April and much of May. Then the injury bug hit. Player after player went down, and the Reds plunged all the way to fifth place. The Reds had counted on Rijo being a big winner. He had a record of 7-6 with a 2.84 ERA on July 17 when he suffered a stress fracture in his lower back, which sidelined him for the remainder of the season.

After the 1989 season ended Rosie and José became parents of a baby boy, José Jr., called Josie. But their marriage was already beginning to come apart. "She didn't want me to visit my friends, go out and have a drink, whatever. She wanted me to let her know everything I do, where I spend my money and what I spend it on. ... It's tough having someone trying to control you," he said. "When the woman wants to take control, you know, it ain't going to work. You know a man is a man. And I wear the pants in the house. I bring the food into the house, so I should have control."[17] Despite marital discord, the union endured throughout the 1990 season.

How Cincinnati would fare in 1990 depended, among other things, on how the wounded troops recovered from their injuries and how the players responded to their new manager, Lou Piniella. The results were positive on both fronts. Most of the players recovered from their injuries, and most of them responded well to Piniella's fiery leadership. The Reds got off to a terrific start, winning nine consecutive games to start the season, and were never headed, leading their division wire-to-wire. Although Rijo had been expected to be the club's ace, he was unable to contribute to the streak, suffering from tendinitis in his throwing shoulder. However, other pitchers picked up the slack. When Rijo won his first game of the season, on the last day of April, Cincinnati's record was 13-3. Of course, they couldn't keep winning at that pace, but they held onto first place. On June 29 Rijo went on the disabled list with a muscle strain in his right shoulder. The Reds were 45-26 at that point, and Rijo was 5-3. When Rijo returned on July 21 the Reds were 57-32. Rijo won his first game back after being reinstated, but lost three of next five decisions.

During the dog days of August the Reds were losing more often than winning. They lost five in a row from August 17 to 20. On August 21 pitching coach Stan Williams lit a fire under Rijo. He called the starting pitchers together and told them he was thinking about going to a four-man rotation. "Awesome," Rijo said.[18] "Well, good, José, because you're not one of them," replied the coach.[19] Piniella said the rotation would include Tom Browning, Danny Jackson, Norm Charlton, and either José Rijo or Jack Armstrong – "whoever is pitching well."[20]

In fact, Williams and Piniella did not go to a four-man rotation. If the gambit was intended as a motivational ploy, it worked. Over his next nine starts, Rijo went 6-2 with a 1.27 ERA. Sportswriters John Erardi and Joel Luckhaupt wrote that Rijo put the Reds on his back and carried them to the finish line.[21]

The Reds won the division and faced the favored Pittsburgh Pirates in the National League Championship Series. As the ace of the staff, Rijo drew the assignment to start the first game of the NLCS at Riverfront Stadium. He pitched 5⅓ innings, being relieved by Norm Charlton with two on and one out and the score tied, 3-3, in the top of the sixth inning. Charlton escaped the jam, but lost the game, 4-3, on a double by Andy Van Slyke in the seventh inning. After the series moved to Pittsburgh, Rijo started Game Four at Three Rivers Stadium. He picked up the victory this time, pitching seven innings in a 5-3 Cincinnati win. The Reds won the NLCS in six games for their first National League pennant since 1976.

The Reds faced the defending world champion Oakland Athletics in the 1990 World Series. Led by the "Bash Brothers," Mark McGwire and José Canseco, and featuring an outstanding pitching staff, the A's were overwhelming favorites. Manager Lou Piniella chose Rijo to start Game One, and Rijo was masterful, pitching seven shutout innings before turning the game over to Nasty Boys Rob Dibble and Randy Myers to nail down the 7-0 win. The Reds won Game Two, 5-4, and took Game Three, 8-3. It was Rijo's turn again in Game Four and he wrapped up the world championship for Cincinnati with another outstanding performance, pitching 8⅓ innings and giving up only one run. Myers came in to shut the door and the Reds claimed the game, 2-1. Rijo was named the Most Valuable Player of the World Series.

In the Series Rijo had twice defeated Dave Stewart, the ace of the Oakland staff. Stewart was not a gracious loser. He implied the Reds win was a fluke. "It's not always the best team that wins. It's the team that plays the best," he said. "I didn't take anything away from Cincinnati. I just wouldn't admit they were a better team than we were. I don't feel they were. I don't feel that now. They were just better than us in four games. It wasn't me that made the odds for the World Series. Someone else said we were going to win, we were the better team. Even the Cincinnati fans thought the Reds were going to lose."[22]

Less than two months after the end of the World Series, Rijo filed for divorce from his wife, Rosie. He alleged in the suit, filed in the Hamilton County (Ohio) Court of Common Pleas, that he and Rosie were incompatible and that Rosie was guilty of gross neglect of duty. Rosie denied the charges. "My husband, José, is a wonderful baseball player and a world-class athlete, but he has a lot to learn about marriage. José does not understand that a successful marriage, like a winning ballclub, requires the efforts of more than one player."[23] Rosie claimed that José never told her he was planning to sue for divorce. She said she learned about the divorce proceedings from news reports. "I'm in shock," she said. "We just came back from a cruise, and I'm pregnant."[24] (The Rijos' daughter, Sasha, was born the following summer.)

"I did tell her," José said, "but I think she always thought I was joking. She never thought I was going to do it. ... I love Rosie. I love my wife. I don't think I'm ever going to find anyone better than her. She's a beautiful wife. She's the best cook I've ever seen. I treasure her a lot. She's a very reliable person.

I just think her attitude was a little tough to deal with. She thought she was boss."[25]

Marge Schott, owner of the Reds, had tried to save the marriage. "There has been a problem that I worked very hard on with Rijo and his wife. ... I got into their thing about a year ago. They've got a child, she's pregnant again. There's nothing I want more than Rijo and his wife to stay together."[26]

For his part, José resented Schott's interference. When her efforts to bring about a reconciliation failed, Schott provided a lawyer to look out for Rosie's financial interests. "She recommended her a lawyer," Rijo said. "That's personal life. Nobody should interfere with my personal life. But she tried to talk to me about getting back together. She didn't want me to get a divorce."[27]

"I don't want to be changing wives liked I've changed uniforms," Rijo said. "But a man's got to do what he's got to do."[28]

With divorce proceedings under way, it appeared the marriage was irretrievably doomed. Then, surprisingly, the couple quietly reconciled. Many pages had been written about the pending divorce, but no newspaper articles heralded the reconciliation. It was mentioned briefly in *USA Today Baseball Weekly*,[29] but otherwise ignored by the press. Apparently, news sources considered it a nonstory. Anyway, José and Rosie were back together again.

After his stellar performance in the 1990 World Series, Rijo had good reason to believe he deserved a large pay raise. In order to avoid arbitration, the Reds signed him to a three-year, $9 million contract. Dave Stewart, perhaps still smarting from his World Series losses, had some comments. "The money has gotten ridiculous in the game for mediocre players. I'm not saying he's not worth $3 million. I'm saying I don't think his statistics right now indicate he should be paid that kind of money. Maybe they're paying him on potential. You look at his statistics the last two, three years and I don't see $3 million worth. ... If you can get it, that's great. I can appreciate that. But a lot of guys are getting a lot of money when they haven't quite earned it yet. But if the owners want to give it, O.K. It works out good for players like myself who have earned it.[30]

Schott was asked if she thought Rijo was worth $3 million a year. Even though she was the one who authorized his salary, she replied. "He only had one really good year – last year. No, I don't, but I'm as guilty as the rest of the owners. I mean, who's worth that kind of money anyway? A person who runs General Motors doesn't get that kind of money. The president of the United States doesn't get that kind of money. Plus (pitchers) only play part-time."[31] Rijo, of course, thought he was worth every cent he was paid.

During the offseason Rijo spread some of his money around in the Dominican Republic. The World Series star was accorded a new status in his homeland. "I became a king," he said. "I was like some kind of hero, which I'm not. I'm just a very lucky person."[32] "I had 30 people a day asking me for money," he said. "And people started calling me El Millionario. Even my friends started looking at me differently, which made me feel sad."[33]

"People weren't just asking me for $100," he said. "I had people asking me for 2 million pesos to make a business. One person wanted to sell me a hotel. Everybody had a different problem. Some people said, 'I need medicine for my baby.' Other people said, "I need some money to buy rum. ... It's sad. I like to help people who really need help. But people were trying to use me. And I hate to be used."[34] He built a fence around his mother's house to keep solicitors out.

In some ways Rijo was generous with his new-found wealth. When he returned to the Dominican, he took a load of gloves, bats,

T-shirts, and tennis shoes to give to children. He spent about $60,000 for two ambulances, one for the police department, one for his hometown's hospital. "They deserve it," he said. "They need it. They suffer a lot. I've seen a lot of people die there because they didn't have transportation to a hospital. I figure as long as I've got the money, I can help them."[35]

Rijo didn't give all his money away. He spent plenty on his passion for classic automobiles. In 1989 he had purchased a cherry-red Porsche 960 Turbo from Pete Rose. By 1991 he was proudly driving a white BMW 750IL, one of seven cars he kept in his three residences in Florida, Ohio, and the Dominican Republic.[36]

During spring training in 1991 Rijo discussed his prospects for the future. "I'm capable of doing a lot of things if I can stay healthy for a full season," he said. "That's what I'm praying for, to be healthy for one full year and see what I can do. I've got one goal in mind, being in the All-Star Game and being the Cy Young winner."[37]

When asked about his inability to stay healthy, he replied: "It bothers me big time. It's happened the last three years and now you wonder if it's going to happen again."[38]

Rijo couldn't stay healthy. Shortly before Opening Day, he had some wisdom teeth removed, which contributed to manager Lou Piniella's decision to start Tom Browning rather than Rijo in the season's first game. Rijo was irate about the manager's action. "I don't think it's fair," he said.[39]

Injuries continued to haunt Rijo. In a game against the Montreal Expos at Riverfront Stadium on June 20, he broke an ankle while trying to steal second base. He missed six weeks, not returning to action until August 5. Meanwhile, dissension disrupted the clubhouse. The togetherness and camaraderie that had marked the championship season of 1990 was gone. Rijo contributed to the rancor. After a 13-0 loss in San Diego on August 11, he said, "It's hard to comprehend the situation, but when you see it, you believe it. I see a losing team. I see a team giving up with two months to go. Look at the game today. If you'd said we'd play like that, I'd have said 'No way.'"[40]

Four days later Rijo was pitching a shutout in the early innings of a game at San Francisco's Candlestick Park until Reds third baseman Chris Sabo committed an error that led to two unearned runs. After the Reds lost the game, 4-1, Rijo confronted Sabo in the dugout and took a swing at him. It took the efforts of six players to separate the two and prevent a real knockdown fight.[41]

His problems with his teammates were soon patched over. Around the first of September his elbow started hurting again, Rijo pitched through the pain and pitched some of the best baseball of his life. Seven shutout innings against Houston on September 15 earned him his sixth win in a row and brought his season record to 14-4. There was talk about Rijo as a candidate for the Cy Young Award. Piniella said, "José is developing into the best pitcher in the National League, pure and simple. He's really got it all together out there. ... As far as the best pitcher in the league, he's got my vote."[42]

José said, "I'm right at the top in almost every category. I don't know if they're going to take that (broken ankle) into consideration, but if they do, I'll have a fair shot. ... I think I'm quickly developing into the luckiest pitcher in the league, the way my elbow feels."[43]

Alas, Rijo lost two of his last three starts and came in fourth in Cy Young voting. Nevertheless, he had a great season. Despite missing six weeks with a broken ankle, he won 15 games for the first time in his major-league career. He led the league in won-lost percentage and WHIP (walks plus hits per innings pitched), and was second in earned-run average and strikeouts per innings pitched.

In 1992 Rijo won 15 games again, despite another stint on the disabled list. He was on the DL from April 18 to May 3 because of an inflammation of his right elbow. When he returned, Piniella, with the advice of Dr. Frank Jobe and Dr. James Andrews, placed him on a pitch count of 65-70 pitches for the next six or seven starts. He was afraid Rijo would break down again if he tried to come back too quickly. When Rijo protested the pitch count, Piniella advised him to keep his mouth shut. "He's being paid to pitch. He'll do what we tell him. We're doing what's best for him."[44] According to Retrosheet, over the next seven games Rijo pitched, his lowest pitch count was 83; three times he exceeded 100 pitches.

While he was on the DL, Rijo was taking four capsules of a powerful anti-inflammatory drug daily. Because of possible dire effects, the drug, Butazolidin, commonly called Bute, was given only in cases of severe pain. Dr. Mark Siegel of the Cincinnati Sportsmedicine and Orthopaedic Center said, "It's kind of a drug of last resort. It's usually used in cases where you need a good response quickly because it's usually this or possibly surgery.[45]

Rijo hedged his bets on which religion could help him most. For a long time he kept a voodoo doll and a bottle of snake oil in his locker. In 1991 he looked for a new source of help. He started carrying a picture of Pope John Paul II in his shaving kit. Before a start in Pittsburgh, he removed the picture from the case and propped it on a hook in his locker. He told himself, "If he falls off the hook, we lose. And if he hangs in there, we win."[46] Perhaps papal intervention paid off. At any rate, on July 2 Rijo pitched seven innings of six-hit ball, and the Reds beat Pittsburgh, 2-1, to end a three-game losing streak.

Rijo made it through the 1992 season without recourse to surgery, but it was extremely difficult. In July he didn't know if he could make it. His sore elbow was a major concern. "All I know is it's not getting any better. I'm trying to take it like a man. But I'm not having any fun even though we're winning. ... I'm trying. I'm doing my best. It's bad, but I've been able to swallow my pain and go out and pitch. ... but it's getting harder and harder."[47]

Somehow Rijo made it through the season. It may have been the Bute, or voodoo, or snake oil, or the pope, or just sheer determination on his part. His numbers weren't quite as good as they had been in '91, but they were still good. His strikeouts-to-walks ratio was second best in the National League.

The Cincinnati chapter of the Baseball Writers Association of America yearly presents the Joe Nuxhall Good Guy Award to a player who shows exemplary conduct on and off the field. The 1992 recipient was José Rijo. (Ten years later he won the award again, the first Red to be so honored twice.)

For the first time in six seasons with the Reds, Rijo avoided a stay on the DL in 1993. He won 14 games again. He could have won several more had he received a little more help from his teammates. Five potential victories were blown by the bullpen in the ninth inning and three more were lost by relievers in the eighth. In eight of his losses the Reds had scored a total of seven runs. He had good reason for his claim. "Given the lineup (Atlanta) had last year, and I probably would have won 25. It definitely would have been at least 20."[48]

Rijo led the league in strikeouts in 1993. He ranked second in ERA and third in WHIP. He led the league in games started and ranked second in innings pitched. Rijo finished fifth in balloting for the Cy Young Award in 1993. Despite those stellar numbers, Rijo was not a happy camper in 1993. He and Rosie had marital problems and broke up again. (This breakup appeared to be permanent.) The Reds were beset with troubles. Owner Marge Schott was suspended from Organized Baseball for a year because of inappropriate remarks. Manager Tony Pérez was fired. Rijo clashed with some of his teammates, including one expletive-filled tirade when he thought they were not supporting Pérez. "To me he is the best manager we've ever had here. He lets us have fun, and he lets us know when we've done something wrong. He's been great.[49] After Pérez was fired, Rijo said, "We've definitely reached the highest level of embarrassivity."[50]

The Reds lost 89 games, the most they had lost in a season since 1984. "There was no happiness," Rijo said. "There were no good times at all. It was all aggravation, irritation. To lose every day is not fun. Even though you're throwing the ball good, it's no consolation because you're supposed to do that. You've got to win. That's the most important thing."[51]

The Reds turned things around in 1994. They got off to a good start and led their division almost every day until the season came to an abrupt halt. Rijo's slider was one of the principal reasons for the Reds' success. While José was still a teenager, Pascual Pérez taught him how to throw the pitch. The slider is typically so hard on the elbow that some clubs refuse to teach it to their young hurlers. Perhaps overuse of the slider is partially responsible for the elbow and shoulder injuries that plagued Rijo throughout much of his career. He refrained from throwing sliders between starts and in early exhibition games, but when the season started he was willing to throw sliders at any time. By 1994 he was throwing the slider 50 percent of the time. In a poll conducted by *The Sporting News*, Rijo's slider was voted best in the National League by an overwhelming margin. He received 43 votes; John Smoltz and Larry Andersen tied for second with four votes each.[52]

Rijo achieved one of his goals by being selected for the 1994 All-Star Game, although he did not pitch in the game. His record was 8-4 at the time. He won only one more game after the break. His hopes of competing in another World Series were thwarted when the baseball season was ended by a strike on August 12. Although the Reds were in first place at the time, there was no postseason for them or any other team. Rijo had a record of 9-6, with an ERA of 3.08. He led the league in games started and was second in strikeouts.

The work stoppage ended when US District Judge Sonia Sotomayor issued a preliminary injunction against the owners on March 31, 1995. After an abbreviated spring training, the season began in late April. The Reds were again expected to win the National League Central. Sportswriter Bob Nightengale foresaw Rijo winning the Cy Young Award that he had coveted for so long.[53] Instead Rijo's world came crashing down on him again.

On June 2 Rijo was placed on the DL with tendinitis in his right elbow. He came off the DL on June 17 and attempted to pitch again, but even with the help of cortisone shots the pain was too much. The bone spurs that had troubled him for years were getting worse. By 1995 the bone spurs were 2½ times larger than when he was 17. On July 19 he was put on the DL again in the hope that rest would relieve the pain and enable him to pitch effectively again. It didn't work. Magnetic resonance imaging (MRI) showed a partially torn ulnar collateral ligament (UCL) as well as some bone formation within the ligament. Some bleeding was detected.

On August 22, 1995, Tommy John surgery was performed on Rijo's right elbow by Dr. James Andrews in Birmingham, Alabama. The surgery consisted of removing a UCL and replacing it with a tendon from elsewhere in the body. Andrews estimated Rijo would be able to pitch again in about one year. He thought there was an 80 percent probability that Rijo would regain his full pitching capability. He cautioned that physical recovery after surgery is but a fraction of the recovery process. "What we're really talking about here is mind over matter," Andrews said. "We're talking about six months to a year or even more in recovery, and a player has to prepare for that mentally even more than what he has to endure physically. Surgery is just the first step in a long journey."[54]

Rijo was soon ready mentally to pitch, but the surgery did not end his physical problems. Rijo has been cited as one of the greatest failures of Tommy John surgery.[55]

Rijo was expected to miss most, if not all, of the 1996 season, but in early spring he appeared to be making great progress and was already throwing sliders in addition to fastballs. The Reds were not eager to reactivate him; not only did they not want to jeopardize his recovery by rushing him back too soon, but it was also to their financial advantage to keep him on the DL. Their insurance company was picking up all of his

$5.9 million salary. They were right. Rijo did push himself too soon. During spring training he developed excruciating pain. He had to undergo a second surgery on his right shoulder on April 4, 1996. It was an arthroscopic procedure to remove elbow calcification, bone formation in his elbow and scar tissue. He started throwing again in late May, but he couldn't handle the strain. He had to undergo surgery again on November 20 to repair a ruptured flexor tendon, his third time under the knife in 15 months. There seemed no chance that he could pitch in 1997. By early March of that year, it seemed likely that Rijo would never pitch in the majors again.[56] On April 7 Dr. Andrews removed some sutures and scar tissue. However, Rijo kept trying. In August he severely injured the flexor tendon in his right elbow. The tendon was torn completely off the bone. The result was a fourth elbow surgery by Dr. Andrews on August 27.

The Reds granted Rijo free agency on October 29. On January 8, 1998, they signed him to a minor-league contract for 1998, but it was doubtful that he could pitch.

Rijo reported to the Reds' 1998 spring-training camp in Sarasota able to throw, but was told to wait a few weeks before pitching off a mound. He agreed to stay with the club as a scout if his comeback failed. He was told that the position of scout could lead to a role in management or as a pitching coach.[57] Nothing came of this agreement. He was granted free agency again on October 15, 1998.

In the spring of 1999, Rijo opened a baseball academy he built on a hillside on the southern coast of the Dominican Republic, near his hometown of San Cristobal. *Loma del Sueño,* he called it, Hill of Dreams. "I know a lot of dreams are going to come true there," he said.[58] The complex included seven baseball fields, 10 indoor batting cages, a track, two weight rooms, two dining rooms, four locker rooms, and housing for 600 youngsters. "This is my biggest pitch of my whole life. I can pass on all the knowledge that I learned about the game to those kids," he said.[59] In its first two years, his academy helped nearly 100 youths sign minor-league contracts.

For five years Rijo worked very hard at rehabilitation. He kept trying to come back but met setback after setback. In 2000 he said, "I'm going to lay off for a whole year, start traveling, eat steak, drink wine, have fun and forget about baseball for a year. ... I was resting my mind and my arm both."[60] To keep himself in shape, the 35-year-old Rijo played basketball with the youngsters at his academy.

As he had so many times in the past, Rijo tried to make a comeback in 2001. His slider had lost some of its bite, but he had developed a forkball that dropped almost straight down, and he still had an effective fastball. In May he traveled to Cincinnati for medical exams to see if his rehabilitation had been complete enough for him to resume pitching. He passed the tests; On July 1 Rijo signed a free-agent contract with Cincinnati. The Reds sent him to Dayton of the Class-A Midwest League. He started one game for the Dragons, pitched three innings in which he allowed only one run, and was ready to move on. His next stop was at Chattanooga in the Double-A Southern League. He pitched three innings for the Lookouts, struck out three, walked one, and allowed one hit, but no runs. "Those were three good innings," he said. "My arm feels outstanding. My mechanics were good. ... I feel ready (for the major leagues.)"[61]

In order to prove that he was indeed ready for the big leagues, Rijo needed to be tested at the highest minor-league level. He made four starts and two relief appearances for the Louisville Riverbats of the Triple-A International League before Jim Bowden, Cincinnati's general manager, pronounced him ready for prime time. He was called up on August 17. He pitched the eighth and ninth innings of a loss to the Milwaukee Brewers that evening. In two innings he gave up two hits, walked two, and struck out two. It was his first major-league appearance since 1997. Rijo became the first pitcher to return to the majors after having been out of Organized Baseball for five seasons.

Rijo's joy at returning to the majors was almost more than he could express. "I cannot describe with words how I feel right now. It's beyond anything in my life that I ever accomplished," Rijo said. "No moment could beat this moment today, until I die and go to heaven and meet Jesus. This feeling is that close. ... I never thought it would take this long. Nobody has any idea how hard it was to be here today."[62]

After posting a 2.12 ERA in 13 appearances with the Reds in 2001, Rijo joined the Florida Instructional League to stay in shape so he could pitch in the Dominican Winter League. In January Rijo signed a minor-league contract for 2002, but he fully expected to pitch in the majors. That expectation was fulfilled. In March he was added to the Reds' 40-man roster and given a one-year contract for $500,000. "I feel like I'm a walking miracle right now," he said.[63]

Rijo started the 2002 season as a long reliever, but moved into the starting rotation on April 21. He went 4-3 in eight starts until his shoulder began giving him trouble. He went on the DL on June 7. He returned to action as a reliever on July 13. During the season he made nine starts and relieved 22 times, while compiling a 5-4 record. He didn't know it at the time, but his last major-league appearance came on September 28, 2002. The 37-year-old right-hander pitched the seventh inning of a 6-0 loss at Montreal, giving up one earned run on two hits and a walk.

Rijo received two well-deserved awards at the end of the season. Cincinnati baseball writers presented him with his second Joe Nuxhall Good Guy Award. The Boston Red Sox honored him with the Tony Conigliaro Award, given annually to the major-league baseball player who best overcomes adversity through spirit, determination, and courage.

Rijo was looking forward to another good year in 2003, but again adversity struck. During spring training his elbow began giving him trouble. On March 11 he flew to Birmingham, where Dr. Andrews performed an arthroscopic procedure to remove a bone spur, the sixth surgery on Rijo's elbow. Rijo expected to be back in action in a few weeks, but it didn't happen. By June he was feeling pain in a different part of the elbow. Dr. Andrews told him another operation was not an option. He had two choices – to pitch with the pain or to retire.[64]

Rijo could pitch through pain. He had done it before, and he was willing to do it again. But he couldn't pitch if he couldn't get the ball over the plate. Rijo admitted he couldn't handle any more surgeries.[65] So he really had no choice. He never threw another pitch in Organized Baseball. The Reds granted him free agency on October 15, 2003; his playing career was over at the age of 38.

For the next few years Rijo worked mainly at his baseball academy in the Dominican Republic. On November 1, 2004, Jim Bowden, Cincinnati's general manager, became general manager of the Washington Nationals. He hired Rijo as a special assistant, primarily to increase the organization's ability to attract Latin ballplayers, especially Dominicans. The Nationals developed a special relationship with Rijo's academy. Rijo also spent time in Washington during the season, working with the club's pitchers. "I have a lot of knowledge of the game," he said, "and it means a lot to me to share that knowledge with the young pitchers to help them get better."[66]

Rijo was credited with saving six young Cuban players from deportation. "They had left (Cuba) to look for a better life. They came over in a boat and were caught by the police.

They were very scared. When they learned they were going to be sent back to Cuba, they almost started crying. They said they would rather be shot in the Dominican," Rijo said. "They did not want to go back to receive the punishment they were going to receive."[67]

Rijo appealed to Dominican officials and got the players released so they could live and play at his academy.

Meanwhile, Rijo's career in Cincinnati was not forgotten. On June 11, 2005, he and Eric Davis were inducted into the Cincinnati Reds Hall of Fame. They were the first two players from the world champion 1990 Reds to be so honored. Rijo came back to the Queen City for the ceremony. "There were so many people I was looking forward to seeing here. It reminds you of some people who have left the game. It reminds you of the World Series. It reminds you of how far you've come and how much you can help other people. There are a lot of memories for me here; it has a place in my heart."[68]

Rijo reflected on Dominican baseball. "I think when you play the game in the Dominican, a Dominican kid does a lot with a little, doing the only thing he knows how to do, and that's playing ball. … The desire to become a major-league player is unbelievable. You know that's the only way you're going to make a difference in your country. If I'm healthy, I'm happy. Every day when I wake up, I feel good, and I feel motivated. When I wake up in the morning, I think about the kids in the Dominican. There, 70 percent of the kids don't really have education; they help provide for their families. Some of them don't even know what they're going to eat in the morning."[69]

When asked about his responsibilities with the Nationals, Rijo replied: "Responsibilities? I have too many. I'm assistant GM, I'm a scout, and I'm also a part-time coach at the major-league level. But I'm going to do everything I can to stay around the game."[70]

Those were heady days for José Rijo. He zipped around the Dominican in his fire-engine-red Mercedes convertible, basking in the adoration of his countrymen. Rijo's relationship with the Washington Nationals lasted for more than four years. It came to an unhappy conclusion in February 2009. The Nationals fired Rijo and ended its association with his academy less than a week after it was revealed that prized prospect Esmailyn Gonzalez, who had trained at Rijo's academy before receiving a $1.4 million signing bonus in 2006, had lied about both his name and his age. Rijo denied any knowledge of wrongdoing.[71]

Rijo defended the lengths to which Dominican players will go, including identity fraud, to gain a foothold in North American baseball. Sociologist Alan Klein reported Rijo as saying, "We used to have a factory with 3,000 jobs. It's gone. We used to have a gun factory. Gone. Duty-free, gone. We used to have a hotel in this town. We don't have one anymore. We used to have three movie theaters. We don't have movies anymore. All the job opportunities here are gone. What's people going to do? Be honest? And get a job where?"[72]

Supply and demand outweighed some other considerations. The Dominican has a seemingly inexhaustible supply of young men seeking baseball careers. The major leagues have a demand for more and more talented players. Baseball academies are thriving on the island. Every major-league club now operates an academy. Other academies are operated by entrepreneurs, called *buscones*, who furnish room and board, baseball training, and sometimes English-language instruction to 13- to 15-year-olds, In the expectation of receiving 15 percent of the player's signing bonus, if he is offered a professional contract at age 16.

Soon after Rijo was cleared of any wrongdoing in the Gonzales case, Rijo was back working in an academy as a *buscon*. In 2009 he was still indulging in his passion for automobiles, driving a white Lexus SC430 convertible. But he couldn't avoid suspicion. In December 2011 he was subpoenaed for questioning about his possible involvement in money-laundering for drug traffickers. No concrete evidence was found, and the case was dropped.

Once again Rijo was back in the good graces of his countrymen. How long that would continue remained to be seen.

NOTES

1 *Washington Post,* April 11, 1991.
2 *Washington Post,* April 11, 1991.
3 *Washington Post,* April 11, 1991.
4 *USA Today,* February 28, 1991.
5 Clipping in Rijo's Hall of Fame File, no date.
6 HOF file, April 3, 1985.
7 HOF file, no date.
8 HOF file, no date.
9 *The Sporting News,* March 10, 1986.
10 HOF file, no date.
11 HOF file, no date.
12 *Kansas City Times.,* June 24, 1986.
13 *Washington Post,* April 11, 1991.
14 *The Sporting News,* May 9, 1988.
15 *The Sporting News,* June 20, 1988.
16 *The Sporting News,* June 20, 1988.
17 *Washington Post,* April 11, 1991
18 John Erardi and Joel Luckhaupt, *The Wire-to-Wire Reds.* (Cincinnati: Clerisy Press, 2010), 164.
19 Erardi and Luckhaupt.
20 Erardi and Luckhaupt.
21 Erardi and Luckhaupt.
22 *New York Times,* March 1, 1991.
23 *Washington Post,* April 11, 1991.
24 HOF file, December 14, 1990.
25 *The National Sports Daily,* no date.
26 *USA Today,* February 28, 1991.
27 *New York Times,* March 13, 1991.
28 *USA Today,* February 28, 1991.
29 *USA Today Baseball Weekly,* March 4-10, 1992.
30 *New York Times,* March 1, 1991.
31 *Washington Post,* April 11, 1991.
32 *New York Times,* March 13, 1991.
33 *Washington Post,* April 11, 1991.
34 *Washington Post,* April 11, 1991.
35 *USA Today Baseball Weekly,* March 4-10, 1992.
36 *Washington Post,* April 11, 1991.

37 *New York Times,* March 13, 1991.
38 *New York Times,* March 13, 1991.
39 HOF file, March 22, 1991.
40 *The Sporting News,* August 19, 1991.
41 *The Sporting News,* August 26, 1991.
42 HOF file, no date.
43 HOF file, no date.
44 *The Sporting News,* May 18, 1982.
45 HOF file, June 28, 1992.
46 HOF files, July 13, 1992.
47 *USA Today,* July 26, 1992.
48 HOF file, April 4, 1994.
49 *The Sporting News,* May 3, 1993.
50 *The Sporting News,* June 7, 1993.
51 *The Sporting News,* May 4, 1994.
52 *The Sporting News,* July 11, 1994.
53 *The Sporting News,* May 1, 1995.
54 *The Sporting News,* March 20, 1996.
55 W. Laurence Coker, *Baseball Injuries. Case Studies by Types in the Major Leagues* (Jefferson, North Carolina: McFarland, 2002), 69.
56 *The Sporting News,* March 3, 1997.
57 *The Sporting News,* March 2, 1998.
58 *The Sporting News,* January 5, 2001.
59 *The Sporting News,* January 5, 2001.
60 *USA Today,* March 25, 2002.
61 *Cincinnati Post,* July 10, 2001.
62 *New York Post,* August 18, 2001.
63 *USA Today,* March 25, 2002.
64 Associated Press, June 11, 2003.
65 *Cincinnati Enquirer,* June 11, 2003.
66 *Washington Post,* March 4, 2005.
67 *Washington Times,* March 4, 2005.
68 *Dayton Daily News,* June 9, 2005.
69 *Dayton Daily News,* June 9, 2005.
70 *Dayton Daily News,* June 9, 2005.
71 Espn.go.com, February 26, 2009.
72 Alan Klein, *Dominican Baseball: New Pride, Old Prejudice* (Philadelphia: Temple University Press, 2014), 4.

JUAN SAMUEL

By Thomas J. Brown Jr.

Juan Samuel was a player of many talents. He was also a player who did not quite fit any specific role. Samuel had tremendous talent but was a challenge to put to any kind of real use wherever he played. He had a low batting average, good power, and good speed on the bases so that a team might use him as its leadoff hitter, except that he struck out a lot and didn't draw many walks. Samuel was also not a terrific fielder in spite of his speed.[1] The result is that Samuel never quite found the right role for himself.

Juan Milton Samuel was born on December 9, 1960, in San Pedro de Macoris, Dominican Republic. He learned to play baseball on the sandlots of his hometown. Juan's family eventually moved to Puerto Rico. Juan attended Licey High School in Licey, Puerto Rico. He played amateur baseball in Puerto Rico and the Dominican Republic, where he was discovered by scout Francisco Acevedo.[2] He signed with the Philadelphia Phillies on April 29, 1980.

Samuel was 19 years old when he joined the Phillies organization. He was sent to the Central Oregon (Bend, Oregon) Phillies of the low Class-A Northwest League. In 69 games, Samuel stole 26 bases and hit 17 home runs

Photo courtesy of the National Baseball Hall of Fame

and 11 doubles, finishing the season with a .503 slugging percentage.

Samuel's success that first year earned him a promotion to Spartanburg of the low Class-A South Atlantic League for the 1981 season. He continued to show promise when he hit 22 doubles and 11 home runs. Samuel's 53 stolen bases showed that he was a threat whenever he got on base.

The Phillies continued to believe in their young infielder by promoting him to the high Class-A Carolina League in 1982. Samuel played in 135 games for the Peninsula Pilots and was one of the stars on a team that went 90-47. Samuel batted .320 with 28 home runs, 29 doubles, a slugging percentage of .573, and 64 stolen bases.

After his success with the Pilots, Samuel started the 1983 season with the Reading Phillies of the Double-A Eastern League. He continued his hitting ways. In just 47 games with Reading, Samuel had 10 doubles and 11 home runs. This led to his promotion in early June to the Triple-A Portland Beavers. Facing the higher caliber of pitchers did not slow him down. In 65 games with the Beavers, Samuel had 86 hits, including 15 home runs and 14 doubles, and 33 stolen bases. The Phillies were so impressed with Samuel's progress that they called him up in August.

Samuel made his major-league debut on August 24, 1983. He was the leadoff hitter for the Phillies and his first major-league hit was a triple off Mark Davis of the San Francisco Giants in the third inning. Samuel scored when Giants center fielder Chili Davis made an error as he tried to field the ball. Samuel played in 18 games for the Phillies after his call-up, and the club kept him on the roster for the postseason and Samuel got into three games for the Phillies in the World Series, twice as a pinch-runner and once as a pinch-hitter. His overall performance that year led many observers to predict that he would become a Phillies starter in 1984.

Samuel did well in 1984 spring training, and stuck with the Phillies when the season began. Manager Paul Owens said that Samuel had all the tools to be a superstar in the field with his speed, range, soft hands, and a quick release. "With most rookies, there is almost always an element of doubt in some area," Owens said, "but the way this kid got to balls in the field and stayed aggressive at the plate, you knew he had the stuff to make it."[3]

Samuel played in 160 games in 1984, all at second base, and finished second to Dwight Gooden in the voting for the NL Rookie of the Year Award. He came in 21st in the voting for MVP honors, impressive for a rookie. He was a double threat for the Phillies whenever he came to bat. Samuel showed that he could hit for power by finishing the season with 15 home runs, 36 doubles, and an astonishing 19 triples, the most in the National League that season. He stole 72 bases, breaking Tim Raines' rookie record of 71 that had been set three years earlier. He also set a major-league record for most at-bats by a right-handed hitter, 701. (He had 737 plate appearances.)

Samuel was named to the National League team for the All-Star Game, but didn't play in the game.

Samuel did not show any signs of slowing down during his sophomore season. He continued to be a threat whenever he came to bat, hitting 19 home runs, stealing 53 bases, and finishing the season with a .264 batting average and a .436 slugging percentage.

Samuel was an important part of the Phillies lineup from 1985 through 1987. Many observers thought that he might become one of the best players in the game as he continued to put up impressive statistics. In 1987 Samuel led the league again with 15 triples. He also led the NL with 80 extra-base hits. He put up solid defensive statistics when he led all second basemen in putouts (374) and was second in assists (434). He was the first major leaguer to reach double figures in doubles, triples, home runs, and stolen bases in each of his first four seasons.

Samuel's solid play earned him a spot on the NL All-Star team in 1987. Playing six innings, he was hitless but made several key defensive plays to help the NL win 2-0. Samuel also earned his only Silver Slugger award in 1987 and came in 13th in the voting for MVP. Although he finished the season with some of his best batting numbers, Samuel also led the league in strikeouts. This distinction tied him with Hack Wilson (1927-30) and Vince DiMaggio (1942-45) for the major-league record for consecutive strikeout titles with four.

Samuel's statistics dropped off after 1987. Although he was still productive, he did not produce as consistently as in his first four years. In 1988 the Phillies moved Samuel to center field. The reason may have been that Samuel led the league in errors by second baseman in 1984, 1986, and 1987.

Midway through the 1989 season, Samuel was sent to the New York Mets. He was traded for Lenny Dykstra and Roger McDowell as the Mets revamped their team. Samuel replaced Dykstra and became the Mets' center fielder and leadoff hitter. Mets manager Davey Johnson said, "Juan Samuel is an impact player. Whenever I thought about the Phillies the last four or five years, I thought about Juan Samuel. He reminds me of Bobby Bonds. People don't realize what kind of impact player he is."[4] While Samuel may have been surprised by the trade, he was optimistic and said, "It's hard for me and good for me. I gained 10 games in the standings in one day. I think the Mets are suited to my kind of baseball. I'm a winner."[5]

After he joined the Mets, Samuel continued to struggle offensively. The Mets introduced him after the trade as the impact player they needed to rescue their sluggish offense. But Samuel did not enjoy being the center of attention and he allowed his sensitivities and his anxieties to hinder his athletic skills.[6] He hit only three home runs and stole 31 bases after his arrival in New York.

The Mets, disappointed in Samuel's lack of productivity, traded him to the Los Angeles Dodgers after the season for Mike Marshall and Alejandro Peña. Samuel became more productive as he split time between second base and center field for the Dodgers in 1990 and 1991. He played well enough in his second season in Los Angeles to earn a spot on the All-Star team. He hit a single, his only hit in three appearances in the midsummer classic.

After 2½ seasons with the Dodgers, Samuel was released by the team on July 30, 1992, as he struggled to produce at the plate. He was signed by the Kansas City Royals. Samuel played in 29 games for the Royals at second base and left field. He became a free agent at the end of the season.

Samuel signed with the Cincinnati Reds in the offseason. He played in 103 games for the Reds, in 1993, mostly in a utility role, and was released after the season. In April of 1994 Samuel signed a contract with the Detroit Tigers. The Tigers used him primarily as a backup in 1994 and 1995; he played in a total of 135 games, splitting his playing time between second base and the outfield. Near the end of the 1995 season, the Tigers traded Samuel back to Kansas City for Phil Hiatt.

When the Royals released Samuel after the 1995 season, he signed with the Toronto Blue Jays. He played there for three years as a utilityman and designated hitter. He retired as a player after the 1998 season.

Samuel jumped immediately into coaching after he finished his playing career. He was the Tigers' first-base coach from 1999 to 2002, then the third-base coach from 2002 to 2005.[7]

Samuel tried his hand at managing in 2006. The Mets hired him to take charge of the Double-A Binghamton Mets. He led the team to a second-place finish in the Eastern League in his lone season as the manager.[8]

Samuel returned to the major leagues in 2007 when he was hired to coach third base for the Baltimore Orioles. When manager

Dave Trembley was fired in June 2010, Samuel was named interim manager.[9] He took over a team that had the worst record in baseball at the time and said he had "full intention to take advantage of this opportunity and see how far we can push these guys."[10] Despite a pair of four-game winning streaks, the Orioles went 17-34 with Samuel as the manager and he was replaced by Buck Showalter on August 3.[11]

Samuel was offered a position as a coach on Showalter's staff but declined, saying that it would have been uncomfortable staying on. He said: "It would have been confusing at times for the guys, and they have already been through so much. Sometimes it's just time to move on."[12]

Samuel did not leave the Orioles organization altogether. He returned to his native Dominican Republic, where he spent the rest of the season working as a talent evaluator for the Orioles academy there.

Samuel joined the Phillies coaching staff for 2011. He became the third-base coach when Sam Perlozzo was moved to the first-base coaching position. Samuel was also responsible for working with the team's outfielders. In 2012 he moved to the first-base coaching box when Ryne Sandberg became the third-base coach. He shifted back to third base after Sandberg was promoted to interim manager near the end of the 2013 season.[13] Samuel also took over as the baserunning instructor as well as outfield instructor in 2012.

Reflecting on his work as a coach, Samuel said the biggest challenge to coaching the outfielders was "recognizing, reading the swing, understanding what the hitter's trying to do, and focusing. I tell the outfielders that, even if we say we're usually going to play somebody on the pull side, in general, if we get a report that he has trouble against the pitcher he's facing tonight, he might not pull this guy. You need to read his swing if you see that he's behind a little bit."[14]

Sandberg moved Samuel back to the first-base coach's box for the 2014 and 2015 seasons. When Pete Mackanin was named the interim manager late in the 2015 season, Samuel again moved across the diamond to third base. As of the 2018 season that remained his post.

Samuel said in 2015 that he looked forward to having another opportunity to manage in the major leagues. "I think that I'm capable of doing it, I'm prepared and I'm ready to do it," he said. "I got a taste of it in Baltimore and I enjoyed it. It's something that is my ultimate goal. Before I hang it up I would like to get a shot whether it's here [in Philadelphia] or somewhere else."[15]

Samuel was the third-base coach for the 2013 World Baseball Classic championship team from the Dominican Republic.[16] The team defeated Puerto Rico in each of the three rounds, including the Gold Medal game, to become the first WBC champion from the Western Hemisphere, as well as the first team to complete the tournament undefeated.

During his playing career, Samuel collected 1,578 hits and 396 stolen bases, and reached double figures in home runs nine times.

Samuel was a popular player with the Phillies. He was enshrined on the Phillies Wall of Fame in 2008. In an interview in 2016, he tried to make light of his achievements, saying, "Did I really make that much impact in the short time I was there? I think about the other folks on the Wall of Fame – it's great. I'm glad somebody remembered."[17] Samuel was inducted into the Reading Phillies Hall of Fame in 2004, and into the San Pedro de Macoris Hall of Fame in 2015. In September 2006, in a ceremony at Citizens Bank Park, he received the Phillies Latino Legend Award.

He has three children, a son, Samuel, and daughters Alexa and Noemy.

Samuel demonstrated throughout his long career that he didn't fit any one mold. First as a player with many talents, he never found one role that suited them appropriately as he played different positions for different teams. Now as a coach, he continues to make his mark. He has learned to adapt in order to help today's players be successful using his personal experience as a major-league player.

SOURCES

In addition to the sources cited in the Notes, the author used the Baseball-Reference.com and Retrosheet.org websites for box scores, player, team, and season pages, pitching and batting game logs, and other pertinent material. FanGraphs.com provided individual statistical information.

NOTES

1. Dave Fleming, "14 Players," Bill James Online, May 25, 2009. billjamesonline.com/article1145/.
2. Stephen Falk, "The Interview: Juan Samuel Is a Stickler for … Well, Everything," Phillies.com, August 5, 2016.
3. Phil Elderkin, "Young Speedster Juan Samuel Looks Like NL's Top Rookie of 1984," *Christian Science Monitor*, June 4, 1984.
4. Joséph Durso, "Mets Get Samuel for McDowell, Dykstra," *New York Times*, June 19, 1989.
5. Durso.
6. Tom Verducci, "Pendulum Swings for Juan Samuel," *Newsday*, June 18, 1990.
7. Tyler DiSalle, "Phillies 2016 Coaching Staff: Juan Samuel," ThatBall'sOuttaHere.com, March 11, 2016.
8. DiSalle.
9. DSalle.
10. Brittany Ghiroli, "Trembley Dismissed; Samuel in as Interim," MLB.com, June 4, 2010.
11. Tyler DiSalle, "Phillies 2016 Coaching Staff."
12. "Samuel Declines Post, Will Remain with Club," MLB.com, August 1, 2010.
13. Tyler DiSalle, "Phillies 2016 Coaching Staff."
14. Stephen Falk, "The Interview."
15. Jim Salisbury, "Juan Samuel Eager for Shot to Manage in Majors," CSNPhilly.com, September 23, 2015.
16. "Phillies Manager and Coaches," Phillies.MLB.com.
17. Stephen Falk, "The Interview."

Pedro Alejandro San

By Julio M. Rodriguez

In 1945 Montecristi was a village of maybe 4,000 inhabitants, located on the shore of the Atlantic Ocean in the northwest corner of the Dominican Republic and near the border with Haiti. The local baseball park was named for Pedro Alejandro San. There were many who were not familiar with San.

The ballpark's grandstand was a wooden structure that could hold around 300 fans.[1] It was known that San was a pitcher who could throw a submarine ball that would anesthetize batters. He was born in Montecristi and was one of the first Dominicans to play in other countries of the Caribbean where baseball was played, and in the United States.

In the part of town called Pueblo Abajo (low part of town) there was a man who lived with a large family; his nickname was El Mono (the monkey). He had lost one eye and was very proud of it. Why? Because he had lost that eye in a baseball game, while catching San without a mask.

It was a tale perhaps difficult to believe, but nobody in town claimed the story was false, not even Pinto Santos, the most popular sportsman in Montecristi at the time.[2]

In 1945 the idol of most kids in the area was Bombo Ramos, also a pitcher. Bombo was not a submariner, but stymied batters with his fastball.

One boy, 8 years old, often traveled the 6 kilometers from his home in the small community of Laguna Verde to watch Bombo pitch. He decided that he would become a pitcher himself. His ambition brought him to the Baseball Hall of Fame in Cooperstown. His name was Juan Marichal.

Almost three years later, Bombo, Miguel A. Rodriguez (also a pitcher), and José Jimenez, a shortstop, died when a plane carrying the Santiago baseball team crashed in Rio Verde, near Yamasa, on January 11, 1948, during a national baseball tournament in the Dominican Republic.

In 1946 electricity came to Montecristi and radio broadcasts of the Cuban winter league games could be heard. In the summer, these stations would retransmit major-league games from the United States.

People in town began to wonder why San, if he was so good that he had a baseball field named after him, did not play in those leagues.

When Pinto Santos was asked about this, he remained silent. Then, in 1947, came big news in the baseball world that for the first time a man of color, Jackie Robinson, would play in the major leagues, with the Brooklyn Dodgers.

In 1948 the Dodgers, along with their Montreal Royals Triple-A affiliate, trained in Santo Domingo (called Trujillo City in those days). At the swimming pool of the Jaragua Hotel, where the Dodgers were staying, Robinson was in a pool with white people for the first time.

In 1959 a picture of San was published in a sport publication in Santo Domingo and finally the young people of Montecristi realized why San had not been able to play in the major leagues. He was a black man.

The following year, 1960, a fellow from Montecristi went to St. Louis for his internship after finishing medical school in Santo Domingo. He saw in the news that Ernie Banks, a famous black ballplayer, could not stay at the Chase Hotel, then the best in the city, along with the rest of his Chicago Cubs teammates, because of his race.

Then he thought of San and said to himself, "Well, at least Banks could play in the major leagues, things are getting better."[3]

Pedro Alejandro San was born in Montecristi in 1895. The actual date of his birth is unknown. It is also not known what sort of work his parents may have done, but they were of very low standing in the class structure of the day. It is possible that they were of Haitian background, but this is not known for sure.

By 1916, when the first twentieth-century American military intervention in the Dominican Republic took place and the game of baseball became fashionable in the country, San was 21 and showed great ability as an outfielder with an arm that was so good that he was converted into a right-handed pitcher.

By the age of 26, San had earned national recognition as a pitcher, famous because of his "submarine pitch," which rose when reaching home plate. He made his debut in Santo Domingo on July 31, 1921, pitching for the Licey Tigers and losing 1-0 to the Escogido Lions and their star Fellito Guerra, in spite of San striking out 11 batters, including all three he faced in the second, fifth, and eighth innings.

On November 5, 1921, pitching again for Licey, he faced the all-star team of the US Marines in Santo Domingo. In 10 innings, he won the game, 7-3. The Marines were held to nine hits.

A few months later, on January 21, 1922, San was even better. In nine innings he allowed the Marine all-stars only two runs and four hits, winning by a score of 6-2. With that victory Licey won the series between the two teams.

That same year, 1922, was the first time an all-star team of Dominican players went abroad to play baseball. They went to Puerto Rico and San was one of the four pitchers on the team.

On September 24, San worked nine innings against Ponce and allowed only one run and three hits while striking out eight, winning the game, 2-1. At the plate, he hit a single and a triple.

In the Dominican Republic in 1923, San pitched for Escogido, and in the opening game of the season, on April 2, threw a three-hit shutout, defeating Santiago, 5-0. Santiago's starting pitcher was Francisco Chicharrón, relieved in the fifth by Felicito Gallardo. San's record for the year was 7-2, leading all pitchers in the league.

San's record for 1924 and 1925 remains unknown.

From 1926 through 1928 San played in the United States for Alex Pompez's Cuban Stars East of the Eastern Colored League. During the 1926 season, his record was 2-3 in two starts and several relief appearances totaling $33^{1}/_{3}$ innings of work. He started nine games

The Concordia Eagles of 1934. Back row, L to R: Marcelino Blondet, Tetelo Vargas, Martin Dihigo, Jimmy Jordan, Balbino Espinosa, Francisco Quevedo, Josh Gibson, and (in street clothes) Arturo Lopez, delegate. Front row, kneeling L to R: Cesar Nieves, Luis Aparicio (Senior), Manuel Malpica, Rap Dixon, Luis Jimenez, Silvino Ruiz, and Pedro Alejandro San.

Photo courtesy of Cuqui Cordova

in 1927, with an 8-4 record, working a total of 85 innings. In 1927 he started 10 games but worked only 48 2/3 innings; he was 3-5.

In 1929 San was back in the Dominican Republic, pitching again for Licey.

In the Caribbean it is widely felt that the best baseball team ever assembled in the region was the Eagles of Concordia, built through the efforts of the family of Venezuelan dictator Juan Vicente Gomez, a rabid baseball fan.

From 1932 through 1935, the Eagles visited all the countries in the area, winning every series in which they participated. Some of the names on this team give us an idea of how good Concordia was: Martin Dihigo, Pedro Alejandro San, Josh Gibson, Johnny Mize, Rap Dixon, Tetelo Vargas, and Luis Aparicio (father of the future Hall of Famer Luis Aparicio.)

The peak years of San's career are said to have been 1930 through 1935, years in which he played in Puerto Rico, the United States, Colombia, Cuba, and Venezuela. Unfortunately, there is no detailed record available showing what he did during those years. The best-documented games are two in which he faced Dihigo in Venezuela.

The first game took place on August 21, 1932, Dihigo throwing for Concordia and San for a team called Cincinnati, made up mostly of Cuban players who named the team that way because most Cuban players in the major leagues had entered baseball in the United States with Cincinnati. Dihigo threw a no-hit, no-run game and beat San.

The second game was on April 17, 1933, at Barquisemeto, Venezuela. Some of the Concordia players had been distributed to the teams of different cities. San pitched for a team called "Japan" and Dihigo pitched for "America." This time San beat Dihigo, 1-0. He allowed only two hits and fanned 14 batters.

In January 1934 Concordia visited the Dominican Republic. Because Johnny Mize left the team and went back to the United States, Concordia brought Rap Dixon and Josh Gibson to replace him. Probably the best of all the Concordia teams, they defeated Dominican opponents Licey and Escogido. Pitching for Concordia, San won two games during this visit, one against Licey and the other against Escogido, each time allowing only two runs.

The Dominicans assembled an all-star team with the best players of Licey and Escogido, and Concordia also beat them, winning the Presidente Rafael Leonidas Trujillo Cup without suffering even one loss.

San's last season was in 1936, pitching for the Eagles of Santiago in the tournament in the Dominican Republic won by las Estrellas Orientales (the Oriental Stars) of San Pedro de Macoris, in the eastern part of the country. His record was 3-3

Because La Romana was then a prosperous place built around the sugar mill industry, San went to live there and died relatively young at 48 years of age, on January 12, 1943.[4]

Two years later, in 1946, San was selected by the Sociedad Pro Deportes as a member of the best Dominican baseball team of all time. In 1967 he was inducted into the Salon de la Fama del Deporte Dominicano (Dominican Sports Hall of Fame).

NOTES

1. The ballpark in Montecristi still bears San's name. The old park was destroyed in 1954 to build a hospital, but the new park, which can hold around 600 fans, was built of concrete blocks in another part of town.

2. Much of the information for this biography comes from two sources – personal conversations with Pinto Santos in Montecristi and a series of columns about San by Cuqui Cordova, in *Listin Diario*. The columns were titled "Beisbol de Ayer" and were published from July 26 through October 8, 2011.

3. The medical intern was this author.

4. Cuqui Córdova, "Pedro Alejandro San, el hombre de la submarina," *Listin Diario*, July 23, 2011. listindiario.com/el-deporte/2011/07/23/196909/pedro-alejandro-san-el-hombre-de-la-submarina . The cause of death is not known.

ELÍAS SOSA

By Rory Costello

Righty Elías Sosa was a useful reliever for eight different big-league teams. He appeared in 601 games at the top level from 1972 through 1983. He posted 83 saves, with a high of 18 in both 1973 and 1979. Though Sosa was never a big strikeout pitcher, "he's got a good fastball and excellent slider," said one opponent, Ted Simmons. "He comes at you."[1]

The Dominican's delivery featured a kick, modeled after that of his boyhood idol and future teammate, the great Juan Marichal. Sosa learned it in high school from the man who scouted them both, Horacio "Rabbit" Martínez. "I couldn't kick as high and still can't," said Sosa in 1973, "but from then on I used that kind of a windup."[2]

Elías Sosa Martínez was born on June 10, 1950, in La Vega. It is a large city in the Dominican Republic and the capital of La Vega province in the center of the nation. The names of Sosa's parents are not at present available, but his father worked in gold mines as a mechanic.[3] Elías was one of nine children.[4]

Sosa grew up in Bonao, a city in what is now Monseñor Nouel province (which was split off from La Vega in 1982). "We played with taped-up balls," he recalled in 1973. "Until I was 13 or so I had to play barehanded.

Photo courtesy of the National Baseball Hall of Fame

Then I got hold of an old small glove." Sosa attended Liceo Elías Rodríguez in Bonao. There he played volleyball as well as baseball.[5]

"Pitching in the big leagues was my dream," said Sosa, "but I always thought it would be impossible for me."[6] He got his first foot on the ladder when Horacio Martínez signed him for the San Francisco Giants in

1968. The bonus was $2,000.[7] Martínez had been a slick-fielding shortstop in the Negro Leagues and various Caribbean leagues in the 1930s and '40s. Hall of Famer Alex Pómpez, who had employed Martínez with the New York Cubans, went to work for the Giants in 1950 (when the team was still based in New York). Pómpez hired Martínez as a bird dog, and Rabbit helped to bring in the first wave of Dominican major leaguers – men like Marichal, the Alou brothers (Felipe was also a hero to Sosa), and Manny Mota.

Sosa's first professional season, with Salt Lake City in the Pioneer Rookie League, was rough. In eight games (five starts), he was 0-5 with an 8.00 ERA. Wildness was a problem – although he struck out 15 batters in 18 innings, he walked 14. He also gave up 33 hits.

In the winter of 1968-69, Sosa made his debut in Dominican winter ball. He joined Leones del Escogido, one of the nation's two longest-running clubs. The 18-year-old must have been nervous. He faced two batters, walking one, hitting the other, and throwing two wild pitches. It was his only appearance that winter. He went on, however, to pitch in 10 more seasons at home. Seven of those were with Escogido.

Sosa's next two minor-league seasons appeared nondescript on the surface: 0-3, 5.33 and 6-8, 4.96. Yet his promise was evident: he reached Double A briefly in 1970 and cut down markedly on his walks.

Sosa spent all of the 1971 summer season at Class A with Fresno of the California League. He continued to develop, posting a 12-9 record with a much-improved 3.32 ERA. The latter mark ranked second in the league, and he also received honorable mention as a league all-star.

The following year, Sosa jumped to Triple-A Phoenix. There the Giants organization focused him on the bullpen. In his first four years as a prospect, Sosa had started in 44 of his 86 games. With Phoenix, just four of his 55 outings were starts. He was 10-2 with a 2.93 ERA. He benefited greatly in spring training that year from the tutelage of the Giants' minor-league pitching coach, Gordy Maltzberger.[8]

Thus, when the rosters expanded in September 1972, Sosa got his first call to the majors. He never pitched again in the minors until he made a brief comeback 15 years later.

Sosa's first appearance as a big leaguer came on September 8 at San Francisco's Candlestick Park. The Houston Astros had knocked starter Jim Barr out of the box in the third inning, and when Sosa entered, there were runners on second and third with two outs. He got Doug Rader to ground out to shortstop and then pitched a scoreless fourth inning. He pitched seven more times over the rest of the season, picking up saves in his last three outings.

The 1973 season was one of Sosa's best. He finished in a tie for third in the voting for NL Rookie of the Year. (The award went to teammate Gary Matthews.) He pitched in a career-high 71 games, which tied the franchise record set by Hoyt Wilhelm in 1952. "I like to pitch almost every day," said Sosa that August. "I feel strong. I don't mind pitching four or five days in succession."[9]

Sosa won 10 games, which was also a career high, and his 18 saves led the Giants. Among other things, he appeared in the same game as his hero Juan Marichal for the first time on April 15, and got his first of two saves for Marichal on May 28 (the other came on July 20). With his good sinker, Sosa gave up just seven home runs in 107 innings. Over the course of his big-league career, opponents homered against him once every 14⅓ innings.

Sosa got into 68 more games with San Francisco in 1974. Though he had nine wins, his save total dropped to six. Shortly after the '74 season ended, the Giants traded Sosa and catcher Ken Rudolph to the St. Louis Cardinals for another catcher, Marc Hill. Jerry Donovan, assistant to Giants President Horace Stoneham, called Hill "the best young catcher in baseball."[10] *The Sporting News* wrote that the Cardinals were "trying to add some muscle to their relief corps."[11]

St. Louis general manager Bing Devine called Sosa "one of the topflight relievers in baseball" and went so far as to put him in the same class as iron man Mike Marshall, who was then at his best.[12] Bill Madlock, who went on to win the first of his four batting titles in 1975, agreed.[13]

Sosa's first wife, Stephanie Berner, was a native of San Francisco. They had two children: a son named Brandon and a daughter named Anjelica. Sosa thought that Stephanie would like St. Louis.[14] Yet he didn't stay there long enough to find out. On May 28, 1975, the Cardinals traded him and Ray Sadecki to the Atlanta Braves for Ron Reed and a player to be named later (who turned out to be Wayne Nordhagen). Braves general manager Eddie Robinson said, "While we hate to give up Reed, we felt that we should get a good left-handed pitcher and a relief pitcher."[15]

Sosa's stay in Atlanta was also rather brief, just over a year, and mediocre. A couple of months after he joined the Braves, he entered manager Clyde King's office, apologized for his performance, and promised better things. "And he'll deliver too," said King.[16] That did eventually come true, but not with the Braves. On June 23, 1976, they sent Sosa and Lee Lacy to the Los Angeles Dodgers.

Though Los Angeles acquired their contracts for cash, the transaction was related to another deal, for none other than Mike Marshall. Earlier that month, the prickly Marshall had openly criticized his teammates' fielding. A group of Dodgers went to general manager Al Campanis and asked him to trade the 1974 Cy Young Award winner for the good of the team.[17] Marshall was put on waivers, and the Braves claimed him for $20,000.[18]

Six days later, against Atlanta at Dodger Stadium, Sosa got one of his most memorable saves. LA was leading 2-1 when manager Walter Alston summoned him with the bases loaded and one out in the top of the ninth – and with a 3-and-1 count inherited from Charlie Hough. "I told him not to try to aim the ball," said Alston, "but just cut loose as hard as he could." Sosa got Rod Gilbreath to hit into a game-ending 5-2-3 double play. "I can't remember being in a spot like that before," said Sosa. "But I'm happy it turned out that way. I like to do a job whenever I pitch. I went up there with the idea of throwing a fastball to the plate to make him hit it. As soon as he did, I knew it was a double-play ball."[19]

Tommy Lasorda, who was then the Dodgers' third-base coach, had a funny line. "That's like getting caught red-handed robbing a bank with 18 guys shooting at you, and still getting away with the money."[20] Lasorda knew Sosa from his days as Escogido's manager in the 1970-71 season. They'd also been on opposing sides of a war of "duster" pitches." It started when Lasorda was managing Escogido's archrival, Licey, in the 1972-73 season – and carried over to Los Angeles vs. San Francisco in 1973. As a result, Lasorda and Giants manager Charlie Fox got into a fight.[21]

Lasorda, who became LA's manager at the tail end of the '76 season, used Sosa sparingly in the first half of 1977. He got more action down the stretch, though, and was quite effective overall (2-2, 1.98 in 44 games). An amusing moment came on September 17, when Lasorda invited comedian Don Rickles to put on a Dodgers uniform and sit in the dugout. The Dodgers were up 5-1 in the ninth inning and Sosa was on the mound when Lasorda decided to have a little fun. He sent "Mr. Warmth" (wearing number 40 but no name) out to the mound to give the pitcher the hook. Sosa wouldn't leave, telling Rickles, "You're not the manager; you're not even a coach. You can't pull me out of the game." Home-plate umpire John McSherry then came to the mound, said, "I'll be damned, Don Rickles," and proceeded to ask for tickets to a Las Vegas show. After that, Sosa set the Braves down in order to finish the game.[22]

That year Sosa made it to the postseason in the United States for the first time. In the National League Championship Series against Philadelphia, he pitched twice, taking the loss in Game One. He also got into two games in the World Series. In Game Six at Yankee Stadium, he gave up the second of Reggie Jackson's three home runs that night. "I wanted him to throw a strike on the first pitch, try to get ahead," recalled "Mr. October" in 1993. "He threw me a fastball right down Broadway."[23] Reggie had an idea what to look for because he got on the phone to Yankees scout Gene Michael as soon as Sosa came in.[24]

The month after the World Series, Los Angeles signed reliever Terry Forster as a free agent. Thus, the well-traveled Sosa was soon on the move again. "They [the Dodgers] told me I wasn't going to be No. 1 in the bullpen under any circumstances. So I told them, I wasn't going to sign under any circumstances. I took it personally. I wasn't asking for a lot of money, not the kind they paid [Forster]." Sosa set up an arbitration case, but Al Campanis got mad and refused to go to arbitration. Los Angeles promptly put Sosa on waivers, and on January 31 the Pittsburgh Pirates—the team that Forster had left—acquired the Dominican.[25]

Before Opening Day, however, Sosa was traded again. On April 4 he went with countryman Miguel Diloné and a player to be named later (Mike Edwards) to the Oakland A's; Pittsburgh reacquired the very popular veteran Manny Sanguillen. Pirates GM Pete Peterson said, "Diloné didn't have any options left and he didn't want to play in this organization. And with Sosa, we felt at the time, based on what he showed in spring training, well, we weren't that impressed with him."[26]

Yet as it turned out, Sosa was in good form with Oakland in 1978: 8-2, 2.64 with 14 saves. That August, Dodgers outfielder Glenn Burke – an outspoken critic of Campanis and Lasorda – said, "He's sticking it to them now. I bet they wish they had him back." Sosa himself was gracious, saying, "I am not mad at anybody. To me, the Dodgers were the best organization in baseball when I played with them and they're the best organization in baseball today."[27]

That November, Sosa became a free agent. Interest in him was high; the maximum 13 teams selected him in the re-entry draft. In January 1979 he signed a five-year contract with the Montreal Expos for $1.2 million. Montreal's general manager, John McHale, had hoped to sign both Mike Marshall and Sosa. After Marshall signed with the Minnesota Twins, though, McHale focused on Sosa. Jack McKeon, who had managed Sosa in Oakland for most of 1978, had joined the Expos to manage their Triple-A club in November. He filed a positive report.

"McKeon said that Sosa is definitely at his best when the game is on the line," said McHale. "He said that Sosa had a tendency to be less effective in a two- or three-run ballgame but that when the games were at stake, then he was a helluva pitcher." McHale had received other good reports – including one from Felipe Alou, who was then managing Montreal's Double-A team in Memphis.[28]

Not long after the signing, Sosa himself said, "There's more than money. I wanted to go to a team that has a chance to win the pennant. I think the Expos are a good young team." He added, "I like cold weather. I've pitched in Oakland and San Francisco and I've been very successful in the cold. I can pitch just about every day in the cold."[29]

Sosa's longest period with one team in the majors ensued. The 1979 season was his best overall. He was 8-7, with a 1.96 ERA, a career-low WHIP of 1.18, and just two homers allowed in 96 2/3 innings pitched. He matched his big-league high with 18 saves; that number also led the Expos, who came in second behind the Pirates in a hard-fought race for the National League East title. Expos beat writer Ian MacDonald commented, "He did all that could have been asked as their main stopper in the bullpen."[30]

Sosa dropped off to just nine saves in 1980, though, as Montreal turned more to 40-year-old Woodie Fryman in those situations. Sosa's ERA looked good at 3.07, but late that summer, Ian MacDonald wrote, "The Expos were hoping desperately for Elías Sosa to become consistently solid. Too often, Sosa was flashing top form after a stray pitch had permitted a previous pitcher's runners to score."[31] Sosa himself acknowledged, "I'm not concentrating as I did last year. ... When a pitcher doesn't concentrate he loses his rhythm. When that happens he makes mistakes and he gets hurt."[32]

In May 1981 Montreal obtained hard-throwing young reliever Jeff Reardon, which reduced Sosa's role. The Expos made it to the postseason for the only time in that strike-split season. Sosa pitched twice in the divisional series against the Phillies, and after the Expos advanced, he made one brief appearance in the championship series against the Dodgers.

Sosa, who had skipped winter ball for five straight years after the 1975-76 season, returned in the winter of 1981-82. He joined Estrellas Orientales and spent two seasons with that club.

The Expos and Sosa parted ways near the end of spring training in 1982. Personal reasons were a big factor. His wife, Stephanie, was not happy in Montreal and had often said she wanted to be closer to family business interests in Phoenix. Sosa also said that his income tax was much more than he was told it would be. It all added up to the desire for a fresh start. He said, "You don't want to spend your life working in the same place. You have to move around and you have to make changes. You change your car and you change your house. The Expos are a good team and a fine organization ... [but] I simply think that it is time for a change. My arm is strong. I have never been injured. I can help a team."[33]

"We will not trade Sosa just because he wants to be traded," said John McHale." When and if we trade Sosa it will be to benefit the Expos."[34] Soon thereafter, though, he was sent to the Detroit Tigers in a cash transaction. Detroit pitching coach Roger Craig said, "I haven't seen him pitch in a while. But I know he throws everything hard. He has a good hard curve and hard slider. I also know he can take the ball a lot, he can throw almost every day – if need be."[35]

Sosa spent just one undistinguished year in Detroit. The most telling statistic was that he allowed 11 homers in 61 innings pitched. Shortly after that season ended, the San Diego Padres purchased his contract. Two of his backers were in San Diego: The manager was Dick Williams, Sosa's skipper with the Expos, and the general manager was Jack McKeon.

During Sosa's 12th and final season in the majors, he got into 41 games with the Padres. In the nightcap of a doubleheader on August 29, he made his last of just three starts in the majors, going five innings and getting no decision. He got his 59th and last big-league win on June 19 at San Diego's Jack Murphy Stadium. His final big-league save came at New York's Shea Stadium on September 4.

Sosa concluded his winter-ball career in the winter of 1983-84, pitching in 17 games for Azucareros del Este. Over his 11 seasons in the Dominican League, he pitched in 175 games, starting 18 of them. He won 21, lost 28, saved 25, and had a 3.64 ERA in 366 innings pitched. His teams made it into the league playoffs in four years, reaching the finals twice, but Sosa never had the fortune to play for a champion at home.

Sosa became a free agent again after the 1983 season but did not attract any offers. San Diego released him in mid-February 1984, but his original team, the Giants, invited him to their camp as a nonroster player.[36] That didn't pan out, and so, at age 33, Sosa retired as a player.

Three years later, at age 37, Sosa made a comeback. The San José Bees, an unaffiliated team in the California League, signed him in May.[37] *The Hardball Times* later described this club as "part Japanese farm team, part independent league, and part … well, I don't know what the third part was, but it was fun."[38] Quite a few former big leaguers suited up for the Bees in 1986 and '87.

Sosa got into three games with San José, allowing 12 hits and nine walks in 6⅓ innings. He also pitched in the summer of 1987 for Yucatán in the Mexican League—notably, all eight of his appearances came as a starter. He went 1-2 with a 4.50 ERA in 50 innings.

Sosa served as a minor-league pitching coach for the Expos in 1988 and the Braves in 1989, but he still wasn't quite through pitching himself. When the Senior Professional Baseball Association began play in the fall of 1989, he joined the St. Petersburg Pelicans. He was effective as a swingman, posting a record of 3-4 with a 2.90 ERA in 59 innings pitched across 20 games. The Pelicans were the SPBA's champions in the league's only full season. He returned to St. Petersburg for the second season, but the SPBA folded in late December 1990.

Sosa remained active in baseball as a minor-league pitching coach at various levels with at least two other different organizations, the Giants and Cardinals, until 2000. He became a member of *El Pabellón de la Fama del Deporte Dominicano* – the Dominican Sports Hall of Fame – in 2001. That year, he also joined Major League Baseball as coordinator for the Latin American division of MLB's International Baseball Envoy program. The job led Sosa to travel extensively throughout the region – even to destinations one would not normally associate with baseball, such as Guyana.[39]

On his profile page at LinkedIn.com, Sosa stated, "We send coaches to work with Baseball Federations. We also conduct seminars for coaches covering topics including physical development, baseball instruction, player motivation, character development, teamwork and sports medicine. Our program includes classroom instruction followed by practical application on the field."

A quote from 2008 captured Sosa's feelings about his work. He said, "I have been very fortunate in my career. I just feel strongly that at my age I still haven't done enough to help. Doing this job brings me so much happiness and satisfaction. … I feel that I need to give and help build kids' skills and work ethic. If I can help, by using baseball as a means to inspire a kid to become a better player and citizen of his country, then it's all worth it. Who knows, I may help someone who will become a major-leaguer someday."[40]

At some point around 2016, Sosa departed his envoy position.[41] He and his second wife, Robin Trent (whom he married on December 9, 2012), make their home in Matthews, North Carolina, a suburb of Charlotte.

SOURCES

In addition to the sources cited in the Notes, the author also consulted:

Treto Cisneros, Pedro, ed., *Enciclopedia del Béisbol Mexicano* (Mexico City: Revistas Deportivas, S.A. de C.V.: 11th edition, 2011).

history.winterballdata.com/ (Dominican statistics).

LinkedIn.com.

Facebook.com.

NOTES

1. Neal Russo, "Simmons-[Al] Hrabosky Duo Off-Season Hit on Radio," *The Sporting News*, February 1, 1975: 38.
2. Pat Frizzell, "Giants Getting Big Kick Out of Sosa's Work," *The Sporting News*, August 25, 1973: 7.
3. Neal Russo, "Nothing So-So About Sosa's Love for New Card Pals," *The Sporting News*, January 11, 1975: 30.
4. Neal Russo, "Sosa Says St. Louis Is 'Wish Come True,'" *St. Louis Post-Dispatch*, December 24, 1974: 10.
5. Frizzell, "Giants Getting Big Kick Out of Sosa's Work."
6. Frizzell, "Giants Getting Big Kick Out of Sosa's Work."
7. Russo, "Sosa Says St. Louis Is 'Wish Come True.'"
8. Frizzell, "Giants Getting Big Kick Out of Sosa's Work."
9. Frizzell, "Giants Getting Big Kick Out of Sosa's Work." Gary Lavelle broke the franchise record for appearances in 1977.
10. Associated Press, "Cards Obtain Elías Sosa, Ken Rudolph," *Decatur* (Illinois) *Daily Review*, October 15, 1974: 10.
11. "Giants' Sosa, Rudolph to Cardinals for Hill," *The Sporting News*, October 26, 1974: 21.
12. Neal Russo, "Devine Defends His Deals, Gloats Over Sosa," *The Sporting News*, November 2, 1974: 15.
13. Bob Hallstrom, "Madlock Elects Cardinals as Team to Beat," *Decatur Herald*, November 7, 1974: 25.
14. Bob Broeg, "Fans Will Get a Kick Out of Sosa," *St. Louis Post-Dispatch*, March 3, 1975: 13.
15. United Press International, "Braves Trade Reed to Cards," *Pocono Record* (Stroudsburg, Pennsylvania), May 29, 1975: 14.
16. Wayne Minshew, "King Sees a Rainbow in Atlanta Gloom," *The Sporting News*, August 30, 1975: 14.
17. United Press International, "Braves Obtain Marshall from L.A. for Lacy, Sosa," *Fremont* (California) *Daily Argus*, June 24, 1976: 17.
18. Gordon Verrell, "Dodgers Bid Marshall Adieu Without a Kiss," *The Sporting News*, July 10, 1976: 11.
19. United Press International, "Dodgers' Sosa Preserves Win," *Van Nuys* (California) *Valley News and Green Sheet*, July 1, 1976: 59.
20. Gordon Verrell, "[Rick] Rhoden Dazzles as All-Star Scholar," *The Sporting News*, July 24, 1976: 10.
21. Melvin Durslag, "A Duster Artist," *The Sporting News*, August 25, 1973: 7.

22 Like many such stories, this one has been told in a variety of ways over the years. Don Rickles with David Ritz, *Rickles' Book* (New York: Simon & Schuster, 2007), 221-222. T.J. Simers, "Don Rickles Is a Hotter Ticket Than the Dodgers," *Los Angeles Times*, October 24, 2011. Mark Langill, *Dodger Stadium* (Charleston, South Carolina: Arcadia Publishing, 2004), 63.

23 Mike Lupica, "Reggie's Triple-Header," *New York Daily News*, April 19, 1993: 160.

24 Bruce Lowitt, "Mr. October Lives Up to Star Billing," *Tampa Bay Times*, November 28, 1999: 46.

25 Bruce Isphording, "New Pirate Sosa Raps Move by L.A.," *Sarasota Journal*, March 24, 1978: 10C.

26 Ed Rose Jr., "Peterson Insists Trades Weren't Bad," *Beaver County* (Pennsylvania) *Times*, May 24, 1978: C-1.

27 United Press International, "Ex-Dodger Sosa Is Now Mainstay of A's Bullpen," *Galveston Daily News*, August 11, 1978: 30.

28 Ian MacDonald, "Expos Give Pitcher Sosa Five-year Pact," *Montreal Gazette*, January 9, 1979: 17.

29 Ian MacDonald, "'More than Money' Says Newest Expo," *Montreal Gazette*, January 20, 1979: 24.

30 Ian MacDonald, "Expos Redouble Hunt for Hurlers," *The Sporting News*, December 8, 1979: 48.

31 Ian MacDonald, "Sun Always Shines for Expos' [Bill] Gullickson," *The Sporting News*, September 6, 1980: 41.

32 Ian MacDonald, "Big 3 a 4-Star Show on Expo Hill," *The Sporting News*, October 4, 1980: 7.

33 Ian MacDonald, "Elías Sosa Unhappy in Montreal; Asks Trade So He Can Start Again," *Montreal Gazette*, March 2, 1982: C2.

34 MacDonald,"Elías Sosa Unhappy in Montreal; Asks Trade So He Can Start Again."

35 Associated Press, "Tigers Acquire Reliever Sosa from Expos," *Poughkeepsie* (New York) *Journal*, March 31, 1982: 40.

36 United Press International, "Sosa Reports to Giants," *Arizona Republic* (Phoenix), February 23, 1984: 58.

37 "San José Bees Sign Elías Sosa," *San Bernardino* (California) *Sun*, May 17, 1987: 43.

38 Brandon Isleib, "Weird History: 1987 San José Bees," *The Hardball Times*, August 27, 2010.

39 "MLB Coach to Conduct Training in Georgetown," *Guyana Times*, April 26, 2014.

40 Raymond Sarracino, "Charlotte Resident Elías Sosa Tours with U.S. Southern Command All-Stars in Latin America," press release, U.S. Southern Command Public Affairs, Panama City, Panama, May 1, 2008.

41 Telephone conversation, Rory Costello with Chris Haydock (international development director, Major League Baseball), December 4, 2018.

Sammy Sosa

By Eric Hanauer

Who is the real Sammy Sosa? Is he the charismatic slugger whose home-run race with Mark McGwire brought baseball's fandom back from the ruins of the 1994 strike? Is he the Dominican shoeshine boy from a poverty-stricken family who became a hero in his country and the United States? Is he a steroid cheater who has never confessed? Is he the egotistical clubhouse cancer who walked out on his team during the last game of the 2004 season? This complex man was one of the most popular and controversial players of his time.

Nobody else has hit 60 home runs in three different seasons. Yet he didn't lead the league in any one of them. In the five-year period from 1998 through 2002 he hit 292 home runs, an average of 58 a year. Nobody has even come close, either clean or chemically assisted. He had seasons of 158 and 160 RBIs, and 10.3 WAR. He was an All-Star seven times and an MVP. His 609 home runs are the ninth highest of all time. Yet he's never been selected on more than 17 percent of Hall of Fame ballots, which he attained in 2021, his next to final year of eligibility.

Samuel Peralta Sosa was born on November 12, 1968, in Consuelo, Dominican Republic, one of seven children. His father, Juan Bautista Montero, drove a tractor clearing sugar-cane fields. He died of a cerebral hemorrhage when Sammy was 6 years old. After Juan's death, his mother, Mireya, reverted to her maiden name, Sosa. She had dropped out of school in her teens and worked as a maid and a cook. Sammy and his brothers washed cars and shined shoes to bring in pesos for the family. All of them slept in a single room in the barrio.[1]

When Sammy was 13, Mireya moved to San Pedro de Macoris, where she married Carlos Maria Peralta. Conditions improved a bit, but Sammy, who was called Mikey by family and friends, prioritized work over school. He and older brother Luis established a business shining shoes for middle-class businessmen. One of them was Bill Chase, an American who was opening a shoe factory. He hired Sammy and became a surrogate father. He bought Sammy his first bicycle, and his first baseball glove.[2]

Although baseball is the national passion in the Dominican Republic, Sammy wanted to be a boxer. He trained seriously, but when Mireya found out, she made him promise to give it up. That's when he turned his focus to baseball.[3] At 14, he attracted the attention of a *buscon*, or informal agent, quit school, and

Photo courtesy of the National Baseball Hall of Fame

joined a traveling team with real uniforms. At 15 he signed with the Phillies, but the contract was voided because he was underage. The following year was a parade of tryouts and rejections from other teams. Finally Omar Minaya and Amado Dinzey of the Texas Rangers signed him for $3,500.

Sosa made his official pro debut in 1986 at the age of 17, with the Gulf League Rangers in Sarasota, Florida. At the time he was lean and lithe, about 165 pounds, with speed rather than power his greatest asset. In 61 games he hit .275 with 4 home runs and 11 stolen bases. One of his teammates and best friends on the team was Juan Gonzalez.

The following year they moved up together to Class-A Gastonia, North Carolina. Sosa hit .279 with 11 home runs and 59 RBIs. He was also learning English, primarily by hanging with his American teammates.[4] By the end of the season, Sosa and Gonzalez were ranked one and two in the Rangers' farm system.

The next step was Charlotte in the High-A Florida State League. At 19, Sammy was one of the youngest players, hit only .229 and struck out 106 times. Yet he stole 42 bases and drove in 51 runs. At times his behavior roused the ire of some coaches, who were not used to dealing with Latin players, but Minaya protected him.[5] A strong season in Dominican winter ball brought an invitation to major-league spring training in 1989.

At this time, the Rangers were heavily invested in Latin players. Among them were Rafael Palmeiro, Ivan Rodriguez, Julio Franco, and Ruben Sierra. Sosa and Gonzalez were sent to Tulsa in the Double-A Texas League to start the season. By June, Sammy was hitting .297 with seven home runs, and made the All-Star team. On the parent club, Pete Incaviglia was placed on the disabled list with a sore neck, and Sosa was called up to replace him. He was 20 years old, and had been playing baseball for six years. He flew first class to New York, and on June 16, 1989, hit leadoff in Yankee Stadium, where he singled against Andy Hawkins in his first major-league at-bat. In the sixth inning he doubled off Hawkins and scored his first run.

The next stop for the Rangers was Fenway Park, with Roger Clemens on the mound. He struck out Sosa in the first inning, but in the fifth, Sammy hit one of Clemens's offerings over the Green Monster for his first major-league home run. After a hot start, Sosa started seeing more breaking balls, and his average plummeted to .238. The Rangers sent him to Triple-A Oklahoma City, where he moped a bit and wasn't hitting. However Larry Himes, then general manager of the White Sox, saw something he liked. He projected Sosa as a Minnie Minoso-type player, with speed and a strong outfield arm. So Himes traded aging Harold Baines and Fred Manrique to the Rangers for Sosa, Wilson Alvarez, and Scott Fletcher.

Sammy was sent to Triple-A Vancouver, where he hit .367 in 13 games. The White Sox called him up and he joined the team in Minnesota. In his White Sox debut, Sosa walked twice and went 3-for-3 with a two-run homer as Chicago won, 10-2. In 33 games he hit .273 with an OPS of .765. The first thing he did when he returned home was to buy a house for his mother, partly with a loan from Bill Chase, his businessman friend.

In 1990, the 21-year-old outfielder displayed both his raw talent and inexperience. He hit .233 made 13 errors, and struck out 150 times. Yet he hit 15 home runs, stole 32 bases, and drove in 70 runs. Walt Hriniak, the White Sox hitting coach, had some rigid ideas that conflicted with Sammy's free-swinging approach. It worked for some, but totally frustrated Sosa.[6] Although the team had a good year, Himes was fired at the end of the season because of conflicts with owner Jerry Reinsdorf. A year later, he would be the GM of the Cubs and trade for Sosa again.

Sammy married an American woman in 1990. It lasted only eight months before ending in divorce. By spring training 1991 he was still sorting through the resulting legal mess, his stepfather died, and the conflicts with Hriniak continued. Though he hit two homers on Opening Day, the White Sox platooned him with Cory Snyder. By July 19, he was hitting .200 and was demoted to Triple A. Recalled in August, he hit only .203 in 116 major-league games. About the only redeeming aspect of that lost season was meeting Sonia Rodriguez. They married the following year, and as of 2018 had six children.

Sosa went to spring training with the White Sox in 1992 amid trade rumors and reports that he was uncoachable. On March 30, Himes pulled the trigger on the best trade of his checkered Cubs tenure. He sent George Bell and $400,000 cash to the White Sox for Sosa and pitcher Ken Patterson. (A year later he made his worst transaction, by failing to meet Greg Maddux's reasonable demands and letting him sign with the Braves.) Sammy was ecstatic. On his way out, he told his White Sox teammates, "Okay boys. I'm out of here. You guys will see me again. I'm going to be the best player in this game."[7]

At age 23, Sosa was listed at 6 feet tall and a lithe 185 pounds. The Cubs played him in center field, because Andre Dawson was established in right, and hit him at the top two slots in the order because he was the fastest runner on the team. That didn't fit with Sammy's free-swinging style, and when he slumped, manager Jim Lefebvre moved him down in the lineup. He began to hit with power. On June 10 in St. Louis he hit two home runs, for the first time since Opening Day 1991. But a few days later a Dennis Martínez fastball broke a bone in Sosa's right wrist. That put him on the disabled list for six weeks.

He returned on July 27 and hit a home run in his first at-bat. The Cubs swept a three-game series against the Pirates at Wrigley Field. Sammy played a key role with clutch hits. In the final game, his 11th-inning home run won it, and for the first time the chant, "Sam-my, Sam-my" rang down from the stands. In nine games coming off the DL, he hit .385 with three home runs. But the next day fate struck again. He fouled off a pitch that broke a bone in his ankle. Sosa's season was finished. He had only 262 at-bats, hit .260 with 8 home runs and 15 stolen bases. But his hustle, speed, youth, and potential had made him a favorite with Cubs fans.

The next season, 1993, was Sosa's breakout year. Hitting coach Billy Williams and Lefebvre adopted a hands-off approach, encouraging him to just be himself. With Dawson gone, he returned to his natural position, right field. Sosa responded with 33 home runs, 93 RBIs, and 36 stolen bases, the first Cub to make the 30-30 club. At the time, only nine other players had achieved it. The highlight of the season came in Denver on the Fourth of July weekend. He went 6-for-6, giving him nine hits in a row, one short of the National League record. At the end of the season the Cubs signed Sosa to a new contract, for $2,950,000. He bought his mother another new house, and one for himself and Sonia in Santo Domingo.

In 1994 Tom Trebelhorn replaced Lefebvre as Cubs manager. He couldn't have got off to a worse start, losing 12 straight home games. By early May, the Cubs were 6-18. A toxic aura in the clubhouse labeled Sosa as a selfish player. He didn't help matters by sporting a gaudy gold necklace with a 30-30 pendant.[8] On the field he led the Cubs in nearly every offensive category. When the season was cut short in August by the players strike and the owners lockout, the Cubs were in last place. Sosa hit .300 with 25 homers, 70 RBIs, and 22 stolen bases in 105 games.

Before the strike was finally settled, there was some confusion about Sosa's free-agent status. His agent, Adam Katz, was in serious discussions with the Red Sox, but in the end Sosa remained a Cub. Himes and Trebelhorn were gone, replaced by Ed Lynch and Jim Riggleman. The Cubs were in the playoff race for a while. Sosa played in the All-Star Game for the first time, won a Silver Slugger Award, and finished eighth in the MVP balloting. He hit .268 with 36 homers, 119 RBIs, and 34 stolen bases.

On the eve of free agency in January 1996, the Cubs signed Sammy to a three-year, $16 million contract. He had bulked up to a listed 200 pounds, and was swinging for the fences. The fans in the right-field bleachers responded to his daily sprint and wave, but the reputation as a selfish player continued. At the All-Star break he was leading the league in home runs, but was not selected on the team. That stung, but Sosa continued to mash. On August 20 he led the league with 40 home runs and had 100 RBIs. But that day he was hit on the right hand by pitcher Mark Hutton of the Florida Marlins. His pisiform bone was broken, and surgery was required. Sosa's season was over. Despite missing the last six weeks, he finished fifth in the NL in home runs.

The Cubs' 1997 season was over by the third week. They lost their first 14 games, a club record. Sammy's contract status was in limbo, as his opt-out clause was being negotiated. Finally, on June 27, he signed a four-year, $42 million contract, making him the third-highest-paid player in baseball. The Cubs limped home with 94 losses, tied for the worst in the National League. Sosa's year yielded 36 home runs, 119 RBIs, and a .251 batting average with a league-leading 174 strikeouts. In and outside the clubhouse, he was labeled as a flop. Jeff Pentland was the new Cubs hitting coach in 1997. He spent that year getting to know Sosa, studying his approach, and formulating a plan. That plan came to fruition in 1998.

Pentland convinced Sammy that he didn't have to swing so hard to hit home runs. He also lowered Sammy's hands and introduced a foot tap as a timing device. Sosa was coached to become more selective, take walks, and hit to right field when that was all the pitcher gave him. Sosa wrote, "Of all the coaches I've had in my life, he is the one who has gotten the most out of me...."[9]

Sammy started the 1998 season slowly. By May 22 he had only eight home runs. The drought was broken with a 440-foot shot to center field off Maddux. By the end of the month he had 13, still 14 behind McGwire and trailing several others. In June, Sosa made history with 20 home runs, breaking Rudy York's 1937 major-league record of 18 in one month. At month's end the gap with McGwire was down to four, and the national media began to notice. Sammy's homer hop, heart tap, and kisses blown to his mother from the dugout, became staples on ESPN's *SportsCenter* and *Baseball Tonight*. On July 27 at Phoenix he hit the first grand slam of his career, driving in all the Cubs runs with two homers in a 6-2 win. It was the 247th of his career, which broke Bob Horner's record (207) for the most home runs before the first grand slam. Making up for lost time, Sosa hit another the next day. On August 19 he hit homer number 48 against the Cardinals to take the lead for the first time. It didn't last long, as Big Mac hit two in the same game. Later in the game, after Sosa walked, McGwire turned to him and said, "Hey, I think we're going to do it."[10]

As the pressure built, McGwire seemed to feel it more. Sosa embraced it, maintaining a happy face with the press and the fans, who in turn embraced him. When a bottle of Androstenedione was spotted in McGwire's locker, Sosa attributed his own physique to Flintstones Vitamins. Number 57 broke the Cubs' single-season record set by Hack Wilson in 1930. When Big Mac hit number 62 against the Cubs, Sosa ran in from right field and hugged him. In a dramatic September series at home against the Brewers, Sammy hit numbers 59 to 62 to tie McGwire. Number 63 in San Diego tied the race again. The overflow crowd gave Sammy a standing ovation on each trip to the plate. In the eighth inning the Padres were ahead, 3-2. The bases were loaded, Sammy got another standing O, then hit one into the upper deck for a 6-3 win. He took a curtain call as the San Diego management set off fireworks. Padres players later complained. On September 25, Sosa hit number 66 to take the lead for the final time. That lasted about a half-hour as Mac connected against Montreal. McGwire hit four the last two games of the season to finish with 70. Sosa hit .308 with 66 home runs, a league-leading 158 RBIs, 134 runs scored, 416 total bases, and 171 strikeouts. With the Cubs making the playoffs (and quickly eliminated by the Braves) Sammy was the winner of the MVP Award. He and McGwire were selected co-Sportsmen of the Year by *Sports Illustrated*. The Cubs had a day for Sosa in September and gave him a purple Plymouth Prowler. McGwire received a classic red 1962 Corvette from the Cardinals on his day.

The offseason brought more recognition and honors. President Leonel Fernandez of the Dominican Republic made Sammy an ambassador. When a hurricane hit his country, Sosa sparked humanitarian aid with money, publicity, and personally distributed food, water, and medicine. At the State of the Union address, President Bill Clinton introduced him and acknowledged his accomplishments. Endorsements and offers flooded his agent.

Sosa and McGwire repeated their race in 1999, but this time a jaded public wasn't nearly as excited. Rumors about performance enhancing drugs were swirling not only around them, but about the entire generation of sluggers that suddenly made 30 to 50 home runs commonplace. Sosa briefly addressed PEDs in his autobiography: "I have never used Andro, nor do I plan to. ... While it's true that I tried the food supplement Creatine once or twice, I never saw it have any particular impact on my body or development. ... I attribute my physical development to many years of strict weight training and proper nutrition. ..."[11]

The Cubs crashed in 1999, beset with injuries and bad vibes, losing 95 games and finishing last in their division. Some players resented Sosa's ego, his entourage, and his loud salsa music in the tiny clubhouse. Regardless, he had another banner year. On September 18 he became the first player to hit 60 home runs in more than one season. McGwire quickly caught up and finished with 65 to Sosa's 63. Sammy hit .288 and drove in 141 runs. He led the league in games played, 162, total bases, 397, and strikeouts, 171. Riggleman was fired and replaced by Don Baylor.

Sosa hit only 50 home runs in 2000, but led the league for the first time. He became more selective at the plate, hitting .320 with a higher OBP, .406, and OPS, 1.040, than in his 60-home-run years. He also won the Home Run Derby at the All-Star Game. The Cubs limped home in last place again.

In many ways, Sosa's 2001 season was better than his MVP year. He hit a career-high .328, led the league with 146 runs, 160 RBIs, 37 intentional walks, and 425 total bases. With 64 home runs, he became the only player in history to hit 60 three times. He finished strong, hitting .377 in his final 57 games. He was 10-for-15 with the bases loaded, including two grand slams, totaling seven for his career. In MVP voting he finished second behind Barry Bonds, who hit 73 homers in his monster year.

Sammy made cameo appearances in two movies that year: *Hardball* and *On the Line*. In 1997 he had appeared in *Kissing a Fool*. Each had low ratings on the Rotten Tomatoes website.[12]

Sosa won his second home run crown in 2002, with 49. On August 10 he hit three three-run homers in consecutive innings. It was the sixth three-homer game of his career, tying Johnny Mize's major-league record. Sosa's 122 runs scored led the league for the third time, to go along with a .288 average and .399 OBP. Sosa made his fourth All-Star Game start and won his sixth Silver Slugger. By now, rumors of steroid use and clubhouse dissension were rampant. But throughout the losing years, Cubs management promoted and indulged Sosa, as he kept putting people in the seats.

Dusty Baker took over as manager in 2003. The Cubs won the Central Division, and advanced to the League Championship Series, eventually blowing a three-games-to-one lead to the Florida Marlins. Sammy pitched in with 40 homers and 103 RBIs. At age 34, his bat was slowing down but he kept achieving milestones. On April 4 he became the 18th player to hit 500 home runs, and the first NL player with six consecutive 40-home-run seasons. In the playoffs that year, Sosa hit his first two postseason home runs. One came in the ninth inning of the first NLCS game against the Marlins, sending it into extra innings.

Two incidents that year may have contributed to Sosa's decline. On April 20, he was hit in the head by a Salomon Torres fastball that smashed his helmet. Concussion protocols weren't in place then, and Sammy played the next game. But he hit only one home run in his next 98 plate appearances. Then on June 3, his bat broke on a swing against the Tampa Bay Rays. Home-plate umpire Tim McClelland found cork in the center of the shattered club. Sosa was kicked out of the game, and eventually suspended for seven games. Sammy claimed it was a batting practice bat that he accidentally picked up. Sosa's other bats were X-rayed with no evidence of cork. But his credibility took a major hit. Whether the bats, or the concussion, or age, or backing off PEDs contributed to Sammy's decline is still a subject for debate.[13] During that season, random anonymous drug tests were administered to major-league players. In 2009 a list of players who failed was leaked to the *New York Times*. Sosa's name was on that list. A summary article was published in July.[14]

The 2004 season marked the closing of Sosa's era with the Cubs. He passed Ernie Banks for the team's career home-run record with 545. Other than that, it wasn't pretty. He went on the disabled list when a violent sneeze caused back spasms. He hit only .253 with 35 homers and 80 RBIs. During the final week of the season, the Cubs blew a wild-card lead and missed the playoffs. On the final day, Sammy asked Dusty Baker not to play him. He disappeared from the bench, and security cameras showed him driving away shortly after the game started. When his teammates found out, they vented their anger on his boombox. When Cubs management released the security tape to the press, it became evident that he couldn't return.

Trading from a position of disadvantage, the Cubs didn't get much. The Baltimore Orioles sent them Mike Fontenot, Jerry Hairston, and Mike Crothers for Sosa and cash. Sammy played in only 102 games in 2005, hitting .221 with 14 homers and 45 RBIs. His biggest headline came when he testified before a congressional committee in the PED investigations. Speaking in Spanish with a translator, he denied ever using steroids. Sosa and McGwire were excoriated for their testimony. To this day, the only actual link of Sosa with PEDs is that leaked report of a failed test in 2003.

Only one team offered Sammy a contract in 2006, and he didn't like the terms, so he sat out that year. Still, there was one more milestone to pursue. So he signed with the Texas Rangers in 2007 for the major-league minimum salary and a spring training invitation. On June 20, he hit his 600th career home run, off Cubs pitcher Jason Marquis. Ironically, Marquis was wearing Sammy's old number, 21. At age 38, Sosa hit .252 with 21 homers and 92 RBIs. It was a far more fitting finish than the down year with Baltimore.

With nothing left to prove, Sammy told his agent not to seek another contract. Since then, Sosa has mostly stayed out of the limelight. Occasionally there are reports of extravagant overseas birthday celebrations.[15] He has invested in and lent his name to several business ventures. His net worth is estimated at $70 million. That's a long way from shining shoes on the streets of San Pedro de Macoris.

The remaining loose thread is Sosa's relationship with the Cubs. He hasn't been invited to Cubs Conventions or historic Wrigley Field celebrations, or had his number 21 retired, although ownership and management from his playing days is gone. Other sluggers of the steroid era like Barry Bonds, Mark McGwire, and Manny Ramírez have been welcomed back like prodigal sons. Sosa hasn't. History is a major element of the Cubs' appeal. With the passing of Ernie Banks and Ron Santo, they are running low on iconic figures. Occasional rumors surface of contact between representatives, a need for apologies, and statements from bloggers and fans.[16] But as of 2021 Sosa remained in limbo with the organization where he spent the best years of a historic career.

SOURCES

In addition to the sources cited in the Notes, the author also consulted the following:

Baseball-Reference.com.

Chicago Tribune. Sammy's Season (Chicago: Contemporary Books, 1998).

Chicago Cubs Information Guides, 1993 and 2004.

Davis, Ryan. "Despite Cloud of Suspicion, Sammy Sosa's Career Is Still Hall-Worthy," January 7, 2015, cubsinsider.com/despite-cloud-suspicion-sammy-sosas-career-still-hall-worthy/.

Bernard, Zach Bernard. "Redefining Sammy Sosa's Baseball Legacy," January 4, 2016, baseballessential.com/news/2016/01/04/redefining-sammy-sosas-baseball-legacy/.

NOTES

1. Sammy Sosa with Marcus Breton, *Sosa, an Autobiography* (New York: Warner Books Inc. 2000), 24-25.
2. Sosa with Breton, 31-32.
3. Sosa with Breton, 41-42.
4. Sosa with Breton, 74.
5. Sosa with Breton, 86.
6. Sosa with Breton, 118.
7. Sosa with Breton, 126.
8. Joséph A. Reaves, "What Makes Sammy a Star?" *Chicago Tribune*, June 16, 1995.
9. Sosa with Breton, 183.
10. Sosa with Breton, 190.
11. Sosa with Breton, 191.
12. rottentomatoes.com/celebrity/sammy_sosa/.
13. Bradley Woodrum, "The Three Declines of Sammy Sosa," January 29, 2015, hardballtimes.com/the-three-declines-of-sammy-sosa/.
14. Michael S. Schmidt, "Sosa Is Said to Have Tested Positive in 2003," *New York Times*, June 16, 2006.
15. Brendan Maloy, "Sammy Sosa Held His 47th Birthday Party in Dubai," si.com, November 17, 2015. si.com/extra-mustard/2015/11/17/sammy-sosa-birthday-party-dubai.
16. Scott Miller, "Sammy Sosa in Exile: There's Silence Rather Than Apology From Former Cubs Star," February 25, 2015. bleacherreport.com/articles/2368638-sammy-sosa-in-exile-theres-silence-rather-than-apology-from-former-cubs-star.

Mario Soto

By Gregory. H. Wolf

With a population of just over 10 million, the Dominican Republic has produced approximately 450 big-league pitchers as of 2021. Hall of Famers Juan Marichal and Pedro Martínez are easily the most famous, and most successful; however, no hurler from the Caribbean nation had a reputation as a harder thrower than Mario Soto. A converted catcher, Soto caught on with the Cincinnati Reds on his fourth try, in 1977, and emerged over a six-year stretch (1980-1985) as one of the best right-handers in the majors, averaging 208 strikeouts per season while surrendering 6.8 hits per nine innings, the lowest of any starter active in those years.[1] In his 12-year career, prematurely ended by arm and shoulder injuries, Soto (100-92) became just the third Dominican hurler to win at least 100 games, following Marichal and Joaquín Andújar.

Mario Melvin Soto was born on July 12, 1956, in Bani, the capital city of Peravia province, located on the south-central coast, about 35 miles southwest of the nation's capital, Santo Domingo. When Soto was about 8 years old, his parents separated. His mother, Marta, raised Soto and his two siblings by working as a laundress. "We used to go down to the river at 6 in the morning, baskets of laundry

Photo courtesy of the National Baseball Hall of Fame

on our heads," recalled Soto of growing up with limited means, "and not come back until the evening."[2] Melvin, as Soto was called as a youth, quit school at the age of 14 and worked full-time in construction to help support the family.

Like many kids growing up in the baseball-crazed Dominican Republic, Soto idolized the country's most accomplished player in the big leagues, Juan Marichal. Soto played baseball on local sandlots whenever he could, practicing in the evenings and playing games on Sundays. He started out as a catcher despite his tall and skinny stature, but had one flaw: "I couldn't hit a lick."[3] Juan Melo, a longtime member of the Dominican national team, took note of Soto's strong right arm and converted him to a pitcher at the age of 17. "I think [catching] helped me a little bit as far as pitching," said Soto about his transition, which was easier than many expected. "I knew how the motion worked."[4] Soto immediately raised a few eyebrows with his bullets, but most major-league scouts combing the island for talent were uninterested in such an inexperienced hurler. One exception was Johnny Sierra, a bird-dog scout for the Cincinnati Reds. Sierra alerted team scout George Zuraw who traveled from the United States to check out the teenage Soto, who had been pitching for just two months. At a Reds tryout camp near Santo Domingo, Soto piqued Zuraw's curiosity with his mechanics, delivery, and rhythm despite a fastball topping out in the low 80s and augmented by only a curveball. In late 1973 Soto accepted Zuraw's offer of a $1,000 bonus and signed with the Reds. "Frankly, I wasn't impressed," said Zuraw years later, after Soto had become an All-Star with the Reds. "We signed him strictly on a projection basis. I'd be lying to you if I said I thought he would be great."[5]

Soto's transition to professional baseball in the United States was anything but smooth. Thrust into a country where he didn't speak the language, know the customs, or have friends and family, Soto contemplated quitting and returning home on several occasions. To make matters worse, he broke his elbow at the Reds' minor-league spring camp in 1974 and missed the entire season. In 1975, Soto was still plagued by arm pain and made only five appearances for the Eugene (Oregon) Emeralds in the Low-A Northwest League. Finally healthy in 1976, Soto discarded his curveball, which hurt his elbow, and rode his fastball, now in the low 90s, to a breakthrough season with the Tampa Tarpons, leading the Class-A Florida State League in ERA (1.87), innings (197), and strikeouts (124), while posting a 13-7 record. Mike Moore, general manager in Tampa, described Soto as "one of the best players ever to go through [the Reds'] organization."[6]

The reigning two-time world champion Reds fast-tracked Soto to the big leagues, much to the pitcher's detriment. He was added to the club's 40-man roster after the 1976 season, and participated in his first big-league spring training in 1977. The Reds elevated the 20-year-old two levels, assigning him to Triple-A Indianapolis, where he was the fourth youngest hurler in the American Association. Facing mature players, many of whom had big-league experience, Soto blazed a trail, winning 11 of 16 decisions in 18 starts. When 37-year-old Reds starter Woody Fryman unexpectedly retired in early July to deplete an already thin staff, Soto was promoted. His debut on July 21 at Pittsburgh's Three Rivers Stadium was uninspiring; he yielded three hits and two runs in two innings of relief against the Pirates. Six days later, Soto tossed a complete game and struck out nine to win his first start, 6-2, against the Chicago Cubs. On August 7 he flashed his mid-90s heater to blank the Pirates, 9-0, leading skipper Sparky Anderson to gush, "Unless I'm totally crazy, the kid will be outstanding."[7] In that shutout, the first of 13 in his career, Soto also gave an inkling of the type pitcher he would become by knocking down Bill Robinson on consecutive brushback pitches in the first inning and letting one sail over the batter's head in the sixth, precipitating a bench-clearing incident. A fatigued Soto (2-6, 5.34 ERA) pitched erratically thereafter and lost his next five decisions as the Big Red Machine finished in second place in the NL West.

Inconsistency, wildness, and injuries defined Soto's next two seasons. He spent the 1978 campaign with Indianapolis, where he seemingly regressed (9-12, 5.01, 95 walks in 160 innings), followed by a brief September call-up. At the Reds spring training in 1979, he came down with severe back pain, necessitating hospitalization in late March. Back with Indianapolis to start the season, Soto was converted into a reliever and was recalled by the Reds in late June. His results for Cincinnati were disappointing: 30 walks and a 5.30 ERA in 37⅓ innings (25 appearances). Soto also made his one and only postseason appearance, tossing two scoreless innings against the Pittsburgh Pirates in Game Three in the NLCS. Soto's status as a rising star was fading fast, as a quartet of 26-and-under right-handers had secured spots in the staff. Mike LaCoss won 14 games in 1979; 25-year-old Paul Moskau looked like a dependable starter, 21-year-old rookie Frank Pastore pitched well in the final two months of the season, and Tom Hume had been converted into one of the NL's most dependable closers.

As he had after the previous four seasons, Soto joined the Leones del Escogido in the Dominican Winter League in 1979-80. He had spent the offseasons in Bani living with his mother, and seemed more relaxed and at ease pitching in Santo Domingo than in the United States. Hurling primarily out of the bullpen for manager Matty Alou, Soto posted a stellar 2.46 ERA in 80⅓ innings over 25 appearances. Nonetheless few predicted that Soto would translate that success to the Reds in 1980.

Cincinnati sportswriter Peter King suggested that if a film had been made about Soto's 1980 campaign, it would be called "The Maturation of Mario Soto";[8] while Ray Buck of the *Cincinnati Enquirer* described Soto as the "sleeper of the staff."[9] Indeed, Soto's midseason transformation from a meddling reliever, mop-up artist, and target of jeering fans' anger and frustration to one of the most effective swingmen in baseball was stunning. The turning point came on July 5 when skipper John McNamara called on Soto (4.92 ERA at the time) to replace starter Bruce Berenyi, who had been knocked out after yielding six runs in one-third of an inning to the Houston Astros. Soto yielded three hits over 8⅔ scoreless innings, including setting down 16 batters in a row, to pick up his first victory in 10 months, 8-6. In his next outing, six days later, Soto was informed by McNamara just minutes before the game that he'd be starting in place of Frank Pastore. Soto tossed 130 pitches, scattering five hits over 8⅔ innings to pick up a 5-3 victory against the Atlanta Braves. He struck out 10 batters, the first of 27 times in his career that he whiffed 10 or more in a game.

Sportswriter Buck noted that the most difficult aspect for Soto was adjusting to role of never knowing when he'd pitch, either as a starter or reliever.[10] Reds pitching coach Bill Fischer was unequivocal in his praise of Soto, calling him "probably the best pitcher in the National League from July on."[11] Over the last six weeks of the campaign (beginning on August 13), Soto was "awesome," according to teammate Johnny Bench.[12] Soto seemed unhittable during that stretch, yielding just 35 hits (.147 batting average) and 11 earned runs (1.41) ERA in 70⅓ innings. Included were an overpowering complete-game 7-1 victory over the Braves on September 9 with a career-best 15 punchouts (one off the nine-inning team record set by Noodles Hahn in 1901 and tied by Jim Maloney in 1963; Maloney also fanned 18 in an 11-inning start in 1965) and a five-hit shutout against Houston in his next start. While Queen City sportswriter Lonnie

Wheeler suggested that a strong case could be made for Soto as the team's MVP instead of Ken Griffey, the lanky hurler settled for the Johnny Vander Meer Award, given by the Cincinnati chapter of the Baseball Writer Association of America to the team's top hurler. It was well deserved as Soto (10-8, 3.07 ERA in 190⅓ innings) led the majors by allowing the fewest hits (6.0) and striking out the most batters (8.6) per nine innings.

Soto's extraordinary emergence as one of the NL's top hurlers can be directly attributed to his changeup, which players, coaches, sportswriters, and statisticians, including Bill James, considered not only one of the game's best, but one of the best in history.[13] "There's no doubt that his changeup and his offspeed pitches with his fastball make him one of the best pitchers in all of baseball," opined veteran Rusty Staub.[14] Scott Breeden, the Reds' minor-league roving pitcher instructor, is widely credited with teaching Soto the career-altering pitch. "Velocity is great, but movement on the ball is 90 percent of the battle," said Ray Shore, a Reds scout. "[Soto] throws his changeup with perfect motion … but that thing drops right off the table. It's almost like a spitter."[15]

Soto relied essentially on two pitches, a fastball and changeup, throughout his career; he also occasionally showed a slider. His changeup, which was typically 10 to 15 mph slower than his mid-90s heater, froze batters and buckled their knees, leading to what sportswriter Tim Sullivan called "embarrassing" strikeouts.[16] Bench once claimed that when Soto was in a groove and had command of both pitches, his fastball "looks like 120 [mph]."[17] It was impossible for batters to tell Soto's changeup and fastball apart when each left his hand. "I throw the changeup with the same motion that I throw the fastball," said Soto.[18] By 1980 he had enough trust in his changeup that it became his go-to pitch to either right- or left-handed hitters. "I get most of my strikeouts with the changeup," said Soto bluntly."That's the pitch that's made the difference for me."[19] Standing just 6 feet tall and weighing about 170 pounds, Soto might not have looked menacing like Bob Gibson and Don Drysdale, but he commanded the plate just as they did, and never shied away from throwing inside. Said batterymate Joe Nolan, "[Soto's] just a little bit wild enough to keep batters from digging in."[20] All of those characteristics together made Soto one of the dominant strikeout pitchers in baseball. "If I had to build a pitching staff from scratch, I'd start with Soto," said St. Louis Cardinals skipper Whitey Herzog, not known for hyperbole.[21]

Soto began the 1981 season widely hailed as the best pitcher from the Dominican Republic since Marichal. "We're just going to turn him loose," replied pitching coach Fischer when asked about his plans for Soto.[22] Poor run support contributed to Soto's rough start (1-5) despite pitching well. He won five of his next six decisions, each by complete game, punctuated by a stellar six-hit shutout with 12 punchouts against the New York Mets at Shea Stadium on June 10. Two days later the season was interrupted by the players' strike, the fourth work stoppage in baseball since the players' strike in 1972. When play resumed on August 9 with the All-Star Game, just over one-third of the season had been canceled. Soto picked up where had had left off, winning six of nine decisions. On the last day of the season, October 4, he spun a one-hit shutout against Atlanta at Riverfront Stadium with little motivation other than pride and honor. "Soto's brilliance," suggested beat writer Tim Sullivan, "was obscured by … the cloud of bitterness that hung over the Reds clubhouse."[23] Soto's gem marked the Reds' major-league-best 66th victory, but no one on the team rejoiced. Baseball owners had decided to split the season into two halves with the division winner in each half squaring off in a best-of-five playoff series. The Reds finished in second place in each half and were thus shut out of the playoffs. Prior to Soto's performance the Reds salvaged some measure of dignity (and revenge) by unfurling a banner declaring "Baseball's Best Record 1981."[24] Soto's name was plastered among the NL leaders; he finished tied for third in wins (12), strikeouts (151), and innings (175), while tying for second in complete games (10) and first in starts (25). Soto and 36-year-old teammate Tom Seaver (14-2) formed the most potent one-two punch in baseball.

An aging Reds team hit rock bottom in 1982, setting a dubious franchise record with 101 losses. The NL's worst team and the lowest-scoring club in the majors made pitching, and winning, a monumental task, all of which underscores Soto's season as one of the best in Reds history. Named Opening Day starter for the first of five consecutive seasons, Soto displayed a performance that was an omen for what would unfold: He picked up the loss despite yielding just two runs in seven innings and fanning 10. Soto's campaign reads like a highlight reel. He fanned 10 or more in a game nine times in 34 starts. On August 17 he equaled his career best with 15 punchouts, and did not issue a walk in a complete-game four-hit victory against the Mets.

Soto was durable, too. He went the distance 13 times; however, one of the best outings in his career, a 10-inning, three-hit, scoreless masterpiece, was good enough for just a no-decision in a 2-0 loss to Atlanta in 14 innings on June 27. Soto finished the season with a misleading 14-13 record, as the Reds scored two runs or less (18 total) in each of his losses. With a career-most 274 strikeouts, Soto broke Luis Tiant's record for the most strikeouts in a season by a Latino player (264 in 1968) and eclipsed Maloney's team record of 265 set in 1963. In a demonstration of control and power, Soto led the majors in strikeouts per nine innings (9.6), in the fewest hits/walks per inning (1.060) and in strikeout-to-walk ratio (3.86). Selected to his first of three consecutive All-Star Games, Soto tossed two scoreless innings, whiffing four. In the offseason he was named the Vander Meer winner by the BBWAA for the second time in three seasons.

Soto had a fiery and sometimes violent temperament on the mound. Despite his emergence as one of the best right-handers in baseball, he had a tendency to blow up after bad pitches, poor calls by umpires, hits, and runners on base. Recognizing Soto's Achilles heel, opponents mercilessly bench-jockeyed him, further inflaming his rage. "[Soto] has the tendency to get mad and lose concentration, especially in close games," said batterymate Alex Trevino.[25] Hall of Famer Johnny Bench, who had caught his share of firebrands and loose cannons, such as Pedro Borbón and Ross Grimsley, tried to keep Soto level-headed and focused. "Sometimes he gets too fired up thinking of the strikeout title," said Bench. "I try to get him to calm down. I say, 'Stay back and figure out what you're trying to do instead of starting to think in the middle of your windup.'"[26] Soto's temper got the best of him on May 31, 1982, against the Philadelphia Phillies at Veterans Stadium. He had yielded just one hit over six innings, but had also plunked two batters. When Phillies starter Ron Reed retaliated with Soto at bat in the seventh, an enraged Soto appeared as if he would sling the bat at the hurler, resulting in a benches-clearing brawl. Soto was ejected, but his reputation as a dirty player was cemented; however, Soto's most publicized incidents were still two years off. His volatile on-field personality contrasted sharply with what Lonnie Wheeler of the *Cincinnati Enquirer* described as a soft-speaking, loner type persona away from the game.[27]

While Reds finished in the NL West cellar again in 1983, Soto fashioned yet another dominating season. Sportswriters noticed a change in his demeanor as the 26-year-old hurler won three of his first four starts despite a tender elbow in spring training and then blisters on his right fingers. "[M]aturity is his biggest asset now," praised Lonnie Wheeler. He's willing to handle some adversity."[28] In May, Soto went nine innings in each of his five starts, winning four of them by complete game, yielding just 22 hits (.148 batting average) and seven earned runs (1.40 ERA). "This is the best I've pitched over a long period," said Soto, capping it off with a five-hit, 9-0 whitewashing of Pittsburgh. "[N]ot since the great double 'play" combo of Gilbert and Sullivan has anyone made the Pirates look so silly as Mario Soto," wrote Sullivan ebulliently.[29] On June 12 Soto flirted with a no-hitter, holding the Los Angeles Dodgers hitless for 6 1/3 innings before Pedro Guerrero, his teammate with Escogido in winter ball, lined a single; Soto settled for a three-hitter.

Selected to start the All-Star Game at Comiskey Park in Chicago, Soto yielded two hits, two walks, and two unearned runs to pick up the loss. Days after he blanked Atlanta on three hits on September 13, the Reds announced that they had inked the hard-throwing righty to a five-year contract, widely reported to be the richest in Reds history at $6 million.[30] The runner-up to Philadelphia's John Denny for the Cy Young Award, Soto finished second in innings (273 2/3) and strikeouts (242) to the Phillies ace Steve Carlton, and led the NL with 18 complete games, the most by a Reds hurler since Bob Purkey's 18 in 1962. Soto was indeed the toast of town and the unequivocal center of Cincinnati's baseball world. "He's the kind of pitcher who intimidates hitters," said Reds skipper Russ Nixon.[31] A darling of the media, Soto pulled off a double at the annual BBWAA banquet in the Queen City, capturing his third Vander Meer award and the Ernie Lombardi Award as team MVP.

Buoyed by a multimillion-dollar contract, Soto jumped out of the gates in 1984, winning seven of his first eight decisions. On May 12 he was just one out from a no-hitter when George Hendrick of the St. Louis Cardinals spoiled it with a home run; Soto settled for a one-hitter as part of a career-best six straight winning starts. Everything changed for the emotional pitcher in a fateful start against Chicago at Wrigley Field on May 27, which Dave Parker of the Reds called "chaos and beyond."[32] Though Soto had shown signs of keeping his temper in check the previous season, he always appeared just a few bad calls away from a meltdown. In the bottom of the second, the Cubs' Ron Cey belted a deep fly toward the left-field foul pole. Third-base umpire Steve Rippley ruled it a home run, beginning an ugly brouhaha that interrupted the game for 31 minutes.[33] Soto immediately protested and had to be restrained by teammates. As the umpiring crew met to discuss the call, tempers on both sides simmered to a boiling point. About 20 minutes into the melee, Soto rushed into a scrum of players and coaches, heading for one of the umpires. At the last moment Reds catcher Brad Gulden tackled the outraged pitcher, hurling him into Cubs coach Don Zimmer; both benches simultaneously erupted into a nasty brawl. "If [Soto] had hit the umpire the way he was coming," said Gulden, he probably wouldn't play another game in his life."[34] When Soto was finally pulled away and led to the dugout, he was belted with ice from the stands. Soto went ballistic again, grabbed a bat, and attempted to climb into the box seats to confront the unruly spectator. Cey's hit was ultimately ruled a foul, but the damage to Soto had been irrevocable.

When the NL suspended Soto for five days and fined him $1,000, it was the *Cincinnati Enquirer's* turn to go ballistic. In a scathing editorial, the paper lambasted the Peñalty as "ridiculous" and harshly criticized Soto for his "intent on crude slugfest violence."[35] If Soto had a chance to redeem himself to the Cincinnati media and fans, it was lost three starts later, on June 16 in Atlanta, when he was inexplicably involved in another revolting incident that sportswriter Greg Hoard described as an "extraordinarily senseless act" and "out-and-out insanity."[36] The Braves' Claudell Washington, already on edge from two brushback pitches from Soto earlier in the game, sent a not-so-subtle message when his bat opportunistically slid out of his hands and sailed toward the pitcher after a strike. Washington walked to the mound to confront Soto and a fight erupted.[37] Soto's inexcusable transgression occurred when the benches cleared. He violently tossed the baseball into the crowd on the mound; amazingly, no one was seriously injured. "When a pitcher fires the ball into the stack," said home-plate umpire Lanny Harris after the game, "and hits an umpire and a coach, I think it is serious."[38] Soto was once again suspended for five days, and fined $5,000.

The two events marked a profound shift in the media's portrayal of Soto, whose mental stability members of press openly questioned. Playing in a small market for mainly bad teams, Soto had undeservedly not gotten the national exposure he should have had. Now the national spotlight was on him, but for all of the wrong reasons. "I don't care what they say about me," said Soto unremorsefully. "Everybody is entitled to a few mistakes. Nobody is perfect."[39] Manager Vern Rapp defended his much-maligned hurler, and cautioned the media to consider Soto's perspective. "I wish people knew where Mario comes from, how he had to fight to achieve what he has," said the renowned player's manager. "He still has to learn self-control, to act like a professional. Mario and I have sat down and talked about this. What he did this year had no malicious intent to it as far as I can see. I think he just became frightened, more than anything else. Somebody was trying to take away his livelihood."[40] Despite those words of encouragement, Soto retreated into a shell, finishing the season with a career-high 18 victories (seven losses) despite battling shoulder inflammation over the last six weeks of the season. He once again led the NL in complete games (13), but his ERA rose to 3.53 and his strikeouts dipped to 185 in 237⅓ innings.

Extremely sensitive to the fans' and media's criticism, Soto dug in during spring training. "If they're going to hate me, they're going to hate me," he said.[41] On the mound, Soto seemed to prosper in the four-man rotation ushered in by skipper Pete Rose and pitching coach Jim Kaat. He overcame some elbow tenderness and an altercation in an Atlanta nightclub to post an 8-3 record with a 2.48 ERA by June 4. Behind the scenes, it was a different story. "Yeah, I'm mad," said Soto, directing his vehemence toward Rose and Kaat. "Why can't I pitch on five days' rest?"[42] Claiming his fastball and changeup lost their effectiveness on less rest, Soto went into a tailspin beginning on June 9, losing eight straight decisions and 12 of his 16, while posting an uncharacteristically high 4.25 ERA. Equally noticeable to teammates and sportswriters was a profound change in Soto's personality. "Somehow, some way, through a series of events and circumstances that only he knows," opined beat writer Greg Hoard, "[Soto] has become withdrawn where he was once outgoing, and dispirited in performance, where he was formerly a vigorous competitor."[43] Soto took a me-against-the world posture, refusing any suggestion that he speak to the media about his slump. "When

I pitch, this is my career," he said defiantly. "I have to handle it. I have to work it out myself. I don't have to talk to anyone about it."[44] While the Reds unexpectedly challenged the Dodgers for the West crown, Soto missed several pivotal starts over the last five weeks of the season with toe and shoulder injuries. "There's no reason to try [to pitch] when you're not 100 percent," he said.[45] Sportswriters took Soto's attitude for insouciance, and continued to bash the ailing hurler. "Soto's legacy for the 1985 season," wrote Hoard in an undeservedly scathing commentary, "will be that he and no one else lost the Western Division title for the Reds; that he lost heart, lost too many games."[46] Critics unfairly pointed to Soto's losing record (12-15) as a sign of failure, while overlooking his durability (256⅔ innings) and strikeouts (214).

Soto's ongoing battle with Cincinnati sportswriters continued to 1986. "[Y]ou just can't keep going out there and have good years," he said, trying to deflect incessant criticism, yet the comment only exacerbated the situation.[47] Soto, a proud player who knew firsthand the personal sacrifice required to be a big leaguer, vowed not to speak to the press all season. By May 17, after his fifth consecutive loss, it was obvious that he was hurting, and not the same pitcher he was 12 months earlier. After he landed on the disabled list three times with shoulder pain, Soto's career took another irreversible turn in late August when he underwent shoulder surgery by Dr. Frank Jobe in Los Angeles. Jobe diagnosed "erosion" in the pitcher's wing, and not a rotator-cuff tear, but the damage to Soto proved to be permanent and career-altering.[48] Soto (5-10, 4.71 ERA) missed the rest of the season.

Once one of the most overpowering pitchers in baseball, Soto was reduced to just 20 combined starts over the next two seasons. His velocity was noticeably down in 1987, and he spent much of season on the DL. After an unexpectedly productive spring training in 1988, Soto was tabbed by Rose to start his sixth Opening Day. He enjoyed a brief renaissance over the first six weeks, tossing a four-hit shutout against San Francisco in his second start and wining three of his first five decisions. With his last victory, a five-hitter against Chicago at Riverfront Stadium on May 20, Soto became the 17th Reds pitcher to notch 100 victories. Pain resurfaced in his shoulder thereafter, and he lost five straight starts, surrendering 34 hits and 21 earned runs in 23 ⅔ innings. On June 20, 1988, Cincinnati released him outright. Soto took offense to Rose's disparaging remarks in the press, but otherwise saw the writing on the wall. A week later he signed as a free agent with the Los Angeles Dodgers. After just one outing with Bakersfield in the High-A California League, Soto was shelved for the remainder of the campaign.

Days after signing a minor-league contract with the Dodgers in December, Soto had second thoughts and announced his retirement. "I will definitely not recover," he told *El Caribe*, a newspaper in Santo Domingo. "[I]t looks like my shoulder will not get better. I've already gone as far as I can go."[49] In parts of 12 seasons, Soto fashioned a 100-92 record with a 3.47 ERA in 1,730⅓ innings. His 1,449 strikeouts ranked second behind Maloney's (1,592) as of 2021.

Since his retirement after the 1988 season, Soto has dedicated his life to helping young Dominican and Latino prospects realize their dream of making it to the big leagues. He organized a developmental baseball school near his hometown of Bani in 1991, and remained a staunch supporter of the Dominican Winter League, serving as GM of Leones del Escogides, a club he played on for 11 seasons.

In 2001 Soto was inducted into the Cincinnati Reds Hall of Fame, located in Great

American Ball Park. He remained close to the Reds after his retirement, serving as a spring-training instructor, scout, and director of the team's Dominican operations. In 2009 he was named a special assistant to the GM, and began working closely with Latino prospects in the Reds farm system, serving as a mentor, and helping them transition to a new country, language, and culture.

As of 2016, Soto still resided near Bani, in the Dominican Republic.

SOURCES

In addition to the sources cited in the Notes, the author also accessed the *Encyclopedia of Minor League Baseball*, Retrosheet.org, Baseball-Reference.com, the SABR Minor Leagues Database, accessed online at Baseball-Reference.com, and *The Sporting News* archive via Paper of Record, and relied heavily on the *Cincinnati Enquirer*, accessed through newspapers.com. Special thanks to Bill Mortell for his assistance with genealogical research.

NOTES

1. Nolan Ryan ranked second with 7.1 hits per nine innings. Dwight Gooden debuted in 1984 and surrendered 6.5 hits per nine innings over two seasons.
2. Steve Wulf, "His Bad Rap Is a Bad Rap," *Sports Illustrated*, July 23, 1984. si.com/vault/1984/07/23/620158/his-bad-rep-is-a-bad-rap.
3. Tim Sullivan, "Some Changes Certain With Soto Pitching Today," *Cincinnati Enquirer*, April 5, 1982: D1.
4. Sullivan, "Some Changes Certain With Soto Pitching Today."
5. Lonnie Wheeler, "The Changes in the 'Two' Lives of Soto," *Cincinnati Enquirer*, July 6, 1983: B1.
6. Jim Kaplan, "Soto Isn't So-So Anymore," *Sports Illustrated*, July 5, 1982. si.com/vault/1982/07/05/624641/soto-isnt-so-so-anymore
7. Bob Hertzell, "Reds Just Need a Few More Marios," *Cincinnati Enquirer*, August 8, 1977: 25.
8. Peter King, "Reds KO Braves Again as Soto Strikes Out 15," *Cincinnati Enquirer*, September 10, 1980: B1.
9. Ray Buck, "Magic-Man Soto Mystifies Dodgers, 6-5," *Cincinnati Enquirer*, August 18, 1980: B1.
10. Ray Buck, "Soto Cheered Not Jeered as Reds Rally to Whip Astros," *Cincinnati Enquirer*, July 6, 1981: C1.
11. Tim Sullivan, "Reds' Plans for Soto Are Simple: Turn Him Loose," *Cincinnati Enquirer*, March 1, 1981: C1.
12. Peter King.
13. Bill James and Rob Neyer, *Neyer/James Guide to Pitchers*, (New York: Fireside, 2004), 35.
14. Peter King, "Soto Strikes Again! Marion Just Keeps Right On Whiffing," *Cincinnati Enquirer*, August 18, 1982: E1.
15. Tim Sullivan, "An Ace Isn't an Ace When Soto Deals," *Cincinnati Enquirer*, February 20, 1982: B1.
16. Tim Sullivan, "Soto Whiffs 11, Reds Zap Bucs," *Cincinnati Enquirer*, May 8, 1982: B1.
17. Peter King, "Reds KO Braves Again as Soto Strikes Out 15."
18. Tim Sullivan, "Some Changes Certain With Soto Pitching Today."
19. Tim Sullivan, "Soto Whiffs 11, Reds Zap Bucs."
20. Tim Sullivan, "Soto Hurls Reds Past Mets, 2-0," *Cincinnati Enquirer*, June 11, 1981: B1.
21. Wulf.
22. Tim Sullivan, "Reds Plans for Soto Are Simple: Turn Him Loose."

23 Tim Sullivan, "It's Over and the Best Team Watches," *Cincinnati Enquirer*, October 5, 1981: D1.

24 Ed Reinke, AP Photo, *Cincinnati Enquirer*, October 5, 1981: D3.

25 Kaplan.

26 Kaplan.

27 Lonnie Wheeler, "The Changes in the 'Two' Lives of Soto."

28 Wheeler.

29 Tim Sullivan, Soto Beats Bucs to Tune of 9-0," Cincinnati Enquirer, May 28, 1983: B1.

30 Wulf.

31 Lonnie Wheeler, "The Changes in the 'Two' Lives of Soto."

32 Greg Hoard, 'Suspension Looms for Soto After Brawl," Cincinnati Enquirer, May 28, 1984: D1.

33 A 33-minute clip of the entire melee can be found on You Tube. youtube.com/watch?v=qAhzFOBKrE8

34 Greg Hoard, 'Suspension Looms for Soto After Brawl."

35 "The National League Fell Short of Giving Soto What He Deserved," Cincinnati Enquirer, June 6, 1984: A16.

36 Greg Hoard, "Reds Will Appeal Soto's Suspension This Time," Cincinnati Enquirer, June 21, 1984: B1.

37 The ruckus can be seen on You Tube. youtube.com/watch?v=bt0ftk6kFoA.

38 Lonnie Wheeler, "Reds Wind Up Winners, but Soto May be the Loser," Cincinnati Enquirer, June 17, 1984: C1.

39 "Soto Smiles Again With Giants Help," Cincinnati Enquirer, June 28, 1984: C8.

40 Wulf.

41 "Reds Notebook," Cincinnati Enquirer, March 5, 1985: B4.

42 Greg Hoard, "Soto Demands More Rest, Muddles Reds Pitching Scheme," Cincinnati Enquirer, May 16, 1985: D4.

43 Greg Hoard, "Soto Keeps His Troubles to Himself," Cincinnati Enquirer, June 30, 195: C1.

44 "Reds Notebook," Cincinnati Enquirer, August 22, 1985: B7.

45 "Reds Notebook," Cincinnati Enquirer," September 16, 1985: B5.

46 Greg Hoard, "Soto's Certain He'll Make a Comeback in 1986," Cincinnati Enquirer, October 8, 1985: D1.

47 Tim Sullivan, "Soto Embarks on a New Start," Cincinnati Enquirer, April 7, 1986: B4.

48 "Reds Notebook," Cincinnati Enquirer, August 24, 1986: C3.

49 Associated Press, "Shoulder Forces Soto to Retire," Cincinnati Enquirer, December 11, 1988: D1.

Fernando Tatis

By Chad Moody

Fernando Tatis's journey began with a childhood bedtime story. It was a journey on which family, faith, and baseball all intersected. Although it was filled with injuries and struggles, the journey contained moments of triumph – both professionally and personally. Early in the 1999 season, Tatis accomplished one of the most memorable feats in baseball history: hitting two grand slams in one inning. And baseball also enabled Tatis to accomplish the personal triumphs of finding his father and building a church.

Fernando Tatis (pronounced TAH-teese) was born on January 1, 1975, in San Pedro de Macorís, Dominican Republic, to Fernando Antonio Tatis and Yudelca Tatis.[1] His father was a minor-league infielder in the Houston Astros organization from 1969 to 1978, advancing as high as the Triple-A level, but was released after his play began to suffer in part due to the lingering effects of a shoulder injury. These struggles on the diamond affected his father's personal life, resulting in a divorce with Yudelca in the late 1970s. Although the elder Tatis did continue in baseball as an Astros minor-league coach and scout into the early 1980s, the pain and suffering of a difficult failed second marriage caused him to quit baseball and disappear, having no further

Photo courtesy of Dreamstime

contact with his ex-wife, Yudelca (with whom he had remained friendly), or his young son.

As a child, Tatis's primary memory of his absent father was from a favorite bedtime story he would have his mother often recite. The story involved the time when "Fernandito"

(Tatis's childhood nickname) was brought home from the hospital at two days old. As the story goes, when he was placed in his crib for the first time, his father smiled and laid a miniature baseball bat across his newborn son's chest and said, "God bless you, Fernandito; someday you will be a baseball player just like your father."[2] This story stoked Tatis's love for baseball, and provided motivation to succeed in reaching the big leagues where his father had failed.

Growing up with only his mother in the Miramar neighborhood of San Pedro de Macorís, Tatis cultivated his love for the game by following the Dominican big leaguers of the day. He recalled, "We grew up watching those guys play – Pedro Guerrero, Alfredo Griffin, George Bell, Tony Fernández. When we watch those people, how could we not love baseball?"[3] Tatis also noted the close connection these Dominican stars had with the local community: "It's not that unusual to see ballplayers, to be able to talk to them. They're still a part of where they came from."[4]

Tatis played baseball on the streets as a child, learning to bat and throw right-handed like his father. He tore up blankets, rolled the pieces into balls, and sewed them together to make baseballs. Tatis loved the game so much that he would "play with anything."[5] As he got older, he began playing organized amateur ball, improving his skills, and attended the same San Pedro de Macorís high school that generated much big-league talent over the years, including stars Rico Carty, Alfonso Soriano, and Sammy Sosa. Tatis's potential did not go unnoticed by big-league scouts in this baseball-rich area. After a tryout camp in the Dominican Republic in which he "(distinguished) himself from the pack almost immediately," the 17-year-old infielder was signed by the Texas Rangers as an amateur free agent on August 25, 1992, receiving a signing bonus of $8,000.[6] Tatis was scouted by fellow Dominican Omar Minaya, who later went on to attain notable executive-level positions in the Montreal Expos, New York Mets, and San Diego Padres organizations. Minaya recalled, "Fernando was young and lean, but he also had a loose arm, good hands, and he was a good athlete. He wasn't as big in his upper body as he is now, but he had good body definition. He had a muscular frame for a little guy. Plus, you could tell there was something else about him. He knew how to play the game."[7]

Assigned by the Rangers to the Dominican Summer League in 1993 to accelerate his development, Tatis had a solid season, hitting .273 with 4 home runs and 27 RBIs in 59 games.[8] His first taste of minor-league ball in the United States came the next season in the Gulf Coast League. Primarily playing third base for the Rangers' rookie-league affiliate, Tatis hit an impressive .330 in 60 games, and was rewarded with a promotion to the low Class-A Charleston RiverDogs of the South Atlantic League in 1995. Settling in at the third-base position, Tatis had another successful season. Leading the RiverDogs in average (.303), home runs (15), and RBIs (84), Tatis was named the Rangers' Minor League Player of the Year. Continuing his upward trajectory, Tatis began the 1996 season with the Port Charlotte Rangers of the advanced Class-A Florida State League. Although a broken wrist in spring training delayed his regular-season debut, he posted another solid season in Port Charlotte, hitting .286 with 12 home runs and 53 RBIs in 85 games.[9] Tatis finished the season playing in two games for the Oklahoma City 89ers of the Triple-A American Association.

The 1997 season proved to be a watershed for Tatis. Beginning the season for the Double-A Tulsa Drillers of the Texas League, he continued his offensive productivity, hitting .314 and swiping 17 bases. Although not a particularly large man, the 5-foot-11, 185-pound

Tatis displayed some power, hitting 24 home runs for the Drillers, good for second place in the league. Three of those home runs came in a single game in a 19-8 victory over Shreveport on June 19, making Tatis the first Driller to accomplish that feat.[10] Also noted as having "good defensive range," Tatis was touted as being a Texas League top 10 prospect.[11] His strong performance at Tulsa resulted in a Texas League All-Star Game start at third base, and a second Rangers Minor League Player of the Year Award – the Rangers' first-ever two-time winner.[12] It also resulted in Tatis attaining the goal he dreamed of as a child – a promotion to the big leagues.

Replacing Rangers starting third baseman Dean Palmer, who had been traded to the Kansas City Royals, Tatis made his big-league debut on July 26, 1997, in Chicago against the White Sox (less than four months after his cousin Ramón Tatis became the first player named Tatis ever to appear in the major leagues).[13] He singled in his first major-league at-bat – getting his first RBI in the process – and hit his first big-league home run the following night, a solo shot off the White Sox' Danny Darwin. Tatis started 60 of the Rangers' 61 remaining games at third base, finishing the season eighth among American League rookies in both home runs (8) and RBIs (29), despite the limited playing time.

In addition to being a watershed year professionally, 1997 was also an extremely important year for Tatis personally. Since the inception of his minor-league journey in the United States, he had searched unsuccessfully for his long-lost father, who was rumored to have settled in Florida. Thanks to the prodding of Minaya, he decided to divulge the story of his missing father to a reporter in August, hoping that it would aid in his search.[14] Numerous newspapers around the country picked up the story, including one in Sarasota, Florida, where his father had been living and working as a contract painter. His father saw the article, reached out to the Rangers organization, and in September father and son had an emotional reunion in Texas. Upon seeing his father after their long separation, Tatis said, "It's like a big pain is gone. I feel so much better, like I can breathe again."[15] The following day, Tatis capped this happy occasion by hitting two home runs in a game against the Minnesota Twins with his father in attendance.

Tatis began the 1998 season as the Rangers' starting third baseman, having a solid first half. Attempting to collect the personnel pieces needed to win the AL West, however, the Rangers reluctantly dealt the promising Tatis to the St. Louis Cardinals in July.[16] For the remainder of the season, he started at third for the Cardinals. After having hit only three home runs in 95 games for the Rangers, Tatis experienced a power surge in St. Louis, hitting eight home runs in 55 games. This was a harbinger of things to come.

Building off his strong finish in 1998, Freddie (as he was nicknamed by teammates) had a career year in St. Louis in 1999 – with some very memorable early-season success. On April 23 against the Dodgers in Los Angeles, Tatis accomplished one of the most notable feats in baseball history. With his team down 2-0 in the top of the third inning and the bases loaded, Tatis hit a pitch from Chan Ho Park into the left-field bullpen for a grand slam. Later in the inning, after his teammates continued to reach base safely via a series of walks, hits, and an error, Tatis again stepped to the plate with the bases loaded. Having worked the count full, he once again delivered, driving an offering from Park over the fence in left-center field for his second grand slam of the inning. In accomplishing this feat, Tatis became the first major leaguer ever to hit two grand slams in the same inning.[17] His eight

RBIs in one inning were also a major-league record, leading the Cardinals to a 12-5 victory. Tatis continued his strong performance throughout the season, ending the year hitting .298 with 34 home runs, 107 RBIs, 104 runs, and 21 steals. His 34 home runs broke Ken Boyer's 1960 club record for the most home runs (32) by a St. Louis third baseman.[18] He also played solid defense, committing only four errors after the All-Star break.

The beginning of the 2000 season saw Tatis continue his hot hitting for the Cardinals. He hit .375 with six home runs and a National League-leading 28 RBIs in April, hitting safely in 18 of his 21 games during that span. A strained left groin suffered in late April, however, caused Tatis to miss two months of action.[19] Upon finally returning to the lineup, Tatis was unable to regain his early-season momentum. Although he finished the season hitting .253 with 18 home runs and 64 RBIs in 96 games, Tatis struggled mightily down the stretch, going 5-for-46 in his final 14 games. Because of those late-season struggles, Tatis found himself benched in favor of Plácido Polanco throughout the National League Division Series against the Atlanta Braves. Although unhappy about this, he admitted, "I've got to have more concentration (at the plate). I've got to hit the ball."[20] An injury to Polanco got Tatis his first taste of major-league postseason action. He played in all five games of the Championship Series, going 3-for-13 with two doubles and two RBIs in the series loss to the New York Mets.

Seeking to bolster their pitching staff, the Cardinals dealt Tatis to Montreal after the season. Questions surrounding possible poor work habits and conditioning after his groin injury also were rumored to have played a role in the decision to make Tatis expendable. Being upset over these rumors and how the trade was handled, he took the news particularly hard, noting that the Cardinals were "my team, what I played for, where I put up really good numbers."[21]

Tatis played the next three seasons for the Expos, signing his first sizable contract ($2.75 million) there. During that time, he was able to reunite with Minaya, who became Montreal's general manager in 2002. "It's going to be great for us, especially for the Latin guys. We're going to feel pretty confident. Not that we didn't feel confident with an American guy, but it just feels great to have somebody from your country be a GM," Tatis said of Minaya's hiring.[22] But Tatis battled numerous injuries all along the way in Montreal, limiting him to 41, 114, and 53 games in the 2001-2003 seasons respectively. Tatis also battled poor play. His batting average declined precipitously each year, finally bottoming out at .194 in 2003. Additionally, Tatis's perceived bad attitude caused a strained relationship with Expos manager Frank Robinson, and also alienated him from some teammates. And his overweight and listless appearance resulted in embittered Expos fans calling him "Fatis."[23] This difficult time in Montreal culminated in Tatis spending the final 3½ months of the 2003 season on the disabled list due to panic attacks, with one teammate commenting, "I think he's done."[24] In October 2003 the Expos granted him free agency. In reflecting back on his experience in Montreal, Tatis admitted, "I don't miss the Expos, no. In Montreal, they don't like baseball. When I was there, they lost the feeling for baseball."[25]

Hoping for a new start, Tatis signed with the Tampa Bay Devil Rays, but was released during 2004 spring training. Disappointed, he returned home to the Dominican Republic with his wife and children. He spent the 2004 and 2005 seasons out of professional baseball. A devout Christian since his childhood and noted for his charitable actions during his baseball career, Tatis decided to shift his focus toward construction of a church for the community in his hometown of San Pedro de Macorís.[26] Needing funds to get the church built, Tatis realized that if he was able to sign a new major-league contract, he would earn the money necessary to help bring the project to fruition. Tatis told his family quite presciently that he was going to return to the big leagues. Indeed, the Baltimore Orioles contacted him, and in November 2005 the club signed him to a contract, making his goal of building the new church attainable.

In an effort to prepare Tatis for his attempted comeback, the Orioles assigned him to the Ottawa Lynx of the Triple-A International League for the 2006 season. He regained his stroke there, hitting .298 in 90 games. This was good enough to get Tatis a promotion to the big-league club in late July. Playing in 28 games for the Orioles, he reinvented himself as a utility player, splitting time at first base, second base, third base, and the outfield. Tatis failed to impress, however, hitting .250 in his time with the big-league club. He was granted free agency in December.

The Dodgers decided to take a gamble on the fading 32-year-old for the 2007 season, but released him in March after his poor performance in spring training. All was not lost for Tatis, however, as he again reconnected with Minaya, now the Mets' general manager, whom he once described as being "like my big brother."[27] The Mets signed Tatis on March 23 and assigned him to the New Orleans Zephyrs of the Triple-A Pacific Coast League. "I thought he still had something left," Minaya said.[28] Although Tatis had a relatively productive season in New Orleans (hitting .276 with 21 home runs, 67 RBIs, and 90 runs in 131 games), he did not get a call-up to the big-league club. In addition to battling on the field in his unsuccessful attempt to return to big leagues in 2007, Tatis also had to battle off-the-field issues. Early in the year, it was reported that Major League Baseball had requested medical files from Tatis in its investigation of the use of steroids and other illegal performance-enhancing substances by players.[29] But when the Mitchell Report was released in December, he was not implicated in any wrongdoing.[30]

Finding himself back with the Zephyrs at the beginning of the 2008 campaign, Tatis enjoyed a power resurgence, hitting 12 home runs in his first 37 games for New Orleans. This, plus a season-ending injury in May to Mets outfielder Ángel Pagán, opened the door for Tatis to return to the big leagues. He made the most of his opportunity, experiencing a rebirth of sorts in New York. Playing solid defense in the outfield and delivering several clutch hits for the team early on, Tatis quelled any doubts about his work habits and commitment to the game that beleaguered him in St. Louis and Montreal. Mets teammate David Wright said, "Obviously, he's come up with some big hits for us, he's played some outstanding defense, but just as important, he's given us a lot of energy. He goes out there and plays hard, plays the game the right way and I think that rubs off on a lot of players. Players see his excitement, passion, his intensity, and they want to go out there and match it."[31] Injuries to Mets outfielders Moisés Alou and Ryan Church solidified a starting outfield spot for Tatis. He continued his strong play into midseason, leading the major leagues in hitting for the month of July with a .397 batting average. Although he suffered a season-ending shoulder separation in September, Tatis finished his first season in New York in fine fashion, posting a .297 batting average, 11 home runs, and 47 RBIs in 92 games. He was named *The Sporting News* NL Comeback Player of the Year.[32] Tatis capped the year by returning home to San Pedro de Macorís in November to visit Jerusalem First Church, the church he helped construct, which had opened in the spring. Remaining humble about his role in the project, Tatis said, "Most people down here do not know I was involved in building the church. I tried to keep it a secret down here. I told my wife I don't want anyone to know what we did for this church. The more we can keep it a secret, the better I feel."[33]

Extending his feel-good comeback into the following year, Tatis spent spring training representing his home country in the 2009 World Baseball Classic. As the Mets' season kicked off, however, a logjam of healthy returning starters and newly acquired outfielders left Tatis without a clear position. Still, his offensive ability and defensive versatility won him a roster spot. Even as a utility player, Tatis managed to appear in 125 games for New York, the most he had played in a season since his breakout year in 1999. During the course of the season, Tatis played all four infield positions, left field, and right field. Offensively, he finished the year hitting a solid .282 with 8 home runs and 48 RBIs.

Back with the Mets for the 2010 season, age and injuries began to catch up to Tatis. He struggled early on, posting a .185 batting average after 41 games. Still suffering the lingering effects of the shoulder injury he sustained in 2008, Tatis was placed on the disabled list in July. Shortly thereafter, he had surgery to repair a labrum tear and clean out the AC joint.[34] It was too much for the 35-year-old to overcome, and Tatis never returned to the major leagues. He finished his big-league career with a .265/.344/.442 slash line, 113 home runs, and 448 RBIs.

Nevertheless holding onto his baseball career, Tatis continued to play in the Dominican Winter League from 2011 to 2013, as he had done each year since 2006. He noted how seriously Dominicans take baseball: "In the Dominican, everybody knows you. Everybody's there, every day. They live for this stuff, man. We're crazy about baseball. Everyone knows about baseball in the Dominican, and everywhere you go, people talk to you about the same thing over and over again. And if you screwed up, watch out. They love you, but they'll criticize you, because they want you to win. No matter what, they want you to win. At all costs."[35] In 2014 Tatis signed with the Vaqueros de la Laguna of the Mexican League, but was released a month later. Later that year, he retired from professional baseball.

The record holder for most grand slams and RBIs in an inning settled in the Dominican Republic on a farm in Juan Dolio with his wife, María, and their five children, Fernando Gabriel, Fernando Joshua, Elijah, María Fernanda, and Daniel Fernando.[36] All five children were given biblical names, according to Tatis.[37] Son Fernando Gabriel (popularly known as Fernando Jr.) followed in his father's footsteps as a highly-touted infield prospect, signing a minor-league contract with the Chicago White Sox in 2015 for a reported bonus of $700,000. In 2016 the White Sox dealt the youngster to the San Diego Padres organization, where he progressed to becoming the club's "unquestioned top prospect" after finishing the 2017 season at the Double-A level.[38]

In addition to following his son's exploits on the diamond, Tatis himself has remained close to the game. He conducted "marathon" offseason training sessions with Twins slugger Miguel Sanó to prepare him for the 2017 campaign; this culminated in Sanó using Tatis as his pitcher during that season's MLB Home Run Derby.[39] Tatis also has coached in the Dominican Winter League, and was added to the Boston Red Sox organization in 2018 as the manager of one of their clubs in the Dominican Summer League.[40]

NOTES

1. During Tatis's playing career, he and his father were sometimes referred to as Fernando Jr. and Sr., respectively. Tatis's son – now popularly also known as Fernando Jr. – has himself begun gaining in renown with his recent success in professional baseball. Tatis, his father, and his son are therefore now often referred to as Fernando II, I, and III, respectively, when it is needed to distinguish between the three consecutive generations of Fernando Tatises who have played in Organized Baseball.

2. Tim Crothers, "In the Name of the Father: To Find His Dad, Fernando Tatis Jr. Had to Make It to the Big Leagues," *Sports Illustrated*, June 14, 1999.

3. Tim Wendel, *The New Face of Baseball: The One-Hundred-Year Rise and Triumph of Latinos in America's Favorite Sport* (New York: HarperCollins, 2003), 180.

4. Wendel, 183.

5. Mark Kurlansky, *The Eastern Stars: How Baseball Changed the Dominican Town of San Pedro de Macorís* (New York: Riverhead Books, 2010), 130.

6. Mike Berardino, "A Friend of the Family," *South Florida Sun-Sentinel*, March 3, 2002.

7. Mike Berardino, "A Friend of the Family."

8. Ben Badler, "Mining for Prospects in the DSL," *Baseball America*, March 17, 2009, baseballamerica.com/today/prospects/international-affairs/2009/267777.html, accessed August 16, 2016.

9. *2006 Baltimore Orioles Information & Record Book* (Baltimore: Baltimore Orioles, 2006), 226.

10. Barry Lewis, "Saying Goodbye to Drillers Stadium: The Top Moments in Stadium History," *Tulsa World*, June 24, 2016.

11. Barry Lewis, "Ward, Tatis Head List of Texas League Stars," *Tulsa World*, August 24, 1997.

12. Barry Lewis, "Tonight's Game," *Tulsa World*, June 23, 1997.

13. Murray Chass, "Hirschbeck Is Back in an Unwelcome Spotlight," *New York Times*, August 24, 1997.

14. Murray Chass, "Tatis Finally Hears, 'We Found Your Father,'" *New York Times*, August 20, 1997.

15. Tim Crothers, "In the Name of the Father."

16. Murray Chass, "Baseball: Notebook; Tatis Has Blossomed as Cardinal Slugger," *New York Times*, May 9, 1999.

17. Mike Huber, "April 23, 1999: Fernando Tatis Hits Two Grand Slams in One Inning," SABR Baseball Games Project, sabr.org/gamesproj/game/april-23-1999-fernando-tatis-hits-two-grand-slams-one-inning, accessed August 16, 2016.

18. *2006 Baltimore Orioles Information & Record Book*, 226.

19. *2006 Baltimore Orioles Information & Record Book*, 226.

20. Rick Hummel, "Tatis Returns to Third," *St. Louis Post-Dispatch*, October 13, 2000.

21. Mike Eisenbath, "Tatis Is Still Upset Over How Trade Was Handled," *St. Louis Post-Dispatch*, April 26, 2001.

22. Mike Berardino, "A Friend of the Family."

23. Jonah Keri, "Tatis the Unlikely Catalyst of the Resurgent Mets," *New York Sun*, August 21, 2008.

24. Stephanie Myles, "Panic Attacks Strike Out an Expo," *Montreal Gazette*, August 4, 2003.

25. David Brown, "Q&A with Fernando Tatis, MLBPA's Comeback Player of the Year," Yahoo! Sports, October 25, 2008, sports.yahoo.com/mlb/blog/big_league_stew/post/Q-amp-A-with-Fernando-Tatis-MLBPA-s-Comeback-Pl?urn=mlb,115797, accessed on August 16, 2016.

26. "Fernando Tatis: In God's Moment," The Christian Broadcasting Network, 1.cbn.com/sports/fernando-tatis%3A-in-god%27s-moment, accessed August 16, 2016.

27. Mike Berardino, "A Friend of the Family."

28. Kevin Kernan, "Amazin' Surprise Star Tatis Builds Church," *New York Post*, November 29, 2008.

29. Duff Wilson, "Sosa and Palmeiro Cited in Steroid Investigation," *New York Times*, May 9, 2007.

30. George J. Mitchell, "Report to the Commissioner of Baseball of an Independent Investigation into the Illegal Use of Steroids and Other Performance Enhancing Substances by Players in Major League Baseball," Office of the Commissioner of Baseball, December 13, 2007.

31. Kristie Ackert, "Fernando is Marvelous Once Again," *New York Daily News*, May 31, 2008.

32. *2010 New York Mets Media Guide* (New York: Sterling Mets, 2010), 217.

33. Kevin Kernan, "Amazin' Surprise Star Tatis Builds Church."

34. Adam Rubin, "Tatis Has Surgery," ESPN.com, July 15, 2010, espn.com/blog/new-york/mets/post/_/id/6753/tatis-has-surgery, accessed August 16, 2016.

35　Alden Gonzalez, "Former Major Leaguers Keep Playing in Caribbean Ball: Tatis Still Active in Dominican Republic, Garcia Plugging Away in Mexico," MLB.com, m.mlb.com/news/article/41400422/former-major-leaguers-fernando-tatis-karim-garcia-keep-playing-in-caribbean-leagues, accessed August 16, 2016.

36　Jeff Sanders, "Fernando Tatis Jr. Groomed for Big Future in Baseball," *San Diego Union-Tribune*, September 28, 2017, sandiegouniontribune.com/sports/padres/sd-sp-padres-fernando-tatis-jr-groomed-for-big-future-in-baseball-20170928-story.html, accessed January 10, 2018.

37　"Mi Gente: Fernando Tatis," *Listín Diario*, February 26, 2012.

38　Jeff Sanders, "Postseason Awards Rolling in for Fernando Tatis Jr.," *San Diego Union-Tribune*, September 8, 2017, sandiegouniontribune.com/sports/padres/sd-sp-padres-fernando-tatis-minor-league-awards-20170908-story.html, accessed January 10, 2018.

39　Mike Berardino, "Fernando Tatis on Star Pupil Miguel Sano: 'I'm Always Going to Be There for Him,'" *St. Paul Pioneer Press*, July 11, 2017, twincities.com/2017/07/11/fernando-tatis-on-star-pupil-miguel-sano-im-always-going-to-be-there-for-him/, accessed January 10, 2018.

40　"Tatis Asegura Lake Retomará Su Forma," Estrellas Orientales, December 9, 2017, estrellasorientales.com.do/2017/12/09/tatis-asegura-lake-retomara-forma/, accessed January 12, 2018; Jason Mastrodonato, "Red Sox Minor League Coaching Staffs Get Little Change," *Boston Herald*, January 10, 2018, bostonherald.com/sports/red_sox/2018/01/red_sox_minor_league_coaching_staffs_get_little_change, accessed January 10, 2018.

JOSÉ URIBE

By William H. Johnson

Born on January 21, 1959, in San Cristobal, Dominican Republic, José Uribe found a path from the pockmarked, rock-and-dirt baseball fields of the Dominican Republic to international baseball success. Named the All-Decade Shortstop of the 1980s for the San Francisco Giants,[1] he played well in an unforgettable World Series with the team in 1989. In 2006, though, he died tragically in an automobile accident in his native country.

José Altagracia Gonzalez's father, Eligio Gonzalez, was a career member of Rafael Trujillo's army, and his mother, Luz Maria, kept home and tended to the array of domestic responsibilities attendant to supporting a military family lifestyle.[2] After a youth spent partially in school, but mostly playing baseball on the empty fields around San Cristobal, José Uribe signed his first professional baseball contract with the New York Yankees organization as an amateur free agent, at the age of 18,[3] on February 18, 1977, on the recommendation of Epy Guerrero.[4] He signed that contract as José Gonzalez, but after spending parts of the next four months on the disabled list, he was released on July 5. Three years later, the 20-year-old signed with the St Louis Cardinals, and at age 22 made his professional debut in 1981 with their Class-A minor-league club in St. Petersburg, Florida.

The following season, 1982, Gonzalez hit .247 for the Double-A Arkansas Travelers, and then .357 in an eight-game stint with Triple-A Louisville at the end of the season. He was assigned to the Louisville out of 1983 spring training, where he hit .284 with 26 stolen bases in 122 games. A late-season call-up to the Cardinals in 1984 after making the International League All-Star team that season, he made his major-league debut against the Philadelphia Phillies on September 13, 1984, starting at shortstop and going 0-for-4 in a loss to Philadelphia.

On February 15, 1985, Uribe was traded, along with David Green, Dave LaPoint, and Gary Rajsich, to the San Francisco Giants for slugger Jack Clark. He had signed his contracts and played in the minor leagues as José Gonzalez, since Gonzalez was his father's surname. At some point in 1985, he changed his professional name from José Gonzalez Uribe to José Uribe. This meant he was using his mother's maiden name, instead of his father's, because "There are too many Gonzalezes in baseball." Rocky Bridges later joked that Uribe was "the ultimate player to be named later."[5]

Just after the 1985 season began, Uribe's defensive prowess and offensive aptitude forced incumbent San Francisco Johnnie LeMaster to the bench.[6] After a winter playing for Licey, in the Dominican winter league, Uribe with his defense and his ability to switch-hit eventually afforded new manager Roger Craig the latitude to consider moving the young player to second base. "Although veteran Brad Wellman and rookie Mike Woodard are the prime candidates for the San Francisco Giants second base job," *The Sporting News* reported, "Manager Roger Craig said he was not averse to shifting José Uribe from shortstop if newcomer Dave Owen looks good at that position."[7] Uribe remained at short, though, and in 1986 posted then-career highs of 43 runs batted in, 22 stolen bases, and 61 walks.

Given a raise from $133,000 to $195,000 for the 1987 season,[8] Uribe posted his best year in professional baseball, batting .291 for the year and going 7-for-26 in the National League Championship Series. Nick Peters, writing in *The Sporting News*, observed, "The San Francisco Giants' front office took a lot of heat when slugger Jack Clark was traded to St. Louis for Dave LaPoint, David Green, Gary Rajsich, and José Gonzalez. While Clark powered St Louis to a pennant in 1985, the Giants lost a franchise-record 100 games. Two years later, Green is back with the Cardinals, LaPoint is pitching for the Chicago White Sox, Rajsich is playing in Japan, and Gonzalez is Uribe. ... San Francisco wouldn't have been on the verge of the National League West title without Uribe. A slick fielder obscured by Ozzie Smith in St Louis, Uribe has been San Francisco's most consistent shortstop since Chris Speier. 'You're not going to find a better double-play combination than Uribe and (Robby) Thompson,' said Speier. ... Manager Roger Craig said, 'They're as good a double-play combination as I've seen. They make routine (plays) on balls that would be hits against other clubs.'"[9]

The following February, Uribe signed a one-year deal for $535,000,[10] which was, presumably, a harbinger of good things to come. It was not.

In 1983 Uribe had married, Sara Reyes,[11] also from San Cristobol, and she gave birth to their daughters Luz Adriana in 1984 and Jacqueline in 1985. On June 1, 1988, Sara suffered a heart attack, due to chronic pulmonary hypertension and not the rigor of childbirth, and died while prematurely delivering their son, Rique José."[12]

Uribe was a fan favorite, and when he would come to bat at home in Candlestick Park, would be greeted by the "U-Reebee" cheer, in which one side of the stadium chanted "OOH," and the other "REEBAY" immediately after. After the 1988 season he won the Giants' Willie Mac Award, a prestigious honor named for Giants star Willie McCovey that is voted on by peers and fans and which recognizes the cumulative value of a player not only on the field but in the community as well. But Uribe was in perpetual agony. "This season was like 20 years for me," he said. "It sometimes seemed like it would never end. My body was sore and my mind was so tired. There were times when I felt like I didn't want to play."[13]

Uribe returned home to the Dominican Republic for the winter, but the team was not sure how he would respond in the future. "Second baseman Robby Thompson, who is probably closer to Uribe than any other player, said his double-play partner's mind sometimes wandered, said an article in *The Sporting News*. " 'At times, José wasn't himself out there. ... There was a game when he started running off the field when there were only two outs. Another time I flipped to him at second base for the third out and he threw to first. I'm sure he was distracted at times, but that's understandable.'"[14]

Photo courtesy of Dreamstime

The 1989 season began with more turmoil. Uribe was arrested on a rape charge in the Dominican Republic, and was forbidden to depart the island until after the trial. According to *The Sporting News,* a local woman accused Uribe of "threatening her with a gun and raping her." The woman alleged that Uribe "drugged her beer while she was at a discotheque he owned, and then took her to a hotel and raped her. Uribe denied the charge, but spent three days in jail before being released on his own recognizance."[15] Less than four weeks later, the charges were dismissed after a blood test performed on the complainant "indicated that there was no foundation for the charge."[16]

Despite another raise, this time to $687,500, Uribe's performance understandably declined in 1989, when he batted .221 and slugged at a paltry .280 clip. The Giants won the National League pennant for the first time since 1962, and faced the Oakland Athletics in the World Series. That Series is remembered for two primary reasons: The Series was interrupted by the Loma Prieta earthquake that devastated the Bay Area; and when it resumed, the A's swept the Giants.

After another winter in the Dominican Republic, Uribe returned to San Francisco and performed at a higher level than he had in 1989. Unfortunately for the shortstop, though, his personal struggles persisted. In December 1990, he was arrested and charged with assaulting two women with a baseball bat. Santo Domingo newspapers said he denied the charged and was released after posting $26,000 bail.[17] Again, the charges were dropped for lack of evidence.[18]

The 1991 and 1992 campaigns proved to be the beginning of the end of Uribe's major-league career. His batting average fell to .241 in 1992, and with the rise of young shortstop Royce Clayton in San Francisco, the Giants released him. He spent the winter in the Dominican Republic again, this time delivering shoes and donated equipment for young ballplayers on the island.[19] When he returned to the United States, he did so as a Houston Astro, having signed with the club on January 5, 1993. Houston had a young hopeful of their own, in Andújar Cedeño, but envisioned Uribe as an experienced hand and willing to accept a role as a backup infielder with major-league experience. According to Houston general manager Bill Wood, "We didn't want someone who was a backup and only a backup. We wanted someone who could handle the everyday job if Andújar doesn't get the job done."[20]

Uribe played only 45 games in 1993, with his final appearance on October 3 against the Cincinnati Reds. He got two hits in four at-bats. On October 29 the Astros released him. At 34, Uribe was through as a major-league player.

For his career, Uribe posted a lifetime batting average of .241, with 74 stolen bases and 307 runs scored. He was never more than a weak power hitter, but his glove work and speed had allowed him to succeed in the big leagues for a decade.

Out of baseball, Uribe – known as "Uvita," or "the black grape" in San Cristobal[21] -- returned to his neighborhood in the Juan Baron section of Sabana Grande de Palenque, about 30 miles west of Santo Domingo. He had remarried, this time to Wendy Guerrero, with whom he had four more children, and he managed a pawn shop/hardware store while operating the José Uribe Youth League for young Dominican players. On December 8, 2006, it all came to an abrupt end.

According to the Associated Press, the 47-year-old was driving a sport-utility vehicle on a highway 30 miles west of Santo Domingo, and wasn't wearing a seatbelt when his SUV crashed on a mountainous road. An unidentified passenger with him was reportedly not injured. Uribe's death was confirmed by Glovis Reyes, a longtime friend of the ballplayer and a former member of the Dominican Congress. "Uribe was a very loved person in Juan Baron. He was like the lord of the town," Reyes said.[22]

The outpouring was immediate and sincere. Hall of Fame outfielder Vladimir Guerrero led mourners through the streets of Juan Baron, a group that included Uribe's second cousin Juan Uribe. "I was very saddened to hear the news of José's passing this morning," Giants owner Peter Magowan said. "He meant so much to the Giants during his playing days. He was such an important part of the team's success in the late 1980s. When you saw José on the field, he exuded happiness and pure joy for the game and life. Personally, I was really looking forward to catching up with him this season during the 20th reunion of the 1987 NL West championship team."[23]

NOTES

1. Tom Schott and Nick Peters, eds., *The Giants Encyclopedia* (Champaign, Illinois: Sports Publishing, LLC, 2003), 247-248.
2. Email exchange with Luz Uribe, José's eldest child, on August 31 and September 2, 2017.
3. Steve Wulf, "Standing Tall at Short," *Sports Illustrated*, February 9, 1987.
4. sports.yahoo.com/blogs/mlb-big-league-stew/epy-guerrero-super-scout-helped-open-dominican-baseball-221957739.html.
5. Associated Press, *Gettysburg Times*, April 8, 1985: 7.
6. Nick Peters, "Top Notch Pitching Wasted by the Giants," *The Sporting News*, May 13, 1985: 20.
7. *The Sporting News*, March 10, 1986: 41.
8. https://www.baseball-reference.com/players/u/uribejo01.shtml
9. Nick Peters, "Uribe May Give Giants Last Laugh," *The Sporting News*, October 5, 1987: 18.
10. *The Sporting News*, February 15, 1988: 40.
11. Ancestry.com.
12. "Uribe's Wife Dies of Heart Attack," *New York Times*, June 2, 1988: nytimes.com/1988/06/02/sports/uribe-s-wife-dies-of-heart-attack.html.
13. *The Sporting News*, November 28, 1988: 52.
14. . *The Sporting News*, November 28, 1988: 52.
15. *The Sporting News*, February 20, 1989: 31.
16. *The Sporting News*, February 27, 1989: 34.
17. *The Sporting News*, December 10, 1990: 38.
18. *The Sporting News*, December 31, 1990: 33.
19. *The Sporting News*, October 5, 1992: 19.
20. *The Sporting News*, January 18, 1993: 26.
21. "Standing Tall at Short."
22. Jonathan Katz, Associated Press, "José Uribe Killed in Car Crash," *Colorado Springs Gazette*, December 9, 2006: Sports 3.
23. Katz.

Juan "Tetelo" Vargas

By Joséph Gerard and Julio M. Rodriguez

During the 1953 season, a 47-year-old dominated the Dominican Republic's professional baseball summer league.[1] His .355 batting average led all hitters (he was 66-for-186), playing center field for Estrellas Orientales of San Pedro de Macoris. He could do things other players half his age were unable to. He was so fast that he had earned the nickname El Gamo (the buck, or Dominican deer); even at age 47, he could outrun most of the players in the league. He would bunt successfully, spread singles all over the field, steal bases, and was an excellent outfielder.

He was the ultimate gentleman, on and off the field. His complexion kept him on the wrong side of the major leagues' color barrier – he was 41 when Jackie Robinson arrived. Yet Tetelo Vargas accomplished much in more than three decades of professional baseball (1923-1956), a career that took him from his homeland to Puerto Rico, Venezuela, Cuba, Canada, and the US Negro Leagues.[2] He also played in the United States for the Havana Red Sox, the Cuban House of David, and the New York Cubans. He is unequivocally recognized as the greatest Dominican player of his era. As Peter Bjarkman, historian of Latin American baseball, wrote, "The slender, wiry outfielder and shortstop ... is without doubt the most

Photo courtesy of Cuqui Cordova

accomplished Dominican native never to spend a single day in the majors."[3]

Juan Esteban Vargas Marcano was born on April 11, 1906. His father, Isaías Vargas, was a shoemaker who resided in Santo Domingo with his wife, Baudilia Marcano. His parents had six other children, two of whom also played baseball. Like many young boys on the island at that time, Juan learned the game on the local backyards and empty lots, playing in many sandlot pickup games with his friends. A maternal uncle who was known as Tetelo began to call the young boy Tete, and from there everyone called him Tetelo, too.

In 1911 the first stadium for baseball was inaugurated in Santo Domingo. It was a wooden structure, double-decked along the third-base line.[4] The Gimnasio Escolar was the first center for sports activities in the country and local baseball players began to develop their talent. Many of the older children formed club teams and battled for local bragging rights. Two of the better-known club teams Tetelo played for were Gimnasio Escolar and Capotillo. But the most renowned of these club teams was created one night in November 1907 by a group of boys in the home of Vicente Maria Vallejo on La Calle El Conde in Santo Domingo. El Club Licey, as they called themselves, soon settled on blue-and-white-striped flannel uniforms that led to their becoming known as Los Azules, and later, Los Tigres.

In 1921 young Vargas had his first involvement in organized baseball as a batboy for Licey; the team went on to become one of the two most famous in the history of Dominican baseball.

Licey had started in 1906, the same year Tetelo was born. It routinely beat all the other clubs in the city. In 1921 Escogido, built around the best players of three other teams, was formed to beat Licey. In 1922 Tetelo became the batboy of Escogido and began to show his athleticism. This was during the years of the American occupation of the Dominican Republic (1916-24), and baseball became the national pastime. In 1923, at age 17, Tetelo began playing shortstop for Escogido and continued playing without a break for the next 34 years, until 1956, when he retired at the age of 50.

In addition to playing for Escogido in 1923, Vargas also made his professional debut for the Humacao club in Puerto Rico that same season. He continued to play ball in Puerto Rico for Ribosch de Cayey in 1924, the Arecibo Lobos in 1925, and the Guayama Stars in 1926. During this same period in the Dominican Republic, he played for Escogido in 1923-24 and Central Romana in 1926. In 1925 he played for the Atlas team in Colombia.

The year 1927 was a seminal one in the development of Vargas's career, as he played in both the United States and Venezuela for the first time. Being dark-skinned, Vargas was excluded from consideration for organized white baseball in the States. But having been recruited by Alex Pómpez, one of the most significant figures in the history of organized black baseball, Vargas played that summer for the New York Cuban Stars in what turned out to be the final full season of the Eastern Colored League. He also got married that year, to a Puerto Rican woman named Celia Amaro.

Due to his relationship with the powerful booking agent Nat Strong and bankrolled by his lottery empire, Pómpez had procured a lease at the Dyckman Oval outside Harlem, securing a permanent home for his team. With this advantage, he was able to avoid the instabilities that faced many owners of Negro League teams, who were totally dependent on the magnates of organized white baseball who controlled the access to ballparks. Pómpez scoured Latin America and the United States for the best Latin players, and he spent lavishly to secure their services. In addition to Vargas, players on the 1927 Cuban Stars roster included Martín Dihigo, Alejandro Oms, Manuel "Cocaína" Garcia, and Bernardo Baro.

After the season, Vargas barnstormed throughout the United States and Canada for the Havana Red Sox of Ramiro Ramírez. That same winter, Vargas made his debut in Venezuela for the Santa Marta club; he went on to become one of the most enduring players in that country, competing for various clubs for 13 consecutive seasons.

Vargas did not return to the United States in 1928, but instead played for the Guayama Brujos in Puerto Rico. During the winter he returned to the Dominican Republic to play for Escogido, and subsequently returned to the United States to once again play for the Cuban Stars, as the traveling team joined with four other clubs from the now-defunct Eastern Colored League to form the American Negro League, which folded after only one season.

In the winter of 1929 Vargas made his first trip to Cuba, where he hit .316 for the Habana Leones. In the summer of 1930 he returned to play for the Havana Red Sox, which by this time had been purchased by Syd Pollock, the legendary owner and promoter of black barnstorming teams. Pollock went on to achieve fame with the Indianapolis Clowns in the 1940s and '50s, for whom he signed Hank Aaron to his first professional contract in 1952.

In the winter of 1930, Vargas returned to Cuba for a second term with Habana, but the season was shortened due to a dispute over rent between the league and the owners of La Tropical Stadium. Perhaps disillusioned by this turn of events, Vargas did not return to play in Cuba again until 1942.

In 1931 Pollock changed the name of the Havana Red Sox to the Cuban House of David, one of many impersonators of the original Israelite commune's barnstorming team from Benton Harbor, Michigan. After a brief appearance with Abel Linares' Western version of the Cuban Stars, Vargas hooked up with Pollock's team for the remainder of the 1931 season. In September in Sioux City, Iowa, Vargas was credited with breaking the world record by running the bases in 13.25 seconds, apparently unencumbered by the full set of whiskers he and his teammates donned to mimic their forebears. Pollock also made the claim that during this season Vargas hit seven home runs in as many plate appearances against a semipro team in Omaha, Nebraska.

Vargas's greatest asset was his speed, which became the stuff of legend. It is said he often scored from first base on a single, that he would routinely beat out infield grounders, and that he never once grounded into a double play. A story is told about a 1931 race in Cincinnati with Jesse Owens, later an Olympic champion, and a number of ballplayers. As the story goes, Owens was dressed in his shorts, while Vargas and the other players wore their usual baseball uniforms. Taking this into account, Owens gave them a five-meter lead in the 100-meter race. When the race began, Vargas outraced them all. It is said that Tetelo was once asked to run around the bases from home plate and he was clocked at 13.25 seconds.

Vargas was also an excellent hitter, several times hitting over .400. Playing for Escogido in 1929, he was 15-for-37 (a .405 average).

In the winter of 1931 Vargas returned to the Santa Marta club, beginning a period of relative stability in which he played the better part of six seasons in Venezuela. From 1932 to 1934, he played for the Concordia Eagles, a traveling team sponsored by Gonzalo Gómez, the son of President Juan Vicente Gómez. The 1934 Concordia roster included Martín Dihigo, Josh Gibson, Rap Dixon, and Luis Aparicio Sr., and is considered to be one of the greatest clubs in the history of baseball in Venezuela.

Vargas moved on to play for the Royal Criollos in 1935 and Gavilanes in 1936-37. At home in 1936, he played for Estrellas Orientales.

In the summer of 1937, the Dominican dictator Rafael I. Trujillo fused the Santo Domingo teams Licey and Escogido and named them the Trujillo City Dragons. He had just changed the name of the city from Santo Domingo to Trujillo City. The Trujillo City team could not be allowed to lose the championship. When the Dragons were not doing well in the early part of the season, Trujillo dispatched Dr. José Enrique Aybar to the United States to acquire the best available players available for the team. White major-league players being reasonably well-paid, Aybar selected several of the best players from the Negro Leagues – Satchel Paige, Josh Gibson, Cool Papa Bell, Sam Bankhead, Robert Griffith, and Bill Perkins. The other owners, their pride hurt, mounted their own efforts and brought in a number of other players. Aguilas Cibaeñas of Santiago brought in Chet Brewer, Bert Hunter, Clarence Pamm, and Martin Dihigo. Estrellas Orientales from San Pedro de Macoris (the 1936 championship team) imported Ernest Carter, George Tubby Scales, Cocaina Garcia, Alejandro Oms, and Ramon Bragaña, the pitcher who had given them the 1936 championship. This was clearly baseball being played at a very high level. Tetelo Vargas played for Estrellas Orientales; he had 30 hits in 106 at-bats, for a .283 average.

The Dragons won with an 18-13 record, but the financial and emotional stress for the owners of the clubs was so great that there was not another professional baseball tournament in the country for 14 years, until 1951.

The following year, 1938, was another pivotal one for Tetelo. He returned to the United States to play for Pómpez's New York Cubans, who barnstormed that summer before joining the Negro National League the following year. In addition, Vargas joined the Guayama club in the fledgling Liga de Béisbol Profesional de Puerto Rico (LBPPR), which became one of the most prominent winter leagues for decades to come. Vargas hit .405, second on the team to Perucho Cepeda's .465 average, and slugged a league-leading .677 as Guayama won the championship with a 27-12 record.

Vargas went on to play the next three winters for Guayama. In the 1939-40 season, he led the team in runs scored with 69 and stolen bases with 33. The latter still is still the league's fourth best single-season total. To put the mark in perspective, only the top-ranked basestealers surpassed Vargas in their annual totals, and the schedules were somewhat longer in the number of games played. The record holder is Rickey Henderson, who swiped 44 in the 1980-81 winter season. Number two is Carlos Bernier, the all-time leader in the LBPPR, with 41 in 1949-50. Number three is Ron LeFlore, with 34 in 1977-78. Guayama won its second consecutive championship, compiling a record of 39-17 – Satchel Paige contributed 19 of those wins.

In the United States, while for the Cuban Stars and the Havana Red Sox from 1927 through 1941, in 93 recorded at-bats during league games, Vargas had 46 hits, for a .495 average.

The 1940 census shows Vargas and Celia living in Guayama, with two children, Carmen (aged 11) and Juan Esteban Jr. (9). Tetelo did not play for the New York Cubans that year, returning to play his last season in Venezuela, but returned in 1941, when he shared the outfield with the great Puerto Rican player Francisco "Pancho" Coimbre. The Cubans won the second-half title that season but lost the championship series to the Homestead Grays. The following spring, the Cubans played an exhibition series against the Brooklyn Dodgers in Havana, winning three out of the five games.

Playing for Estrellas Orientales in 1941, Vargas had another .400 season, 13-for-29, for a .448 average.

Vargas played the balance of his Negro League career, through 1944, for the Cubans, including a remarkable performance in the 1943 season, when he batted .450 and slugged .580 in league play.[5] General comments in the day focused on his speed, calling him "the fastest man in colored baseball today" – or simply "the fastest man in baseball," without qualification.

Vargas returned to Cuba for the last time to play for the Habana Leones in the 1942-43 winter season. Beginning in the winter of 1943, at the age of 37, he embarked on an extraordinary string of 12 consecutive seasons in the LBPPR. Playing for Santurce in the 1943-44 season, he hit .420 (55-for-134.) The last nine of those 12 seasons were spent with his old Guayama club, which now shared their team with the town of Caguas to the north. The Caguas/Guayama Criollos won three LBPPR championships during this period: 1947-48, 1949-50, and 1953-54. As a result, Vargas went to two Caribbean Series. (The tournament was established in 1949.)

In 1947 Puerto Rico hosted a three-game exhibition series against the world champion New York Yankees; in 14 at-bats, Vargas had seven hits for a .500 average.

When the Dominican Summer League was established in 1951, Vargas joined the Estrellas Orientales and played for four seasons. He beat out Negro League great Ray Dandridge for the batting title in 1953 at the age of 47, and led his team to the league championship in 1954. After the league switched to a winter schedule, Vargas played the 1955-56 season at the age of nearly 50. His playing career then concluded at last.

Vargas, who weighed only 160 pounds despite standing 5-feet-10-inches tall, played shortstop and second base early in his career. His move to the outfield can be estimated to have occurred around the age of 33, when the New York Cubans moved him to center field in 1939. In large part because of his exceptional speed, Vargas won plaudits from many of his peers. Millito Navarro, a friend and rival during the 1930s and '40s, said, "He was reliable and produced in the clutch. I saw him score from first on a single. Another time he made it home from second on a long fly ball to right field. He was one of my idols in baseball, a very complete ballplayer."[6]

Charlie Dressen, who visited Puerto Rico in 1936 while serving as manager of the Cincinnati Reds, said, "He could fly. He's just a very good ballplayer."[7] Mickey Owen managed Vargas at Caguas in 1953-54; even though Vargas was then in his late 40s, Owen said, "He ran like a deer and could outrun Jim Rivera and Hank Aaron."[8]

In Puerto Rico, Vargas won the LBPPR batting title three times, led the league in runs scored on four occasions and in triples twice, and, in perhaps his most notable achievement, led the league in slugging percentage twice – eight years apart – the second coming at the age of 40. He finished with a career batting average of .321, which was sixth best in league history, despite playing for a total of 16 seasons, until he reached the age of 49.

After the 1947-48 season, when he was 41 years old, Vargas's performance in Puerto Rico tailed off considerably. A better view of his true batting skills comes from the first nine seasons of his career in the LBPPR – through the age of 41 – when he hit for a combined average of .357, better than the .350 average achieved by the all-time LBPPR batting champion, legendary Negro League star Willard Brown, who was posthumously elected to the National Baseball Hall of Fame in 2006.

During his career in the Negro Leagues, Vargas compiled a batting average of .332 and a slugging percentage of .447, and was selected to play in three East-West All-Star games, two in 1942 and one in 1943. He was 2-for-7 with two RBIs in the All-Star Games.[9]

In limited opportunities against major league pitching, Vargas batted .409, including a 7-for-14 performance in exhibition games against the New York Yankees that were played in San Juan in 1947.

Vargas played much less frequently in the Dominican Republic, as there was no professional league between 1937 and 1951. His only consistent period of play occurred with the creation of the Dominican Summer League in 1951, when he was 45 years old. Vargas finished play in his native country with a batting average of .325 and slugging percentage of .401.

Unfortunately, detailed records are not available for much of the time that Vargas spent playing in Venezuela, during what should have been his peak years. The records that do exist are consistent with his performance elsewhere, including a lifetime batting average of .310.

Perhaps the greatest testament to his talent, and the regard in which he is held in his home country, took place in 1961. The two-year-old ballpark in San Pedro de Macorís – home of the Estrellas Orientales, Vargas's former team in the Liga del Béisbol Profesional Dominicana – was renamed Estadio Tetelo Vargas in his honor. Subsequently, the Estrellas retired his uniform number.

After he retired from baseball, Vargas worked for some time as a scout for the Pittsburgh Pirates. A widower after the death of his first wife, Vargas was married in Puerto Rico to Violeta Incháustegui in 1954. Despite being revered in the Dominican Republic as well as Venezuela, Vargas settled in Guayama after his retirement from baseball. Vargas had two more children, daughters Ana and Iris. (Celia may have been the mother of one, but sources differ.)

In 1967 Vargas was inducted into the Dominican Republic Baseball Hall of Fame.

Juan Esteban Vargas died on December 30, 1971, at the age of 65 after a battle with lung cancer (though Dominican author Héctor Cruz cited prostate cancer). He is buried next to his wife in El Cementerio Municipal de Guayama. The Puerto Rican Baseball Hall of Fame inducted Vargas in 1992 as part of its second class; the Cuban Baseball Hall of Fame (in exile) followed suit in 1998. In 2010 Vargas was honored in his native country with selection to El Salón de la Fama del Béisbol Latino in La Romana.

SOURCES

Books:

Córdova, Cuqui. *Tetelo Vargas: El Gamo* (Santo Domingo, Dominican Republic: Revista Histórica del Béisbol, 2004).

Crescioni Benítez, José A. *El BéisbolProfesional Boricua* (San Juan, Puerto Rico: Aurora Comunicación Integral, 1997).

Holway, John. *The Complete Book of Baseball's Negro Leagues* (Winter Park, Florida: Hastings House, 2001).

Klein, Alan M. *Sugarball: The American Game, the Dominican Dream* (New Haven, Connecticut: Yale University Press, 1993).

Kurlansky, Mark. *The Eastern Stars: How Baseball Changed the Dominican Town of San Pedro de Macoris* (New York: The Penguin Group, Inc., 2010).

McNeill, William F. *Black Baseball Out of Season: Pay for Play Outside of the Negro Leagues* (Jefferson, North Carolina: McFarland & Company, 2007).

Revel, Dr. Layton, and Luis Muñoz. *Forgotten Heroes; Juan "Tetelo" Vargas* (Carrollton, Texas: Center for Negro League Baseball Research, 2008).

Riley, James A. *The Biographical Encyclopedia of the Negro Baseball Leagues* (New York: Carroll & Graf Publishers, 1994).

Magazines and newspaper articles

Morrison, Heriberto. "Tetelo Vargas: fuesuperastro sin jugaren las grandesligas," *Rumbo* (Santo Domingo, Dominican Republic), May 2, 1994, 54.

Vargas, Juan E. Jr. obituary, *Connecticut Post*, September 12, 2011.

Internet sources:

Cruz, Héctor J. *El BéisbolDominicano* (scribd.com/doc/25085233/EL-BEISBOL-DOMINICANO-2).

McKenna, Brian. "Tetelo Vargas, the Dominican Deer," Baseballhistoryblog.com, May 8, 2010.

Ancestry.com.

Baseballthinkfactory.org.

Fultonhistory.com.

NOTES

1. The league operated from 1951 through 1954.
2. By some accounts, Vargas played in Colombia and Panama. These appear to refer to another Dominican player, Ramón "Tetelito" Vargas. There is also no visible historical support for accounts stating that Vargas played in Mexico. *La Enciclopedia del Béisbol Mexicano* shows no evidence that he played there in the summer, and his winters are all accounted for elsewhere.
3. Peter C. Bjarkman, *Diamonds Around the Globe: The Encyclopedia of International Baseball* (Westport, Connecticut: Greenwood Press, 2005), 182.
4. The ballpark was located near the coast, but was destroyed by Hurricane San Zenon that hit Santo Domingo on September 3, 1930.
5. Totals differ. The figures here come from Baseball-Reference.com, but Seamheads reports him as batting .471 and slugging .587 in league play. See seamheads.com/NegroLgs/player.php?playerID=varga01tet.
6. Thomas E. Van Hyning, *Puerto Rico's Winter League* (Jefferson, North Carolina: McFarland & Company, 2004), 80.
7. Van Hyning, 80.
8. Van Hyning, 80.
9. Larry Lester, *Black Baseball's National Showcase: The East-West All-Star Game 1933-1953* (Lincoln: University of Nebraska Press, 2001).

OZZIE VIRGIL

By Ryan Brecker

Ozzie Virgil was the first Dominican to play in the major leagues, as well as the first player of color for the New York Giants and for the Detroit Tigers. Spending parts of nine seasons in the major leagues as a utility player, Virgil forged a lifelong career in baseball by transitioning to coaching. "Virgil should be for my country as important as [Jackie] Robinson [is] to the African-American, I'd place his legacy up there that of those who established our republic," Dominican slugger David Ortiz said in 2006.[1]

Osvaldo José Virgil Pichardo was born on May 17, 1932, in the small coastal town of Monte Cristi, near the Dominican Republic's border with Haiti. During his playing career, his birth date was commonly listed as May 7, 1933; immigration paperwork would place his birth year as 1934.[2]

Virgil grew up with his father Henry Virgil, who worked as a boat pilot in the harbor of Monte Cristi.[3] Seeking better conditions, Henry emigrated to the United States when Ozzie was still young. In the United States, "(h)e was a merchant marine, carrying cargo and stuff for troops overseas," Virgil said. After the war was over, he sent for my brother Carlos and me."[4]

The family included his mother, Isabel Pichardo, and older sibling, Carlos. Virgil's father was a vocal opponent of the Dominican dictator, Rafael Trujillo, which led to the Virgils fleeing the Dominican Republic in 1947 for safety. They went briefly to Puerto Rico and settled in the Bronx later that same year.

Despite living in the Bronx, Virgil became a Brooklyn Dodgers fan primarily after his father secured World Series tickets in 1947. Virgil said, "I saw the great catch that Dodger outfielder Al Gionfriddo made against the Yankees in the 1947 World Series. My first baseball game was a World Series game!"[5]

Virgil attended the integrated Dewitt Clinton High School in the Bronx, but did not play any sport for the school.[6] He noted, "I did not make the baseball team in high school but did play sandlot ball. I played in a Puerto Rican league, which had eight or nine teams."[7] After graduating in 1950, Virgil joined the US Marine Corps. He was called up to active duty and served until 1952. He played baseball while in the military, for the team at Camp LeJeune, North Carolina.[8]

After his time with the Marines, Virgil went back to playing sandlot ball in the Bronx, where he was discovered by New York Giants

Photo courtesy of the National Baseball Hall of Fame

scout George Mack, who signed Virgil to a contract for the 1953 season, with a $300 signing bonus.[9] Virgil made his professional debut in Minnesota in 1953 with the Class-C St. Cloud Rox of the Northern League, batting .259.

Promoted to the Class-B Danville Leafs of the Carolina League for the 1954 season, Virgil got his first taste of the Jim Crow South. He later recalled, "When I played in Danville, Virginia, we couldn't eat in the hotels, we couldn't sleep in the hotels; we went to somebody's home. Even in the major leagues, we couldn't eat in St Louis in the restaurants. We had to get room service."[10] With Danville, Virgil displayed aptitude at the hot corner and increased his batting average to .291.

On January 29, 1955, Virgil married Maria Lopez. They had three children, including Ozzie Virgil Jr. in 1956; he later became a two-time All-Star catcher while playing parts of 11 years in the major leagues. Ozzie Virgil Jr.'s son, José, also played one year of minor-league baseball, after being drafted in the 18th round out of Oklahoma State University in 2003.

Ozzie Sr. advanced to the Double-A Texas League for the 1955 season, manning the hot corner for the league champion Dallas Eagles. He was named to the league all-star team and led the league's third basemen in fielding percentage at .975. He was beginning to draw notice as a prospect, with Jack Schwarz of the Giants noting, "There never was any question about his fielding. I guess playing winter ball in Puerto Rico has helped Ossie's (sic) hitting."[11] The *New York World Telegram and Sun* promoted him as the future solution to the Giants' third-base needs.[12]

Virgil continued his ascent through the minor leagues in 1956, playing for the Triple-A Minneapolis Millers. He led American Association third basemen in putouts, assists, and double plays. He earned a late-season call-up to the Giants and made his major-league debut on September 23, 1956, at the Polo Grounds, becoming the majors' first Dominican-born player. There are no known contemporaneous reports noting this achievement. Virgil later recalled of his debut:

"I can still remember my blood streaming furiously through my veins and adrenaline almost choking me on my first day in the majors. It was very hot and we were playing the last game of a series of three against

Philadelphia. I was placed on third base and went 0-4, but felt as if I'd finished 4-4. I had been upgraded from the minors two or three days before, and I knew I would be the first of my small country to arrive in the best baseball league in the world. But what I never suspected was that in time, it would become something ordinary."[13]

Virgil played in two more games that year, with a total of five hits in 12 at-bats. His strong showing was enough to keep him on the Giants roster for all of the 1957 season, although he was unable to break into the lineup as an everyday player. Virgil played in 96 games and began to highlight his versatility with appearances at both shortstop and the outfield in addition to third base. On April 27, 1957, he hit the first home run of his career, off future Hall of Famer Robin Roberts. He was noted in the local papers as "a polite, good looking chap" who "seems to be a good ballplayer, but not the kind that makes a big impression."[14]

The offseason brought a change of scenery as Virgil was traded to the Detroit Tigers along with first baseman Gail Harris for Jim Finigan and $25,000. Somewhat bewildered by the trade, Virgil later recalled, "I thought the Giants needed a third baseman at that particular time. I knew that the Tigers did not have any black players on their roster nor had never invited one to spring training. I wondered what they were going to do with me."[15] The Tigers, along with the Boston Red Sox, were the only teams to have not integrated yet.

Virgil found himself back in the American Association to start the 1958 season with the Charleston Senators. He got off to a hot start, batting .293 with a league-leading 34 RBIs through early June to earn a promotion to the Tigers on June 5.

Virgil was entering a racially charged situation in Detroit, amid increased protests over the Tigers' lack of Black players, initially led by a Black newspaper, the *Michigan Chronicle*. A group led by the Reverend George Hill, known as the Boycott Committee, was formed as a result and met with Tigers leadership, advocating for integration. When the Tigers would not commit to a timeline, the Boycott Committee developed plans to picket Briggs Stadium starting May 31, 1957.[16] The leaders of the *Chronicle* objected to this approach, and pushed for collaborative solutions instead, which led to a split in the Boycott Committee and cancellation of the picketing.

Less than a week after the planned picketing date, Virgil was recalled to the Tigers, though all parties denied that the timing was anything but coincidental. The Tigers' general manager, John McHale Sr., said, "Look at the standings, we needed help at third base. Virgil is the best third baseman and has more experience than anyone else we have in our system."[17] This is supported by both a slump by Tigers third baseman Reno Bertoia and an injury to Harvey Kuenn, with the *Michigan Chronicle* noting, "The injury to Kuenn, Bertoia's slump, and the club's lowly position created the need for re-evaluation and immediate action."[18] The *Chronicle* also credited this move with avoiding the picketing: "Virgil's elevation brought to a halt the boycott plans of two groups evolving from a larger organization which called itself the Briggs Stadium Boycott Committee."[19]

Virgil joined the team in Washington, and was widely reported as the first Negro to play for the Tigers.[20] His experience has been later recalled with some melancholy, with Virgil noting the challenge of the situation. "Unfortunately most of the people in Detroit did not accept me as a black player. They said I was a Dominican player and they wanted one of their own."[21] Virgil, like many Latino players of the time, found himself isolated from multiple sides. "One of the hardest parts was that we weren't accepted within the black community, the African-American community. It was hard being ignored by both the white people and the African-Americans, who didn't always consider us Latinos as black. We had to stick together."[22] For his part, Virgil attempted to stay above labels and focus on the game, remarking, "If they called me black, fine. If they called me white, fine. If they called me Latino, fine. I didn't care what they called me – I just wanted to play."[23]

Virgil made his Tigers debut in Washington on June 6, batting sixth and going 1-for-5. He acquitted himself well and was bumped up to the second spot in the batting order after two games. The road trip continued through Boston and New York before Virgil's Briggs Stadium debut on June 17. With 11 days having passed since his promotion, a larger than usual crowd of 29,794 welcomed the Tigers home and Virgil did not disappoint. In what he often cited as his foremost baseball thrill, he went 5-for-5 in his home debut, earning a standing ovation.[24]

Virgil was unable to keep up his hot start with the bat, and after hitting .244 in the 1958 season found himself back in the American Association in 1959, where he was once again an all-star, this time as a utility infielder. He earned his way back to Detroit in 1960 after hitting .381 in 59 games with the Denver Bears.

Traded to Kansas City in August of 1961, Virgil spent the majority of the remainder of his playing career in the minor leagues, finding himself back in Triple A with the Rochester Red Wings for the 1962 and 1963 seasons; he had a one-game appearance for the Baltimore Orioles.

Virgil grew into his role as a veteran player, and was recognized for his baseball acumen. Playing for rookie manager Sparky Anderson in Toronto of the International League in 1964, he was named a player-coach midway through the season at Anderson's request, starting Virgil's coaching career. He was also recognized in a poll of International League managers as a co-winner of the smartest player in the league.

Virgil signed with the Washington Senators before the 1965 season, but wound up spending the year with Pittsburgh after being selected in the minor-league draft. The following offseason saw him shipped back to his original team – the Giants – along with Joe Gibbon for fellow Dominican Matty Alou.

Virgil began the 1966 season in the minors, but returned to the big-league team in May. He went 0-for-3 in his first three pinch-hitting appearances; but getting the chance to start for the Giants for the first time in nine years, Virgil responded by getting three hits, including a home run, along with a stolen base, two runs, and two RBIs, in a 6-4, series-sweeping victory over the Chicago Cubs.

He stayed with the Giants organization in Triple A for the 1967 and 1968 seasons. Showing he wasn't quite finished as a player, he made the 1967 Pacific Coast League all-star first team as a utility player, and also was named the Phoenix Giants' most popular player. In 1968 he was named player-coach for Phoenix under manager Clyde King.

King was promoted to manage the San Francisco Giants for the 1969 season and, familiar with Virgil's high baseball IQ, made him his third-base coach. The 1969 season also saw Virgil's last appearance as a player, as he made one pinch-hitting appearance while filling a roster spot for catcher Bob Barton while Barton was on a two-week tour of active duty in the Army Reserve.

Virgil remained the Giants' third-base coach through the 1972 season, keeping busy in the winters managing winter-league teams, winning the Dominican League pennant with Aguila in the winter of 1970-1971, and managing Caracas in the Venezuelan winter league the following offseason.

Virgil left the ballfield for the first time since his initial signing with the 1973 season, working as a Giants scout in Latin America. He missed the game action, however, and was brought back to coach third base for the Giants in the 1974 and 1975 seasons; he left for the same position with the Montreal Expos for the 1976 season.

Virgil remained with the Expos in 1977 as manager Dick Williams took the helm. They forged a fast friendship, and Virgil was Williams's third-base coach for the next decade, following him to San Diego in 1982 and Seattle in 1986 before Williams's retirement in 1988. Highlights during Virgil's tenure as Williams's top lieutenant include winning the 1984 National League pennant with the Padres, and coaching third base in the 1985 All-Star Game. A particular highlight of the All-Star Game was the chance to coach his son, Ozzie Virgil Jr., who was named to the game as a reserve catcher and had a two-run single in the National League's victory.

While 1988 was Virgil's last season as a major-league coach, he remained active in the game, coaching in the short-lived Senior Professional Baseball Association, and continuing to coach and manage in Latin American leagues. Starting in 2007, Virgil worked part time for the Mets, primarily overseeing catching instruction in the Dominican Summer League.

Virgil has become increasingly recognized for his role as the first Dominican in major-league baseball. He was elected to the Latino Baseball Hall of Fame in 2014 and the Rochester Red Wings Hall of Fame in 2015. He was an honorary coach for the New York Mets late in the 2018 season. In 2006 the Osvaldo Virgil National Airport opened in his hometown of Monte Cristi.

Extremely humble, Virgil always expressed gratitude and respect for his role as a pioneer, looking back on his trailblazing career and noting:

"I have always felt grateful and fortunate to have been chosen by God to open the doors of MLB for my countrymen, considering that hundreds with more talent than me hadn't been given the chance."[25]

Another time he said, "I may not have been the most talented, and I may not hold the records or any huge numbers, but I'll always have a special number: number one! And I'm glad that I was able to be that person that opened the door for many other Dominicans after me, especially considering there are many others more talented than me."[26]

SOURCES

In addition to the sources cited in the Notes, the author consulted Baseball-Reference.com.

NOTES

1. Enrique Rojas, "50 Years Ago, Ozzie Virgil Made Baseball History," ESPN.com, September 22, 2006. espn.com/espn/hispanichistory/news/story?id=2598606, accessed October 4, 2018.

2. National Baseball Hall of Fame Player File; Topps Baseball Cards. For the 1934 date, see the Statue of Liberty-Ellis Island Foundation, libertyellisfoundation.org/passenger-details/czoxMzoiOTAxMTg2NTkxNTkwOSI7/czo5Oi-JwYXNzZW5nZXIiOw==, accessed November 17, 2018.

3. Interview with Ozzie Virgil by Julio Rodriguez on December 13, 2018.

4. William Anderson, "Ozzie Virgil Breaks the Color Line with the Detroit Tigers," *Michigan History Magazine*, September/October 1997: 50.

5. Anderson.

6. Biographical information included in Virgil's National Baseball Hall of Fame player file.

7. Anderson.

8. Anderson.

9. See Virgil's player file at the National Baseball Hall of Fame and Enrique Rojas.

10. Kevin Oklobzija, "Ozzie Virgil Sr. Made History in MLB and with the Wings," *Rochester* (New York) *Democrat and Chronicle*, August 14, 2015: D2,

11. Zander Hollander, "Next Stop Peoria!" *New York World Telegram and Sun*, July 26, 1955.

12. Hollander

13. Rojas.

14. Bill Roeder, "Virgil New Forgotten Man at PG," *New York World Telegram and Sun*, May 2, 1957.

15. Anderson: 49.

16. Anderson.

17. Anderson.

18. Bill Matney, "Exclusive Report on Tigers' Hiring Policy!" *Michigan Chronicle* (Detroit), July 14, 1958.

19. Matney.

20. *Detroit News*, June 6, 1958; *Michigan Chronicle*, June 21, 1958; *Detroit Free Press*, June 6, 1958.

21. Anderson, 53.

22. "Living History: Ozzie Virgil." sportsmbablog.com/living-history-ozzie-virgil/, accessed 10/3/2018.

23. Jodie Valade, "Like Jackie, Virgil Just Wanted to Play," *Detroit Free Press*, July 5, 1997.

24. Rob Edelman, "Ozzie Virgil Biography," biography.jrank.org/pages/2436/Virgil-Ozzie.html, accessed October 3, 2018.

25. Rojas.

26. "Living History: Ozzie Virgil."

Dominican Passion and Pride on Display in Sweep of 2013 World Baseball Classic

By Richard Cuicchi

Since their embarrassing first-round knockout in the 2009 World Baseball Classic, the Dominican Republic team had been determined to make an improved showing in 2013.

In the first WBC competition, in 2006, and again in 2009, Dominican Republic teams had fielded their best players, but many fans felt that they did not take the series seriously. That changed in 2013, when public pressure encouraged the team to put forth a better showing. The team responded with a spirit that became the standard for the competitors. The Dominicans, many of whom were major-league all-stars, became the first team to go undefeated in the WBC.

While the WBC was sponsored by Major League Baseball to provide an international stage for competition among the world's best players, some major-league clubs discouraged their better players from taking part. They feared the tournament would interrupt the players' normal spring-training preparation the regular season. They also worried that players might be injured.

The Dominican players tended to downplay those possibilities and embraced opportunities to showcase their talent and put their country in the international limelight. In 2013 they seemed particularly fixated on redeeming themselves after their disastrous outcome in 2009. Some of the players trained all winter to prepare for the WBC.

The Dominican Republic is known for its passion for baseball, which it considers its national pastime. Its fans are considered among the most rabid in the sport. A Mardi Gras-like atmosphere is typical at Dominican games. Singing, horn-playing, drum-beating, and flag-waving complement the fans' cheering activities. The players seem to feed off their fans' high energy.[1]

The country relished taking on the world in international competition. It was as though the Dominican Republic wanted to prove to the rest of the world that its players were among the most talented in professional baseball.

Manager Tony Peña, who was then the bench coach for the New York Yankees and had been named the American League Manager of the Year in 2003 with Kansas City, boasted a squad with 17 active major leaguers, two former major leaguers, and eight minor-league prospects. The position players included All-Stars Robinson Cano, Carlos Santana, José Reyes, Hanley Ramírez, Nelson Cruz, Miguel Tejada, and Edwin Encarnacion.[2]

Carlos Santana #41 and Nelson Cruz #17 celebrate after scoring against Venezuela during the first round of the World Baseball Classic at Hiram Bithorn Stadium on March 7, 2013 in San Juan, Puerto Rico.

Photo by Al Bello/Getty Images

If the team had a weakness going into the tournament, it was perceived to be the starting pitching. Edinson Volquez and Wandy Rodriguez, who were middle-of-the-rotation pitchers on their major-league clubs, led a relatively inexperienced staff. However, the bullpen was strong with Santiago Casilla, Octavio Dotel, Kelvin Herrera, Fernando Rodney, and Pedro Strop.[3]

The Dominican Republic opened the tournament in the first-round Pool C, hosted by San Juan, Puerto Rico. Their opponents were Puerto Rico, Venezuela, and Spain. The Dominicans won all three games and advanced, along with Puerto Rico.[4]

In the Pool 2 second round played in Miami, the Dominicans defeated Italy, the United States, and Puerto Rico again. The Dominican and Puerto Rican teams advanced to the semifinals.[5]

In the semifinal round, played in San Francisco, the unbeaten Dominicans defeated the Netherlands, 4-1, while Puerto Rico advanced to the finals by defeating Japan, the 2006 and 2009 champion.[6]

For the third time in the series, the Dominican Republic defeated Puerto Rico, 3-0, in an all-Caribbean final game. On a cold, dreary night in San Francisco during which it rained for the final six innings, the Dominicans got out front in the first inning. Encarnacion doubled in two runs, with Reyes and Cano scoring. Erick Aybar drove in the Dominicans' other run when he doubled in Alejandro de Aza in the fifth inning.[7]

Starter Samuel Deduno and four relievers shut down the Puerto Rican offense. They scattered three hits and four walks, but only three baserunners advanced past first base.

Deduno gave up two hits in five innings, struck out five, and issued three walks.[8]

Rodney pitched a scoreless ninth inning to claim the save, his seventh of the tournament. The Dominican bullpen didn't allow a run over 20⅔ innings during the last five games.[9] Overall, the Dominican pitching staff allowed just 14 runs in eight games.

It was the second time the Dominican Republic shut out Puerto Rico – the first was a 2-0 whitewash in Miami – and became the first team to go undefeated in a WBC tournament. The Dominican pitching staff held the Puerto Rican lineup scoreless for the last 23 innings of their three contests.

After the final out, the Dominican and Puerto Rican teams stayed on the field to party together, setting off a wild celebration in the Dominican Republic. Cano and Puerto Rico's Yadier Molina had agreed before the game that the teams would celebrate together regardless of which team won.[10]

Asked about how he would return to the normal spring-training routine with the Yankees, Cano said, "I'll tell you one thing. Tonight, we're gonna celebrate. Tomorrow, we're going to celebrate. And Thursday, we'll worry about spring training."[11] Because of the spring-training schedule, the Dominican champions didn't have time to go back to Santo Domingo for a triumphal parade, as their fans had expected. Instead, a celebration was held for them after the regular major-league season, although it drew less attention by that time.

Reyes commented on his team's accomplishment, "We have to understand this is the third Classic. Thank God we're finally able to accomplish what everyone wanted and expected of the D.R., which was a trophy as champions. We did it all together."[12] His remarks reflected the redemption the Dominican team felt after their poor showing in 2009.

Cano was named the tournament MVP. He batted .469 with two home runs and six RBIs, including three hits in each of the first four games.[13] He was named to the all-WBC team along with teammates Reyes and Rodney.[14]

Throughout the tournament the Dominican players celebrated on the field when their teammates excelled, although not in a way that provoked their opponents. They did the type of things you normally see with youth baseball teams, including chanting and singing in the dugout. Fernando Rodney was the keeper of a rally plantain used to spur their efforts in tight game situations. After the final out of the championship game, the Dominican players visited the Puerto Ricans' dugout to exchange handshakes and hugs in a strong display of sportsmanship.[15]

The Dominican players' behavior, with their passion and exuberance, pushed the limits of baseball traditionalists. Cano remarked about his team's style of play, "It's like you're playing winter ball. You play your way and have fun, something you don't do in the big leagues."[16]

The Dominican Republic's championship in 2013 showed the world what national pride looked like. Their passion spawned a return to national pride for the USA team in 2017, when more of the top-flight American players embraced roster spots and ultimately won their first-ever WBC title.

Following are the line scores for the Dominican Republic's eight 2013 WBC games.

March 7, 2013   Pool C   San Juan, Perto Rico   Hiram Bithorn Stadium

Dominican Republic 9, Valenzuela 3

	1	2	3	4	5	6	7	8	9	R	H	E
VEN	0	0	2	1	0	0	0	0	0	3	6	1
DOM	3	2	0	0	1	0	3	0	–	9	13	0

W: Strop (1-0)   L: Sanchez (0-1)

Full boxscore: mlb.mlb.com/wbc/2013/gameday/index.jsp?gid=2013_03_07_venint_domint_1&mode=box

March 9, 2013   Pool C   San Juan, Perto Rico   Hiram Bithorn Stadium

Dominican Republic 6, Spain 3

	1	2	3	4	5	6	7	8	9	R	H	E
DOM	0	2	3	0	0	0	0	1	0	6	9	1
ESP	0	0	0	0	0	0	1	0	1	3	9	1

W: Deduno (1-0)   L: Negrin (0-1)   SV: Rodney (1)

Full boxscore: mlb.mlb.com/wbc/2013/gameday/indexjsp?gid=2013_03_09_domint_espint_1&mode=box

March 10, 2013   Pool C   San Juan, Perto Rico   Hiram Bithorn Stadium

Dominican Republic 4, Puerto Rico 2

	1	2	3	4	5	6	7	8	9	R	H	E
DOM	1	0	0	0	1	1	1	0	0	4	12	1
PUR	0	0	0	2	0	0	0	0	0	2	7	2

W: Barcelo (1-0)   L: Berrios (0-1)   SV: Rodney (2)

Full boxscore: mlb.mlb.com/wbc/2013/gameday/index.jsp?gid=2013_03_10_domint_purint_1&mode=box

March 12, 2013   Pool 2   Miami, Florida   Marlins Park

Dominican Republic 5, Italy 4

	1	2	3	4	5	6	7	8	9	R	H	E
ITA	4	0	0	0	0	0	0	0	0	4	4	0
DOM	0	0	1	0	0	1	3	0	–	5	10	0

W: Strop (1-0)   L: Venditte (0-1)   SV: Rodney (1)

Full boxscore: http://mlb.mlb.com/wbc/2013/gameday/index.jsp?gid=2013_03_12_itaint_domint_1&mode=box

March 14, 2013   Pool 2   Miami, Florida   Marlins Park

Dominican Republic 3, United States 1

	1	2	3	4	5	6	7	8	9	R	H	E
DOM	0	2	0	0	0	0	0	0	2	3	9	1
USA	1	0	0	0	0	0	0	0	0	1	6	0

W: Strop (2-0)   L: Kimbrel (0-1)   SV: Rodney (2)

Full boxscore: mlb.mlb.com/wbc/2013/gameday/index.jsp?gid=2013_03_14_domint_usaint_1&mode=box

March 16, 2013   Pool 2   Miami, Florida   Marlins Park

Dominican Republic 2, Puerto Rico 0

	1	2	3	4	5	6	7	8	9	R	H	E
PUR	0	0	0	0	0	0	0	0	0	0	3	0
DOM	0	0	0	0	1	1	3	1	–	2	6	1

W: Rodriguez (1-0)   L: Roman (0-1)   SV: Rodney (3)

Full boxscore: mlb.mlb.com/wbc/2013/gameday/index.jsp?gid=2013_03_16_purint_domint_1&mode=box

March 18, 2013   Semifinals   San Francisco, California   AT&T Park

Dominican Republic 5, Italy 4

	1	2	3	4	5	6	7	8	9	R	H	E
NED	1	0	0	0	0	0	0	0	0	1	4	1
DOM	0	0	0	0	4	0	0	0	–	4	9	0

W: Volquez (1-0)   L: Markwell (0-1)   SV: Rodney (1)

Full boxscore: mlb.mlb.com/wbc/2013/gameday/index.jsp?gid=2013_03_18_nedint_domint_1&mode=box

March 19, 2013   Semifinals   San Francisco, California   AT&T Park

Dominican Republic 3, Italy 4

	1	2	3	4	5	6	7	8	9	R	H	E
PUR	0	0	0	0	0	0	0	0	0	0	3	0
DOM	2	0	0	0	1	0	0	0	–	3	8	1

W: Deduno (1-0)   L: Alvarado (0-1)   SV: Rodney (1)

Full boxscore: mlb.mlb.com/wbc/2013/gameday/index.jsp?gid=2013_03_19_purint_domint_1&mode=box

SOURCES

In addition to the sources cited in the Notes, the author also consulted:

David, Craig. "National Pride at Stake as World Baseball Classic Returns to Miami," Sun Sentinel (Fort Lauderdale, Florida), March 7, 2017. sun-sentinel.com/sports/miami-marlins/fl-sp-world-baseball-classic-overview-20170307-story.html. Accessed June 20, 2018.

Thanks to Julio Rodriguez for his perspective.

NOTES

1. Matt Whitener. "The Dominican Republic, Pride and Its Will on the World," *The Sports Fan Journal*, March 15, 2013. thesportsfanjournal.com/sports/baseball/dominican-republic-and-the-love-of-the-game/. Accessed June 20, 2018.

2. Rick Weiner. "Dominican Report World Baseball Classic 2013: Schedule, Roster, and Predictions," *Bleacher Report*. bleacherreport.com/articles/1552567-dominican-republic-world-baseball-classic-2013-schedule-roster-and-predictions. Accessed June 20, 2018.

3. Weiner.

4. "World Baseball Classic Results," *The Sporting News*, March 19, 2013. sportingnews.com/mlb/news/4481866-world-baseball-classic-2013-results-scores-tv-schedule-pool-standings. Accessed June 20, 2018.

5. "World Baseball Classic Results."

6. "World Baseball Classic Results."

7. Ben Martin, "Dominican Republic Completes Perfect Run to Claim WBC Title," *San Francisco Examiner*, March 19, 2013. sfexaminer.com/dominican-republic-completes-perfect-run-to-claim-wbc-title/. Accessed June 20, 2018.

8. Martin.

9. Martin.

10. Bill Shaikin. "Dodgers' Ramírez Is Hurt in WBC Final," *Los Angeles Times*, March 20, 2013: C3.

11. Martin.

12. Martin.

13. Phil Rogers. "Cano Simply 2nd to None," *Chicago Tribune*, March 20. 2012: 3:2.

14. Associated Press via *San Francisco Examiner*, March 30, 2013. sfexaminer.com/cano-reyes-rodney-and-wright-make-all-wbc-team/. Accessed June 20, 2018.

15. Tom Verducci, "Dominicans Win WBC, Help Set Sportsmanship Standard," *Sports Illustrated*, March 20, 2013. si.com/mlb/2013/03/20/verducci-wbc-final. Accessed June 20, 2018.

16. Rogers.

Contributor Biographies

Malcolm Allen is an Orioles fan from Baltimore. Now he lives in Brooklyn, New York with his wife, Sara, and daughters, Ruth and Martina. He met Joaquín Andújar a handful of times at Memorial Stadium and is seeking a publisher for his full-length book about "One Tough Dominican."

Mark Armour is a researcher and writer living in Corvallis, Oregon.

Richard Bogovich is the author of *Kid Nichols: A Biography of the Hall of Fame Pitcher* and *The Who: A Who's Who,* both published by McFarland & Co. He has contributed to such SABR books as *Pride of Smoketown: The 1935 Pittsburgh Crawfords* and *Bittersweet Goodbye: The Black Barons, the Grays, and the 1948 Negro League World Series.* He works for the Wendland Utz law firm in Rochester, Minnesota.

Ryan Brecker has been a SABR member since 2004 and is Chair of the Luke Easter SABR Chapter. An Emergency Medicine physician by night; he lives in Penfield, New York with his wife Stephanie and two girls, Cadence and Quinn.

Thomas J. Brown Jr. is a lifelong Mets fan who became a Durham Bulls fan after moving to North Carolina in the early 1980s. He was a national board certified high school science teacher for 34 years. Tom still volunteers with ELL students, serving as a mentor to those students while they are in school as well as after graduation. He is also a resource for ELL teachers in the local school system. Tom has been a member of SABR since 1995 after learning about the organization during a visit to Cooperstown on his honeymoon. He became active in the organization after his retirement and has written numerous biographies and game stories, mostly about the New York Mets. Tom also enjoys traveling as much as possible with his wife and has visited major league and minor league baseball parks across the country on their trips. He loves to cook, making the meals for his family as well as writing about the recipes that he cooks on his blog, Cooking and My Family.

Ralph Carhart is the head of the Society for American Baseball Research's 19th Century Baseball Gravemarker Project. He is the recipient of the SABR 19th Century Committee's 2015 Chairman's Award and the Baseball Reliquary's 2019 Hilda Award. His historical interests include baseball's pioneer days, the Negro Leagues, the Hall of Fame, Brooklyn, Cuba, and the New York Mets.

Alan Cohen has been a SABR member since 2010. He serves as Vice President-Treasurer of the Connecticut Smoky Joe Wood Chapter and is datacaster (MiLB First Pitch stringer) for the Hartford Yard Goats, the Double-A affiliate of the Colorado Rockies. Since December 13, 2020, Alan has served as Chairperson of the Fact-Checking Committee for the SABR BioProject. His biographies, game stories and essays have appeared in more than 50 SABR publications. Since his first *Baseball Research Journal* article appeared in 2013, Alan has continued to expand his research into the Hearst Sandlot Classic (1946-1965) from which 87 players advanced to the major leagues. He has four children and eight grandchildren and resides in Connecticut with wife Frances, their cats Morty, Ava, and Zoe, and their dog Buddy.

Rory Costello has written bios of Dominican players as part of his broader interest in Latin America. He counts Estadio Quisqueya in Santo Domingo as one of the most enjoyable ballparks he has visited. Rory lives in Brooklyn, New York, with his wife Noriko and son Kai.

Joe Cox has written or contributed to 10 sports books. His most recent solo offering, *A Fine Team Man: Jackie Robinson and the Lives He Touched*, was published by Lyons Press in 2019. Joe practices law and lives near Bowling Green, Kentucky, where he's looking forward to being able to return to rooting on the Class-A Bowling Green Hot Rods.

Reynaldo Cruz is the founder and head editor of the Cuban-based magazine *Universo Béisbol*, which is hosted in MLBlogs. He is a language graduate of the University of Holguin, in his hometown, and has been leading the aforementioned magazine since March 2010. A SABR member since the summer of 2014, he writes, translates, and photographs baseball and was in the first row of the Barack Obama game in Havana, shooting from the Tampa Bay Rays dugout. In spite of the rich history of Cuban baseball, his favorite player happens to be no other than Ichiro Suzuki, whom he expects to meet and interview. A retro lover, he envisions Fenway Park, Wrigley Field, Koshien Stadium, and Estadio Palmar de Junco as the can't-miss places in baseball.

Richard Cuicchi joined SABR in 1983 and is an active member of the Schott-Pelican Chapter. Since his retirement as an information technology executive, Richard authored *Family Ties: A Comprehensive Collection of Facts and Trivia about Baseball's Relatives*. He has contributed to numerous SABR BioProject and Games publications. He does freelance writing and blogging about a variety of baseball topics on his website TheTenthInning.com. Richard lives in New Orleans with his wife Mary.

Scott Cummings worked as a special education teacher for both public and private schools. He holds a bachelor's degree in Mathematics from the University of Minnesota as well as a Masters in Education with an emphasis in Mathematics Education. He also holds teaching licensure in Special Education Academic and Behavioral Strategist (K-12) and Mathematics (5-12). He keeps active by skiing, running, biking, and doing yoga to help train for the American Birkebiner every year. The "Birkie" is a 50K cross country ski race from Cable to Hayward, Wisconsin with about 14,000 other skiers. He is a big Minnesota Twins fan and follows them as much as he can. He also shares Minnesota Gopher football season tickets with his father, and likes to cook.

John DiFonzo grew up in Somerville, Massachusetts where he was the sports editor for his high school newspaper, *The Radiator*. He is a lifelong Red Sox fan and season-ticket holder since 2004 currently living in Boston with his wife Gabriella. John graduated from Tufts University with a bachelor's degree in Electrical Engineering, holds a Master of Science in Global Financial Analysis from Bentley University and is a CFA charterholder.

Charles F. Faber was a retired public high school and university teacher and administrator who lived in Lexington, Kentucky. He was a frequent contributor to SABR and edited the SABR book *The 1934 St. Louis Cardinals: The World Champion Gas House Gang*. Among his publications are dozens of professional journal articles, encyclopedia entries, and research reports in fields such as school administration, education law, and country music. In addition to textbooks, he has written 10 books (mostly on baseball) published by McFarland.

A retired English professor, **Jan Finkel** lives in Pittsburgh, directly across the Allegheny River from PNC Park. He joined SABR in 1994, has contributed to several SABR publications, and served as chief editor of the Biography Project from 2002 to 2015. Juan Marichal is one of his favorite pitchers.

Paul Geisler serves as pastor of Christ Lutheran Church in Lake Jackson, Texas, where he and his wife Susan are actively involved with the local community theater. They have three grown children. For his entire life, Paul has enjoyed all aspects of baseball – playing, watching, coaching, researching, and writing. He has written several articles for SABR and has worked with MLB on pitch tracking and for the Texas Rangers at the Ballpark in Arlington.

A SABR member since 2014, **Paul Goodson** is a librarian and a longtime Cubs fan. His research interests include defunct minor league teams and leagues, ballpark and franchise histories, as well as baseball simulations. When not focused on baseball he enjoys reading science fiction and mysteries. He lives in New Bern, North Carolina with his wife Michele.

Eric Hanauer is a widely published writer and underwater photographer, with nearly 1,000 magazine articles and five books. His scuba diving adventures have taken him to some 50 countries around the world. In 2019 he received a NOGI, the dive industry's equivalent of an academy award for lifetime achievement. For 35 years his day job was Associate Professor of Kinesiology at California State University Fullerton, where he also coached swimming and water polo, and founded the scuba diving program. His main claim to fame was developing the grab start. He owes all of this to lack of baseball skill as a youth, which led him into the water as a second choice. Hanauer is a lifelong Cubs fan, ever since his first Wrigley Field game at the age of 9. He was finally rewarded in 2016 when they won the World Series.

Tom Hawthorn is a journalist and author who lives in Victoria, B.C., Canada. He was a utility writer on the Blue Jays beat for the Toronto *Globe and Mail* from 1987-89. He has been a member of the selection committee of the B.C. Sports Hall of Fame and the Canadian Baseball Hall of Fame. He is an honorary member of the Peña Deportiva Parque Central in Havana, Cuba.

Leslie Heaphy is an Associate professor of history at Kent State University at Stark. Author and/or editor of a number of books, book chapters and articles on the Negro Leagues, Women's baseball, and the New York Mets. Currently serving as VP for SABR and as a board member for the IWBC (International Women's Baseball Center).

Paul Hofmann, a SABR member since 2002, is a frequent contributor to SABR publications. Paul is a native of Detroit, Michigan and lifelong Detroit Tigers fan. He enjoys collecting baseball cards during his free time. He currently resides in Folsom, California.

Jorge Iber currently serves as Associate Dean in the Student Division of the College of Arts and Sciences and Professor of History at Texas Tech University in Lubbock. He is the author/co-author/editor of 13 books and numerous scholarly and encyclopedic articles. Recent projects include a biography of Mexican American former MLB pitcher, Mike Torrez; an anthology covering key moments in the history of the Pittsburgh Pirates; and a junior-high level biography on Mariano Rivera. He has just completed a biography of former Texas Tech All American nose tackle, Gabe Rivera.

William H. "Bill" Johnson is the author of a full-length biography, *Hal Trosky: A Baseball Biography* (McFarland & Co., 2017), along with more than two dozen essays for the Society for American Baseball Research's BioProject. He retired from the US Navy in 2006 after a 24-year career in naval aviation. He has also presented papers at several baseball-history conferences. He graduated from the University of California (Berkeley) with a degree in rhetoric, and has subsequently earned a master of arts in military history from Norwich University and a masters in aeronautical science from Embry-Riddle Aeronautical University. He is currently teaching unmanned aviation at Embry-Riddle.

Norm King lived in Ottawa. Ontario and was an active SABR member. He edited the SABR book *Au Jeu / Play Ball – The 50 Greatest Games in the History of the Montreal Expos* (SABR, 2016). Norm also contributed to a number of other SABR books including *Thar's Joy in Braveland: The 1957 Milwaukee Braves* (2014), *Winning on the North Side: The 1929 Chicago Cubs* (2015), and *A Pennant for the Twin Cities: The 1965 Minnesota Twins* (2015).

Justin Krueger hopes to one day own a Nokona baseball glove. He has also published articles in Multicultural Perspectives, the Journal of Educational Controversy, and The History Teacher. His all-time favorite ballpark to watch a game at is Kokernot Field in Alpine, Texas - home of the Sul Ross State University Lobos.

Len Levin is a longtime newspaper editor in New England, now retired. He lives in Providence with his wife, Linda, and an overachieving orange cat. He now (Len, not the cat) is the grammarian for the Rhode Island Supreme Court and edits its decisions. He also copyedits many SABR books, including this one. He is just down the interstate from Fenway Park, where he has spent many happy hours.

Seth Moland-Kovash is a lifelong passionate baseball fan and amateur historian. He grew up in Minnesota and his love of the game and the Twins has carried through many years, many moves, and many Twins eras. During the day, Seth is a Lutheran pastor in suburban Chicago where he lives with his wife Jennifer and their son Carl. Carl has also inherited the love of baseball and plays whenever the fields are not covered by snow. Seth's favorite teams are the Twins and whatever team Carl is on.

Wynn Montgomery is a retired bureaucrat and educator and a recovering workaholic. He has been a SABR member since 1983. As a member of the Magnolia Chapter in Atlanta, Wynn served as co-editor *Baseball in the Peach State*, SABR's 2010 Atlanta convention journal. He has contributed five biographies to the BioProject. Since moving to Colorado in 2011, he has become a Rockies fan while continuing to follow the Braves from afar. His baseball interests include the art and history of the game, minor league and college baseball, and the Negro Leagues. With two other SABRites, he takes an annual "B-4" Road Trip that feeds his passion for Baseball, Battlefields (mostly Civil War), Burial Grounds (historic cemeteries), and Barbeque. He has seen every major-league team play a home game and has visited more than 100 minor-league and college ballparks.

Chad Moody is a nearly lifelong Detroit-area resident, where he has been a fan of the Detroit Tigers from birth. An alumnus of the University of Michigan and Michigan State University, he has spent 30 years working in the automotive industry. From his humble beginning of having a letter published in *Baseball Digest* as a teenager, Chad has since contributed to numerous SABR and Professional Football Researchers Association projects. He and his wife, Lisa, live in Northville, Michigan, with their dog, Daisy.

Frank Morris is an associate professor at UMass Lowell and Endicott College, where he teaches a class in sport and American culture. A Red Sox and Dodgers fan with a deep appreciation for Dwight Evans and Pedro Guerrero, Frank is the author of a sports trivia book series titled *Ask Your Uncle Trivia* and lectures on sports history in the greater Boston area.

Bill Nowlin enjoyed an opportunity to see the Boston Red Sox play a couple of exhibition games in Santo Domingo back in March 2000, against the Houston Astros. Born in Boston, he has been a Red Sox fan through thick and thin. He has been active with SABR since helping host the Boston convention in 2002 and on the board of directors since 2004. As a volunteer with SABR, he has written over 1,000 research articles.

Gregg Omoth has been a SABR member since 2000. He is a lifelong Minnesota Twins fan. Gregg and his wife Dianne live in Otsego, Minnesota with their three children – Amelia, Nolan, and Emma.

Carl Riechers retired from United Parcel Service in 2012 after 35 years of service. With more free time, he became a SABR member that same year. Born and raised in the suburbs of St. Louis, he became a big fan of the Cardinals. He and his wife Janet have three children and he is the proud grandpa of two.

Julio M. Rodriguez, MD is a board certified pediatrician born in Montecristi, Dominican Republic.(DR). Montecristi is also the birthplace of hall of fame Juan Marichal and Osvaldo Virgil, the first Dominican to play in the major leagues.Because he had part of his training in St. Louis, he is a Cardinal fan and a friend of Julian Javier, the regular second baseman of the Cardinals through the 1960s. He is the head of the Juan Marichal chapter of SABR in Santo Domingo, D:R. He has contributed to this book with reviews of the biographies of the players published in it and feels happy about it.

Blake W. Sherry is a lifelong Pittsburgh Pirates fan who resides in Dublin, Ohio. A retired Chief Operations Officer of a public retirement system, he has been a member of SABR since 1997. He co-leads the Hank Gowdy SABR Chapter in Central Ohio, and currently runs that chapter's quarterly baseball book club. He contributed to several previous SABR books, including *Moments of Joy and Heartbreak: 66 Significant Episodes in the History of the Pittsburgh Pirates*.

J.W. Stewart is the author of biographies of Josie Heard and Harry Staley as well as a history of early baseball's mascots and bat boys. He holds a master's degree in history from Sam Houston State University. J.W. currently lives in Frisco, Texas where he teaches American history.

John Struth has been a member of SABR for 20-plus years. He fell for baseball at an early age and that blossomed to love during the Miracle Mets championship in 1969. He has contributed several bios for SABR publications and has presented at the Jerry Malloy conference.

Josh Sullivan was born in Houston, Texas and grew up watching the Astros at the Dome and the Braves on TBS. It only makes sense that he has actually been a diehard Padres' fan since 1987. Baseball, with its beautiful history, is the sport he loves. Both he and his wife, Shari, are school teachers, though Josh would rather be writing and telling stories. The Sullivans have five children and live in Tomball, Texas.

Cosme Vivanco is a Chicago-based writer who received his Masters of Fine Arts in Creative Writing from Columbia College in 2010. As a small child, he developed an incredible passion for baseball history. His other areas of interest are politics and music. He has participated in the Chicago Marathon on four different occasions and hopes to do it again in 2022. His biography on Steve Carlton was included in SABR's *20 Game Losers*. He also contributed to *Met-rospectives: A Collection of the Greatest Games in New York Mets History*. And his biography on Jason Schmidt was included in *Braves Win! Braves Win! Braves Win!: The 1995 World Champion Atlanta Braves*.

Joseph Wancho lives in Brooklyn, Ohio, and is a lifelong Cleveland Indians fan. He has been a SABR member since 2005 and serves as the vice chair of SABR's Baseball Index Project Committee. He was the editor of *Pitching to the Pennant: The 1954 Cleveland Indians* (University of Nebraska Press, 2014) and *The Sleeping Giant Awakes: The 1995 Cleveland Indians* (SABR, 2019).

Gregory H. Wolf was born in Pittsburgh, but now resides in the Chicagoland area with his wife, Margaret, and daughter, Gabriela. A professor of German studies and holder of the Dennis and Jean Bauman Endowed Chair in the Humanities at North Central College in Naperville, Illinois, he has edited a dozen books for SABR. He is currently working on projects about Shibe Park in Philadelphia and Ebbets Field in Brooklyn. Since January 2017 he has been co-director of SABR's BioProject, which you can follow on Facebook and Twitter.

New Books from SABR

Part of the mission of the Society for American Baseball Research has always been to disseminate member research. In addition to the *Baseball Research Journal*, SABR publishes books that include player biographies, historical game recaps, and statistical analysis. All SABR books are available in print and ebook formats. SABR members can access the entire SABR Digital Library for free and purchase print copies at significant member discounts of 40 to 50% off cover price.

JEFF BAGWELL IN CONNECTICUT:
A Consistent Lad in the Land of Steady Habits
This volume of articles, interviews, and essays by members of the Connecticut chapter of SABR chronicles the life and career of Connecticut's favorite baseball son, Hall-of-Famer Jeff Bagwell, with special attention on his high school and college years.
Edited by Karl Cicitto, Bill Nowlin, & Len Levin
$19.95 paperback (ISBN 978-1-943816-97-2)
$9.99 ebook (ISBN 978-1-943816-96-5)
7"x10", 246 pages, 45 photos

1995 CLEVELAND INDIANS:
The Sleeping Giant Awakens
After almost 40 years of sub-500 baseball, the Sleeping Giant woke in 1995, the first season in the Indians spent in their new home of Jacob's Field. The biographies of all the players, coaches, and broadcasters from that year are here, sprinkled with personal perspectives, as well as game stories from key matchups during the 1995 season, information about Jacob's Field, and other essays.
Edited by Joseph Wancho
$19.95 paperback (ISBN 978-1-943816-95-8)
$9.99 ebook (ISBN 978-1-943816-94-1)
8.5"X11", 410 pages, 76 photos

TIME FOR EXPANSION BASEBALL
The LA Angels and "new" Washington Senators ushered in MLB expansion in 1960, followed by the Houston Colt .45s and New York Mets. By 1998, 10 additional teams had launched: the Kansas City Royals, Seattle Pilots, Toronto Blue Jays, and Tampa Bay Devil Rays in the AL, and the Montreal Expos, San Diego Padres, Colorado Rockies, Florida Marlins, and Arizona Diamondbacks in the NL. *Time for Expansion Baseball* tells each team's origin and includes biographies of key players.
Edited by Maxwell Kates and Bill Nowlin
$24.95 paperback (ISBN 978-1-933599-89-7)
$9.99 ebook (ISBN 978-1-933599-88-0)
8.5"X11", 430 pages, 150 photos

BASE BALL'S 19TH CENTURY "WINTER" MEETINGS 1857-1900
A look at the business meetings of base ball's earliest days (not all of which were in the winter). As John Thorn writes in his Foreword, "This monumental volume traces the development of the game from its birth as an organized institution to its very near suicide at the dawn of the next century."
Edited by Jeremy K. Hodges and Bill Nowlin
$29.95 paperback (ISBN 978-1-943816-91-0)
$9.99 ebook (ISBN978-1-943816-90-3)
8.5"x11", 390 pages, 50 photos

MET-ROSPECTIVES:
A Collection of the Greatest Games in New York Mets History
This book's 57 game stories—coinciding with the number of Mets years through 2018—are strictly for the eternal optimist. They include the team's very first victory in April 1962 at Forbes Field, Tom Seaver's "Imperfect Game" in July '69, the unforgettable Game Sixes in October '86, the "Grand Slam Single" in the 1999 NLCS, and concludes with the extra-innings heroics in September 2016 at Citi Field that helped ensure a wild-card berth.
edited by Brian Wright and Bill Nowlin
$14.95 paperback (ISBN 978-1-943816-87-3)
$9.99 ebook (ISBN 978-1-943816-86-6)
8.5"X11", 148 pages, 44 photos

CINCINNATI'S CROSLEY FIELD:
A Gem in the Queen City
This book evokes memories of Crosley Field through detailed summaries of more than 85 historic and monumental games played there, and 10 insightful feature essays about the history of the ballpark. Former Reds players Johnny Edwards and Art Shamsky share their memories of the park in introductions.
Edited by Gregory H. Wolf
$19.95 paperback (ISBN 978-1-943816-75-0)
$9.99 ebook (ISBN 978-1-943816-74-3)
8.5"X11", 320 pages, 43 photos

MOMENTS OF JOY AND HEARTBREAK:
66 Significant Episodes in the History of the Pittsburgh Pirates
In this book we relive no-hitters, World Series-winning homers, and the last tripleheader ever played in major-league baseball. Famous Pirates like Honus Wagner and Roberto Clemente—and infamous ones like Dock Ellis—make their appearances, as well as recent stars like Andrew McCutcheon.
Edited by Jorge Iber and Bill Nowlin
$19.95 paperback (ISBN 978-1-943816-73-6)
$9.99 ebook (ISBN 978-1-943816-72-9)
8.5"X11", 208 pages, 36 photos

FROM SPRING TRAINING TO SCREEN TEST:
Baseball Players Turned Actors
SABR"s book of baseball's "matinee stars," a selection of those who crossed the lines between professional sports and popular entertainment. Included are the famous (Gene Autry, Joe DiMaggio, Jim Thorpe, Bernie Williams) and the forgotten (Al Gettel, Lou Stringer, Wally Hebert, Wally Hood), essays on baseball in TV shows and Coca-Cola commercials, and Jim Bouton's casting as "Jim Barton" in the *Ball Four* TV series.
Edited by Rob Edelman and Bill Nowlin
$19.95 paperback (ISBN 978-1-943816-71-2)
$9.99 ebook (ISBN 978-1-943816-70-5)
8.5"X11", 410 pages, 89 photos

To learn more about how to receive these publications for free or at member discount as a member of SABR, visit the website: sabr.org/join

Friends of SABR

You can become a Friend of SABR by giving as little as $10 per month or by making a one-time gift of $1,000 or more. When you do so, you will be inducted into a community of passionate baseball fans dedicated to supporting SABR's work.

> Friends of SABR receive the following benefits:
> - ✓ Annual Friends of SABR Commemorative Lapel Pin
> - ✓ Recognition in This Week in SABR, SABR.org, and the SABR Annual Report
> - ✓ Access to the SABR Annual Convention VIP donor event
> - ✓ Invitations to exclusive Friends of SABR events

SABR On-Deck Circle - $10/month, $30/month, $50/month
Get in the SABR On-Deck Circle, and help SABR become the essential community for the world of baseball. Your support will build capacity around all things SABR, including publications, website content, podcast development, and community growth.

A monthly gift is deducted from your bank account or charged to a credit card until you tell us to stop. No more email, mail, or phone reminders.

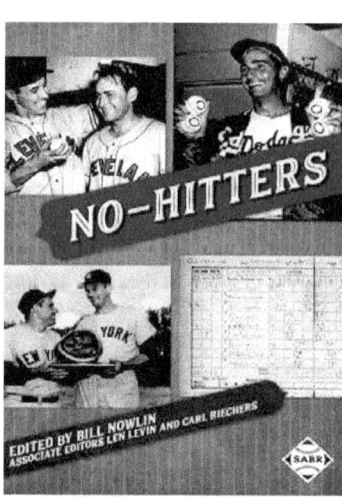

Join the SABR On-Deck Circle

Payment Info: _____ Visa _____ Mastercard   ○ $10/month

Name on Card: _____   ○ $30/month

Card #: _____   ○ $50/month

Exp. Date: _____ Security Code: _____   ○ Other amount _____

Signature: _____

Go to sabr.org/donate to make your gift online

www.ingramcontent.com/pod-product-compliance
Lightning Source LLC
Chambersburg PA
CBHW081342070526
44578CB00005B/697